Communications
in Computer and Information Science

T0092651

Azizah Abd Manaf   Akram Zeki
Mazdak Zamani   Suriayati Chuprat
Eyas El-Qawasmeh (Eds.)

Informatics Engineering and Information Science

International Conference, ICIEIS 2011
Kuala Lumpur, Malaysia, November 14-16, 2011
Proceedings, Part II

 Springer

Volume Editors

Azizah Abd Manaf
Advanced Informatics School (UTM AIS)
UTM International Campus
Kuala Lumpur, 54100, Malaysia
E-mail: azizah07@ic.utm.my

Akram Zeki
International Islamic University
Kulliyah of Information and Communication Technology
Kuala Lumpur, 54100, Malaysia
E-mail: akramzeki@yahoo.com

Mazdak Zamani
Advanced Informatics School (UTM AIS)
UTM International Campus
Kuala Lumpur, 54100, Malaysia
E-mail: mazdak@utm.my

Suriayati Chuprat
Advanced Informatics School (UTM AIS)
UTM International Campus
Kuala Lumpur, 54100, Malaysia
E-mail: suria@ic.utm.my

Eyas El-Qawasmeh
King Saud University, Information Systems Department
Riyadh, Saudi Arabia
E-mail: eyasa@usa.net

ISSN 1865-0929   e-ISSN 1865-0937
ISBN 978-3-642-25452-9   ˙e-ISBN 978-3-642-25453-6
DOI 10.1007/978-3-642-25453-6
Springer Heidelberg Dordrecht London New York

Library of Congress Control Number: 2011941089

CR Subject Classification (1998): C.2, H.4, I.2, H.3, D.2, H.5

Typesetting: Camera-ready by author, data conversion by Scientific Publishing Services, Chennai, India

Printed on acid-free paper

Springer is part of Springer Science+Business Media (www.springer.com)

Message from the Chair

The International Conference on Informatics Engineering and Information Science (ICIEIS 2011)—co-sponsored by Springer—was organized and hosted by Universiti Teknologi Malaysia in Kuala Lumpur, Malaysia, during November 14–16, 2011 in association with the Society of Digital Information and Wireless Communications. ICIEIS 2011 was planned as a major event in the computer and information sciences and served as a forum for scientists and engineers to meet and present their latest research results, ideas, and papers in the diverse areas of digital information processing, digital communications, information security, information ethics, and data management, and other related topics.

This scientific conference comprised guest lectures and 210 research papers for presentation over many parallel sessions. This number was selected from more than 600 papers. For each presented paper, a minimum of two reviewers went through each paper and filled a reviewing form. The system involves assigning grades to each paper based on the reviewers' comments. The system that is used is open conference. It assigns grades for each paper that range from 6 to 1. After that, the Scientific Committee re-evaluates the paper and its reviewing and decides on either acceptance or rejection.

This meeting provided a great opportunity to exchange knowledge and experiences for all the participants who joined us from all over the world to discuss new ideas in the areas of data and information management and its applications. We are grateful to Universiti Teknologi Malaysia in Kuala Lumpur for hosting this conference. We use this occasion to express thanks to the Technical Committee and to all the external reviewers. We are grateful to Springer for co-sponsoring the event. Finally, we would like to thank all the participants and sponsors.

Azizah Abd Manaf

Preface

On behalf of the ICIEIS 2011 conference, the Program Committee and Universiti Teknologi Malaysia in Kuala Lumpur, I have the pleasure to present the proceedings of the International Conference on Informatics Engineering and Information Science' (ICIEIS 2011).

The ICIEIS 2011 conference explored new advances in digital information and data communications technologies. It brought together researchers from various areas of computer science, information sciences, and data communications to address both theoretical and applied aspects of digital communications and wireless technology. We hope that the discussions and exchange of ideas will contribute to advancements in the technology in the near future.

The conference received more than 600 papers of which 530 papers were considered for evaluation. The number of accepted papers 210. The accepted papers were authored by researchers from 39 countries covering many significant areas of digital information and data communications. Each paper was evaluated by a minimum of two reviewers.

Organization

General Chair

Azizah Abd Manaf   Universiti Teknologi Malaysia, Malaysia

Program Chair

Ezendu Ariwa   London Metropolitan University, UK
Mazdak Zamani   Universiti Teknologi Malaysia, Malaysia

Program Co-chairs

Yoshiro Imai   Kagawa University, Japan
Jacek Stando   Technical University of Lodz, Poland

Proceedings Chair

Jan Platos   VSB-Technical University of Ostrava,
         Czech Republic

Publicity Chair

Maitham Safar   Kuwait University, Kuwait
Zuqing Zhu   University of Science and Technology of China,
         China

International Program Committee

Abdullah Almansur   King Saud University, Saudi Arabia
Akram Zeki   International Islamic University Malaysia,
         Malaysia
Ali Dehghan Tanha   Asia Pacific University, Malaysia
Ali Sher   American University of Ras Al Khaimah, UAE
Altaf Mukati   Bahria University, Pakistan
Andre Leon S. Gradvohl   State University of Campinas, Brazil
Arash Habibi Lashkari   University Technology Malaysia (UTM),
         Malaysia
Asadollah Shahbahrami   Delft University of Technology,
         The Netherlands
Chantal Cherifi   Université de Corse, France
Craig Standing   Edith Cowan University, Australia

Radhamani Govindaraju   Damodaran College of Science, India
Ram Palanisamy   St. Francis Xavier University, Canada
Riaza Mohd Rias   University of Technology MARA, Malaysia
Salwani Mohd Daud   Universiti Teknologi Malaysia, Malaysia
Sami Alyazidi   King Saud University, Saudi Arabia
Shamsul Mohd Shahibudin   Universiti Teknologi Malaysia, Malaysia
Talib Mohammad   University of Botswana, Botswana
Valentina Dagiene   Institute of Mathematics and Informatics,
                                 Lithuania
Viacheslav Wolfengagen   JurInfoR-MSU Institute, Russia
Waralak V. Siricharoen   University of the Thai Chamber of Commerce,
                                 Thailand
Wojciech Mazurczyk   Warsaw University of Technology, Poland
Wojciech Zabierowski   Technical University of Lodz, Poland
Yi Pan   Georgia State University, USA
Zanifa Omary   Dublin Institute of Technology, Ireland
Zuqing Zhu   The University of Science and Technology
                                 of China, China
Zuqing Zhu   University of Science and Technology of China,
                                 China
Zuraini Ismail   Universiti Teknologi Malaysia, Malaysia

Reviewers

Morteza Gholipour Geshnyani   University of Tehran, Iran
Asadollah Shahbahrami   University of Guilan, Iran
Mohd Faiz Hilmi   Universiti Sains Malaysia, Malaysia
Brij Gupta   Indian Institute of Technology, India
Naeem Shah   Xavor Corporation, Pakistan
Shanmugasundaram Hariharan   B.S. Abdur Rahman University, India
Rajibul Islam   University Technology Malaysia, Malaysia
Luca Mazzola   Università della Svizzera Italiana, Italy
K.P. Yadav   Acme College of Engineering, India
Jesuk Ko   Gwangju University, Korea
Mohd Wahab   Universiti Tun Hussein Onn Malaysia, Malaysia
Luca Mazzola   Università della Svizzera Italiana, Italy
Anirban Kundu   West Bengal University of Technology, India
Hamouid Khaled   Batna University, Algeria
Muhammad Naveed   Iqra University, Pakistan
Yana Hassim   Universiti Tun Hussein Onn Malaysia, Malaysia
Reza Moradi Rad   University of Guilan, Iran
Rahman Attar   University of Guilan, Iran
Zulkefli Bin Mansor   Universiti Teknologi MARA, Malaysia
Mourad Amad   Bejaia University, Algeria
Reza Ebrahimi Atani   University of Guilan, Iran
Vishal Bharti   Dronacharya College of Engineering, India

Thaweesak Yingthawornsuk	University of Technology Thonburi, Thailand
Chusak Thanawattano	Thailand
Ali AL-Mazari	AlFaisal University, Kingdom of Saudi Arabia
Amirtharajan Rengarajan	SASTRA University, India
Nur'Aini Abdul Rashid	Universiti Sains Malaysia, Malaysia
Mohammad Hossein Anisi	Universiti Teknologi Malaysia (UTM), Malaysia
Mohammad Nazir	University Technology of Malaysia, Malaysia
Desmond Lobo	Burapha University International College, Chonburi, Thailand
Salah Al-Mously	Koya University, Iraq
Gaurav Kumar	Chitkara University, India
Salah Eldin Abdelrahman	Menoufia University, Egypt
Vikram Mangla	Chitkara University, India
Deveshkumar Jinwala	S V National Institute of Technology, India
Nashwa El-Bendary	Arab Academy for Science, Technology & Maritime Transport, Egypt
Ashish Rastogi	Guru Ghasidas Central University, India
Vivek Kumar Singh	Banaras Hindu University, India
Sude Tavassoli	Islamic Azad University, Iran
Behnam Dezfouli	University Technology Malaysia (UTM), Malaysia
Marjan Radi	University Technology Malaysia (UTM), Malaysia
Chekra Ali Allani	Arab Open University, Kuwait
Jianfei Wu	North Dakota State University, USA
Ashish Sitaram	Guru Ghasidas University, India
Aissa Boudjella	Jalan Universiti Bandar Barat, Malaysia
Gouri Prakash	HSBC Bank, USA
Ka Ching Chan	La Trobe University, Australia
Azlan Mohd Zain	Universiti Teknologi Malaysia, Malaysia
Arshad Mansoor	SZABIST, Pakistan
Haw Su Cheng	Multimedia University (MMU), Malaysia
Deris Stiawan	Sriwijaya University, Indonesia
Akhilesh Dwivedi	Ambedkar Institute of Technology, India
Thiagarajan Balasubramanian	RVS College of Arts and Science, India
Simon Ewedafe	Universiti Tun Abdul Rahman, Malaysia
Roheet Bhatnagar	Sikkim Manipal Institute of Technology, India
Chekra Allani	The Arab Open University, Kuwait
Eduardo Ahumada-Tello	Universidad Autonoma de Baja California, Mexico
Jia Uddin	International Islamic University Chittagong, Bangladesh
Gulshan Shrivastava	Ambedkar Institute of Technology, India
Mohamad Forouzanfar	University of Ottawa, Canada

Kalum P. Udagepola	BBCG, Australia
Muhammad Javed	Dublin City University, Ireland
Partha Sarati Das	Dhaka University of Engineering, Bangladesh
Ainita Ban	Universiti Putra Malaysia, Malaysia
Noridayu Manshor	Universiti Putra Malaysia, Malaysia
Syed Muhammad Noman	Sir Syed University of Engineering and Technology, Pakistan
Zhefu Shi	University of Missouri, USA
Noraini Ibrahim	Universiti Teknologi Malaysia (UTM), Malaysia
Przemyslaw Pawluk	York University, Canada
Kumudha Raimond	Addis Ababa University, Ethiopia
Gurvan Le Guernic	KTH- Royal Institute of Technology, Sweden
Sarma A.D.N	Nagarjuna University, India
Utku Kose	Afyon Kocatepe University, Turkey
Kamal Srivastava	SRMCEM, India
Marzanah A. Jabar	Universiti Putra Malaysia, Malaysia
Eyas ElQawasmeh	King Saud University, Saudi Arabia
Adelina Tang	Sunway University, Malaysia
Samarjeet Borah	Sikkim Manipal Institute of Technology, India
Ayyoub Akbari	Universiti Putra Malaysia, Malaysia
Abbas Mehdizadeh	Universiti Putra Malaysia (UPM), Malaysia
Looi Qin En	Institute for Infocomm Research, Singapore
Krishna Prasad Miyapuram	Università degli Studi di Trento, Italy
M.Hemalatha	Karpagam University, India
Azizi Nabiha	Annaba University of Algeria, Algeria
Mallikarjun Hangarge	Science and Commerce College, India
J. Satheesh Kumar	Bharathiar University, India
Abbas Hanon AlAsadi	Basra University, Iraq
Maythem Abbas	Universiti Teknologi PETRONAS, Malaysia
Mohammad Reza Noruzi	Tarbiat Modarres University, Iran
Santoso Wibowo	CQ University Melbourne, Australia
Ramez Alkhatib	AlBaath University, Syrian Arab Republic
Ashraf Mohammed Iqbal	Dalhousie University, Canada
Hari Shanker Hota	GGV Central University, India
Tamer Beitelmal	Carleton University, Canada
Azlan Iqbal	Universiti Tenaga Nasional, Malaysia
Alias Balamurugan	Thiagarajar College of Engineering, India
Muhammad Sarfraz	Kuwait University, Kuwait
Vuong M. Ngo	HCMC University of Technology, Vietnam
Asad Malik	College of Electrical and Mechincal Engineering, Pakistan
Anju Sharma	Thapar University, India
Mohammad Ali Orumiehchiha	Macquarie University, Australia
Khalid Hussain	University Technology Malaysia, Malaysia

Valentina Emilia Balas	University of Arad, Romania
Muhammad Imran Khan	Universiti Teknologi PETRONAS, Malaysia
Daniel Koloseni	The Institute of Finance Management, Tanzania
Jacek Stando	Technical University of Lodz, Poland
Yang-Sae Moon	Kangwon National University, Korea
Mohammad Islam	University of Chittagong, Bangladesh
Joseph Ng	University Tunku Abdul Rahman, Malaysia
Umang Singh	ITS Group of Institutions, India
Sim-Hui Tee	Multimedia University, Malaysia
Ahmad Husni Mohd Shapri	Universiti Malaysia Perlis, Malaysia
Syaripah Ruzaini Syed Aris	Universiti Teknologi MARA, Malaysia
Ahmad Pahlavan	Islamic Azad University, Iran
Aaradhana Deshmukh	Pune University, India
Sanjay Singh	Manipal University, India
Subhashini Radhakrishnan	Sathyabama University, India
Binod Kumar	Lakshmi Narain College of Technology, India
Farah Jahan	University of Chittagong, Bangladesh
Masoumeh Bourjandi	Islamic Azad University, Iran
Rainer Schick	University of Siegen, Germany
Zaid Mujaiyid Putra Ahmad	Universiti Teknologi MARA, Malaysia
Abdul Syukor Mohamad Jaya	Universiti Teknikal Malaysia Melaka, Malaysia
Yasir Mahmood	NUST SEECS, Pakistan
Razulaimi Razali	Universiti Teknologi MARA, Malaysia
Anand Sharma	MITS, LAkshmangarh, India
Seung Ho Choi	Seoul National University of Science and Technology, Korea
Safoura Janosepah	Islamic Azad University, Iran
Rosiline Jeetha B	RVS College of Arts and Science, India
Mustafa Man	University Malaysia Terengganu, Malaysia
Intan Najua Kamal Nasir	Universiti Teknologi PETRONAS, Malaysia
Ali Tufail	Ajou University, Korea
Bowen Zhang	Beijing University of Posts and Telecommunications, China
Rekha Labade	Amrutvahini College of Engineering, India
Ariffin Abdul Mutalib	Universiti Utara Malaysia, Malaysia
Mohamed Saleem Haja Nazmudeen	Universiti Tunku Abdul Rahman, Malaysia
Norjihan Abdul Ghani	University of Malaya, Malaysia
Micheal Arockiaraj	Loyola College, India
A. Kannan	K.L.N.College of Engineering, India
Nursalasawati Rusli	Universiti Malaysia Perlis, Malaysia
Ali Dehghantanha	Asia-Pacific University, Malaysia
Kathiresan V.	RVS College of Arts and Science, India
Saeed Ahmed	CIIT,Islamabad, Pakistan
Muhammad Bilal	UET Peshawar, Pakistan

Ahmed Al-Haiqi	UKM, Malaysia
Dia AbuZeina	KFUPM, Saudi Arabia
Nikzad Manteghi	Islamic Azad University, Iran
Amin Kianpisheh	Universiti Sains Malaysia, Malaysia
Wattana Viriyasitavat	University of Oxford, UK
Sabeen Tahir	UTP Malaysia, Malaysia
Fauziah Redzuan	UiTM, Malaysia
Mazni Omar	UUM, Malaysia
Quazi Mahera Jabeen	Saitama University, Japan
A.V. Senthil Kumar	Hindusthan College of Arts and Science, India
Ruki Harwahyu	Universitas Indonesia, Indonesia
Sahel Alouneh	German Jordanian University, Jordan
Murad Taher	Hodieda University, Yemen
Yasaman Alioon	Sharif University of Technology, Iran
Muhammad Zaini Ahmad	Universiti Malaysia Perlis, Malaysia
Vasanthi Beulah	Queen Mary's College, India
Shanthi A.S.	Loyola College, Chennai, India
Siti Marwangi Mohamad Maharum	Universiti Teknologi Malaysia, Malaysia
Younes Elahi	UTM, Malaysia
Izzah Amani Tarmizi	Universiti Sains Malaysia, Malaysia
Yousef Farhang	Universiti Teknologi Malaysia, Malaysia
Mohammad M. Dehshibi	IACSIT, Iran
Ahmad Kueh Beng Hong	Universiti Teknologi Malaysia, Malaysia
Seyed Buhari	Universiti Brunei Darussalam, Brunei Darussalam
D. Christopher	RVS College of Arts and Science, India
NagaNandiniSujatha S	K.L.N. College of Engineering, India
Jasvir Singh	Guru Nanak Dev University, India
Omar Kareem	Alma'arif University College, Iraq
Faiz Asraf Saparudin	Universiti Teknologi Malaysia, Malaysia
Ilango M.R.	K.L.N. College of Engineering, India
Rajesh R.	Bharathiar University, India
Vijaykumar S.D.	RVS College of Arts and Science, India
Cyrus F. Nourani	AkdmkR&D, USA
Faiz Maazouzi	LabGED Laboratory, Algeria
Aimi Syamimi Ab Ghafar	Universiti Teknologi Malaysia, Malaysia
Md. Rezaul Karim	Kyung Hee University, Korea
Indrajit Das	VIT University, India
Muthukkaruppan Annamalai	Universiti Teknologi MARA, Malaysia
Prabhu S.	Loyola College, India
Sundara Rajan R.	Loyola College, India
Jacey-Lynn Minoi	Universiti Malaysia Sarawak, Malaysia
Nazrul Muhaimin Ahmad	Multimedia University, Malaysia
Anita Kanavalli	M.S. Ramaiah Institute of Technology, India
Tauseef Ali	University of Twente, The Netherlands

Hanumanthappa J.	University of Mangalore, India
Tomasz Kajdanowicz	Wroclaw University of Technology, Poland
Rehmat Ullah	University of Engineering and Technology, Peshawar, Pakistan
Nur Zuraifah Syazrah Othman	Universiti Teknologi Malaysia, Malaysia
Mourad Daoudi	University of Sciences and Technologies Houari Boumediene, Algeria
Mingyu Lee	Sugnkyunkwan University, Korea
Cyriac Grigorious	Loyola College, India
Sudeep Stephen	Loyola College, India
Amit K. Awasthi	Gautam Buddha University, India
Zaiton Abdul Mutalip	Universiti Teknikal Malaysia Melaka, Malaysia
Abdu Gumaei	King Saud University, Saudi Arabia
E. Martin	University of California, Berkeley, USA
Mareike Dornhöfer	University of Siegen, Germany
Arash Salehpour	University of Nabi Akram, Iran
Mojtaba Seyedzadegan	UPM, Malaysia
Raphael Jackson	Kentucky State University, USA
Abdul Mateen	Federal Urdu University of Science and Technology, Pakistan
Subhashini Ramakrishnan	Dr G.R. Damodaran College of Science, India
Randall Duran	Singapore Management University, Singapore
Yoshiro Imai	Kagawa University, Japan
Syaril Nizam	University Technology Malaysia, Malaysia
Pantea Keikhosrokiani	Universiti Sains Malaysia, Malaysia
Kok Chin Khor	Multimedia University, Malaysia
Salah Bindahman	Universiti Sains Malaysia, Malaysia
Sami Miniaoui	University of Dubai, United Arab Emirates
Intisar A.M. Al Sayed	Al Isra University, Jordan
Teddy Mantoro	International Islamic University Malaysia, Malaysia
Kitsiri Chochiang	PSU University, Thailand
Khadoudja Ghanem	University Mentouri Constantine, Algeria
Rozeha A. Rashid	Universiti Teknologi Malaysia, Malaysia
Redhwan Qasem Shaddad	Taiz University, Yemen
MuhammadAwais Khan	COMSATS Institute of Information and Technology, Pakistan
Noreen Kausar	Universiti Teknologi PETRONAS, Malaysia
Hala Jubara	UTM, Malaysia
Alsaidi Altaher	Universiti Sains Malaysia, Malaysia
Syed Abdul Rahman Al-Haddad	Universiti Putra Malaysia, Malaysia
Norma Alias	Universiti Teknologi Malaysia, Malaysia
Adib M. Monzer Habbal	University Utara Malaysia, Malaysia
Heri Kuswanto	Institut Teknologi Sepuluh Nopember, Indonesia

Asif Khan	FAST NUCES Peshawar Campus, Pakistan
Tufail Habib	Aalborg University, Denmark
Amin Shojaatmand	Islamic Azad University, Iran
Yasser K. Zahedi	Universiti Teknologi Malaysia, Malaysia
Vetrivelan N.	Periyar Maniammai University, India
Khalil Ullah	National University of Computing and Emerging Sciences, Pakistan
Amril Syalim	Kyushu University, Japan
Habib Ullah	COMSATS Institute of IT, Pakistan
Michal Kratky	VSB-Technical University of Ostrava, Czech Republic
Suyeb Khan	Electronics and Communication Engineering, India
Heng Yaw Ling	Multimedia University, Malaysia
Zahid Mahmood	COMSATS, Institute of Information Technology, Pakistan
Sebastian Binnewies	Griffith University, Australia
Mohammadreza Khoei	Universiti Teknologi Malaysia, Malaysia
Zahid Mahmood	COMSATS IIT, Pakistan
Thawanrat Puckdeepun	Universiti Teknologi PETRONAS, Malaysia
Wannisa Matcha	Universiti Teknologi PETRONAS, Malaysia
Sureena Matayong	Universiti Teknologi PETRONAS, Malaysia
Sapna Mishra	Dayanand Academy of Management Studies, India
Qaim Mehdi Rizvi	SRMCEM, India
Habib Ullah	COMSATS Institute of Information Technology, Wah Campus, Pakistan

Table of Contents – Part II

Image Processing

Algorithms

Artificial Intelligence and Soft Computing

E-commerce

Data Mining

Performance Study of Two-Dimensional Orthogonal Systolic Array Matric Multiplication

A.H.M. Shapri, N.A.Z. Rahman, and M. Mazalan

School of Microelectronic Engineering,
Universiti Malaysia Perlis,
Blok A, Kompleks Pusat Pengajian Jejawi 1,
02600 Jejawi, Perlis, Malaysia
{ahmadhusni,azeani,mazleemazalan}@unimap.edu.my

Abstract. The systolic array implementation of artificial neural networks is one of the ideal solutions for communication problems generated by highly interconnected neurons. A systolic array is an arrangement of processors in an array where data flows synchronously across the array between neighbours, usually with different data flowing in different directions. The simulation of systolic array for matrix multiplication is the practical application in order to evaluate the performance of systolic array. In this paper, a two-dimensional orthogonal systolic array for matrix multiplication is presented. Perl scripting language is used to simulate a two-dimensional orthogonal systolic array compared to conventional matrix multiplication in terms of average execution time. The comparison is made using matrices of size 5xM versus Mx5 which M ranges from 1 to 10, 10 to 100 and 100 to 1000. The orthogonal systolic array results show better average execution time when M is more than 30 compared to conventional matrix multiplication when the size of the matrix multiplication is increased.

Keywords: orthogonal systolic array, matrix multiplication, perl scripting.

1 Introduction

Matrix multiplication is the operation of multiplying a matrix with either a scalar in which a single number is multiplied with every entry of a matrix or multiplication of an entire matrix by another entire matrix. In the scalar variety, every entry is multiplied by a number, called a scalar. For the multiplication of an entire matrix, the two matrices can be multiply if and only if, the number of columns in the first matrix equals the number of rows in the second matrix. Otherwise, the product of two matrices is undefined. The product matrix's dimensions are (rows of first matrix) × (columns of the second matrix). The ordinary matrix product is most often used and the most important way to multiply matrices. Multiplying the $m \times n$ matrix with $n \times p$ matrix will result in $m \times p$ matrix. If many matrices are multiplied together and their dimensions are written in a list in order, e.g. $m \times n, n \times p, p \times q$ and $q \times r$, the size of the result is given by the first and the last numbers which is $m \times r$. The values surrounding each comma must match for the result to be defined.

A. Abd Manaf et al. (Eds.): ICIEIS 2011, Part II, CCIS 252, pp. 1–13, 2011.

A number of systolic algorithms are available for matrix multiplication, the basic computation involved in the operation of a neural network. Using these, many systolic algorithms have been formulated for the implementation of neural networks [1]. A systolic array is composed of matrix-like rows of data processing units called systolic cells or processing elements. Each cell shares the information with its neighbours immediately after processing. The systolic array is often rectangular where data flows across the array between neighbour cells, often with different data flowing in different directions [2]. Systolic arrays are suited for processing repetitive computations. Although this kind of computation usually involves a great deal of computing power, such computations are parallelizable and highly regular. The systolic array architecture exploits this parallelism and regularity to deliver the required computational speed. In a systolic array, all systolic cells perform computations concurrently, while data, such as initial inputs, partial results, and final outputs, is being passed from cell to cell. When partial results are moved between cells, they are computed over these cells in a pipeline manner. In this case the computation of each single output is separated over these cells.   This contrasts to other parallel architectures based on data partitioning, for which the computation of each output is computed solely on one single processor [3-4].

When a systolic array is in operation, computing at cells, communication between cells and input from and output to the outside world all take place at the same time to accomplish high performance. This is analogous to the circulatory system; data is pulsed through all cells where it is processed. Being able to implement many operations simultaneously is one of the advantages of systolic arrays. Other advantages include modular expandability of the cell array, simple and uniform cells, efficient fault-tolerant schemes and nearest-neighbor data communications.

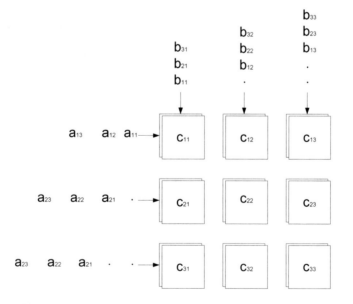

Fig. 1. Two-dimensional systolic array for matrix multiplication

Fig. 1 illustrates a two-dimensional systolic array capable of performing matrix multiplication, C = A x B for 3x3 matrices $A = (A_{ij})$, $B = (B_{ij})$ and $C = (C_{ij})$. As indicated, entries in A and B are shifted into the array from left and top, respectively. It is easy to see that the C_{ij} at each cell can accumulate all its terms $a_{i1}b_{1j}$, $a_{i2}b_{2j}$ and $a_{i3}b_{3j}$ while A and B march across the systolic array. Kung *et. al.* have proposed a unified systolic architecture for the implementation of neural network models [5]. It has been shown that the proper ordering of the elements of the weight matrix makes it possible to design a cascaded dependency graph for consecutive matrix multiplication, which requires the directions of data movement at both the input and the output of the dependency graph to be identical. Using this cascaded dependency graph, the computations in both the recall and the learning iterations of a back-propagation algorithm have been mapped onto a ring systolic array.

A similar mapping strategy has been used in [6] for mapping the recursive back-propagation network and the hidden Markov model onto the ring systolic array. The main disadvantage of the above implementations is the presence of spiral communication links. In [5], a two-dimensional array is used to map the synaptic weights of individual weight layers in the neural network. By placing the arrays corresponding to adjacent weight layers side by side, both the recall and the learning phases of the back-propagation algorithm can be executed efficiently. But, as the directions of data movement at the output and the input of each array are different, this leads to a very non-uniform design.

A large number of systolic array designs have been developed and used to perform a broad range of computations. In fact, recent advances in theory and software have allowed some of these systolic arrays to be derived automatically [7]. There are numerous computations for which systolic designs exist such as signal and image processing, polynomial and multiple precision integer arithmetic, matrix arithmetic and nonnumeric applications [8].

Scripting languages such as perl represent a very different style of programming than system programming languages such as C or Java. Scripting languages are typeless approaches to achieve a higher level of programming and more rapid application development than system programming languages. Increases in computer speed and changes in the application are mixes together making scripting languages more and more important for applications of the future [9].

Perl was originally designed as a glue programming language which is a language used to fill in the gaps between other programming languages, systems and interfaces. It has offers features such as the ability to program in the object oriented, a rich feature set by encompassing all of the good parts of other programming languages, a full set of data reduction and manipulation operators, file system manipulation abilities, process and procedure management, database functionality, client-server programming capabilities and secured programming. Perl borrows heavily features from other programming languages such as C, C++, Java, awk, BASIC and Python. It is possible to start writing perl code almost immediately if the users know at least one other programming language beforehand. It is also possible for any programmer to read some well written perl code.

The objective of this paper is to do the simulation of two-dimensional orthogonal systolic array and conventional approach for matrix multiplication by using perl scripting language. The determination is to evaluate the performance of both approaches in terms of average execution time. The comparison is made using matrices of size 5xM versus Mx5 which M ranges from 1 to 10, 10 to 100 and 100 to 1000. The execution time is crucial for high performance of computations or load balancing of the resources. Hence, the results of this simulation can be used to select the best matrix multiplication approach with a significant improvement in process execution speed.

2   Background

There are also other applications of the systolic array multiplication which are finite impulse response (FIR) filter [7], matrix polynomial and powers of a matrix [10]. FIR filter implementing a simple systolic array multiplication. Given inputs X_i and weights W_j, the filtering problem is to compute outputs Y_i, defined by $Y_i = W_1X_i +W_2X_{i+1} + \bullet\bullet\bullet + W_kX_{i+k-1}$. Fig. 2. depicts a one-dimensional systolic array for a FIR filter with k = 3 weights, each of which is preloaded into a cell. During computation, both partial results for Y_i and inputs Xi flow from left to right, where the former move twice as fast as the latter. More precisely, each X_i stays inside every cell it passes for one additional cycle, and thus each X_i takes twice as long to march through the array as does a Y_i. One can check that each Y_i, initialized to zero before entering the leftmost cell, is able to accumulate all its terms while marching to the right. For example, Y_1 accumulates W_3X_3, W_2X_2 and W_1X_1 in three consecutive cycles at the leftmost, middle, and rightmost cells, respectively.

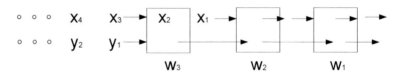

Fig. 2. One-dimensional systolic array for implementing FIR filter

Although each output Y is computed using several inputs X and several weights W, and each input and each weight is used in computing several outputs, the systolic array described here uses no global communication. More accurately, data communication at each cycle is always between adjacent cells.

A matrix polynomial is a matrix whose elements are univariate or multivariate polynomials. A slight modification of the design allow the creation of matrix multiply-and-add step of the form $X^{(n)} \leftarrow X^{(n-1)}A+B$. The accumulation of B can be done on the fly when the values $X^{(n-1)}A$ reach the left row of the array, as depicted by Fig. 3. Consider the calculation of the matrix polynomial $P=\sum_{k=0}B_kA^k$ where B_k and A are $n \times n$ matrices. The algorithm is also valid when the matrices are $n \times p$, or when the coefficients B_k are vectors. Using Horner's rule, P can be computed by the following iterative scheme:

$$X^{(0)} = B_N \tag{1}$$
$$X^{(k)} = X^{(k-1)}A+B_{N-k} \tag{2}$$
$$P \equiv X^{(N)} \tag{3}$$

Therefore, P can be computed in exactly $2n(N+1)-1$ steps on the systolic array of Fig. 3. A well-known efficient algorithm for the computation of matrix powers $P = A^N$ is described by Knuth [11] and Lamagna [12]. It consists in using the binary representation of N to control a sequence or multiply by A steps. Although this method is not optimal, it has the greatest advantage, compared to others, that is does not require an important storage. This property makes it well-suited for a systolic realization.

More precisely, let $N^P N^{p-}...N^0$ be the binary representation of N, and let $C_q, C_{q-1},...C_0$ be the new sequence obtained by rewriting each N_k as SX if $N_k = 1$ or as S if $N_k = 1$ or as S if $N_k = 0$, and by discarding the first pair of letters SX. C is used to control a sequence of operations and is interpreted from the left to right, each S meaning square the current matrix and each X equal to multiply the current matrix by A. For example, decimal 19 is equal to binary 10011 will be rewritten as $SSSXSX$ and the sequence of computations will be $A^2, A^4, A^8, A^9, A^{18}, A^{19}$. Then the following iteration scheme

$$X^{(0)} = A \tag{4}$$

$$X^{(n)} = (X^{(n-1)})^2 \ if \ C_{q-r} = S \ else \ X^{(n-1)} A \tag{5}$$

$$P \equiv X^{(q)} \tag{6}$$

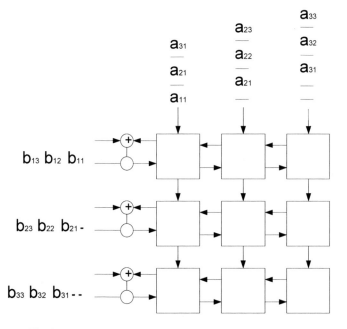

Fig. 3. Systolic array for the matrix polynomial calculation

The basic calculation to be done is either a square or a matrix multiplication. Again, a simple modification of our design enables us to square a matrix. The basic idea is to route the result to the upper row of the array too. Depending on the value of C_{q-1}, A or $X^{(n-1)}$ will be fed into the array from the top to bottom. Elementary movements along the vector $(1, 0, -1)$ is compatible with the timing-function, t

$$t(i, j, k) = i+j+k-3 \tag{7}$$

and the resulting design is shown by Fig. 4. As the binary representation of N has Equ. 8 bits, q is majored by Equ. 9. Hence, the calculation of A^N takes a maximum of Equ. 10 steps on a n^2 mesh connected array.

$$N = [log_2 N]+1 \tag{8}$$

$$q = 2[log_2+N] \tag{9}$$

$$A^N = 2n(2Log_2 N+1)-1 \tag{10}$$

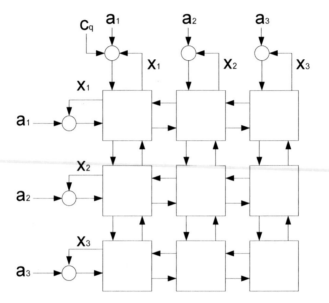

Fig. 4. Systolic array for the powers of matrix calculation

3   Methodology

We have created a simulation program using perl scripting language that simulates the orthogonal systolic array and conventional matrix multiplication. The goal of the simulator design is to develop an accurate, fast and stable simulator based on an orthogonal systolic array and conventional matrix multiplication.

3.1   Perl Scripting Language

Scripting languages such as perl, tcl, tk and python are the main achievement of the open source movement. Perl is a popular and widely used cross-platform programming language. In particular, its flexibility can be fully utilized to become a powerful simulator. There are no rules about indentation, newlines, etc. Most lines end with semicolons, but not everything has to. Most things do not have to be declared, except for a couple of things that do [13]. Perl only has three basic data types: scalars, arrays and hashes. It stores numbers internally as either signed integers or double-precision, floating-point values.

Perl is an open source interpreted programming language. It is a control program that understands the semantics of the language and its components, the interpreter executes program components individually as they are encountered in the control flow. This is usually done by first translating the source code into an intermediate representation called bytecode and then interpreting the bytecode. Interpreted execution makes perl flexible, convenient and fast for programming, with some penalty paid in execution speed.

One of the major advantages of perl scripting language is the support for regular expressions. Regular expressions are the key to powerful, flexible, and efficient text processing. Regular expressions are used in several ways in perl. They are used in conditionals to determine whether a string matches a particular pattern, to find patterns in strings and replace the match with something else. Regular expressions themselves with a general pattern notation allow the designer to describe and parse text [14].

3.2 Two-Dimensional Orthogonal Systolic Array

Systolic array designs have two main characteristics: a) they are flow-simple, where each processor element is used once every clock-cycle and they are locally connected   and   b) where each processing element   is connected to   the nearest neighbour. Matrix-multiplication systolic array is well known as the matrix multiplication, $C = AB$ as shown in Fig. 5 can be implemented on two-dimensional arrays using orthogonal arrangement in Fig. 6. Numerous designs can be used depending on whether one wants C, A or B to move. Here we consider the simple design where C stays in place. Coefficient c_{ij}, where $1 \leq i, j \geq n$ thus is calculated by cell i, j of a mesh connected array of multiply-and-add processors, as depicted by Fig. 6. Cell i, j contains a register c which is first reset to zero and then accumulates successively products $a_{ik} b_{kj}$ where k varies from 1 to n. However this implementation suffers from the drawback that the results do not move and consequently a systolic output scheme has to be designed in order to recover them.

$$\begin{bmatrix} a_{11} & a_{12} & a_{13} \\ a_{21} & a_{22} & a_{23} \\ a_{31} & a_{32} & a_{33} \end{bmatrix} \times \begin{bmatrix} b_{11} & b_{12} & b_{13} \\ b_{21} & b_{22} & b_{23} \\ b_{31} & b_{32} & b_{33} \end{bmatrix} = \begin{bmatrix} c_{11} & c_{12} & c_{13} \\ c_{21} & c_{22} & c_{23} \\ c_{31} & c_{32} & c_{33} \end{bmatrix}$$

Fig. 5. Matrix multiplication $C = AB$

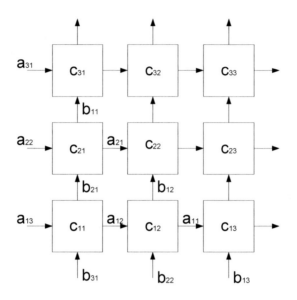

Fig. 6. Orthogonal systolic array for the multiplication of matrices

4 Implementation Details

The simulation program consists of two main scripts which are run.pl and systolic.pl. The run.pl has been developed in order to get the average execution time as shown in Fig. 7 below. The while loop has been used to execute the systolic.pl in a batch mode.

```
for($h=100; $h<=200; $h=$h+100){ #for M value
`touch tmp.txt`;

$g=0;
while ($g<2){ #takes 10 value for each
        `perl systolic.pl 5 $h 5 1`;
        print "count $g : L:5 M:$h N:5\n";
        $g+=1;}
```

Fig. 7. Pseudocode of run.pl

The systolic.pl is the core of the simulation program. It has five parts, which are listed in Table 1. The purpose of this script is to execute the systolic.pl in batch mode, which is to get 10 values of execution time for each matrix multiplication. These values can be used to calculate the average execution time. All scripts are executed in Windows® environment by using Cygwin™ terminal.

Table 1. Five parts of systolic.pl

No	Part	Functions
1	random matrix generator	to generate the value for matrices or select the files for matrix inputs.
2	systolic array	to apply systolic array matrix multiplication using orthogonal arrangement.
3	conventional	to apply matrix multiplication using conventional approach.
4	execution time	to capture the execution time for each approach.
5	result	to display the result on screen and record it to files.

```perl
#!/bin/perl
print "\n SIMULATION OF MATRIX MULTIPLICATIONS\n";
.
.
.
# populate array
@inputA = ();
for ($j=0; $j<$total0; $j++) { push(@inputA,
int(rand($range)));
}

@inputB = ();
for ($j=0; $j<$total1; $j++) { push(@inputB,
int(rand($range)));
}
```

Fig. 8. Pseudocode of systolic.pl (random matrix generator)

Fig. 8 shows the random matrix generator part. Operation for two-dimensional orthogonal systolic array has been accomplished by using the for loop. The rand function has been used to generate the values based on the seed given. The array arrangement is done by referring to the orthogonal arrangement. The pseudocode for the systolic array operation is depicted in Fig. 9. The pseudocode of conventional approach calculation is shown in Fig. 10. It is done by following the conventional matrix multiplication steps which are multiply the elements of each row of the first matrix by the elements of each column in the second matrix and finally adds the products.

```
#operation for systolic array
for($g=0; $g<$c; $g=$g+1){
   $valueA = $valueA + $inA[0][$g] * $inB[0][$g];
   $valueB = $valueB + $inA[1][$g] * $kananA;
   $valueE = $valueE + $inA[2][$g] * $kananB;
   $valueM = $valueM + $inA[3][$g] * $kananE;
   $valueU = $valueU + $inA[4][$g] * $kananM;
   $valueC = $valueC + $bawahA     * $inB[1][$g];
   $valueD = $valueD + $bawahB     * $kananC;
   $valueF = $valueF + $bawahE     * $kananD;
   .

   .
}
```

Fig. 9. Pseudocode of systolic.pl (systolic array)

```
#operation for conventional approach
for ($e=0; $e<$Lslice; $e++){
  for ($y=0; $y<$Nslice; $y++){
    $array_out[$e][$y]=0;
      for ($z=0; $z<$Mslice; $z++){
         $array_out[$e][$y]= $array_out[$e][$y]+
         ($inA1[$e][$z]*$inB1[$y][$z]);}
      }
}
```

Fig. 10. Pseudocode of systolic.pl (conventional)

Fig. 11 shows the pseudocode of systolic.pl for execution time part. The execution time has been captured by using Time::HiRes module. The Time::HiRes module implements a perl interface to the high resolution time and timers. The differences between $t1 and $t0 give a floating point value, representing number of seconds between them. The execution times are collected for both systolic array and conventional matrix multiplication.

```
use Time::HiRes qw(gettimeofday);
$t0 = gettimeofday;
.

.
$t1 = gettimeofday;

#$elapsed is a floating point value, representing
number of seconds between $t0 and $t1
$elapsed = $t1-$t0;
```

Fig. 11. Pseudocode of systolic.pl (execution time)

```
#time comparison for both approaches
printf "\n For %dx%d matrix multiplication\n",
$Lslice,$Nslice,;

$diff = abs($elapsed1-$elapsed);
printf "Execution time differences : %.6f s",$diff;

#record to file
open(OUT,">tmp.txt")||die "Can't open file:$!\n";
printf OUT "%d %.6f%.6f\n",$Mslice,$elapsed,
$elapsed1;
close OUT;
```

Fig. 12. Pseudocode of systolic.pl (result)

The result for both approaches has being displayed on screen and recorded into files as depicted in Fig. 12. The maximum size of output matrix is 5x5. Hence, the matrix size for the simulation is 5xM versus Mx5, where the M value can be divided into three parts which is from 1 to 10, 10 to 100 and 100 to 1000 and the number of processing elements or systolic cells used in the simulation is 25.

5   Result

Fig. 13 shows the average execution times for a matrix multiplication using orthogonal systolic array and conventional approach for matrix values, M, from 1 to 10. At M=1, a big differences of average execution time occurs between these two approaches by 61%. While at M=10, only 1.5% difference is seen between the two approaches. From here, we noticed that the orthogonal systolic array needs more time to compute the matrix multiplication for a small matrix size compare to the conventional approach because the matrix was been multiplied using reusable processing elements, which introduced delays.

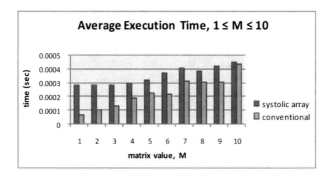

Fig. 13. Average execution time for $1 \leq M \leq 10$

For matrix size with value M from 10 to 100, as shown in Fig. 14, the average execution times for matrix multiplication using conventional approach is increased. For M=10, the average execution time required for orthogonal systolic array to complete the matrix multiplication is 11.9% higher than conventional approach. When M=20, the differences became smaller and slightly equal to conventional approach. After M=30 and above, the average execution time for conventional approach is higher than the orthogonal systolic array approach.

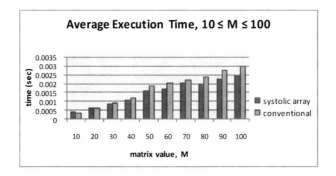

Fig. 14. Average execution time for $10 \leq M \leq 100$

In Fig. 15, the average execution time for matrix multiplication using orthogonal systolic array is lower than the conventional approach. The total average execution time for orthogonal systolic array is 150 ms while that for the conventional approach is 174 ms. The percentage increase is up to 7.4% for $100 \leq M \leq 1000$. The orthogonal systolic array approach is much better than conventional approach for large size matrix multiplications.

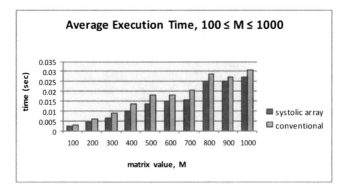

Fig. 15. Average execution time for $100 \leq M \leq 1000$

6   Conclusion

This paper evaluates the performances of two-dimensional orthogonal systolic array compared to conventional approach for the multiplication of matrices. Three series of evaluation has been completed for M in range of 1 to 10, 10 to 100 and 100 to 1000. From the results, the average execution time was examined and the orthogonal systolic array show a better results compared to the conventional approach. When M=30 and above, the orthogonal systolic array shows less average execution time, which performed better. When M=20, the average execution time between orthogonal systolic array and conventional approach is slightly same and at M=1, major differences of value occurred. The main advantage of the orthogonal systolic array is the processing elements can be reused for a new multiplication without the need of intermediate storage. In conclusion, an orthogonal systolic array can be used perfectly in order to handle large sizes of matrix multiplication with better performance than conventional approach.

References

1. Sudha, N., Mohan, A.R., Meher, P.K.: Systolic array realization of a neural network-based face recognition system. In: IEEE International Conference on Industrial Electronics and Applications (ICIEA 2008), pp. 1864–1869 (2008)
2. Shapri, A.H.M., Rahman, N.A.Z., Wahid, M.H.A.: Performance Study of Two-Dimensional Orthogonal Systolic Array. In: Zain, J.M., Wan Mohd, W.M.b., El-Qawasmeh, E., et al. (eds.) ICSECS 2011, Part II. CCIS, vol. 180, pp. 567–574. Springer, Heidelberg (2011)
3. Chung, J.H., Yoon, H.S., Maeng, S.R.: A Systolic Array Exploiting the Inherent Parallelisms of Artificial Neural Networks. Micro-processing and Microprogramming 33 (1992)
4. Kane, A.J., Evans, D.J.: An instruction systolic array architecture for neural networks. International Journal of Computer Mathematics 61 (1996)
5. Kung, S.Y., Hwang, J.N.: A unified systolic architecture for artificial neural networks. J. Parallel Distrib. Comput. 6, 358–387 (1989)
6. Hwang, J.N., Vlontzos, J.A., Kung, S.Y.: A systolic neural network architecture for hidden markov models. IEEE Trans. on ASSP 32 12, 1967–1979 (1989)
7. Kung, H.T., Leiserson, C.E.: Systolic arrays (for VLSI). In: Duff, I.S., Stewart, G.W. (eds.) Sparse Matrix Proceedings 1978, pp. 256–282. SIAM (1979)
8. Muroga, C.: On a Case of Symbiosis between Systolic Arrays. Integration the VLSI Journal 2, 243–253 (1984)
9. Ousterhout, J.K.: Scripting: Higher Level Programming for the 21st Century. IEEE Computer Magazine (1998)
10. Rahman, N.A.Z., Shapri, A.H.M.: Performance Evaluation of Two-Dimensional Systolic Array using Orthogonal Arrangement. In: IEEE International Conference on Intelligent Network and Computing (ICINC 2010), vol. 1, pp. 10–13 (2010)
11. Knuth, D.: The Art of Computer Programming. Seminumerical Algorithms 2, 398–422 (1969)
12. Lamagna, E.A.: Fast Computer Algebra. 43 (1982)
13. Spainhour, S., Siever, E., Patwardhan, N.: Perl in a Nutshell, 2nd edn., pp. 43–45. O'Reilly Media (2002)
14. Friedl, J.E.F.: Mastering Regular Expressions. O'Reilly & Associates, Inc. (1998)

Computational Approaches for Gene Prediction: A Comparative Survey

Israa M. Al-Turaiki, Hassan Mathkour,
Ameur Touir, and Saleh Hammami

Department of Computer Science,
College of Computer and Information Sciences,
King Saud University, Riyadh, Saudi Arabia
{ialturaiki,mathkour,touir,shammami}@ksu.edu.sa

Abstract. Accurate gene structure prediction plays a fundamental role in functional annotation of genes. The main focus of gene prediction methods is to find patterns in long DNA sequences that indicate the presence of genes. The problem of gene prediction is an important problem in the field of bioinformatics. With the explosive growth of genomic information there is a need for computational approaches that facilitate gene location, structure and functional prediction. In this paper, we survey various computational approaches for gene predictions.

Keywords: Bio-informatics, Gene Prediction, Bio-Computation, Promoter Identification.

1 Introduction

The main focus of gene prediction methods is to find patterns in long DNA sequences that indicate the presence of genes. The problem of gene prediction is an important problem in the field of bioinformatics [5]. It presents many difficulties especially in eukaryotes where exons (coding regions) are interrupted by introns (non-coding regions).The gene prediction problem can be defined formally as:

Input: DNA sequence $X = \{x_1, x_2, \ldots . x_n \in \Sigma^*$ where $\Sigma = \{A, T, G, C\}$

Output: correct labeling oof each element of x as coding, noncoding or intergenic [4].

Although researchers continue to devise new algorithms for gene prediction, the satisfactory accuracy is still far from reach. According to [2], 90% of genes are accurately predicted at the nucleotide level, 45% at the exon level and only 20% on the gene level. This explains the reason why the number of genes in the human genome cannot be precisely estimated (between 30,000 and 100,000). Current gene prediction methods are based on exploiting two gene features: content sensors and signal sensors [3]. Content sensors try to distinguish protein coding and non-protein coding regions. On the other hand, signal sensors try to predict the presence of functional sites. Many algorithms are used for gene prediction including: dynamic programming, hidden Markov models (HMMs), artificial neural networks (ANNs) and linear discriminate analysis.

A. Abd Manaf et al. (Eds.): ICIEIS 2011, Part II, CCIS 252, pp. 14–25, 2011.

2 Gene Prediction

Gene prediction problem can be divided into two sub-problems: prediction of protein coding regions and prediction of functional sites [5, 20]. The development of gene prediction programs have evolved in four generations [1]. In the first generation the programs such as GRAIL [10] and TestCode [11], were designed to identify approximate locations of protein coding regions. According to [1] such programs were not able to produce precise location predictions. In the second generations, programs such as SORFIND [12] and Xpound [13] combined splice signal and coding region identification to predict exons. However, the programs did not attempt to produce complete genes by assembling the predicted exons. The task of predicting complete gene structures was addressed by the third generation programs such as GeneID [14], GeneParser [15] ,GenLang [16] and FGENEH [17]. All those programs were based on the unrealistic assumption that the input sequence contains a single complete gene. The fourth generation programs came to solve this shortcoming and improve the prediction accuracy. They include GENSCAN [18] and AUGUSTUS[19].

Gene prediction methods rely on exploiting two types of gene information: content and signal. Contents refer to variable-length features such as exons or introns. On the other hand, signals are local sites such as splice sites, start and stop codons, branch points, promoters and terminators polyadenylation sites, ribosomal binding sites and transcription binding sites. Accordingly, Haussler [21] classified gene prediction methods into three categories: content sensors, signal sensors and integrated methods. Content sensors are methods that predict coding and non coding regions. Signal sensors refer to methods that try to detect the presence of functional sites. Integrated gene finding methods combine content and signal sensors in order to predict complete gene structure.

Mathe et al. [3] divided gene finding approaches into finding the evidence for a gene and combining the evidence in order to predict gene structure. Fig. 1 depicts Gene Finding Approachs. Content sensors and signal sensors are used to look for the evidence of a gene. Content sensors are either *extrinsic* or *intrinsic* [3]. In extrinsic content sensors, local alignment methods such as Smith-Waterman, BLAST and FASTA are used to detect similarity between a sequence and DNA or protein sequence in a database. This approach is based on observing that exons are more conserved that introns and intergenic regions. Three types of sequences may be used in such case: protein sequences, ESTs, or genomic DNA. One limitation in ETS-based similarity search is that only small parts of a gene correspond to ESTs which makes it difficult to predict the complete gene structure [1]. The strength of this similarity-based method lies in fact that prediction is based on accumulated annotated sequences. The presence of a gene can be detected even with a single match. However, this method is highly dependent on the content of the database. The database may contain poor quality sequences or it may not have sequences similar to the query sequence. Moreover, only half of the genes being discovered are significantly homologous to database sequences.

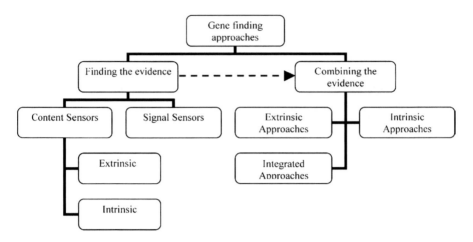

Fig. 1. Gene Finding Approachs [4]

Intrinsic content sensors use different measures in order to classify a region as protein coding. In protein coding regions nucleotide composition and codon composition is different from non-protein regions. Protein coding regions are (C+G) rich. While non coding regions are more (A+T) rich. Hexamer frequency is higher in protein coding regions than in non-protein coding regions and is the most discriminative feature between coding and non-coding regions. It is one of the main features used in SORFIND [12], Geneview2 [23] and MZEF[24]. Statistical models such as HMM and ANN can be used to derive intrinsic features.

Signal sensors try to predict the presence of functional sites. The presence of functional sites can be detected simply by searching using a consensus sequence obtained by multiple sequence alignment. This simple signal prediction method is implemented in SPLIECVIEW [33] and SplicePredictor [34]. Signals may also be represented using positional weight matrices (PWMs) computed from a multiple alignment of functionally related sequences. The PWM indicates the probability of a given base appearing in specific position of the functional sites. Weight matrices sensors return a score that is the sum of individual residue matches over the siteq Algorithms which use PWM rely on previously known motif sequences and assume independence between adjacent nucleotides. PMWs can be regarded as a perceptron which a simple neural network. They can be also defined as one zero order Markov model per position. Dependences between adjacent nucleotides can be captured using higher order Markov models called Weight Array Models (WAMs). To take insertions and deletions into account, one can use Hidden Markov Models (HMM).

In combining the evidence for gene prediction, rather than looking for independent exons, gene prediction programs try to identify the complete gene structure [3]. Using signal sensors, one can detect the presence of translation starts and stops and splice sites. These signals are the most important signs of the presence of genes. According to stop and start codons, exon can be classified as single exon gene which starts with a start codon and ends with a stop codon, an initial exon that begins with a start codon and ends with a donor site, a terminal exon that starts with an acceptor site and ends with a stop codon and an internal exon that starts with an acceptor site and ends with a donor site [6]. Fig. 2 depicts exon classifications. Each of the four exon types present different challenges and the ability of gene prediction programs to predict each type is different. Evidences can be combined to predict the complex structure of a gene. "In theory, each consistent pair of detected signals defines a potential gene region" [3]. If one takes into consideration all possible gene regions to build a gene model, the number of possible gene models grow exponentially with the number of predicted exons.

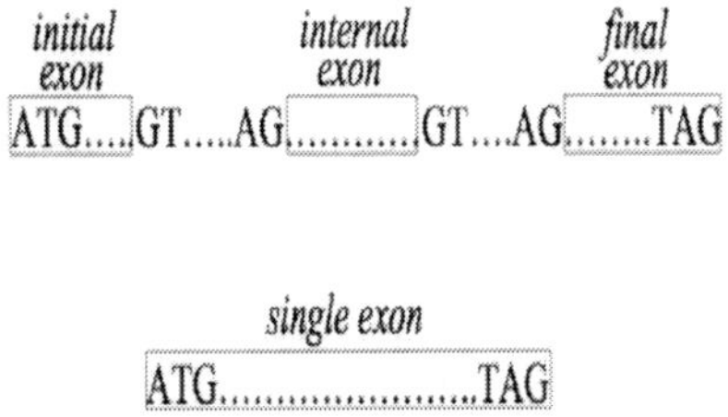

initial   *internal*   *final*
exon   *exon*   *exon*

ATG....GT.....AG............GT....AG........TAG

single exon

ATG.......................TAG

Fig. 2. Exon Classifications [29]

According to [3] the method that try to predict the whole gene structure can be classified into: extrinsic, intrinsic or integrated. The classification is based on the way these methods use to asses contents. Programs that follow the extrinsic approach are based on combining similarity information and signal information. This information is used to refine region boundaries. Such programs inherit the strengths and weaknesses of the sensors used. Intrinsic programs try to locate all gene elements in a genomic sequence. Dynamic programming is used to identify the high scoring gene structures. Integrated methods combine both extrinsic and intrinsic methods.

2.1 Prokaryotic Gene Prediction

Prokaryotic organism, like bacteria and Archaea, are known to have small genomes with size ranging from 0.5 to 10 Mbp. They have high gene density, where coding sequences make more than 90% of the genome. DNA sequences in prokaryotes are transcribed into mRNA and translated to protein without significant modifications. The main characteristic of prokaryotic genes is the absence of introns. Several conserved patterns are found in prokaryotic genes. Gene prediction can make use of gene regulatory sequences. The start codon of most bacterial genes is ATG. But sometimes, GTG and TTG are used as start codons. However the start codon alone is not enough to identify a gene since there could be more than one start codon at the beginning of a frame. The ribosomal binding site which is located directly after the transcription initiation site and before the translation start codon is used to help in locating the start codon. In many bacteria the ribosomal binding site has a consensus motif of AGGAGGT. At the end of protein coding region a stop codon is found. There are three possible stop codons and they are easy to identify.

Conventionally, a prokaryotic gene can be identified manually using the longest open reading frame (ORF) and the major prokaryotic gene signals. One limitation of this approach is the possibility of missing very small genes. Although prokaryotic genomes have small intergenic regions and lack introns, genes may overlap and makes it difficult to predict translation starts [3]. Early gene prediction algorithms relied on examining the nucleotide distribution in DNA sequences. One method observes the composition of the third position in a codon. In coding sequences it is more likely that this position will be G or C. Statistical features of encoding regions can be analyzed using Markov Models and Hidden Markov Models. This approach may be statistically limited when there are no enough hexamers. The solution to such problem is to use an alternative option called interpolated *Markov models* (IMM). A program that finds potential genes in microbial DNA – Bacteria and Archaea is Glimmer [9]. It is based on IMM. Other HMM/IMM programs include ECOPARSE [7], GENMARK [8] and are able to predict genes with good specificity.

2.2 Eukaryotic Gene Prediction

Gene prediction is more difficult in eukaryotes than in prokaryotes. Eukaryotic organisms have large genomes with size falling in the range between 10Mbp and 670Gbp. They have low gene density. For example, only 3% of the human genome actually codes for protein. The structure of eukaryotic genes is more complicated. Many repetitive sequences appear between genes. A eukaryotic gene consists of coding regions called exons and non-coding regions called introns.   Introns are removed by splicing mechanism that results in mRNA. Splice junctions have no strong consensus and it is not clear how exons are identified in long DNA stretches. The main issue in gene prediction is the identification of exons, introns and functional sites. Gene prediction distinguishes between coding and non-coding regions by exploiting many features such as nucleotide composition, codon bias , ployA site signal and hexamer frequency.

3 Computational Approaches for Gene Prediction

In 1984, Staden [31] developed a program with graphic interface that displayed signal information and content measures. From the user interface the user could make exon combinations that likely make a gene. In 1999 a truly automated gene prediction was developed by Fields and Soderlund [32]. GeneModeler combined many content and signal measures. It was able to identify all exons that with a score exceeding a certain threshold and generate all possible genes. Similarly another program, GeneID [14], was developed to for vertebrate sequences. The main limitation of the programs was the extremely large number of possible combinations.

3.1 Dynamic Programming

In order to deal with the extremely large number of possible gene models, dynamic programming methods are used in gene finding applications. In terms of gene finding, grammatical rules of gene structure are used. They provide constraints on the order on which gene segments can appear. For example, an internal intron appears between two exons. Giving a set of rules and scored introns and exons it is possible to scan the sequence once and determine the highest scoring gene structure. This approach although guaranteed to produce the highest scoring gene structure it does not always produce correct predictions. However, researchers can focus on improving the predicted gene structure and improve the score assigned to them. GeneParser [15] is a gene prediction program that employs dynamic programming in order to compute optimal combination of introns and exons.

3.2 Neural Networks

Neural networks are capable of finding complex patterns and relationships between sequence residues. In gene finding a neural network is composed of input, output and hidden layers. The input to the network is a gene sequence. The output is the probability of exon. A neural network is trained using known gene structures. Gene structure is composed of several features: hexamer frequencies splice sites, GC composition. The weights of the ANN are adjusted to recognize different patterns. After training an artificial neural network (ANN) will be able to apply the rules learned in the training phase to recognize unknown sequences. Fig. 3 depicts ANN for Gene Prediction in Eukaryotes.

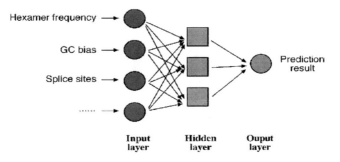

Fig. 3. ANN for Gene Prediction in Eukaryotes [24]

GRAIL is an example of a gene prediction program based on artificial neural networks. It is a web based program that provides analyses of protein coding regions, ploy(A) sites, promoters and gene model construction. GRAIL is available at http://compbio.ornl.gov/Grail-1.3/. GrailEXP is a newer version of GRAIL. It is a software package that predicts exons, genes, promoters, poly(A)s, CpG islands, EST similarities, and repetitive elements within DNA sequence.

Fogel et al. [25] developed an approach that uses genetic algorithms to evolve artificial neural networks (ANNs) for identifying coding and non coding regions in a DNA sequence. A DNA sequence was obtained using a window of 99 nucleotides. The ANN was used to classify the nucleotide in the center of the window as coding or non-coding. The ANN architecture consisted of 9 input nodes corresponding to 9 features, 14 hidden layers and one output node. The output ranged from -1 (non coding) to 1 (coding). The interconnection weights and biases were evolved using GA. This approach is superior to traditional ANN since evolving ANNs can adapt to various inputs with less involvement of the operator.

In [26] [27], ANNs were employed in the prediction of regions that overlap with the first exon of a gene or exists close to it. First, a promoter finder is used to predict transcription start site (TSS). Then another system is used to predict the presence of CpG islands. Then a four-layer ANN is used to predict the presence of a gene based on the predicted TSS and CpG islands.

3.3 Pattern Discrimination Methods

Discrimination methods are statistical methods used to classify sequences based on one or more observed patterns. Some gene prediction use linear discrimination analysis (LDA) or quadratic discrimination analysis (QDA) to improve the accuracy of prediction. Discrimination methods try to define boundaries between coding and no coding sequences based on sequence features. Fig. 4 depicts two discriminant analysis, LDA and QDA. FGENES and MZEF [22] [28] are two program for exon prediction. The programs are based on LDA and QDA respectively. FGENES is available at www.softberry.com.

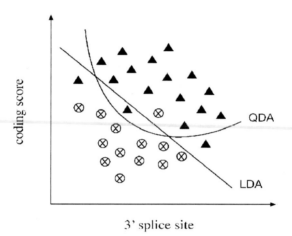

Fig. 4. Two discriminant analysis, LDA and QDA. ▲ coding features; ⊗ noncoding[24]

3.4 Hidden Markov Models

Hidden Markov models are designed to process sequences of data. They are widely used in computational biology for analyzing DNA and protein sequences. They have been already used in multiple sequence alignment, motif finding and protein structure prediction. A Markov model is a one that assumes that the probability that a given character will appear at a specific position depends on the previous k characters. k is called the order of Markov model. The model is defined using conditional probability $P(X/k\ previous\ nucleotides)$ where $X = \{A, T, C, G\}$ for DNA sequences. In order to build a Markov model a set of sequences is required to estimate the probabilities. Using the built Markov model, it is easy to compute the likelihood that a given sequence is generated by this model. A HMM is made of a number of states each of which has two parameters: *symbol-emission probabilities*, and *state-transition probabilities*. Symbol-emission probabilities indicate the probability of emitting each possible symbol from a state. The state-transition probabilities determine the probabilities of moving from one state to the next. Sequences can be generated by beginning at some initial state and moving from state to another according to the state-transition probabilities until an end state is reached. Each state then emits symbols according to that state's emission probability distribution, creating a sequence of residues.

There are three attributes of HMMs that led to their popularity in gene finding. They have intuitive analogy to the gene structure. They have consistent mathematical formalism on which rigorous analysis can be made. There are many algorithms that allow for efficient determination of their properties [6]. According to [4] there is no HMM system that can deal with the size and complexity required in gene finding. A full gene finding HMM model is divided into three smaller models one for each class of DNA nucleotides: exons, introns and integenic regions.

The HMM is first trained using the expectation maximization algorithm. It is used to determine reasonable values for all HMM probabilities. Emission and state transition probabilities are initialized to random values. Sometimes it is good to use prior estimations of those probabilities if available. When it receives a DNA sequences the EM algorithm re-estimate the probabilities. It runs each training sequence through the model and calculates the posterior probability $P(s/\lambda)$ for each sequence s. The $P(s/\lambda)$ are multiplied to produce $P(S/\lambda)$ where S is the set of all sequences. The probabilities are adjusted in order to maximize the value of $P(S/\lambda)$. The procedure continues to run data through the model and adjust probabilities according to $P(S/\lambda)$ until the value is maximized. The EM algorithm is guaranteed to produce the local optimal estimates of all probabilities. After training the HMM it becomes ready to interpret sequences. For this purpose a dynamic programming algorithm called Viterbi algorithm is often used. It can efficiently align any sequence to a trained HMM. It finds the most likely sequence of states of the model for the given sequence.

GENESCAN [18] is an online gene prediction program based on fifth-order HMM. The program allows for predicting the locations and exon-intron structures of genes in genomic sequences from a variety of organisms. It combines hexamer frequencies with coding signals in prediction. Putative exons are assigned a score of being true exons. If the score exceeds 0.5 the prediction is considered reliable. This program has been used in annotating the human genome. It is available at http://genes.mit.edu/GENSCAN.html.

HMMgene available at http://www.cbs.dtu.dk/services/HMMgene/ is another online HMM based gene prediction program. It distinguishes coding regions from non-coding regions using a unique measure called conditional maximum likelihood. If a sequence contains sub-regions that have been already identified as coding regions (by similarity search) the regions are locked as coding regions. Then the HMM prediction is made with bias to locked regions. The program tries to extend locked regions to predict the remaining coding parts of a gene.

4 Promoter Identification

Promoters are DNA sequences found at the 5́ side of a gene. They regulated transcription by binding regulatory proteins to specific binding sites. Protein interactions can either induce or repress the transcription process. Traditionally promoters and regulatory proteins are determined by experimental analysis which is time consuming and laborious. Computational promoter identification is required to replace a great deal of experimental analysis. Identifying promoters is a difficult task. This is mainly due to the shortness of binding sites and their variability. More over these short sequences can be found in any sequence by chance.

In prokaryotes, transcription is initiated by RNA polymerase. The small unit of RNA polymerase recognizes specific sequence upstream of a gene called, promoter, and then allows the larger unit to bind. The promoter includes segments located 35 and 10 base pairs upstream from the transcription start site. For the E. coli the -35 box has a consensus of TTGACA. The -10 box has a consensus of TATAAT. In addition to the RNA polymerase, there are other DNA binding proteins that play a fundamental role in the transcription process. These proteins are called *transcription factors*. They bind to specific DNA sequences either to enhance RNA polymerase or to inhibit its function. The specific DNA sequences to which transcription factors bind are called *regulatory elements*.

In eukaryotes, transcription is more complex since there are three different types of RNA polymerase(*I, II III*). Each polymerase transcribes different set of genes. RAN polymerase II is responsible for transcribing protein coding genes. Unlike prokaryotes where genes many share a common promoter, each eukaryotic gene has its own promoter. In eukaryotes, more transcription factors are required to initiate the transcription process. RNA polymerase requires a dozen or more transcription factors to recognize and bind to the promoter in a specific order. After that it can bind itself to the promoter. Many eukaryotic promoters contain a sequence called TATA box having the consensus TATA(A/T)A. It is located 30 base pairs upstream from transcription start site. Although not always present in promoters, the TATA box is often used as an indicator of presence of a promoter.

5 Computational Approaches for Promoter Identification

According to [24] promoter identification algorithms can be either ab initio based or homology based also called Phylogenetic footprinting. Most algorithms focus on the prediction of RNA polymerase II promoter and its associated regulatory elements.

5.1 Ab Initio-Based Algorithms

Using this type of algorithms, both eukaryotic and prokaryotic promoters can be predicted. The prediction process is based on characteristic patterns for promoters and regulatory elements. The idea of predicting promoters and regulatory sites is based in match consensus sequence patterns. Ab initio algorithms require training and thus trained algorithms are species specific. Using ab initio algorithms it is difficult to predict unknown motifs.

In prokaryotes the most important aspect of promoter prediction is the prediction of the operon structure. Within an operon linked genes share a common promoter located upstream from the first gene. Knowing the operon structure, only prediction of one promoter is required. The most accurate method for operon prediction was developed in 2004 [30] but it is not yet available as a computer program. The most widely used promoter prediction program for prokaryotes is BPROM. BPROM is a bacterial sigma70 promoter recognition program with about 80% accuracy and specificity. It uses LDA with signal and content information. First operon structure is predicted using 100 base pairs as a distance for genes in an operon. Then promoter prediction takes place. The program is available at http://linux1.softberry.com/berry.phtml?topic=bprom&group=programs&subgroup=gfindb

For eukaryotes a unique feature of eukaryotic promoter, CpG islands, is used to increase the prediction accuracy. By predicting the presence of CpG islands near the promoter region overlapping the transcription start site promoters can be traced on the upstream of the island. CpGProD is a program for predicting promoters containing high density of GpC islands in mammalian sequences. CpGProD is available either via a web server, useful for a small dataset, or as a standalone application for a larger dataset. The online version of the program can be found at http://pbil.univ-lyon1.fr/software/cpgprod_query.html .

5.2 Phylogenetic Footprinting Algorithms

Promoter and regulatory elements from closely related organisms are highly conserved. The conservation can be observed at both sequence and element organization levels. This makes it possible to predict promoters based on comparative analysis. Phylogenetic footprinting refers to the identification of functionally important noncoding DNA sequences. These methods can be applied to both eukaryotic and prokaryotic sequences. In this type of comparative analysis, the choice of organisms is very important. If the two organisms are closely related (human and chimpanzee for example) it would be difficult to extract functional elements. On the other hand, if the evolutionary distance between two organism is very long (for example between human and fish) detecting promoters and other elements would be very difficult. A good choice is usually using human and mouse sequences. Using Phylogenetic footprinting algorithms no training of probabilistic models is required, thus this approach is widely applicable. It is also possible to discover new regulatory elements that are common to both organisms. However, this approach puts restrictions on the evolutionary distance among organisms. ConSite is an online Phylogenetic footprinting program. It finds promoters by comparing two sequences using global alignment algorithm. The program is available at http://asp.ii.uib.no:8090/cgi-bin/CONSITE/consite/ . Similar programs include rVISTA at http://rvista.dcode.org/ and PromH(W) from www.softberry.com.

6 Conclusion

Gene prediction is an important problem in bioinformatics. Different approaches have been used to tackle this problem including: dynamic programming, HMM, ANN and GA. In prokaryotes gene prediction is much easier than in eukaryotes. On the nucleotide level more than 90% of nucleotides can be classified as coding or non-coding. But the exact exon boundaries are still very difficult to predict. Some problems in gene finding are still open. According to [1], it is difficult to locate short exons because discriminative characteristics are not apparent in short sequences. The problem is worse when a coding exon is a multiple of three. Missing such exon will not affect the gene assembly. Another problem that has not been solved effectively is the alternative splicing which results in genes having more than one possible exon assembly. Although programs like GENESCAN and MZEF tried to solve the problem by identifying sub-optimal exons, the problem remains open [1]. Moreover, there is no current method that can predict overlapping eukaryotic genes. There prediction of multiple genes in a single sequence is still difficult. With the wide variety of gene prediction programs there is a need for comprehensive criteria for assessing the quality of gene prediction programs.

References

1. Wang, Z., Chen, Y., Li, Y.: A Brief Review of Computational Gene Prediction Methods. Geno. Prot. Bioinfo. 2, 216–221 (2004)
2. Zhang, M.Q.: Computational Prediction of Eukaryotic Protein-Coding Genes. Nature Reviews Genetics 3, 698–709 (2002)
3. Mathe, C., Sagot, M., Schiex, T., Rouze, P.: Current Methods for Gene Prediction, Their Strengths and Weakness. Nucleic Acid Research 30, 4103–4117 (2002)
4. Bandyopadhyay, S., Maulik, U., Roy, D.: Gene Identification: Classical and Computational Intelligence Approaches. IEEE Transactions On Systems, Man, And Cybernetics—Part C: Applications And Reviews 38, 55–68 (2008)
5. Mount, D.W.: Bioinformatics: Genome and Sequence Analysis. Cold Spring Harbor Laboratory Press, New York (2004)
6. Stormo, G.D.: Gene-Finding Approaches in Eukaryotes. Genome Research 10, 394–397 (2000)
7. Krogh, A., Mian, I.S., Haussler, D.: A hidden Markov model that finds genes in E. coli DNA. Nucleic Acids Res. 22, 4768–4778 (1994)
8. Borodovsky, M., McIninch, J.: GENMARK: parallel gene recognition for both DNA strands. Comput. Chem. 17, 123–133 (1993)
9. Salzberg, S.L., Delcher, A.L., Kasif, S., White, O.: Microbial gene identification using interpolated Markov models. Nucleic Acids Res. 26, 544–548 (1998)
10. Uberbacher, E.C., Mural, R.J.: Locating protein-coding regions in human DNA sequences by a multiple sensor-neural network approach. Proc. Natl. Acad. Sci. USA 88, 11261–11265 (1991)
11. Fickett, J.W.: Recognition of protein coding regions in DNA sequences. Nucleic Acids Res. 10, 5303–5318 (1982)
12. Hutchinson, G.B., Hayden, M.R.: The prediction of exons through an analysis of spliceable open reading frames. Nucleic Acids Res. 20, 3453–3462 (1992)
13. Thomas, A., Skolnick, M.H.: A probabilistic model for detecting coding regions in DNA sequences. IMA J. Math. Appl. Med. Biol. 11, 149–160 (1994)
14. Guigo, R., Knudsen, S., Drake, N., Smith, T.: Prediction of gene structure. J. Mol. Biol. 226, 141–157 (1992)
15. Snyder, E.E., Stormo, G.D.: Identification of coding regions in genomic DNA sequences. J. Mol. Biol. 248, 1–18 (1995)
16. Dong, S., Searls, D.B.: Gene structure pre-diction by linguistic methods. Genomics 23, 540–551 (1994)

17. Solovyev, V.V., Salamov, A.A., Lawrence, C.B.: Predicting internal exons by oligonucleotide composition and discriminate analysis of spliceable open reading frames. Nucleic Acids Res. 22, 5156–5163 (1994)
18. Burge, C., Karlin, S.: Prediction of Complete Gene Structure in Human Genomic DNA. J. Mol. Biol. 268, 78–94 (1997)
19. Stanke, M., Waack, S.: Gene Prediction With A Hidden Markov Model and A New Intron Submodel. Bioinformatics 19, 215–225 (2003)
20. Burge, C., Karlin, S.: Finding the Genes in Genomic DNA. Curr. Opin. Struct. Biol. 8, 346–354 (1998)
21. Haussler, D.: Computational Genefinding. Trends Biochem. Sci., 12–15 (1998)
22. Zhang, M.Q.: Identifcation of protein coding regions in the human genome by quadratic discriminate analysis. Proc. Natl. Acad. Sci. USA 94, 565–568 (1997)
23. Milanesi, L., Kolchanov, N.A., Rogozin, I.B., Ischenko, I.V., Kel, A.E., Orlov, Y.L., Ponomarenko, M.P., Vezzoni, P.: GenView: a computing tool for protein-coding regions prediction in nucleotide sequences. In: Second International Conference on Bioinformatics, Supercomputing and Complex Genome Analysis, pp. 573–588. World Scientific Publishing, Singapore (1993)
24. Xiong, J.: Essential Bioinformatics. Cambridge University Press, New York (2006)
25. Fogel, D.B., Chellapilla, K., Fogel, D.B.: Identification of Coding Regions in DNA Sequences Using Evolved Nueral Networks. In: Fogel, G.B., Corne, D.W. (eds.) Evolutionary Computation is Bioinformatics, pp. 195–218. Morgan Kaufmann, USA (2003)
26. Bajic, V.B., Seah, S.H.: Dragon gene start finder: An advanced system for finding approximate locations of the start of gene transcriptional units. Genome Res. 13, 1923–1929 (2003)
27. Bajic, V.B., Seah, S.H.: Dragon gene start finder identifies approximate locations of the 5' ends of genes. Nucleic Acids Res. 31, 3560–3563 (2003)
28. http://www.cshl.edu/OTT/html/mzef.html
29. http://www.geneprediction.org/book/overview.pdf
30. Wang, L., Trawick, J.D., Yamamoto, R., Zamudio, C.: Genome-Wide Operon Prediction in Staphylococcus Aureus. Nucleic Acids Res. 32, 3689–3702 (2004)
31. Staden, R.: Graphic Methods to Determine the Function of Nucleic Acid Sequences. Nucleic Acids Research, 521–538 (1984)
32. Fields, C.A., Soderlund, C.A.: Gm a practical tool for automating DNA Sequence Analysis. Comput. Appl. Biosci. 6, 263–270 (1990)
33. Rogozin, I.B., Milanesi, L.: Analysis of Donor Splice Signals in Different Organisms. J. Mol. Evol. 45, 50–59 (1997)
34. Kleffe, J., Hermann, K., Vahrson, W., Wittig, B., Brendel, V.: Logitlinear Models for the Prediction of Splice Sites in Plant pre-mRNA Sequences. Nucleic Acid Research 24, 4709–4718 (1996)

Retinal Feature-Based Registration Schema

Heba M. Taha[1], Nashwa El-Bendary[2], Aboul Ella Hassanien[1],
Yehia Badr[3], and Vaclav Snasel[4]

[1] Faculty of Computers and Information, Cairo University,
5 Ahmed Zewal St., Orman, Giza, Egypt
heba_memy@hotmail.com, aboitcairo@gmail.com
[2] Arab Academy for Science,Technology, and Maritime Transport,
23 Dr. ElSobki St., Dokki, 12311, Giza, Egypt
nashwa_m@aast.edu
[3] National Institute of Laser Enhanced Sciences, Cairo University,
Natio Sudan St., Mohandseen, 12613, Giza, Egypt
ybadr@niles.edu.eg
[4] Faculty of Electrical Engendering and Computer Science,
VSB-Technical University of Ostrava,
17. listopadu 15, 708 33 Ostrava-Poruba, Czech Republic
vaclav.snasel@vsb.cz

Abstract. This paper presents a feature-based retinal image registration schema. A structural feature, namely, bifurcation structure, has been used for the proposed feature-based registration schema. The bifurcation structure is composed of a master bifurcation point and its three connected neighbors. The characteristic vector of each bifurcation structure consists of the normalized branching angle and length, which is invariant against translation, rotation, scaling, and even modest distortion. The proposed schema is composed of five fundamental phases, namely, input retinal images pre-processing, vascular network detection, noise removal, bifurcation points detection in vascular networks, and bifurcation points matching in pairs of retinal images. The effectiveness of the proposed schema is demonstrated by the experiments with 12 pairs retinal images collected from clinical patients. The registration is carried out through optimizing a certain similarity function, namely, normalized correlation of images. It has been observed that the proposed schema has achieved good performance accuracy.

Keywords: Retinal image, Bifurcation structure, Image registration, Feature extraction, Normalized correlation (NCOR).

1 Introduction

A great number of methods have been developed for helping ophthalmologists to diagnose various diseases. Fundus camera imaging of the retina is widely used to document ophthalmologic disorders including diabetic retinopathy, glaucoma, and age-related macular degeneration [1], [2].

Fast and accurate image registration techniques become increasingly important in clinical human retina diseases diagnosis and treatment [3], however, it still a

A. Abd Manaf et al. (Eds.): ICIEIS 2011, Part II, CCIS 252, pp. 26–36, 2011.
© Springer-Verlag Berlin Heidelberg 2011

challenging task due to the great content, complexity, and low image quality of the unhealthy retina [4].

Another fundamental reason, which counts retinal images registration as a challenging problem [5], is that the retina is a curved surface; nonlinear deformation may occur when using a weak-perspective camera. So, multiple images are to be joined together using image registration technique to form a mixture with a larger field of view. A variety of methods for retinal image registration have been proposed, but evaluating such methods objectively is difficult due to the lack of a reference standard for the true alignment of the individual images that make up the mixture.

In view of this, a new structural feature has been presented for feature-based retinal image registration. Different from point-matching techniques, the proposed schema in this paper applies a structure-matching approach.

This paper presents a retinal feature-based registration schema. The rest of this paper is organized as follows. Section 2 introduces the proposed retinal registration schema and its phases. Experiments and results are presented in section 3. Finally, Section 4 addresses conclusions and discusses future work.

2   Retinal Feature-Based Registration Schema

The proposed schema is composed of five phases. (1) Pre-processing that means manipulating each retinal image in such way that it later performs the basic standards (dimensions of the image, color, and illumination) for the following processing. The result is a grayscale image with improved contrast. (2) Vascular network detection that means detecting the vascular network on retina images by implementing a highpass Gaussian filter, which attenuates low frequencies while sharpening high frequencies. (3) Noise removal that means removing the produced noise from previous processes through finding the skeleton of the segmented image, then implementing size thresholding to delete small objects from the image. Afterward, removing noise outside the perimeter with a mask filter that hard-thresholding the initial image so that every non-zero value becomes white. (4) Bifurcation points detection that means shrinking retina vessel tree images, which have been produced from previous steps, for each pair of images, in order to detect bifurcation points. Bifurcation points are prominent visual features that can be recognized by 3 surrounding branches. And (5) bifurcation points matching that means associating features across each pair of images through using the eigen-decomposition methods that exploit spatial relations between features with the aid of the coordinate proximity matrices in order to verify the initial correspondence.

Figure 1 illustrates the general structure of the proposed retinal feature-based registration schema.

2.1   Pre-processing

Before we enter the dominant processing stages, we manipulate a retinal image in such way that it later performs the basic standards for the following processing. The standards that should be fulfilled are the dimensions of the image, color and the illumination standard. The result is a grayscale image with improved contrast.

To overcome the problem of a poor intensity image we normalize the image to can rescaling or offsetting the data as necessary.

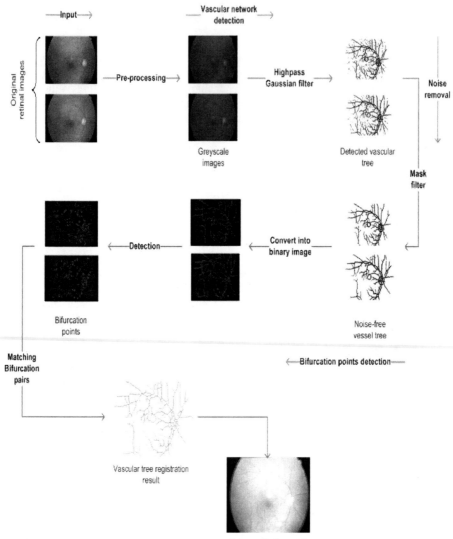

Fig. 1. Retinal feature-based registration schema architecture

2.2   Vascular Network Detection

To detect the vascular network on the retina images, the system implements a highpass Gaussian filter which attenuates low frequencies while sharpening high [5]. The form of a highpass Gaussian filter in two dimensions is given by equation (1).

$$H(u,v) = 1 - e^{-D^2(u,v)/2D_0^2} \tag{1}$$

Where D is the distance between the points u and v.

After implementing the median and the highpass Gaussian filters, image segmentation algorithm takes part. Pixels were removed to generate an object without holes in order to shrink the vessel tree in the retinal image to a minimally connected stroke. The thresholding value is calculated using equation (2).

$$thresh = median(gs) - a \cdot std(gs) \qquad (2)$$

Where 'gs' denotes the statistical median of the image, 'std' is the standard deviation, and 'a' is a multiplier that is adjusted through observation of the sample behavior. It can be noticed that apart from the vascular network there are little objects that add noise to the image. To overcome the problem, length filtering [5] has to be applied.

2.3 Noise Removal

To remove the produced noise from previous processes the system implements several techniques. First of all, the objects are now described by thin lines and their size (in pixels) has reduced. The algorithm implements size thresholding to delete small objects from the image. After this phase noise outside the perimeter has to be removed with a mask filter, so, the skeleton of the segmented image has resulted. This mask has been created by hard-thresholding the initial image so that every non-zero value becomes white.

2.4 Bifurcation Points Detection

This phase is applied for the vascular network in order to detect bifurcation points of each pair of images, which has been produced from previous noise removal phase. Bifurcation points are prominent visual features and can be recognized by 3 surrounding branches [6]. The bifurcation point can be detected if 3 neighbors in 3*3 windows belongs the foreground. To detect these points each blood vessel image has to be converted into a binary image. Then, indexes of each binary image should have at least 3 neighbors. After that, each point has to be linked with its neighbors and select the points with 3 different links that are not in same path.

2.5 Bifurcation Points Matching

Associating features across two images is critical to image registration, where features may be matched with one-, none-, or multiple-correspondence. To verify and correct the initial correspondence, the eigen-decomposition methods exploit spatial relations between features with the aid of the coordinate proximity matrices. Here, an efficient correspondence verification scheme is developed.

It is well known that the minimum points requirement for linear transformation is 2 pairs, and affined is 3 pairs. Therefore, one matched bifurcation structure pair is enough to estimate the parameters of low-order transformation model for it provide 4 point pairs. The correspondence refinement and transformation estimation can be simultaneously implemented by equation (3).

$$e_{(pq,mn)} = d\left(M(x_p,y_q),N(x_m,y_n)\right) \qquad (3)$$

In contrast to 3 angles of single bifurcation point, the characteristic vector for the proposed bifurcation structure contains ordered length and angle.

3 Experimental Results

The proposed retinal registration schema is composed of five fundamental phases, namely, input retinal images pre-processing, vascular network detection, noise removal, bifurcation points detection in vascular networks, and bifurcation points matching in pairs of retinal images.

All the results reported in this paper were obtained on a PC with Windows 7 Home Premium, Pentium 4, CPU 3.80GHz, using MATLAB version 7.5.5 [7] with the Digital Image Processing Toolbox. The computational time of the whole process of the proposed schema takes approximately 10 seconds for the comparison of two retinal images. The images are of size 519x346. The coverage percentage (the numerical criterion of identification process) is close to 90% for retinal images taken from the same eye and around 10% for images taken from different eyes.

Figure 2 shows the retinal images resulted from the pre-processing phase, while figure 3 shows the vascular network detection using Gaussian filter for input images of figures 2 (a) and 2 (b), respectively. Figure 4 shows the results of thresholding for images of figure 3. Figure 5 presents results of noise removal for images in figure 4. Figure 6 shows bifurcation points detection from figure 5. Figures 7 and 8 show the registered vascular network and registered retinal image, respectively.

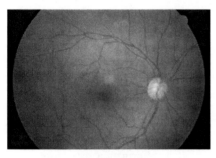

(a) Input image (1)

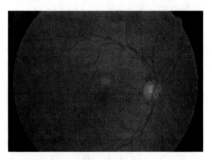

(c) Resulted image of (a)

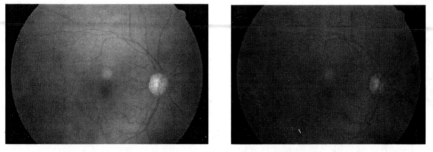

(b) Input image (2)

(d) Resulted image of (b)

Fig. 2. Results of pre-processing phase

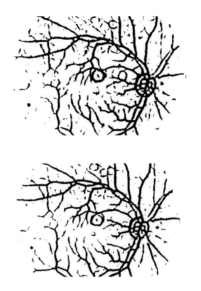

Fig. 3. Vascular network detection using Gaussian filter for input images of figures 2 (a) and 2 (b), respectively

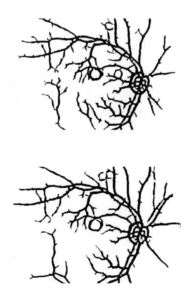

Fig. 4. Results of thresholding for images of figure 3

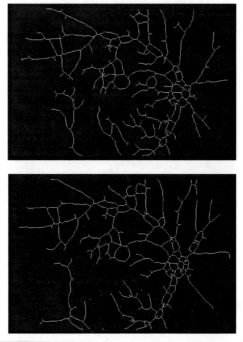

Fig. 5. Results of noise removal for images in figure 4

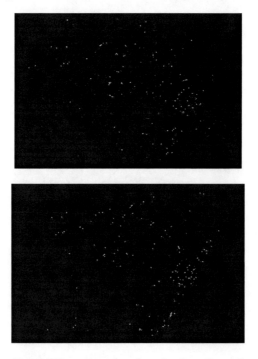

Fig. 6. Bifurcation points detection from figure 5

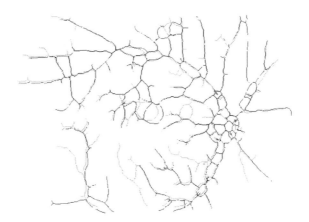

Fig. 7. Registered vascular network

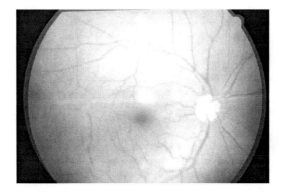

Fig. 8. Registered retinal image

The proposed retinal registration schema is evaluated using the Normalized Correlation (NCOR) [8], [9] assessment criteria. NCOR has been commonly used as a metric to evaluate the degree of similarity (or dissimilarity) between two compared images.

Normalized Correlation (NCOR) is defined as shown in equation (4):

$$\text{NCOR}\,[R, T] = \frac{\sum\limits_{x} R(x) \cdot T(x)}{\sqrt{\sum\limits_{x} R(x)^2 \cdot \sum\limits_{x} T(x)^2}}. \tag{4}$$

Where R stands for reference image, T for template image and x for two related points in R and T and this measure increases with the degree of similarity [9].

The performance of the proposed registration schema, described using the normalized correlation metric, is visually demonstrated in Figure 9. Table 1 summarizes the comparative experiment results (max. peak of NCOR) of twelve template retinal images with a reference retinal image. According to the results presented in table 1, it has been observed that most of the results for maximum peak of the NCOR, of the reference image and all template images, are close to 100%, which means that the registration accuracy of the proposed retinal registration schema is accepted.

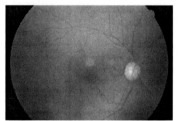

Ref. image

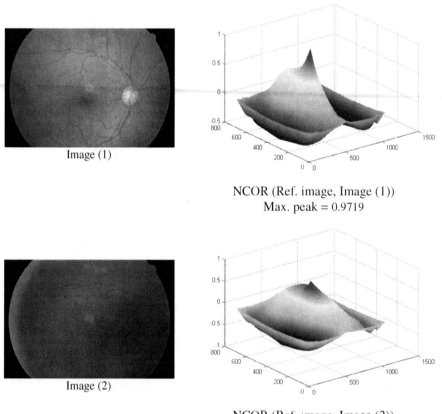

Image (1)

NCOR (Ref. image, Image (1))
Max. peak = 0.9719

Image (2)

NCOR (Ref. image, Image (2))
Max. peak = 0.7760

Fig. 9. Some image registration results for the maximum peak of the NCOR of reference image and template images

Table 1. The comparative experiment results (max. peak of NCOR) of twelve template retinal images

Registering image	Max. peak (NCOR)
Image (1)	0.9719
Image (2)	0.7760
Image (3)	0.9388
Image (4)	0.9287
Image (5)	0.7962
Image (6)	0.8522
Image (7)	0.7888
Image (8)	0.8723
Image (9)	0.8403
Image (10)	0.8021
Image (11)	0.8970
Image (12)	0.9135

4 Conclusions and Future Work

This paper presents a vascular network detection and feature-based retinal image registration schema based on bifurcation structure matching. The bifurcation structure is composed of a master bifurcation point and its three connected neighbors. Bifurcation structure is invariant against translation, rotation, scaling, and even modest distortion. It can deal with the registration of retinal images when vascular-like pattern is identifiable, even partially. The simplicity and efficiency of the proposed schema enable it to be willingly applied alone or incorporated with other existing systems in order to formulate hybrid or hierarchy schemes. It has been observed that the proposed schema has achieved good performance accuracy.

In the future work we want to improve the thresholding techniques and the vascular network detection phase. Also, a graph-based algorithm framework could be implemented for retinal image registration through utilizing hierarchical retinal features.

References

1. El-Bendary, N., Hassanien, A.E., Corchado, E., Berwick, R.C.: ARIAS: Automated Retinal Image Analysis System. In: Corchado, E., Snášel, V., Sedano, J., Hassanien, A.E., Calvo, J.L., Ślęzak, D. (eds.) SOCO 2011. AISC, vol. 87, pp. 67–76. Springer, Heidelberg (2011)
2. Lee, S., Reinhardt, J.M., Abramoff, M.D.: Validation of Retinal Image Registration Algorithms by a Projective Imaging Distortion Model. In: Proc. IEEE Eng. Med. Biol. Soc., vol. 1, pp. 6471–6474 (2007)
3. Deng, K., Tian, J., Zheng, J., Zhang, X., Dai, X., Xu, M.: Retinal Fundus Image Registration via Vascular Structure Graph Matching. International Journal of Biomedical Imaging, vol. 2010, Article ID 906067, 13 pages (2010)
4. Zheng, J., Tian, J., Dai, Y., Deng, K., Chen, J.: Retinal Image Registration Based on Salient Feature Regions. In: The IEEE International Conference of Engineering in Medicine and Biology Society 2009, Minneapolis, Minnesota, USA, September 2-6 (2009)

5. Petsatodis, T., Diamantis, A., Syrcos, G.P.: A Complete Algorithm for Automatic Human Recognition based on Retina Vascular Network Characteristics. In: 1st International Scientific Conference e RA, Tripolis, Greece, pp. 41–46 (2004)
6. Chen, L., Zhang, X.L.: Feature-based Image Registration Using Bifurcation Structures. Matlab Central (2009)
7. Image Processing Toolbox (MATLAB), http://www.mathworks.com
8. Tsai, D., Lin, C.: Fast Normalized Cross Correlation for Defect Detection. Pattern Recognition Letters, 2625–2631 (2003)
9. Yoo, T.: Insight into images: Principles and Practice for Segmentation, Registration and Image Analysis. AK Peters Ltd. (2004)

Exploring Particle-Based Caricature Generations

Somnuk Phon-Amnuaisuk

Perceptions and Simulation of Intelligent Behaviours,
Universiti Tunku Abdul Rahman, Petaling Jaya, Malaysia
`somnuk@utar.edu.my`

Abstract. Computer generated caricatures are commonly created using either line drawing or image warping technique. Two main paradigms employed to automate the caricature generation process are variance exaggeration which exaggerates facial components that deviate from norms; and example-based generation which exaggerates facial components according to provided templates. In this paper, we explore a novel application of an interactive particle-based technique for generating a caricature of a given face. This does not require prior examples but relies on users' feedback to explore the caricature face space. In this approach, facial feature points are represented as particles and their movements are used to incrementally warp a given face until the desired exaggerations are achieved. We have shown that the proposed approach could successfully provide an interactive means for generating good quality facial caricatures.

Keywords: Automated caricature generation, Particle-based system.

1   Background

The term *particle* refers to a small discrete object. It has been used to describe different computing paradigms, for example, the Particle Swarm Optimisation (PSO) system and a physics model of particles in computer graphics. PSO is attributed to Kennedy and Eberhart [5], and has been successfully employed to solve optimisation problem. In this paradigm, each particle in a swarm is encoded as a plausible solution and each particle moves over the search space in search for a better solution. The basic mechanisms of PSO are based on the exploitation of the swarm's group knowledge and of each individual particle's personal knowledge. It is a heuristic search which does not rely on the guidance gradient of the search landscape.

In this paper, we explore the warping technique to automate the generation of a caricature from a given celebrity face. In brief, the given face is marked with coordinates corresponding to predefined points (face model). The face model comprises of 84 points which represent 84 particles, these particles move in a 2D space and the particles' positions are used to warp the image. However, at each time step, there could be many possible next states from the current state (i.e., the particles could move to many different combinations). Here, the system explores the caricature face space in a depth first search fashion, by generating

A. Abd Manaf et al. (Eds.): ICIEIS 2011, Part II, CCIS 252, pp. 37–46, 2011.

six possible next states (the branching factor is arbitrarily decided to be six here). The user interactively identifies one or more faces that she likes and the system generates a new six possible next states from the chosen image (or the average of the chosen images). The user terminates the generation process when the desired caricature is produced. Details of this implementation will be discussed in section 3.

This paper is organised into the following sections. Section 2 gives an overview of related works. Section 3 discusses our proposed concept and gives the details of the techniques behind it. Section 4 provides the output of the proposed apprach. Finally, the conclusion and further research are presented in section 5.

2   Literature Review

In principle, caricatures express concepts rather than physical similarities. The figure of *Venus of Willendorf* (see Figure 1, left)[1] could be argued as a carica-ture of a woman with an exaggeration to her fertility. Similarly, the concept of femininity is exaggerated in the sculpture of the Hindu goddess named *Parvathi* (see Figure 1, middle). The figure exaggerates her femininity through the pos-ture and body characteristics such as a narrow waist, full breasts, and a wide hip. This kind of conceptual exaggeration is universal in most cultures, if not all. It is suggested by Ramachandran [13] that this is the *peak shift* effect in which the brain favours an exaggerated concept more than a non-exaggerated version.

The art of facial caricature is a much-neglected gem despite the fact that expressing a concept in an exaggerated manner is common in all communica-tion modes. Caricaturists do not really receive recognition in the art scene. Your colleague may raise an eyebrow if you want to touch this area. Nevertheless, the science of caricature has received some attention from the researchers in the facial recognition community in recent years. From the literature, an article about *Rules for Drawing Caricatures* was published in 1791 by Francis Grose (see discussion in [2]). It is generally accepted that caricatures are exaggerations of distinct features. There are a few accepted scientific hypotheses that explain why a distorted image could still be recognised. Perkins suggests that a cari-cature is recognised because we recognise *selected attributes* that are common between the caricature and the real person. The other common explanation of caricatures is that a successful caricature exaggerates features that are different from the norm features. Ramachandran explains that this results from the peak shift effect hypothesis [13]. This school of thought is also backed up by Leopold et al.'s findings that the face-recognizing neurons seem to strongly respond to the caricature version of the same faces [7]. At present, we still do not fully understand this issue. An understanding of the cognitive process behind facial recognition is important and could be beneficial to many applications, e.g., art and entertainment, face recognition, and facial animation. It is interesting to note that the area of facial animation is closely related to caricature generation in terms of representation and processing techniques.

---

[1] All images are retrieved from http://en.wikpedia.org

Fig. 1. Exaggerating concepts, (left) Venus of Willendorf: the concept of fertility is exaggerated using oversized breasts and abdomen; (middle) Parvati: her femininity is exaggerated through her posture and properties such as a narrow waist and full breasts; (right) Ancient Pompeiian graffiti caricature of a politician: take note of the exaggerated nose and chin

Brennan [2] was one of the pioneers who applied the computer to generate caricatures. Her methodology was based on interactive amplification of the features that were different from the averaged norms. The *caricature generator* program altered the line drawing of a given face by exaggerating the metric differences between the subject and the prototype norm. In her experiments, the averaged norms were taken from a group of male population from Aspen, Colorado, USA., as well as some accepted anatomical ideals after Leonardo da Vinci. It is interesting to note that she also reported that good caricature results frequently came from *any two pictures* which *just seem different* e.g., Elizabeth Taylor and John F. Kennedy in her experiment [2].

Caricature generation method by Brennan could be described as semi-automated. Users' control played a crucial role in controlling the caricature generation process. In order to automate the process, the system must possess knowledge about the common features on a face and how to exaggerate those features. The application of artificial intelligence (AI) techniques in line drawing was investigated in Librande's example-based character drawing [10], where examples of drawings were analysed and corresponding interpolation functions were learned. The generation of line drawing caricatures was also investigated in PICASSO [6] and implemented in a robot that would draw the face of a customer into a *shrimp rice cracker* [15]. Another work that followed the line drawing approach was the facial sketch from Chen et al. [3]. Later, Liang et al. [8] expanded facial sketch techniques in [3] to line-drawing caricatures.

A deformation-based approach is another popular approach employed to generate caricatures. Morphing/warping was employed by Akleman [1]. Note that this is from a different perspective as compared to Brennan's line drawing approach, though the deformation was also based on moving reference points in the 2D space. Akleman's approach to caricature generation was semi-automated where user interactions were very important in the generation process.

The process employed in computer generated caricatures above share the same tactic. In essence, the caricature was generated by exaggerating the attributes that deviated from the prototypes. We have seen two main computer generated caricature genre: (i) line drawing; and (ii) pixels morphing. Our work in this report explores an interactive particle-based approach which could be described as semi-automated pixels morphing. The details of the system are introduced in the next section.

3   An Interactive Particle-Based Caricature Generation

It is our interest here to explore the interactive caricature generation of a given face. Here, the face is modified by the particle movements where each particle represents a reference point in a *facial feature model* (will be discussed later in this section). Our approach interactively and incrementally modifies the image using the information from the particles' movements. In each step, a user selects one or more caricatures produced by the system. If more than one images are selected, the average of all the images will be used. The position and velocity of the particles would be employed in the next iteration. This can be seen as a depth-first search strategy with a modified tree expansion tactic since the information from different child nodes are allowed to be combined before branching onto the next level. Next, the two important theoretical backgrounds in this study are discussed: (i) the representation of a facial feature model using particles, and (ii) the warping of an image when the particles move.

3.1   Representing a Face Model Using Particles

MPEG4 has a standardised facial feature points with the aim to support facial animation with a low bit rate. MPEG4 defines 84 facial feature points in its facial model as well as face animation parameters. Instead of sending the whole animation frame by frame, only control information to instruct facial model would be sent over the network. Although MPEG4 has suggested facial feature points in its specification, apparently, it is not adopted in most caricature generation works. Researchers usually devise their own face model where variations in reference feature points in their models are common. This is understandable. Although caricature generation and facial animation share many common grounds, they are not exactly the same. In this work, we also propose our own facial model. The design of the face model is to support facial deformation. This involves the deformation of components such as mouth, nose, eyes, eyebrows, etc. Figure 2 displays the facial feature points in our face model. The deformation of a face could be obtained by warping the image from the current facial points to new facial points.

In this paper, the concept of particles is applied to our problem domain. The coordinates in a 2D space are represented as particles. Let a vector of particles $\mathbf{f} = (x_{11}, ..., x_{ij})$ represents a facial model where feature points $x_{ij} \in \mathcal{R}$ denotes

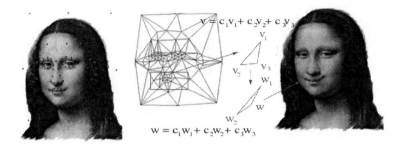

Fig. 2. A conceptual illustration showing that particles movements alter each triangular mesh and this results in a warped image. From left to right: (i) Mona Lisa's face, red dots (gray in BW) show corresponding particle positions on her face; (ii) Triangular mesh is formed using the particles' positions as vertices; and (iii) Her facial features are interactively warped as particles traverse the facial space. In this example, she has a bigger smile.

the position of particle i in a j dimension. Particles at time point t, $\mathbf{f}(t)$ could be transformed across time to $t+1$ as a new vector $\mathbf{f}(t+1)$ as follow:

$$x_{ij}(t+1) = x_{ij}(t) + v_{ij}(t+1)$$

where v_{ij} is the velocity of particle i in dimension j.

$$v_{ij}(t+1) = wv_{ij}(t) + c_1 r_{1j}(p_{ij}(t) - x_{ij}(t)) + c_2 r_{2j}(g_{ij}(t) - x_{ij}(t))$$

where w is the inertia weight that seeds particular movement units (e.g., eyes, nose, mouth, etc). The v_{ij} is the velocity of a particle i in a j dimension. The $c_1 r_{1j}$ and $c_2 r_{2j}$ are weight parameters that combine the influence of the local best position p_{ij}, global best position g_{ij} and the current velocity to determine the velocities of the particles in the next step.

3.2   Generating Caricature Using Particles' Positions:

Allowing particles to move freely in a 2D space would generate all kinds of facial deformations. Unfortunately, many of the deformations obtained in this way would be useless. It is likely that some kind of control mechanisms must be incorporated to control particle movements. In our implementation, 48 primitive movements are created as seed-movements for *face shape, eyes, eye brown, nose*, and *lips*. These seed movements are either *expanding/shrinking* particles' movement from a reference point, or *vertically/horizontally* push/pull particles in certain degrees and directions. As it is our interest to explore interactive feedback from users, these seeds provide search-guides. During the caricature generation process, movements of the particles derived from different primitive seed-movements could be combined and this helps generate diversity while curbing exploration at the same time. Figure 3 provides some examples of the seeding and Table 1 shows the flow of the caricature generation process.

Fig. 3. Examples of the applications of seed-movements to face shape, mouth and eyes (column two, three and four respectively). The original image marked with particles' positions is shown on the left top row.

Table 1. Caricature Generation

Outline of important conceptual steps
// create a particle vector **f** for an input image
f ← initParticle(image);
0 ← t;
while not Termination_Criterion(**f**(t)) **do**
// determine particles velocity (see sub-section 3.1)
$\mathbf{v}_{pso}$ ← interactiveSession(**f**(t));
// generate six variations of a given face based on PSO and primitive
// seed movements
f(t)[6] ← applyPSO(**f**(t), $\mathbf{v}_{seed}$);
// a user guides the search by choosing one or more preferred images
f(t) ← interactiveSession(**f**(t + 1)[6]);
t ← t + 1;
endwhile

Warping Techniques. In this paper, the warping technique is used to deform facial components to generate the caricature of a given image. Firstly, a triangular mesh is formed using the coordinates from the facial feature points. For any triangle in the mesh, three vertices $\mathbf{u}_1, \mathbf{u}_2, \mathbf{u}_3$ of an original triangle could be warped to a new triangle formed by the vertices $\mathbf{w}_1, \mathbf{w}_2, \mathbf{w}_3$ such that

$$\mathbf{w}_i = M\mathbf{u}_i + \mathbf{b}$$

where M is a 2×2 matrix and $\mathbf{b}$ is a vector. It is known that there is a uniquely affine transformation that maps $\mathbf{u}_1, \mathbf{u}_2, \mathbf{u}_3$ to $\mathbf{w}_1, \mathbf{w}_2, \mathbf{w}_3$ respectively and any point $\mathbf{u}$ in the triangle formed by $\mathbf{u}_1, \mathbf{u}_2, \mathbf{u}_3$ would map to a point $\mathbf{w}$ in the triangle formed by $\mathbf{w}_1, \mathbf{w}_2, \mathbf{w}_3$ if $\mathbf{u} = c_1\mathbf{u_1} + c_2\mathbf{u_2} + c_3\mathbf{3}$, $\mathbf{w} = c_1\mathbf{w}_1 + c_2\mathbf{w}_2 + c_3\mathbf{w}_3$ and $c_1 + c_2 + c_3 = 1$.

4   Results and Discussion

This subsection provides an overview of the caricature generation process in our approach. We work with the famous Mona Lisa face in this example. The aim of this exercise is to give readers a walk through a typical generation process in our approach.

1. The first step is to prepare an input image. All images used are downloaded from public domains via Google. The position of particles are manually marked to each face.
2. For each iteration the particles move to new points as described in subsection 3.1. In this implementation, the branching factor is set at six.
3. Users then select one or more generated caricatures and further explore the search space in that direction. If more than one caricatures are selected, then the positions and the velocities of the particles would be averaged and the search would continue from the averaged output.
4. Although the branching factor is fixed at six, users could repeatedly generate various output before making their choices.
5. The process continues until the desired caricature effects are achieved.

Figure 4 shows examples of various smiles generated by the system. Figure 5 shows the caricature of sixteen celebrities. As the evaluation function is subjective, we provide an insight on how the search space is guided in generating these output. Our strategy used in creating these caricatures could be summarised in the following simple heuristics: (i) examine the face and think about the impression you have of the face; (ii) exaggerate that part; (iii) modify the neighboring components to agree with the exaggeration you intend to achieve, for example,

Fig. 4. Examples of plausible smiles produced from warping different degrees of particle movements

Fig. 5. Caricature examples produced by our approach. All celebrity faces are retrieved from public domain from the Internet. No special treatment other than removing the background and some smudging on the shirts are applied to the input images.

a bigger smile may go well with slightly bigger nose and slightly smaller eyes. Explore those face space. Repeat steps i, ii, iii until the desired distortion is obtained.

The issue of computational aesthetics in evolutionary art has been addressed by many researchers before [11], [4], [9]. It is a challenge to find features that could capture the aesthetic dimension. Choices of these features, at a fine granularity level, such as sound frequency spectra or histograms of color could throw away many semantics (i.e., semantics could emerge from a hierarchical composition of lower level units). At a coarse granularity such as universal I-V-I progressions in music, or fractal parameters, it could be too high-level and too abstract. For faces, it has been suggested that pleasing faces are those which are symmetrical. Although many males are also attracted to pouty lips and sometimes non-symmetrical female smiles, many pleasing visual experiences do coincide with symmetry. Unfortunately, caricatures are also about distortion. It is difficult to propose an objective fitness functions for the task.

5   Conclusion and Future Work

We have shown that an interactive particle-based approach could be used to generate convincing caricatures. The particles movements in a 2D space are guided by interactive fitness evaluation to create a caricature of a given celebrity face. The particle-based approach supports both the mutation and breeding concepts. Mutation can be seen as particles' movements in the face space and breeding can be seen as the averaged velocity update of many leaf nodes during the search tree expansion step. This guarantees that the particles have a means to explore the face space and useful information could be shared among particles (i.e., good solutions breed). Future work could be extended in the following areas: (i) investigation of the automated aesthetic evaluation criteria, (ii) devising more primitive seed movements to explore various areas of the face space, (iii) breeding inherited facial features from parents, and (iv) animating facial emotional expressions. There are many interesting applications in the emerging creative industries that could benefit from this line of research.

References

1. Akleman, E.: Making Caricatures with Morphing. In: Proceedings of the International Conference on Computer Graphics and Interactive Techniques ACM SIGGRAPH 1997 Visual Proceedings: The Art and Interdisciplinary Programs of SIGGRAPH 1997, Los Angeles, California, United States, p. 145 (1997) ISBN:0-89791-921-1
2. Brennan, S.E.: Caricature Generator: The Dynamic Exaggeration of Faces by Computer. Leonardo 18(3), 170–178 (1985)
3. Chen, H., Xu, Y.Q., Shum, H.Y., Zhu, S.C., Zheng, N.N.: Example-based Facial Sketch Generation with Non-parametric Sampling. In: Proceedings of the Eighth International Conference on Computer Vision (ICCV 2001), Vancouver, Canada, July 7-14, pp. 433–438 (2001)
4. den Heijer, E., Eiben, A.E.: Comparing Aesthetic Measures for Evolutionary Art. In: Proceedings of the 9th European Event on Evolutionary and Biologically Inspired Music, Sound, Art and Design (EvoMusart), EvoApplication 2010, Istanbul, Turkey, April 7-9 (2010)
5. Eberhart, R.C., Kennedy, J.: A New Optimizer using Particle Swarm Theory. In: Proceedings of the Sixth International Symposium on Micromachine and Human Science, Nagoya, Japan, pp. 39–43 (1995)

6. Koshimizu, H., Tominaga, M., Fujiwara, T., Murakami, K.: On KANSEI Facial Image Processing for Computerized Facial Caricaturing System PICASSO. In: Proceedings of 1999 IEEE International Conference on Systems, Man, and Cybernetics, Tokyo, Japan, vol. 6, pp. 294–299 (1999) ISBN: 0-7803-5731-0

7. Leopold, D., Bondar, I., Giese, M.: Norm-based Face Encoding by Single Neurons in the Monkey Inferotemporal Cortex. Nature 442(7102), 572–575 (2006)

8. Liang, L., Chen, H., Xu, Y.Q., Shum, H.Y.: Example-based Caricature Generation with Exaggeration. In: Proceedings of the 10th Pacific Conference on Computer Graphics and Applications, pp. 386–389 (2002)

9. Li, Y., Hu, C.J.: Aesthetic Learning in an Interactive Evolutionary Art System. In: Proceedings of the 9th European Event on Evolutionary and Biologically Inspired Music, Sound, Art and Design (EvoMusart), EvoApplication 2010, Istanbul, Turkey, April 7-9 (2010)

10. Librande, S.E.: Example-based Character Drawing, MSc in Visual Studies Thesis, Massachusetts Institute of Technology. U.S.A.

11. Machado, P., Romero, J., Manaris, B.: Experiments in Computational Aesthetics: An Iterative Approach to Stylistic Change in Evolutionary Art. In: The Art of Artificial Evolution. Natural Computing Series, Part V, pp. 381–415 (2008)

12. Mauro, R., Kubovy, M.: Caricature and Face Recognition. Memory and Cognition 20, 433–440 (1992)

13. Ramachandran, V.S.: A Brief Tour of Human Consciousness. PI Press, New York (2004)

14. Staake, B.: The Complete Book of Caricature. North Light Books, Cincinnati (1991)

15. Tokuda, N., Hoshino, T., Watanabe, T., Funahashi, T., Fujiwara, T., Koshimizu, H.: Facial Caricaturing Robot COOPER Exhibited at EXPO2005 and Its Improvements. In: Proceedings of the 2007 International Conference on Machine Vision Applications (MVA2007 IAPR), Tokyo, Japan, May 16-18, pp. 512–515 (2007)

16. Tversky, B., Baratz, D.: Memory for Faces: Are Caricatures Better than Photographs. Memory & Cognition 13(1), 45–49 (1985)

17. Yang, T.T., Lai, S.H.: A Learning-based System for Generating Exaggerative Caricature from Face Images with Expression. In: Proceedings of the 2010 IEEE International Conference on Acoustics Speech and Signal Processing (ICASSP), Dallas, Texas, March 14-19, pp. 2138–2141 (2010) ISSN: 1520-6149 ISBN: 978-1-4244-4295-9

Towards Automatic Forensic Face Recognition

Tauseef Ali, Luuk Spreeuwers, and Raymond Veldhuis

Faculty of Electrical Engineering, Mathematics and Computer Science,
University of Twente, The Netherlands
{T.ali,L.J.Spreeuwers,R.N.J.Veldhuis}@utwente.nl

Abstract. In this paper we present a methodology and experimental results for evidence evaluation in the context of forensic face recognition. In forensic applications, the matching score (hereafter referred to as similarity score) from a biometric system must be represented as a Likelihood Ratio (LR). In our experiments we consider the face recognition system as a 'black box' and compute LR from similarity scores. The proposed approach is in accordance with the Bayesian framework where the duty of a forensic scientist is to compute LR from biometric evidence which is then incorporated with prior knowledge of the case by the judge or jury. In our experiments we use a total of 2878 images of 100 subjects from two different databases. Our experimental results prove the feasibility of our approach to reach a LR value given an image of a suspect face and questioned face. In addition, we compare the performance of two biometric face recognition systems in forensic casework.

Keywords: LR, Evidence, Similarity score, Bayesian framework.

1 Introduction

Output of a score-based biometric system is not suitable for forensic applications where the objective is to obtain degree of support for one hypothesis (prosecution) against other (defense). This issue is discussed in detail in previous literature on forensic speaker recognition [1-3], forensic voice comparison [4] and some other fields of forensic science such as DNA [5]. Systems using a threshold to decide between two classes are not acceptable in forensic domain [3]. For forensic applications, Bayesian interpretation framework is an agreed upon standard way to report evidence value from a biometric system. However, less effort has been done to utilize this framework in forensic face recognition in contrast to forensic speaker, voice, fingerprints, and DNA etc. There are very few published works [6] which focus on the forensic aspects of face recognition and there is an utmost need for a reliable facial comparison and recognition systems which can assist law enforcement agencies in investigation and whose output can be readily used in judicial system. In [6] the author performs preliminary experiments to reach to LR values for forensic face recognition. However, the approach lacks suitable modeling of Within-Source Variability (WSV) and Between-Source Variability (BSV) before LR computation.

A. Abd Manaf et al. (Eds.): ICIEIS 2011, Part II, CCIS 252, pp. 47–55, 2011.
© Springer-Verlag Berlin Heidelberg 2011

In a typical forensic face recognition scenario, a forensic expert is provided with two face images; one of a suspect (usually obtained from a mugshot database) and other face image is of a person whose identity is in question (the perpetrator). The duty of forensic expert is to reach to a LR value which is interpreted as a degree of support for one hypothesis against the other. The first hypothesis, called prosecution hypothesis, states that the suspect is the source of unknown face. Second hypothesis, called defense hypothesis, states that someone else in potential population (not the suspect) is the source of unknown face. Usually as a part of forensic face recognition, forensic experts also have to compare a questioned face to a database of mugshots. It is highly desirable to automate the process of forensic facial comparison which will not only speed up comparison but will also standardize the process.

The remaining of the paper is organized as follows: In section 2 we discuss general idea of Bayesian framework. Section 3 presents the computation process of LR from a similarity score. Section 4 reviews briefly our employed face recognition systems. Section 5 shows experimental results and finally in section 5 we conclude our work and show future research directions.

2   Bayesian Interpretation Framework

Bayesian framework (or the likelihood ratio framework) is a logical approach to evaluation of evidence from a biometric system and can be applied to any biometric system without change in the underlying theory. A general description of this framework can be found in [7]. A description of this framework in context of forensic speaker recognition, voice comparison, and DNA analysis can be found in [1-5]. In this framework the task of a forensic scientist is to compute LR based on evidence from a biometric system. This LR assessed from a score based biometric system is then provided to judge or jury where they combine it with the prior knowledge about the case (I) to reach to a conclusion. The basic idea of this framework is that evidence does not consist uniquely of scientific data [8] and the forensic scientist while evaluating evidence from a biometric system should report a soft decision in the form of LR. While in commercial biometric systems, the objective is to make decision in binary form, in forensic applications, the objective is to find the degree of support for one hypothesis against the other. Using the Bayes theorem, given the prior odds (prior knowledge of case) and LR, the posterior odds can be calculated as:

$$\frac{\Pr(H_p \mid E,I)}{\Pr(H_d \mid E,I)} = \frac{\Pr(E \mid H_p,I)}{\Pr(E \mid H_d,I)} \times \frac{\Pr(H_p \mid I)}{\Pr(H_d \mid I)} \tag{1}$$

where H_p and H_d are the prosecution and defense hypothesis respectively and E represents forensic information (evidence) while I is background information on the case at hand. The prosecution hypothesis H_p states that the suspect is the source of the questioned face while the defense hypothesis H_d states that someone else in the relevant population is the source of the questioned face.

In this framework, the likelihood ratio

$$\frac{\Pr(E \mid H_p, I)}{\Pr(E \mid H_d, I)}$$

gives a measure of degree of support for one hypothesis H_p against the other H_d based on the scientific analysis of the questioned face. It calculates the conditional probability of observing a particular value of evidence with respect to two competing hypotheses. The task of a forensic scientist in this framework is to compute LR value from the evidence (similarity score) which is then used by the judicial system to reach to a decision. A LR greater than one support prosecution hypothesis, for instance, if LR is 10, it will be interpreted as 10 times stronger belief that the suspect is the perpetrator regardless of the prior information about the case. Similarly a LR less than 1 support defense hypothesis. A LR of 1 supports both hypothesis equally or in other words no additional information can be derived from biometric evidence.

3   Computation of LR

The numerator of LR is the probability of observing evidence (score value) given the prosecution hypothesis is true. It states that the two images being compared is coming from the same source, i.e., suspect is the perpetrator. It requires WSV of the suspect to be computed. The denominator of the LR is the probability of observing the same evidence (score value) given the defense hypothesis is true. It states that someone else in relevant population is the source of the questioned face i.e., someone else is the perpetrator. It requires BSV to be estimated from relevant population. Figure 1 illustrate general approach of LR computation when evidence (similarity score) of a biometric system is used for forensic investigation.

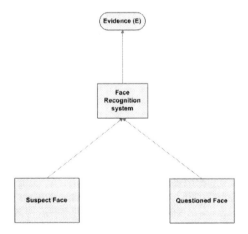

Fig. 1. Evidence from a face recognition system

Estimation of WSV. WSV is estimated by obtaining similarity scores using a database of a number of images of the suspect. This database is called 'control database' and contain images of suspect taken under similar conditions as that of the image obtained in crime scene (questioned face image). There are two approaches to computing WSV. First one is suspect-dependant and it requires that all images in control database must be of the suspect which is under investigation. The second approach called suspect-independent allow for accumulating a number of different subjects each having several images taken under similar conditions. Face images of each subject are then compared with other images of that subject to estimate WSV. Due to the difficulty of obtaining enough number of images from one subject to estimate WSV, the suspect-independent approach is generally followed.

Estimation of BSV. To estimate BSV we need a large scale database of relevant population. This database referred to as 'potential population database' should be made of a large number of facial images taken under similar conditions to that of the questioned image. Generally it is hard to decide as to the exact number of images to be used in this database as it should ideally be dependent on the case at hand. However once a system is employed and tested on sample database it can be easily adjusted to the particular case at hand by changing the size and nature of relevant population in the potential population database.

Modeling WSV and BSV. Once WSV and BSV of similarity scores are obtained, the next step is to model distributions of score using a probability density function. In our work we use Kernel Density Estimation (KDE) [9] for WSV and BSV modeling. The use of KDE to model WSV and BSV is also demonstrated by Meuwly [10] for forensic speaker recognition. KDE smooth out the contribution of each observed data point over a local neighborhood of that data point. The contribution of data point s_i to the estimate at some point s depends on how apart si and s are. The extent of this contribution is dependent upon the shape of the kernel function adopted and the width (bandwidth) accorded to it. If we denote the kernel function as K and its bandwidth by h, the estimated density at any point s is

$$f(s) = \frac{1}{n} \sum_{i=1}^{n} K\left(\frac{(s - s_i)}{h}\right) \tag{2}$$

The size of kernel function can be optimally computed as:

$$h = \left(\frac{4\sigma^5}{3n}\right) \tag{3}$$

where σ is the sample standard deviation of the samples and n is the size of samples. Once the background probability density function (pdf) of WSV and BSV are in hands, LR is simply computed by dividing pdf of WSV by pdf of BSV at point value of evidence (similarity score).

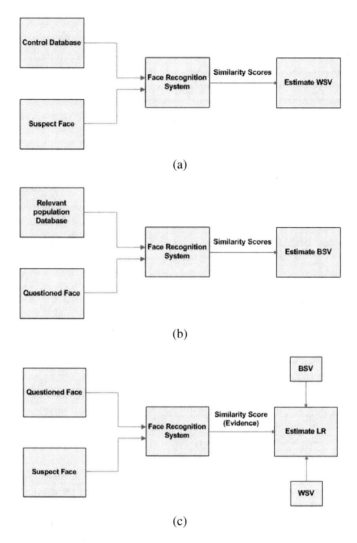

Fig. 2. (a) Estimation of WSV (b) Estimation of BSV (c) Computation of LR

4   Face Recognition Systems

We use two face recognition systems in our experiments. Both systems are used as a 'black box' however a general description of each system is presented in this section.

System A. This system is based on AdaBoost [11] algorithm with LDA [12] as a week learner is used for feature selection in LDA subspace while classification is performed using a classic nearest center classifier. This approach is based on the work of [13] and is partially inspired by Viola's and Jone's [14] work as boosting is used for feature extraction and not for classification. The performance of traditional LDA-based approach is improved by incorporating it in boosting framework. Each round of boosting generalizes a new LDA subspace particularly focusing on examples which are misclassified in previous LDA subspace. The final feature extractor module is an ensemble of several specific LDA solutions. This kind of ensemble based approach take advantage of both LDA and boosting and outperforms only LDA based systems in complex face recognition tasks such as the case where less number of training samples for each subject are available compared to number of dimensions of samples (small-sample-size problem) [15] and when non-linear variations are present in facial images. Refer to [13] for a detailed description of this employed face recognition system.

System B. This system used in our experiments is Cognitec [16] commercial face recognition system. This system has better discriminative ability and handles the pose and illumination problem better than system A. Detail about the Cognitec system can be found here [16].

Both systems are essentially used as a 'black box' and the main objective is to explore and evaluate their use in forensic framework.

5   Experimental Results

In our experiments we use a total of 2878 images of 100 different subjects. Images are collected from two public databases: BioID [17] and FRGC [18]. Variation in terms of facial expression and lighting conditions exist in both databases. Mostly images are frontal and only small variation exist in pose of facial images. Fig 3 shows some example images used in our experiments. 60% images of each subject are used for training and remaining 40% for testing the face recognition system. Depending on the number of test images available for each subject, 1 to 3 images in the testing set are used for suspect trails. This corresponds to a total of 1736 training images, 954 testing images and 188 suspect images. Each test results in 100 similarity scores corresponding to each of the subject in the database. For each test image, the target similarity score is used for WSV estimation and the remaining 99 similarity scores are used for BSV estimation. Following this procedure for 954 test images we get a total of 954 similarity scores for WSV and to 94446 (954 X 100 – 954) similarity scores for estimation of BSV. Fig 4 show histograms of similarity scores obtained for target matches or WSV and non-target matches or BSV using system A.

Fig. 5 shows the pdfs of WSV and BSV estimated from histograms of similarity scores in fig. 4 using KDE. LR is then computed by dividing pdf of WSV by pdf of BSV at value of similarity score for which we want to find LR. Fig. 5 also illustrates calculation of LR for an evidence value (similarity score) of 20. LR of 18.79 implies that a suspect image whose similarity score with the questioned face is 20 is 18.79 times more likely to be the source of the questioned face compared to the hypothesis that someone else is the source of questioned face.

The LR value of 18.79 can be multiplied to prior odds (prior knowledge of the case) by the judicial system to reach to posterior odds (conclusion).

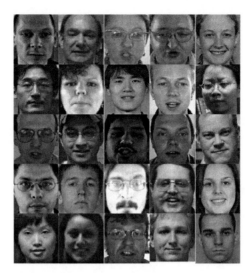

Fig. 3. Example images from BioID and FRGC database used in experiments

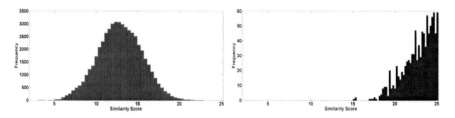

Fig. 4. (a) Histogram of similarity scores obtained for non-target matches (BSV); (b) Histogram of similarity scores obtained for target matches (WSV)

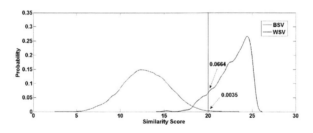

Fig. 5. Probability density functions of WSV and BSV estimated using KDE. To comoute LR value for similarity score of 20, pdf of WSV is divided by pdf of BSV at point value 20, 0.0664 / 0.0035 = 18.79.

Fig. 6 shows result of modeling WSV and BSV of similarity scores using same dataset for system B. Score range of System B is from 0 to 1, however, for easy comparison it is scaled to match score range of System A. As can be seen from fig 6, system B better separates WSV and BSV scores values which shows better discriminative ability of the system.

The performance of a forensic system is better evaluated using Tippet plot. Fig. 5 shows the tippet plot when 50000 non-target and 1000 target LR values are computed using both systems. Greater separation between the curves of target and non-target LR values is desirable and shows the system reliability in computing LR values.

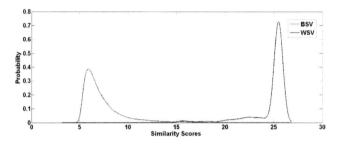

Fig. 6. Probability density functions of WSV and BSV estimated using similarity scores obtained from System B

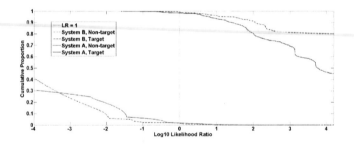

Fig. 7. Tippet plot computed for 1000 target and 50000 non-target LR values

6   Conclusion and Future Work

This work focused on the use of existing biometric face recognition systems in forensics. The process of LR computation is explained in face recognition context. Large numbers of face images from two public databases are used to estimate WSV and BSV. Target and non-tart LRs for two different face recognition systems are evaluated for same set of face data and compared using tippet plot. Future research will include better methods of LR computation and working with facial data taken under forensic conditions.

Acknowledgment. This research is funded by the European Commission as a Marie-Curie ITN-project (FP7-PEOPLE-ITN-2008) under Grant Agreement number 238803.

References

1. Champod, C., Meuwly, D.: The Inference of Identity in Forensic Speaker Recognition. Speech Commun. 31, 193–203 (2000)
2. Gonzalez-Rodriguez, J., Fierrez-Aguilar, J., Ortega-Garcia, J.: Forensic Identification Reporting Using Automatic Speaker Recognition Systems. In: Proc. ICASSP (2003)
3. Aitken, C.G.G.: Statistics and Evaluation of Evidence for Forensic Scientists. John Wiley & Sons (1997)
4. Morrison, G.S.: Forensic Voice Comparison. In: Freckelton, I., Selby, H. (eds.) Expert Evidence. Thomson Reuters, Sydney (2010)
5. Buckleton, J.: A Framework for Interpreting Evidence. In: Buckleton, J., Triggs, C.M., Walsh, S.J. (eds.) Forensic DNA Evidence Interpretation, pp. 27–63. CRC, Boca Raton (2005)
6. Peacock, C., Goode, A., Brett, A.: Automatic Forensic Face Recognition from Digital Images. Sci. Justice. 44, 29–34 (2004)
7. Robertson, B., Vignaux, G.A.: Interpreting Evidence. Wiley, Chichester (1995)
8. Lewis, S.R.: Philosophy of Speaker Identification. Police applications of Speech and Tape Recording Analysis. Proc. of the Institute of Acoustics 6(1), 69–77 (1984)
9. Silverman, B.W.: Density Estimation for Statistics and Data Analysis. Chapman and Hall, London (1986)
10. Meuwly, D., Drygajlo, A.: Forensic Speaker Recognition based on a Bayesian Framework and Gaussian Mixture Modeling (GMM). In: Proc. Odysse 2001, pp. 145–150 (2001)
11. Freund, Y., Schapire, R.: A decision-theoretic Generalization of On-line Learning and an Application to Boosting. J. Comput. Syst. Sci. 55, 119–139 (1997)
12. Belhumeur, P.N., Hespanha, J.P., Kriegman, D.J.: Eigenfaces vs. Fisherfaces: Recognition using Class Specific Linear Projection. IEEE Trans. Pattern Anal. Mach. Intell. 19, 711–720 (1997)
13. Lu, J., Plataniotis, K.N., Venetsanopoulos, A.N., Li, S.Z.: Ensemble-Based Discriminant Learning with Boosting for Face Recognition. IEEE Trans. Neural Networks 17, 166–178 (2006)
14. Viola, P., Jones, M.J.: Robust Real-time Face Detection. Int. J. Comput. Vis. 57, 137–154 (2004)
15. Raudys, S.J., Jain, A.K.: Small Sample Size Effects in Statistical Pattern Recognition: Recommendations for practitioners. IEEE Trans. Pattern Anal. Mach. Intell. 13, 252–264 (1991)
16. http://www.cognitec-systems.de/FaceVACS-SDK.19.0.html
17. Kirchberg, K.J., Jesorsky, O., Frischholz, R.W.: Genetic Optimization for Hausdorff-Distance based Face Localization. In: Intl. Workshop on Biometric Authentication, Denmark, pp. 103–111 (2002)
18. Phillips, P.J., Flynn, P.J., Scruggs, T., Bowyer, K.W., Chang, J., Hoffman, K., Marques, J., Min, J., Worek, W.: Overview of the Face Recognition Grand Challenge. In: Proceedings of IEEE Conference on Computer Vision and Pattern Recognition (2005)

Occurrence Order Detection of Face Features Deformations in Posed Expressions

Khadoudja Ghanem[1] and Alice Caplier[2]

[1] Laboratory MISC, Mentouri University, Rue Ain El Bey, Constantine, Algeria
gkhadoudja@yahoo.fr
[2] Gipsa Laboratory, 961 Rue de la Houille Blanche, F-38402 St Martin, France
alice.caplier@gipsa-lab.grenoble-inp.fr

Abstract. Timing, duration, speed and occurrence order of facial actions are different parameters related to dynamic analysis. These parameters are crucial in human behavior understanding and in distinguishing posed from spontaneous expressions. In this paper, the occurrence order parameter is analyzed. Motion information is extracted from image sequence by tracking characteristic facial points. Extracted information is got in the form of multi time series. Allen's Logic Algebra is used to model the occurrence order parameter in these time series. A rule based method is used to learn order rules. These rules are evaluated in the classification of new examples into one of five facial expressions namely: Joy, Disgust, Anger, Sadness or Unknown. The system is evaluated in terms of recognition accuracy. High rates have been obtained when classifying new unseen examples.

Keywords: Facial expression, temporal parameters, occurrence order, classification, time series, association rule.

1 Introduction

Current approaches to automated facial expression analysis typically attempt to recognize facial expressions from either static facial images or image sequences. The vast majority of past work considering sequence images does not take the dynamics of facial expressions into account when analyzing facial behavior.

Timing, duration, speed and occurrence order of facial actions are crucial parameters related to dynamic behavior [8]. According to [9, 10, 11], the parameters cited below are highly important cues for distinguishing posed from spontaneous facial expressions. Timing, duration and speed have already been analyzed in several studies [9,12,13,14]. Little attention has been given to occurrence order [12,14]. The work in [14] clearly shows that the differences between spontaneous and deliberately displayed smiles are in the order of dynamics of shown behavior (e.g., the movement order of head and body) rather than in the configuration of the displayed expression.

The contributions of this paper are as follows:

• Analyze the "Occurrence Order" attribute of facial deformations to understand facial behavior of posed expressions. The usefulness of this analysis will be in a future work to use the learned occurrence order of facial deformations to deal with spontaneous expressions.

A. Abd Manaf et al. (Eds.): ICIEIS 2011, Part II, CCIS 252, pp. 56–66, 2011.
© Springer-Verlag Berlin Heidelberg 2011

The integration of relationships or correlations and dynamics with measurements improve expression recognition. Allen's logic algebra [19] is introduced to model "Occurrence Order" in time.

• Represent the sequence of observations over time by time series to identify the occurrence order pattern.
• Evaluate the "One association rule", a rule based method. This method is known by its large ability in taking all possible configurations (in our case of displayed expressions) into consideration. Also, Rule based methods in contrast to most existing approaches, allows representing blend expressions.

The remainder of this paper is organized as follows. Section 2 provides some related works which are the most closely related to our problematic. In section 3, the proposed method is presented. Experimental studies are discussed in section 4. Finally, section 5 concludes the paper.

2 Related Work

The most interesting works in facial expression analysis field can be found in [1, 2 and 3]. Only few studies analyze explicitly the temporal dynamics of facial expressions [4, 5, 6, 7]. In [6] Valstar et al proposed a geometric based approach, they were the first authors who addressed the problem of action unit (AU) temporal segments recognition. They used motion history for facial action detection. In [7], Koelestra et al, proposed an appearance-based approach to facial expression recognition, they were the second group to propose a dynamic texture based method to detect all AUs and their temporal segments.

Rule based methods are basic methods to describe the relations between input and output and to predict the consequence in classification. Many emotion synthesis systems apply rule-based models for emotion recognition. However, because of the constraints in representation and modeling capability of IF-THEN rule structure, researchers intend to ignore rule-based systems during feature-extraction and pattern recognition. They concentrate on statistic, ensemble or probabilistic methods such as support vector machine (SVM), Gentleboost or Hidden Markov Models (HMM).

The first surveyed rule based method is the one proposed by Black & Yacoob [15]. In [16], a rule-based system containing 20 rules is used to recognize the AUs defined in the Facial Action Coding System (FACS). The method is based on the extracted mid-level feature parameters describing the state and motion of the feature points and their shapes from the face profile contour.

In [17] a fuzzy rule based system was proposed. A set of 41 rules is created to characterize a user's emotional state in terms of the activation emotion space in the whissel's wheel.

Our work explore the "One association rule", to describe facial dynamics in terms of the dynamic parameter which is the "Occurrence order" of facial deformations.

3   Proposed System

The proposed system consists of several stages, it treats videos. 18 characteristic facial points are located manually on the first frame of each video. These points correspond to eye, eyebrows and mouth corners (Fig. 1). Selected points allow calculating the following distances:

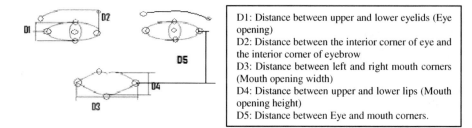

D1: Distance between upper and lower eyelids (Eye opening)
D2: Distance between the interior corner of eye and the interior corner of eyebrow
D3: Distance between left and right mouth corners (Mouth opening width)
D4: Distance between upper and lower lips (Mouth opening height)
D5: Distance between Eye and mouth corners.

Fig. 1. Characteristic distances

Characteristic points are then tracked from frame to frame using Lucas-Kanade's algorithm [18] and new distances are calculated. This leads to a multivariate time series of distances.

To analyze occurrence order of facial feature deformations, Allen's Logic algebra is used. This algebra allows modeling order in multi time series.

3.1   Allen's Interval Logic Algebra

Allen [19] proposed an interval algebra framework to represent hierarchical and possibly indefinite and incomplete temporal information. Events are represented by time intervals. There are basic relations between time intervals. The basic relations are disjoint and exhaustive (Fig. 2).

Relation	Symbol	Inverse	Meaning
X before Y	b	bi	
X meets Y	m	mi	
X overlaps Y	o	oi	
X starts Y	s	si	
X during Y	d	di	
X finishes Y	f	fi	
X equals Y		eq	

Fig. 2. The basic relations between time intervals

In this work we are not interested in breaking the time series into intervals and in labeling each interval, to look for similarities between these intervals. We consider each time series as a unique interval and, we look for occurrence order between obtained time series.

Example: Fig. 3 shows an example of obtained data from tracking features in an image sequence of 200 frames with 'joy expression' and its transformation by using two basic relation (Before, After) from Allen's algebra:

Before Transformation

S1	D1	D2	D3	D4	D5
Frame1	...	...	...	...	...
Frame2	...	...	...	...	...
....	...	...	<>	...	...
....	...	...	...	<>	...
....	<>	...	...	...	...
Frame200	...	...	...	...	...

(a)

$\Rightarrow$

After Transformation

S1	D1	D2	D3	D4	D5
	3	/	1	2	/

(b)

Fig. 3. Data (a) before transformation , (b) after transformation

From Fig. 3, <> = Changed; 1= the first changed distance is D3; 2 = the second changed distance is D4; 3 = the third changed distance is D1. So D3 is Before D1, D4; D4 is After D3 and before D1 and, D1 is After D3, D4.

We suppose that considering only the first three modified facial distances is enough to build a specific dynamic description for each expression. Fig. 4 shows an example of two image sequences for Joy and Anger with occurrence order of facial features deformations.

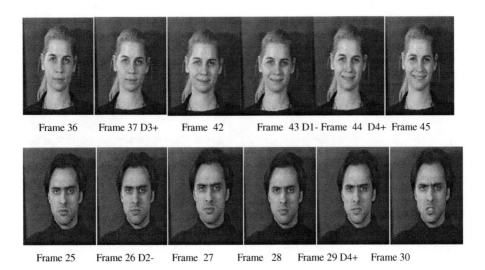

Frame 36   Frame 37 D3+   Frame 42   Frame 43 D1- Frame 44 D4+ Frame 45

Frame 25   Frame 26 D2-   Frame 27   Frame 28   Frame 29 D4+   Frame 30

Fig. 4. Occurrence order of facial features deformations of two subjects from MMI Database {First line: Joy: the first changed distance is D3+ (frame 37), the second changed distance is D1- (frame 43) and then the third changed distance is D4+ (frame 44). Second line: Anger: the first changed distance is D2- (frame 26), the second changed distance is D4+ (frame 29)}.

3.2 Transformation Algorithm in Terms of Occurrence Order

The aim, in this stage, is to transform data which are in the form of multivariate time series in terms of Allen's Logic Algebra. This algebra uses different terms related to occurrence order which are: before, meets, overlaps, starts, during, finishes (and their opposites) besides equals. In our case, we are interested by only one pattern which is "Before" and its opposite "After". This pattern is used to formulate the temporal order of facial deformation either in the eye region or in the mouth area. The raison of this choice (a single pattern) is that we have chosen as a rule based classifier a method which only uses one attribute in the IF part of the rule.

```
For each facial expression Ei: i=1..5
    For each actor Sj: j=1..N
1.   Find the distance witch change before all other
distances (First order);
2.   Find the distance witch change after the first one
(Second order);
3.   Find the distance witch change after the second one
(third order);
    End
End
```

Ei is a facial expression; Sj is a subject and N is the number of subjects in the database.

To detect changed distances, the current distance is compared to the first distance of the time series because each video from tested databases starts with a neutral face. If the ratio is larger (or lower) than a threshold, the distance is considered to be changed. To confirm that this distance modification is not due to an error's detection, the distances in two consecutive frames are compared in the same way and the modification is validated only if change has been detected in the two consecutive frames.

In the scope of learning new knowledge from occurrence order analysis and at once constructing a new dynamic classifier, we use "The one Association Rule" method.

3.3 One Association Rule Based Classification Method Principle [20]

The One association rule is a major paradigm of the Rule induction algorithm. It is a popular and well known method for extracting relationships between variables and it is considered as potentially useful for knowledge discovery purposes since rules are easily understood by humans. Its principle is to consider a set of training sample cases (S). Each case is composed of the observed features and the true classification. The goal is to find the best rule set RS_{best} such that the error rate on new cases is minimum.

Algorithm (2) is defined as follows:

```
For each attribute A
    For each value V of attribute (A), create a rule:
        1. Count how often each class appears
        2. Find the most frequent class, c
        3. Make a rule "if A==V then C=c"
    end
```

```
        Calculate the error rate of this rule
    end
    Pick the attribute whose rules produce the lowest
error rate.
```

4 Experimental Studies

4.1 Training Step

Training examples come from emotional databases (Dafex and Cohn & Kanade databases [21,22]) and are in the form of video sequences. These examples represent several actors displaying expressions with non rigid head motion. Each video contains from 10 to 400 frames. Each frame is characterized by the five distances (See Fig. 1). Four facial expressions plus Unknown are studied; E1:*Joy*, E2:*Disgust*, E3:*Anger*, E4:*Sadness* and E_{un}: *Unknown*.

8 subjects with the four facial expressions from Dafex database, and 10 subjects for *Joy*, 6 subjects for *Disgust*, 13 subjects for *Anger* and 18 subjects for *Sadness* from Cohn and Kanade database are considered.

The attribute set is {D1+,D1-,D2+,D2-,D3+,D3-,D4+,D4-,D5+,D5-}/

'+' = Distance Increases; '-' = Distance decreases;

Each attribute can take one of the three values {1,2,3} / 1=First order, 2=Second order, 3=Third order.

Algorithm (1) is first used to transform data in term of occurrence order, and then Algorithm (2) is used to deduce association rules. For example, deduced rules for attribute D3+ are presented in table 1.

Table 1. Deduced rules for Attribute D3+

Attribute	Values	Class appearance	Freq. class	Deduced rule	Error	Accuracy	Comment
D3+	1	E1	E1	If D3+=1 then Exp=E1	0/18 records	18/18 = 100%	
	2	E2,E3, E4	E4	If D3+=2 then exp=E4 If D3+=2 then exp=E3	2/4 records	2/4 = 50%	25%exp=E2 25%exp=E3
	3	E2,E4	E2,E4	If D3+=3 then exp =E2	1/2 records	½ = 50%	50% exp=E4
Total					**3/24 records**		

From table 1, we can see that D3+ is the first changed distance, it means that it is Joy expression because all considered examples (18/18) have D3+ as first changed distance. The deduced rule (in column 5) has full accuracy, (because there is no case with first changed distance D3+ that does not represent Joy, column 7).

Another value taken by the same attribute D3+ is '2'. In this case, 2/4 examples have D3+ as the second changed distance, it means that it can be 'Sadness' with accuracy=50%, or it can be Disgust or Anger with accuracies= 25%.

The last value taken by the same attribute is '3'. In this case, 2 examples have D3+ as the third changed distance, it means that it can be 'Disgust' with accuracy=50%, and it can be 'Sadness' with accuracy= 50%.

At the end, 27 rules are deduced. To select the most pertinent rules, additional information must be considered. For example, since we have four classes, we need at least four rules, each rule describing one class. If a given expression is recognized by using the "First order" without any doubt with another expression, rules concerning the "second order" are ignored. The presence of more than one rule to recognize (Ei) based on different attributes means that each person has his own way to express a facial expression and we keep all the rules. Finally, if any rule from the selected ones can be used, the studied expression is classified as unknown (Eun).

After considering these points, and accuracy's rule and after eliminating redundant rules, only 13 rules are selected. These rules are given in Table 2.

Table 2. Selected rules

Attri bute	Rules	Errors	Accur acy	Insta nces	Recognized expressions
D1+	(1) If D1+=1 then Exp=E3	0/2	100%	2	E3
D1-	(2) If D1-=1 then Exp=E4	19/53	100%	7	E4
D2+	(3) If D2+=1 then Exp=E4	0/10	100%	4	E4
D2-	(5) If D2- =1 then Exp =E2	15/30	50%	14	E2:50%;
	(6) If D2- =1 then Exp =E3				E3: 50%
D3+	(7) If D3+=1 then Exp=E1	3/24	100%	18	E1
D3-	(8) If D3- =1 then Exp=E3	0/8	100%	5	E3
D4+	(9) If D4+ =1 then Exp=E2	0/25	100%	7	E2
D4-	(11)If D4- =1 then Exp=E3	4/24	100%	7	E3
	(12)If D4- =2 then Exp −E3		73,33 %	11	E3:73,33% E4:26,67%
D5+	(13)If D5+=1 then Exp =E4	0/11	100%	11	E4
D5-	(14) If D5-=1 then Exp =E4	0/3	100%	3	E4
	(15) If D5-=2 then Exp =E2	2/16	62,5%	8	E2:62,5%;E1:12,5%,E4: 25% (E1,E4 recognized in first order) =>E2:100%

As we have said before, in most surveyed studies the classification of an expression is generally performed into basic emotion categories. When using dynamic classifiers like rule based methods (which are sensitive to person dependant expression), we can recognize blended expressions. For instance, in the case of the rule with attribute D2-, there is a doubt in the expression recognition, it can be Disgust or Anger.

MPEG-4 gives facial expressions description in static context, by introducing the "occurrence order" attribute, we bring something new in facial expression analysis, and some semantic information about facial expressions can be deduced. Indeed, Table 3 gives the static facial expression rules enriched by dynamic temporal rules.

Table 3. Static and dynamic descriptions

Expressions	Description of facial Expression in static context	Description of facial Expression in dynamic context
Joy	Eyes are slightly closed and mouth is opened, its corners are pulled backward to ears;	First facial deformation: Mouth corners are pulled backward to ears.
Disgust	Lower lip is turned down, upper lip is raised, mouth is opened;	First facial deformation: either Upper lip can be raised, OR Inner corner of eyebrow is lowered
Anger	Mouth is compressed, brows are furrowed and eyes are wide opened or slightly closed;	First facial deformations: either Eyes are opened OR Mouth is compressed OR Eyebrows Inner corners are lowered
Sadness	Mouth corners are depressed and eyebrows inner corners are raised;	First facial deformations :either Eyes are slightly closed OR Eyebrows inner corners are raised OR Mouth corners are depressed.

From table 3, we can see in the second column the classical facial expression description, and in the third column the same description but with the consideration of occurrence order attribute. For instance, joy is described by: eyes are slightly closed, mouth is opened, its corners are pulled backward to ears. With dynamic description, the expression is recognized by considering the first order of facial changes. This change corresponds to the mouth corners which are pulled backward to ears.

4.2   Test and Deployment

4.2.1   Test on Cohn and Kanade Database

To evaluate the efficiency of learned rules, we tested different datasets. Examples coming from Cohn and Kanade database which have not been used in the training step are tested. There are 40 subjects for *Disgust*, 19 subjects for *Anger*, 74 subjects for *Joy* and 40 subjects for *Sadness*.

In the case of Disgust, we found that 8 subjects verify rule (9) and 29 subjects verify rule (5). In the case of Anger, 1 subject verifies rule (8), 7 subjects verify rule (11) and 8 subjects verify rule (6). In case of Sadness, 32 subjects verify rule (13), 6 subjects verify rule (3), 1 subject verifies rule (14) and 1 subject verifies rule (2). These findings reflect the variety of displaying these expressions. Obtained rates are estimated and presented in table 4.

Columns of table 4 present expressions recognized by an expert and lines present expressions recognized by the proposed system. We can see that *Joy* and *Sadness* can be recognized without any doubt, but *Disgust* and *Anger* are sometimes confused (like in the study with static data). The obtained rates for unknown expression are due to the absence of any rule of "First or Second order" with the corresponding changed attribute.

To show the difference between classification between static and dynamic data, we compared the proposed system to systems proposed in [25, 26]. The two systems use different methods but are evaluated on the same database Cohn-Kanade. We can see that the obtained results with our proposed system are better even if we consider the singleton results or if we take into account the doubt between expressions.

Table 4. Classification rates of Cohn and Kanade database (Per %)

Sys/ Exp	Proposed System				Proposed System in [25] on the Cohn and Kanade database				Proposed System in [26] on Cohn and Kanade database			
	Joy	Disg.	Ang.	Sad	Joy	Disg.	Ang.	Sad	Joy	Disg.	Ang.	Sad
Joy	100				72,64				97,5			
Disg		92,5				80,35				97,5		
Ang			84,4				75,86				85,1	
Sad				100				82,79				74,7
Disg Or Ang		7,5%	10,5									
Unknown			5,26									
Total Known	100	100	94,74	100	72,64	80,35	75,86	82,79	97,5	97,5	85,1	74,7

4.2.2 Test on H_C Database

Another database has been tested. It is the H_C database [23] which contains 21 subjects, Joy and Disgust expressions are considered. Each subject has a video with more than 200 frames. Obtained results are presented in Table 5.

Table 5. Classification rates of Hammal-caplier database

System/Expert	Our System		System in [24] on H_C database	
	Joy	**Disgust**	**Joy**	**Disgust**
Joy	100%		76.36%	
Disgust		90,48%		43,10%
Disgust Or Anger		4,76%		
Joy Or Disgust			10,90%	8,62%
Unknown		4,76%	6,06%	
Total Recognized	**100%**	**95,24%**	**87,26%**	**51,72%**

Table 5 summarizes the recognition rates for the two facial expressions Joy and Disgust. When comparing our results with the results presented in [24], we can see that these results are better even if we consider the singleton results or when we take into account the doubt between expressions.

4.2.3 Test on MMI Database

With MMI database [27] we have tested 35 videos for Joy, 32 videos for *Disgust*, 28 videos for *Anger and* 26 videos for *Sadness*. The obtained results are presented in table 6.

From table 6, we can see that classification rates have decreased compared with those obtained on the other databases. New expert system based methods suggest adding examples which represent new rules with significant rates in the training step, in order to extract all possible new rules and improve the recognition rates.

Table 6. Classification rates of MMI database

System/Expert	Joy	Disgust	Anger	Sadness
Joy	**100%**			
Disgust		**87,5%**		
Anger			25%	3,57%
Sadness		12,5%	3,57%	**96,16%**
Disgust Or Anger			67,86%	
Unknown				
Total Known	**100%**	**87,5%**	**96,16%**	**96,16%**

To compare with other relevant studies, we examined the best results of other facial classification studies that use the MMI database. The studies in [26] achieved 86.9%. In these studies, recognition performance on the MMI database decreases too, compared to that on the Cohn- Kanade database.

5   Conclusion

In this paper, we have presented and evaluated a rule based method to improve the analysis of facial temporal dynamics in terms of classifying a studied facial expression by using occurrence order attribute. Four facial expressions were considered: Joy, Disgust, Anger, Sadness and Unknown. The method is evaluated in terms of recognition accuracy. As future work, we aim at analyzing occurrence order attribute with spontaneous expressions to distinguish posed from spontaneous ones.

References

1. Pantic, M.: Automatic Analysis of Facial Expressions: The State of the Art. IEEE Transactions on Pattern Analysis and Machine Intelligence 22(12) (2000)
2. Fasel, B., Luettin, J.: Automatic facial expression analysis: a survey. The Journal of Pattern Recognition Society 36, 259–275 (2003)
3. Zeng, Z., Pantic, M., Roisman, I., Thomas, S.: A survey of affect recognition Methods: Audio,Visual, and Spontaneous Expressions. IEEE Trans. Pattern Analysis & Machine Intelligence 31(1) (2009)
4. Tong, Y., Liao, W., Ji, Q.: Facial action unit recognition by exploiting their dynamics and semantic relationships. IEEE Trans. Pattern Analysis & Machine Intelligence 29(10), 1683–1699 (2007)
5. Pantic, M., Patras, I.: Detecting facial actions and their temporal segments in nearly frontal-view face image sequences. In: Proc. IEEE Int'l. Conf. Systems, Man & Cybernetics, pp. 3358–3363 (2005)
6. Valstar, M., Pantic, M., Patras, I.: Motion History for Facial Action Detection from Face Video. In: Proc. IEEE Conf. Systems, Man, and Cybernetics, pp. 635–640 (2004)
7. Koelstra, S., Pantic, M., Patras, I.: A Dynamic Texture-Based Approach to Recognition of Facial Actions and Their Temporal Models. IEEE Trans on Pattern Analysis and Mach. Intelligence 32 (2010)
8. Ekman, P., Rosenberg, E.L.: What the Face Reveals: Basic and Applied Studies of Spontaneous Expression Using the Facial Action Coding System (2005)

9. Cohn, J.F., Schmidt, K.L.: The timing of facial motion in posed and spontaneous smiles. J. Wavelets, Multi-resolution and Information Processing 2(2), 121–132 (2004)
10. Ekman, P.: Darwin, deception, & facial expression. Annals N.York Ac. Sciences 1000, 105–221 (2003)
11. Valstar, M.F., Pantic, M., Ambadar, Z., Cohn, J.F.: Spontaneous vs. posed facial behavior: automatic analysis of brow actions. In: Proc. ACM Intl. Conf. on Multimodal Interfaces, pp. 162–170 (2006)
12. Valstar, M.F., Pantic, M., Ambadar, Z., Cohn, J.F.: Spontaneous versus Posed Facial Behavior: Automatic Analysis of Brow Actions. In: Proc. ACM Int'l. Conf. Multimodal Interfaces, pp. 162–170 (2006)
13. Bartlett, M.S., Littlewort, G., Frank, M., Lainscsek, C., Fasel, I., Movellan, J.: Recognizing Facial Expression: Machine Learning and Application to Spontaneous Behavior. In: Proc. IEEE Int'l. Conf. Computer Vision and Pattern Recognition, pp. 568–573 (2005)
14. Valstar, M.F., Gunes, H., Pantic, M.: How to Distinguish Posed from Spontaneous Smiles Using Geometric Features. In: Proc. ACM Int'l. Conf. Multimodal Interfaces, pp. 38–45 (2007)
15. Black, M.J., Yacoob, Y.: Recognizing Facial Expressions in Image Sequences Using Local Parameterized Models of Image Motion. In: Intl Conf. on Computer Vision, pp. 374–381 (1995)
16. Pantic, M., Rothkrantz, L.: Expert System for Automatic Analysis of Facial Expressions. Image and Vision Computing 18(11), 881–905 (2000)
17. Ioannou, S.V., Amaryllis, T., et al.: Emotion recognition through facial expression analysis based on a neurofuzzy network. Journal of Neural Networks 18, 423–435 (2005)
18. Lucas, B.D., Kanade, T.: An Iterative Image Registration Technique with an Application to Stereo Vision. In: Proceedings of Imaging Understanding Workshop, pp. 121–130 (1981)
19. Allen, J.F.: Maintaining knowledge about temporal intervals, pp. 832–843. ACM Press (1983)
20. Hu, X., Song, I.-Y., et al.: Temporal rule induction for clinical outcome analysis. Intl. Journal of Business Intelligence and Data Mining 1(1), 122–136
21. Dafex Database, http://tcc.itc.it/research.i3p/dafex/index.html
22. Kanade, T., Cohn, J.F., Tian, Y.: Comprehensive database for facial expression analysis. In: Proc. the 4th IEEE Intl. Conf. on Automatic Face and Gesture Recognition, France, pp. 46–53 (2000)
23. H_C database, http://www.lis.inpg.fr/pages_perso/caplier/english/emotionnelle.html.en/emotionnelle_2.html.en.html
24. Hammal, Z.: Facial Features Segmentation, Analysis and Recognition of Facial Expressions using the Transferable Belief Model, PHD thesis, France (2006)
25. Datcu, D., Rothkrantz, L.: Facial Expression Recognition in still pictures and videos using Active Appearance Models. A comparison approach. In: Intl. Conf. on Comp. Systs. and Tech., vol. 285, p. 112 (2007)
26. Shan, C., Gong, S., McOwan, P.W.: Facial expression recognition based on local binary patterns: A comprehensive study. Image and Vision Computing 27(6), 803–816 (2009)
27. MMI Database, http://www.mmifacedb.com/

A Study on Speech Coders for Automatic Speech Recognition in Adverse Communication Environments

Seung Ho Choi

Department of Electronic and Information Engineering, Seoul National University of Science and Technology, Seoul 139-743, Korea
shchoi@seoultech.ac.kr

Abstract. In this research work, we present the effects of several standard speech coders on automatic speech recognition in adverse communication environments such as tandem, frame erasure, and noisy conditions. The adverse conditions were chosen to simulate the operations of mobile communication environments. The comparative results can provide a guideline for selecting a speech coder when a speech recognition service is needed in digital communication networks.

Keywords: Speech recognition, speech coder, adverse communication environments.

1 Introduction

Interests and needs for speech recognition in communication networks are rapidly growing [1]. However, the communication environments often cause some degradation of speech signal, which results in low speech recognition performance. In mobile communication environments, especially, the speech signal can be severely distorted by ambient noises, encoding-decoding processes, and channel distortions. Hence, these adverse environments have to be considered when a speech recognition service is implemented in digital mobile communication systems. Fig. 1 shows a simplified block diagram of digital communication system and describes the adverse environments for speech recognition. The adverse environments include background noises added to the input speech signal, spectral distortions by the speech coders, and channel distortions over a communication channel.

Several researchers have addressed the problems of speech recognition systems in digital mobile communication environments [2]-[5]. Lilly and Paliwal showed that the performance of a speech recognizer degrades when a synthesized speech of the speech coder is used as an input of the recognition system [2]. Mokbel, *et al.* proposed an equalization technique in the preprocessing stage and hidden Markov model (HMM) parameter adaptation approaches in order to improve the robustness of speech recognition systems [3]. Moreover, some useful approaches which utilize quantized spectral representations such as line spectrum pairs and

A. Abd Manaf et al. (Eds.): ICIEIS 2011, Part II, CCIS 252, pp. 67–75, 2011.

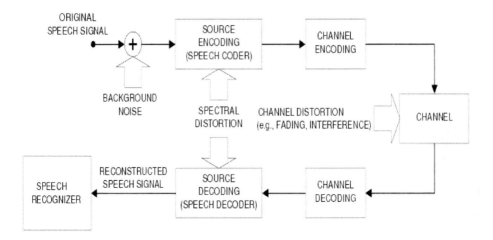

Fig. 1. An illustration of adverse environments for speech recognition in a digital communication system

log area ratios were investigated [4][5]. In [6] and [7], the effects of the parameterization of different codecs in communication networks on automatic speech recognition are studied.

As another viewpoint, speech recognition performance can be improved by a proper selection or design of a speech coder in digital communication systems. Since low bit-rate speech coders are designed by using a perceptual criterion, the performance of the coders is evaluated by subjective quality tests such as mean opinion score [8]. However, in view of an application to a wireless man-machine interface, other performance measure of the coders must be considered. In this respect, the recognition accuracy is one of the feasible measures to evaluate the performance of the speech coders.

The purpose of this paper is to suggest a guideline for selecting a speech coder applicable to adverse communication networks where a speech recognition service is considered. Five coders - IS-96A (variable 8 kbps QCELP) [9], variable 13 kbps QCELP [10], IS-127 (variable 8 kbps EVRC) [11], ITU-T G.729 (fixed 8 kbps CS-ACELP) [12], and GSM-EFR (fixed 12.2 kbps) [13] - are chosen in the following recognition experiments. Since the adverse conditions such as background noise, tandem, and frame erasure, which can severely degrade the speech signal, often exist in digital communication networks, recognition performances of the speech coders need to be measured under these adverse conditions.

We will briefly address the adverse conditions for speech recognition in Section 2. In Section 3, the recognition system used in this work is explained and then we will describe how the communication environments are simulated. We will show the recognition results under various adverse environments in Section 4 and conclude this paper in Section 5.

2   Adverse Conditions for Speech Recognition

A multitude of terrestrial or wireless telecommunication circuits are usual in a long distance telephone connection. Each of them may utilize a different speech coder and thus a telephone connection is formed by tandeming of these different coders. As the number of tandem connections increase, the speech quality is more degraded.

Fig. 2 shows an example of the speech degradation caused by tandeming of the IS-96A coder. In this figure, one can observe that speech signal is more degraded as the number of tandems increases, especially, in the first transitional part from unvoiced to voiced regions.

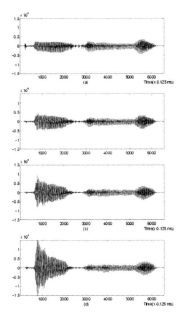

Fig. 2. An example of speech degradation by tandeming (/gu-il-yug/): (a) original (b) one tandem (c) two tandems (d) three tandems

The channel distortions caused by interference and fading are frequently occurred on digital mobile channels. Channel degradation is generally separated in two classes, random errors and burst errors. Most linear prediction-based analysis-by-synthesis coders are robust to random bit errors. When burst errors are sufficiently long, or in a packet network, it is possible to lose all information for a frame, and this condition is referred to as *frame erasure* [8].

When burst errors are common, as an error detection strategy, it is usual to inform the speech decoder whether a frame erasure is occurred or not.

Some authors introduced frame reconstruction techniques that can be used to alleviate the degradation caused by frame erasure [14]. In general, lost frames are

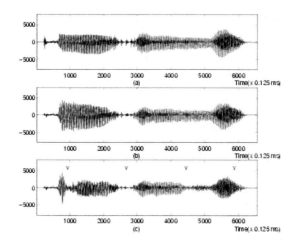

Fig. 3. An example of speech degradation by frame erasure (/gu-il-yug/): (a) original (b) reconstructed (one tandem) (c) reconstructed with the FER of 10%

reconstructed by repeating the parameters of the previous frame with gains that are scaled down. Actually, every speech coders have a solution for constructing lost speech frames.

Fig. 3 shows an example of speech degradation caused by random frame erasure of 10% frame erasure rate (FER). We also used the IS-96A coder. In this figure, "v" indicates the position that frame erasure is occurred. One can notice the ill effect of frame erasure on speech signals at the subsequent frames as well as at that frame.

In mobile communication environments, the speech signal can be severely degraded by ambient noises such as the babble noise at public places and the driving car noise within or outside a car. Moreover, the distortions are often nonstationary. Some of the speech coders have an optional scheme to tackle these distortions. For example, the IS-127 coder has a noise suppression scheme that works optionally.

3   Experimental Setup

For the experiments, we used a connected Korean digit database that consists of 90 male and 50 female speakers. Utterances from 93 speakers were used as training data, and those from the other 47 speakers were used as test data. Each speaker pronounced 40 digit strings generated randomly by varying the number of digits from three to seven. The speech signals were preemphasized with the factor of 0.95. They were hamming windowed with a length of 30 ms and then the feature parameters were extracted once every 10 ms. Twelve mel-frequency cepstral coefficients (MFCCs), frame energy, and the corresponding their time derivatives, resulting in a 26-dimensional observation vector, were used as a feature vector. Each digit was modeled by a left-to-right, seven-state, continuous density HMM having three Gaussian mixtures per state. The HMM parameters were trained by the segmental K-means algorithm, and the Viterbi search algorithm was used for decoding. This work aims at investigating the relative performance of speech coders, and thus the HMMs trained under clean environment were used for obtaining recognition accuracies under all the conditions. We computed the word recognition rate by counting each insertion, deletion, and substitution errors, and also we used an unknown-length grammar.

Fig. 4 shows how to process speech signals to simulate the mobile communication environments. The network has to be able to serve a traffic between the users plugged in the public switched telephone network (PSTN). This condition was simulated by connecting each speech coder several times, as shown in Fig. 4(a). We also assumed that the transmission channel is ideal except bringing a burst error that was modeled by frame erasure as shown in Fig. 4(b). Severe noisy condition causes degradation of speech recognition performance. Some speech coders employ a noise suppression scheme as an internal processing block. This paper also examines the effect of this internal block on speech recognition in tandem and background noise conditions.

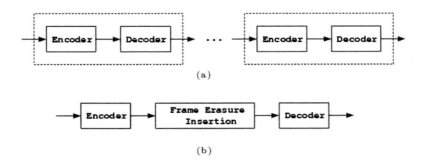

Fig. 4. Schematic diagrams for speech signal processing to simulate (a) tandeming and (b) frame erasure conditions

4   Recognition Results and Discussions

Fig. 5 shows the word recognition rates of each speech coder according to the number of tandems, where the recognition rate at the zero tandem is a result obtained from the system using original speech.

In other words, the baseline system throughout this work has a recognition rate of 93.2%. As the number of tandem increases, the recognition accuracy decreases fast. As a matter of fact, the quality of reconstructed speech signal is much degraded by increasing the number of tandems. Also, the recognition rates show a wide variance among the coders. In this respect, we can expect that the speech quality is closely related with the the speech recognition performance that may be a measure of the speech quality by a machine. The experimental results show that the recognition rate is considerably related with the average bit-rate.

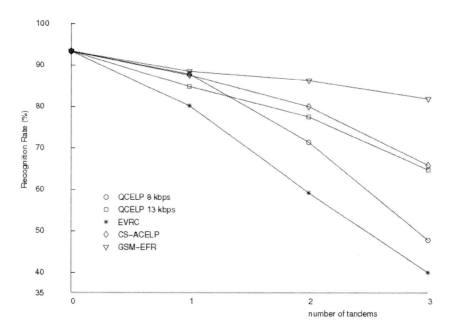

Fig. 5. Comparison of recognition accuracies according to different number of tandems

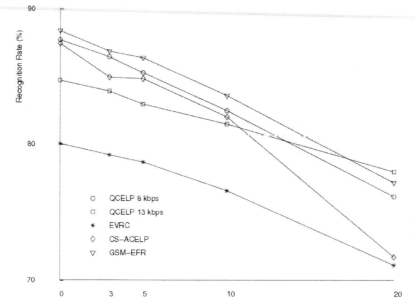

Fig. 6. Comparison of recognition accuracies according to different frame erasure rates (FERs)

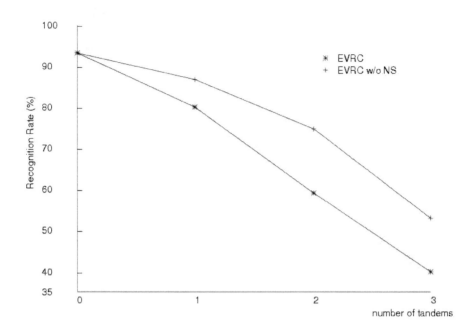

Fig. 7. Recognition accuracies of EVRC with and without noise suppression (NS) scheme in tandem environments

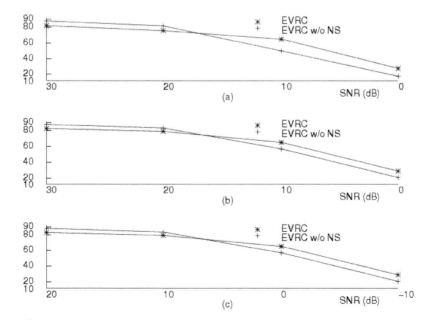

Fig. 8. Recognition accuracies of EVRC with and without noise suppression scheme (NS) in additive noise environments: (a) white noise (b) babble noise (c) car noise

Two variable rate coders of IS-96A and IS-127 show worse performances than others because they have the lower average bit-rates than 8 kbps. On the other hand, GSM-EFR gives the best performance since GSM-EFR has the highest average bit-rate of 12.2 kbps.

Fig. 6 shows the recognition rates by varying the FER from 3% to 20%. The FER of 20% can give a sufficient simulation environment of a burst error for mobile communications. For every speech coder, the recognition rate decreases as the FER increases, but frame erasure condition is not as critical to the speech recognition accuracy as tandem case does. The frame erasure has a crucial effect on the spectral envelope of reconstructed speech. From the figure, one can find that the recognition rate grows higher as the number of bits assigned to the spectral envelope is larger on the average. This is because the spectral distortion can be reduced by increasing the number of the bits. GSM-EFR quantizes the spectral envelope at a rate of 38 bits per 20 ms, which is the largest in the coders, while CS-ACELP assigns 18 bits per 10 ms and the number of bits assigned to the spectral quantizer for the other variable rate coders averages smaller than GSM-EFR does.

Finally, we examined whether the noise suppression (NS) scheme in the IS-127 coder is effective for speech recognition in tandem and background noise conditions. In tandem conditions, the NS scheme in IS-127 coder causes considerable degradation of speech recognition performance as shown in Fig. 7. From the recognition results shown in Fig. 8, the NS slightly improves the robustness of speech recognition in low signal-to-noise ratios (SNRs), but rather deteriorates it in high SNRs.

In view of reconstructed speech quality, we can similarly state that the intelligibility of reconstructed speech is diminished in high SNRs while is increased in low SNRs by the NS scheme. From the recognition results of IS-127 coder with and without NS scheme, we know that an optional scheme must be carefully selected or designed considering speech recognition.

5   Conclusions

In this paper, we described the effect of several standard speech coders on speech recognition for a digital communication network service. We selected some adverse environments such as tandem, frame erasure, and noisy conditions, which are expected to simulate the environments being occurred in a network. The experiment gives that there is a close relationship between speech recognition rate and the average bit rate in tandem condition. Also, the recognition accuracy of a speech coder will not be much decreased if the speech coder is designed to assign more bits to spectral envelope quantization. A noise suppression module in a speech coder can degrade speech recognition performance. Thus, we showed that it is necessary to carefully adopt or design an optional scheme of a speech coder.

Acknowledgments. This work was supported in part by Electronics and Telecommunication Research Institute in 2011.

References

1. Tan, Z.H., Lindberg, B.: Automatic speech recognition on mobile devices and over communication networks. In: Tan, Z.H., Lindberg, B. (eds.). Springer, Heidelberg (2008)
2. Lilly, B.T., Paliwal, K.K.: Effect of speech coders on speech recognition performance. In: Proc. ICSLP, Philadelphia, PA, pp. 2344–2347 (1996)
3. Mokbel, C., Mauuary, L., Karray, L., Jouvet, D., Monne, J., Simonin, J., Bartkova, K.: Towards improving ASR robustness for PSN and GSM telephone applications. Speech Communication 23(1-2), 141–159 (1997)
4. Choi, S.H., Kim, H.K., Lee, H.S., Gray, R.M.: Speech recognition method using quantised LSP parameters in CELP-type coders. Electron. Lett. 34(2), 156–157 (1998)
5. Huerta, J.M., Stern, R.M.: Speech recognition from GSM codec parameters. In: Proc. ICSLP, Sydney, Australia, pp. 1463–1466 (1998)
6. Turunen, J., Vlag, D.: A Study of speech coding parameters in speech recognition. In: Proc. EUROSPEECH, Scandinavia, pp. 2363–2366 (2001)
7. Carmen, P.M., Ascension, G.A., Diego, F.G.C., Fernando, D.M.: A comparison of front-ends for bitstream-based ASR over IP. Signal Processing 86(7), 1502–1508 (2006)
8. Kleijn, W.B., Paliwal, K.K.: Speech coding and synthesis. In: Kleijn, W.B., Paliwal, K.K. (eds.). Elsevier Science, Amsterdam (1995)
9. TIA/EIA IS96A: Speech service option standard for wideband spread spectrum digital cellular system (1994)
10. Qualcomm: High rate speech service option for wideband spread spectrum communication systems (1996)
11. TIA/EIA IS127: Enhanced variable rate codec, speech service option 3 for wideband spread spectrum digital systems (1995)
12. ITU-T G.729: Coding for speech at 8 kbit/s using conjugate-structure algebraic-code-excited linear-prediction (CS-ACELP) (1996)
13. Jarvinen, K., Vainio, J., Kapanen, P., Honkanen, T., Haavisto, P., Salami, R., Laflamme, C., Adoul, J.-P.: GSM enhanced full rate speech codec. In: Proc. ICASSP, Munich, Germany, pp. 771–774 (1997)
14. Kondoz, A.M.: Digital speech: Coding for low bit rate communications systems. In: Kondoz, A.M. (ed.). John Wiley (1994)

On Robustness of Multi Fractal Spectrum to Geometric Transformations and Illumination

Samir H. Abdul Jauwad[1] and Rehmat Ullah[2]

[1] Deptt of Electrical Engg, King Fahd Univ of Petroleum & Minerals Dhahran, Saudi Arabia
[2] Deptt of Computer Systems Engg, Univ of Engg & Technology Peshawar, Pakistan
samara@kfupm.edu.sa, rehmatkttk@nwfpuet.edu.pk

Abstract. Regular region based segmentation approaches utilize color or intensity information to distinguish between different regions. The performance of such procedures is acceptable for man-made objects, since they mainly consist of regular shapes and smooth surfaces. Most natural objects such as mountains, trees or clouds on the other hand are typically formed of complex, rough and irregular surfaces in 3-D, which are transformed into textured regions on the 2-D image plane through the image formation process. If we want to segment or classify images of such surfaces in an automatic fashion, we need to find a way to capture the essence of their structure succinctly. This can be achieved by making use of the 3-D information in combination with the texture of the corresponding region on the image plane. One possible way to model this relationship is through fractal analysis, which has proven to be a good representation of natural objects.

This paper is based on the work of Xu et al. [1]. The aim is to explain a way of efficiently representing natural objects by the use of the multi fractal spectrum (MFS), which is an extension of the regular fractal analysis. Section 1 of this paper will present the concepts of image texture. Then section 2 will briefly introduce the fractal theory and section 3 will elaborate on the concept of fractal dimension (FD). Section 4 is the main part of the paper, which will explain the MFS as a robust and invariant texture descriptor. The final section will present the experimental results obtained by Xu et al. [1] and provide conclusions.

Keywords: Image Texture, Fractal analysis, Fractal dimension (FD), Multi fractal spectrum (MFS), Bi-Lipschitz transformations.

1 Image Texture

Several image properties such as smoothness, coarseness, depth, regularity, etc. can be intuitively associated with textures. However there is no accepted formal definition for texture. Many researchers have described texture as a descriptor of the local brightness variation from pixel to pixel in a small neighbourhood around a central pixel. Alternatively, texture can be described as an attribute representing the spatial arrangement of the gray levels of the pixels in a region. Texture analysis has played an important role in many areas including medical imaging, remote sensing and

A. Abd Manaf et al. (Eds.): ICIEIS 2011, Part II, CCIS 252, pp. 76–95, 2011.

industrial inspection, and its tasks are mainly classification, segmentation, synthesis, compression and scene description. Human touch is a useful way of interpreting texture, since we naturally relate surface structure to touch. In that sense a texture can be rough, silky, bumpy, etc.

Textures can be categorized into repetitive, stochastic, mixed and fractal patterns. Examples of that are illustrated in Fig. 1. Fig. 1(a) shows a repetitive texture, which is obtained by replicating a texture primitive (brick) in the image X and Y directions. Fig. 1(b) shows a stochastic texture, which is generated by sampling a random process. Fig. 1(c) illustrates that different combinations of texture types can be present in the same image. Fig. 1(d) shows a fractal texture, which will be introduced in further detail in section 2.

A texture descriptor is a discriminant metric to quantify the perceived texture of a surface. A good descriptor should have the following properties:

- o   Rich informative surface description
- o   Spatial invariance to geometrical transformations
- o   Illumination invariance
- o   Efficient computation (especially for real time systems)

(a) Repetitive texture   (b) Stochastic texture

(c) Mixed texture   (d) Fractal texture

Fig. 1. Texture categories

There are several techniques to obtain a descriptor for a textured image, which can be divided into two main categories. The first one follows a structured approach, which sees an image as a set of primitive texels in a regular or repeated pattern. This approach is particularly useful for describing artificial textures. The second one is a statistical approach, which computes a quantitative measure of the arrangement of the intensities in a region. In general this approach is easier to compute and is more widely used, since natural textures consist of irregular sub-elements. Popular techniques in this category are the *gray level co-occurrence matrices*, *laws masks*, *autocorrelation coefficients* and *fractal analysis*. The latter rather new technique will be discussed in the next section.

2 Fractal Theory

A fractal is a self-similar geometric shape, i.e. it is made up of reduced size copies of itself. Fractals are defined recursively and can be constructed in an iterative fashion. The roots of the fractal theory go back to the 17th century; however the mathematical concepts were developed one century later. The term fractal was coined by Benoit Mandelbrot in 1975 and was derived from the Latin word fractus, which means "broken" or "fractured". A key property of fractals is that they comprise finite area, but have an infinitely long boundary. No small segment along the boundary of fractal is line-like and the distance between any two distinct points on the boundary is infinite. There are two classes of fractals, depending on the level of self-similarity. Exact self-similar fractals consist exclusively of exact copies of itself. On the other hand quasi self-similar fractals are made up of several structures that are repeated recursively. Two popular examples for the fractal classes are shown in Fig. 2.

As mentioned earlier fractals are constructed iteratively. In order to illustrate this process iterations 0 to 4 of the Koch curve are shown in Fig. 3. The construction starts

(a) Koch curve   (b) Mandelbrot set

Fig. 2. Fractal classes

at iteration 0 with an equilateral triangle. Then in every iteration the middle third of every straight line segment is replaced by a pair of line segments that form an equilateral bump (inclination angles of 60^0 and 120^0). If this process is repeated forever, the boundary will become infinitely long. The Koch curve is a good approximation of the physical formation of snowflakes. Another popular example is the Sierpinski triangle.

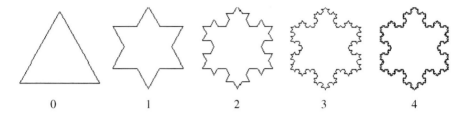

0   1   2   3   4

Fig. 3. Koch curve: demonstration of fractal construction

3 Fractal Dimension

The fractal dimension (FD) is a key quantity in the field of fractal texture analysis. It is an indicator of how completely a fractal fills the surrounding space and it is also a measure of the irregularity of the point distribution of an object. The mathematical formulation for computing the FD of a point set $E \in \Re$ is

$$\dim(E) = \lim_{\delta \to 0} \frac{\log N(\delta, E)}{-\log \delta} \qquad (1)$$

where δ is the measurement scale, $N(\delta, E)$ is the number of copies of the original object when going to a smaller scale and $\dim(E)$ is the fractal dimension of the point set. For each δ, an object is measured in a way that ignores irregularities of size less than δ. The fractal dimension is then obtained by observing how these measurements change as δ approaches 0. One way to illustrate the measurement scale is to think of δ as being the length of a ruler that is used to measure the boundary of the object in question. Fig. 4 shows an example of measuring the length of the coast line of Great Britain using rulers of decreasing sizes. As can be seen the smaller the ruler is, the more detail can be captured, i.e. the better the approximation of the coast line is. No matter at what scale we look at the coast line there will always be scalloping smaller than that scale. This means that the estimated length of the coast line increases as the ruler size decreases. Hence the length of the coast line (or in general the outline of an object) does not just depend on the length of the coast line itself, but also on the length of the measurement tool. In order to obtain a consistent measurement of the coast line, the notion of dimension must be generalized to include fractional dimensions. In this way the unique fractional power that yields consistent estimates of the object's metric properties is that object's fractal dimension (reason for the limit in Eqn. 1).

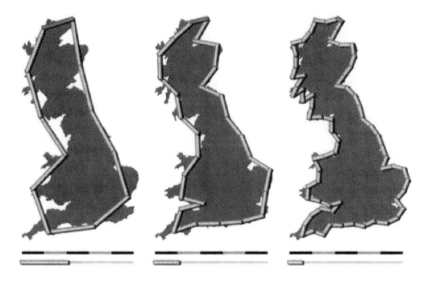

Fig. 4. Measuring the coast line of Great Britain using a ruler

However when analysing image textures the theoretical way of computing the fractal dimension demonstrated above cannot be applied, since digital images are recorded at a finite resolution and it is not possible to go beyond single pixel resolution. That's why in practice the so-called box-counting dimension is used. Fig. 5 shows the same example of measuring the coast line of Great Britain, using circular disks of decreasing radius r. In general the box-counting dimension is computed by covering the space with a mesh of boxes with side length r, called the r mesh boxes (r squares in 2-D) and then counting how many boxes are needed to cover the whole structure.

Fig. 5. Measuring the coast line of Great Britain using circular disks

3.1 Computation of the FD

In order to illustrate the concept of FD more clearly, we will show the computation of the FD of the primitive objects that cover up the whole 1-D, 2-D and 3-D space respectively and in contrast to that the FD of a real fractal. Fig. 6-8 have the following structure: the left subfigure shows the original object, the right one shows the result when doubling its extent (scaling factor k of 2) in all dimensions. This scaling factor k determines the number of replications of the object in one dimension. The measurement scale δ on the other hand determines the reduction in length of the ruler. Since they describe the same concept in two opposite ways, their mathematical relation is $k = \dfrac{1}{\delta}$. In Fig. 6 it can be seen that the number of copies of the original object after the dilation is 2 and hence $\delta = 0.5$. So the FD can be computed using Eqn. 1 as

$$\dim(L) = \lim_{\delta \to 0} \frac{\log N(\delta, L)}{-\log \delta} = \frac{\log 2}{-\log 0.5} = 1$$

(a) Original line   (b) Dilated line

Fig. 6. Fractal dimension of a 1-D line

Fig. 7 shows that the original square is replicated four times when both dimensions are doubled. So the number of copies $N = 4$. The measurement scale δ is still 0.5 and hence the FD can be computed as

$$\dim(S) = \lim_{\delta \to 0} \frac{\log N(\delta, S)}{-\log \delta} = \frac{\log 4}{-\log 0.5} = 2$$

(a) Original square   (b) Dilated square

Fig. 7. Fractal dimension of a 2-D square

As can be seen in Fig. 8 the original cube is replicated eight times when all three dimensions are doubled and so the number of copies $N = 8$. The measurement scale did not change and hence the FD is as follows

$$\dim(C) = \lim_{\delta \to 0} \frac{\log N(\delta, C)}{-\log \delta} = \frac{\log 8}{-\log 0.5} = 3$$

From the examples given above we can conclude that regular geometrical objects

- have an integer fractal dimension
- have a fractal dimension which is equal to their topological dimension

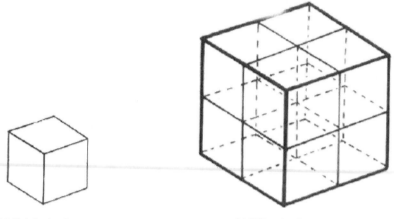

(a) Original cube   (b) Dilated cube

Fig. 8. Fractal dimension of a 3-D cube

As an example of the FD of a real fractal we show the Koch curve. The scaling factor $k = 3$, so $\delta = \frac{1}{3}$. As can be seen in Fig. 9 the number of copies of the original object (shown in black) is $N = 4$. So its fractal dimension can be computed as

$$\dim(K) = \lim_{\delta \to 0} \frac{\log N(\delta, K)}{-\log \delta} = \frac{\log 8}{-\log \frac{1}{3}} \approx 1.2619$$

In contrast to regular objects the fractal dimension of an irregular object is always a fractional number (hence the name fractal dimension).

Another way of illustrating the concept of fractal dimension is to increase gradually the roughness of a 3-D plane from a completely smooth surface to a highly irregular one and observing how its FD changes (as shown in Fig. 10). The 3-D surface irregularities are projected as texture on the 2-D image plane through the image formation process. By computing the FD of the texture, we can see that it is directly proportional to the roughness of the corresponding surface: the higher the roughness, the higher the FD and vice versa.

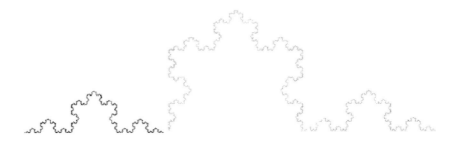

Fig. 9. Fractal Dimension of the Koch Curve

3.2 Fractal Dimension of Images

Up till now we have only discussed how to compute the fractal dimension of differently shaped objects. In order to utilize the FD for texture analysis we need to extend the concept to the space of images. A crucial property of shapes is that for every point in space, we know if it belongs to the shape or not. Hence it is possible to compute its fractal dimension. However images consist of a dense matrix of RGB or intensity values. So a pre-processing step is necessary to binarize the images. Then the FD of the binary images can be computed, where white means that a pixel belongs to the shape (logical true) and black means that it does not (logical false). This binarization (or categorization) can be achieved in various ways, depending on the task at hand and the input image

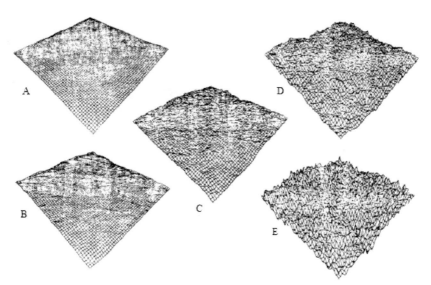

A: FD ≈ 2.0, B: FD ≈ 2.1, C: FD ≈ 2.5, E: FD ≈ 2.8

Fig. 10. Surfaces of increasing fractal dimension

class. In order to illustrate the concept we will start by simple thresholding. Fig. 11 shows the original color image of a tree and its binarized version obtained by thresholding the blue channel[1]. All pixels with blue channel intensities below 80 are set to white, the rest of the pixels are set to black. The binary version clearly shows the shape of the object of interest (tree) in relation to the background.

(a) Original tree image   (b) Binarized tree image

Fig. 11. Binarization of an RGB image for computation of its FD

Fig. 12 shows the fractal dimension of the binarized tree image from Fig. 11(b) as a function of the box size used to cover the shape. The first thing to observe is that the fractal dimension for a box size of 2000 pixels or more is 2, i.e. that the full image is covered by a single box and hence the FD corresponds to the topological dimension. But we know from Eqn. 1 that the FD is defined for the box size r going to zero. As the box size approaches zero, we get different values for the FD. Since an image is

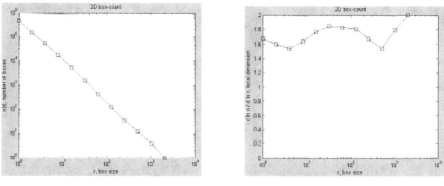

(a) Number of boxes   (b) Fractal dimension

Fig. 12. Functions w.r.t. the box size of the tree image

---

[1] The binary image just contains a centred, reduced size version of the original image, because it represents the most descriptive part of the tree shape.

recorded at a final resolution the minimum box size is one pixel (at the left border of the graph). The final FD is obtained by taking the average of the finite differences of the number of boxes with respect to the box size. For the tree image it is approximately 1.801 ± 0.06394. The FD can just be estimated, because of two reasons: firstly, the finite resolution of the image just allows for finite differencing and not for an analytical derivative and secondly, if the image size is not an integer power of 2, the boxcount[2] function pads the remaining space with zeros (e.g. a 320x200 image is padded to 512x512) and hence that region is not considered to be part of the shape.

Fig. 13 shows the computation of the fractal dimension for a binary image that contains a fractal-like shape. We can observe that the line evolves differently w.r.t. the previous figure.

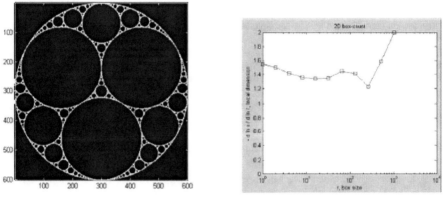

(a) Original fractal image   (b) Fractal dimension

Fig. 13. FD of a fractal gray scale image

3.3 Issues with the FD

The fractal dimension analysed up to now has several advantages. It is insensitive to image scaling, it is close to the human perception of surface roughness and it is a good representation of natural objects. But there are also two main drawbacks, namely that the FD just gives a single value for a texture and that different textures can have the same FD. Hence it is not a unique and very rich descriptor. A possible solution to overcome the mentioned limitations is the extension to the multi fractal spectrum (MFS), which will be covered in the following section.

4 Multi Fractal Spectrum

The MFS is a vector of the fractal dimensions of some categorization of the image. Here, a categorization is a way of creating binary sub images from the original image

---

[2] A Matlab function.

using some thresholding criteria (as shown in the tree example in the previous section). A more general way to do this is intensity thresholding: divide the overall range (e.g. 0-255) in N bins, and for every bin compute a binary image by setting all the pixels in the bin to black and all others to white. In this way N binary images are obtained. Fig. 14 shows this process for a grass texture.

 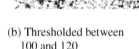 

(a) Original Image   (b) Thresholded between   (c) Thresholded between
                              100 and 120   80 and 100

Fig. 14. Binarization of grass texture

The computation of the MFS is a three step process, which is illustrated in Fig. 15. It consists of the following stages:

  I.   Extract N binary images from the original image
  II.   Compute the fractal dimension of all the binary images
  III.   Concatenate all the computed FDs into one vector, called the Multi Fractal Spectrum

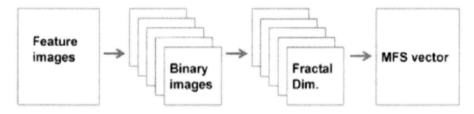

Fig. 15. Overview of the FSM computation

An important aspect of this process is the way how the categorization is achieved. The classical approach in the MFS literature (which was also followed in [1]) introduces a local density function for this task. It is also called Hölder exponent or local fractal dimension, since its formula resembles the one for computing the normal FD. The crucial difference is that instead of having the number of boxes in the numerator, a measurement function is used.

4.1 Local Density Function

The local density function for an image pixel x is defined as:

$$d(x) = \lim_{r \to 0} \frac{\log \mu(B(x,r))}{\log r} \tag{2}$$

where $d(x)$ is the local density at the image pixel x; x is a two element vector containing the (x, y) position of the central pixel, r is the radius of the circle or the side length of the square used to define the neighbourhood around the central pixel, $B(x,r)$ is the area with center x and radius r, μ is a measurement function that returns a single, representative value for the given area. The density function describes how locally the measurement function μ satisfies the power law behaviour. It measures the "non-uniformness" of the intensity distribution in the region neighbouring the measured point. In practice, the local density is obtained as the slope of the line fitted to the data $\{\log r, \log \mu(B(x,r))\}$, where r takes on several discrete values in a fixed range. When the local density is computed for every pixel in the input image a density image is obtained. Fig. 16 shows the original grass texture and the corresponding density image.

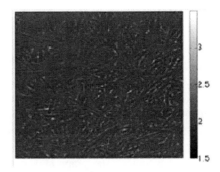

(a) Original grass texture   (b) Density image

Fig. 16. Computing the local density image from a texture

There are several possibilities to define the measurement function μ. The first approach is to work directly on the intensity domain. Denoting with $I(x)$ the intensity of pixels x, $\mu(B(x,r))$ is defined as:

$$\mu_1(B(x,r)) = \iint_{B(x,r)} (G_r * I)dx \tag{3}$$

where "$*$" is the 2-D convolution operator and G_r is a Gaussian smoothing kernel with variance r.

$$G_r = \frac{1}{r\sigma\sqrt{2\pi}} e^{\frac{-\|x\|^2}{2\sigma^2 r^2}} \tag{4}$$

where σ is a predefined parameter. In other words, $\mu(B(x,r))$ is the sum of average intensity values inside the disk $B(x,r)$. Since the variance of the Gaussian kernel depends on the neighbourhood size r, it encodes how the intensity at a point changes over scale. When using this measurement function, the final MFS vector contains the fractal dimension for multiple values of the density of the intensity.

The measurement function shown in Eqn. 3 is simple to compute but not robust to large illumination changes. To overcome this problem, several meaningful definitions of μ can be introduced. One possibility is to take the differential operators along the four main directions (horizontal, vertical, diagonal, anti-diagonal). The new measurement function

$$\mu_2(B(x,r)) = \left(\iint_{B(x,r)} \sum_K (f_k(G_r * I))^2 \right)^{\frac{1}{2}} dx \tag{5}$$

is illumination invariant, since the finite differencing due to the differential operators removes the effects of linear additive illumination changes. Another variant for the measurement function is

$$\mu_3(B(x,r)) = \int\int_{B(x,r)} \left| \left(\frac{\partial^2}{\partial x^2} + \frac{\partial^2}{\partial y^2} \right)(G_r * I) \right| dx \tag{6}$$

which is the sum of the Laplacians of the image inside $B(x,r)$. The definition of the measurement function is important, since it directly affects the final MFS vector. A combined MFS vector obtained by using different measurement functions leads to a better representation of the texture. Fig. 17 shows the output images obtained by using different definitions of the measurement functions and a graph illustrating the three corresponding MFS vectors. As can be seen the vectors are substantially different from each other. The graph shows the fractal dimension $f(\alpha)$, where $\alpha \in \Re$ is a level of local density.

Fig. 18 shows the four different textures and a graph with their corresponding MFS. It demonstrates that the MFS vectors of different textures are significantly different. The MFS of the carpet texture is completely different from the other MFS vectors. This is due to the fact that the carpet texture is stochastic (is comprised by a random pattern), whereas the other three textures show natural images of plants that are more similar to each other. We can also observe that as the surface roughness decreases from 18(a) to 18(d), the shape of the main bump of the MFS vectors becomes gradually narrower.

4.2 Properties of the MFS

The most relevant property of the MFS texture descriptor is its invariance to geometrical transformations under the Bi-Lipschitz map. A Bi-Lipschitz transform is a general class of spatial transformation including translation, rotation, projective transformation and texture warping on regular surfaces. It is defined as a function $g : \Re^2 \rightarrow \Re^2$, if there exists two constants $c_1 > 0, c_2 > 0$ such that for any $x, y \in \Re^2$ the following relation holds:

$$c_1 \|x - y\| < \|g(x) - g(y)\| < c_2 \|x - y\| \tag{7}$$

This spatial invariance is a very powerful feature and it has been mathematically proven for images with infinite resolution. In practice we are dealing with finite resolution images, but the MFS has shown to be very robust to perspective transformations and warping of the surface. Usually four to five levels of resolution (radius r used to compute the FD) are sufficient for a good estimation of the fractal dimension. Fig. 19 shows an example of the grass texture, shown earlier in Fig. 14(a),

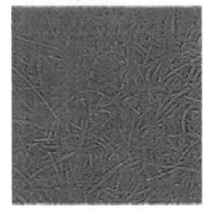

(a) μ_1 - Intensity

(b) μ_2 - Gradients

(c) μ_3 - Laplacians

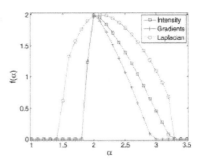

(d) Resulting MFS Vectors

Fig. 17. Comparison of different measurement functions

(a) Carpet

(b) Grass

(c) Leaf

(d) Tree

(e) Multi Fractal Spectra of the density of the four textures above

Fig. 18. Comparison of the MFS vectors of different textures

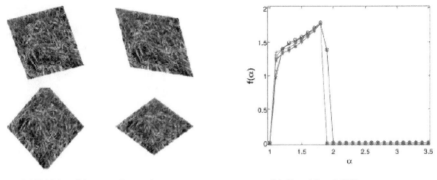

(a) Bi-Lipschitz transformations   (b) Resulting MFS vectors

Fig. 19. Four perspective views of a foliage texture and the corresponding MFS vectors of the density of intensity

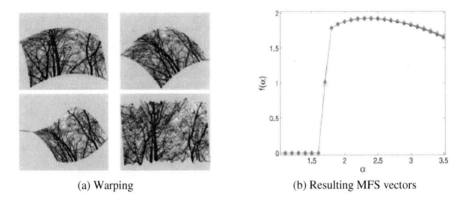

(a) Warping   (b) Resulting MFS vectors

Fig. 20. Perspective images of tree texture on different general smooth surfaces and the corresponding MFS vectors

which has been deformed using Bi- Lipschitz transformations. The resulting MFS vectors are displayed next to it. As can be seen they are very similar and hence the different images would be matched to the same texture prototype.

Fig. 20 shows another type of Bi-Lipschitz transform, namely the warping of a perspective transformation of the texture onto a smooth surface. As can be observed the resulting MFS vectors are nearly identical and hence the MFS is very robust to this type of transformations.

In addition to the spatial invariance the MFS descriptor is invariant to local multiplicative changes in image illumination, if the intensity measurement function μ_1 is used, and also to local linear changes in illumination if μ_2 or μ_3 are used. The first invariance is due to the fact that the ratio of logarithms in Eqn. 1 does not change due to multiplicative changes (transformed into additive changes). The second invariance is due to the principle of finite differencing, namely that image derivatives always compensate for additive illumination changes.

4.3 Comparison of MFS and Histogram

The most used statistical texture descriptor is the histogram. It is efficient and simple to compute, since it just counts the number of elements in a bin according to a categorization of the image. However in this process all the information about the spatial distribution of the elements is lost. Hence it is not invariant to perspective transformations. It is also very sensitive to changes in illumination.

The multi fractal spectrum on the other side estimates the exponential changing ratio of the number of elements in a bin over multiple resolutions (different radii r in the computation of the local density). Accordingly it incorporates more geometrical information and is, as mentioned before, invariant to perspective transformations.

5 Experimental Results

In the paper of Xu et al. [1] the performance of the MFS descriptor was evaluated using classical texture retrieval and classification tasks. The MFS is compared with three other methods:

LSP: was presented by Lazebnik et al. [2] in 2005 and is a sophisticated interest-point based texture representation. The main concept is to use elliptic clusters for characterizing a texture. It represents an image texture by its frequency of texture elements. It is robust to geometric transformations; however it is affected by changes in scale and viewpoint. Additional drawbacks of this method are: sophisticated pre-processing, K-means clustering and a large number of parameters. Hence it is complex and computationally expensive.

VZ-J: was presented by Varma and Zisserman [3] in 2003 and uses a dense set of textons for the description task. It is very simple and non-invariant, but it has shown to outperform complex texton descriptors, based on the output of certain filters.

VG-F: was presented by Varma and Garg [4] in 2007 and also makes use of the local density function. They apply the MR8 filter bank in a pre-processing step and their final feature vector contains 13 values. The descriptor for each image is a normalized histogram of the pixel texton labellings. The main difference to MFS is that they only use fractal geometry locally and do not integrate the standard global fractal dimension.

The experimental configuration of the MFS descriptor was obtained by using a combination of SVM cross-validation and the Fisher-score. The final vector had 33 dimensions and consisted of 13 intensity, 10 gradient and 10 Laplacian values (obtained by computing the local density images using μ_1, μ_2 and μ_3 respectively).

A weighing of $\frac{1}{5}.(1,2,2)$ was applied to compose the vector. The distance between the vectors was computed using the absolute sum (L_1 norm). A nearest neighbour algorithm was used to classify the images, which were fetched from the UIUC

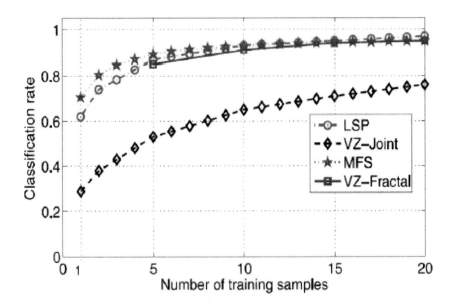

Fig. 21. Mean classification rate of 25 texture classes of MFS in comparison to three other methods

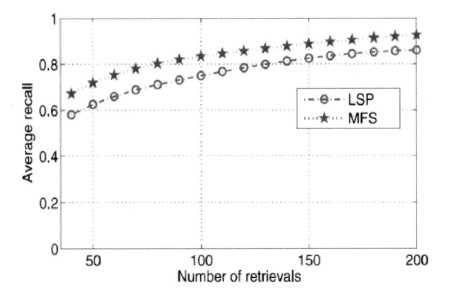

Fig. 22. Retrieval curves for the UIUC dataset for the MFS and LSP methods

repository. Fig. 21 shows the classification outcome of the MFS classifier as described before in comparison to the other three methods. It can be observed that the MFS classifier is clearly better than the VZ-Joint and comparable to the other two methods. The MFS performs better for a small number of training samples; however as the number of training samples (X-axis) increases the LSP method is more accurate. This is due to the fact that the LSP method is more robust to large illumination changes as compared to MFS.

Fig. 22 shows the retrieval curves on the UIUC dataset. Here just the performance of the LSP method is shown as a reference, since it is the most competitive one to the MFS. As can be seen the MFS accuracy is better by a noticeable margin. It is also necessary to mention that MFS uses a very small number of parameters as compared to LSP.

Fig. 23 shows a comparison between the performance of MFS and LSP on high resolution images taken from the UIUC dataset. The overall performance is very similar; however as the number of retrievals increases the performance of MFS is slightly better than LSP.

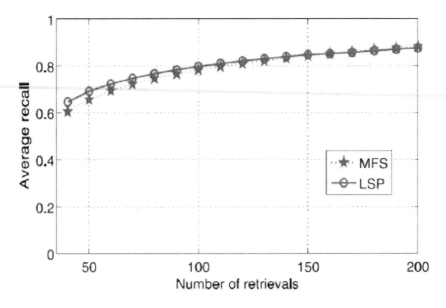

Fig. 23. Retrieval curves for high resolution images of the UIUC dataset for the MFS and LSP methods

6   Summary and Conclusions

In conclusion it can be said that the MFS is a promising texture descriptor. Its invariance to transformations under the Bi-Lipschitz map and illumination changes is proven mathematically and results in a robust descriptor. As shown in the experimental results it can be efficiently employed for texture retrieval and classification and its performance is similar or in some cases even better than comparable state-of-the-art texture classifiers.

A noticeable advantage w.r.t. to the other methods is that no feature detection, clustering or other pre-processing is required. Hence its computation is very efficient. It was also shown that the MFS is capable of utilizing the extra details that are present in high resolution images to create a more accurate texture description.

Acknowledgment. The authors wish to gratefully acknowledge *King Fahd University of Petroleum & Minerals Dhahran, Saudi Arabia,* for providing the funds to complete this work.

References

1. Xu, Y., Ji, H., Fermüller, C.: Viewpoint Invariant Texture Description Using Fractal Analysis. International Journal on Computer Vision (83), 85–100 (2009)
2. Lazebnik, S., Schmid, C., Ponce, J.: A Sparse Texture Representation Using Local Affine Regions. IEEE Transactions on Pattern Analysis and Machine Intelligence 27(8), 1265–1278 (2005)
3. Varma, M., Zisserman, A.: Texture Classification: Are Filter Banks Necessary? In: Proceedings of the IEEE Conference on Computer Vision and Pattern Recognition, Madison, Wisconsin, vol. 2, pp. 691–698 (June 2003)
4. Varma, M., Garg, R.: Locally Invariant Fractal Features for Statistical Texture Classification. In: Proceedings of the IEEE International Conference on Computer Vision, Rio de Janeiro, Brazil (October 2007)
5. Chaudhuri, B.B., Sarkar, N.: Texture segmentation using Fractal Dimension. IEEE Transactions on Pattern Analysis and Machine Intelligence 17(1), 72–77 (1995)
6. Pentland, A.P.: Fractal-based description of natural scenes. IEEE Transactions on Pattern Analysis and Machine Intelligence 6(6), 661–674 (1984)

A New SIFT-Based Camera Calibration Method for Hybrid Dual-Camera

Yi-Qian Low, Sze-Wei Lee, Bok-Min Goi, and Mow-Song Ng

Faculty of Engineering and Science
Universiti Tunku Abdul Rahman
Kuala Lumpur, Malaysia
lowyq1@mail2.utar.edu.my, {leeszewei,goibm,ngms}@utar.edu.my

Abstract. Camera networks, consisting of various types of camera systems, play an important role in security surveillance system. This paper presents a new calibration method for hybrid multi-camera system; particularly, a video surveillance system with a static camera and a dynamic camera which is used for environment-monitoring and security purpose. The first static wide angle camera covers the complete scene, whereas the second dynamic camera, Pan-Tilt-Zoom (PTZ) camera provides multi-view-angle and multi-resolution images of the complete scene. The new proposed calibration method is based on Lowe's Scale invariant Feature Transform (SIFT) algorithm and keypoints are selected based on the measurement of their stability. To improve the accuracy and robustness, a simple noise (unwanted keypoints) filtering technique using trigonometry theorem has also been adopted in the proposed system. From the obtained experimental results, it is shown that great improvement, in term of the determination and detection rate (from 55.71% to 94.87%) in camera networks calibration, has been achieved.

Keywords: Camera Calibration, SIFT Algorithm, Mutli-camera System.

1 Introduction

Surveillance is the monitoring of the behaviour, activities, or changing information, usually of people and often in a surreptitious manner. Nowadays, video surveillance has become an important tool to help to reduce crime and protect public spaces. System surveillance reduced crime statistics, but there are drawbacks in the use of classic video camera; it obtains low resolution information and lack of flexibility to observe the complete scene. To overcome these problems, we propose a method which uses two different types of cameras; namely, a static wide angle camera and an active Pan-Tilt-Zoom (PTZ) camera. The static wide angle camera is used to observe a complete scene at a distance to provide a global view and used to detect and track multiple objects. Accuracy of the camera intrinsic and extrinsic parameter will affect and improve the measurement accuracy[1].

Camera calibration is much more complex when handling different kinds of cameras. Assuming that all cameras are linked in a camera networks, undergo a planer to control PTZ camera and object detection in static camera. But, background

A. Abd Manaf et al. (Eds.): ICIEIS 2011, Part II, CCIS 252, pp. 96–103, 2011.
© Springer-Verlag Berlin Heidelberg 2011

appearance is not stationary and camera parameters are kept on changing throughout the time while the PTZ cameras pan, tilt and zoom. Hence, it is difficult to compute and justify the spatial position of the object[3]. The traditional calibration methods need a known structure, high precision calibration object as a space reference and some tailor-designed algorithms to get the parameters of the cameras. This is to relate each others between the space point and the image point. These two principal sources of difficulty in performing the task are: (a) different appearance of the object from different viewpoints and illuminations; and (b) partial occlusion of the object of interest by other object[4]. Therefore, in order to overcome the shortcoming of the traditional methods, the Lowe's Scale invariant Feature Transform (SIFT) algorithm has been used to perform self-calibration in camera networks. It does not need any calibration object as the calibration can be done directly relying on the relationship of corresponding points of the number of image solely[1].

Fig. 1. The Hybrid Dual-Camera System

In this paper, we made three contributes:

a) Setup a testbed – the hybrid dual-camera systems, to collect data and fine tuning the parameters of PTZ camera, as shown in Fig. 1.
b) Propose, implement and test the new SIFT-based camera methods, with various parameter sets.
c) Introduce a novel filtering method by using trigonometry theorem. For proof of concept, this method has been adopted in the proposed methods and the empirical results showed that the detection rate of the calibration has been improved dramatically.

2   Background and Literature Review

The purpose of the dual camera calibration is to determine the coordinate of the region of interest on two camera images, and calibrate it to obtain a higher accuracy coordinate of the region of interest. Feature-based approach has been widely used in computer vision image processing. Hence, the most common image features in previous work are image contour, corner, region of interest or interest point and etc. Featured-based algorithms involve the extraction of regions of interest in the image and then identification of the counterparts in individual images of the sequence [5]. The well execution of feature extraction will reduce the amount of workload to be proceeded and also obtaining a higher level of understanding of scene as these features are matched between the frames. Meanwhile, Lowe's Scale Invariant Feature Transform (SIFT) features allows to transform an image into a large collection of local feature vectors, each of which is invariant to image translation, scaling, and rotation, and partially invariant to illumination changes and affine or 3D projection [6].

2.1   SIFT Theory

SIFT algorithm performs efficiently by using staged filtering approach [6]. The first stage identifies key locations in scale space by looking for locations that are maxima or minima of a difference-of-Gaussian function. Each point is used to generate a feature vector that describes the local image region sampled relative to its scale-space coordinate frame. The features achieve partial invariance to local variations, such as affine and 3D projections by blurring image gradient locations. The resulting vectors are called SIFT keys. The SIFT keys derived from an image are used in a nearest-neighbour approach to indexing to identify candidate object models. The feature extraction can be computed efficiently by building an image pyramid with re-sampling between each level.

  According to Lowe's method [8], SIFT algorithm detects keypoints using a cascade filtering approach to identify locations and scales that can be repeatedly assigned under differing views of the object.

  a) **Scale-space extrema detection:** The first stage of computation searches over all scales and image locations. Difference-of-Gaussian is being used to identify potential interest points that are invariant to scale and orientation.

  b) **Keypoint localization:** At each potential interest point, a detailed model is fit to determine location and scale. Keypoints are selected based on measures of their stabilities.

  c) **Orientation assignment:** One or more orientations are assigned to each keypoint location based on local image gradient directions. All future operations are performed on image data that has been transformed relative to the assigned orientation, scale, and location for each feature, thereby providing invariance to these transformations.

  d) **Keypoints descriptor:** The local image gradients are measured at the selected scale in the region around each keypoint. These are transformed into a representation that allows for significant levels of local shape distortion and change in illumination.

The SIFT algorithm computes for each keypoint and its location in the image as well as a distinctive 128-dimension descriptor vector associated with it [8, 9]. Matching a keypoint to a keypoints database is usually done by identifying its nearest neighbour in that database. The nearest neighbour is defined as the keypoint with minimum Euclidean distance to the keypoint descriptor [8]. To reduce the lag in the matching process, the ratio of the distance of the closest neighbour to that of the second closest neighbour is computed.

In matching processing, it is an exhaustive search due to high dimensionality of the keypoint. In order to increase the processing speed, k-dimensional tree [12] provide an efficient search for more than about 10-dimensional spaces. The tolerance threshold value is $0 < \chi < 1$. The smaller value χ, the higher similarity rate is needed to match each keypoint.

2.2 Theorem Trigonometry Filter (TTF)

In plane geometry, is about shape that can be show in 2-dimentional image. While we captured both images at the same time by using hybrid dual-camera system, it contains high similarity information. This image-to-image homology makes matching process much simpler. So, it is assume there are no rotations around and there is only one orientation. It is a good assumption to calculate the gradient of pairs' keypoints and classified them into either positive or negative orientation.

Theorem Trigonometry Filter playing the role to calculate and classified the orientation of the images. The threshold allow in the filter is $0 < \theta < 90$ degree of gradient. While the keypoints' gradient is greater or smaller than certain threshold for example, average degree of gradient ± 5 will be discarded.

Fig. 2. The setup of PTZ and Wide-Angle Cameras

3 Proposed Calibration Method

In our approach, different value was set for the PTZ. With each value, images were captured from each of the camera and build a camera network database. The construction of the database was built from frame-to-frame of the current view in wide angle camera and PTZ camera. Then, it is proceed with image extraction by using SIFT algorithm. In SIFT algorithm, each image was computed and keypoints information were gathered. After collected all the keypoints from both cameras, both images were matched according to nearest search in the feature descriptor space, k-d tree. Yet, Theorem Trigonometry Filter was being used in order to increase the detection rate of the matching process. Lastly, we localized the respected view to the scene. These processes will keep looping until the PTZ camera covered entire environment while matching with wide angle camera.

Through these processes, we stored the entire coordinate's value in to database. These large databases are useful while tracking the region of interest in future enhancement, for example, object tracking from one place to the other.

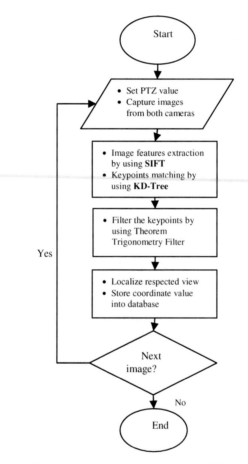

Fig. 3. Flowchart of the Processing Steps of the Proposed Hybrid Dual-Camera system

4   Experiment Results

Two different types of cameras which were used in this project were Samsung Mini SmartDome (PTZ) and a normal wide angle camera. PTZ camera consists of

10Megapixels resolution and 10 times optical zoom while wide angle camera has 2Megapixels resolution and 1 times optical zoom. Both of them were placed at the corner of the room, at about 2.5 meters height and 0.3 meter from each other. Images from both cameras were taken at 320x240 pixels of resolution.

Fig. 4 shows an example of current-frames from the PTZ camera were captured with different values of pan, tilt and zoom. The images stored inside the database. The large database will matched with the wide angle camera image. Fig. 5 shows the matching process between wide angle camera and PTZ camera with SIFT algorithm.

Fig. 4. Multiple Frames by the PTZ Camera with Different Values of Pan, Tilt and Zoom

In Fig. 4, the matching process was conducted to identify location of the image from wide angle camera using the PTZ camera's image as a model. Both images were captured from cameras and cascaded side by side. Then, matching process using SIFT algorithm and Theorem Trigonometry Filtering were demonstrated. The red solid lines show the correct matches while the blue lines are not in the TTF threshold value. Lastly, we localize the respected view which was a yellow box and only truth keypoints selected were shown in the images. The red box was the region of interest when matching process was completed.

Fig. 5. SIFT-based Keypoint Detection and Matching between Wide Angle Camera (Left) and PTZ Camera (Right)

Table 1. The accuracy(%) by using different threshold values

Kd-tree matching threshold	Positive Matching Pairs	Negative Matching Pairs	Without Filter (%)	With Filter (%)
0.4	39	31	55.71	94.87
0.5	55	46	54.46	90.90
0.6	75	67	52.81	90.67

In this experiment, different kd-tree matching threshold value applied to a sample image. Through the process in Fig. 3, the threshold value 0.4 computed 39 pairs of positive and 31 pairs of negative gradient keypoints that are found at matching locations. With the larger vote of positive pairs, we defined positive gradient consist more region of interest in the image. So, the calculation of matching percentage is 55.71%. Apparently, the rate of accuracy is increase from 55.71% to 94.87% after applied the Theorem Trigonometry filter.

5   Conclusion and Future Works

In this paper, the proposed calibration method for both different appearance of the object from different viewpoint and illumination has been presented, based on the basic PTZ camera networks. The empirical results showed that the proposed method could increase accuracy of calibration from 55.71% to 94.87%. Furthermore, our proposed algorithm does not require any 3D pre-processing in order to identify the region of interest from the view of PTZ camera. This approach produces a better solution in camera calibration in different scenarios. However, there are some limitations of the proposed approach, i.e. the detection rate of the image will be affected by the objects with high similarity located nearby. For future works, we are going to further reduce computational time and fine tune the internal and external parameters which cause the imperfection of the system.

References

1. Liu, R., Zhang, H., Liu, M., Xia, X., Hu, T.: Stereo Cameras Self-calibration Based on SIFT. In: 2009 International Conference on Measuring Technology and Mechatronics Automation (2009), doi:10.1109/ICMTMA.2009.338
2. de Agapito, L., Hayman, E., Reid, I.D.: Self-calibration of rotating and zooming cameras. International Journal of Computer Vision 45(2) (November 2001)
3. Del Bimbo, A., Dini, F., Lisanti, G., Pernici, F.: Exploiting distinctive visual landmark maps in pan–tilt–zoom camera networks. Computer Vision and Image Understanding 114, 611–623 (2010)
4. Bo, W., Nevatia, R.: Detection and Tracking of Multiple,Partially Occluded Humans by Bayesian Combination of Edgelet based Part Detectors. International Journal of Computer Vision, doi:10.1007/s11263-006-0027-7
5. Zhou, H., Yuan, Y., Shi, C.: Object tracking using SIFT features and mean shift. Computer Vision and Image Understanding 113, 345–352 (2009)
6. Lowe, D.G.: Object Recognition from Scale-Invariant Features. In: Proc. of International Conference on Computer Vision, Corfu, pp. 1150–1157 (September 1999)
7. Lindeberg, T.: Scale-space theory: a basic tool for analysing structures at different scales. J. Appl. Statist. 2(2), 224–270 (1994)
8. Lowe, D.G.: Distinctive Image Features from Scale-Invariant Keypoints. International Journal of Computer Vision (2004)
9. Liu, J., Hubbold, R.: Automatic Camera Calibration and Scene Reconstruction with Scale-Invariant Features. In: Bebis, G., Boyle, R., Parvin, B., Koracin, D., Remagnino, P., Nefian, A., Meenakshisundaram, G., Pascucci, V., Zara, J., Molineros, J., Theisel, H., Malzbender, T. (eds.) ISVC 2006. LNCS, vol. 4291, pp. 558–568. Springer, Heidelberg (2006)
10. Beis, J.S., Lowe, D.G.: Shape indexing using approximate nearest-neighbour search in high-dimensional spaces. In: CVPR, p. 1000 (1997)
11. Ke, Y., Sukthankar, R.: PCA-SIFT, A more distinctive representation for local image descriptors. In: CVPR, pp. 506–513 (2004)
12. Friedman, J.H., Bentley, J.L., Finkel, R.A.: An algorithm for finding best matches in logarithmic expected time. ACM Transactions on Mathematical Software 3(3), 209–226 (1977)

Performance Evaluation of Density Based Graph Cuts Segmentation Technique of Mammograms

Nafiza Saidin[1,*], Harsa Amylia Mat Sakim[1], Umi Khaltum Ngah[1],
and Ibrahim Lutfi Shuaib[2]

[1] School of Electrical and Electronic,
Universiti Sains Malaysia, 14300, Nibong Tebal, Penang, Malaysia
ns.1d09@student.usm.my
[2] Advanced Medical and Dental Institute,
Universiti Sains Malaysia, No 1-8 (Lot 8), Persiaran Seksyen 4/1,
Bandar Putra Bertam, 13200 Kepala Batas, Penang, Malaysia

Abstract. This paper involves the study of density based segmentation of mammograms using the graph cut technique. The focus of this research is for the segmentation of the dense area with regards to the breast anatomical structure for visualization, such as location of nipple if possible, skin-air interface, fatty tissue, glandular tissue and pectoral muscle. Previous related research has used rough ground truth, whereas this work emphasizes on using detail and precise ground truth in performance evaluation. In this paper, a comparison between the two is presented. It can be deduced that the comparison of performance evaluation for segmentation results by using different ground truths is not comparable, unless an objective ground truth is used or a clear definition and explanation of ground truth is stated for this kind of research in the future.

Keywords: Image processing, Image segmentation, Medical imaging, Breast Density, Mammography, Performance Evaluation.

1 Introduction

Breast cancer is the leading cause of cancer deaths in Asia, and it has become the commonest female malignancy in the developing Asian Countries [1]. Patients in developing countries are a decade younger compared with patients in developed and western countries [2, 3]. Younger patients' means that the mammographic images involved would be denser and thus are more difficult to diagnose [4]. Therefore, prognosis rate could be poor. In a dense breast, the sensitivity of mammography for early detection of breast cancers is reduced. This may be due to the fact that the tell-tale signs have similar x-ray attenuation properties are embedded in the dense tissue and therefore, become obliterated. So, it is most appropriate to focus on density based segmentation studies among Asian women.

Breast cancer usually occurs in the glandular part of breast tissue. The dense structure of the glandular tissue gives a measure of the breast density. The breast density portion contains ducts, lobular elements, and fibrous connective tissue of the

---

[*] Corresponding author.

A. Abd Manaf et al. (Eds.): ICIEIS 2011, Part II, CCIS 252, pp. 104–116, 2011.
© Springer-Verlag Berlin Heidelberg 2011

breast. Breast density is an important factor in the interpretation of a mammogram. The proportion of fatty and fibroglandular tissue of the breast region is evaluated by the radiologist during the process of interpretation of mammographic images. The result is subjective and varies from one radiologist to another. Breast Imaging Reporting and Data System (BIRADs), which was developed by the American College of Radiology (ACR) is the recent standard in radiology for categorizing the breast density [5]. BIRADs classify breast density into four major categories: (1) predominantly fat; (2) fat with some fibroglandular tissue; (3) heterogeneously dense; and (4) extremely dense. In the study done by Martin *et al.* [6], hormone therapies, including estrogen and tamoxifen treatments have been found to be able to change mammographic density [7-10] and alter the risk of breast cancer [11-14]. Therefore, a method for breast density detection can provide as a tool for investigating breast cancer risk. Subsequently, the association of breast density with the risk of breast cancer can be more definitive and will allow better monitoring response of a patient as preventive or interventional treatment of breast cancers.

Despite the fact that only a small group of researchers has done segmentation based on breast tissue anatomy. It was sound that by doing segmentation based on the anatomy, more detailed divisions can be made. For example, with the detection of the breast edge, distortion in breast structure and the nipple position in the breast will be detectable. This will also help in the diagnosis. The segmentation method proposed by Karssemeijer [15] allowed the subdivision of a mammogram into three distinct areas: breast tissue, pectoral muscle and background. Adel *et al.* proposed segmentation of breast regions into pectoral muscle, fatty and fibroglandular regions using Bayesian techniques with adaptation of Markov random field for detecting regions of different tissues on mammograms [16]. Aylward *et al.* segmented the breast into five regions using a combination of geometric (Gradient magnitude ridge traversal) and statistical (Gaussian mixture modeling) method [17]. The five regions that they segmented are the background, uncompressed fat, fat, dense tissue and muscle. El-Zaart segmented mammogram image into three regions, which are fibroglandular disc, breast region and background [18]. In this study, graph cut technique is able to segment the breast regions into the background, skin-air interface, fatty, glandular and pectoral muscle [19]. In many segmented images, the outline of the breast region is positioned more inwardly than the actual boundary, perhaps because the skin line was hardly visible. The previous segmentation research by Oliver *et al.* resulted in a minor loss of skin-air regions in the breast area [20]. This work has attempted to avoid this situation by preserving the skin line position and if possible, nipple location. This is important because it assists the practitioner in the detection of architectural distortion. Moreover, according to Karssemeijer [15], it is important to preserve the skin line position for feature selection. As a continuation of previous work [19], a performance evaluation of the segmentation results will be presented in this paper.

2   Methodology

A proper understanding of the breast anatomical regions on a mammogram is essential before actually executing the segmentation process. A mammogram consists of two different regions, which are the breast regions and non breast regions. The breast anatomical regions on a mammogram are illustrated in Fig. 1.

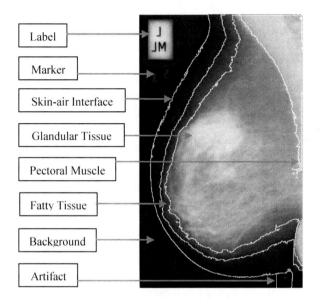

Fig. 1. A mammogram image composes of the image background, label, marker, artifact, skin-air interface, fatty tissue, pectoral muscle and denser glandular tissue

Breast regions can be partitioned into:

1. Skin-air interface region which contains uncompressed fatty tissue positioned at the periphery of the breast, near-skin tissue where the breast is poorly compressed.
2. Fatty region which is composed of fatty tissue is positioned next to the uncompressed fatty tissues and surrounds the denser region of fibroglandular tissue.
3. Glandular region which is composed of non uniform breast density tissue with heterogeneous texture that surrounds the hyperdense region of the fibroglandular tissue.
4. Hyperdense region which is represented by high density portions of the fibroglandular tissue, or may be that of a tumor.

Non breast regions contain unexposed air background regions such as the background, artifacts (scratches), bright rectangular label and opaque markers.

Most of the previous works were focused on the detection of masses and microcalcification. The niche of this study is the application of the Graph Cuts technique for detecting breast anatomical regions, including the glandular regions on the digitized mammograms. Usually, mass is represented by hyperdense structure. Overlapped fibroglandular tissue also has similar intensity with mass [21]. Hence, focusing on the glandular area and highlighting the hyperdense regions of the glandular area, may assist and act as a second opinion for experts in diagnosis. In using graph cuts, the user only needs to put labels on the desired regions to perform segmentation regardless of values to be set for thresholding. This is considered as a hard constraint (clues) that is imposed by the user. The graph cuts algorithm was developed with the aid of the software library developed by Olga Veksler. The graph cut equation is modified and represented as follows:

$$E(f) = \lambda \cdot \sum_{p \in P} D_p(L_p) + \mu \cdot \sum_{\{p,q\} \in N} V\{p,q\} \cdot \delta(L_p \neq L_q) \qquad (1)$$

$E(f)$ is an energy function and $L = \{L_p \mid_{p \in P}\}$ is a labeling of image P. The first term of this equation is called datacost or also known as the regional properties term by Boykov and Funka-Lea. $D_p(L_p)$ is a data penalty function and it indicates individual label preferences (hard constraint) of pixels based on observed intensities and pre-specified likelihood function [23]. The second term is called the smoothcost or also called boundary properties. $V_{\{p,q\}}$ is an interaction potential and it encourages spatial coherence by penalizing discontinuities between neighboring pixels. There are two constants, λ and μ, which correspond to datacost and smoothcost, purposely to obtain the optimal segmentation. Only four to six mark labels will be chosen, depending on how many different breast tissues need to be highlighted. After marking, the graph cuts algorithm is compiled and run. The user can repeat the process by repositioning the labels marks until the user is satisfied with the results. In this work, the value for data cost constant (λ) is set to 10 and smooth cost constant (μ) is set to 20.

The most essential requirement from a radiologist point of view for image processing algorithms is the ability to achieve enhanced visualizations of anatomical structure, while preserving the details of the structure [24]. Usually, the performance of the segmentation results is compared with the ground truth by the radiologists. Ground truth in this research means, a correct marking of the glandular tissue by the radiologist in a digital mammogram. The terms and formula used in evaluating the segmentation result is stated below:

1. True Positive (TP) means breast segmented or classified as glandular/dense tissue that proved to be glandular/dense tissue.
2. False Positive (FP) means breast segmented or classified as glandular/dense tissue that proved to be other tissues.
3. False Negative (FN) means breast segmented or classified as other tissues that proved to be glandular/dense tissue.
4. True Negative (TN) means breast segmented or classified as other tissues that proved to be other tissues.

Three performance metrics that are used in this evaluation are completeness (CM), correctness (CR) [25, 26] and quality (ρ) [25, 16]. Completeness is the percentage of the ground truth region which is explained by the segmented region. Correctness is the percentage of correctly extracted breast region type. A single metric which is quality (ρ), can be obtained by combining completeness and correctness [25, 16]. The optimum value for both metrics is 1.

$$Completeness \approx \frac{TP}{TP + FN} \qquad (2)$$

$$Correctness \approx \frac{FP}{FP + TN} \qquad (3)$$

$$Quality \approx \frac{TP}{FN + FP + TP} \tag{4}$$

The problem here is that the qualitative response of the radiologist is very subjective and varies hugely [24, 26, 27]. The ground truth by each radiologist may be different from one radiologist to another. Markings for ground truth depend on hands-on capability and skill. For example, a radiologist who is very careful, meticulous and experienced may give more detailed ground truth markings distinguishing ducts and lobules. On the flip side however, a radiologist who is not too diligent may give a rough outline by considering the whole glandular region. This practice may give rise to the inclusion of the fatty regions in the area of interest.

3 Results

In this study, the segmentation technique using graph cut have been tested on 40 images from mini-MIAS (Mammographic Image Analysis Society) Database [28] with normal cases, 10 images for fat and glandular breast types and 20 images for dense breast type. The relationship of each breast type and its BIRADs categories is also taken into consideration. More images are selected for the dense breast types. This is because those types of images can usually represent images for BIRADs 3 and BIRADs 4 categories. The confusion matrix of the breast types and BIRADs categories are shown in Table 1.

Table 1. Confusion matrix of breast types and birads categories

		BIRAD 1	BIRAD 2	BIRAD 3	BIRAD 4
TRUTH	FAT	10	0	0	0
	GLANDULAR	1	9	0	0
	DENSE	0	0	10	10

As stated before, the focus of this research is not only for the segmentation of density area but also considering the other breast anatomical structure for visualization such as the location of nipple if possible, the skin-air interface, fatty tissue, glandular tissue and pectoral muscle. Although there are other researchers who segment the breast region into fatty and dense regions [16, 18], the technique in this study has the capability of segmenting the image into its anatomical regions up to six regions. There are also studies, which concentrate on the detection of breast boundary or localization of nipple [25]. However, they have not considered the detection of dense areas. On the other hand, previous works which concentrate on the detection of breast density, have not considered on the preservation of breast boundary or localization of nipple [20]. Our approach here would be to take into consideration, the detection of breast density as well as to preserve if possible, the breast boundary or localization of nipple position.

For evaluating performance evaluation of the proposed method, ground truth sketching from an expert radiologist is obtained by using MIPAV software. Most of the previous research used a rough and simple ground truth [16, 29]. On the other hand, in this study, the ground truth is detailed and precise, which can also delineate lobule and ducts of the breast. The ground truths are done by an expert radiologist who has more than 20 years of experience. From his point of view, a sketching of ground truth is not enough to present heterogeneous region (BIRADs 1, 2 and 3), but it can be used to represent a homogeneous region (BIRADs 4). By using a rough ground truth to represent the heterogeneous or homogenous region, most probably, the fatty tissues will also be included inside the regions. On the experimental results, the ground truth is represented by sketching with red in color. Although the graph cuts technique has the capability to segment breast region into its anatomical regions, the performance evaluation in this research is focusing only on the glandular tissue, which involves the dense area omitting the pectoral muscle region. The dense area, which is represented with the yellow region in color labeled graph cuts and brightest region in the gray labeled graph cuts technique, is compared with the ground truth and then the performance evaluation metrics is calculated.

Performance evaluation has been evaluated on the mammograms with different breast tissue type or BIRADs categories, which are fatty (Fat), fatty-glandular (GL) and dense-glandular (D) breast type. Overall, for the 40 normal images, the mean value for completeness (CM), correctness (CR) and quality (ρ) were 0.702, 0.635 and 0.513. For fatty breast tissue type, the mean values for completeness, correctness and quality were 0.334, 0.426 and 0.189. For fatty-glandular breast tissue type, the mean values for completeness, correctness and quality were 0.839, 0.488 and 0.447. And for dense-glandular breast tissue type, the mean values for completeness, correctness and quality were 0.818, 0.814 and 0.707. Performance evaluation results of graph cuts technique are shown on Fig. 2, where y axis represented mean values using completeness, correctness and quality metrics for different breast tissue type and overall image, in x axis.

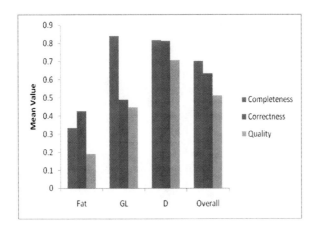

Fig. 2. Performance evaluation results of graph cuts using completeness, correctness and quality technique for different breast tissue type and overall image

The first experiment deals with a mammogram which is predominantly comprised of fatty tissues. The BIRADs category for this case is 1. Fig. 3 shows the original image with ground truth and graph cuts (GC) segmentation results for MIAS image mdb079 compared with the ground truth. The performance evaluation result for MIAS image mdb079 was obtained using CM=0.582, CR= 0.271 and ρ= 0.227.

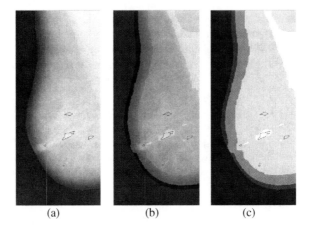

(a)   (b)   (c)

Fig. 3. (a) Fatty image mdb079 with radiologist ground truth (red outline), segmentation of image mdb079 using GC and output segmented image with (b) color label and (c) grayscale label superimposed with radiologist ground truth

The second experiment deals with a mammogram which is predominantly comprised of glandular tissue. Here, the BIRADs category is 2. Fig. 4 shows the original image with ground truth and graph cuts (GC) segmentation results for MIAS image mdb041 compared with ground truth. The performance evaluation result for MIAS image mdb041 was obtained using CM=0.936, CR−0.919 and ρ=0.865.

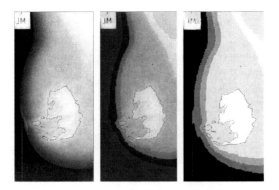

Fig. 4. (a) Dense image mdb041 with radiologist ground truth (red outline), segmentation of image mdb041 using GC and output segmented image with (b) color label and (c) grayscale label superimposed with radiologist ground truth

The third experiment deals with a mammogram which is predominantly comprised of dense tissue and for this, the BIRADs category is 3. Fig. 5 shows the original image with the ground truth and graph cuts (GC) segmentation results for MIAS image mdb106 compared with ground truth. The performance evaluation result for MIAS image mdb106 was obtained using CM=0.965, CR=0.627 and ρ= 0.614.

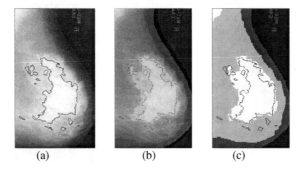

(a)   (b)   (c)

Fig. 5. (a) Dense image mdb106 with radiologist ground truth (red outline), segmentation of image mdb106 using GC and output segmented image with (b) color label and (c) grayscale label superimposed with radiologist ground truth

The fourth experiment deals with a mammogram which is predominantly comprised of dense tissue and here, the BIRADs category is 4. Fig. 6 shows the original image with the ground truth and graph cuts (GC) segmentation results for MIAS image mdb003 compared with ground truth. The performance evaluation result for MIAS image mdb003 was obtained using CM=0.877, CR=0.940 and ρ= 0.831.

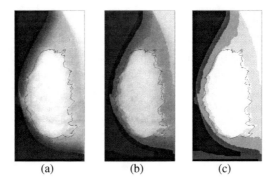

(a)   (b)   (c)

Fig. 6. (a) Dense image mdb003 with radiologist ground truth (red outline), segmentation of image mdb003 using GC and output segmented image with (b) color label and (c) grayscale label superimposed with radiologist ground truth

The fifth experiment deals with a mammogram which is predominantly comprised of fatty tissues and BIRADs category is 1. Fig. 7 shows the original image with ground truth and graph cuts (GC) segmentation results for MIAS image mdb009 compared with ground truth. The performance evaluation result for MIAS image mdb009 was obtained using CM=0.501, CR= 0.149 and ρ= 0.130.

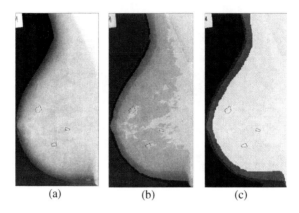

(a)   (b)   (c)

Fig. 7. (a) Fatty image mdb009 with radiologist ground truth (red outline), segmentation of image mdb009 using GC and output segmented image with (b) color label and (c) grayscale label superimposed with radiologist ground truth

According to Nishikawa *et al.* [27], it is not meaningful to compare different techniques if the techniques are tested on different databases. Therefore, we have compared our findings with other studies that used images from the same database. However, there are very few techniques that have been tested using quantitative performance evaluation involving ground truth from a radiologist. We have compared the performance evaluation of our technique with the previous technique by Adel *et al.* [16], whereby Bayesian technique with an adaptation of Markov random field was used. Adel *et al.* [16] evaluated their performance evaluation using quality metric and the results of the metric for mdb003 (dense-glandular breast type), mdb009 (fatty breast type) and mdb041 (fatty-glandular breast type) were 0.58, 0.185 and 0.77 respectively; whereas our results for the same images are **0.831, 0.130** and **0.865**. For the dense-glandular and fatty-glandular breast types, our method produced better results of quality metric compared with the previous method. Although ours result are found to be poor for the fatty image mdb009, the segmented output image is quite similar, if we compare the segmented image with the previous segmented image by Adel *et al* [16]. This means that the difference in quality metric is caused by the difference in ground truths. With the different ground truths, it will affect the reliability of the performance evaluation of the segmentation result. Therefore, it is absolutely necessary to find a way to obtain an objective ground truth.

4 Discussion

The graph cut segmentation technique can segment image into the respective background, i.e. the skin-air interface, fatty, glandular and pectoral muscle regions. It can also preserve the nipple position, if need be. The performance evaluation result is good for dense breast type, which usually has homogeneous regions. This is because the homogenous region only needs one sketching of the ground truth similar with the other research. The performance evaluation results using correctness and quality metrics decreases in the fatty-glandular breast type (which involve heterogeneous region). In fatty breast type, the computerized method has difficulty in detecting the dense structure if the intensity is quite similar. Fortunately, a fully experienced radiologist can delineate the dense structure of duct and lobule in the detail ground truth although the intensity is not obviously different. However, with the detail and precise ground truth, the problem faced is that the completeness, correctness and quality metrics of the proposed method will be low for the fatty breast type. It is because by using detailed ground truth that involves multiple regions, the false positive and false negative values will be increased. Subsequently, it will affect the performance evaluation results of completeness, correctness and quality. For the fatty breast type with similar intensity normally there is no probability or sign for mass, unless there is a distinct intensity. Therefore, in generally this will not affect the diagnosis.

In this paper, a comparison of this study which uses detailed ground truth with existing works that used rough ground truth is also presented. The completeness, correctness and quality of the proposed method are better or comparable to the previous research for fatty-glandular and dense-glandular type of breast (BIRADs 2, 3 and 4). However, the performance evaluations which involve fatty images produce poor results compared with the previous researches. This is because; the more detailed ground truth of glandular breast type involves multiple locations of density area to represent the heterogeneous region and previous researches' only considered one location spread over a large area as their ground truths. The different ground truths will affect the performance evaluation result, although the segmentation result is quite similar.

It is very difficult to compare manual ground truth sketching with the computerized results. This is because; a radiologist's sketch is based on his or her own interpretation of the detailed breast anatomical structure, while computerized results are based on the intensity. A computerized method may be powerful enough to discriminate pixel values based upon the intensity; a radiologist on the other hand, uses his or her own naked eyes in the differentiation of intensity. However, a fully experienced radiologist has the capability to make interpretations based on detailed anatomical structure compared with the computerized method whose workings are only based upon the intensity. Ground truths can be accepted as guidance in performance evaluation; however, it is not an absolute evaluation. There are still restrictions and limitations in the performance evaluation of segmentation results and there is a necessity for further improvement.

5   Conclusion and Recommendations

The experimental results are promising; indicating that the graph cuts technique can delineate the breast tissue region in mammograms, including the skin-air interface, the fatty, the glandular and the pectoral muscle region. This study has emphasized on using detailed and precise ground truths in performance evaluation. The performance evaluation results show the robustness of the graph cut method, especially for the dense glandular breast type of images. This research has tried to highlight that the comparison of performance evaluation for segmentation results by using different ground truth is not comparable.

In the performance evaluation, there is still no standard measurement or an objective ground truth for the mammogram images that had been segmented as yet. Hence, future research should try to identify the same ground truth in order to compare the computer assisted system that will be developed. A standard definition or explanation of ground truth is deemed necessary, so that an objective ground truth can be sketched correctly according to the criteria derived. The next direction of this work would be to make the classification of breast mammograms into BIRADs categories. The segmentation and classification methods would extensively be tested on a large number of mammogram images. Therefore, future work will combine all the steps in the Computer Aided Diagnosis System.

Acknowledgment. The authors would like to acknowledge USM-RU-PGRS under Grant 1001/PELECT/8042038 for providing financial support for this work.

References

1. Agarwal, G., Pradeep, P.V., Aggarwal, V., Yip, C.-H., Cheung, P.S.Y.: Spectrum of Breast Cancer in Asian Women. World Journal of Surgery 31(5), 1031–1040 (2007)
2. GLOBOCAN 2008: Cancer Incidence and Mortality Worldwide in 2008. The International Agency for Research on Cancer (IARC), http://globocan.iarc.fr/
3. Hisham, A.N., Yip, C.-H.: Overview of Breast Cancer in Malaysian Women: A Problem with Late Diagnosis. Asian Journal of Surgery 27(2), 130–133 (2004)
4. Subashini, T.S., Ramalingam, V., Palanivel, S.: Automated Assessment of Breast Tissue Density in Digital Mammograms. Computer Vision and Image Understanding 114(1), 33–43 (2010)
5. American College of Radiology. American College of Radiology Breast Imaging Reporting and Data System (BIRADS). 4th ed., American College of Radiology, Reston, VA (2003)
6. Martin, K.E., Helvie, M.A., Zhou, C., Roubidoux, M.A., Bailey, J.E., Paramagul, C., Blane, C.E., Klein, K.A., Sonnad, S.S., Chan, H.-P.: Mammographic Density Measured with Quantitative Computer-aided Method- Comparison with Radiologists' Estimates and BI-RADS Categories. Radiology 240, 656–665 (2006)
7. Heine, J.J., Malhotra, P.: Mammographic Tissue, Breast Cancer Risk, Serial Image Analysis, and Digital Mammography. Acad. Radiol. 9, 298–335 (2002)
8. Stomper, P.C., Van Voorhis, B.J., Ravnikar, V.A., Meyer, J.E.: Mammographic Changes Associated with Postmenopausal Hormone Replacement Therapy: a Longitudinal Study. Radiology 174, 487–490 (1990)
9. Laya, M.B., Gallagher, J.C., Schreiman, J.S., Larson, E.B., Watson, P., Weinstein, L.: Effect of Postmenopausal Hormonal Replacement Therapy on Mammographic Density and Parenchymal Pattern. Radiology 196, 433–437 (1995)

10. Son, H.J., Oh, K.K.: Significance of Follow-up Mammography in Estimating the Effect of Tamoxifen in Breast Cancer Patients Who Have Undergone Surgery. AJR Am. J. Roentgenol. 173, 905–909 (1999)
11. Colditz, G.A., Hankinson, S.E., Hunter, D.J., Willett, W.C., Manson, J.E., Stampfer, M.J., Hennekens, C., Rosner, B., Speizer, F.E.: The Use of Estrogens and Progestins and the Risk of Breast Cancer in Postmenopausal Women. N. Engl. J. Med. 332, 1589–1593 (1995)
12. Ross, R.K., Paganini-Hill, A., Wan, P.C., Pike, M.C.: Effect of Hormone Replacement Therapy on Breast Cancer Risk: Estrogen Versus Estrogen Plus Progestin. J. Natl. Cancer Inst. 92, 328–332 (2000)
13. Fisher, B., Costantino, J.P., Wickerham, D.L., Redmond, C.K., Kavanah, M., Cronin, W.M., Vogel, V., Robidoux, A., Dimitrov, N., Atkins, J., Daly, M., Wieand, S., Tan-Chiu, E., Ford, L., Wolmark, N.: Tamoxifen for Prevention of Breast Cancer: Report of the National Surgical Adjuvant Breast and Bowel Project P-1 Study. J. Natl. Cancer Inst. 90, 1371–1388 (1998)
14. Rossouw, J.E., Anderson, G.L., Prentice, R.L., et al.: Risks and Benefits of Estrogen Plus Progestin in Healthy Postmenopausal Women: Principal Results from the Women's Health Initiative Randomized Controlled Trial. JAMA 288, 321–333 (2002)
15. Karssemeijer, N.: Automated Classification of Parenchymal Patterns in Mammograms. Phys. Med. Biol. 43, 365–378 (1998)
16. Adel, M., Rasigni, M., Bourennane, S., Juhan, V.: Statistical Segmentation of Regions of Interest on a Mammographic Image. EURASIP Journal on Advances in Signal Processing 2007, Article ID 49482, 1–8 (2007)
17. Aylward, S.R., Hemminger, B.M., Pisano, E.D.: Mixture Modeling for Digital Mammogram Display and Analysis. In: Karssemeijer, N., Thijssen, M.A.O., Hendriks, J.H.C.L., Van Erning, L.J.T.O. (eds.) Digital Mammography. Computational Imaging and Vision Series, vol. 13, pp. 305–312. Kluwer Academic Publishers, Dordrecht (1998)
18. El-Zaart, A.: Expectation–maximization technique for fibro-glandular discs detection in mammography images. Comput. Biol. Med. 40(4), 392–401 (2010)
19. Saidin, N., Ngah, U.K., Sakim, H.A.M., Siong, D.N., Hoe, M.K.: Density Based Breast Segmentation for Mammograms Using Graph Cut Techniques. In: TENCON (IEEE Region 10 Conf.), pp. 1–5 (2009)
20. Oliver, A., Freixenet, J., Martí, R., Pont, J., Pérez, E., Denton, E.R., Zwiggelaar, R.: A Novel Breast Tissue Density Classification Methodology. IEEE Trans. Inf. Technol. Biomed. 12(1), 55–65 (2008)
21. Pierre, M.: Combining Assembles of Domain Expert Markings. M. Sc. Thesis, Department of Computing Science, Ume°a University, Sweden (2010)
22. Wolfe, J.N.: Breast Patterns as an Index of Risk for Developing Breast Cancer. Journal of Roentgenology 26, 1130–1139 (1976)
23. Boyd, N.F., Rommens, J.M., Vogt, K., Lee, V., Hopper, J.L., Yaffe, M.J., Paterson, A.D.: Mammographic Breast Density as an Intermediate Phenotype for Breast Cancer. Lancet Oncology 6, 798–808 (2005)
24. Wirth, M.A.: Performance Evaluation of CADe Algorithms in Mammography. In: Suri, J.S., Rangayyan, R.M. (eds.) Recent Advances in Breast Imaging, Mammography, and Computer-Aided Diagnosis of Breast Cancer, pp. 640–671. SPIE Press, Bellingham
25. Wirth, W., Nikitenko, D., Lyon, J.: Segmentation of Breast Region in Mammograms using a Rule-Based Fuzzy Reasoning Algorithm. ICGST Graphics, Vision and Image Processing Journal 5(2), 45–54 (2005)

26. Wirth, M., Lyon, J., Fraschini, M., Nikitenko, D.: The Effect of Mammogram Databases on Algorithm Performance. In: Proceedings of the 17th IEEE Symposium on Computer-Based Medical Systems (2004)
27. Nishikawa, R.H., Giger, M.L., Doi, K., Metz, C.E., Yin, F.F., Vyborny, C.J., Schmidt, R.A.: Effect of Case Selection on the Performance of Computer-aided Detection Schemes. Medical Physics, AAPM, 265–269 (1994)
28. Heath, M., Bowyer, K., Kopans, D., Moore, R., Kegelmeyer, P.: The Digital Database for Screening Mammography. In: Proceedings of the Fifth International Workshop on Digital Mammography, pp. 212–218 (2001)
29. Olsén, C., Georgsson, F.: Assessing Ground Truth of Glandular Tissue. In: Astley, S.M., Brady, M., Rose, C., Zwiggelaar, R. (eds.) IWDM 2006. LNCS, vol. 4046, pp. 10–17. Springer, Heidelberg (2006)

User Acceptance of Panoramic Views as a Technique for Virtual Tour in an Educational Environment

Asma Hanee Ariffin[1] and Abdullah Zawawi Talib[2]

[1] Faculty of Art, Computing and Creative Industry,
Universiti Pendidikan Sultan Idris, Tanjong Malim, Perak, Malaysia
asma@fskik.upsi.edu.my
[2] School of Computer Sciences, Universiti Sains Malaysia,
Penang, Malaysia
azht@cs.usm.my

Abstract. Different levels of knowledge and expertise of the audience may lead to different levels of acceptance of the chosen technology. This paper presents a study on user acceptance of different groups of users of panoramic views as a presentation tool of the landscape of an educational environment which is Universiti Pendidikan Sultan Idris. Basically, the panoramic views were developed using mosaicking which is one of the Image-Based Rendering techniques (IBR). The evaluation of the user acceptance of this image-based approach in a virtual tour was on behavioral intention (perceived usefulness and perceived ease of use) based on Technology Acceptance Model (TAM) by Davis which is determined by acceptance criteria requirement specifications as suggested by Southern Idaho Society for Software Quality Assurance (SISQA). Additionally, a new determinant which is perceived enjoyment which is adapted from the original two determinants was also used in the evaluation. Based on the interviews and hands-on sessions, the participants found that panoramic views can be accepted as a presentation tool although several recommendations were suggested from different groups of participants. The result has established preliminary evidence that indicates the sign of readiness and suitability in using Virtual Reality (VR) technology for creating innovative learning environment.

Keywords: user acceptance, panoramic view, Technology Acceptance Model.

1 Introduction

Presenting and visualizing interesting places and workplaces, or promoting products require the organization or presenter to deliver information as close as it could possibly be to the targeted audience. If the presentation finally grasps their attention that is they can immersively blend into the idea being presented, it will definitely increase the benefit to the organization. When delivering or presenting the information virtually, creating a variety of ways of grasping the first impression of various levels of users (novice to expert users) is crucial and needs to be emphasized. The conventional ways of using still images and texts need to be enhanced and enlightened up by using other interactive or immersive technologies.

A. Abd Manaf et al. (Eds.): ICIEIS 2011, Part II, CCIS 252, pp. 117–127, 2011.

Using panoramic images as a tool in a virtual tour can alternatively replace simple and conventional ways such as using single images, or more complicated ways such as using 3-D computer graphics model of the specific virtual environment [1]. When the targeted landscapes are marked, linked and compressed together, a picture-based virtual tour that allows the users to look around and move forward to the next scene nodes is created [2]. However, the acceptance and motivation of targeted users may vary based on certain criteria, such as behavioural intention in using the system [3]. In this paper, user acceptance towards the image-based approach is measured qualitatively based on user interactions with a picture-based virtual tour of an academic institution which is Universiti Pendidikan Sultan Idris (UPSI).

UPSI is an academic institution that typically aims towards producing excellent and innovative educators. Therefore, staff as well as students in UPSI must be aware of suitable delivery technologies in order to create more attractive teaching and learning sessions. In order to invite users to use technology, an application developer needs to exploit virtual environment where the users can freely interact and capture the feel as if they are in the actual place. Panoramic view of UPSI is a prototype developed with an attempt to present landscapes of lab facilities in UPSI using a picture-based virtual tour.

As a preliminary study, an organized measure to evaluate the user acceptance towards this image-based approach must start somewhere and this paper aims to fulfil that call. We first review picture-based virtual tour approach with a brief introduction on mosaicking, its application in education and user acceptance criteria, which is based on technology acceptance model (TAM). The next section comprised two different methodologies of measuring user acceptance and constructing the prototype for the panoramic view application. This is followed by a discussion on the findings pertaining to users' evaluation based on the interview and presentation sessions conducted during the study.

2 Background and Related Work

This section describes the basic ideas and related work on the technique of mosaicking and its applications, and the user acceptance criteria.

2.1 Mosaicking: Panoramic View from Stitching Sequence of Images

Creating virtual environment can best be associated with three-dimensional (3-D) elements. However, constraints in creating 3-D computer graphics using traditional 3-D model-based rendering lead to extensive research work on Image-Based Rendering (IBR). 3-D model-based rendering is generally referred to as explicit use of complex geometric 3-D models, and it is time-consuming and requires sophisticated, fragile and expensive software and hardware for realisms. On the other hand, IBR relies on a collection of images or photographs, and is economical as it is based on the extensive use of digital cameras available in the mass market. It is time savvy compared to fine-grained geometric modeling ([4], [5], [6], [7], [8], [9]).

In a survey conducted by [4] on IBR techniques, there are three types of panoramic image and ways of generating 'mosaics' which are stitched images that form a larger view of an image. Types of panoramic images are based on the field of view and parts of scene to be included (eg. top and bottom view). For instance, rectilinear panoramic images are suitable for a relatively small field of view (less than 180º) rather than cylindrical panoramic images which are suitable for a wide scene view. If part of the scene involved top and bottom view, spherical images are recommended where camera with fisheye lens are required [4].

2.2 Applications of Panoramic View

Interactive and immersive elements of panoramic viewing technology have successfully attracted several application domains. Basically, it is suitable for exploration of real or imaginary scenes in many areas which include tourism, e-commerce, entertainment as well as education [9].

Education, a field that is specifically related to this study can utilize this technology in two different ways. Firstly, the panoramic view and IBR approaches are the cheaper and easier ways of using Virtual Reality (VR) in schools since the use of high-end VR with head displays such as VR goggles, data gloves and sensors is costly and too complex to most students and teachers [10]. As a variation of using a map, watching video and site-visit while teaching subjects like Geography and History, panoramic view would be able to provide a similar excitement of immersiveness and experiences. It may not be as good as real visit, but it may provide a better impression rather than using single still images and text books.

Secondly, academic institutions can embed virtual tours in their portals in an effort to attract visitors to view their campus and also as a way to present the location of every building within the campus. For examples, as shown in Fig.1, an academic

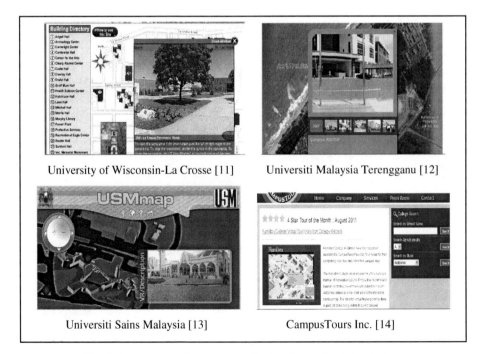

University of Wisconsin-La Crosse [11]   Universiti Malaysia Terengganu [12]

Universiti Sains Malaysia [13]   CampusTours Inc. [14]

Fig. 1. Examples of virtual tour application for academic institutions

institution can be compressed in a virtual campus tour project as in CampusTours Inc., an interactive map that combines panoramic views of the University of Wisconsin-La Crosse, and campus virtual tours of Universiti Malaysia Terengganu and Universiti Sains Malaysia.

Recent advances in this area especially in education have inspired us to develop a virtual tour of computer labs in UPSI using panoramic views. Currently, the facilities offered can be viewed in still images. Panoramic viewing is one of the most attractive methods that can be introduced in addition to the traditional still images presentation via the web. Furthermore, once the academics and computer administration staff as well as the students are prepared to accept this approach, the technique could be further adopted in teaching and learning activities.

2.3 User Acceptance Criteria

Several measures have been studied in different prominent literature on user acceptance of Information System applications. Of all factors that may influence user acceptance, determinants which were suggested based on Technology Acceptance Model (TAM) as shown in Fig. 2, have been highly regarded by many researchers ([15],[16],[17]).

The determinants used in this study are Perceived Usefulness (PU), Ease of Use (PEOU) and Enjoyment (PEnjoy). Perceived usefulness (PU) is defined as "the degree to which an individual believes that using a particular system would enhance his or her job performance [3]". The system that is considered to be useful may also in return, assists the user in many beneficial ways such as job reinforcement and providing time-and-cost-savvy task.

Perceived ease of use (PEOU) is defined as the degree to which an individual believes that using a particular system would be free of difficulty or great effort. Mostly, an application that is perceived to be easier to use than another is more likely to be accepted by users [19].

In addition to the above determinants, Davis [18] was aware that user acceptance may be influenced by not only extrinsic motivation as highlighted in TAM, but it may

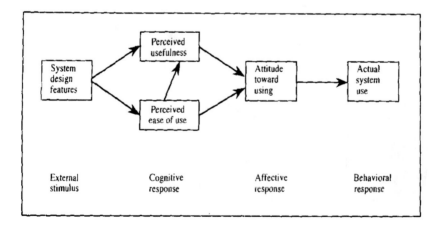

Fig. 2. Technology acceptance model [18]

also be caused by intrinsic motivation, which is relevant to perceived enjoyment from using the system as stated by Malone [20]. Therefore, some researchers extended TAM by including other determinants, such as TAM3 which includes Perceived Enjoyment (PEnjoy) ([21],[22]).

Perceived enjoyment is "the extent to which the activity of using a specific system is perceived to be enjoyable in its own right, aside from any performance consequences resulting from system used" [23]. Hence, this study also includes PEnjoy as the determinant of behavioural intention that is influenced by the two previous determinants, which are PU and PEOU.

As suggested by The Southern Idaho Society for Software Quality Assurance (SISQA), for every determinant that is listed, there are definitions on acceptance criteria that will be the basis for evaluating every determinant. The following four acceptance criteria were highlighted by Langley [24];

- Functionality Requirements which relate to the business rules that the system must execute.
- Performance Requirements which relate to operational aspects, such as time or resource constraints.
- Interface Quality Requirements which relate to connections from one component to another component of processing.
- Overall Software Quality Requirements which specify limits for factors or attributes such as reliability, testability, correctness and usability.

3 Research Methodology and Implementation

This section presents a more detailed picture for evaluating different group of users' acceptance towards the panoramic view prototype and the steps involved in the authoring process to construct the prototype.

3.1 Research Model and Hypotheses

Since technological and social changes may lead to a major impact in teaching and learning, there is a need for parallel learning styles that suits our current generation of students who are more enthusiastic with virtual technologies [25]. As a preliminary study, this research aims to study three different groups of users' acceptance (lab administration staff, academic staff and undergraduate students) towards panoramic view by utilizing a qualitative research design. As mentioned earlier, realizing the fact that TAM has been a great influence and inspiration to previous researchers and in order to suit the panoramic view application in this research, the two determinants which are Perceived Usefulness (PU) and Perceived Ease of Use (PEOU) are adapted to form a new determinant which is Perceived Enjoyment (PEnjoy) which is used in this study in addition to PU and PEOU.

Qualitative analysis was conducted from application presentations, observations and interviews with all the three groups of users. Interview questions were derived based on four themes which are labelled as acceptance criteria from [24].

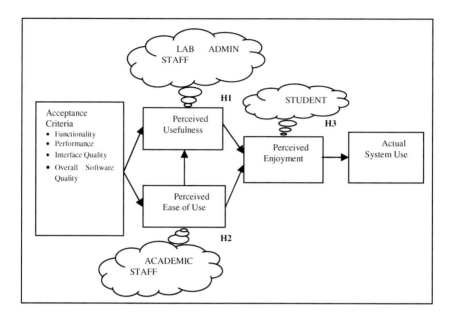

Fig. 3. Research model for different group of users' acceptance towards panoramic view

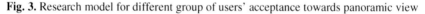

Based on Fig.3, the hypotheses are formulated as follows:

H1:   The computer lab administration staff are influenced to use *Panoramic View of UPSI* based on Perceived Usefulness (PU) criteria.

H2:   The academic staff are influenced to use *Panoramic View of UPSI* based on Perceived Ease of Use (PEOU) criteria.

H3:   The undergraduate students are influenced to use *Panoramic View of UPSI* based on Perceived Enjoyment (PEnjoy) criteria.

The interview question sets as derived based on the four acceptance criteria are used to measure the hypotheses. The criteria are as follows:

- Functionality Requirements part for determining PU criteria of the application for computer lab administration staff (**H1**).
- Performance Requirements part for determining PEOU criteria of the application for academic staff (**H2**).
- Interface Quality Requirements part for determining PEnjoy criteria of the application for undergraduate students (**H3**).
- The overall Software Quality Requirements part as supportive evidence for all hypotheses and users. (**H1,H2,H3**).

3.2 Panoramic View of UPSI

To construct the protoype for the panoramic view application, this research adopted the authoring process adapted from [9]. For the ease of viewing, the panoramic views are combined into a virtual tour and uploaded in the UPSI official portal.

Node Selection. There are four main nodes selected which are the four locations of the lab facilities; *Bangunan Teknologi Maklumat*, *Bangunan KDP*, *Makmal* IT and *Bangunan Sains dan Teknologi*. As mentioned by [9], "the nodes are selected in such way that visual consistency is maintained when moving from one to another". Since no panoramic professional equipments are available, a normal digital camera was used by placing it on a tripod and rotating it in sequence in one direction.

Stitching. After transfering the sequence of images into the computer, this mosaicking process was completed by using a stitching software to stitch the images together into panoramic views. Based on the surroundings of the location, two types of panoramic views are produced which are rectilinear (less than 180° views) by using Realviz StitcherExpress 2, and cylindrical panoramic views (360° views) by using Ulead Cool 360 1.0. The panoramic view images were saved into two formats which are Quick Time movie to be viewed in Quick Time Player, and JPEG format that combines the images for virtual tour production.

Hot Spot Marking and Linking. By using Tourweaver 1.30, it is easier to generate the virtual tour by just planning, arranging and publishing the still images and panoramic images (JPEG format). The software offers an easy step-by-step development process to produce the virtual tour. Adobe Photoshop CS is used to touch up and resize the images into the required sizes. Once the skin was prepared, the selected still images and panoramic images were arranged with suitable text, audio and linked to the UPSI location map. All the images were then marked with suitable hot spots that link different nodes as selection to user. Once the virtual tour was published, the virtual tour file was uploaded to Joomla!, an open source content management system to allow viewing via UPSI portal. Dice and compress process were automatically done by the software used while publishing the virtual tour.

4 Evaluation

The panoramic views were presented to ten staff members (including Information Technology lecturers, Information Tecnology officers and computer lab technicians) and ten students as internal respondents to evaluate the user acceptance of this application. A set of questions adapted based on four themes from [24] were asked during the interview session while the respondents tried to view the panoramic views and virtual tour. The responses were compiled and summarized.

The panoramic view as shown in Fig.4 were presented and viewed by 20 randomly selected respondents. The test was conducted to evaluate the preliminary acceptance of this approach compared to the current presentation. The user acceptance test consists of four themes which are the functionality requirements (related to H1) which are concerned with a manageable system that can be an additional way of presenting the information and facilities of UPSI, the performance requirements (related to H2) which pertain to the operational aspects based on the ease of use by academic staff as presenter to the application, the interface quality requirements (related to H3) which focus on elements that bring forms of enjoyment especially to the undergraduate students (aspects of virtual tour - location map with hot spots, slide show, slide information, sound and thumbnails), and the overall approach of the quality requirements which specify limits for factors or attributes that relate to all three hypotheses such as reliability, testability, correctness, and usability of the application.

Fig. 4. Panoramic view of UPSI

5   Results and Discussion

The results of the evaluation are summarized in Table 1. For the functionality requirements (H1: PU), all the respondents agreed on these requirements since the virtual tour contains non-stop slide show that can easily be plugged-in by the computer lab administration staff in applications such as a presentation tool to visitors. For the performance requirements (H2:PEOU), six respondents complained on the time constraints of the approach. The virtual tour is quite slow and often stucked when clicking on the map's hot-spot while running the slide show. This may be due to the different types of browser being used by the users. Seven respondents complained on the lack of assistance while navigating the virtual tour. Seven respondents focused on the slow speed and resource constraints of plugging-in in Quick Time Player. For the interface quality requirements (H3:PEnjoy) All twenty respondents agreed that there were no broken link between the hot spots but they agreed that the size of the still images is not suitable with the slide show.

Furthermore, they did not noticed the scroll bar. For the final requirements (all three hypotheses such all of them agreed on the reliability, testability, correctness, and usability of the approach although there are rooms for improvement as suggested by the lecturers and Information Technology officers.

Table 1. Results Based on Targeted Hypotheses and Interview Questions

Hypotheses	Relevant Criteria	Results (Total Respondents = 20)
H1: PU	**Functionality** Requirements: Computer lab administration staff	**All respondents** agreed. **Reason:** The virtual tour contains non-stop slide show that can easily be plugged-in.
H2: PEOU	**Performance** Requirements: Academic staff	**6 respondents** complained on the time constraints of the approach. **Reason:** The virtual tour is quite slow and often stucked when clicking on the map's hot-spot while running the slide show. This may be due to the different types of browser being used. **7 respondents** complained on the lack of assistance. **Reason**: Problem while navigating the virtual tour. **7 respondents** focused on resource constraints of plugging-in in Quick Time Player.
H3: PEnjoy	**Interface Quality** Requirements: Undergraduate students	**All respondents** agreed but with **Reason**: There were no broken link between the hot spots BUT the size of the still images is not suitable with the slide show AND they did not noticed the scroll bar.
All Hypotheses	**The Overall Software Quality** Requirements: All users	**All respondents** agreed but with the above comment for improvement.

5   Conclusion

Based on users' feedbacks and findings during the evaluation we can conclude the followings for a personalised and adaptive tool to strengthen the users' chain:

- Lab administration staff perceived usefulness since they can deliver the application as a useful tool for the academic staff.
- Academic staff perceived ease of use since they can deliver the application as an easy way to learn and teach.
- Students perceived enjoyment since they can deliver the application as an interesting and fun tool for teaching and learning environment in schools.

Also based on this study, it has been proven that there are economical and simple ways of creating virtual environment without ignoring the immersiveness of the environment and flexibility offered by the technique of panaromic images to the audience.

Acknowledgments. We express our thanks to UPSI for the Short-term Research Grant and the equipment provided to complete this research.

References

1. Paul Debevec Homepage, http://ict.debevec.org/~debevec/#Resources
2. Geng, W., Pan, Y., Li, M., Yang, J.: Picture-Based Virtual Touring. Int. J. VR. 4(3) (2000)
3. Davis, F.D.: A technology acceptance model for empirically testing new end-user information systems: theory and results. Ph.D in Management thesis, Massachusetts Institute of Technology (1985)
4. Kang, S.B.: A survey of image-based rendering techniques. Technical report, Cambridge Research Lab (1997)
5. Mcmillan, L., Gortler, S.J.: Image-Based Rendering: A New Interface Between Computer Vision and Computer Graphics in Applications of Computer Vision to Computer Graphics. Proc. ACM SIGGRAPH 33(4) (1999)
6. Popescu, G.V.: Forward Rasterization: A Reconstruction Algorithm for Image-Based Rendering. Ph.D. Dissertation, University of North Carolina (2001)
7. JHU Department of Comp. Science Homepage,
   http://www.cs.jhu.edu/~cohen/RendTech99/Lectures/
   Image_Based_Rendering.bw.pdf
8. Gong, Z., Lu, D., Pan, Y.: Dunhuang Artcave presentation and Preserve using VE. In: 4th International Conference on Virtual Systems and Multimedia, pp. 612–617. IOS Press, Netherlands (1998)
9. Chen, S.E.: QuickTime® VR–An Image-Based Approach to Virtual Environment Navigation. In: Proceedings of Computer Graphics and Interactive Techniques Conference, pp. 29–38. ACM Press, New York (1995)
10. Barron, A.E.: Technologies for Education: A Practical Guide. Libraries Unlimited, Greenwood Village USA (2002)
11. University of Wisconsin-La Crosse,
    http://www.uwlax.edu/campus-map/index2.htm
12. Universiti Malaysia Terenggan,
    http://www.umt.edu.my/v8/kampus_maya.php
13. Universiti Sains Malaysia, http://www.cs.usm.my/usmmap/vtour.php
14. CampusTours, Inc., http://www.campustours.com/
15. Legris, P., Ingham, J., Collerette, P.: Why do People Use Information Technology? A Critical Review of the Technology Acceptance Model. Information and Management 40, 191–204 (2003)
16. Ndubisi, N.O., Jantan, M., Richardson, S.: Is the Technology Acceptance Model Valid for Entrepreneurs? Model Testing and Examining Usage Determinants. Asian Academy of Information Journal 62, 31–54 (2001)
17. Yi, M.Y., Hwang, Y.: Predicting the Use of Web-based Information System: Self-efficacy, Enjoyment, Learning Goal Orientation and the Technology Acceptance Model. Int. J. Human-Computer Studies 59, 431–449 (2003)

18. Davis, F.D.: User Acceptance of Information Technology: System Characteristics, User Perceptions and Behavioural Impacts. Int. Journal of Man-Machines Studies 38, 475–487 (1993)
19. Davis, F.D.: Perceived Usefulness, Perceived Ease of Use and User Acceptance of Information Technology. MIS Quarterly 13(3), 319–340 (1989)
20. Malone, T.W.: Toward a Theory of Intrinsically Motivating Instruction. Cognitive Science 5(4), 333–369 (1981)
21. Bertrand, M., Bouchard, S.: Applying the Technology Acceptance Model to VR With People Who are Favorable to Its Use. Journal of Cybertherapy & Rehabilitation 1(2), 200–211 (2008)
22. Venkatesh, V., Bala, H.: Technology Acceptance Model 3 and a Research Agenda on Interventions. Decision Sciences 39, 273–315 (2008)
23. Viswanath Venkatesh Homepage,
    `http://www.vvenkatesh.com/it/organizations/`
    `theoretical_models.asp`
24. SISQA Homepage,
    `http://www.sisqa.com/Training/`
    `2006_CSTE_CBOK_Skill_Category_7b.ppt`
25. Proserpio, L., Gioia, D.A.: Teaching the Virtual Generation. Academy of Management Learning & Education 6(1), 69–80 (2007)

Hybrid Intelligent System for Disease Diagnosis Based on Artificial Neural Networks, Fuzzy Logic, and Genetic Algorithms

Hamada R.H. Al-Absi[1], Azween Abdullah[1],
Mahamat Issa Hassan[1], and Khaled Bashir Shaban[2]

[1] Department of Computer and Information Sciences, Universiti Teknologi PETRONAS,
Bandar Seri Iskandar, 31750 Tronoh, Perak, Malaysia
[2] Computer Science and Engineering Department, College of Engineering, Qatar University,
P.O. Box: 2713, Doha, Qatar
hamada.it@gmail.com,
{azweenabdullah,mahamat.hassan}@petronas.com.my,
khaled.shaban@qu.edu.qa

Abstract. Disease diagnosis often involves acquiring medical images using devices such as MRI, CT scan, x-ray, or mammograms of patients' organs. Though many medical diagnostic applications have been proposed; finding subtle cancerous cells is still an issue because they are very difficult to be identified. This paper presents an architecture that utilizes a learning algorithm, and uses soft computing to build a medical knowledge base and an inference engine for classifying new images. This system is built on the strength of artificial neural networks, fuzzy logic, and genetic algorithms. These machine intelligence are combined in a complementary approach to overcome the weakness of each other. Moreover, the system also uses Wavelet Transform and Principal Component Analysis for pre-processing and feature to produce features to be used as input to the learning algorithm.

Keywords: Computer Aided Diagnosis, Soft Computing, Artificial Neural Networks, Fuzzy Logic, Genetic Algorithms.

1 Introduction

Disease diagnosis is an important process in healthcare. This essential process is conducted by physicians before giving medical treatments to the patients. The diagnosis is often based on results of blood tests, urine tests and so forth. In cases that required an examination of internal organs of the patient, physician would refer them to radiologists to acquiring vital images using devices such as MRI, CT scan, x-ray, or mammograms, depending on the organ and the suspected disease. In the past, the radiologists or the physicians undertook themselves the reading and interpreting these images. Later, computer aided diagnosis (CAD) was introduced in aid of diagnosing the complex cases. However, the images produced by imaging devices such as for breast cancer, could be affected by noise and distortion which consequently affect the

A. Abd Manaf et al. (Eds.): ICIEIS 2011, Part II, CCIS 252, pp. 128–139, 2011.
© Springer-Verlag Berlin Heidelberg 2011

diagnosis of the radiologists [1]. The noises or distortions in the image could also cause errors during the diagnosis procedure. For instance, by missing tumors or wrongly detecting tumors that in fact are non presence (false positives). These mistakes would certainly influence the final assessment and lead to the wrong treatment / therapy.

CAD systems such as [2-4] are utilized to support the decision of radiologist in diagnosing images. Such systems have been reported to increase the performance of detecting cancer by 19.6% compared to the sole diagnosis taken by a radiologist [5]. CAD systems highlight certain regions that enclose cancer or any sort of abnormalities that might be overlooked by radiologists. Computer aided diagnosis systems are often built with algorithms based on artificial neural networks, support vector machines classifiers and others [3]. However, apart from the success of CAD systems application, the issue of finding subtle cancerous cells remains cumbersome as these cells are very difficult to be identified. In addition, [6] reported that some radiologists tend to pay no attention to detected cancers highlighted by CAD systems. Those radiologists might have had experiences with CAD systems that wrongly diagnosed cases which highly affected their trust towards these systems. In this regard, systems capable to produce accurate detection results (especially for hidden cancerous cells) are needed.

This paper presents an architecture of a CAD system that utilizes soft computing technique to analyze images and identify abnormalities. This architecture combines artificial neural networks, fuzzy logic and genetic algorithms for the learning and classification tasks. Section 2 presents some related work in this area. Section 3 explains the proposed architecture and the hybrid learning algorithm, and section 4 discusses an experiment to evaluate the hybrid learning algorithm. Finally, the conclusion and a discussion on future work directions are presented in section 5.

2   Related Work

In computer aided diagnosis, many applications have been developed to assist radiologists in diagnosing diseases. Most of the applications are focusing on the diagnosis of cancer, since it is one of the main causes of deaths in the world. Diagnosing or detecting cancers, as well as other diseases in early stages bring an impact on the cure at later treatment.

Ramirez et al. [7] presented a system aimed at diagnosing *Alzheimer*'s disease and detecting it in its early stage using support vector machine classifier and classification tree. The proposed method attained 96% accuracy in the classification task. Azvine et al. [8] experimented the usage of expert system method to design a clinical decision support system to aid the diagnosis in otology. They experimented with some of the soft computing algorithms (neural network and fuzzy logic) and they support these algorithms in future medicine applications. Economou et al. [9] designed a computer aided diagnosis for pulmonary disease in which the system aimed to support physicians in their diagnosis and gave them a trust factor to make decisions. Another system developed by Nazmy et al [10] was to diagnose focal liver lesions based on CT images. Features were extracted and feed to a neural network classifier. The system was based on 2D images and as some abnormalities were hidden, a 3D image was needed to enable the detection. A system introduced by Raja et al. [11] is aimed for a computer aided system for early diagnosis of *Alzheimer* disease based on single-photon emission computed tomography (SPECT) image feature selection and random forest classifier. The project achieved 96% classification accuracy. The above applications are considered successful in the area of computer aided systems CAD to diagnose different diseases. However, diagnosing subtle cancer cells is still an issue that need to be addressed by developing better algorithms capable of revealing these cells.

2.1 Soft Computing and Disease Diagnosis

Soft computing aims at solving uncertain, imprecise or partially true problems [12]. Fuzzy Logic (FL), Neural Network (NN) and Genetic Algorithm (GA) etc. are some techniques for soft computing. The idea of hybrid intelligent systems is to combine more than one methodology to complement each other [13]. Nazmy et al. [14] for instance developed an adaptive neuro-fuzzy inference system (ANFIS) for classification of ECG signals. The performance of this classifier has been tested and the result achieved a rate of 97% accuracy. Raja et al. [15] meanwhile developed a computer aided diagnosis system using NN-FL hybrid technique for diagnosing ultrasound kidney images. Another application of NN-FL technique in detecting tumors in medical images was developed by [16]. This system used a hybrid combination of NN-FL with expert system to classify tumors in images. A breast cancer diagnosis system proposed in [17] was based on FL-GA to detect the Wisconsin breast cancer diagnosis (WBCD). The system has been tested and show average accuracy of 97%. In addition, [18] proposed a FL-GA approach for the classification of epilepsy risk level from EEG signals. This technique performed well with the accuracy reaching more than 90%. A system has been developed to predict the lung sounds using a hybrid system of NN-GA [19]. Another application of NN-GA was also developed to analyze digital mammograms [20]. A soft computing methodology is demonstrated when NN, FL and GA were combined in one system to solve a specific problem. A system that combined the three methodologies was proposed in [21]. The purpose of the system was to interpret medical images by classifying and detecting any abnormalities. Other systems in [22] and [23] utilized the same methodology and the results of all systems have been reported to be very good.

Methodologies such as NN-FL, NN-GA and FL-GA have been used in many applications. However, in regard to the technique where the three methodologies are combined in a hybrid system, there are still limited applications of this approach. According to [24], NN-FL-GA has the smallest number of published papers. Only 5 papers in the period 1995-2007. NN-FL-GA methodology has a great advantage either in complementing each other or in solving each others' limitation. Hence, more applications should be developed in computer aided diagnosis where the accuracy is the most important issue.

The various forms of combining soft computing methodologies forming hybrid systems are discussed in Yardimci papers [24]. Table 1 summarizes the most common soft computing combinations.

Table 1. Common soft computing combination in hybrid systems

Combination	Description
NN-FL	• NN controlled by FL
	• FL controller tuned by NN
NN-GA	• GA used to pre-process the input parameters that train the NN
FL-GA	• GA controlled by FL
	• FL controller tuned by GA

3   A Proposed Hybrid System Based on ANN, FL, and GA

In this section, an intelligent system based on hybrid soft computing methodology is presented. The system integrates artificial neural networks, fuzzy logic and genetic algorithms by combining the strength and features of the three methods with regard to disease diagnosis requirements in the context of learning capability.

The system is developed wtih two phases, learning phase and diagnosis phase. The system goes through a learning procedure before diagnosing the diseases. An image dataset which represents the suspected disease is required for the learning task. The dataset is subject to a noise reduction procedure using wavelet transform and PCA-Wavelet method to extract its features. Then, GA will be utilized to select the most significant features to be used in training the algorithm. We introduce a learning algorithm which is based on the combination of artificial neural networks, fuzzy logic and genetic algorithms.   The algorithm (discussed in section 3.3) will produce a knowledge base (KB) that shall be consulted when diagnosing new images. In the event of KB cannot diagnose a new image, the algorithm will re-train itself to learn this new case (after the new case has been classified by an expert). This will enhance the KB and increase its ability to diagnose more cases. Figure 1 shows an activity diagram that demonstrates the flow of the first phase of the system.

In diagnosis phase, new images (different from the images used to train the system) are used as inputs. The knowledge base that was built during the learning phase will provide a diagnostic decision for new images. In this phase, each image will be subjected to a noise removal process. This process is to reduce the amount of noise or distortion in the image to produce a better outcome. After that, the de-noised treated image will be subjected to feature extraction and segmentation and can be input to the classification algorithm to make a diagnostic decision. Figure 2 shows an activity diagram of the second phase of the system.

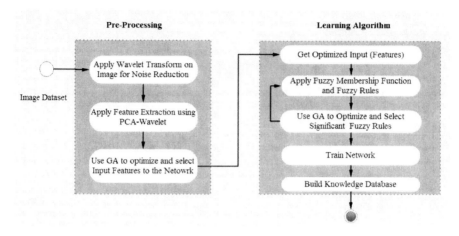

Fig. 1. Activity diagram of the first phase (learning phase) of the system

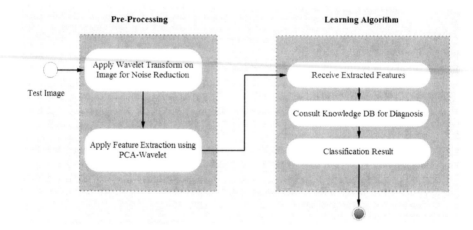

Fig. 2. Activity diagram of the second phase (diagnosis phase) of the system

The architecture of the proposed system is in figure 3 which shows the integration of the training phase and the diagnosing phase.

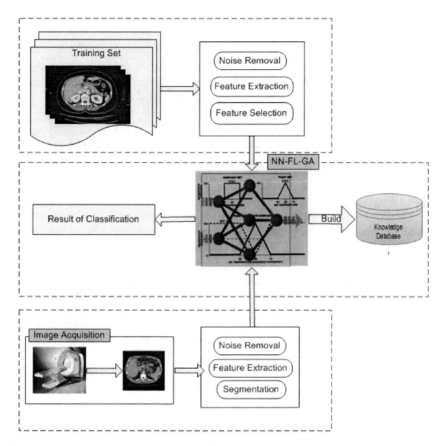

Fig. 3. The proposed architecture of a hybrid disease diagnosis system using neural network, fuzzy logic and genetic algorithm

3.1 Noise Reduction

The acquired image(s) will be filtered by the system to reduce the noises acquired during the acquisition process. In this project, Wavelet Transform (WT) is one of the techniques that is used in signal processing to suppress noise. WT can be defined as follows [25]:

$$P_m = \sum_n f_m[n]\phi_{mn}(x), \qquad \phi_{mn}(x) = 2^{-\frac{m}{2}}\phi(2^{-m}x - n) \tag{1}$$

$$Q_m = \sum_n d_m[n]\psi_{mn}(x), \qquad \psi_{mn}(x) = 2^{-\frac{m}{2}}\psi(2^{-m}x - n) \tag{2}$$

Where the P_m is a signal that is the approximation of the f(x) at a resolution m, and the Q_m is a signal that is the difference between the approximation $P_m - 1$ and P_m.

3.2 Feature Extraction

After the images have been de-noised, a feature extraction process will be applied to extract the most important features for image classification. Texture features will be extracted here to obtain descriptors that can lead to better performance. It has been proven that texture descriptors are more effective than shape descriptors in providing more information of the images [26]. PCA-Wavelet technique will be used to extract the features and to segment the image(s). The feature extraction process is conducted in which 2D-Discrete wavelet transform decomposes an image to reduce its resolution and then the PCA uses eigenfeatures to extract object features from the image [27].

3.3 Learning Algorithm

After the features extraction, the next step is to use these features as input to the learning algorithm. The algorithm combines the strength of the three methodologies to form a strong algorithm. The strengths include the optimization of GA, the learning capability of ANN, and the uncertainty and imprecision tolerance of FL that will be utilized in the learning of the ANN.

Since the system is expected to be able to retrain itself if it is not being able to decide whether an image contains abnormalities or not, and since retraining the whole network is time consuming and not practical, the network type that will be used in this system must have some sort of memory that stores the output weights of the network after training, which to be combined with the new data. Recurrent Neural Network (RNN) [28] is a type of artificial neural networks that enclose a memory or a context layer that memorizes / keeps the outputs weights of the hidden layer. The context layer uses these weights as an input to the hidden layer after a period of time (small delay in time) [28] this can be utilized to retrain the network once new data is presented and a retraining of the system is needed.

In this hybrid system, the first step is selecting the most significant features out of a huge number of features that were extracted. Genetic algorithm performs feature selection in order to reduce the amount of features used to train the algorithm. In addition to that, GA is used to optimize the initial weights of the neural network. Although artificial neural networks' capability in learning has made it applicable in many applications, however, the network deals only with crisp values which make it not suitable in application that are based on imprecision or uncertainty. For that, in order to enhance the capability of ANN under uncertainty or partially truth situation, it is combined with fuzzy logic to improve the performance. Fuzzy rules are represented in if-then approach, e.g. they can be expressed in the form *if x is A, then y is B*. The role of fuzzy here is to deal with uncertainty and imprecision and combine those features with the learning ability of neural network. Therefore, by combining these two methods in a medical imaging application (which has lots of uncertainties due to the nature of images and information enclosed in them i.e. organs, abnormalities...etc); the system would contribute to minimize errors and maximize the diagnosis accuracy. On the other hand, in fuzzy logic, not all fuzzy rules would contribute to the best results. Therefore, they need to be refined. For this, GA is used to optimize the fuzzy rules by selecting the most significant rules making the performance of the algorithm better. Figure 4 shows the learning algorithm using the combined soft computing techniques of NN-FL-GA.

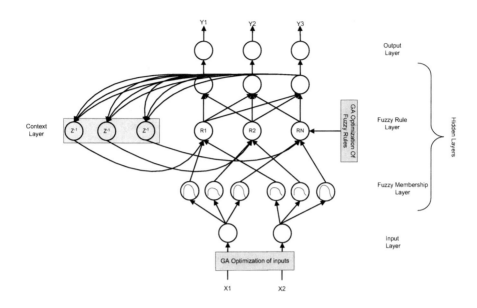

Fig. 4. The components of the learning algorithm

4 Experiments

4.1 Experiments Set Up

For the purpose of evaluating the accuracy of the hybrid learning algorithm presented in the preceding section, experiment was conducted using NeuroSolutions software to test the algorithm. NeuroSolutions is a simulation environment that provides a platform for the development of neural network applications.

Table 2. Sample data

Col1	Col2	Col3	Col4	Col5	Col6	Col7	Col8	Col9	Col10	Col11
63375	9	1	2	6	4	10	7	7	2	4
76389	10	4	7	2	2	8	6	1	1	4
95719	6	10	10	10	8	10	7	10	7	4
128059	1	1	1	1	2	5	5	1	1	2
142932	7	6	10	5	3	10	9	10	2	4
144888	8	10	10	8	5	10	7	8	1	4
145447	8	4	4	1	2	9	3	3	1	4
160296	5	8	8	10	5	10	8	10	3	4
167528	4	1	1	1	2	1	3	6	1	2
183913	1	2	2	1	2	1	1	1	1	2

A dataset of breast cancer developed by the University of Wisconsin Hospitals [29] was utilized in this experiment. The dataset contains 699 instances with 10 attributes for each instance. As shown in table 2, the first column in the dataset represents the instance ID, the columns 2-10 represent the instances which have 2 possible outputs: benign or malignant. Column 11 represent the desired outputs where 2 is for benign and 4 for malignant.

In this test, three different experiments were performed with different methods which are neural network with fuzzy logic, neural network with genetic algorithms and the presented learning algorithm.

4.2 Experiments Results

The hybrid learning algorithm was built using the NeuroSolutions graphical interface tool. All parts of the system were connected to form the learning algorithm for the three methods experimented. Figure 5 illustrates the NeuroSolutions Breadboard of the hybrid learning algorithm presented in this paper.

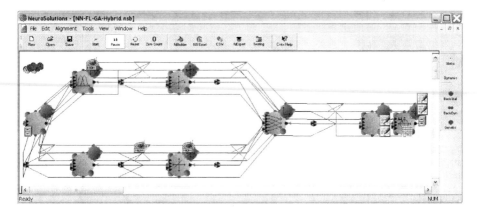

Fig. 5. The Hybrid method developmented on NeuroSolution simulation environment

To evaluate the hybrid learning algorithm and comparing it with other methods, 699 samples were used in each experiment, where 60 % is for training, 20% is for cross validation and 20% for testing (139 samples). Table 3 reports the results obtained from the experiments.

As shown in the table, the performance of the proposed method is better than the neural network with fuzzy logic, however, neural network with genetic algorithm is better than the hybrid method. This could be due to the amount of the sample data that was used for the training phase. Neural network applications require large dataset for the training phase to produce better performance and with the combination of the three methodologies in a hybrid system, the sample data for training should be larger than the data that was used in this experiment.

Generally, the performance reported in these experiments shows some evidences that the hybrid system may perform better than other methods which were discussed in the previous sections.

Table 3. Results of the experiments on the breast cancer dataset

Method	No. of Testing samples	Correct	Incorrect	Accuracy
Neural Network with Fuzzy Logic	139	134	5	96.40
Neural Network with Genetic Algorithms	139	136	3	97.84
Hybrid Method (Neural Network, Fuzzy Logic and Genetic Algorithm)	139	135	4	97.12

5 Conclusions and Future Work

This paper presents an architecture of a hybrid disease diagnosing system. The system integrates soft computing methodologies (artificial neural networks, fuzzy logic and genetic algorithms) to build the diagnostic software application. As shown in the architecture, the system has a learning capability to accumulate knowledge, which can be utilized in diagnosing new images. Currently, the system is in the design phase. An experiment to evaluate the performance of the hybrid learning algorithm was carried out, and the preliminary results suggest that it is performing better than other methods. However, the results can be improved by testing the hybrid system with a larger dataset and by fine tuning the NeuroSolution's breadboard of the hybrid learning algorithm.

Future direction of this work includes implement and assess the whole components of the system using benchmark data. This system is expected to contribute to the advancement of automated healthcare system by providing accurate diagnoses of illnesses and revealing the hidden/subtle regions that might contain cancerous cells.

Acknowledgement. The authors would like to thank the University of Wisconsin Hospitals, Madison;Dr. William H. Wolberg for providing the breast cancer dataset that was used in this work.

References

1. Rangayyan, R.M., Ayres, F.J., Desautels, J.E.L.: A review of computer-aided diagnosis of breast cancer: Toward the detection of subtle signs. Journal of the Franklin Institute 344(3-4), 312–348 (2007)
2. Chen, D.-R., Hsiao, Y.-H.: Computer-aided Diagnosis in Breast Ultrasound. J. Med. Ultrasound 16(1), 46–56 (2008)
3. Huang, Y.-L.: Computer-aided Diagnosis Using Neural Networks and Support Vector Machines for Breast Ultrasonography. J. Med. Ultrasound 17(1), 17–24 (2009)

4. Marcela, X.R., Pedro, H.B., Caetano, T.J., Paulo, M.A.M., Natalia, A.R., Agma, J.M.: Supporting content-based image retrieval and computer-aided diagnosis systems with association rule-based techniques. Data and Knowledge Engineering 68(12), 1370–1382 (2009)
5. Nishikawa, R.M.: Current status and future directions of computeraided diagnosis in mammography. Computerized Medical Imaging and Graphics 31, 224–235 (2007)
6. Nishikawa, R.M.: Current status and future directions of computer-aided diagnosis in mammography. Computerized Medical Imaging and Graphics 31(4-5), 224–235 (2007)
7. Salas-Gonzalez, D., Górriz, J.M., Ramírez, J., López, M., Álvarez, I., Segovia, F., et al.: Computer aided diagnosis of Alzheimer's disease using support vector machines and classification trees. Phys. Med. Biol. 55, 2807–2817 (2010)
8. Goggin, L.S., Eikelboom, R.H., Atlas, M.D.: Clinical decision support systems and computeraided diagnosis in otology. Otolaryngology–Head and Neck Surgery 136, S21–S26 (2007)
9. Economou, G.-P.K., Lymberopoulos, D., Karvatselou, E., Chassomeris, C.: A new concept toward computer-aided medical diagnosis–A prototype implementation addressing pulmonary diseases. IEEE Trans. Inform. Technol. Biomed. 5, 55–66 (2001)
10. Stoitsis, J., Valavanis, I., Mougiakakou, S.G., Golemati, S., Nikita, A., Nikita, K.S.: Computer aided diagnosis based on medical image processing and artificial intelligence methods. Nuclear Instruments and Methods in Physics Research 569, 591–595 (2006)
11. Ramirez, J., Chaves, R., Górriz, J.M., López, M., Álvarez, I., Salas-Gonzalez, D., Segovia, F., Padilla, P.: Computer aided diagnosis of the Alzheimer's Disease combining SPECT-based feature selection and Random forest classifiers. In: IEEE Nuclear Science Symposium Conference Record (NSS/MIC), Orlando, FL, pp. 2738–2742 (2009)
12. Azvine, B., Azarmi, N., Tsui, K.C.: An introduction to soft computing — A tool for building intelligent systems. LNCS, pp. 191–210. Springer, Heidelberg (1997)
13. Negnevitsky, M.: Artificial intelligence: A Guide to Intelligent Systems, 2nd edn. Addison Wesley (2005)
14. Nazmy, T.M., El-messiry, H., Al-bokhity, B.: Adaptive neuro-fuzzy inference system for classification of ecg signals. Journal of Theoretical and Applied Information Technology (2005)
15. Raja, K.B., Madheswaran, M., Thyagarajah, K.: A Hybrid Fuzzy-Neural System for Computer-Aided Diagnosis of Ultrasound Kidney Images Using Prominent Features. Journal of Medical Systems 32 (2008)
16. Benamrane, N., Freville, A., Nekkache, R.: A Hybrid Fuzzy Neural Networks for the Detection of Tumors in Medical Images. American Journal of Applied Sciences 2(4), 892–896 (2005)
17. Andreś, C., Penã-Reyes, Sipper, M.: A fuzzy-genetic approach to breast cancer diagnosis. Artificial Intelligence in Medicine 17, 131–155 (1999)
18. Harikumar, R., Sukanesh, R., Bharathi, P.A.: Genetic algorithm optimization of fuzzy outputs for classification of epilepsy risk levels from EEG signals. In: Conference Record of the Thirty-Eighth Asilomar Conference on Signals, System and Computer (2004)
19. Guler, I., Polat, H.u., un, U.m.E.: Combining Neural Network and Genetic Algorithm for Prediction of Lung Sounds. Journal of Medical Systems 29(3) (2005)
20. Verma, B., Zhang, P.: A novel neural-genetic algorithm to find the most significant combination of features in digital mammograms. Applied Soft Computing 7, 612–625 (2007)
21. Benamrane, N., Aribi, A., Kraoula, L.: Fuzzy Neural Networks and Genetic Algorithms for Medical Images Interpretation. In: Proceedings of the Geometric Modeling and Imaging–New Trends (2006)

22. Ozekes, S., Osman, O., Ucan, O.N.: Nodule Detection in a Lung Region that's Segmented with Using Genetic Cellular Neural Networks and 3D Template Matching with Fuzzy Rule Based Thresholding. Korean Journal of Radiology (2008)
23. Das, A., Bhattacharya, M.: GA Based Neuro Fuzzy Techniques for Breast Cancer Identification. In: International Machine Vision and Image Processing Conference (2008)
24. Yardimci, A.: Soft computing in medicine. Applied Soft Computing 9, 1029–1043 (2009)
25. Satish Chandra, D.V.: Image Enhancement and Noise Reduction Using 'Wavelet Transform. In: Proceedings of the 40th Midwest Symposium on Circuits and Systems (1997)
26. Muhammad, M.N., Raicu, D.S., Furst, J.D., Varutbangkul, E.: Texture versus Shape Analysis for Lung Nodule Similarity in Computed Tomography Studies. In: Andriole, K.P., Siddiqui, K.M. (eds.) Medical Imaging 2008: PACS and Imaging Informatics. Proceedings of the SPIE, vol. 6919 (2008)
27. Kim, K.-A., Oh, S.-Y., Choi, H.-C.: Facial feature extraction using PCA and wavelet multi-resolution images. In: Sixth IEEE International Conference on Automatic Face and Gesture Recognition (2004)
28. Elman, J.L.: Finding structure in time. Cognitive Sci. 14(2), 179–211 (1990)
29. Mangasarian, O.L., Wolberg, W.H.: Cancer diagnosis via linear programming. SIAM News 23(5), 1–18 (1990)

An Implementation of Hybrid Algorithm for Diagnosing MRI Images Using Image Mining Concepts

A. Kannan[1], V. Mohan[2], and N. Anbazhagan[3]

[1] Department of MCA,
K.L.N. College of Engineering,
Sivagangai District, Tamilnadu, India
kannamca@yahoo.com
[2] Department of Mathematics,
Thiagarajar College of Engineering,
Madurai, Tamilnadu, India
vmohan@tce.edu
[3] Department of Maths, Alagappa University,
Karaikudi, Tamilnadu, India
anbazhagan_n@yahoo.co.in

Abstract. Images play a major role in every nature of problems today. Especially, Medical and Space Images play vital role in the field of research. Image mining is the leading technology where general collection of images will be processed instead of concentrating on a single image not as in image process concept. In this paper, MRI images have been classified to diagnosis the nature of tumor in the human brain based on the concept of image mining techniques. There are several algorithms for image classifications in the field of image processing concepts. Here, we have designed a hybrid algorithm for classifying MRI images using KNN and SVM concepts to detect the brain tumor.

Keywords: Gray Level Co-occurrence Matrix (GLCM), KNN, SVM.

1 Introduction

Images play a major role in every nature of problems today. Especially, Medical and space images play vital role in the field of research. Image mining is the leading technology where general collection of images will be processed instead of concentrating on a single image not as in image process concept. In this paper, MRI images have been classified to diagnosis the nature of tumor in the human brain based on the concept of image mining techniques. There are several algorithms for image classifications in the field of image processing concepts. Here, we have designed a hybrid algorithm for classifying MRI images using KNN and SVM concepts to detect the brain tumor.

Normally, the Bidirectional Associative Memory (BAM), Portable Neural Network (PNN), Support Vector Machine (SVM), and K-Nearest Neighbor are the popular image classification algorithms. The BAM is having high accuracy rate, but, it consumes more time to classify the images even for low number and it consumes

A. Abd Manaf et al. (Eds.): ICIEIS 2011, Part II, CCIS 252, pp. 140–150, 2011.

more memory spaces. The PNN is the fastest one, but, produces low accuracy rate. The SVM and KNN will be the fastest in processing as well as slightly high accurate compared to BAM.

However, both SVM and KNN have their own drawbacks. Hence, we have designed a hybrid algorithm by combing the SVM and KNN for classifying MRI images to conclude whether the brain is affected by tumor or not. The result will be benign, normal and malignant.

In other end, image mining is the fastest growing and challenging research area with regard to both still and moving images. Image mining normally deals with the extraction of implicit knowledge, image data relationship, or other patterns not explicitly stored from the low-level computer vision and image processing techniques. i.e.) the focus of image mining is the extraction of patterns from a large collection of images. The focus of computer vision and image processing techniques will be gathering or extracting specific features from a single image. [1]

Hence, the image mining is rapidly gaining more attention among the researchers in the field of data mining, information retrieval and multimedia databases.

2 Problem Definition

As we have seen earlier, the medical images play major role in order to identify the heterogeneous types of diseases in human beings. Especially, MRI images will be very useful to identify the formation of tumour in human brain and necessary remedial actions can be taken immediately. Unfortunately, we are not able to classify those images in a right manner at right time. If we analyze those images with proper classification algorithms, it will reveal useful information to physicians whether the stage of formation of tumour in the human brain is Benign, Normal or Malignant. The fig.1 shows that the pre-processed MRI images of various stages of tumour formation in human brain.

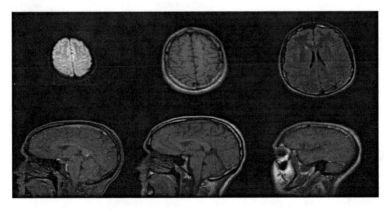

Fig. 1. The Stages of tumour formation

The concept of image mining system provides collection of various classification algorithms to classify images in different dimensions. The most popular algorithms are Bidirectional Associative Memory (BAM), K-Nearest Neighbour (KNN), Portable Neural Network (PNN) and Support Vector Machine (SVM). Of these, the KNN and SVM will be more user-friendly and faster than the rest. Although these two have very good feedback, they have their own drawbacks compared to others.

The efficiency and accuracy of the KNN algorithm will be low when the numbers of samples are increased. i.e) KNN-distance functions are anticipated to have poor classification performance as the dimensionality of the noisy data increases. In SVM, there is lower classification accuracy if the sample data of the two classes in a binary classification are all close to the separating hyper plane. [3]

2.1 Problem Description

In this study, we have two major tasks such as training process and testing process. In the training process, the MRI images have already been collected in the form of grey level images. The Grey Level Co-occurrence Matrix (GLCM) features will be extracted from the collected stored images (training) and those features will be kept in a database for future processes (2). Then, the features of the training images will be optimized to certain level using Sequence Forward Selection (SFS) method. Here, we have got the optimized features as Cluster Prominence and Entropy. Finally, we have to identify the neighbors of each sample using the KNN Sample Selector method. The fig.2 shows the block diagram of the Hybrid KNNSVM process.

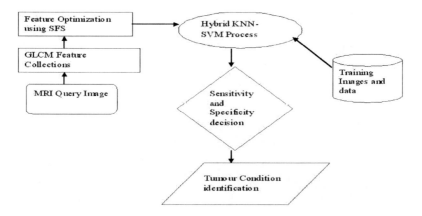

Fig. 2. Block Diagram of Hybrid KNN-SVM Process

In the testing process, the test image i.e., the patient's MRI image will be received and the GLCM features of that image will be extracted in terms of feature vectors. Here, we have to extract about 12 features from the given test image. Of these, only the optimized features of the image will be used for our test such as Entropy, Cluster Prominence etc. Based on these features, the KNN feature space can be formed.

The K-Nearest-Neighbour (KNN) algorithm measures the distance between a test sample and a set of training samples in the features space. The training samples have already been labelled based on some criteria. K-nearest neighbours for this test sample will be determined. If the testing sample is same as the label of the majority of its k-nearest neighbours, then the test sample will be grouped to the concerned category of the classification. [3] Here, the distances of the neighbours are calculated using the Euclidean distance method. The fig.3 shows the sample 12 GLCM features that we have extracted from the training set of images.

Contrast	Correlatio	Clus.Prom	Clus.Shac	Dissimilar	Energy	Entropy	Homogen	Homop	Max.Prob	Sosvh	Auto.Corr
0.076978	0.955866	295.6385	30.12207	0.061946	0.834309	0.536679	0.971382	0.970524	0.913014	2.318267	2.317603
0.166851	0.531982	10.97391	1.853608	0.15269	0.656248	0.7828	0.925562	0.925021	0.802967	1.463509	1.405617
0.119304	0.856217	132.3281	13.22594	0.080142	0.826696	0.516733	0.965198	0.963728	0.908386	1.657289	1.632714
0.087816	0.89289	90.48805	11.14623	0.060364	0.853755	0.464491	0.973639	0.972528	0.923576	1.659678	1.650949
0.135047	0.898226	189.7629	20.72418	0.076582	0.828986	0.537348	0.968734	0.967142	0.909929	2.025196	1.994383
0.166377	0.898959	255.5011	26.4797	0.091139	0.803471	0.629785	0.962908	0.96114	0.895728	2.277108	2.231843
0.143117	0.906357	183.9123	21.68506	0.081487	0.802866	0.622724	0.96882	0.965064	0.895411	2.227421	2.193908
0.152848	0.919698	294.6303	30.70965	0.093196	0.787922	0.672409	0.960849	0.959027	0.886946	2.48507	2.447587
0.126741	0.918725	180.2494	21.49874	0.085601	0.78399	0.68227	0.962829	0.9612	0.884731	2.284015	2.259217
0.096734	0.914628	78.51145	12.31779	0.067326	0.816186	0.56975	0.970778	0.969362	0.902868	2.004524	1.992722
0.182278	0.906026	175.5874	23.39528	0.113449	0.73595	0.813125	0.952453	0.949936	0.856764	2.661172	2.610916
0.115111	0.913163	68.13628	11.99739	0.078797	0.760548	0.703486	0.965531	0.96408	0.870807	2.238183	2.220095
0.113291	0.931624	101.8365	16.34958	0.079589	0.747661	0.745594	0.965069	0.963542	0.863212	2.514127	2.498299
0.16962	0.962881	634.0849	68.79708	0.11693	0.680062	0.933774	0.948824	0.946696	0.822429	4.693464	4.657397
0.159652	0.96161	616.2992	65.40447	0.114399	0.705172	0.878222	0.949332	0.947265	0.838133	4.299983	4.26697
0.16962	0.962881	634.0849	68.79708	0.11693	0.680062	0.933774	0.948824	0.946696	0.822429	4.693464	4.657397
0.169652	0.96161	616.2992	65.40447	0.114399	0.705172	0.878222	0.949332	0.947265	0.838133	4.299983	4.26697
0.13663	0.959732	498.4454	53.62866	0.1	0.734265	0.797713	0.955268	0.953618	0.855617	3.674399	3.650277
0.112816	0.957732	427.2246	44.46549	0.087975	0.776689	0.695554	0.959712	0.95848	0.880538	3.057198	3.042049

Fig. 3. Sample features of set of images

2.2 Classification Details

After receiving the test MRI image, the features of the image have to be collected in terms of feature vectors. Let we define training images be as $TR=\{tr_1, tr_2, tr_3 \ldots tr_n\}$. The feature vectors of the training samples are $TF=\{(tf1_{s1}, tf1_{s2}, tf1_{s3}, tf1_{s4,\ldots} tf1_{si}), (tf2_{s1}, tf2_{s2}, tf2_{s3}, tf2_{s4,\ldots} tf2_{sj}),\ldots\ldots\ldots(tfn_{s1}, tfn_{s2}, tfn_{s3,\ldots} tfn_{sm},)\}$.

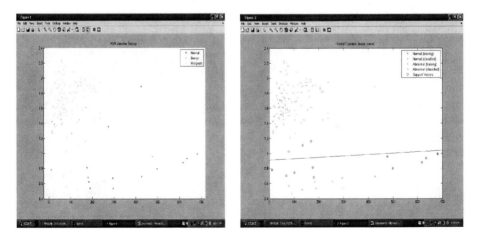

Fig. 4. a) KNN Feature Classification b) SVM Feature Classification

The Query image of the patient will be received from the user. Let the features of the test image be QF={f1,f2.....fn}. As we have mentioned earlier, the 12 prominent features of the MRI image will be extracted from the given query image. Then, the features those collected from the image will be optimized to certain level. Here, the Cluster Prominence and Entropy can only be the received features after optimization. The sample with the optimized features will be taken into account for KNN classification. KNN creates a feature space where the features of the training samples will be scattered. Likewise, the SVM Features samples are created. The fig.4 a & b show the classification of training samples using KNN and SVM methods separately.

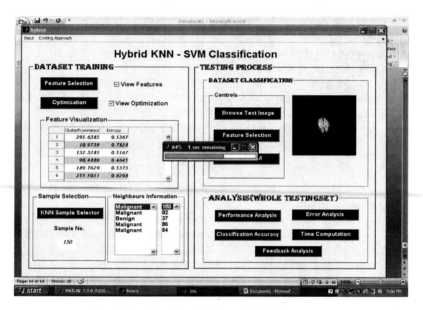

Fig. 5. Loading the Query MRI Image

Here, the algorithm starts. At first, the KNN tries to analyze whether the test sample falls in the majority of the training samples or not. The Euclidean distance of the test sample and the training samples will be compared, so that, the neighbourhood of the test sample can be identified (3). Otherwise, the pair-wise distances of the samples have to be calculated to identify the neighbours. The fig.5 shows the selection of query image for testing process.

$$d_2(a_1, a_2) = \sqrt{\sum_{j=1}^{k}(a_{1,j} - a_{2,j})^2} \qquad \text{Euclidean or } L_2 \text{ distance} \qquad (3)$$

If so, then the result of the given query image will be concluded either as Benign, Normal or Malignant based on the majority ratio of the categories. It means that the KNN considers only the majority of the neighbour samples. If KNN fails, then the control of classification will be transferred to the binary SVM classification. In binary SVM1, the optimized hyper plan will be defined between Normal and

Abnormal conditions of category. If the given test sample falls in the category of Normal, then the classification is concluded with that category. Else, the optimized hyper plane will be defined between Benign and Malignant categories in the binary SVM2. Then the classification will be concluded based on the classification of the result.

In our study, the given query image is not classified by the KNN because of not satisfying the majority constraints of the KNN. So, the process is switched to SVM1. The fig.6 shows that the failure of KNN classification and switched over to SVM1.

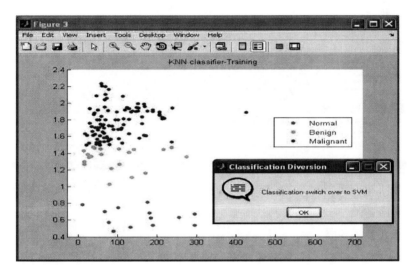

Fig. 6. Failure of KNN classification for the given query image

The optimized hyper plan is to be formed in order to split the sample features in a right way.

Expression for hyper plane
w.x+b = 0…. [6]

x – Set of training vectors
w – Vectors perpendicular to the separating hyper plane
b – Offset parameter which allows the increase of the margin

As we have spoken earlier, we analyze whether the test sample of the given image falls in the category of 'Normal' or 'Abnormal' in SVM1. In this, the given query image is concluded as 'Normal' in the SVM1 Classification stage1 itself. The fig.7 proves that the given query image belongs 'Normal' category below. The rounded circle indicates the result. The fig.8 indicates that the classification result of another given query image which falls in the category of 'Benign' in SVM2 binary classification and which is indicated by a rounded circle.

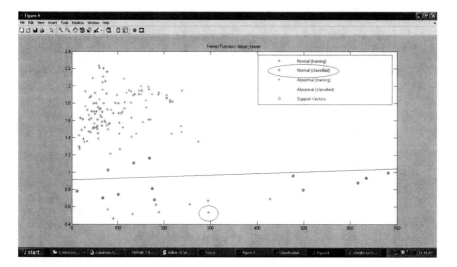

Fig. 7. SVM classification result for the given query image

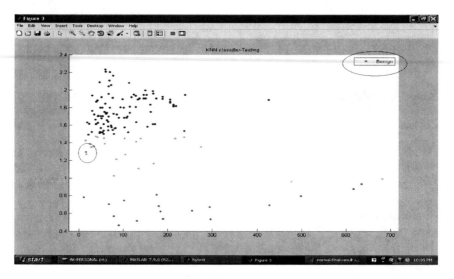

Fig. 8. KNN Classification result for the given query image

Furthermore, in order to justify the result, the conventional sensitivity and specificity examination to be done. Sensitivity and specificity are two statistical measurements to be used for identifying the performance of a binary classification test. Sensitivity measures the proportion of actual positives which are correctly identified. Specificity measures the proportion of negatives which are correctly identified. Hence, we have plotted the conventional Partest Graph based on the following criteria.

True Positive (TP)   - Sick people correctly diagnosed as sick (TP)
False Positive (FP)   - Healthy people incorrectly identified as sick (FP)
True Negative (TN) - Healthy people correctly identified as healthy (TN)
False Negative (FN) - Sick people incorrectly identified as healthy (FN) .....[4]

Hence, the values of the TP and TN should always be high. The fig.9 shows the Partest-graph of our classification where the rate of FP and FN are highly reduced and the rate of TP and TN are highly increased.

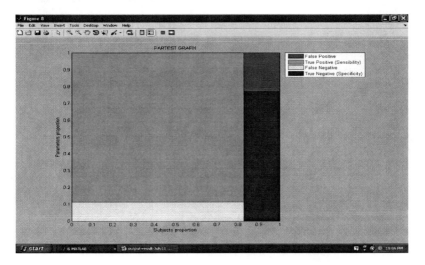

Fig. 9. Partest Graph for Sensitivity and Specificity Analysis

Sensitivity

Probability that test is positive on unhealthy subject
Sensitivity = TP/ (TP+FN)*100 %...[5]

Specificity

Probability that test is negative on healthy subject
Specificity = TN/ (TN+FP)*100 %....[5]

The fig.10 shows that the time consumed by Hybrid KNNSVM compared to KNN and SVM classifications processed separately. HKNNSVM consumes an average time of KNN and SVM. The time has been compared at regular intervals in the rate of twenty five, fifty, seventy five, hundred and one fifty images. The fig.11 shows that the overall classification accuracy rate of testing images compared to training set. Here, we have taken both the training and test images as same. So, the accuracy has been improved in the test stage compared to training stage. Though the algorithm improves the accuracy of the classification result, it also produces certain misclassification calculations in the execution. Hence, we have analysed the error rate calculations at every rate of 25 images. However, the error rate for every 25 images is very low. The fig.12 shows the error rate at each and every twenty images classification processes. The % of error rate shows that the misclassification of our algorithm at regular interval. Hence, we have got the accuracy rate as 86.7% and misclassification rate as 13.3% as shown in the figure 13.

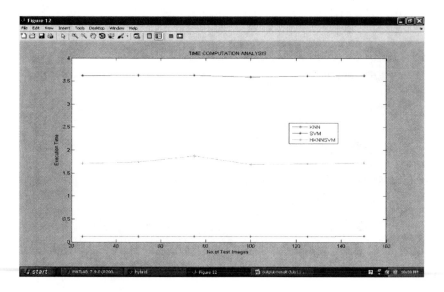

Fig. 10. Time comparison of SVM, KNN and Hybrid SVMKNN

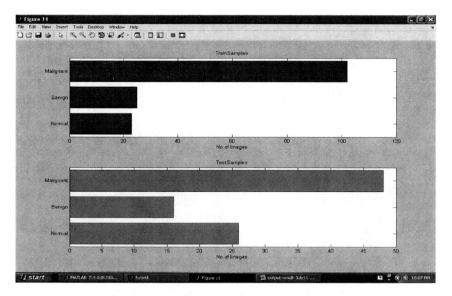

Fig. 11. Classification Accuracy of HKNNSVM

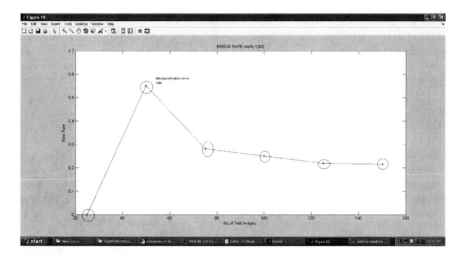

Fig. 12. Error Rate Analysis

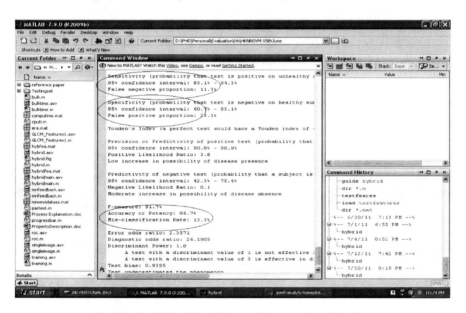

Fig. 13. Sensitivity, Specificity and Accuracy Justifications

3 Conclusion

In this paper, we have classified 150 MRI images in order to diagnosis the tumour stages as 'Normal', 'Benign' and 'Malignant' in human brain based on the classification algorithms of KNN and SVM. In general, either KNN or SVM will be used to classify the images. But, here, on considering their drawbacks in certain situations, it has jointly been applied in our application. Here, the SVM has also been designed as binary classifications as SVM1 and SVM2. Hence, the accuracy of the result has been consistently increased and the error rate has been consistently reduced. In future, we have an idea to propose an application to implement CBIR concepts along with this application to retrieve similar features images based on the given query MRI images.

References

1. Image Mining: Trends and Developments, Ji Zhang Wynne Hsu Mong Li Lee
2. Image Texture Classification using Combined Grey Level Co-occurrence Probabilities and Support Vector Machines. Hee-Kooi Khoo, Hong-Choon Ong, Ya-Ping Wong, School of Mathematical Sciences, Universiti Sains Malaysia, 11800 Gelugor, Penang, Malaysia, Faculty of Information Technology, Multimedia University, 63100 Cyberjaya, Selangor, Malaysia, 978-0-7695-3359-9/08
3. A Review of Nearest Neighbor-Support Vector Machines Hybrid Classification Models. Lam Hong, Lee, Chin Heng, Wan, Tien Fui, Yong and Hui Meian, Kok, Faculty of Information and Communication Technology, Universiti Tunku Abdul Rahman, Jalan Universiti, Bandar Barat, 31900 Kampar, Perak, Malaysia
4. Sensitivity and Specificity- Wikipedia,
   http://en.wikipedia.org/wiki/Sensitivity_and_specificity
5. An Improved Objective Evaluation Measure for Border Detection in Dermoscopy Images. M. Emre Celebi_Dept. of Computer Science Louisiana State Univ., Shreveport, LA, USA, Gerald Schaefer School of Engineering and Applied Science Aston Univ., Birmingham, UK, Hitoshi Iyatomi Dept. of Electrical Informatics Hosei Univ., Tokyo, Japan, William V. Stoecker Stoecker & Associates, Rolla, MO, USA, Joseph M. Malters The Dermatology Center, Rolla, MO, USA, James M. Grichnik Dept. of MedicineDuke Univ. Medical Center, Durham, NC, USA, July 13 (2009)
6. Data Classification Using Support Vector Machine. Durgesh K. Srivastava, Ass. Prof., Department of CSE/IT, BRCM CET, Bahal, Bhiwani, Haryana, India-127028, LEKHA BHAMBHU, Ass. Prof, Department of CSE/IT, BRCM CET, Bahal, Bhiwani, Haryana, India-127028. Journal of Theoretical and Applied Information Technology (2005-2009)

Biclique Cover of Complete Graph K_n and Honeycomb Network $HC(n)$

Jasintha Quadras and Vasanthika S.

Department of Mathematics, Stella Maris College, Chennai, India
vasanthika.s@gmail.com

Abstract. A biclique of a simple graph G is a complete bipartite subgraph of G. A biclique cover of a graph G is a family of complete bipartite graphs (or bicliques) such that every edge of the graph G belongs to at least one of these subgraphs. *The minimum biclique cover* of G is a collection of minimum number of bicliques which covers E(G). We represent K_n in a $\lceil \log_2 n \rceil$-dimensional hypercube in $R^{\lceil \log_2 n \rceil}$ space and we prove that the cardinality of minimum biclique cover of complete graph K_n is $\lceil \log_2 n \rceil$. We have proved that the cardinality of minimum biclique cover of honeycomb network HC(n) is $3n^2$.

Keywords: Biclique, honeycomb network, edge cover, hyperplane.

1 Introduction

A number of graph algorithms depend on finding all subgraphs of certain type in a larger graph. Covering the edges of a graph by cliques, matchings, cycles etc. is one of the basic problems in graph theory. Let G be a simple undirected graph with vertex set $V(G)$ and edge set $E(G)$. A *biclique* of G is a complete bipartite subgraph of G. A *biclique cover* of a graph G is a collection of bicliques covering $E(G)$ (every edge of G belongs to at least one biclique of the collection). The *minimum biclique cover* of G is a collection of minimum number of bicliques which covers $E(G)$. The *cardinality of minimum biclique cover* of G is $b(G)$. The biclique cover problem of a graph G is to determine $b(G)$.

Various problems on minimal coverage of graphs have been investigated. Amilhastre [1] show that for bipartite domino-free graphs, minimum biclique cover can be computed in polynomial time. Bipartite domino-free graphs include bipartite C_4- free graphs, bipartite distance-hereditary graphs and bipartite convex graphs. For bipartite chordal graphs the biclique cover problem is *NP*-complete. Tuza [12] proved that the edge set of an arbitrary simple graph G on n vertices can be covered by at most $n - \lfloor \log_2 n \rfloor + 1$ complete bipartite subgraphs of G, for all n. Tverberg [13] has given a proof of impossibility of decomposing the complete graph on n vertices into n - 2 or fewer complete bipartite graphs. Archdeacon [2] give a characterization of all bipartite coverings in terms of factoring the covering map through the canonical double covering and described regular bipartite graphs in terms of voltage assignments. Fishburn and Hammer [5] show that $b(G)$ equals the Boolean interval

A. Abd Manaf et al. (Eds.): ICIEIS 2011, Part II, CCIS 252, pp. 151–158, 2011.

dimension of the complementary graph of G. Orlin [9] shows that the calculation of $b(G)$ is NP-complete for general bipartite graphs and Muller [8] proved that the biclique cover problem remains NP-complete when restricted to chordal bipartite graphs. Harary [6] proved that the minimum number of bipartite graphs required to cover a graph G is $\lceil \log_2 \chi(G) \rceil$, $\chi(G)$ is the chromatic number of G and according to the Four color theorem the minimum number of bipartite graphs required to cover a plannar graph is 2. Cornaz [4] derived a 0-1 linear programming formulation to find the maximum weighted biclique in a graph and proved that the continuous relaxation of this integer program can be solved in polynomial time and also given a continuous relaxation method for minimum biclique cover. Jukna [7] proved that, if a bipartite graph with e edges contains n vertex-disjoint edges, then $\frac{n^2}{e}$ complete bipartite subgraphs are necessary to cover all its edges and has noted $b(\hat{K}_n) \leq \lceil \log_2 n \rceil$.

A hyperplane is a concept in geometry. It is a generalization of the plane into a different number of dimensions. A *hyperplane* in R^n space is a flat subset with dimension $n-1$. In Cartesian co-ordinates, a hyperplane can be described with a linear equation

$$a_1 x_1 + a_2 x_2 + \cdots + a_n x_n = b$$

Where at least one $a_i \neq 0$, $i = 1,2,\dots,n$, which separates (disconnects) the R^n space into two spaces, which are the two connected components of the complement of the hyperplane $a_1 x_1 + a_2 x_2 + \cdots + a_n x_n = b$, and are given by

$$a_1 x_1 + a_2 x_2 + \cdots + a_n x_n < b$$

$$a_1 x_1 + a_2 x_2 + \cdots + a_n x_n > b$$

A real line is a hyperplane in 2-dimensional space. A plane is a hyperplane in 3-dimensional space.

For a positive integer q, we define the $(q-1)$-dimensional hyperplanes in the q-dimensional space R^q $\Pi_1, \Pi_2, \Pi_3, \dots, \Pi_q$ as follows

$$x_1 = \tfrac{1}{2}, \quad x_2 = \tfrac{1}{2}, \quad x_3 = \tfrac{1}{2}, \dots, x_q = \tfrac{1}{2}.$$

A vertex transitive graph is a graph G such that, given any two vertices v_1 and v_2 of G, there is an automorphism

$$f : V(G) \to V(G), \quad \text{such that } f(v_1) = v_2.$$

A *honeycomb network* can be built in various ways. The honeycomb network $HC(1)$ is a hexagon; see Fig. 1(a). The honeycomb network $HC(2)$ is obtained by adding a layer of six hexagons to the boundary edges of $HC(1)$ as shown in Fig. 1(b). Inductively honeycomb network $HC(n)$ is obtained from $HC(n-1)$ by adding a layer of hexagons around the boundary of $HC(n-1)$. Alternately the size n of $HC(n)$ is the number of hexagons between the center and boundary of $HC(n)$ (both inclusive) and the number of vertices and edges of $HC(n)$ are $6n^2$ and $9n^2 - 3n$ respectively [10].

The honeycomb networks are wildly used in computer graphics, cellular phone base station [11], and image processing [3] and in chemistry as representation of benzenoid hydrocarbons [10].

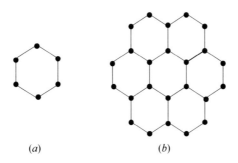

(a)   (b)

Fig. 1. (a) HC (1) (b) HC (2)

2 Biclique Cover of Complete Graph

Lemma 1. Let K_n be a complete graph. Let q be the least integer such that $n \leq 2^q$. Then K_n has a biclique cover of cardinality q.

Proof. Suppose $n = 2^q$. Represent K_n in a q-dimensional hypercube in the q-dimensional space R^q. The vertices here are given binary representation as in the hypercube and all the vertices are adjacent to each other. The vertices $v_1, v_2, v_3, \ldots, v_{n-2}, v_{n-1}, v_n$ of K_n are represented by the q-dimensional co-ordinate system in the q-dimensional space R^q as

v_1	000............000
v_2	000............001
v_3	000............010
.	.
.	.
.	.
v_{n-2}	111............101
v_{n-1}	111............110
v_n	111............111

Let H_i, $i = 1, 2, \ldots, q$ be the q number hyperplanes in the q-dimensional space R^q. The induced subgraph of the edges traversing through the ith hyperplane H_i is a biclique B_i of K_n. Here each B_i is isomorphic to $K_{2^{q-1}, 2^{q-1}}$. Since $B_1 \cup B_2 \cup B_3 \cup \ldots \cup B_q = K_n$, $\{B_1, B_2, B_3, \ldots, B_q\}$ is a biclique cover of K_n with cardinality q. Fig. 2 shows K_8 in 3-dimensional space with their 3 hyperplanes.

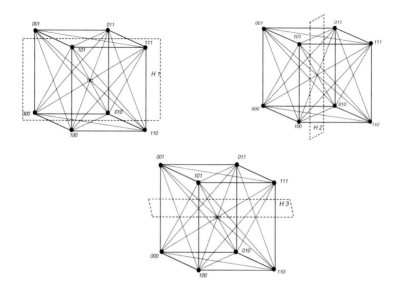

Fig. 2. K_8 in 3-dimensional space with the 3 hyperplanes H_1, H_2, H_3

When $n \leq 2^q$, K_n is a subgraph of K_{2^q}. The edges of K_n through the hyperplane H_i is a biclique B_i. Since $B_1 \cup B_2 \cup B_3 \cup \dots \cup B_q = K_n$, $\{B_1, B_2, B_3, \dots, B_q\}$ is also a biclique cover of K_n with cardinality q.   □

Lemma 2. Let K_n be a complete graph. If $n = 2^q$ where q is a positive integer then $b(K_n) = q$.

Proof. Let H_i, $i = 1,2,\dots,q$ be the q number of (q - 1)-dimensional hyperplanes in the q-dimensional space R^q defined by $x_i = \frac{1}{2}$, $i = 1,2,\dots,q$. The edges traversing through the ith hyperplane H_i induces a biclique $K_{2^{q-1},2^{q-1}}$ in K_n. Hence through the q number of (q - 1)-dimensional hyperplanes, q bicliques cover K_n with cardinality q and is minimum.

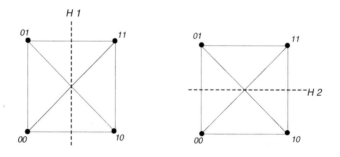

Fig. 3. K_4 in the 2-dimensional space with the 2 hyperplanes H_1, H_2

Suppose it is not minimum, then there is at least one biclique, say $K_{l,m}$ whose edges do not traverse through any of the hyperplanes H_i, $i = 1, 2, ..., q$. In this case $l \neq m \neq 2^{q-1}$. Without loss of generality let $l < m$. Clearly $l < 2^{q-1}$ and $m > 2^{q-1}$. Then there are cliques $K_{2^{q-1}}$, which are not covered by $K_{l,m}$ in K_n, need more than q bicliques to cover K_n. Therefore the cardinality of biclique cover of K_n is greater than q, which is not minimum. Hence $b(K_{2^q}) = q$.   □

Illustration of Lemma 2 is shown in Fig. 3. When $n = 4$. $b(K_4) = 2$, where the edges of the bicliques are considered through the two hyperplanes H_1 and H_2 (H_1 and H_2 are straight lines $x = \frac{1}{2}$ and $y = \frac{1}{2}$ respectively in the XOY plane) in the space R^2. In this case the bicliques are $K_{2,2}$ and $K_{2,2}$.

On the other hand, consider a star biclique $K_{1,3}$ in K_4, then at least two more bicliques are needed to cover the remaining edges of K_4 (which are not covered by $K_{1,3}$). Here the cardinality of biclique cover of K_4 is 3, which is not the minimum cardinality. See Fig. 4.

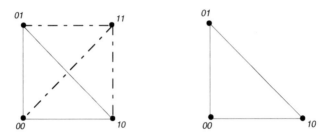

Fig. 4. K_4 in the 2-dimensional space with a biclique $K_{1,3}$ and remaining uncovered edges of K_4

Theorem 1. K_n has minimum biclique cover, where all the bicliques are isomorphic to each other iff there exists a positive integer q such that $n = 2^q$.

Proof. Let K_n has minimum biclique cover of cardinality q, that is $b(K_n) = q$, where all the bicliques are isomorphic to each other. Suppose $n \neq 2^q$, then $n > 2^q$ or $n < 2^q$. If $n > 2^q$ then $b(K_n) \geq q + 1$, which is a contradiction that $b(K_n) = q$. If $n < 2^q$ then there exists a $H_i, i = 1, 2, ..., q$, traversing through the edges of a biclique, which is not balanced, which is a contradiction that all the bicliques are isomorphic to each other. Hence $n = 2^q$. Conversely assume that there exists a positive integer q such that $n = 2^q$. Since K_n is symmetric without isolated vertices it is vertex transitive and edge transitive, and since K_n is complete graph on 2^q vertices, the q number of bicliques whose edges traversing through the q different hyperplanes $H_i, i = 1, 2, ..., q$ are q copies of $K_{2^{q-1}, 2^{q-1}}$, and hence all the bicliques are isomorphic to each other. By Lemma 2, it is the minimum biclique cover of K_n. □

Lemma 3. $b(K_{2^q+1}) = q + 1$.

Proof. K_{2^q+1} is a complete graph which contains two disjoint cliques K_{2^q} and K_{2^q}. By Lemma 2, $b(K_{2^q}) = q$. The edges through the q hyperplanes H_i traversing through both the cliques K_{2^q} and K_{2^q} induces q number of bicliques $K_{2^q, 2^q}$ in K_{2^q+1}. The edges between both the cliques K_{2^q} and K_{2^q} in K_{2^q+1}, considered through the $q + 1^{th}$ hyperplane H_{q+1} induces the $q + 1^{th}$ biclique $K_{2^q,2^q}$ in $K_{2^{q+1}}$. Hence $q+1$ bicliques ($q+1$ numbers of $K_{2^q,2^q}$) cover $K_{2^{q+1}}$ with minimum cardinality $q+1$.   □

Lemma 4. $b(K_{2^q+1}) = q + 1$.

Proof. K_{2^q+1} is a complete graph which contains a clique K_{2^q} as subgraph. By Lemma 2, $b(K_{2^q}) = q$. The edges through the q hyperplanes H_i traversing through the clique K_{2^q} induces q bicliques in K_{2^q+1} . The edges between the clique K_{2^q} and the $2^q + 1^{th}$ vertex is considered through the $q + 1^{th}$ hyperplane H_{q+1} induces the $q + 1^{th}$ star biclique $K_{1,2^q}$ in K_{2^q+1} . Hence $q+1$ bicliques cover K_{2^q+1} with minimum cardinality $q+1$.   □

Lemma 5. The cardinality of minimum biclique cover of K_n , $2^q < n \leq 2^{q+1}$ is $q+1$, where q is a positive integer.

Proof. By Lemma 2, $b(K_{2^q}) = q$, by Lemma 3, $b(K_{2^q+1}) = q + 1$, by Lemma 4, $b(K_{2^q+1}) = q + 1$ and since K_n , $2^q + 1 \leq n \leq 2^{q+1}$ is a clique of K_{2^q+1} , the cardinality of minimum biclique cover of K_n is $q+1$.   □

Jukna [7] noted $b(K_n) \leq \lceil \log_2 n \rceil$, is now proved in the following theorem.

Theorem 2. Let K_n be a complete graph on n vertices. The cardinality of minimum biclique cover of K_n is $\lceil \log_2 n \rceil$.

Proof. By Lemma 1, K_n has a biclique cover of cardinality q, where q is a positive integer such that $n \leq 2^q$. The proof is by induction. $b(K_2) = 1$, $b(K_n) = 2$, $2^1 < n \leq 2^2$ (since $b(K_3) = 2$, $b(K_4) = 2$). Suppose $b(K_n) = q$, $2^{q-1} < n \leq 2^q$, by Lemma 5, $b(K_n) = q + 1$, $2^q < n \leq 2^{q+1}$. Hence minimum biclique cover of K_n is $\lceil \log_2 n \rceil$.   □

The following algorithm finds the minimum biclique cover of any complete graph on n vertices. Here the vertices are labelled as $v_1, v_2, v_3, ... , v_{n-2}, v_{n-1}, v_n$. Given the input n, the algorithm gives the bipartite cover $B_1, B_2, B_3, ..., B_q$ as $[V_1', V_1''] , [V_2', V_2''] , ..., [V_p', V_p'']$ respectively. The outer loop is on $\lceil \log_2 n \rceil$ times and the inner loop is on n times. The complexity of the above algorithm is $o(n \log_2 n)$.

Algorithm: Minimum biclique cover of K_n.

    begin

        for $i \leftarrow 1$ *to* $\lceil \log_2 n \rceil$ *do*

        $V_i' \leftarrow \{null\}$

        $V_i'' \leftarrow \{null\}$

            for $N \leftarrow 1$ *to* n *do*

                if $\left\lceil \frac{N}{2^{i-1}} \right\rceil = odd$

              then $V_i' \leftarrow V_i' \cup V_N$

              else $V_i'' \leftarrow V_i'' \cup V_N$

$$endfor$$

$$endfor$$

$$end$$

3 Biclique Cover of Honeycomb Network

Lemma 6. $b(P_{2n+1}) = n$, where n is a positive integer.

Proof. $b(P_n) = \lfloor \frac{n}{2} \rfloor$ as $K_{1,2}$ is the largest (with maximum number of edges) biclique in P_n . $b(P_{2n+1}) = \lfloor \frac{2n+1}{2} \rfloor = \lfloor n + \frac{1}{2} \rfloor = n.$ □

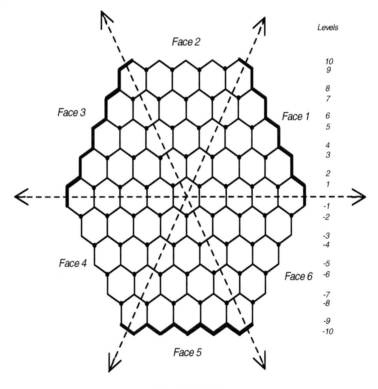

Fig. 5. $HC(5)$

Theorem 3. $b(HC(n)) = 3n^2$.

Proof. $K_{1,3}$ is the largest (with maximum number of edges) biclique in $HC(n)$. When m is a positive odd integer, every 3-degree vertex in the level m (highlighted by dots in the Fig. 5) and their 3 incident edges form a biclique $K_{1,3}$. In the same way, when m is a negative even integer, every 3-degree vertex in the level m (highlighted by dots in the Fig. 5) and their 3 incident edges also form a biclique $B_{1,3}$. See Fig. 5.

When m is a positive odd integer, there are $\frac{3n(n-1)}{2}$ 3-degree vertices, and when m is a negative even integer, there are $\frac{3n(n-1)}{2}$ 3-degree vertices. Hence there are $3n(n-1)$ star bicliques $K_{1,3}$ in $HC(n)$. Now the edges of the 3 number of P_{2n+1} (highlighted in the Fig. 5), which are located in the 3 alternate faces 1, 3 and 5 of $HC(n)$ need to be covered by minimum $3n$ bicliques $K_{1,2}$, by Lemma 6. Therefore $3n(n-1)$ number of $K_{1,3}$ and $3n$ number of $K_{1,2}$ cover $HC(n)$. Hence $b(HC(n)) = 3n^2$.   □

Remark 1. Since $|E| = 9n^2 - 3n = 3 \times n(n-1) + 2 \times 3n$, the minimum star cover number is $3n^2$ and the minimum biclique decomposition number is also $3n^2$. The above proof holds for both these problems.

4 Conclusion and Further Work

In this paper we study minimum biclique cover of complete graphs and honeycomb network. Minimum biclique cover and maximal biclique problems on interconnection networks are under investigation.

References

1. Amilhastre, J., Vilarem, M.C., Janssen, P.: Complexity of Minimum Biclique Cover and Minimum Biclique Decomposition for Bipartite Domino-Free Graphs. Discrete Appl. Math. 86, 125–144 (1998)
2. Archdeacon, D., Kwak, J.H., Lee, J., Sohn, M.Y.: Bipartite Covering Graphs. Discrete Math. 214, 51–63 (2000)
3. Bell, S.B.M., Holroyd, M.D.C.: A Digital Geometry for Hexagonal Pixels. Image and Vision Computing 7, 194–204 (1989)
4. Cornaz, D., Fonlupt, J.: Chromatic Characterization of Biclique Covers. Discrete Math. 306, 495–507 (2006)
5. Fishburn, P.C., Hammer, P.L.: Bipartite Dimensions and Bipartite Degrees of Graphs. Discrete Math. 160, 127–148 (1996)
6. Harary, F., Hsu, D., Miller, Z.: The Biparticity of a Graph. J. Graph Theory 1, 131–133 (1977)
7. Jukna, S., Kulikov, A.S.: On Covering Graphs by Complete Bipartite Subgraphs. Discrete Math. 309, 3399–3403 (2009)
8. Muller, H.: On Edge Perfectness and Classes of Bipartite Graphs. Discrete Math. 149, 159–187 (1996)
9. Orlin, J.: Contentment in Graph Theory: Covering Graphs with Cliques. Indag. Math. 39, 406–424 (1977)
10. Stojmenovic, I.: Honeycomb Networks: Topological Properties and Communication Algorithm. IEE Transactions on Parallel and Distributed Systems 8(10), 1036–1042 (1997)
11. Tajozzakerin, H.R., Sarbazi-Azad, H.: Enhanced-Star: A New Topology Based on the Star Graph. In: Cao, J., Yang, L.T., Guo, M., Lau, F. (eds.) ISPA 2004. LNCS, vol. 3358, pp. 1030–1038. Springer, Heidelberg (2004)
12. Tuza, Z.: Covering of Graphs by Complete Bipartite Subgraphs; Complexity of 0-1 Matrices. Combinantorica 4(1), 111–116 (1984)
13. Tverberg, H.: On the Decomposition of K_n into Complete Bipartite Graphs. J. Graph Theory 6, 493–494 (1982)

Could Aura Images Can Be Treated
as Medical Images?

R. Rajesh[1], B. Shanmuga Priya[2], J. Satheesh Kumar[1], and V. Arulmozhi[3]

[1] Bharathiar University, Coimbatore, Tamil Nadu, India
[2] CMS College of Science & Commerce, Coimbatore, Tamil Nadu, India
[3] Tiruppur Kumaran College for Women, Tiruppur, Tamil Nadu, India
{kollamrajeshr,jsathee}@ieee.org, shanmugapriyaa.b@gmail.com
arultkc@yahoo.co.in

Abstract. Aura is the electromagnetic field that surrounds the human body and every organisms and objects in the universe. Illness may be represented by characteristic defects in the finger based aura images which correspond to the main organs of the body. The main focus of this paper is to exemplify the role of aura image in medical diagnosis. Experiments have done with nearly 40 subjects(both normal and abnormal). It clearly shows that the state of imbalanced energy in the concerned organs which may leads to cause diseases. The result shows that the aura images are effectively treated as medical images in predicting and diagnosing diseases.

Keywords: Aura, Energy, Human organs, Medical diagnosis, Chakras.

1 Introduction

Human is one of the wonderful model created by God. Physically, the human body is created with organs related with energy field. Depending on the human characteristics and behaviours, the energy imbalance in the concerned organ may causes diseases. In medical, usually when a patient is examined by a doctor, he begins an interaction with patients and examines their medical history and records, then interviews the patient and finally does physical examinations and medical tests. In physical examination, the doctor used to examine the flow of blood on the nails by holding the finger and pressing the tip of the finger. For example, If the blood flow in the nail is less, it indicates the person is anemic. If the color of the hand is yellowish, then he is prone to jaundice. Various medical imaging techniques are used to create images of the human body for clinical purposes or medical science such as x-rays, MRI, CT etc.

Recently, aura images are used to find out the energy levels of the body which is then used to diagnose diseases. It is possible by use of Kirlian camera which captures an aura images that measures human energy levels and examine changes in the subtle energy distribution of the individual [6]. Effectively, the aura is a safeguard that keep our body healthy and joyful when it is stable.

A. Abd Manaf et al. (Eds.): ICIEIS 2011, Part II, CCIS 252, pp. 159–170, 2011.

Aura images are useful for predicting the ailments through energy field weeks or months before it appears in the body.

The main focus of this paper is to show the relationship of Aura image with various organs disease. Experiments show the effectiveness of the aura in diagnosing diseases. This paper is organized as follows. Section 2 presents the medical image based diagnosis. Section 3 presents the review of aura image. Section 4 presents arua-based diagnosis. Section 5 presents the experimental results and section 6 concludes the paper.

2   Medical Image Based Diagnosis

In medicine, diagnosis is the process of identifying a medical condition or disease by its signs, symptoms, and from the results of various diagnostic procedures. It is defined by two distinct dictionary definitions. The first is "the recognition of a disease by its signs and symptoms". The second is "the analysis of the underlying physiological/ biochemical causes of a disease". It began in earnest from the ancient times of Egypt & Greece. The practice of diagnosis continues by theories in the early 20th century [1] [2] [3] [4].

In clinical practice, a doctor begins an interaction with an examination of the patient's medical history, record, interview, physical examinations and medical tests [5]. Basic diagnosis medical devices such as stethoscope, depressor etc., are typically used. There are four diagnostic methods used namely, inspection, auscultation, Olfaction, Interrogation, palpation for the disease of infection, uremia, diabetic etc.

Medical imaging refers to techniques and processes used to create images of the human body for clinical purposes or medical science. It is generally associate with radiology or Clinical Imaging like x-rays. Medical imaging uses a set of techniques to produce images of the internal phase of the body. Image processing techniques are developed for analyzing remote sensing data that are modified to analyze the outputs of medical imaging systems to analyze symptoms of the patients easily [10]. When the digital data is reproduced any number of times, it will not change and retains the originality of the data. It is further used by the doctors for giving demonstrations and presentations over patients health.

3   Aura Image – A Review

The Human Energy Field as a collection of electro - magnetic energies of varying densities that permeate through and emit or exit from the physical body of a living person. These particles of energy are suspended around the healthy human body in an oval shaped field. This "auric energy" emits out from the body approximately 2-3 feet on all sides. It extends above the head and below the feet into the ground. The aura is sensitive to colour. It reacts to the colours of clothing and to that of its surroundings. This accounts for our natural likes and dislikes when it comes to choosing the colours that surround us.

The aura consist of seven levels/layers/auric bodies . Each one of the subtle bodies that exist around the physical body, has its own unique frequency. They are interrelated, and affect one another and the person's feelings, emotions, thinking, behaviour, and health as well. Therefore a state of imbalance in one of the bodies leads to a state of imbalance in the others. Aura is related with human chakras. The Chakras are said to be "force centers" or whorls of energy permeating, from a point on the physical body, the layers of the subtle bodies in an ever-increasing fan-shaped formation.

An aura imaging technique is used to capture the energy field by an instrument /device called Kirlian camera. Kirlian camera captures an aura images that measures human energy levels and examine changes in the subtle energy distribution of the individual. This Kirlian photograph gives information on the subject of the psychological, emotional and physical stipulation [7]. Professor K. Korotkov, inventor and Russian scientist has proved that the energy fields from electrophotographic device of the fingertips afford an image which shows the function of the whole mind- body system [8] [9]. Kirlian images quantify the person stressed, tired and conclude bio-energic electro photonic performance of the body and mind. Recently, it has become a diagnostic tool in medical science.

Aura healing is also known as spiritual healing, energy healing, or psychic healing. Many physical problems have their root cause on an energy level. In other words, physical problems can be a symptom of energetic, emotional, psychic, or spiritual issues. Rather than focussing on the body symptom, spiritual healing can work with problems at their energetic root cause.

4   Aura-Based Diagnosis

Aura imaging system captures the frequency levels of a person by mapping the energy of five meridian points of the hand. The human body contains psychic energy centres called chakras. There are seven major chakras namely, mooladhara, swadhisthana, manipura, anahata, vishuddha, ajna and saharara. The abnormalities of the energy states various ailments like improper digestion, weak liver function etc [11].

The basic difference between the modern medicine and the energy systems is that, the modern medicine gives importance to the physical body and microorganisms like viruses; whereas the aura scanning image is based on mental, emotional and spiritual and give importance to energy at cellular levels, chakras and meridians. The captured energy is translated in the form of color spectrum. The various colors show the characteristics of the person based on mental and spiritual energy.

Researchers found that the changes in the color, brightness and patterns of light detect the changes in the emotional conditions of humans [12]. The ability of software to take the sector of all fingers of a person gives the appearance of an aura [8] [9]. For example, a person's left ring finger with kidney trouble shows outburst type of defect in the kidney sector indicates the region of pain or acute inflammation. A person's right thumb with teeth trouble shows gaps specify the

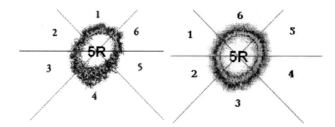

Fig. 1. (a) Abnormal Subject : Energy levels in the right little finger with problem in respiratory system and right kidney, (b) Normal Subject

region of weak energy in jaw. Fig. 1, 2, 3 shows (i) finger, (ii) chakra and (iii) organs of abnormal & normal subjects.

Energy medicine including magnetic therapy, millimeter wave therapy, sound energy therapy, light therapy, homeopathy, distance healing, herbal medicine, acupuncture, acupressure, moxibustion and cupping are used to restore the flow of energy from the vital energy through meridians.

5   Experiments and Results

Experiments have been conducted for 40 subjects. Most of the subjects have shown abnormal energy levels. The results of only one subject with abnormal energy level who is prone to get deseases are shown in this paper due to space constraints. The results in Fig. 4, 5 show the energy level of the ten fingers of the abnormal subject.

The energy levels of various organs represented by the left finger as shown in fig. 4 can be explained as (a) Left Thumb Finger: 1-Right eye,2-Right side nose; ear, 3-Right side Jaw; Teeth, 4-Thorat; Larynx; Trachea; Thyroid gland, 5-Left side Jaw; Teeth, 6-Left side nose; ear, 7-Left eye, 8-Cerebral zone, (b) Left Index Finger : 1-Descending colon, 2-Sigmoid colon, 3- Rectum, 4-Coccyx; Pelvis minor zone, 5-Sacrum, 6-Spiral column Lumbar zone, 7-Spiral column Thorax zone, 8-Spinal column Cervical zone, 9-Transverse colon, (c) Left Middle Finger : 1-Cardiovascular system,2-Left Kidney, 3-Liver, 4-Abdomenal zone, 5-Immune system, 6-Thorax zone; Respiratory system, 7-Cerebral zone (vessels), (d) Left Ring Finger : 1-Hypothalamus, 2-Nervous system, 3-Spleen, 4-Urinogenital system, 5-Adrenal gland, 6-Pancreas, 7-Thyroid gland, 8-Hypophysis, 9-Epiphysis, (e) Left Little Finger(5L.jpg): 1-Left part of Heart, 2-Left Kidney, 3-Mammary gland; Respiratory system, 4-Jejunum, 5-Right part of Heart, 6-Coronary vessels.

The energy levels of various organs represented by the right finger as shown in fig. 5 can be explained as (a) Right Thumb Finger: 1-Right eye, 2- Right side nose; ear, 3-Right side Jaw; Teeth, 4- Throat; Larynx; Trachea; Thyroid gland, 5-Left side Jaw; Teeth, 6- Left side nose; ear, 7-Left eye, 8-Cerebral zone(cortex), (b)Right Index Finger : 1-Spinal column Cervical zone, 2-Spiral column Thorax zone, 3-Spiral column Lumbar zone, 4-Sacrum, 5-Coccyx; Pelvis minor zone,6-Blind gut, 7-Appendix, 8-Ascending colon, 9- Transverse colon, (c) Right Middle

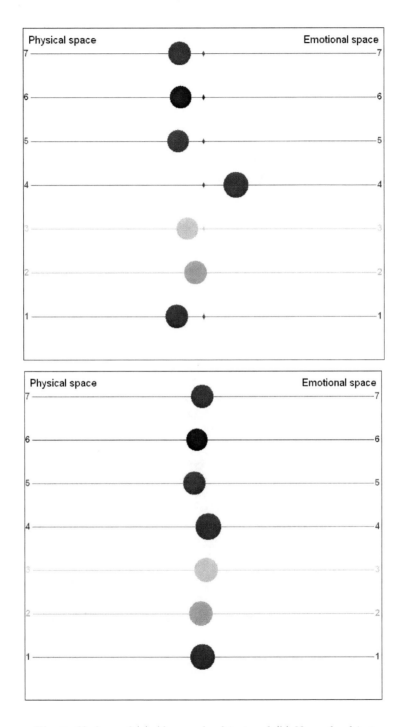

Fig. 2. Chakras of (a) Abnormal subject and (b) Normal subject

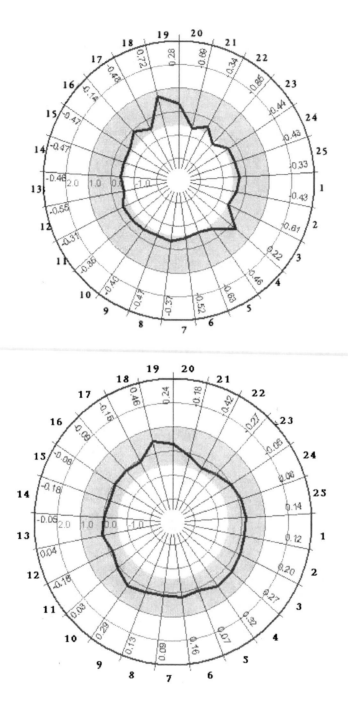

Fig. 3. Right Organ of (a) Abnormal subject (read curve touching central white region) and (b) Normal subject

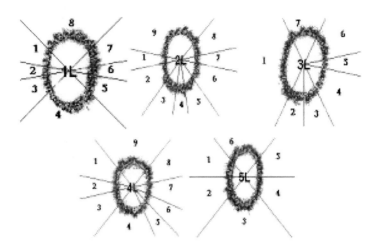

Fig. 4. Energies in left hand fingers: (a) Thumb (1L), (b) Index (2L), (c) Middle (3L), (d) Ring (4L), (e) Little (5L)

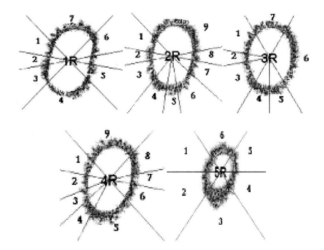

Fig. 5. Energies in right hand fingers: (a) Thumb (1R), (b) Index (2R), (c) Middle (3R), (d) Ring (4R), (e) Little (5R)

Finger : 1-Thorax zone; Respiratory system, 2-Immune system, 3-Gall-bladder, 4-Liver, 5-Right kidney, 6-Cardiovascular system, 7-Cerebral zone (vessels), (d) Right Ring Finger: 1-Hypophysis, 2-Thyroid gland, 3-Pancreas, 4-Adrenal gland, 5-Urino-genital system, 6-Spleen, 7-Nervous system, 8-Hypothalamus, (e) Right Little Finger :1- Duodenum, 2-IIeum, 3- Mammary gland; Respiratory system, 4-Right kidney, 5-Heart, 6-Coronary vessels.

If there is high energy field in the regions, then the organs corresponding to that region may/might have defects. Figure 6,7 show problems in throat, maxillary sinus, cerebral zone (cortex), blind gut, respiratory system, right kidney, cerebral zone (vessels), and abdomenal zone.

Fig. 6 show the overall aura image and also the chakras. The chakras are,1-Muladhara (Spine ending between anus and genitals, perineum area), 2- Svadhisthana (4-6 cm below the navel, at pubic bone level), 3-Manipura (5-7 cm above the navel, solar plexus), 4-Anahata (thorax centre), 5-Vishuddha (base of neck, thymus), 6-Ajna (the centre of brain, epiphysis), 7-Sahasrara (top of the head, vertex). Figure 4 show that the chakras are not properly positioned. One of the chakra is more towards emotional space.

Fig. 7 show the organs system of the body and can be explained as (a) Left side Organ systems: 1-Descending colon, 2-Sigmoid colon, 3-Rectum, 4-Right part of Heart, 5-Liver, 6-Left Kidney, 7-Cervical zone, 8- Thorax zone, 9-Lumber zone, 10-sacrum, 11-Urinogenital system, 12-Nervous system, 13-Immune system, 14-Thyroid gland, 15-Epiphysis, 16-Hypophysis, 17- Hypothalamus, 18-Spleen, 19-Mammary gland, Respiratory system, 20-Coronary vessels, 21-Cerebral zone (vessels), 22-Jaw, Teeth left side, 23-Throat,Larynx, Trachea, Thyroid gland, 24-Cardiovascular system,25-Transverse colon, (b) Right side Organ Systems : 1-Ascending colon, 2-Appendix, 3-Blind gut,4-Duodenum, 5-Liver, 6-Right Kidney, 7-Cervical zone,8- Thorax zone, 9-Lumber zone, 10-sacrum, 11-Urinogenital system, 12-Nervous system, 13-Immune system, 14-Thyroid gland, 15-Epiphysis, 16-Hypophysis, 17-Hypothalamus, 18-Spleen, 19-Mammary gland, Respiratory system, 20-Coronary vessels, 21-Cerebral zone (vessels), 22-Jaw, Teeth right side, 23-Throat, Larynx, Trachea, Thyroid gland, 24-Cardiovascular system, 25-Transverse colon. If the lines are in green area, then the subject is perfectly alright. It can be seen that the subject is having problem in immune system, throat, maxillary sinus, cerebral zone (cortex), blind gut, respiratory system, right kidney, cerebral zone (vessels), and abdomenal zone due to the depletion of the line.

The subject was further studied using traditional medicine and it is found the subject is having 80% of the diseases predicted by aura images. The results show the effectiveness of the aura in diagnosing diseases and it can further extented with automatic feature extraction technique (with features including edge features, segmenatation area, color features, HOG features, etc.) and machine learning techniques (including fuzzy logic [13] [15] [16], neural network [17] [18], genetic algorithm [14], SVM, etc.).

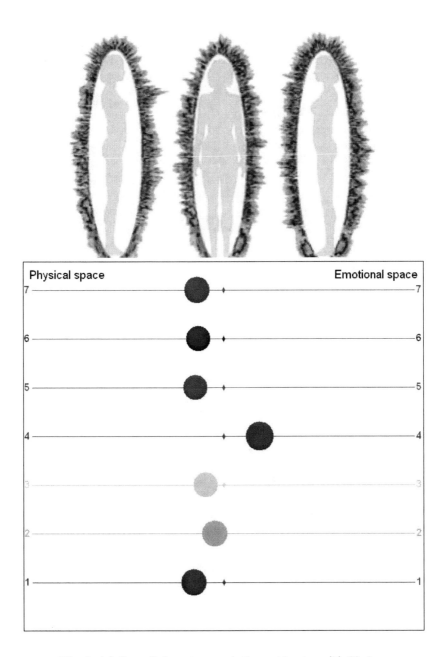

Fig. 6. (a) Overall Aura image A three side view, (b) Chakras

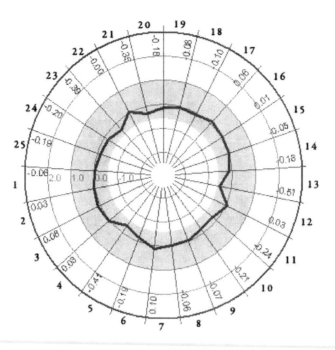

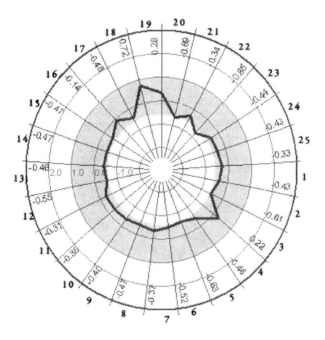

Fig. 7. (a) Left side Organ systems, (b) Right side Organ Systems

6   Conclusion

This paper has shown Kirlian photographic images and its capabilities in detecting diseases. Aura images can capture the human energy levels and examine changes in the subtle energy distribution of the individual. Aura images are similar to medical images which posessess the properties of medical issues. Using Aura images, both emotional and physical problems can be easily classified. The problems like hypertension, sleeping issues, Consious and subconsious problems, blind gunt, kindey problems and problems in various organs can be easily diagnosed. It is one of the powerful method for medical diagnosis without taking blood samples and injecting any medicine. So, Aura images can be effectively treated as medical images. Future work will concentrate on the automatic classification of diseases in aura images using various hybrid methods for more accuracy.

Acknowledgments. The first and third authors are thankful to Bharathiar University authorities for their valuable support. The second author is thankful to CMS College of Science and Commerce and Bharathiar University for their valuable support. The fourth author is thankful to Tiruppur Kumaran College for Women for their valuable support. The authors are also thankful to K.S. Rama Devi, Aura Scanning and Research Centre, Bangalore and Dr.Gomathhi, Aura Scanning Centre, Coimbatore for thier valuable help in getting the scans done at thier centre and for thier valuable suggestions.

References

1. Tierra, M., Tierra, L.: Chinese traditional herbal medicine. Diagnosis & Treatment 1, 195 (1998)
2. Rajesh, R., Kaimal, M.R., Srinivasan, K.: A Note on Medical Image Analysis and Visualization using Matlab. In: ICGST International Journal on Graphics Vision and Image Processing, Special Issue on Medical Image Processing, 352–355 (2006)
3. Satheeshkumar, J., Rajesh, R., Arumugaperumal, S., Kesavdas, C.: A Novel Algorithm for an Efficient Realigning of fMRI Data Series of Brain. ICGST International Journal on Graphics, Vision and Image Processing 9(I), 35–40 (2009)
4. Salem, A.B.M., Roushdy, M., Mahmoud, S.A.: Mining Patient Data based on Rough Set Theory to Determine Thrombosis Disease. Academic Manuscript Central, ICGST-AIML 5(1), 27–31 (2005)
5. Coulehan, J.L., Block, M.R., Davis, F.A.: The Medical Interview: Mastering Skills for Clinical Practice, 5th edn. (2006)
6. Devita, S.: Kinesiology-Energy Medicine and the GDV Kirlian camera. Journal of the ASKUS/CAN-ASK (2003)
7. Halkias, X.C., Maragos, P.: Analysis of Kirlian Images: Feature Extraction and Segmentation. In: Proc. of ICSP, IEEE , vol. 1, pp. 765–768 (2004)
8. Korotkov, K.G.: Aura and Consciousness, 2nd edn. Saint Petersburg (1999)
9. Korotkov, K.G.: Measuring Energy Fields. Saint Petersburg (1999)
10. Serra, J.: Image Analysis and Mathematical Morphology. Academic Press, Inc., Orlando (1983)

11. Priya, B.S., Rajesh, R.: Understanding Abnormal Energy levels in Aura Images. In: Proc. of International Conference on Artificial Intelligence and Machine Learing, Dubai, pp. 75–81 (2011)
12. Olfield, H.: From Kirlian Photography to Polycontrast Interference Photography – PIP (2007)
13. Rajesh, R., Thilagavathy, C., Satheeshkumar, J., Priya, B.S., Priya, K., Sureshkumar, T.: Simple Type-2 T-S Fuzzy Control System for gyros. Proc. of IEEE Fuzzy (2010), doi:10.11.09/FUZZY.2010.5584628
14. Rajesh, R., Kaimal, M.R.: GAVLC: GA with Variable Length Chromosome for the simultaneous design and stability analysis of T-S fuzzy controllers. Proc. IEEE Fuzzy (2008), doi:10.1109/FUZZY.2008.4630553
15. Rajesh, R., Kaimal, M.R.: T-S fuzzy model with nonlinear consequence and PDC controller for a class of nonlinear control systems. Applied Soft Computing 7(3) (June 2007)
16. Rajesh, R., Kaimal, M.R.: Variable Gain Takagi-Sugeno Fuzzy Logic Controllers. Informatica 17(3), 427–444 (2006)
17. Rajesh, R., Rajeev, K., Gopakumar, V., Suchithra, K., Lekhesh, V.P.: On Experimenting with Pedestrian Classification using Neural Network. In: Proc. ICNCS, vol. 1(4), pp. 107–111 (2011)
18. Selvan, A.M., Rajesh, R.: Word Classification Using Neural Network. In: Abraham, A., Mauri, J.L., Buford, J.F., Suzuki, J., Thampi, S.M. (eds.) ACC 2011. CCIS, vol. 192, pp. 497–502. Springer, Heidelberg (2011)

Automatic 3D Image Segmentation Using Adaptive *k*-means on Brain MRI

Luciano Nieddu[1], Giuseppe Manfredi[2], and Salvatore D'Acunto[2]

[1] Universitá LUSPIO, Faculty of Economics,
00145, Rome, Italy
[2] Giustino Fortunato University, Benevento, Italy
l.nieddu@luspio.it

Abstract. The aim of this paper is to present a fully **automatic adaptive k-means segmentation algorithm for MR Images in a 3D space**. We model the gray scale values of the 3D image with a *White Gaussian Process* and superimpose a prior model on the region process in the form of *Markov Random Field*. These assumptions require the use of estimators for the parameters of the two processes. This has been carried out using decreasing size windows.

The Hammersley-Clifford theorem allows us to model the region process in term of a Gibbs Distribution. The Gibbs parameter β is estimated using a correlation-based technique. The segmentation is obtained maximizing the a posterior density function using an Iterated Conditional Modes technique.

The proposed algorithm is fully automatic, i.e. all the parameters of the model are estimated within the segmentation process.

Keywords: Adaptive Estimation, 3D Image Segmentation, *k*-means Algorithm.

1 Introduction

Segmentation algorithms are that part of scene analysis bound for the subdivision of a scene into meaningful and homogeneous regions. In the last few years these techniques have experienced a flowering growth especially in the field of segmentation of Magnetic Resonance Images.

The aim of this paper is to present a new algorithm for segmenting Brain MR Images. In the last years segmentation of MRI has experienced a flowering growth as an aid in medical diagnosis, especially in segmentation of Brain MRI, where these techniques can be used to detect tumors, necrosis and to study the development of brain-size related diseases, like Alzheimer.

Segmentation techniques are not only a pre-processing step to help doctors in disease detection, but can as well be used directly to localize tumors and other diseases as in Clark et al. [4], where a fuzzy clustering technique has been used to detect tumors, edemas and necrosis segmenting and labeling each slice of a 3D Brain MRI by an unsupervised fuzzy c-mean clustering algorithm and then merging them into a volume.

A. Abd Manaf et al. (Eds.): ICIEIS 2011, Part II, CCIS 252, pp. 171–183, 2011.
© Springer-Verlag Berlin Heidelberg 2011

The input of such techniques is usually a gray scale image composed of pixels or voxels (for the 3D case), and as an output, the segmentation algorithm yields another image, where the pixels or voxels are no longer the gray scale values of the underlying image, but are labels indicating the class whom the pixels or voxels of the original image belong to. In some cases [13] clear decision rule that assignes each picture element to one and only one object in the image can not be used because some voxels or pixels could come out to be the result of blending of different tissues. Hence, it could be appropriate to assign a *fuzzy membership values* to each pixel or voxel, indicating the degree of confidence we have for the pixel or voxel to belong to each one object in the image. However in this work we chose to use clear-cut segmentation technique in lieu of fuzzy membership values. Namely we have partitioned the Brain MR image in five zones i.e. **white matter, gray matter, bone, cerebrospinal fluid and background**, and each voxel in the volume data is uniquely assigned to one of the preceding classes.

According to the outbreaking work by Geman and Geman [6], we have modeled the region process as a Markov Random Field imposing a Gibbs distribution on the voxels labels. Besides the intensity value of each region is modeled as a Gaussian Function as in Pappas [9]. The only assumption that needs to be made is that the intensity of the region is a slowly varying function which is an acceptable assumption when there are no texture images involved. The region labels are obtained maximizing the a posterior density function (MAP) via the Iterated Conditional Modes (ICM) technique.

In our work we will show that the estimation of the parameter of the Gibbs distribution (β) is a fundamental step in the process of MRI segmentation and we will introduce a new technique for the estimation of the parameter based on the compatibility function in relaxation labeling algorithm as described in Hummel et al. [8]. This technique is utterly automatic, can be used with any sort of images and does not need any kind of a-priori knowledge on the structure of the clusters in the image. We have embedded our model in 3D space.

The algorithm has been applied on a set of 3D MRI data, yielding a visually good segmentation. In particular, as we will show, our technique manages to deal with noisy data, using the third dimension information and the gibbs model to get rid of noisy spots located on single non adjacent slices.

The outline of the paper is as follow. The model utilized will be introduced in Section 2 while in Section 3 we will present the technique used to estimate the parameters of the Gibbs distribution and of the Gaussian function representing the region process and the intensity value of each region.

In Section 4 we will show the results of the application of our technique on sagittal slices of human brain scans. Finally some conclusions will be drawn in Section 5.

2   Segmentation of 3d Images

The aim of this paragraph is to introduce the theoretical assumptions for the model underlying the volume data. In particular the model for the *a posterior density of the region process* and a neighborhood system will be chosen.

Let consider a volume image defined over a 3D integer lattice of MxN slices forming the volumetric structure of a brain scan, and let y be the observed image. Given a voxel v, y_v will represent the gray scale value of the image at that location; usually y_v will take values in the set $\{0, 1, 2, \ldots, 255\}$.

The aim of a segmentation algorithm is to separate the image into similar and meaningful regions. Let x be a function defined over the same integer lattice of the image, but taking values in a set of K elements representing the labels of each region. If S is a MxN lattice, then:

$$x : S \rightarrow \{1, 2, \ldots, K\} \tag{1}$$

$$y : S \rightarrow \{0, 1, \ldots, 255\} \tag{2}$$

where K is the number of regions in which the image has to be segmented.

The region process x can be modeled as a *Markov Random Field*, [6] and the *Hammersley-Clifford theorem* [2] allows us to write the a priori density function of the region process as a Gibbs distribution

$$p(x) = \frac{1}{Z} e^{-\sum_C V_C} \tag{3}$$

where Z is the *partition function* computed over all the possible values of x and V_C is the clique energy.

The computation of V_C requires the definition of a neighborhood system in 3D and of the corresponding cliques energy. The conditions for a set of subsets of an integer lattice to be a neighborhood system are very loose. Namely, given a set S, a set of subsets of S is a neighborhood system if and only if:

$$\begin{array}{l} 1)\ v \notin N_v\ \forall\, v \in S \\ 2)\ j \in N_v \iff j \in N_v \end{array} \tag{4}$$

where N_v is a subset of S containing the neighboring sites of v. The neighborhood system is the same at every voxel, except for the boundary locations, where a set of different implementation possibilities are available [11]. For images it seems that the *free boundary* neighborhood system is adapt to represent the neighboring interaction more than other systems which use a periodical implementation [6].

Conditions 4 offer us a wide variety of choices for the definition of a 3D neighborhood system. The simplest one in 3D is composed of six neighbors for each voxel and the most complete among the systems accounting for direct neighbors interaction is the 26 neighbors system. Both these systems are depicted in Figure 1.

We are going to consider only two dimensional cliques, i.e. we assume an *a priori uniform distribution for the different regions*. This assumption can be rejected in favor of a more acceptable assumption that assigns to each region of the brain, a probability proportional to the average volume it occupies. Nonetheless this paper wants to build a general and utterly automatic segmentation algorithm, thus we have not considered any assumption that is relative to the particular

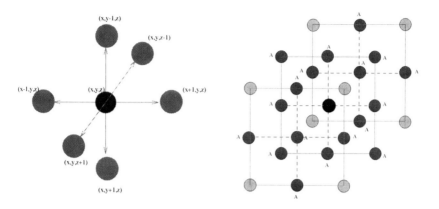

Fig. 1. 3D neighborhood systems

problem at hand. Anyway, it is our belief that the performance of the algorithm can be further improved using also one dimensional cliques, i.e. introducing a priori knowledge on the prior probability of each region.

To model the conditional density of the observed image given the distribution of regions, a Gaussian distribution will be used as in [9].

The mean $\mu_v(x_v)$ is considered as a function of both the voxel v and the cluster x_v that the voxel belongs to. The estimation of the mean is achieved using a 3D adaptive window.

The standard deviation σ for the gaussian distribution is mainly supposed to be known in practical applications: we will drop this assumption embedding the estimation of σ in the segmentation process as presented in Section 4.

The local property of the Markov Random Field allows us to write the a posterior density of the region process only with regards to the neighboring voxels, according to of the neighborhood system adopted.

$$p(x_v \mid y_v) \propto exp\left\{ \frac{1}{2\sigma^2}\left[y_v - m_v(x_v)\right] - \sum_{c \in C} V_C \right\} \tag{5}$$

where $m_v(x_v)$ is the estimation of $\mu_v(x_v)$ at voxel v and the sum $\sum_{c \in C} V_C$ is computed over all the voxels belonging to N_v.

3   Computation of the Smoothness Parameter β

The a posterior density of the region process 5 requires the estimation of $\mu_v(x_v)$ and the computation of $\sum_{c \in C} V_c$. The former will be estimated with a rectangular 3D adaptive windows. The concept is similar to the one espressed for the 2D case in Pappas [9] which we refer the reader to, for more details.

To compute the clique potential, the estimation of the Gibbs parameter β is required. As in [9] the clique energy can be defined as:

$$V_c(x) = \begin{cases} -\beta \text{ if } x_s = x_c \text{ and } s, c \in C \\ +\beta \text{ if } x_s \neq x_c \text{ and } s, c \in C \end{cases} \tag{6}$$

where a positive β will increase the exponent of the 5 for neighboring voxels belonging to the same region, and will lower it for voxels belonging to different regions. Hence a positive β and the MAP estimation will cause neighboring voxels to be more likely to belong to the same region then to different ones. Therefore β can be considered the parameter accounting for the region process. A big value of β will make the neighboring bounds more powerful and then will smooth out small details in the images, while a small value will lessen the bound, making the algorithm tend to the k-mean Maximul Likelihood Estimate (MLE).

Derin and al. [5] have used a recursive algorithm that interleaves parameter estimation and segmentation of images. They found that the performance of the algorithm was relatively independent from the value of the parameter, while the estimation problem was difficult. Other authors [1] [3] [12],[13] agree that the value of β influences the shape and the size of the regions. Pappas has used an ad hoc determination of β in [9].

To test the effect of β on the image segmentation, we applied our segmentation algorithm for varying β on a MR image in 2D. The image used comes from the dataset used in the experimental results and is a 256x256 pixels image with gray values varying from 0 to 256.

In Figure 2 we depict the segmentation of this image using a 2D version of our algorithm for five different values of β ranging from zero to 1.3. The segmentation obtained with $\beta = 0.0$ has been represented in Figure 2 on the top right corner. This model imposes no kind of spatial constraint and, applied to MR images, yields a too noisy segmentation and is, thus, unusable. In Figure 2 on the first image of the second row a value of $\beta = 0.2$ has been used. The segmentation is certainly better then the previous one, but the background and the image itself seem to be still noisy. Increasing the value of β to 0.5 in the second image of the second row of Figure 2, to 0.9 and 1.3 in the first and second image of the last row of Figure 2 respectively, the segmentation gets smoother and smoother; however, with the increment of β some regions start to merge.

Therefore, it seems quite clear that a small value of β yields to a noisy image, while a large value can smooth out important details in the image, thus an accurate way of choosing β is needed. This is particularly true when the image to be segmented is as complex as a Brain MRI, where there are zones with some tissues blending together and a large value of β could smooth out some important details.

As previously stated, β is a parameter indicating how pixels in the same clique can belong to the same cluster or to two different clusters. Then it is likely, for different images, to need different values of β because the structure of the clusters, their shape and size, and the possible neighborhood configurations vary with the image. Nevertheless, assuming a constant β for each couple of clusters is a strong assumption, especially in MR images, where some cluster neighborhoods are very unlikely, as bone and gray matter or CSF and skin [13].

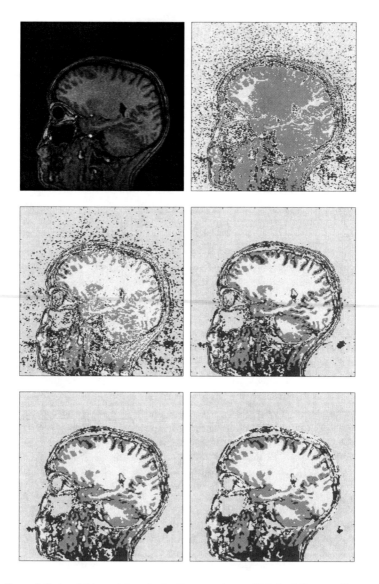

Fig. 2. From left to right and top to bottom we have: Original Image, Segmentation with $\beta = 0.0$, Segmentation with $\beta = 0.2$, Segmentation with $\beta = 0.5$, Segmentation with $\beta = 0.9$, Segmentation with $\beta = 1.3$

Therefore we need to choose different values of β for different classes configurations of pixels or voxels belonging to the same clique. The method we propose satisfies all these conditions and is fully automatic, so that the algorithm adapts the β estimates to the particular kind of image, with no need of human intervention, that can, in certain cases, bias the outcome of the segmentation.

Vandermuelen et. al. in [13] have used a potential function assigning different values of β to different possible combinations of neighboring tissues. Those values were initially determined by trial and error and have been subsequently modified by and expert, who based his choice on the appearance of the segmentation. The technique we are proposing does not require any initialization of the parameter and is completely automatic.

To introduce our estimation technique lets start with an example. Lets suppose that the image we are segmenting is composed of three different kinds of regions and lets label them A, B and C, which could be gray matter, white matter and cerebrospinal fluid. Using the co-occurence matrix the number of occurences of each class (relative frequency) and the number of co-occurrences (relative frequency) of each couple of classes in a clique can be computed.

Those relative frequencies of the occurences of each class are unbiased estimates of the expected value $E(X)$, where X is a multinomial random variable modeling the class of each voxel. The frequencies of the co-occurences can be used to estimate $E(XY)$, where X and Y represent the classes of the voxels belonging to the same clique and together with the occurence matrix can be used to estimate $E(X), X = \{A, B, C\}$, $E(XY), X, Y = \{A, B, C\}$.

Therefore the correlation between two classes can be computed using the formula:

$$cor(X, Y) = \frac{E(XY) - E(X)E(Y)}{\sqrt{(E(X^2) - E^2(X))(E(Y^2) - E^2(Y))}}. \tag{7}$$

The correlation values thus far obtained can be considered as measures of the "likelihood" of combination between different couples of classes (tissues). If this value is negative then it is unlikely for pixels or voxels of those two classes to belong to the same cliques. The other way around is true if the estimate is greater then zero. Then $-cor(X, Y)$ can be used to compute the clique potential in the Gibbs distribution

$$V_C(X) = -\sum_{i \in C} cor(X, Y_i). \tag{8}$$

In the actual computation of correlation for the Brain MR data, we have assigned the classes to the voxels based on an initial segmentation by a simple k-means algorithm. Starting from this initial configuration we scan the image voxel by voxel and we keep trace of the number of voxels belonging to a given class. Besides, for any class i and j we also count the number of couples of neighboring voxels which present the class configuration $< ij >$ according to the neighborhood system that has been adopted.

Once the number of occurrences of all the couples of tissue types are available, by simple computation they are transformed in relative frequencies, that can be considered an unbiased estimator of the probabilities of each class and of the couples of classes. Eventually formula 7 yields values of β for each couple of classes.

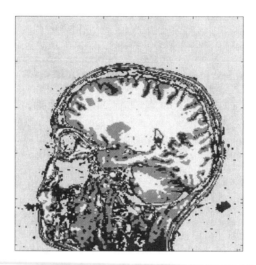

Fig. 3. Segmentation with beta computed according to the proposed method

In Figure 3 we have depicted the segmentation obtained using the proposed β-estimation method on the image of Figure 2 with five clusters.

4   Implementation and Results

The results we are about to show are the outcome of the application of the proposed technique on 3D MRI data. The results obtained with the proposed technique will be compared with the results obtained with an algorithm proposed by Pappas [9] which is also a k-mean based algorithm but works on 2D images and does not carry out any estimate of the β parameter and of the standard deviation of the Gaussian distribution. The implementation of the proposed algorithm is depicted in Figure 4.

The intensity of each region can be modeled as a Gaussian random variable as previously stated. Namely:

$$p(y_v \mid x_v = r) = \frac{1}{\sqrt{2\pi\sigma_r^2}} e^{-\frac{1}{2\sigma_r^2}[y_v - \mu_v(x_v)]^2} \tag{9}$$

where r is the class the voxel v belongs to, y_v is the intensity level of voxel v and $\mu_v(x_v)$ and σ_r are the average and the standard deviation of the class the voxel belongs to. To get a useful segmentation, good estimates of these parameters are necessary.

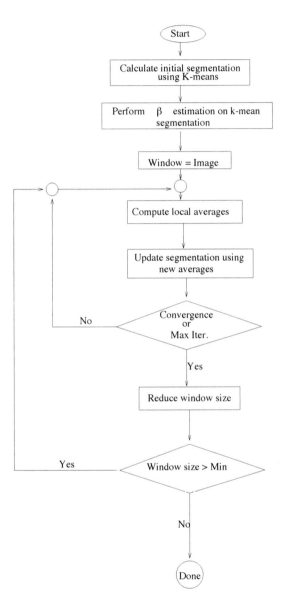

Fig. 4. Flow Chart of the segmentation algorithm

Starting from a k-mean segmentation into 4 classes, the adaptive k-mean algorithm is applied. The estimation of the local mean is achieved, as in [9] for the 2D case, using an adaptive windows which is initially set to the size of the whole 3D image and then decreased adapting to the local characteristics of the image. The implementation of the adaptive windows requires the choice of a lower bound for the size of the adaptive windows, which has been set to 8 pixels in the x and y direction and two pixels in the z direction.

The size of the rectangular windows has been gradually decreased using the formula:

$$(windowsize)_{max}/j \ \ j = 1 \ to \ (windowsize)_{max}/8.$$

The z direction windows size was held at 2 while the size in the x and y directions was reduced.

We have tried other schemes of windows size reduction but very little or no difference has been achieved in terms of the quality of the results obtained.

To obtain and estimate fo σ_r at each iteration the variance of the gray value of each region has been computed according to the formula:

$$\sigma_r^2 = \sum_v (y_v - m(x_v))^2 P(x_v = r|y_v, x_s, s \in N_v),\qquad(10)$$

thus obtaining a value of σ_r for each class. The estimate is updated each time new estimates of the class averages are available and then is used in the MAP estimation of the class process.

The dataset used for the experiments was composed of MR Images of sagittal sections of the human brain. No kind of pre-processing technique has been used on the images. Anyhow, the level of the segmentation could be improved using some artifices, like applying a specific pulse sequence which should enhances the separation between cerebrospinal fluid, gray matter and white matter [10].

To build the 3D volume, 30 slices with the spatial resolution of 256x256 and slice thickness of 1.25 mm have been used. Figure 5 depicts the results of applying our 3D segmentation algorithm to the brain MRI. The figure is organized in three columns. The first column contains arbitrarily picked slices from the original 3D MR data. The third column consists of corresponding slices from the 3D segmentation with the proposed technique and the third colum consists of the corresponding slices from the segmentation obtaned applying Pappas's algorithm on each image with constant $\beta = 0.5$ and $\sigma = 5$.

The segmentation obtained using the proposed technique is smoother than the one obtaned using Pappas' algorithm. Our technique manages to get rid of most of the spots that are located around the skull of the images and near the mouth and the neck.

Particularly intersting is the second row in Figures 5 that depicts the same image previously used in Figure 3 to show the importance of the estimation of β. The new segmentation obtained using the estimation of β together with the

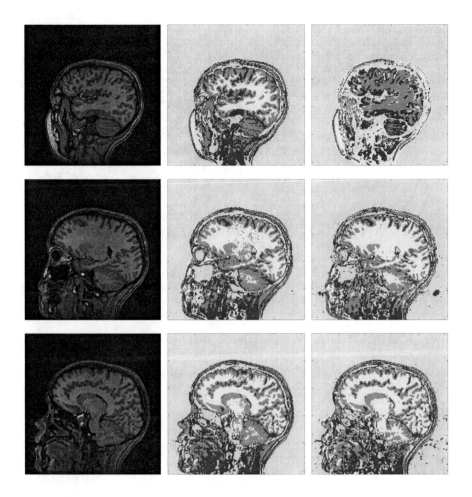

Fig. 5. Results of 3D segmentation: first column:Slices of original data, second column:Corresponding slices from the 3D segmented image, third column:Corresponding slices segmented applying Pappas' algorithm

estimation of μ and σ yields a better yet segmentation than the one obtaned only using estimates for β and μ (Figure 3) as can be more clearly seen in Figure 6, stressing once again the importance of the estimation of parameter in these type of algorithms. Besides, from formula 5 it is easily understendable that σ and β have analogous effect on the MAP estimation of the segmentation, therefore the influence of a good estimate of β can be cancelled by a bad choice for σ made from the expert.

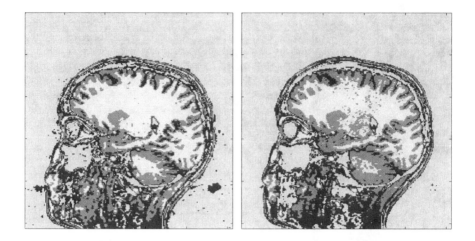

Fig. 6. On the left segmentation obtained using the proposed method with β estimation and constant σ. On the right segmentation obtained using the proposed method with β and σ estimation.

In our experiments, we did not have the input of an expert neurologist in encoding the anatomical knowledge into the prior model. Instead, we relied on the information contained in medical imaging literature.

5   Conclusions

The aim of this paper was to present a 3D volume segmentation technique with application to MR brain scans. The principal features of our algorithm are: an adaptive k-means voxel clustering which manages to consider both general and local characteristics of the 3D image considered, a new fully automatic way of determining the Gibbsian parameter β and the parameters of the Gaussian process which can adapt the estimation to the particular kind of image considered and that does not need any kind of *a priori* initialization.

We have depicted with an example the importance of a good estimation of the parameter of the Gibbs distribution, showing that an ad-hoc determination of β can result in a too noisy segmentation or can smooth out important details of the image.

We have compared the performance of the proposed algorithm to the algorithm proposed by Pappas which is also based on the k-means clustering algorithm but does not perform any estimation for σ and β. Our techinque yields visually better results. However the verification of our segmentation results with the assistance of a neuroanatomy expert is a task that needs to be addressed. Another problem that needs to be addressed regards a technique for the determination of the number of regions that the images should be segmented into.

We are also developing an algorithm which includes all the features of the one depicted in this paper and yet does not need the a-priori determination of the number of clusters and it will be the subject of another paper.

Acknowledgments. The Authors would like to express their gratitude to the Giustino Fortunato University for supporting this research.

References

1. Alfò, M., Nieddu, L., Vicari, D.: A finite mixture model for image segmentation. Statistics and Computing 18(2), 137–150 (2008)
2. Besag, J.: On statistical analysis of dirty pictures. Journal of Royal Statistical Society B 48(3), 259–302 (1986)
3. Celeux, G., Forbes, F., Peyrard, N.: EM procedures using mean field-like approximations for markov model-based image segmentation. Pattern Recognition 36(1), 131–144 (2003)
4. Clark, M.C., Hall, L.O., Golgof, D.B., Clark, L.P., Velthuizen, R.P., Silbiger, M.S.: MRI segmentation using fuzzy clustering techniques. IEEE Engineering in Medicine and Biology 13(5), 730–742 (1994)
5. Derin, H., Elliott, H.: Modelling and segmentation of noisy and textured images using Gibbs random field. IEEE Transactions on Pattern Analysis and Machine Intelligence PAMI-9(1), 39–55 (1987)
6. Geman, S., Geman, D.: Stochastic relaxation, Gibbs distributions, and the bayesian restoration of images. IEEE Transactions on Pattern Analysis and Machine Intelligence PAMI-6(6), 721–741 (1984)
7. Vezina, G., Derin, H., Kelly, P.A., Labitt, S.G.: Modelling and segmentation of speckled images using complex data. IEEE Transactions on Geoscience and Remote Sensing 28(1), 76–87 (1990)
8. Hummel, R.A., Zucker, S.W.: On the foundation of relaxation labelling process. IEEE Transactions on Pattern Analysis and Machine Intelligence 5(3), 267–287 (1983)
9. Pappas, T.N.: An adaptive clustering algorithm for image segmentation. IEEE Transactions on Signal Processing 40(4), 901–914 (1992)
10. Parvin, B., Johnston, W., Roselli, D.: Pinta: A system for visualizing the anatomical structures of the brain from mr imaging. In: Proceedings of the IEEE Computer Society Conference on Computer Vision and Pattern Recognition, July 15-17, pp. 615–616. IEEE Computer Society Press (1993)
11. Kindermann, R., Snell, J.L.: Markov Random Fields and Their Applications, vol. 1. American Mathematical Society, Providence (1999)
12. Rignot, E., Chellappa, R.: Segmentation of polarimetric synthetic aperture radar data. IEEE Transactions on Image Processing 1(3), 281–300 (1992)
13. Vandermeulen, D., Verbeeck, R., Berben, L., Suetens, P., Marchal, C.: Continous Voxel Classification by Stochastic Relaxation: Theory and Application to Mr Imaging and Mr Angiography. In: Barrett, H.H., Gmitro, A.F. (eds.) IPMI 1993. LNCS, vol. 687, pp. 487–506. Springer, Heidelberg (1993)

A Refined Differential Evolution Algorithm for Improving the Performance of Optimization Process

Ahmad Razlan Yusoff[1] and Nafrizuan Mat Yayha[2]

[1] Faculty of Mechancial Engineering
[2] Faculty of Manufacturing Engineering
Universiti Malaysia Pahang, 23300 Pekan, Pahang, Malaysia
razlan@ump.edu.my

Abstract. Various Artificial Intelligent (AI) algorithms can be applied in solving optimization problems. Among the latest Evaluation Algorithm (EA) have been developed is Differential Evolution (DE). DE is developed based on an improved Genetic Algorithm and come with different strategies for faster optimization. However, the population trapped in local optimality and premature convergence to cause in DE algorithm have cause poor performance during optimization process. To overcome the drawbacks, mixed population update and bounce back strategy were introduced to modify and improve current DE algorithm. A Himmelblau function and real case from engineering problem were used to show the performance improvements of refined DE in optimization process.

Keywords: Differential Evolution, missed population, bounce back, Himmelblau function.

1 Introduction

Various Evaluation Algorithm strategies have been developed, such as Genetic Algorithm, Evolutionary Programming and Evolution Strategy. Differential Evolution was introduced by Storn and Price in 1996 [1]. Differential Evolution based on stochastic or non-deterministic approaches for solving polynomial fitting problems. Differential Evolution is developed from an improved Genetic Algorithm with different strategies for faster optimisation. This is similar to other Evaluation Algorithm in which mutation plays the key role with real valued parameters to search for the global optimum. A basic idea in Differential Evolution is that of adapting the search during the evolution process. Differential Evolution advantages are simple structure, ease of use, speed and robustness. In addition, Differential Evolution has been successfully applied in various optimisation applications [2] such as heat exchangers, robotic manipulator design, neural network training, turbo machinery design, production and scheduling, electric motor design, engine and wheel mount identification, diesel engine combustion and machining optimization.

In optimization algorithm, the population improvement processes, including mutation, crossover, objective function assessment and selection. This takes several generations before the global optimal solution is achieved. During the population

A. Abd Manaf et al. (Eds.): ICIEIS 2011, Part II, CCIS 252, pp. 184–194, 2011.
© Springer-Verlag Berlin Heidelberg 2011

process, it is desirable to produce a robust feature and a high convergence rate to create a population with high probability. To achieve trade-off between convergence and robustness, a few attempts have been made by researchers by introducing modified DE, hybrid DE and combined with Particle Swarm Optimization and Ant Colony Optimization.

In modified DE, instead of one array on population update, Babu and Angira [4] applied two population updates during the mutation and crossover process and the original population to ensure each population had equal opportunity. To relocate the violated bound vector to the interior bound, a penalty function was used for avoiding local optimal. A different approach was used by Lee *et al.* [5] to reduce search space, by applying the modified constraint and the local search approach to improve the population. Meanwhile Nearchou and Omirou [6] and Zhang and Xu [7] used random keys encoding to handle discrete variables to produce high performance of the modified DE. By adjusting of minimum space distance, a population's being located in the same area was prevented, as proposed by Hendershot [8]. To accelerate the mutation process and exploration region, Kaelo and Ali [9] recommended a random uniform mutation factor and localisation around best vectors, respectively.

Migration and acceleration strategies were mainly added to the original DE to perform Hybrid DE by Chiou and Wang [10] and Pedchote and Purdy [11]. Migration strategy is used to diversify a population that failed in certain tolerance besides escaping from local optimal and preventing premature convergence. Acceleration reacts to generate fast convergence to improve fitness with population diversity. However, fast convergence leads to obtain a local optimal and a large population region that causes large computational time.

To overcome convergence and robustness, Particle Swarm Optimization was applied by Hendtlass [12] as a main rule for each individual, while DE reacts to search for a better individual. Meanwhile, Ant Colony Optimisation was applied in combination with DE to accelerate search in the mutation process. Besides that, Tasoulis *et al.* [13] and Chiou *et al.* [14] applied parallel processing to make computational time faster without compromising its performance. In applying acceleration and migration region in hybrid DE [13], a local optimal and large population region obtained cause a large computational time. When a violated vectors are modified to inside bound [14], this can solve a local optimal problem and a new population has a wide diversity of searching of the global optimal.

For this paper, DE algorithm really needs to be changed and modified based on poor performance in Himmelblau function. To overcome the problems, mixed population update and bounce back strategy are applied to modify and improve the current DE algorithm.

2   Theory of Differential Evolution

Differential Evolution can solve objective functions that are non-differentiable, non-linear, noisy, flat and multi-dimension, with multi-local minima. Such functions are difficult to solve analytically. This algorithm begins by using initial samples at multiple random chosen initial points. With simple algorithms, Differential Evolution can search for the optimal condition very fast with minimal control parameters such as mutation, crossover, selection and population. The concept is evolved from Genetic Algorithm with a layer population and a special evolutionary strategy of self-adaptive mutation. Instead of a binary encoded population as for a Genetic Algorithm, Differential Evolution deals with a real coded population with its own processes of mutation and crossover. The mutation process is created from three randomly selected population members, using the vector difference between individuals [3]. Although it uses the same evaluation as other Evaluation Algorithm during the crossover process, Differential Evolution applied crossover between any individual population member. Moreover, the population has an equal opportunity to survive in the next generation based on its fitness value.

A strategy that works successfully for a specific problem may not work well when applied to a different problem [2, 15]. However, strategy 7 (DE/rand/1/bin) is the most successful and widely used in many applications [1, 5, 16, 17]. In the current research, the DE source code written by Markus Buehren and available at Matlab Central [18] was used. The code is based on the DE algorithm of Storn and Price [1].

The algorithm of DE is given as follows:

1. Choose strategy (strategy 7) (For other strategy please refer to [1])
2. Initialise the independent parameters' number of dimension, number of population (NP), crossover factor (CR), scaling factor (SF) and maximum generation (NG).
3. Initialise randomly all the dimension with the given upper and lower bound ($x_{j,l}$ and $x_{j,u}$).
4. Evaluate each vector for its function value.
5. Determine the vector with the optimum function value.
6. For each $x_{i,g}$, select three vectors randomly from the current population from other than $x_{i,g}$ to perform mutation.
7. Create $u_{i,g}$ for each $x_{i,g}$ by the crossover with its noisy vector.
8. After the mutation and crossover, the vectors are checked to ensure they are in the bound range. This process will terminate if the vectors are out of bounds.
9. Make selection for each $x_{i,g}$ by comparing its function evaluation with $u_{i,g}$ produced from crossover process. Selected and random $x_{i,g}$ from current population compete with $u_{i,g}$ based on evaluation value. For the next generation, select optimal function value for next generation $x_{i,g+1}$.
10. Repeat 4-9 if termination criteria not met.
11. Print results.

The detailed flow process of DE is presented in Figure 1. For current case, DE setting parameters consist of NP = 10 times number of dimension, CR = 0.9, SF = 0.9 and NG = 70.

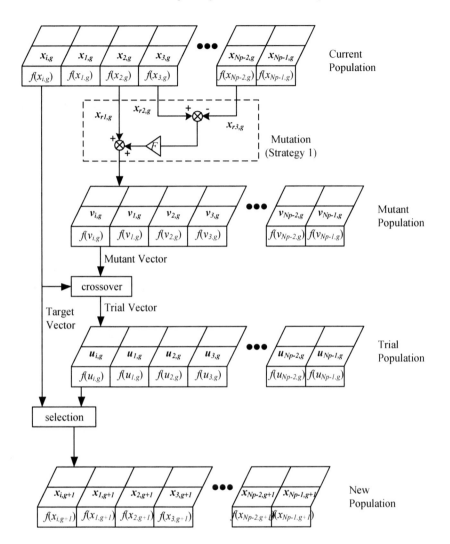

Fig. 1. Process of generating one population to next

3   Method for Refined DE Algorithm

The refined DE consists of mixed population and bounce back boundary are now presented.

3.1   Mixed Population

The initialisation process consists of uniform distribution, randomisation range between (0,1), Gaussian distribution with mean and standard deviation with 0.5 and random without restrictions [2]. Although randomised initialisation was used, the population for every generation is not guaranteed to be updated or changed as shown by previous result (chatter minimisation of variable helix and variable pitch tools' population). As a result, it is suggested that the current population be interrupted by a small amount of random noise population to improve DE process for every generation by encouraging more search space to search for the global optimal and exploring to accelerate the convergence rate. The other population is the best population from the previous generation. This mixed population has a feature of diversity and guarantees to produce a high probability of the global optimal from the introduction of some noise population to the current population as a mixed population.

In every new generation, the next population will consist of 75 percent of the best current population and 25 percent from a randomised population. This randomised population reacts as noise to improve the next population. The pseudo algorithm for the current approach is shown in Figure 2. In every generation, a 25 percent population with additional noise will improve DE performance to overcome premature problem of the population during the optimisation process.

```
D = size (pop,2);
For n = memIndex;
Pop(n,:)  =  0.75  *  baseMem  +  0.25  *rand  (1,D)  *
(XVmax-XVmin);
```

Fig. 2. Introduction of random noise of population to next generation

3.2 Bounce Back Boundary

In constraint optimisation, several methods [2] have been proposed to solve the problem, such as penalty function, random initialisation, bounce back method and rejection of the vectors . Previously, the rejection of the vector was applied; however, the point outside bounds may have a better solution but unfortunately not in the feasible region. A bounce back method function can be used to modify an out of bounds trial parameter with one located on the boundary. Besides escaping from the local optimal, especially at the boundary, this replaces out of bounds vectors to have a highly diverse population.

Figure 3 illustrates the bounce back strategy in a two-dimensional search space. When the population moves outside the bounds, this strategy allows the generation of vectors close to bounds. The pseudocode of the strategy is shown in Figure 4. The violated vector at the upper and lower boundaries is relocated with a trial vector to the each of them, respectively.

The Himmelblau function (Equation (1)) is used as minimisation function to search two variables with wide constraints [7,11].

$$f(x) = \left(x^2_1 + x_2 - 11\right)^2 + \left(x_1 + x^2_2 - 7\right)^2 \quad x_{1,2} \in [-6,6] \tag{1}$$

Next, to demonstrate the DE procedures, Himmelblau function was used with simplicity to give an understanding of how the refined DE solves the optimization problem.

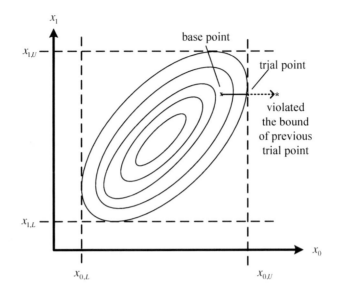

Fig. 3. Bounce back strategy of trial vector to replace out of bounds trial from base vector and violated bound trial point

```
For k = 1 : I_NP % population filled with best member of
last generation
For j =1:I_D
If (u(j,i) < XVmin) % if parameter exceeds lower bound
u(j,i) = Xvmin;
End
If (u(j,i) > XVmax) % if parameter exceeds upper bound
u(j,i) = XVmax;
End
End
```

Fig. 4. Pseudocode for bounce back strategy

4   Results and Discussion

For example, the Himmelblau function (Figure 5a) is used to describe in detail how DE procedure works to optimise the function. In order to make a simple and easy illustration, the constraint of Himmeblau function is [-6,6], as shown in the contour plot of the function in Figure 5b, and DE population is set as 4 and produces only for 10 generations. The other mutation factors and crossover values are the same.

An initialisation process which starts with four populations generated is represented in Figure 5c. Then, four sets of mutated vectors $x_{r1,g}$, $x_{r2,g}$, $x_{r3,g}$ and $x_{r4,g}$ are randomly selected from the population in initialisation. The mutated vectors are introduced and, for example in Figure 5d, $x_{r1,g}$, $x_{r2,g}$ and $x_{r3,g}$ are shown by '×', '×' and 'o', respectively. In this case, $x_{r1,g}$ and $x_{r3,g}$ are located at the same vector and $v_{i,g}$ '*' is out of boundary. Consequently, in the crossover process of Figure 5e, the crossover selects '×' as $u_{i,g}$ from randomised selection of the population as compared to $v_{i,g}$, 'o' to produce a trial population '*' from combination of two $u_{i,g}$ ('×' and 'o'). After that, a $u_{i,g}$ is needed to compete with other randomised vectors to be selected as a new population in the selection process (Figure 5f).

This new vector is introduced into the current generation and each four populations of generation are evaluated, as shown in Figure 5g. The processes is as illustrated before (mutation, recombination and selection), are continued until the criteria meet either maximum population or the fitness value. Figures 5h, 5i and 5j show generations 1, 5 and 10, respectively. Due to the small number of population size and number of generations used, the final value is not achieved, as the purpose of the current example is only to illustrate how DE works.

As in the above example, a Himmelblau function was used to demonstrate how a modified DE improves in optimising the function. For simplicity, the constraint, DE population, number of generation, mutation factor, crossover and strategy are set as in the previous example. The mechanism of bounce back and randomised noise population approaches are now described for a Himmelblau function.

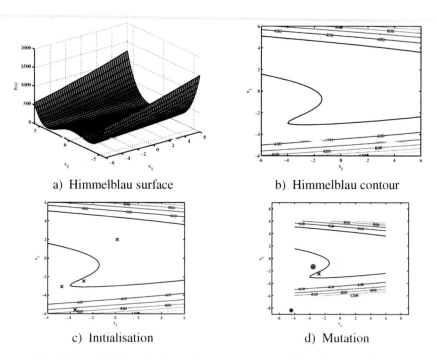

a) Himmelblau surface   b) Himmelblau contour

c) Initialisation   d) Mutation

Fig. 5. Typical Differential Evolution processes using Himmelblau function

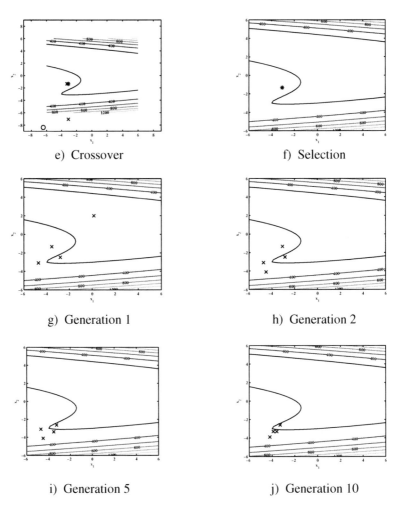

e) Crossover

f) Selection

g) Generation 1

h) Generation 2

i) Generation 5

j) Generation 10

Fig. 5. (*Continued*)

An initialisation process of generating four populations was started similarly to Figure 5c. In the mutation process of Figure 6a, the three mutated vectors are introduced, such as $x_{r1.g}$, $x_{r2.g}$ and $x_{r3.g}$ indicated by '×', '×' and 'o', respectively . Due to '*''s having violated the boundary, the bounce back strategy takes action to propose '+' as a substitute with the violated vector. In previous result, this violated vector was previously terminated. A bounce back reacted to the violated boundary vector during the crossover process to substitute '•' with '+' (Figure 6b). In the previous example, the violated boundary vectors had also been terminated. Again, a bounce back boundary approach made an action to replace the violated vector with the nearest boundary vector. These mutation and crossover processes strongly represented how a bounce back improved the DE algorithm for the Himmelblau example. Figures 6b and 6c show the selection and generation process with substitution vectors during mutation and crossover processes.

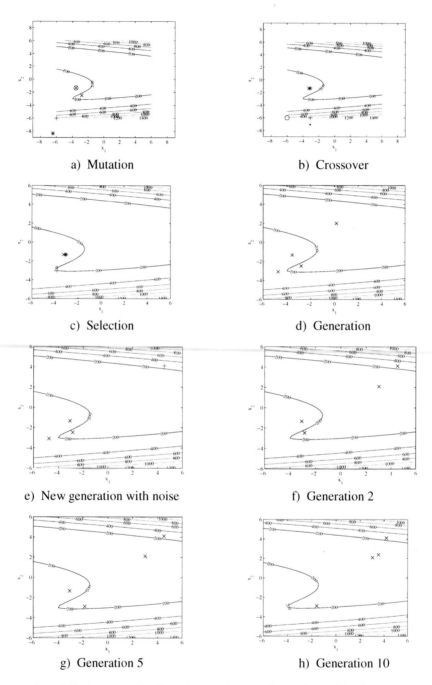

a) Mutation

b) Crossover

c) Selection

d) Generation

e) New generation with noise

f) Generation 2

g) Generation 5

h) Generation 10

Fig. 6. Typical example of how improved DE works on Himmelblau function

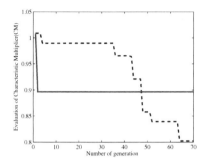

Fig. 7. Performance of DE and refined DE on optimising three-flute variable helix and variable pitch. (—) DE and (---) refined DE

The mechanism of a random noise population approach is now presented. Initially, a generation of four vectors is produced, as shown in Figure 6d. Using a random noise, '+' and 75 percent best population are introduced to update generation (Figure 6e). The 25 percent noise of the new vector is introduced into the current generation to improve optimisation as discussed before. Previously, the generation is taken as proposed by the algorithm without any updating of a new random vector and best vector in the population. Figures 6f, g and h show generations 2, 5 and 10, respectively. Despite a small population size and number of generations, the result of the current population is the 10th generation towards minimum coordinates at 3, 2 location (minimum value vectors). The final value is better than the previous result. This example is only needed to show how bounce back and randomised noise population approaches improved the Himmelblau function when compared to previous example.

In addition to Himmelbalu function example, this refined DE algorithm is also applied to the chatter minimisation problem [12]. DE settings and machining parameters can be referred to ref. [12]. During the optimisation shown (Figure 7), the generation of original DE algorithms cannot be trapped in local optimality and premature convergence at the second iteration. However, the refined DE is significantly better than the original where generation improved to converge at 0.8 evaluation function.

5   Conclusion

The practical implementation of refined DE improves the optimization of Himmeblau function in this paper. It has been indicated that for poor performance and local optimal problem in Himmeblau function, the mixed population and bounce back boundary are introduced to prevent the optimization simulation. Furthermore, current refined DE can also use for optimizing the variable helix tool geometry in suppressing chatter vibrations.

Acknowledgments. Author extend their sincere thanks to the support of the Dr Neil David Sims at Department of Mechanical Engineering, the University of Sheffield.

References

1. Storn, R., Price, K.: Differential evolution – a simple and efficient heuristic for global optimization over continuous spaces. J. Glo. Opt. 11(4), 341–359 (1997)
2. Price, K.V., Storn, R.M., Lampinen, J.A.: Differential evolution a practical approach to global optimization. Springer, Heidelberg (2005)
3. Kurdi, M.H., Schmitz, T.L., Haftka, R.T., Mann, B.P.: Simultaneous optimization of material removal rate and part accuracy in high speed milling. In: ASME International Mechanical Engineering Congress and Exposition (IMECE), Anaheim (2004)
4. Babu, B.V., Angira, R.: Modified differential evolution (mde) for optimization of nonlinear chemical processes. Comp. & Chem. Eng. 30(6-7), 989–1002 (2006)
5. Krishna, A.: Selection of optimal conditions in the surface grinding process using a differential evolution approach. Proceedings of the Institution of Mechanical Engineers, Part B: J. Eng. Man. 221(7), 1185–1192 (2007)
6. Nearchou, A.: Balancing large assembly lines by a new heuristic based on differential evolution method. Int. J. Adv. Man. Tech. 34(9), 1016–1029 (2007)
7. Zhang, J.Z., Xu, J.: A new differential evolution for discontinuous optimization problems. In: Third International Conference on Natural Computation, ICNC 2007 (2007), 0-7695-2875-9/07
8. Hendershot, Z.V.: A differential evolution algorithm for automatically discovering multiple global optima in multidimensional, discontinuous spaces. In: Proc. of the Fifteenth Midwest Artificial Intelligence and Cognitive Science Conference (MAICS 2004), Illinois (2004)
9. Kaelo, P., Ali, M.M.: A numerical study of some modified differential evolution algorithms. Euro. J. Ope. Res. 169(3), 1176–1184 (2006)
10. Chiou, J.-P., Wang, F.-S.: Hybrid method of evolutionary algorithms for static and dynamic optimization problems with application to a fed-batch fermentation process. Com. & Chem. Eng. 23(9), 1277–1291 (1999)
11. Pedchote, C., Purdy, D.: Parameter estimation of a single wheel station using hybrid differential evolution. Proc. Inst. Mech. Eng. Part D: Journal of Auto. Eng. 217(6), 431–447 (2003)
12. Hendtlass, T.: A combined swarm differential evolution algorithm for optimization problems. Eng. Int. Sys., 11–18 (2001)
13. Tasoulis, D.K., Pavlidis, N.G., Plagianakos, V.P., Vrahatis, M.N.: Parallel differential evolution. In: Int. Symposium Parallel Computing in Electrical Engineering (PAR ELEC 2006), pp. 319–329 (2006)
14. Chiou, J.-P., Chang, C.-F., Su, C.-T.: Ant direction hybrid differential evolution for solving large capacitor placement problems. IEEE Transactions on Power Systems 19(4), 1794–1800 (2004)
15. Feoktistov, V.: Differential evolution: In search of solutions. Springer, New York (2006)
16. Saikumar, S., Shunmugan, M.S.: Parameter selection based on surface finish in high speed finish in high speed end milling using differential evolution. Mat. and Man. Pro. 21(4), 341–347 (2008)
17. Yusoff, A.R., Sims, N.D.: Optimisation of variable helix for regerative chatter mitigation. Int. J. Mac. Tools Manu. 51(2), 133–141 (2011)
18. Markus, B.: Differential evolution, http://www.mathworks.com
19. Yusoff, A.R., Sims, N.D.: Optimisation of variable helix end milling tools by self-excited minimisation. J. Physics: Conf. Ser. 181, 012026 (2009)

An Approach to PLC-Based Fuzzy Expert System in PID Control

Jiri Kocian, Jiri Koziorek, and Miroslav Pokorny

Department of Measurement and Control,
VSB-Technical University of Ostrava,
17. Listopadu 15, Ostrava,
Czech Republic
{jiri.kocian,jiri.koziorek,miroslav.pokorny}@vsb.cz

Abstract. Fuzzy control systems have been successfully applied in many cases to which conventional control algorithms are difficult and even impossible to be applied. Fuzzy models have received significant attention from various fields of interest. Especially so called the Takagi-Sugeno-type fuzzy model which superbly describes a nonlinear system. In this paper we present implementation of universal function block of fuzzy expert system and PID regulator for PLC Simatic S7 300/400. Control system with implemented fuzzy expert system and PID regulator and visualization is designed.

Keywords: Fuzzy, Expert System, Regulator, PLC, Visualization, Control System.

1 Introduction

The original idea of fuzzy is from Mamdani. The idea is based on the principle of using language description in the control applications. The aim of this work is design and implementation of universal function block of fuzzy expert system for PLC Simatic S7 300/400.

Many papers deal with fuzzy expert systems or fuzzy supervisors that provide adaptation of standard PID regulator. Fuzzy supervisors generally monitor step responses of closed loop and according measured variables PID regulator constants are recalculated. This approach is in [2], [3]. [4], [5]. Practical case studies of fuzzy gain scheduling as supervisory control function is in [6], [7], [8], [9]. Online stochastic analysis approach of closed loop and case study of adaptive bioreactor control is given in [1].

Generally, there are also a lot of implementations of fuzzy control to the PLC. [11]

Nearly all PLC producers offer fuzzy control functions in their portfolio. But a lot of these solutions do not cover all possibilities that may occur when using, e.g. manual control mode, state indication of the control etc. Therefore, if you need to apply these functions in application programs you have to program it yourself.

The goal of this work is to design own universal fuzzy expert system function block which covers all necessary industrial functions and possibilities mentioned above.

A. Abd Manaf et al. (Eds.): ICIEIS 2011, Part II, CCIS 252, pp. 195–205, 2011.

Many controlled systems are nonlinear systems. Successful control of system with nonlinear characteristic is difficult. Linearization around working point has to be made. If the nonlinear system has to be operated in several different working points or regulated system has significantly nonlinear behavior then constant values of PID regulator parameters cannot lead to good control quality in required operating range.

A method of switching sets of parameter values is one of possible solutions to use in these situations. Several approaches can be used to switch values sets of the PID regulator depending on the working point.

The contribution shows an example of a fuzzy expert system for the adaptation of PID regulator based on the selected working point. The suggested sets of PID regulator parameters are placed into a function block of an expert system. Sets of PID regulator parameters are then sent to PID regulator depending on current working point of the controlled system. This allows a continuous adjustment of PID regulator constants when process value is moving between two working points.

Chapter 2 contains a description of the designed control system with fuzzy expert system in PID control and with the visualization made in Intouch.

Description of implementation details of fuzzy expert system function block and PID regulator function block is in chapter 3.

2   Control System with Fuzzy Expert System

2.1   Control System

Block diagram of the control system is shown on Fig. 1. The control system consists of programmable controller CPU 315-2 DP which is connected to the communication processor CP 343-1 Advanced. Communication processor communicates with the visualization created in InTouch through Ethernet communication interface.

The control loop scheme of the fuzzy expert system with the PID regulator is shown on Fig. 2. Controlled system transfer function is simulated by mathematical blocks of standard library in Step 7 software. Process value is except PID regulator also input for the fuzzy expert system function block.

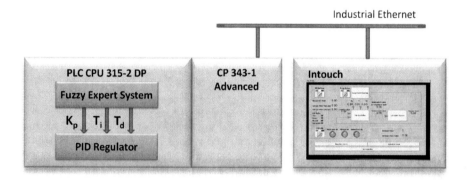

Fig. 1. The block scheme of the control system with the fuzzy expert system

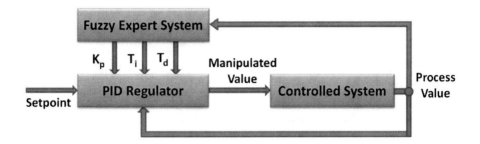

Fig. 2. The principal scheme of the fuzzy expert system with PID regulator

2.2 Configuration of Fuzzy Expert System and PID Regulator

Stable static system with the transfer function (1) is chosen for simulated controlled system.

$$G(s) = \frac{K_S}{(T_1 \cdot s + 1) \cdot (T_2 \cdot s + 1)} = \frac{K_S}{(16 \cdot s + 1) \cdot (2 \cdot s + 1)} \tag{1}$$

Transfer function with changing static gain K_S is chosen to achieve the desired characteristics of the controlled system suitable for testing the fuzzy expert system. The static gain depends on the process variable as is shown in Tab. 1.

Table 1. Controlled system parameters

Process Value	Controlled system parameters		
	K_S	T_1	T_2
<0; 30>	2,0	16,0	2,0
<30; 50>	1,0	16,0	2,0
<50; 70>	0,75	16,0	2,0
<70; 100>	0,5	16,0	2,0

Operation points of regulation are set according Tab. 1: 20.0, 40.0, 60.0 and 80.0.

Coordinates of fuzzy sets and corresponding PID regulator constants dedicated from Tab. 1 are shown in Tab. 2. Coordinates of fuzzy sets are also on Fig. 3. PID regulator constants are calculated according Ziegler-Nichols tuning rules from step response for every value of K_S in transfer function (1).

Implemented PID regulators have purely parallel form with filtration of derivation part (2). Details of implemented PID regulator function block are in Chapter 3.

$$G_R(s) = K_P + \frac{1}{T_I \cdot s} + \frac{T_D \cdot s}{\frac{T_D \cdot s}{\alpha} + 1} \tag{2}$$

Table 2. Fuzzy sets and PID regulator constants

	Fuzzy sets				PID regulator constants		
	1.	2.	3.	4.	K_P	T_I	T_D
Value 1	0,0	0,0	20,0	40,0	8,9274	0,2730	5,2219
Value 2	20,0	40,0	40,0	60,0	17,2548	0,1412	10,0929
Value 3	40,0	60,0	60,0	80,0	22,8065	0,1069	13,3402
Value 4	60,0	80,0	100,0	100,0	33,9097	0,0719	19,8348

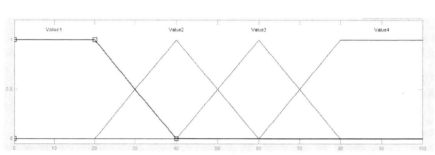

Fig. 3. Coordinates of fuzzy sets according working points

2.3 Visualization

Visualization system is created in InTouch. The visualization application consists of several logically arranged windows. The main window of visualization (Fig. 4) is the central window and displays key information. The main part of the window is control

Fig. 4. Main window

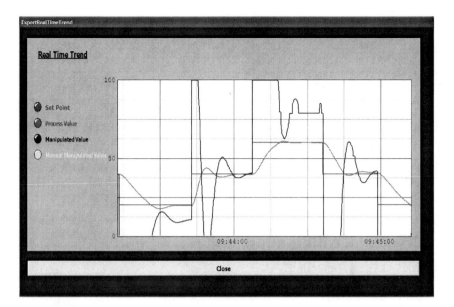

Fig. 5. Real time trend window

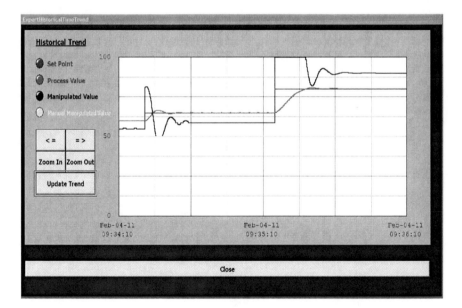

Fig. 6. Historical trend window

loop with control loop values: Set Point, Manipulated Value, Manipulated Value in Test/Direct Mode, Process Value and PID regulator constants set by fuzzy expert system to PID regulator: K_P, T_I and T_D.

Set Point switch switches automatically generated and manual Set Point. There is also a fuzzy expert system switch between manual and automatic mode.

In the middle part of the window there is a switch for initialization procedure of fuzzy expert system. Number of dominant operation point and its value (degree of membership) are displayed in the right panel. From the main window, you can get to the window with real time trend or to the window with historical trend. In addition there are also other windows: window for user's access, window for fuzzy expert system settings, window for simulated control system settings and window with information about the application. Fig. 5 (real time trend window) and Fig. 6 (historical trend window) show sample simulation results of regulation over different working points in regulation range.

3 Implementation Details of the Fuzzy Expert System and PID Regulator

3.1 Fuzzy Expert Function Block

The interface of the implemented function block is shown on Fig. 7.

The implemented fuzzy expert system processes Process Value in its fuzzy algorithm. Process Value can cover the operating range of up to eight fuzzy sets representing up to eight working points. Two fuzzy sets representing two working points are minimum number of fuzzy sets. Fuzzy sets names have general meaning: Value1, Value2, Value3, Value4, Value5, Value6, Value7 and Value8. Each fuzzy set is determined by four coordinates and can be form as trapezoid fuzzy set or triangular fuzzy set.

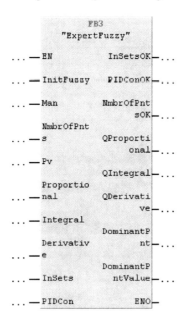

Fig. 7. Implemented function block of fuzzy expert system

PID constants are calculated (3) - (5) by Takagi-Sugeno defuzzification method.

$$K_{P,Q} = \frac{\sum\limits_{i=1}^{r} \alpha_i \cdot K_{P,i}}{\sum\limits_{i=1}^{r} \alpha_i} \tag{3}$$

$$T_{I,Q} = \frac{\sum\limits_{i=1}^{r} \alpha_i \cdot T_{I,i}}{\sum\limits_{i=1}^{r} \alpha_i} \tag{4}$$

$$T_{D,Q} = \frac{\sum\limits_{i=1}^{r} \alpha_i \cdot T_{D,i}}{\sum\limits_{i=1}^{r} \alpha_i} \tag{5}$$

$K_{P,i}$ - Proportional constant of the PID regulator for i fuzzy set

$T_{I,i}$ - Integral constant of the PID regulator for i fuzzy set

$T_{D,i}$ - Derivative constant of the PID regulator for i fuzzy set

$K_{P,Q}$ - calculated value of the proportional constant of the PID regulator

$T_{I,Q}$ - calculated value of the integral constant of the PID regulator

$T_{D,Q}$ - calculated value of the derivative constant of the PID regulator

α_i - Degree of membership of the process value for i fuzzy set

r - Number of fuzzy sets (working points)

Fuzzy controller function block uses auxiliary function "Fuzzification". This function was implemented for degrees of membership evaluation of the Process Value in the case of known sets coordinates.

Function "Fuzzification" is called by internal code of function block. When using fuzzy controller function block, function "Fuzzification" has to be copied to the project.

Coordinates of the fuzzy sets and sets of the PID regulator parameters are inputs of the fuzzy expert system. Fuzzy expert system includes an initialization procedure (input *InitFuzzy*) that will get the coordinates of fuzzy sets and sets of the PID regulator parameters from input structures into static structures of the function block of the fuzzy expert system. Coordinates of fuzzy sets and sets of the PID regulator parameters are also checked during the initialization procedure because wrong coordinates (wrong order of fuzzy sets coordinates etc.) of fuzzy sets can have a fatal impact to manipulated value calculation. If any errors are detected during initialization procedure these errors are then indicated at the output of the function block – outputs *InSetsOK*, *PIDConOK*, *NmbrOfPntsOK* (and shown on visualization).

The input value is fuzzificated by the function "Fuzzification" – degrees of membership of Process Value are calculated depending on coordinates of fuzzy sets.

Furthermore, on the basis of (3) to (5) PID constant calculated and transmitted to the PID regulator function block.

So-called manual control mode is also implemented to expert fuzzy (input *Man*). Fuzzy expert system can be switched to manual control mode and PID regulator parameters from the function block input are directly copied to the output (to the PID regulator).

3.2 PID Regulator

PID algorithm of designed PID regulator operates as a position algorithm. Proportional, integral and derivative actions are connected in parallel form and can be activated or deactivated individually by setting zero to K_P and/or T_I and/or T_D constants. This allows P, PI, PD, and PID regulator to be configured. Pure I and D regulators are also possible but not recommended.

Implemented PID regulators have purely parallel form with filtration of derivation part (2). Although transfer function (2) is not so often implemented in commercial PLC it brings some advantages. [13]

To suppress a small constant oscillation due to the manipulated value quantization (for example due to a limited resolution of the manipulated value by the actuator valve) a dead band is applied to the error signal of the controller. Transfer function of PID regulator is in a component recursion form with filtration of derivate action value by a discrete analogy of continuous low pass filter. The PID regulator implements the control law with two degrees of freedom and anti-wind up.

It is possible to switch over four modes: an automatic, a semiautomatic, a direct and a test mode.

Priorities of modes (1 - the highest priority, 4 - the lowest priority):

1. Test mode

2. Direct mode

3. Semiautomatic mode

4. Automatic mode

The set point (chosen by *RqAuto* from *HmiCmd* UDT) is taken from the function block input *Sp* for calculation of the manipulated value in the automatic mode. The set point *Sp* is established for the set point from the table or list of set points from optimization procedures or from visualisation input of technology in the automatic mode of the control. [10]

In the semiautomatic mode the set point (chosen by *RqMan* from *HmiCmd* UDT) is taken from *HmiSp.ManSp* for automatic manipulated value computation. The set point *HmiSp.ManSp* is established for the set point entered by operator from visualization. [10]

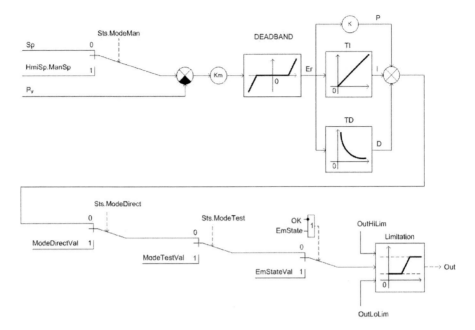

Fig. 8. The simplified function block scheme of the implemented PID regulator

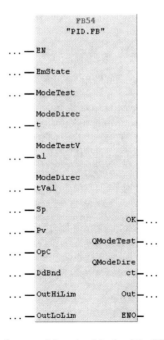

Fig. 9. Implemented function block of the PID regulator

The value *ModeTestVal* is directly copied from the function block input to the manipulated value in the test mode (chosen by *ModeTest* from the function block input). This value is limited according *OutHiLim* and *OutLolim* values. The manual manipulated value *ModeTestVal* is intended for manual manipulated value setting from visualization. This mode corresponds with manual mode in classical PID functions blocks. [10], [12]

The value *ModeDirectVal* is directly copied from the function block input to manipulated value in the direct mode (chosen by *ModeDirect* from the function block input). This value is limited according *OutHiLim* and *OutLolim* values. The manual manipulated value *ModeDirectVal* is intended for the manual manipulated value setting directly from Step 7 software during commissioning. This mode corresponds with manual mode in classical PID functions blocks. [10]

The simplified function block scheme of the implemented PID regulator is on Fig. 8. The interface of the implemented function block of PID regulator is shown on Fig. 9.

4   Conclusion

With the development of PLC, improving the operation speed and function unceasing enhancement, PLC has been applied in many fields, and achieved many functions modular.

The main goal of this work is design and implementation of the universal function block of the fuzzy expert system for PLC Simatic S7 300/400.

The contribution shows an example of the fuzzy expert system for the adaptation of the PID regulator based on the working point. This approach can be appropriate for systems with nonlinear characteristic which have to be controlled in several working points. The suggested sets of PID regulator parameters are placed into the function block of the expert system. Sets of PID regulator parameters are then sent to the PID regulator depending on current working point of the controlled system and according degree of membership of process value to coordinates of fuzzy sets. This allows a continuous adjustment of the PID regulator constants when the process value is moving between two working points.

Implementation details of the fuzzy expert system function block and description of the designed control system with the fuzzy expert system and with the visualization made in Intouch is introduced.

Acknowledgements. This work is supported by project SP2011/45, "Data acquisition and processing from large distributed systems" of Student Grant System, VSB-TU Ostrava and also by the company of Ingeteam a.s. Ostrava.

References

1. Babuska, R., Damen, M.R., Hellinga, C., Maarleveld, H.: Intelligent adaptive control of bioreactors. Journal of Intelligent Manufacturing 14(2), 255–265 (2003), doi:10.1023/A:10229637

2. Chand, S.: On-line, self-monitoring tuner for proportional integral derivative controllers. In: Proceedings of the 30th IEEE Conference Decision and Control, Brighton, UK (1991), doi:10.1109/CDC.1991.261746, ISBN: 0-7803-0450-0
3. Van Nauta Lemke, H.R., de-Zhao, W.: Fuzzy PID Supervisor. In: Proceedings of the 24th IEEE Conference Decision and Control (1985), doi:10.1109/CDC.1985.268559
4. Kanagaraj, N., Sivashanmugam, S., Paramasivam, S.: A Fuzzy Logic Based Supervisory Hierarchical Control Scheme for Real Time Pressure Control. Internation Journal of Automation and Computing 6 (2009) ISSN: 1751-8520
5. Zhen-Yu, Z., Tomizuka, M., Isaka, S.: Fuzzy Gain Scheduling of PID Controllers. IEEE Transactions on Systems and Cybernetics 23(5), 18–9472 (2004) ISSN: 0018-9472
6. Sanjuan, M., Candel, A., Smith, C.A.: Design and implementation of a fuzzy supervisor for on-line compensation of nonlinearities: An instability avoidance module. Journal Engineering Applications of Artifical Inteligence 19(3) (2006), doi:10.1016/j.engappai.2005.09.003
7. Kazemian, H.B.: The SOF-PID Controller for the Control. IEEE Transaction on Fuzzy Systems 10(4) (August 2002)
8. Wang, W., Han-Xiong, L., Zhang, J.: Intelligence-Based Hybrid Control for Power Plant Boiler of a MIMO Robot Arm. IEEE Transaction on Fuzzy Systems 10(2) (March 2002)
9. Kanagaraj, N., Sivashanmugam, P.: Intelligent Fuzzy Coordinated Control Scheme for Pressure Control Process. In: International Conference on Computational Intelligence and Multimedia Applications (2007) ISBN: 0-7695-3050-8
10. Kocian, J., Koziorek, J.: An Outline of Advanced Process Control and Self Tuning Techniques on PLC Background. In: ETFA 2010: Proceedings of IEEE International Conference on Emerging Technologies and Factory Automation, Bilbao, Spain, September 13-16 (2010) ISBN 978-1-4244-6849-2
11. Tutsch, M., Machacek, Z., Krejcar, O., Konarik, P.: Development Methods for Low Cost Industrial Control by WinPAC Controller and Measurement Cards in Matlab Simulink. In: Proceedings of Second International Conference on Computer Engineering and Applications, ICCEA 2010, Bali Island, Indonesia, March 19-21, vol. 2, pp. 444–448. IEEE Conference Publishing Services, NJ (2010), doi:10.1109/ICCEA.2010.235, ISBN 978-0-7695-3982-9
12. Kocian, J., Koziorek, J.: An Outline of Advanced Regulation Techniques on PLC Background and Control Systems with Self Tuning Methods Design. In: PDES 2010: Proceedings of 10th IFAC International Workshop on Programmable Devices and Embedded Systems, Pszczyna, Poland, October 06-08, pp. 143–148 (2010)
13. ÓDwyer, A.: Handbook of PI and PID Controller Tuning Rules, 375 pages. Imperial College Press, London (2003) ISBN: 1-86094-350-0

A Weighted Fuzzy Integrated Time Series
for Forecasting Tourist Arrivals

Suhartono[1], Muhammad Hisyam Lee[2], and Hossein Javedani[2]

[1] Department of Statistics, Institut Teknologi Sepuluh Nopember,
Kampus ITS Sukolilo, Surabaya, Indonesia 60111
[2] Department of Mathematics, Universiti Teknologi Malaysia,
81310 UTM Skudai, Johor, Malaysia
suhartono@statistika.its.ac.id,
mhl@utm.my, h.javedani@gmail.com

Abstract. Literature reviews show that the most commonly studied fuzzy time series models for the purpose of forecasting is first order. In such approaches, only the first lagged variable is used when constructing the first order fuzzy time series model. Therefore, such approaches fail to analyze accurately trend and seasonal time series which is an important class in time series models. In this paper, a weighted fuzzy integrated time series is proposed in order to analyze trend and seasonal data and data are taken from tourist arrivals series. The proposed approach is based on differencing concept as data preprocessing method and weighted fuzzy time series. The order of this model is determined by utilizing graphical order fuzzy relationship. Four data sets about the monthly number of tourist arrivals to Indonesia via four main gates are selected to illustrate the proposed method and compare the forecasting accuracy with classical time series models. The results of the comparison in test data show that the weighted fuzzy integrated time series produces more precise forecasted values than those classical time series models.

Keywords: Differencing, fuzzy time series, seasonality, trend, tourist arrivals.

1 Introduction

The definitions of fuzzy time series were firstly introduced by Song and Chissom (see [1], [2]), and they developed the model by using fuzzy relation equations and approximate reasoning. Furthermore, Song and Chissom [2] divided the fuzzy time series into two types, namely time-variant and time-invariant, whose difference relies on whether there exists the same relation between time t and its prior time $t - k$ (where $k = 1, 2, ..., m$). If the relations are all the same, it is a time-invariant fuzzy time series; likewise, if the relations are not the same, then it is time-variant.

Recently, Liu [3] proposed an integrated fuzzy time series forecasting system in which the forecasted value will be a trapezoidal fuzzy number instead of a single-point value, and effectively deal with stationary, trend, and seasonal time series. Later, Egrioglu et al. [4] proposed a hybrid approach based on SARIMA and partial high order bivariate fuzzy time series for forecasting seasonal data. Additionally,

A. Abd Manaf et al. (Eds.): ICIEIS 2011, Part II, CCIS 252, pp. 206–217, 2011.

Suhartono and Lee [5] also proposed a new hybrid approach based on Winter's method and weighted fuzzy time series for forecasting time series with trend and seasonal pattern.

In this paper, a new weighted fuzzy integrated time series model based on differencing concept as data preprocessing and weighted fuzzy time series are proposed to improve the forecast accuracy in trend and seasonal data. This approach follows the idea of integrated on ARIMA model to make data become a stationary process. In this new model, the weighted fuzzy time series proposed by Chen [6], Yu [7], Cheng [8], and Lee [9] then are applied for these stationary series. This study shows that by using four series of the monthly tourist arrivals to Indonesia, the proposed models with Chen's and Lee's weight outperform other models.

2 Fuzzy Time Series

Chen [6] improved the approach proposed by Song and Chissom (see [1], [2]). Chen's method uses a simple operation, instead of complex matrix operations, in the establishment step of fuzzy relationships. The algorithm of Chen's method can be given as follows:

Step 1. Define the universe of discourse and intervals for rules abstraction. Based on the issue domain, the universe of discourse can be defined as: $U = [starting, ending]$. As the length of interval is determined U can be partitioned into several equally length intervals.

Step 2. Define fuzzy sets based on the universe of discourse and fuzzify the historical data.

Step 3. Fuzzify observed rules.

Step 4. Establish fuzzy logical relationships (FLRs) and group them based on the current states of the data of the fuzzy logical relationships.

Step 5. Forecast. Let $F(t-1) = A_i$.

Case 1: If the fuzzy logical relationship of A_i is empty; $A_i \rightarrow \emptyset$, then $F(t)$, forecast value, is equal to A_i.

Case 2: There is only one fuzzy logical relationship in the fuzzy logical relationship sequence. If $A_i \rightarrow A_j$, then $F(t)$, forecast value, is equal to A_j.

Case 3: If $A_i \rightarrow A_{j_1}, A_{j_2}, ..., A_{j_k}$, then $F(t)$, forecast value, is equal to $A_{j_1}, A_{j_2}, ..., A_{j_k}$.

Step 6. Defuzzify. If the forecast of $F(t)$ is $A_{j_1}, A_{j_2}, ..., A_{j_k}$, the defuzzified result is equal to the arithmetic average of the midpoints of $A_{j_1}, A_{j_2}, ..., A_{j_k}$.

2.1 Yu's Method

Yu [7] proposed weighted models to tackle two issues in fuzzy time series forecasting, namely, recurrence and weighting. The method proposed by Yu applies a linear chronologically weights and produces more accurate forecasts than Chen's first order fuzzy time series method. The steps of the algorithm of the weighted method proposed by Yu [7] can be given below.

Step 1. Define the discourse of universe and subintervals. Based on min and max values in the data set, D_{min} and D_{max} variables are defined. Then choose two arbitrary positive numbers which are D_1 and D_2 in order to divide the interval evenly, $U = [D_{min} - D_1, D_{max} - D_2]$.

Step 2. Define fuzzy sets based on the universe of discourse and fuzzify the historical data.

Step 3. Fuzzify observed rules.

Step 4. Establish fuzzy logical relationships (revised Chen's method). The recurrent FLRs are taken into account by revising Step 4 in Chen's method. For example, there are 5 FLRs with the same LHS, $A_1 \to A_2$, $A_1 \to A_1$, $A_1 \to A_1$, $A_1 \to A_3$, $A_1 \to A_1$. These FLRs are used to establish fuzzy logical relationship group (FLRG) as: $A_1 \to A_2, A_1, A_1, A_3, A_1$.

Step 5. Forecast. Use the same rule as Chen's.

Step 6. Defuzzify. Suppose the forecast of $F(t)$ is $A_{j_1}, A_{j_2}, ..., A_{j_k}$. The defuzzified matrix is equal to a matrix of the midpoints of $A_{j_1}, A_{j_2}, ..., A_{j_k}$:

$$M(t) = [m_{j_1}, m_{j_2}, ..., m_{j_k}],$$

where $M(t)$ represents the defuzzified forecast of $F(t)$.

Step 7. Assigning weights. Suppose the forecast of $F(t)$ is $A_{j_1}, A_{j_2}, ..., A_{j_k}$. The corresponding weights for $A_{j_1}, A_{j_2}, ..., A_{j_k}$ say $w_1', w_2', ..., w_k'$ are specified as:

$$w_i' = \frac{w_i}{\sum_{h=1}^{k} w_h},$$

where $w_1 = 1, w_i = w_{i-1} + 1$ for $2 \leq i \leq k$. We then obtain the weight matrix as

$$W(t) = [w_1', w_2', ..., w_k'] = \left[\frac{1}{\sum_{h=1}^{k} w_h}, \frac{2}{\sum_{h=1}^{k} w_h}, ..., \frac{k}{\sum_{h=1}^{k} w_h}\right]$$

where w_h is the corresponding weight for A_{j_k}.

Step 8. Calculating the final forecast values. In the weighted model, the final forecast is equal to the product of the defuzzified matrix and the transpose of the weight matrix:

$$\hat{F}(t) = M(t) \times W(t)^T$$

$$= [m_{j_1}, m_{j_2}, ..., m_{j_k}] \times \left[\frac{1}{\sum_{h=1}^{k} w_h}, \frac{2}{\sum_{h=1}^{k} w_h}, ..., \frac{k}{\sum_{h=1}^{k} w_h}\right]^T$$

where $\times$ is the matrix product operator, and $M(t)$ is a $1 \times k$ matrix and $W(t)^T$ is a $k \times 1$ matrix, respectively.

2.2 Cheng's Method

Cheng et al. [8] proposed fuzzy time series based on adaptive expectation model for obtain forecasts. The method proposed by Cheng et al. produces more accurate forecasts than Chen's and Yu's method on two real data, namely TAIEX and the enrollments of the University of Alabama. The steps of the algorithm of the method proposed by Cheng et al. [8] are given below.

Step 1. Define the discourse of universe and subintervals as Yu's.

Step 2. Define fuzzy sets based on the universe of discourse and fuzzify the historical data.

Step 3. Fuzzify observed rules.

Step 4. Establish fuzzy logical relationships (revised Chen's method). The FLRs with the same LHSs can be grouped to form of FLR Group. For example, there are 5 FLRs with the same LHS, $A_1 \rightarrow A_2$, $A_1 \rightarrow A_1$, $A_1 \rightarrow A_1$, $A_1 \rightarrow A_3$, $A_1 \rightarrow A_1$. These FLRs are used to establish fuzzy logical relationship group (FLRG) as: $A_1 \rightarrow A_2, A_1, A_1, A_3, A_1$. All FLRs will construct a fluctuation-type matrix. Hence, the fluctuation-type matrix is

$$W(t) = [w_1, w_2, \ldots, w_5] = [1,1,2,1,3].$$

Step 5. Assigning weights. The matrix from Step 4 is further standardized to W_n, and multiplied by the deffuzified matrix, L_{df}, to produce the forecast value. These weights should standardized to obtain the weight matrix, i.e. $W(t) = [w_1', w_2', \ldots, w_k']$. This weight should be normalized by applying the standardize weight matrix equation as follows:

$$W(t) = [w_1', w_2', \ldots, w_k'] = \left[\frac{w_1}{\sum_{h=1}^{k} w_h}, \frac{w_2}{\sum_{h=1}^{k} w_h}, \ldots, \frac{w_k}{\sum_{h=1}^{k} w_h} \right].$$

Step 6. Calculate forecast value.

From Step 5, we can obtain the standardized weight matrix, to get the forecast value by using

$$F(t) = L_{df}(t-1) \times W_n(t-1)^T.$$

where $L_{df}(t-1)$ is the deffuzified matrix and $W_n(t-1)$ is the weight matrix.

Step 7. Employ the adaptive forecasting equation to produce a conclusive forecast.

2.3 Lee's Method

Lee and Suhartono [9] proposed uniform and exponential chronologically weights to tackle two issues in fuzzy time series forecasting, namely, recurrence and weighting, as extension of Yu's method. This method produces more accurate forecasts than Chen's, Yu's, and Cheng's methods. The steps of the algorithm of the weighted method proposed by Lee and Suhartono [9] are given as follows.

Step 1. Define the universe of discourse and partition it into intervals as Yu's method.

Step 2. Establish a related fuzzy set (linguistic value) for each observation in the training dataset.

Step 3. Establish fuzzy relationship.

Step 4. Establish fuzzy relationships groups for all FLRs.

Step 5. Select the best order of FLRs. The graphical orders for FLRs and fluctuation-type matrixes are used to identify the best order of FLRs.

Step 6. Forecast.

Step 7. Defuzzify. Use the same rule as Yu [7].

Step 8. Assigning weights. Suppose the forecast of F(t) is $A_{j_1}, A_{j_2}, ..., A_{j_k}$. The corresponding weights for $A_{j_1}, A_{j_2}, ..., A_{j_k}$, say $w'_1, w'_2, ..., w'_k$ are

$$W(t) = \left[\frac{1}{\sum_{h=1}^{k} w_h}, \frac{c}{\sum_{h=1}^{k} w_h}, \frac{c^2}{\sum_{h=1}^{k} w_h}, \cdots, \frac{c^{k-1}}{\sum_{h=1}^{k} w_h} \right]$$

where $w_1 = 1, w_i = c^{i-1}$ for $c \geq 1, 2 \leq i \leq k$, and w_h is the corresponding weight for A_{j_k}.

Step 9. Calculate the final forecast values. The final forecast is equal to the product of the defuzzified matrix and the transpose of the weight matrix:

$$\hat{F}(t) = [m_{j_1}, m_{j_2}, ..., m_{j_k}] \times \left[\frac{1}{\sum_{h=1}^{k} w_h}, \frac{c}{\sum_{h=1}^{k} w_h}, \cdots, \frac{c^{k-1}}{\sum_{h=1}^{k} w_h} \right]^T$$

where $\times$ is the matrix product operator.

3   Proposed Model and Algorithm

Weighted Fuzzy Time Series (WFTS) models have achieved successes in their own linear or nonlinear domains, particularly for forecasting stationary or seasonal time series with no trend. However, many time series data as tourist arrivals series frequently contain seasonal and trend pattern. Zhang [10] stated that since it is difficult to completely know the characteristics of the data in a real problem, hybrid methodology can be a good strategy for practical use. By combining different models, different aspects of the underlying patterns may be captured.

Liu [3] introduced a combination between decomposition method and WFTS for forecasting trend and seasonal time series. In this paper, we proposed a combination method between differencing as data preprocessing method and WFTS models for forecasting trend and seasonal time series. Differencing is a concept of integrated in ARIMA model to make non-stationary time series become stationary process. Then, we call the proposed method as Weighted Fuzzy Integrated Time Series or WFITS.

Three differencing process are used in this study, i.e. non-seasonal differencing $(d = 1)$ as DP-1, seasonal order 12 differencing $(D = 1, S = 12)$ as DP-2, and both of non and seasonal differencing simultaneously $(d = 1, D = 1, S = 12)$ as DP-3. Hence, the original series become three new series, i.e.

1. DP-1: $Y1(t) = (1 - B)Y(t) = Y(t) - Y(t - 1)$.
2. DP-2: $Y2(t) = (1 - B^{12})Y(t) = Y(t) - Y(t - 12)$.
3. DP-3: $Y3(t) = (1 - B)(1 - B^{12})Y(t)$
$$= Y(t) - Y(t - 1) - Y(t - 12) + Y(t - 13).$$

In summary, the proposed methodology of the WFITS system consists of two steps. In the first step, a differencing is used to make stationary process. In the second step, a WFTS model is developed to model the differencing data. In this second step, we apply four WFTS models proposed by Chen [6], Yu [7], Cheng et al. [8], and Lee and Suhartono [9]. The proposed method exploits the unique feature and strength of WFITS model in determining different patterns. Thus, it could be advantageous to model trend, seasonal, and nonlinear patterns separately by using different models and then combine the forecasts to improve the overall modeling and forecasting performance.

To validate the methodology of the WFITS method for forecasting trend and seasonal time series data, a new algorithm is proposed as follows:

Step 1. Apply differencing to get the stationary process, $Y1_t$, $Y2_t$, and $Y3_t$.

Step 2. Apply WFTS method to model the differencing data and get the forecast component of the stationary process, $\widehat{F1}(t)$, $\widehat{F2}(t)$, and $\widehat{F3}(t)$. In this step, four WFTS methods proposed by Chen [6], Yu [7], Cheng et al. [8], and Lee and Suhartono [9] are applied to find the best forecasted values.

Step 3. Calculate the final forecast values at the same original data scale.

1. For DP-1: non-seasonal differencing data

$$\hat{F}(t) = \widehat{F1}(t) + Y(t-1)$$

2. For DP-2: seasonal differencing data

$$\hat{F}(t) = \widehat{F2}(t) + Y(t-12)$$

3. For DP-3: both of non-seasonal and seasonal differencing data

$$\hat{F}(t) = \widehat{F3}(t) + Y(t-1) + Y(t-12) - Y(t-13)$$

4 Empirical Result

To demonstrate the effectiveness of the WFITS method, we use four data about the number of tourist arrivals to Indonesia, i.e. via Soekarno Hatta airport in Jakarta, Ngurah Rai airport in Bali, Polonia airport in Medan, and via Batam, from January 1998 until December 2009 as case study. Each data are 108 monthly records of the arrivals published by BPS – Statistics Indonesia in *www.bps.go.id*.

The time series plot at Fig. 1a-d illustrate that in general the four data have both trend and seasonal pattern. To assess the forecasting performance of different models, each data set is divided into two samples of training and testing. The training data set that contains 96 records (January 1998 until December 2008) is used exclusively for model development and then the last 12 records (January 2009 until December 2009) as test sample is used to evaluate the established model.

In this study, all WFITS modeling is implemented via two package programs, i.e. MINITAB for differencing and graphical analysis at the first step and MATLAB for WFTS model at the second step. The graphical order of fuzzy logical relationship suggested that two orders of WFTS are appropriate for the data, i.e. the first order non-seasonal (order 1) and the first order seasonal (order 12). The results are compared with ARIMA model. Only the k-step-ahead forecasting is considered. The root mean squared error (RMSE) is selected to be the forecasting accuracy measures. The RMSE is defined as

$$\text{RMSE} = \sqrt{\frac{\sum_{t=1}^{n}(Y_t - \hat{Y}_t)^2}{n}},$$

where n is the number of forecasts.

The results of RMSEs obtained using the WFITS with four methods and a classical
time series ARIMA model at four case studies, both in training and testing data, are
listed in Table 1-4 (in Appendix). Column ratio illustrates the ratio between each
method to the result of ARIMA model. The value is less than 1 show that the result is
better than ARIMA.

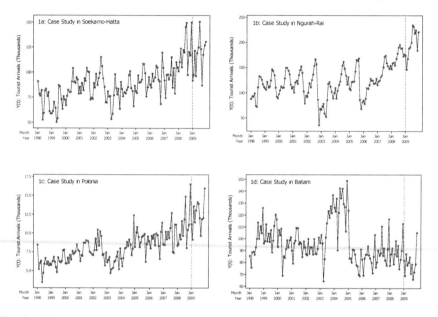

Fig. 1. Monthly tourist arrivals to Soekarno-Hatta airport (1a), Ngurah Rai airport (1b),
Polonia airport (1c), and Batam (1d) from January 1998 – December 2009

These results show that the proposed data preprocessing to make data stationer at
the first step of the algorithm has a significant influence to increase the accuracy of
the forecasted values of each fuzzy time series. In general, the second data
preprocessing (DP-2), namely seasonal differencing yields the most accurate forecast
at two case studies, i.e. at Soekarno-Hatta and Polonia cases. Whereas, the third data
preprocessing (DP-3), namely both of non-seasonal and seasonal differencing yields
the most accurate forecast at two other cases studies, i.e. in Ngurah Rai and Batam.

The performance evaluation in training data shows that ARIMA model always
yields the most accurate forecasted values than all WFITS models. Conversely, the
WFITS models always give better forecasted values than ARIMA at testing data. The
results of comparison also show that the WFITS with exponential weight proposed by
Lee and Suhartono [9] yield the most accurate forecasted values for forecasting tourist
arrivals both in Soekarno-Hatta and Polonia airport. Whereas, the WFITS with Chen's
method [6] give the best forecasted values at Ngurah Rai and Batam. Additionally, in
Soekarno-Hatta case, the best model is WFITS at the first order non-seasonal with
seasonal differencing and $c = 1.3$, whereas WFITS at the first order seasonal with
seasonal differencing and $c = 1.7$ is the best model in Polonia case.

5   Conclusion and Future Works

In this paper, we have proposed WFITS for forecasting trend and seasonal time series, and apply to tourist arrivals data. Four data about the number of tourist arrivals to Indonesia via for main gates have been employed to compare the forecasting accuracy between the proposed WFITS with Chen's, Yu's, Cheng's and Lee's weights a classical time series ARIMA model. The results in testing data show that the proposed WFITS methods, particularly with Chen's and Lee's weights, provide more accurate forecasting values than ARIMA models in term of the RMSE.

This study proposed a data preprocessing (i.e. differencing as a concept of integrated in ARIMA) to make stationary data and weight scheme in WFTS where the more recent ones have higher weights than the older ones as Yu [7]. Other issue could also be further investigated is hybrid method for forecasting data with trend and seasonality as proposed by Zhang [10] and Suhartono and Lee [5]. These hybrid methods could be expanded for resolving other time series patterns such as calendar variation, interventions, outlier's effects, and multi periods of seasonality.

References

1. Song, Q., Chissom, B.S.: Fuzzy Forecasting Enrollments with Fuzzy Time Series-Part 1. Fuzzy Sets and Systems 54(1), 1–9 (1993)
2. Song, Q., Chissom, B.S.: Fuzzy Time Series and Its Models. Fuzzy Sets and Systems 54(3), 269–277 (1993)
3. Liu, H.T.: An Integrated Fuzzy Time Series Forecasting System. Expert Systems with Applications 36, 10045–10053 (2009)
4. Egrioglu, E., Aladag, C.H., Yolcu, U., Basaran, M.A., Uslu, V.R.: A New Hybrid Approach Based on SARIMA and Partial High Order Bivariate Fuzzy Time Series Forecasting Model. Expert Systems with Applications 36, 7424–7434 (2009)
5. Suhartono, Lee, M.H.: A Hybrid Approach Based on Winter's Model and Weighted Fuzzy Time Series for Forecasting Trend and Seasonal Data. Journal of Mathematics and Statistics 7(3), 177–183 (2011)
6. Chen, S.M.: Forecasting Enrollments Based on Fuzzy Time Series. Fuzzy Sets and Systems 81(3), 311–319 (1996)
7. Yu, H.K.: Weighted Fuzzy Time-Series Models for TAIEX Forecasting. Physica A: Statistical Mechanics and its Applications 349, 609–624 (2005)
8. Cheng, C.H., Chen, T.L., Teoh, H.J., Chiang, C.H.: Fuzzy Time Series Based on Adaptive Expectation Model for TAIEX Forecasting. Expert Systems with Applications 34(2), 1126–1132 (2008)
9. Lee, M.H., Suhartono: A Novel Weighted Fuzzy Time Series Model for Forecasting Seasonal Data. In: Proceeding 2nd International Conference on Mathematical Sciences, Kuala Lumpur, Malaysia, pp. 332–340 (2010)
10. Zhang, G.P.: Time Series Forecasting Using a Hybrid ARIMA and Neural Network Model. Neurocomputing 50, 159–175 (2003)

Appendix

Table 1. Comparison of RMSEs both in training and testing at Soekarno-Hatta case study

Differencing & the Order of WFTS	Method	Training		Testing	
		RMSE	Ratio	RMSE	Ratio
DP-1:					
The 1st	Chen's	14.248	1.20	27.597	0.95
	Yu's	13.395	1.13	26.260	0.91
	Cheng's	13.592	1.15	26.395	0.91
	Lee's	13.519	1.14	26.178	0.90
12: seasonal	Chen's	13.677	1.15	26.495	0.92
	Yu's	13.685	1.15	25.323	0.87
	Cheng's	14.645	1.23	19.738	0.68
	Lee's	13.479	1.14	24.526	0.85
DP-2:					
The 1st	Chen's	13.677	1.15	18.316	0.63
	Yu's	12.827	1.08	13.146	0.45
	Cheng's	12.694	1.07	13.502	0.47
	Lee's	15.427	1.30	12.146	0.42
12: seasonal	Chen's	15.306	1.29	14.239	0.49
	Yu's	15.149	1.28	14.009	0.48
	Cheng's	14.993	1.26	12.626	0.43
	Lee's	14.936	1.26	12.869	0.44
DP-3:					
The 1st	Chen's	13.723	1.16	19.473	0.67
	Yu's	13.731	1.16	18.543	0.64
	Cheng's	13.507	1.14	16.841	0.58
	Lee's	13.489	1.14	17.113	0.59
12: seasonal	Chen's	17.251	1.45	19.261	0.67
	Yu's	15.984	1.35	18.735	0.65
	Cheng's	15.757	1.32	17.601	0.61
	Lee's	15.703	1.32	17.859	0.62
ARIMA$(0,1,1)(0,0,1)^{12}$		11.862	1	28.950	1

Table 2. Comparison of RMSEs both in training and testing at Ngurah Rai case study

Differencing & the Order of WFTS	Method	Training		Testing	
		RMSE	Ratio	RMSE	Ratio
DP-1:					
The 1st	Chen's	16.479	1.32	26.319	1.57
	Yu's	15.573	1.25	23.157	1.38
	Cheng's	16.905	1.36	34.184	2.03
	Lee's	15.501	1.24	22.706	1.35
12: seasonal	Chen's	13.561	1.09	22.847	1.36
	Yu's	13.146	1.06	22.361	1.33
	Cheng's	46.374	3.72	24.937	1.48
	Lee's	13.107	1.05	21.581	1.28
DP-2:					
The 1st	Chen's	16.331	1.31	20.579	1.22
	Yu's	15.587	1.25	18.184	1.08
	Cheng's	15.485	1.24	17.304	1.03
	Lee's	18.627	1.50	16.214	0.96
12: seasonal	Chen's	23.831	1.91	32.538	1.94
	Yu's	23.714	1.90	33.376	1.99
	Cheng's	47.465	3.81	19.998	1.19
	Lee's	30.757	2.47	19.071	1.13
DP-3:					
The 1st	Chen's	18.108	1.45	14.832	0.88
	Yu's	16.473	1.32	20.846	1.24
	Cheng's	16.946	1.36	20.779	1.24
	Lee's	16.576	1.33	20.733	1.23
12: seasonal	Chen's	15.017	1.21	22.941	1.36
	Yu's	14.080	1.13	20.793	1.24
	Cheng's	13.950	1.12	20.701	1.23
	Lee's	14.244	1.14	20.698	1.23
ARIMA(0,1,1)(0,0,1)^{12}		12.454	1	16.812	1

Table 3. Comparison of RMSEs both in training and testing at Polonia case study

Differencing & the Order of WFTS	Method	Training		Testing	
		RMSE	Ratio	RMSE	Ratio
DP-1:					
The 1st	Chen's	1.559	1.18	2.811	1.86
	Yu's	1.497	1.13	2.728	1.81
	Cheng's	1.509	1.14	2.718	1.80
	Lee's	2.224	1.68	2.705	1.79
12: seasonal	Chen's	1.490	1.13	2.710	1.79
	Yu's	1.443	1.09	2.721	1.80
	Cheng's	1.440	1.09	2.570	1.70
	Lee's	1.414	1.07	2.706	1.79
DP-2:					
The 1st	Chen's	1.486	1.12	1.982	1.31
	Yu's	1.383	1.04	1.956	1.29
	Cheng's	1.390	1.05	2.001	1.32
	Lee's	1.384	1.05	1.926	1.27
12: seasonal	Chen's	1.645	1.24	1.631	1.08
	Yu's	1.548	1.17	1.919	1.27
	Cheng's	1.557	1.18	2.138	1.41
	Lee's	1.838	1.39	1.474	0.98
DP-3:					
The 1st	Chen's	1.375	1.04	2.674	1.77
	Yu's	1.346	1.02	2.679	1.77
	Cheng's	1.344	1.02	2.682	1.77
	Lee's	1.345	1.02	2.686	1.78
12: seasonal	Chen's	1.479	1.12	2.181	1.44
	Yu's	1.463	1.10	2.256	1.49
	Cheng's	1.458	1.10	2.420	1.60
	Lee's	1.446	1.09	2.353	1.56
ARIMA(0,1,1)(0,0,1)^{12}		1.324	1	1.511	1

Table 4. Comparison of RMSEs both in training and testing at Batam case study

Differencing & the Order of WFTS	Method	Training		Testing	
		RMSE	Ratio	RMSE	Ratio
DP-1:					
The 1st	Chen's	13.084	1.09	13.331	0.71
	Yu's	12.742	1.06	12.815	0.69
	Cheng's	12.679	1.05	12.710	0.68
	Lee's	12.669	1.05	11.022	0.59
12: seasonal	Chen's	12.118	1.00	12.917	0.69
	Yu's	12.121	1.01	11.567	0.62
	Cheng's	13.711	1.14	7.580	0.41
	Lee's	13.150	1.09	10.982	0.59
DP-2:					
The 1st	Chen's	14.415	1.20	9.095	0.49
	Yu's	13.749	1.14	9.969	0.53
	Cheng's	15.138	1.26	10.139	0.54
	Lee's	14.165	1.17	8.588	0.46
12: seasonal	Chen's	20.740	1.72	10.990	0.59
	Yu's	20.335	1.69	14.725	0.79
	Cheng's	25.827	2.14	12.413	0.67
	Lee's	22.290	1.85	9.887	0.53
DP-3:					
The 1st	Chen's	14.254	1.18	9.217	0.49
	Yu's	14.153	1.17	8.722	0.47
	Cheng's	14.104	1.17	8.675	0.47
	Lee's	14.184	1.18	8.666	0.46
12: seasonal	Chen's	14.066	1.17	7.472	0.40
	Yu's	13.459	1.12	9.657	0.52
	Cheng's	13.419	1.11	10.769	0.58
	Lee's	13.584	1.13	9.518	0.51
ARIMA(0,1,1)(0,0,1)^{12}		12.058	1	18.649	1

Security Audit Trail Analysis with Biogeography Based Optimization Metaheuristic

M. Daoudi, A. Boukra, and M. Ahmed-Nacer

Faculty of Electronics and Computer Science, Laboratory LSI, USTHB,
BP 32 16111 El Alia, Bab-Ezzouar, Algiers, Algeria
{dmfinfo,amboukra}@yahoo.fr,
anacer@cerist.dz

Abstract. Information systems and computer networks are essential in nowadays modern society, and computer systems security is crucial as data to store and process becomes more and more important. In this paper, intrusion detection from audit security records is of our interest. As the volume of data generated by the auditing mechanisms of current systems is very large, it is therefore crucial to provide security officers with methods and tools to extract useful information. In this context, we aim at determine predefined attack scenarios in the audit trails. The problem is NP-Complete. Metaheuristics offer an alternative to solve this type of problems. We propose to use the Biogeography Based Optimization (BBO), a new metaheuristic well suited for constrained optimization problems. Experiments and performance measures were performed and a comparison with a Genetic Algorithm based method is made. BBO has proven effective and capable of producing a reliable method for intrusion detection.

Keywords: Intrusion detection, Security audit, Attacks scenario, NP-Complete problem, Biogeography Based Optimization, Genetic Algorithm.

1 Introduction

In Intrusion Detection Systems (IDS) [1]-[8], the volume of data generated by the auditing mechanisms of current systems is very important and it is essential to provide security officers with methods and tools to extract useful information.

Neural networks have been extensively used to detect both misuse and anomalous patterns [9]-[13]. Artificial immune systems have been used to detect intrusive behaviors in a computer network [14-[16]. Other techniques like genetic algorithms [17], [18], Bayesian parameter estimation [19] and clustering [20]-[24] are also used. Lee [25] built an intrusion detection model using association rule and frequent episode techniques on system audit data . Some other researchers try to analyze the problem of intrusion detection by using a multiple fault diagnosis approach. An events-attacks matrix is defined, and the occurrence of one or more attacks is required to be inferred from newly observed events. Such a problem is reducible to a zero-one integer problem, which is NP-Complete [26]. Dass [27] and Me´ [28] both employed GAs as an optimization component. Me´ used a standard GA, while Dass used a micro-GA in order to reduce the time overhead normally associated with a GA.

A. Abd Manaf et al. (Eds.): ICIEIS 2011, Part II, CCIS 252, pp. 218–227, 2011.
© Springer-Verlag Berlin Heidelberg 2011

Our approach consists in a simplified model of intrusion detection from audit security records. It is formalized as a NP-Complete combinatorial optimization problem, where a fitness function defining the incurred risk is constructed from a sum of risks of different attacks. Once formulated suitably a solution representation, change-effecting operator and fitness function, the problem of intrusion detection can be tackled using the Biogeography Based Optimization (BBO) metaheuristic [29], which has proven effective and capable of producing a reliable method for intrusion detection. Experiments and performance measures are performed and a comparison with a Genetic Algorithm based method is carried out.

The rest of the paper is as follows: section 2 is dedicated to the   problem formalization. A presentation of BBO is given in section 3 while section 4 treats of its adaptation to solve the problem. Experimental results are reported in Section 5. Section 6 is conclusions.

2 Problem Formalization

Our goal is to achieve a system that can tell whether an intrusion has occurred or not when analyzing the trace file security audit. Among the different existing approaches to develop such a system, we consider a posterior approach based on attack scenarios recorded in the audit trail. Each attack will be defined by a number of occurrence of auditable events. The audit file for analysis will also be defined by the number of occurrence of auditable events. The temporal order of sequence of events will not be considered (in this case the system can function in a heterogeneous distributed environment where the construction of a common time is impossible). In informal terms, the problem is to find the combination of attacks that maximizes the incurred risk, while possible under number of events of each type recorded in the audit file. Such a model follows.

Let:

- n_e the number of event types
- n_a the number of known potential attacks
- AE a matrix of dimension (n_e x n_a), that gives for each attack the events it generates. $AE_{i\,j} \geq 0$ is the number of events of type i generated by the attack j
- R a vector of dimension n_a where $R_j > 0$ is the weight associated with the attack j. This weight is proportional to the inherent risk of attack scenario j
- O a vector of dimension n_e where O_i is the number of events of type i in the analyzed audit subset. O is the observed audit file
- H a vector of dimension n_a where $H_j = 1$ if attack j is present (based on defined assumptions) and $H_j = 0$ otherwise. H is a subset of possible attacks.

The mathematical model is:

$$\begin{cases} Max \sum_{1}^{n_a} R_j . H_j \\ (AE . H)i \ \leq \ Oi , i \in \{1 \ldots ne\} \end{cases}$$

To obtain the best vector H is a NP-Complete problem. Metaheuristics present an alternative to solve this type of problem when the number of attacks (n_a) is large. We present in the next section the metaheuristic BBO that we propose to use in our approach to solve the problem.

3   Biogeography Based Optimization

Biogeography studies the geographical distribution of biological organisms. It is due to the work of Alfred Wallace [30] and Charles Darwin [31] in the 19th century. This work had a descriptive and historical aspect. In 1960, Robert MacArthur and Edward Wilson have developed a mathematical model for the biogeography [32]. They were interested in the distribution of habitat species. A habitat represents any living space isolated from other spaces. The mathematical model that was developed, describes how some species migrate from one habitat to another. Habitats that are favorable to the residence of biological species are called high *habitat suitability index* (HSI). The parameters influencing the HSI may be rainfall, crop diversity, diversity of terrain ... etc. The variables describing the habitability are called *suitability index variables* (SIV).

Habitats are characterized by the following:

-   A habitat with a high HSI tends to have a high number of species, while those with a low HSI tends to have fewer species.
-   The habitats with high HSI are characterized by a high rate of emigration and low rate of immigration because they are saturated with species.
-   The habitats with low HSI have a high immigration rate and a low emigration rate.

Immigration should result in the modification of the HSI of the habitat. If the HSI habitat remains too long without improving, the species that live there tend to disappear.

Dan Simon introduced in 2008 a metaheuristic based on biogeography [29]. It uses the following analogy:

-   A solution is analogous to a habitat
-   The quality of the solution (fitness) is analogous to the HSI.
-   The variables defining the solution are analogous to SIVs.
-   A good solution is analogous to a habitat with a high HSI, and thus with a high number of species, a high rate of emigration and a low immigration rate.
-   A bad solution is analogous to a habitat with a low HSI, a low number of species, a low emigration rate and a high immigration rate.
-   A good solution tends to share characteristics with a bad solution to improve it (migration of SIVs). This is analogous to the migration of species between habitats. Sharing characteristics does not involve change in the characteristics of good solutions, because migration deals only with a sample of species, so that it does not affect the habitat.
-    The bad solutions accept the characteristics of good solutions in order to improve their quality. This is analogous to the bad habitat that accepts immigration of species from other habitats.

In BBO, the population evolves through migration and mutation processes.

4   Solving the Problem Using BBO

4.1 Solution Representation

To use BBO, we must first find a good encoding for potential solutions: the vectors H, expressed in a form of binary sequence (it takes a value 1 if the attack i is present in the audit file O and a value 0 otherwise). Consequently, a solution of the problem will correspond to a habitat witn n_a SIV. Each SIV value is 0 (no attack) or 1 (presence of an attack) and n_a is the number of attacks. A solution is thus represented with a n_a–uplet $w = (w_1,\ldots, w_n)$ in $\Omega = \{0,1\}^{na}$; It has the disadvantage of not being able to detect the multiple realization of a single attack. However, this does not seem critical [28].

4.2 Change Operators

In BBO algorithm, an initial population of several habitats (binary vector H) is randomly generated. It evolves through a migration (emigration and immigration) and a mutation processes to achieve an optimal solution. The migration process in the biogeography mechanism aims to modify one or more SIV (randomly chosen) in each selected solution, allowing the exchange of information between the good and bad solutions. Different variants of the migration process exist [29]. As part of our work, we opted for the "Partial-Based Immigration BBO". Mutation maintains diversity in the population and explores the search space, avoiding the algorithm to converge too quickly to a local optimum. Mutation comes after the migration process. It will be applied to the lower half of the population, with a very low probability (mutation rate: $p_m = 0.05$), for a great rate can cause destruction of valuable information contained in the solutions. During this process, the characteristics (SIV) of one or more individuals (habitats) of the population will be changed randomly. In other words, one or more characteristics (SIV) are modified to change from one solution to another solution with different value. However, the modified individual will not necessarily be better or worse, but it will bring additional opportunities that could be useful for creating good solutions. During the evolution of the population, it is likely that the best solutions are modified, and therefore lost after the migration process and mutation. To avoid such a situation, an elitism operator is adopted. It copies the p best individuals in the new generation (the value of p has to be fixed by simulation).

4.3 Fitness Function

We are dealing with a maximization problem that seeks for the maximum of the matrix product R.H, under the constraints $((AE.H)_i \leq O_i)$, $1\leq i\leq n_e$. It seems easy to conclude that the selective function F that evaluates the fitness function (HSI) of a given solution H is given by $Max \sum_1^{na} R_j H_j$. However, this selective function ignores the fact we deal with a constrained problem. To represent a possible solution to the problem, a habitat H must verify the inequalities: $(AE.I)_i \leq$ Oi, with $(1 \leq i \leq n_e)$. Solutions which do not satisfy the defined constraints will be penalized by setting their fitness to 0, migration rate μ to 0, and Immigration rate λ to1. As for the solutions satisfying the constraints, they will be sorted in decreasing order of the objective function. A number of species is associated to each solution. P (population size) species are associated to the best solution, (P-1) species to the next solution, and so on.

In this section, we have defined a strategy to use BBO algorithm in solving the problem of analysis of the audit file. The next section will treat of the evaluation measures of the method. Many tests have been performed. Different evaluation measures are used and the results are given and discussed.

5   Performance Evaluation and Results

The effectiveness of an IDS is evaluated by its ability to make correct predictions. According to the real nature of a given event compared to the prediction from the IDS, four possible outcomes may occur [33]. True negatives as well as true positives correspond to a correct operation of the IDS; that is, events are successfully labeled as normal and attacks, respectively. False positives refer to normal events being predicted as attacks; false negatives are attack events incorrectly predicted as normal events.

Our numerical evaluation consists in the following measures of performance:

- True negative rate (TNR): TN / (TN+FP)
- True positive rate (TPR) : TP / (TP+FN)
- False positive rate (FPR) : FP / (TN+FP)
- False negative rate (FNR): FN / (TP+FN)
- Accuracy: (TN+TP) / (TN+TP+FN+FP)
- Precision: TP / (TP+FP).

Experiments were carried out on a 1.86GHz Intel Celeron CPU 540 PC with 1GB memory. We considered first an existing audit trails and a 24x28 matrix AE consisting in a set of 24 attacks scenarios of 28 auditable events known to a Unix system [28], known as "real test". To validate the biogeography approach, we analyzed first the audit file (represented by the vector O), when injecting a certain number of intrusive behaviors, and then we extended our study to larger instances that were randomly generated. Our approach was then compared with a genetic based model using the "real data".

The performance measures (TPR, FPR, Precision, Accuracy and Specificity) are evaluated for 10 different executions, and then the mean value is computed. This evaluation is performed for many values of the different parameters involved in the system such as the generation number (N), the population size (P), the mutation parameter (P_m), the elitism parameter (l) and the number of injected attacks (i_a).

Let (N=100, P=50, P_m =0.005, l=2, i_a =2) be the default values for these parameters. During the tests, they all are maintained fixed to their default value except that we study the influence on the system performance.

5.1 System Performance Evaluation: Real Data

Various tests were performed and the results are given in the tables below.

In Table 1, we observe that for different values of the generations' number parameter N (50, 100, and 200), good results have been obtained: 100% of injected attacks are detected successfully, TPR = Accuracy = Specificity = 100% and no false positive: FPR = 0.

When varying the population size parameter P (50, 100 and 200), same results are obtained as shown in Table 2.

It is not worth increasing the values of these two elements; we retain the default values for both parameters: N=100 and P=50.

In Table 3, we observe the influence of the mutation rate P_m on the system performance. For a mutation rate = 0.005, we get perfect results: no false positive and a rate of injected attacks successfully detected of 100% (specificity= accuracy= precision=100%). Same results are obtained when increasing or decreasing P_m. However, we observe that the system does not detect the attacks when the mutation process is not used. The mutation process is important for better performance of the system. The default value of P_m (0.005) is maintained.

Furthermore, we observe that whatever the number of elites is chosen, the elitism process has no effect on the system performance as shown in Table 4. However, we still keep it with value 2. In the same way, Table 5. shows that the number of injected attacks does not influence the detection performance of the system (TPR=100% and FPT=0%).

Table 1. Influence of the generations' number (N) on the performance of the system

N	TPR	FPR	Precision	Accuracy	TNR
50	100%	0%	100%	100%	100%
100	100%	0%	100%	100%	100%
200	100%	0%	100%	100%	100%

Table 2. Influence of the population size (P) on the performance of the system

P	TPR	FPR	Precision	Accuracy	TNR
50	100%	0%	100%	100%	100%
100	100%	0%	100%	100%	100%
200	100%	0%	100%	100%	100%

Table 3. Influence of the mutation rate (P_m) on the performance of the system

P_m	TPR	FPR	Precision	Accuracy	TNR
0	0	0	-	92%	100%
0.002	100%	0%	100%	100%	100%
0.005	100%	0%	100%	100%	100%
0.006	100%	0%	100%	100%	100%

Table 4. Influence of the elitism number (l) on the performance of the system

l	TPR	FPR	Precision	Accuracy	TNR
0	0	0	-	92%	100%
0.002	100%	0%	100%	100%	100%
0.005	100%	0%	100%	100%	100%
0.006	100%	0%	100%	100%	100%

Table 5. Influence of the number of injected attacks (i_a) on the performance of the system

i_a	TPR	FPR	Precision	Accuracy	TNR
0	-	0%	-	100%	100%
2	100%	0%	100%	100%	100%
10	100%	0%	100%	100%	100%
15	100%	0%	100%	100%	100%

To resume, for the different values given to the two parameters P_m (mutation rate) and l (number of elites), the system has successfully detected the attacks injected in the system, and that, whatever the number of attacks in the file O. Whatever the number of attacks injected there's always a good discrimination between the attacks that are present and those absent. Furthermore, we observe that a population of size 50 and a number of generations equal to 100 are best values.

We note that 96% of the population is in the optimal solution at the hundredth generation. Also, a perfect convergence is reached when using the mutation process and that regardless of other settings.

The execution is very fast, the average time (over 10 runs) is: 70.5ms.

5.2   System Performance Evaluation: Random Data

Several matrices AE of different dimensions have been randomly generated and performance evaluations were performed.

We were considering first a matrix AE of dimension (100x50), randomly generated. The system performance evaluation was carried out in the same manner than in section above, using the same set of default values for the parameters: N=100, P=50, P_m = 0.005, l=2, i_a =2. Same results were obtained when varying the number of generations N or the population size P (TPR = Accuracy = Specificity = 100%, and no false positive: FPR = 0).

The results presented in Table 6 show the influence of the rate P_m on the different evaluating measures. For a mutation rate P_m = 0.005, we obtain a rate of attacks successfully detected equal to 100% and no false positives. The same results were observed with a value of P_m = 0.006. However, when the rate increased more (P_m = 0.05) results deteriorated: we have only a 15% rate of attacks detected successfully and no false positives have been reported. Furthermore, we observe that the system does not detect the introduced attacks when the mutation process is not used. Therefore, the mutation process is important for the good performance of our system in terms of detection. We retain the default value which is 0.005.

Table 6. Influence of the mutation rate (P_m) on the performance of the system

P_m	TPR	FPR	Precision	Accuracy	TNR
0	0	0	-	98%	100%
0.005	100%	0%	100%	100%	100%
0.006	100%	0%	100%	100%	100%
0.05	15%	0%	-	98.4%	100%

As for elitism, once again, it has no effect on the system performance.

When testing the effect of the number i_a of injected attacks on the performance measures of the system, we observed that for a small number of attacks injected into the file we got over 10 executions an average TPR value greater than 90% and FPR= 0%. However, when the number of injected attacks increases, we observe a deterioration of TPR and FPR values. TPR rate stabilizes at 70% and FPR is between 2% and 20%. Some results are given in the following Table 8.

Table 7. Influence of the number of injected attacks (i_a) on the performance of the system

i_a	TPR	FPR	Precision	Accuracy	TNR
0	--	0%	-	100%	100%
2	100%	0%	100%	100%	100%
10	90%	2.2%	0%	97.77%	97%
15	74%	6.3%	0%	90.5%	92.7%

Furthermore, we note that the execution is very fast, the running time is: 565.5ms

5.3 BBO-Based Approach vs. GA-Based Approach

A comparison of the biogeography approach with the genetic approach [27] is made using the same real data (28x24 matrix EA audit trails). In the genetic approach, a number of individuals P=500 and 100 generations were needed to reach (on average over 10 runs) TPR= 99.5% and FPR=0.43%, while in the biogeography approach we obtained better results: TPR = 100% and FPR = 0%, with the parameter values: N = 100, P = 500, P_m = 0.002, l =2, i_a = 2.

When increasing the number of injected attacks, AG-based approach shows even worst results as shown in Table 8.

Table 8. Biogeography-based approach vs GA-based approach

Approach/Measures	TPR	FPR
GA-based	91.5%	2.75%
BBO-based	100%	0%

6 Conclusion

In this paper, we proposed a biogeography-based approach for a detection intrusion system based on a simplified analysis of the audit file. The evaluation of the performance measures performed on real audit trails and signature databases then on large instances that were randomly generated, showed good results and even better than the results obtained in the Genetic Algorithm approach. Another important result is the consistency of performance, regardless of the number of attacks actually present in the matrix of audit analysis. This means that if many attacks occur, the detection system performance is not deteriorated. Similarly, if no attack is launched, it does not detect anything. The processing time is very satisfactory. This allows us to consider building an intrusion detection tool based on BBO approach.

References

1. Amoroso, E.: Intrusion Detection. In: Intrusion.net Books (1999)
2. Mé, L., Alanou, V.: Détection d'Intrusion dans un Système Informatique: Méthodes et Outils. TSI 4, 429–450 (1996)
3. Allen, J., Christie, A., Fithen, W., McHugh, J., Pickel, J., Stoner, E.: State of the Practice of Intrusion Detection Technologies. Technical Report CMU/SEI99 - TR-028. ESC-99-028, Carnegie Mellon, Software Engineering Institute, Pittsburgh Pennsylvania (1999)
4. Axelsson, S.: Intrusion Detection Systems: A Survey and Taxonomy. Technical Report No 99-15, Dept. of Computer Engineering, Chalmers University of Technology, Sweden (2000)
5. Evangelista, T.: Les IDS: Les Systèmes de Détection d'Intrusion Informatique. Edition DUNOD (2004)
6. Lunt, T.: Detecting Intruders in Computer Systems. In: Proceedings of the Sixth Annual Symposium and Technical Displays on Physical and Electronic Security (1990)
7. Majorczyk, F.: Détection d'Intrusions Comportementale par Diversification de COTS: Application au Cas des Serveurs Web. Thèse de Doctorat de l'Université de Rennes 1-N° d'ordre 3827 (2008)
8. Tombini, E.: Amélioration du Diagnostic en Détection d'Intrusions: Etude et Application d'une Combinaison de Méthodes Comportementale et par Scénarios. Thèse de Doctorat de l'Institut National des Sciences Appliquées de Rennes (2006)
9. Cannady, J.: Artificial Neural Networks for Misuse Detection. In: National Information Systems Security Conference, pp. 368–381 (1998)
10. Debar, H., Dorizzi, B.: An Application of a Recurrent Network to an Intrusion Detection System. In: Proceedings of the International Joint Conference on Neural Networks, pp. 78–83 (1992)
11. Debar, H., Becke, B., Siboni, D.: A Neural Network Component for an Intrusion Detection System. In: Proceedings of the IEEE Computer Society Symposium on Research in Security and Privacy, pp. 240–250 (1992)
12. Mukkamala, S., Sung, A.: Feature Selection for Intrusion Detection Using Neural Networks and Support Vector Machines. Journal of the Transport Research Board National Academy, Transport Research Record (1822), 33–39 (2003)
13. Riedmiller, M., Braun, H.: A Direct Adaptive Method for Faster Back Propagation Learning: the RPROP algorithm. In: Proceedings of the IEEE International Conference on Neural Networks, San Francisco (1993)

14. Dasgupta, D., González, F.: An Immunity-Based Technique to Characterize Intrusions in Computer Networks. IEEE Transactions on Evolutionary Computation 6(3) (2002)
15. Harmer, H., Williams, P., Gunsch, G., Lamont, G.: An Artificial Immune System Architecture for Computer Security Applications. IEEE Transactions on Evolutionary Computation 6(3) (2002)
16. Yang, X.R., Shen, J.Y., Wang, R.: Artificial Immune Theory Based Network Intrusion Detection System and the Algorithms Design. In: Proceedings of 2002 International Conference on Machine Learning and Cybernetics, Beijing, pp. 73–77 (2002)
17. Saniee Abadeh, M., Habibi, J., Lucas, C.: Intrusion Detection Using a Fuzzy Genetics-Based Learning Algorithm. Journal of Network and Computer Applications, 414–428 (2007)
18. Ozyer, T., Alhajj, R., Barker, K.: Intrusion Detection by Integrating Boosting Genetic Fuzzy Classifier and Data Mining Criteria for Rule Pre-screening. Journal of Network and Computer Applications 30, 99–113 (2007)
19. Cha, C.S., Sad, S.: Web Session Anomaly Detection Based on Parameter Estimation. Computers & Security 23(4), 265–351 (2004)
20. Xu, B., Zhang, A.: Application of Support Vector Clustering Algorithm to Network Intrusion Detection. In: International Conference on Neural Networks and Brain, ICNN&B 2005, October 13-15, vol. 2, pp. 1036–1040 (2005)
21. Sh, O., Ws, L.: An Anomaly Intrusion Detection Method by Clustering Normal User Behavior. Computers & Security 22(7), 596–612 (2003)
22. Xu, B., Zhang, A.: Application of Support Vector Clustering Algorithm to Network Intrusion Detection. In: International Conference on Neural Networks and Brain, ICNN&B 2005, October 13-15, vol. 2, pp. 1036–1040 (2005)
23. Leon, E., Nasraoui, O., Gomez, J.: Anomaly Detection Based on Unsupervised Niche Clustering with Application to Network Intrusion Detection. In: Proceedings of IEEE Conference on Evolutionary Computation (CEC), pp. 502–508 (2004)
24. Guan, Y., Ghorbani, A., Belacel, N.: Y-MEANS: a Clustering Method for Intrusion Detection. In: Canadian Conference on Electrical and Computer Engineering, pp. 1083–1086 (2003)
25. Lee, W., Salvatore, J., Mok, K.: Mining Audit Data to Build Intrusion Detection Models. In: Proceedings of ACM SIGKDD International Conference on Knowledge Discovery and Data Mining, pp. 66–72 (1998)
26. Dass, M.: LIDS: A Learning Intrusion Detection System. Master of Science, The University of Georgia, Athens, Georgia (2003)
27. Me, L.: GASSATA, A Genetic Algorithm as an Alternative Tool for Security Audit Trails Analysis. In: Proceedings of the 1st International Workshop on the Recent Advances in Intrusion Detection (RAID 1998), Louvain-la-Neuve, Belgium, pp. 14–16 (1998)
28. Mé, L.: Audit de Sécurité par Algorithmes Génétiques. Thèse de Doctorat de l'Institut de Formation Superieure en Informatique et Communication DE Rennes (1994)
29. Simon, D.: Biogeography-Based Optimization. IEEE Trans. on Evol. Comput. 12(6), 712–713 (2008)
30. Wallace, A.: The Geographical Distribution of Animals, vol. 2. Adamant Media Corporation, Boston (2005)
31. Darwin, C.: The Origin of Species. Gramercy, New York (1995)
32. MacArthur, R., Wilson, E.: The Theory of Biogeography. Princeton Univ. Press, Princeton (1967)
33. Wu, S., Banzhaf, W.: The Use of Computational Intelligence in Intrusion Detection Systems: A Review. Computer Science Department, Memorial University of Newfoundland, St John's, NL A1B 3X5, Canada (2008)

Communications in Computer and Information Science: Computational Approaches for Optimization of Sport Rim Parameters

Rahmat Mohd Aris, Azlan Mohd Zain[*], and Mohd Ridhwan Hilmi Mohd Adnan

Department of Modeling and Industrial Computing,
Faculty of Computer Science & Information System,
Universiti Teknologi Malaysia, 81310 Skudai, Johor, Malaysia
azlanmz@utm.my

Abstract. This study considers two computational approaches, mastercam simulation and genetic algorithm (GA) optimization, to estimate the optimal process parameters that lead to the minimum production time of sport rim. The considered process parameters include feed rate, pitch rate, pull rate and spindle speed which represent the fitness function. The results showed that the minimum production time estimated by mastercam and GA are 91.03 and 70.99 minutes, respectively. Subsequently, GA has reduced the minimum production time of mastercam by about 22%.

Keywords: GA optimization, mastercam simulation, minimum production time.

1 Introduction

It is important to estimate optimal process parameters that lead to a minimum production time. Process parameters such as feed rate, pull rate, spindle speed and pitch rate will be optimized in order to make the machining process finish in exceptional time. Traditionally, the machine operators play the major role in selecting the optimal parameters of the cutting conditions so, operator with skill and experience is needed. But in some cases, skilled operators have a hard time to attain optimal process parameters [1]. Alternative to the actual experiment trials, optimization process through computational approaches such as GA are recommended to present the optimal solutions [2-6].

By looking at previous studies, it was found that optimization for optimal process parameters of sport rim design using the GA technique is still lacking. Extending of mastercam simulation, this study considers GA to optimize the process parameters of sport rim design. It was targeted that the GA could estimate a much lower production time when compared to the results of mastercam simulation.

2 Mastercam Solution

The experimental data is a simulation result that was conducted by Rahim [7]. In the experiment, 120 trials were executed in order to find the best process parameters that

---

[*] Corresponding author.

A. Abd Manaf et al. (Eds.): ICIEIS 2011, Part II, CCIS 252, pp. 228–238, 2011.

will return a minimum production time. The experimental trial is executed using mastercam software based on cutting simulation as shown Figure 1. The classification of the process parameters is given in Table 1. Table 2 shows the production time of mastercam simulation and regression model.

Fig. 1. Cutting Simulation

Table 1. Process parameters classification

Process parameters	Lowest	Highest	Average
Feed rate (mm/min)	500	1080	722.5
Spindle speed (RPM)	1600	4500	3012.5
Pitch rate (RPM)	20	165	72.63
Pull rate (mm/min)	600	2050	1306.25

Table 2. Production time of mastercam simulation and regression model

Feed rate (mm/min)	Spindle speed (RPM)	Pitch rate (RPM)	Pull rate (mm/min)	Production time (min)	
				mastercam	regression
500	3000	70	1300	181.93	164.837
520	3000	70	1300	175.43	162.017
540	3000	70	1300	169.4	159.197
560	3000	70	1300	163.8	156.377
580	3000	70	1300	158.6	153.557

Table 2. (*Continued*)

600	3000	70	1300	153.73	150.737
620	3000	70	1300	149.18	147.917
640	3000	70	1300	144.92	145.097
660	3000	70	1300	140.9	142.277
680	3000	70	1300	137.13	139.457
700	3000	70	1300	133.58	136.637
720	3000	70	1300	130.22	133.817
740	3000	70	1300	127.05	130.997
760	3000	70	1300	124.03	128.177
780	3000	70	1300	121.18	125.357
800	3000	70	1300	118.47	122.537
820	3000	70	1300	115.88	119.717
840	3000	70	1300	113.43	116.897
860	3000	70	1300	111.08	114.077
880	3000	70	1300	108.85	111.257
900	3000	70	1300	106.72	108.437
920	3000	70	1300	104.67	105.617
940	3000	70	1300	102.72	102.797
960	3000	70	1300	100.83	99.977
980	3000	70	1300	99.03	97.157
1000	3000	70	1300	97.3	94.337
1020	3000	70	1300	95.65	91.517
1040	3000	70	1300	94.05	88.697
1060	3000	70	1300	92.52	85.877
1080	3000	70	1300	91.03	83.057
700	3000	20	1300	157.82	142.987
700	3000	25	1300	151	142.352
700	3000	30	1300	146.56	141.717
700	3000	35	1300	143.2	141.082
700	3000	40	1300	140.77	140.447
700	3000	45	1300	138.88	139.812
700	3000	50	1300	137.37	139.177
700	3000	55	1300	136.12	138.542
700	3000	60	1300	135.08	137.907

Table 2. (*Continued*)

700	3000	65	1300	134.22	137.272
700	3000	70	1300	133.47	136.637
700	3000	75	1300	132.82	136.002
700	3000	80	1300	132.25	135.367
700	3000	85	1300	131.75	134.732
700	3000	90	1300	131.3	134.097
700	3000	95	1300	130.9	133.462
700	3000	100	1300	130.55	132.827
700	3000	105	1300	130.22	132.192
700	3000	110	1300	129.92	131.557
700	3000	115	1300	129.65	130.922
700	3000	120	1300	129.4	130.287
700	3000	125	1300	129.18	129.652
700	3000	130	1300	128.97	129.017
700	3000	135	1300	128.78	128.382
700	3000	140	1300	128.6	127.747
700	3000	145	1300	128.43	127.112
700	3000	150	1300	128.27	126.477
700	3000	155	1300	128.12	125.842
700	3000	160	1300	127.98	125.207
700	3000	165	1300	127.85	124.572
700	3000	70	600	134	136.637
700	3000	70	650	133.93	136.637
700	3000	70	700	133.88	136.637
700	3000	70	750	133.85	136.637
700	3000	70	800	133.8	136.637
700	3000	70	850	133.77	136.637
700	3000	70	900	133.73	136.637
700	3000	70	950	133.72	136.637
700	3000	70	1000	133.68	136.637
700	3000	70	1050	133.67	136.637
700	3000	70	1100	133.65	136.637
700	3000	70	1150	133.63	136.637
700	3000	70	1200	133.62	136.637

Table 2. (*Continued*)

700	3000	70	1250	133.6	136.637
700	3000	70	1300	133.58	136.637
700	3000	70	1350	133.57	136.637
700	3000	70	1400	133.55	136.637
700	3000	70	1450	133.53	136.637
700	3000	70	1500	133.53	136.637
700	3000	70	1550	133.52	136.637
700	3000	70	1600	133.52	136.637
700	3000	70	1650	133.5	136.637
700	3000	70	1700	133.5	136.637
700	3000	70	1750	133.48	136.637
700	3000	70	1800	133.48	136.637
700	3000	70	1850	133.47	136.637
700	3000	70	1900	133.47	136.637
700	3000	70	1950	133.45	136.637
700	3000	70	2000	133.45	136.637
700	3000	70	2050	133.45	136.637
700	1600	70	1300	133.58	136.637
700	1700	70	1300	133.58	136.637
700	1800	70	1300	133.58	136.637
700	1900	70	1300	133.58	136.637
700	2000	70	1300	133.58	136.637
700	2100	70	1300	133.58	136.637
700	2200	70	1300	133.58	136.637
700	2300	70	1300	133.58	136.637
700	2400	70	1300	133.58	136.637
700	2500	70	1300	133.58	136.637
700	2600	70	1300	133.58	136.637
700	2700	70	1300	133.58	136.637
700	2800	70	1300	133.58	136.637
700	2900	70	1300	133.58	136.637
700	3000	70	1300	133.58	136.637
700	3100	70	1300	133.58	136.637
700	3200	70	1300	133.58	136.637

Table 2. (*Continued*)

700	3300	70	1300	133.58	136.637
700	3400	70	1300	133.58	136.637
700	3500	70	1300	133.58	136.637
700	3600	70	1300	133.58	136.637
700	3700	70	1300	133.58	136.637
700	3800	70	1300	133.58	136.637
700	3900	70	1300	133.58	136.637
700	4000	70	1300	133.58	136.637
700	4100	70	1300	133.58	136.637
700	4200	70	1300	133.58	136.637
700	4300	70	1300	133.58	136.637
700	4400	70	1300	133.58	136.637
700	4500	70	1300	133.58	136.637
			minimum	91.03	83.057

3 Regression Modeling

The mastercam simulation production time measurement of sport rim can be expressed mathematically as follow:

$$y = b_0x_0 + b_1x_1 + b_2x_2 + b_3x_3 + b_4x_4 + \varepsilon \qquad (1)$$

where y is the logarithmic value of production time, b_0, b_1, b_2, b_3, b_4 are process parameters values, x_0 is a constant (k), and x_1, x_2, x_3, x_4 are process parameter of feed rate, spindle speed, pitch rate and pull rate respectively. ε is the logarithmic transformation of experimental error.

Next, Equation (1) can be written as follow:

$$\hat{y} = y - \varepsilon = b_0x_0 + b_1x_1 + b_2x_2 + b_3x_3 + b_4x_4 \qquad (2)$$

where $\hat{y}$ is the logarithmic value of the predictive production time. This equation is required as fitness function for GA optimization. By using SPSS software, the regression model is generated based on the combination of process parameter values given in Table 2. The generated regression model parameters are shown in Table 3.

Based on Table 3, the regression model for predicted production time can be written as follow:

$$\hat{y} = 244.227 - 0.141x_1 - 0x_2 - 0.127x_3 - 0x_4 \qquad (3)$$

Thus can be simplified as:

$$\hat{y} = 244.227 - 0.141x_1 - 0.127x_3 \qquad (4)$$

Equation (4) shows that feed rate and pitch rate give major impact for production time. By using the Equation (4), the prediction production time is calculated as shown in Table 2. The predicted production time of regression model and experimental time of mastercam are compared and as shown in Figure 2.

Table 3. Coefficient value

Model	Unstandardized Coefficients		Standardized Coefficients		
	B	Std. error	Beta	t	Sig.
k	244.227	4.591		53.199	.000
Feed rate	-.141	.004	-.949	-36.663	.000
Spindle speed	.000	.001	-.004	-.156	.877
Pitch rate	-.127	.015	-.214	-8.256	.000
Pull rate	.000	.002	-.009	-.350	.727

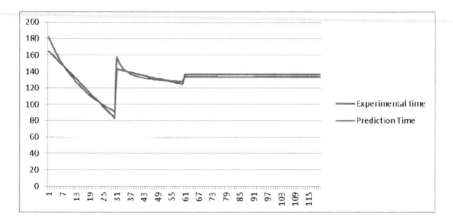

Fig. 2. Results of regression (prediction) vs. mastercam (experimental)

Table 4. Statistic and correlation between mastercam and regression results

Variable	Mean	N	Std. dev.	Std.error mean	Cor.	Sig.
Mastercam	131.66	120	14.16	1.29	0.961	.000
Regression	132.75	120	13.61	1.24		

As shown in Figure 2, the pattern of prediction time is likely same as the mastercam simulation time. It means that the regression model, Equation (4), gives good prediction in estimating the production time. The proof to support this assumption is shown in Table 4, which is regression model and mastercam simulation results are positively correlated (0.961). Subsequently, Equation (4) is considered to be a fitness function of the GA optimization.

4   GA Optimization

GA is based on mechanics of natural selection and natural genetics, which are more robust and more likely to locate global optimum. It is because of this feature that GA goes through solution space starting from a group of points and not from a single point. Before starting the optimization process, the fitness function needs to clearly be identified. Fitness function is required for selecting next generation in GA. Optimum results of process parameters are obtained by comparison of values of objective functions among all individuals after a number of iterations. Figure 3 shows the flow of the GA execution in order to search optimal solution.

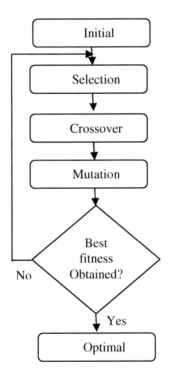

Fig. 3. GA Process Flow

Upper and lower limit values of optimization constraints are defined based on the process parameters classification that is given in Table 1. Considering the predicted regression model, equation (4), the minimization of production time is subjected to the following constraints:

$$500 \leq x_1 \leq 1080 \tag{5}$$

$$20 \leq x_3 \leq 165 \tag{6}$$

In order to find the best optimal solution, numerous trial and error procedures need to be executed. Each trial will consider different values of GA operators. GA operators such as population size, crossover rate and mutation rate must be taken into account. The combinations of the operators' values must be suitable in order to find the optimal solution. In this study, the best combination for the GA operators is shown in Table 5.

Table 5. Combination of GA Operators

Operator	Value
Population Size	100
Crossover	0.8
Mutation	0.7

GA optimization in this study is executed by using Mathlab Toolbox. By using fitness function, Equation (4), and constraints, equations (5) equation (6), the optimal solution is successfully generated as shown in Figure 4.

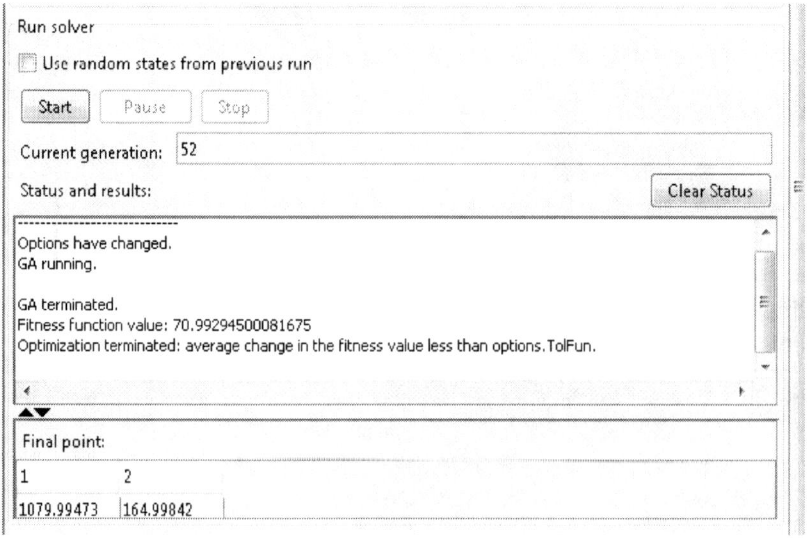

Fig. 4. Matlab Toolbox Result

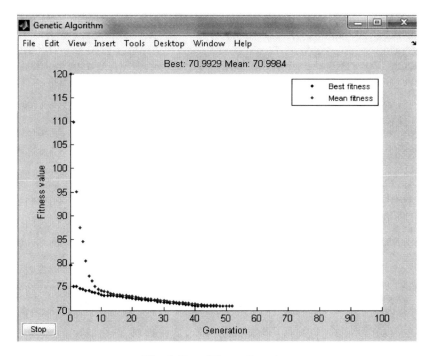

Fig. 5. Plot of Fitness Function

From Figure 4, the optimal solution is obtained at the 52nd iteration. The minimum production time is 70.9929 minutes. The optimal process parameters recommended by GA are 1079.99473mm/min for feed rate and 164.99842mm/min for pitch rate. Figure 5 shows that the mean fitness value is 70.9984 minutes and the best fitness value is 70.9929 minutes.

5   Result Summary and Conclusion

The result that has been obtained from GA optimization are summarised in Table 6. From Table 6, it was obtained that GA has given a much lower minimum production time compared to mastercam simulation and regression model results. GA has reduced the production time value of mastercam and regression by about 22% and 15% respectively. Therefore, it clearly shows that GA has given most significant result.

Table 6. Summary of Study Result

Approaches	Minimum production time (min)
mastercam	91.03
Regression	83.06
GA	70.9929

Acknowledgments. Special appreciative to reviewer(s) for useful advices and comments. The authors greatly acknowledge the Research Management Centre (RMC) Universiti Teknologi Malaysia and Ministry of Higher Education (MOHE) for financial support through the Research University Grant (RUG) No. Q.J130000.7128.01J34.

References

1. Sorace, R.E., Reinhardt, V.S., Vaughn, S.A.: High-speed digital-to-RF converter, U.S. Patent 5 668 842, September 16 (1997)
2. Zain, A.M., Haron, H., Sharif, S.: Estimation of the minimum machining performance in the abrasive waterjet machining using integrated ANN-SA. Expert System with Applications 38(7), 4650–4659 (2011)
3. Zain, A.M., Haron, H., Sharif, S.: Integration of Simulated Annealing and Genetic Algorithm to estimate optimal solutions for minimizing surface roughness in end milling Ti-6AL-4V. International Journal of Computer Integrated Manufacturing 24(6), 574–592 (2011)
4. Zain, A.M., Haron, H., Sharif, S.: Prediction of surface roughness in the end milling machining using Artificial Neural Network. Expert Systems with Applications 37, 1755–1768 (2010)
5. Zain, A.M., Haron, H., Sharif, S.: Application of GA to optimize cutting conditions for minimizing surface roughness in end milling machining process. Expert Systems with Applications 37, 4650–4659 (2010)
6. Zain, A.M., Haron, H., Sharif, S.: Simulated Annealing to estimate the optimal cutting conditions for minimizing surface roughness in end milling Ti-6Al-4V. Machining Science and Technology 14, 43–62 (2010)
7. Rahim, N.H.: Pengoptimuman Penggunaan Mata Alat Mesin Kawalan Berangka Bagi Penghasilan produk Sport Rim. First Degree Thesis, Universiti Teknologi Malaysia, Skudai (2002)

Estimating Minimum Processing Time of Liquid Crystal Display Monitor Hinge in 2D Contouring Machining

Muhammad Firdaus Azman, Nur Asyikin Mohamad Halimin, and Azlan Mohd Zain[*]

Department of Modeling and Industrial Computing,
Faculty of Computer Science & Information System,
Universiti Teknologi Malaysia, 81310 Skudai, Johor, Malaysia
azlanmz@utm.my

Abstract. This study considers mastercam simulation and genetic algorithm optimization to estimate a minimum processing time value of liquid crystal display monitor hinge in two-dimensional (2D) contouring machining. Regression model is developed to formulate the fitness function equation of GA optimization. This study found that GA is capable to estimate the optimal cutting conditions value to minimize the processing time. With high feed rate, high spindle speed rate, high pitch rate and low pull rate of the machining parameter, GA recommended 349.3916 seconds as the minimum processing time. Consequently, GA has reduced the minimum processing time of mastercam simulation by about 6.58 %.

Keywords: process parameters, liquid crystal, optimization.

1 Introduction

Optimisation of process parameters is an important step in machining, particularly for operating CNC machine tools [1]. Conventionally, the optimal process parameters are presented based on experiences and machining handbooks [2]. Unfortunately, the decision was not always the most optimized one because of the constraints. GA is a family of computational approach inspired by evolution. This algorithm encodes a potential solution to a specific problem for recommending optimal process parameters [3,4,5,6,7]. This paper discusses the application of GA to generate the optimal process parameters to minimize the processing time of 2D contouring machining of LCD monitor hinge.

2 Experimental Data

The mastercam simulation was conducted by Din, 2004 [8]. LCD monitor hinge was used as an experiment product and the architecture design of product is shown in Fig 1. 120 experimental trials were executed to find the minimum processing time. According to design of experiment, range of machining process parameters value is given in Table 1. The processing time generated by mastercam simulation is given in Table 2.

---

[*] Corresponding author.

A. Abd Manaf et al. (Eds.): ICIEIS 2011, Part II, CCIS 252, pp. 239–249, 2011.
© Springer-Verlag Berlin Heidelberg 2011

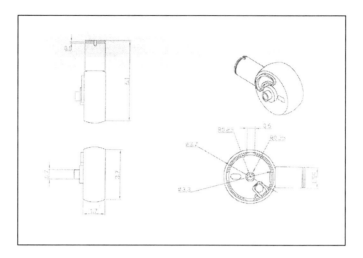

Fig. 1. Architecture design of LCD Monitor Hinge [5]

Table 1. Range of Machining Parameters Values

Cutting Conditions	Low	High
Feed rate	400	690
Spindle speed	1000	3900
Pitch rate	150	440
Pull rate	200	780

Table 2. Processing Time for MasterCAM Simulation and Regression Model

Process parameters				Processing time	
Feed rate (mm/min)	Spindle speed (rmp)	Pitch rate (mm/min)	Pull rate (mm/min)	Mastercam	Regression
400	2000	300	500	535	508
410	2000	300	500	525	503
420	2000	300	500	516	498
430	2000	300	500	508	493
440	2000	300	500	500	488
450	2000	300	500	492	483
460	2000	300	500	530	478
470	2000	300	500	478	473
480	2000	300	500	471	468
490	2000	300	500	464	463
500	2000	300	500	458	458

Table 2. (*Continued*)

510	2000	300	500	452	452
520	2000	300	500	446	447
530	2000	300	500	441	442
540	2000	300	500	436	437
550	2000	300	500	430	432
560	2000	300	500	470	427
570	2000	300	500	430	422
580	2000	300	500	416	417
590	2000	300	500	412	412
600	2000	300	500	407	407
610	2000	300	500	403	402
620	2000	300	500	399	397
630	2000	300	500	395	392
640	2000	300	500	391	387
650	2000	300	500	388	382
660	2000	300	500	384	377
670	2000	300	500	380	372
680	2000	300	500	377	367
690	2000	300	500	374	362
500	1000	300	500	452	460
500	1100	300	500	452	460
500	1200	300	500	452	460
500	1300	300	500	452	459
500	1400	300	500	452	459
500	1500	300	500	452	459
500	1600	300	500	452	459
500	1700	300	500	452	458
500	1800	300	500	452	458
500	1900	300	500	452	458
500	2000	300	500	452	458
500	2100	300	500	452	457
500	2200	300	500	452	457
500	2300	300	500	452	457
500	2400	300	500	452	456
500	2500	300	500	452	456
500	2600	300	500	452	456
500	2700	300	500	452	456
500	2800	300	500	452	455
500	2900	300	500	452	455
500	3000	300	500	452	455
500	3100	300	500	452	455
500	3200	300	500	452	454
500	3300	300	500	452	454
500	3400	300	500	452	454

Table 2. (*Continued*)

500	3500	300	500	452	454
500	3600	300	500	452	453
500	3700	300	500	452	453
500	3800	300	500	452	453
500	3900	300	500	452	453
500	2000	150	500	469	466
500	2000	160	500	468	465
500	2000	170	500	467	465
500	2000	180	500	466	464
500	2000	190	500	465	463
500	2000	200	500	464	463
500	2000	210	500	463	462
500	2000	220	500	462	462
500	2000	230	500	462	461
500	2000	240	500	461	461
500	2000	250	500	460	460
500	2000	260	500	460	460
500	2000	270	500	459	459
500	2000	280	500	459	459
500	2000	290	500	458	458
500	2000	300	500	458	458
500	2000	310	500	457	457
500	2000	320	500	457	456
500	2000	330	500	456	456
500	2000	340	500	456	455
500	2000	350	500	456	455
500	2000	360	500	455	454
500	2000	370	500	455	454
500	2000	380	500	455	453
500	2000	390	500	454	453
500	2000	400	500	454	452
500	2000	410	500	454	452
500	2000	420	500	453	451
500	2000	430	500	453	451
500	2000	440	500	453	450
500	2000	300	200	452	457
500	2000	300	220	452	457
500	2000	300	240	452	457
500	2000	300	260	452	457
500	2000	300	280	452	457
500	2000	300	300	452	457
500	2000	300	320	452	457
500	2000	300	340	452	457
500	2000	300	360	452	457

Table 2. (*Continued*)

500	2000	300	380	452	457
500	2000	300	400	452	457
500	2000	300	420	452	457
500	2000	300	440	452	457
500	2000	300	460	452	457
500	2000	300	480	452	457
500	2000	300	500	452	458
500	2000	300	520	452	458
500	2000	300	540	452	458
500	2000	300	560	452	458
500	2000	300	580	452	458
500	2000	300	600	452	458
500	2000	300	620	452	458
500	2000	300	640	452	458
500	2000	300	660	452	458
500	2000	300	680	452	458
500	2000	300	700	452	458
500	2000	300	720	452	458
500	2000	300	740	452	458
500	2000	300	760	452	458
500	2000	300	780	452	458
			Minimum	374	362.344
			Maximum	535	507.591
			Average	451.642	451.641

3 Regression Modeling

The mathematical equation to develop the regression model for estimating the processing time is given in Equation (1):

$$f = a+b_1x_1+b_2x_2+b_3x_3+b_4x_4 \tag{1}$$

where f is the processing time value, a is constant value of Regression model, b_1,b_2,b_3 and b_4 are the model parameters to be estimated using the experimental data, x_1 is feed rate value, x_2 is spindle speed rate value, x_3 is pitch rate values and x_4 is pull rate value.

Coefficients values for model parameters of 2D contour machining process are given in Table 3. By transferring the values of coefficients values for each machining parameters (independent variable) from Table 3 into equation (1), the Regression model equation can be written as follows:

$$f =728.368-0.501x_1-0.003x_2-0.054x_3+0.002x_4 \tag{2}$$

The Equation (2) is applied to calculate the predicted processing time values, and the results are summarized in Table 2, in the last column, "Processing time (s) (Regression)". Subsequently, this equation will be proposed as the objective function of the optimization solution.

Table 3. Coefficients Values

Independent Variable	Unstandardized Coefficients		Standardized Coefficients	t	Sig.
	B	Std. Error	Beta		
(Constant)	728.368	11.882		61.300	.000
Feed Rate	-.501	.017	-.937	-29.658	.000
Spindle Speed	-.003	.002	-.049	-1.542	.126
Pitch Rate	-.054	.018	-.092	-2.914	.004
Pull Rate	.002	.009	.006	.198	.843

Next, the values of experimental data and predicted values of the Regression model are compared as shown in Fig. 2.

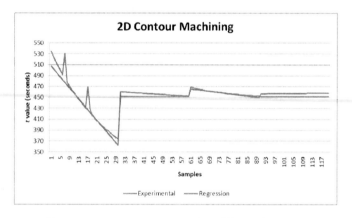

Fig. 2. Experimental vs. Regression of Processing Time

From the Fig. 2, the generated graph shown that the predicted values from Regression Model and experimental data have a similar pattern. To support the result from Fig. 2, the paired sample t test using SPSS software is conducted and results are summarized in Table 4 and Table 5.

Table 4. Statistics and Correlations

Variable	Mean	N	Std. Dev.	Std. Error Mean	Cor.	Sig.
Exp. Data	451.642	120	25.467	2.325		
Reg. Model	451.642	120	24.140	2.204	0.941	0.00

Table 5. Paired Samples Test

Pair	Paired Differences					t	df	Sig. (2-tailed)
	Mean	Std. Devia-tion	Std. Error Mean	95% Confidence Interval of the Difference				
				Lower	Upper			
Exp. – Reg.	0.000	8.590	0.784	-1.553	1.553	0.00	119	1.00

Table 4 shows that both of the data are positively correlated with $r(N=120) = 0.941$. From Table 5, for both of the data there are no difference in value of mean, $t(119) = 0.00$, $p=1.00$. The 95% confidence interval ranges from -1.553 to 1.533 (including zero). From these two tables, the result concluded that Equation (2) is recommended to be a fitness function of the GA optimization.

4 GA Optimization

GA is a technique for solving constrained and unconstrained optimization problems based on natural selection. Fig. 3 shows the flow chart that illustrates how the GA technique works to optimize a problem. The GA algorithm begins with a set of potential solution, chromosomes. The chromosomes are comprised with randomly selected populations. It evolves during several generations. By utilizing the crossover and mutation technique, the new generations or called as offspring are generated. The

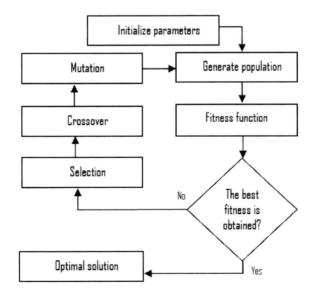

Fig. 3. The Flow of GA Optimization

process of splitting two chromosomes and then combining one-half of each chromosome with the other pair is called as crossover. Mutation involves the process of flipping a chromosome. The GA repeatedly modifies a population of individual solutions. The GA selects individuals randomly from the current population to be parents and generate children for the next generation using selected parents. Over successive generations, the population evolves toward an optimal solution.

Subjected to four process parameters, Equation (2) that is taken as the objective function is written as follows:

$$\text{Minimize: } f(x_1, x_2, x_3, x_4) \tag{3}$$

$$= 728.368 - 0.501x_1 - 0.003x_2 - 0.054x_3 + 0.002x_4$$

The minimization of fitness function value of the Equation (3) is subjected to the boundaries of the machining parameters values. The range values of experimental data given in Table 2 are selected to present the limitations of the optimization solution and given as follow:

$$400 \leq x_1 \leq 690 \tag{4a}$$

$$1000 \leq x_2 \leq 3900 \tag{4b}$$

$$150 \leq x_3 \leq 440 \tag{4c}$$

$$200 \leq x_4 \leq 780 \tag{4d}$$

To obtain the best optimal results, it depends on some factor or criteria. The number of initial population size, the type of selection, the crossover rate and the mutation rate are the major factors that influencing the value of optimal result. These values of parameters setting are set by trial and error to obtain the most optimal result value. The optimal result is generated using MATLAB Optimization Toolbox. Several trials have been conducted to find the most optimal result for minimizing processing time, and the best combination of GA parameters is shown in Table 6.

Table 6. Coefficient Values

Parameters	Setting values
Population size	210
Mutation Rate	1.0
Crossover Rate	0.8

Considering the fitness function in Equation (3), the limitations of machining parameters formulated in Equation (4a), (4b), (4c) and (4d), the best optimal is shown in Fig. 4 and Fig.5. From Fig. 4, the observed minimum processing time is 349.3916 seconds. The values of machining parameters that leads to the minimum processing time are 689.942mm/min for feed rate, 3899.833rmp for spindle speed, 439.986mm/min for pitch rate and 255.973mm/min for pull rate. From Fig.3, the optimal solution is obtained at the 51st iterations of GA. From Fig. 4, the minimum fitness function value is 349.3916 seconds.

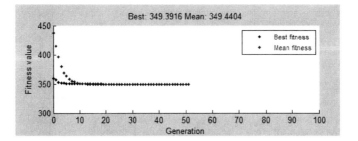

Fig. 4. Results of the MATLAB Optimization Toolbox

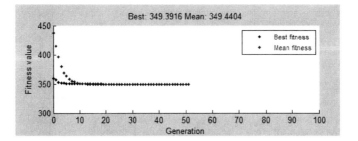

Fig. 5. Plot Functions of the Best Fitness

5   The Evolution of GA Results

Theoretically, to validate the result of the optimal machining parameters values that obtained from GA optimization, these values will be transferred into the Equation (2). With, x_1 is optimal solution value for feed rate, x_2 is optimal solution value for spindle speed rate value, x_3 is optimal solution pitch rate values and x_4 is optimal solution pull rate value, the solution is given as follows:

$$f = 728.368-0.501x_1-0.003x_2-0.054x_3+0.002x_4$$

$$=728.368-0.501(689.942)-0.003(3899.833)$$
$$0.054(439.986)+0.002(255.973)$$

$$=349.3916$$

By transferring the optimal machining parameters values of GA into the best Regression model, it was obtained that the predicted processing time value is 349.3916. This value is compared to the minimum fitness function value of the GA. This value is exactly same as objective function value as shown in Fig. 4.

6 Conclusion

The objective of the optimization process in this study is to determine the optimal values of machining parameters that could lead to the minimum processing time as low as possible. The results of GA compared to regression and mastercam are summarized in Table 7. The minimum processing time of mastercam, regression and GA are 374 seconds, 362.344 seconds, 349.392 seconds respectively. Subsequently, GA reduced the processing time value of mastercam and regression by about 6.58% and 3.57% respectively. Therefore, GA has been the effective technique for estimating the minimum processing time compared to mastercam and regression.

Table 7. Summary of the GA results

Technique	Minimum processing time
Matercam	374
Regression	362.344
GA result	349.392

Acknowledgments. Special appreciative to reviewer(s) for useful advices and comments. The authors greatly acknowledge the Research Management Centre (RMC) Universiti Teknologi Malaysia and Ministry of Higher Education (MOHE) for financial support through the Research University Grant (RUG) No. Q.J130000.7128.01J34.

References

1. Gilbert, W.W.: Economics of machining. Machining Theory and Practice, American Society of Metals (1950)
2. Zhao, X.: Study on numerical machining parameters optimization. Industry University of Shenyang (2006)
3. Zain, A.M., Haron, H., Sharif, S.: Application of GA to optimize cutting conditions for minimizing surface in end milling machining process. Expert Systems with Applications 37, 4650–4659 (2010)
4. Zain, A.M., Haron, H., Sharif, S.: Integration of simulated annealing and genetic algorithm to estimate optimal solutions for minimizing surface roughness in end milling Ti-6AL-4V. International Journal of Computer Integrated Manufacturing 24(6), 574–592 (2011)
5. Zain, A.M., Haron, H., Sharif, S.: Integrated ANN-GA for estimating the minimum value for machining performance. International Journal of Production Research (2011), doi:10.1080/00207543.2011.571454

6. Zain, A.M., Haron, H., Sharif, S.: Optimization of process parameters in the abrasive waterjet machining using integrated SA–GA. Appl. Soft Comput. J. (2011), doi:10.1016/j.asoc.2011.05.024
7. Zain, A.M., Haron, H., Sharif, S.: Genetic algorithm and simulated annealing to estimate optimal process parameters of the abrasive waterjet machining. Engineering with Computers 27(3), 251–259 (2011)
8. Din, M.F.M.: Pengoptimuman penggunaan mata alat mesin kawalan berangka bagi produk engsel monitor LCD, First Degree Thesis, Universiti Teknologi Malaysia (2004)

Ant Based Routing Protocol for Visual Sensors

Adamu Murtala Zungeru[*], Li-Minn Ang, S.R.S. Prabaharan, and Kah Phooi Seng

School of Electrical and Electronics Engineering,
The University of Nottingham,
Jalan Broga, 43500 Semenyih, Selangor Darul Ehsan, Malaysia
{keyx1mzd,kenneth.ang,prabaharan.sahaya,
jasmine.seng}@nottingham.edu.my

Abstract. In routing protocols, sensor nodes tend to route events (images) captured to a particular destination (sink) using the most efficient path. The power and bandwidth required to transmit video data from hundreds of cameras to a central location for processing at a high success rate would be enormous. In this work, captured packets were routed from different sensors placed at different locations to the sink using the best path. Since the captured images (packets) need to be routed to the destination (sink) at regular interval and within a predefined period of time, while consuming low energy without performance degradation, Ant based routing which utilizes the behavior of real ants searching for food through pheromone deposition, while dealing with problems that need to find paths to goals, through the simulating behavior of ant colony is adopted. In this end, we present an Improved Energy-Efficient Ant-Based Routing (IEEABR) Algorithm in Visual Sensor Networks. Compared to the state-of-the-art Ant-Based routing protocols; Basic Ant-Based Routing (BABR) Algorithm, Sensor-driven and Cost-aware ant routing (SC), Flooded Forward ant routing (FF), Flooded Piggybacked ant routing (FP), and Energy-Efficient Ant-Based Routing (EEABR), the proposed IEEABR approach have advantages of reduced energy usage, delivering events packets at high success rate with low latency, increases the network lifetime, and actively performing its set target without performance degradation. The performance evaluations for the algorithms on a real application are conducted in a well known WSNs MATLAB-based simulator (RMASE) using both static and dynamic scenario.

Keywords: Visual sensor networks, Wireless sensor networks, Energy efficiency, Performance Evaluation, Ant based routing.

1 Introduction

The advancement in technology has produced the availability of small and low cost sensor nodes with capability of sensing types of physical, environmental conditions, data processing, and wireless communication [1-5]. The sensing circuitry measures ambient conditions related to the environment surrounding the sensor which transforms them into an electric signal. Processing such a signal reveals some

---

[*] Corresponding author.

A. Abd Manaf et al. (Eds.): ICIEIS 2011, Part II, CCIS 252, pp. 250–264, 2011.

properties about objects located and/or events happening in the vicinity of the sensor. The sensor sends such collected data, usually via radio transmitter, to a command center (sink) either directly or through a data concentration center (a gateway).

A visual sensor network may be a type of wireless sensor network, though much of the theory and application is similar to WSN. The network generally consists of the cameras themselves, which have some local image processing, communication and storage capabilities, and central computers or sinks where image data from multiple cameras is further processed and fused. In some applications, it is usually combined with other sensors for Multimedia applications. Visual sensor networks also provide some high-level services to the user so that the large amount of data can be distilled into information of interest using specific queries [6-8].

More recently, a lot of researchers have being paying attention on optimization of network parameters for WSN as well as VSNs [9] through routing process to provide maximum network lifetime. However, recent developments have forced the gradual drifting from the existing scalar sensing (light, temperature etc.) to a new world of audio-visual applications. As applications to VSNs, video surveillance and traffic control and environmental monitoring are active area of interest.

Ant Based Routing which utilizes the behavior of real ants searching for food through pheromone deposition while dealing with problems that need to find paths to goals, through the simulating behavior of ant colony are treated and surveyed in swarm based routing protocols [10-11]. Though, majority of the routing process are classical routing protocols as surveyed in [12].

The main goals of this study, is to present our proposed routing protocol, while comparing it with its predecessor, and other state-of-the-art Ant-Based routing protocols to see it performance as it meets the requirements of VSNs.

The rest of the paper is organized as follows. Section 2 presents a brief review of the selected ant-based routing protocols for the comparative analysis. In section 3, we describe the experimental and simulation environment. Section 4 discusses the experimental and simulation results. Section 5 concludes the paper with also open research issues.

2 A Brief Review of the Selected Ant-Based Routing Protocols

2.1 Basic Ant Based Routing for WSN

Informally, the basic ant routing algorithm and its main characteristics [13-14], can be summarized as follows:

- At regular intervals along with the data traffic, a forward ant is launched from source node to sink node.
- Each agent (forward ant) tries to locate the destination with equal probability by using neighboring nodes with minimum cost joining its source and sink.
- Each agent moves step-by-step towards its destination node. At each intermediate node a greedy   stochastic policy is applied to choose the next node to move to. The policy makes use of (i) local   agent-generated and maintained information, (ii) local problem-dependent heuristic information, and (iii) agent-private information.

- During the movement, the agents collect information about the time length, the congestion status and the node identifiers of the followed path.
- Once destination is reached, a backward ant is created which takes the same path as the forward ant, but in an opposite direction.
- During this backward travel, local models of the network status and the local routing table of   each visited node are modified by the agents as a function of the path they followed and of its   goodness.
- Once they have returned to their source node, the agents die.

The link probability distribution is maintained by;

$$\sum_{i\in N_k} P_{ji} = 1; \quad j = 1, \dots, N. \tag{1}$$

And other equations governing the behaviors and the simulating operation of Ant based routing are highlighted in [13-14].

2.2   Sensor Driven and Cost-Aware Ant Routing (SC)

In SC [15] it is assumed that ants have sensors so that they can smell where there is food at the beginning of the routing process so as to increase in sensing the best direction that the ant will go initially. In addition to the sensing ability, each node stores the probability distribution and the estimates of the cost of destination from each of its neighbors. Though suffers from misleading when there is obstacle which might cause errors in sensing. Assuming that the cost estimate is Q_n for neighbor n, the cost from the current node to the destination is 0 if it is the destination, otherwise, $C = min_{n\in N}(c_n + Q_n)$, where c_n is the local cost function. The initial probability is calculated according to the expression;

$$P_n \leftarrow \frac{e^{(C-Q_n)\beta}}{\sum_{n\in N} e^{(C-Q_n)\beta}} \tag{2}$$

2.3   Flooded Forward Ant Routing (FF)

FF [15] argues the fact that ants even augmented with sensors, can be misguided due to the obstacles or moving destinations. The protocol is based on flooding of ants from source to the sink. In the case where destination is not known at the beginning by the ants, or cost cannot be estimated, the protocol simply use the broadcast method of sensor networks so as to route packets to the destination. Probabilities are updated in the same way as the basic ant routing, though, FF reduces the flooding ants when a shorter part is transverse.

2.4   Flooded Piggyback Ant Routing (FP)

FP [15] brings a new ant species to forward ants namely data ants whose function is to carry the forward list, though the control of the flooded forward ants is same as in FF. The protocol succeeded in combining forward ants and data ants using constrained flooding to route data and to discover optimal path. The probability distribution constrains the flooding towards the sink node for future data ants. The method is a tradeoff between high success rate and high energy consumption.

2.5 Improved Energy-Efficient Ant-Based Routing Algorithm (IEEABR)

IEEABR as the proposed Algorithm which is an improved version of EEABR [16], consider the available power of nodes and the energy consumption of each path as the reliance of routing selection, improves memory usage, utilizes the self organization, self-adaptability and dynamic optimization capability of ant colony system to find the optimal path and multiple candidate paths from source nodes to sink nodes then avoiding using up the energy of nodes on the optimal path and prolong the network lifetime while preserving network connectivity. This is necessary since for any WSN protocol design, the important issue is the energy efficiency of the underlying algorithm due to the fact that the network under investigation has strict power requirements. As proposed in [17], for forward ants sent directly to the sink-node; the routing tables only need to save the neighbor nodes that are in the direction of the sink-node, which considerably reduces the size of the routing tables and, in consequence, the memory needed by the nodes. As adopted in [16], the memory M_k of each ant is reduced to just two records, the last two visited nodes. Since the path followed by the ants is no more in their memories, a memory must be created at each node that keeps record of each ant that was received and sent. Each memory record saves the previous node, the forward node, the ant identification and a timeout value. Whenever a forward ant is received at any node, it searches for any possible loop with the aid of its identification (ID). For the situation where no record is found, the necessary information is retrieved and timer restarted, hence forwarding the ant to the next node, else, the ant is eliminated if a record containing the ant identification is found. When a backward ant is received, the source ID is search so as to know where to send it to. In this section, we proposed some modifications on EEABR to improve the Energy consumption in the nodes of WSNs and also to in turn improve the performance and efficiency of the networks. We intelligently initialize the routing tables of the nodes, while also giving priority to neighboring nodes of source or routers which falls to be the destination, we also went ahead to reduce the flooding ability of ants in the network for congestion control. The Algorithm of our proposed method is as below.

- Initialize the routing tables with a uniform probability distribution;

$$P_{ld} = \frac{1}{N_k} \tag{3}$$

Where P_{ld} is the probability of jumping from node l to node d (destination), N_k the number of nodes in the network.

- At regular intervals, from every network node, a forward ant k is launched with the aim to find a path until the destination. Where the number of ants lunched at each node is limited to k*5 for network congestion control. The identifier of every visited node is saved onto a memory M_k and carried by the ant.

Let k be any network node; its routing table will have N entries, one for each possible destination.

Let d be one entry of k routing table (a possible destination).

Let N_k be set of neighboring nodes of node k.

Let P_{kl} be the probability with which an ant or data packet in k, jumps to a node l, l∈N_k, when the destination is d ($d \neq k$). Then, for each of the N entries in the node k routing table, it will be n_k values of P_{ld} subject to the condition:

$$\sum_{l \in N_k} P_{ld} = 1; \quad d = 1, ..., N \qquad (4)$$

- At every visited node, a forward ant assigns a greater probability to a destination node d for which falls to be the destination among the neighbor node, d ∈ N_k. Hence, initial probability in the routing table of k is then:

$$P_{dd} = \frac{9N_k - 5}{4N_k^2} \qquad (5)$$

Also, for the rest neighboring nodes among the neighbors for which m ∈ N_k will then be:

$$P_{md} = \begin{cases} \frac{4N_k - 5}{4N_k^2}, & if \ N_k > 1 \\ 0, & if \ N_k = 1 \end{cases} \qquad (6)$$

Of course (5) and (6) satisfy (4). But if it falls to the case where by none among the neighbor is a destination, (3) applies to all the neighboring nodes.

Else,

- Forward ant selects the next hop node using the same probabilistic rule proposed in the ACO metaheuristic:

$$P_k(r, s) = \begin{cases} \frac{[\tau(r,s)]^\alpha \cdot [E(s)]^\beta}{\sum_{u \in M_k}[\tau(r,u)]^\alpha \cdot [E(s)]^\beta}, & s \notin M_k \\ 0, else \end{cases} \qquad (7)$$

where $p_k(r,s)$ is the probability with which ant k chooses to move from node r to node s, τ is the routing table at each node that stores the amount of pheromone trail on connection (r,s), E is the visibility function given by $\frac{1}{(c - e_s)}$ (c is the initial energy level of the nodes and e_s is the actual energy level of node s), and α and β are parameters that control the relative importance of trail versus visibility. The selection probability is a trade-off between visibility (which says that nodes with more energy should be chosen with high probability) and actual trail intensity (that says that if on connection (r, s) there has been a lot of traffic then it is highly desirable to use that connection.

- When a forward ant reaches the destination node, it is transformed in a backward ant which mission is now to update the pheromone trail of the path it used to reach the destination and that is stored in its memory.
- Before backward ant k starts its return journey, the destination node computes the amount of pheromone trail that the ant will drop during its journey:

$$\Delta \tau = \frac{1}{C - \left| \frac{EMin_k - Fd_k}{EAvg_k - Fd_k} \right|} \qquad (8)$$

And the equation used to update the routing tables at each node is:

$$\tau(r, s) = (1 - \rho) * \tau(r, s) + \left[\frac{\Delta \tau}{\emptyset B d_k} \right] \qquad (9)$$

Where ϕ a coefficient and Bd_k is the distance travelled (the number of visited nodes) by the backward ant k until node r. which the two parameters will force the ant to lose part of the pheromone strength during its way to the source node. The idea behind the behavior is to build a better pheromone distribution (nodes near the sink node will have more pheromone levels) and will force remote nodes to find better paths. Such behavior is important when the sink node is able to move, since pheromone adaptation will be much quicker.

- When the backward ant reaches the node where it was created, its mission is finished and the ant is eliminated.
- Else, if it fails to reach the node where it was created, i.e. when a loop is detected, immediately the ant is self destroyed.

By performing this algorithm several iterations, each node will be able to know which are the best neighbors (in terms of the optimal function represented by (9)) to send a packet towards a specific destination.

3 Experimental and Simulation Environment

We use a Routing Modeling Application Simulation Environment (RMASE) [18] which is a framework implemented as an application in the probabilistic wireless network simulator (Prowler) [19] written and runs under Matlab, thus providing a fast and easy way to prototype applications and having nice visualization capabilities.

Prowler is an event-driven simulator that can be set to operate in either deterministic or probabilistic mode. Prowler consists of radio model as well as a MAC-layer model.

The Radio propagation model determines the strength of a transmitted signal at a particular point of the space for all transmitters in the system. Based on this information, the signal reception conditions for the receivers can be evaluated and collisions can be detected. The signal strength from the transmitter to a receiver is determined by a deterministic propagation function, and by random disturbances. The transmission model is given by:

$$P_{rec,ideal}(d) = P_{transmit} \frac{1}{1+d^\gamma} \tag{10}$$

$$P_{rec}(i,j) = P_{rec,ideal}(d_{i,j}).\left(1 + \alpha(d_{i,j})\right).\left(1 + \beta(t)\right) \tag{11}$$

Where $P_{rec,ideal}$ is the ideal reception signal strength, $P_{transmit}$, the transmission signal power, d, the distance between the transmitter and the receiver, γ, a decay parameter with typical values of $2 \le \gamma \le 4$, α and β, random variables with normal distributions $N(0, \sigma_\alpha)$ and $N(0, \sigma_\beta)$, respectively. The MAC layer simulates the Berkeley motes' CSMA protocol, including the random waiting and back-offs.

From several results obtained from our simulation results, we report the following performance metrics for clarity purpose.

Latency: The time delay of an event sent from the source node to the destination node.

Success rate: It is a ratio of total number of events received at the destination to the total number of events generated by the nodes in the sensor network.

Energy consumption: It is the total energy consumed by the nodes in the network during the period of the experiment.

Energy efficiency: it is a measure of the ratio of total packet delivered at the destination (sink) to the total energy consumed by the network's sensor nodes i.e. $\left(\frac{Succes\ rate*total\ packet\ sent\ to\ the\ sink}{Total\ energy\ consumed}\right)$.

4   Experimental and Simulation Results

We use the routing modeling simulation environment (RMASE). We evaluated all the protocols using the metrics defined in section 3 above. In our experiment, the network initially was a 3x3 (9) sensor grid with small random offsets and later increase to 12, 36, 49, 64, and finally 100 nodes, ant ratio set to 2, source rate set to 4, $c1=0.7$, $z=1$, data gain=1.2, reward scale=0.3, ant table size=400, energy level of nodes to be 30 Joules each. We use the default settings of prowler i.e. $\sigma_\alpha = 0.45$, $\sigma_\beta = 0.02$, $P_{error} = 0.05$, transmission signal strength set to 1, maximum radio range about 3d, where d is the distance between two nodes in the grid. The sources where fixed in all simulation as against the fixed camera sensors applications, and generate traffic at a constant bit rate (CBR) of 250kbps. Each experiment was performed for duration of 360 seconds. The experiment was conducted for two situations; when the sink is static, and when it is dynamic (Target tracking).

Static (Sources and Sink in static position)

In the static scenario, all sources and sink are fixed, while the centre of the circle is randomly selected at the start of the experiment.

Latency: Fig 1.a shows the end-to-end delay of the protocols under evaluation. As seen from the figure, IEEABR has the lowest end-to-end delay (latency) followed by its predecessor (EEABR). FF performance was poor, though, the basic ant routing perform worst throughout the period of observation as can be seen in the figure. The poor performance of FF and the basic ant routing is due to the flooding method of ants without control which could cause congestion in the network. As IEEABR limits the number of flooding ants in the network to a fraction of 5 times the number of networks nodes, while also assigning a greater probability to neighboring nodes which falls the same time as the sink, perform better than all the protocols.

Success rate: Fig 1.b shows the success rate of the protocols in other words, the ability of the protocols to deliver successfully to the sink the packets generated at each nodes in the network. Though, FP shows a wonderful performance as it delivered fully all the packets generated in the network to the sink during the period of observation without lost, where as IEEABR having an average of 96% follows. SC has the poorest delivering rate and the basic ant routing the poorer in the experiment. The poor performance of the basic ant routing and SC is due to the flooding of ants without consideration of energy of paths, and path selection based on distance only respectively, in which some nodes of the paths might not be able to deliver the packets given to them for onward delivery.

Energy consumption: Fig 1.c shows the energy consumption of protocols for 9 nodes in the network. Fig 1.e is the energy consumption of protocols for different densities of the network for the variation from 9, 16, 36, 64, and 100 nodes. SC performs better in the lower density network of 9 nodes with 3% difference in performance as against IEEABR, while IEEABR perform better when the network grows higher. The percentage difference between IEEABR and SC when the network grows to 49 nodes is 25%, hence, much performance difference. At the point of 49 nodes, EEABR consumes 31% of energy than IEEABR. Hence IEEABR outperform all the protocols in term of low energy consumption. FP performs worst in that case as almost all the nodes went down due to high energy consumption consuming 719.9J in the network of 100 nodes where as IEEABR consumes 31.6J. The difference in the energy consumption is not comparable, even though it has the highest delivery ratio.

Energy efficiency: Fig 1.d shows the energy efficiency of the protocols. As energy consumption is an important metrics to be consider when designing an efficient protocol, as it is clearly seen, IEEABR not only having low latency in packet delivery, also outperform all the routing protocols in terms of Energy efficiency. The percentage difference between IEEABR and EEABR is 9% and 25%. FP having the highest success rate in the low density network has the poorest result in term of energy efficiency. Though, IEEABR and EEABR are energy aware protocols, and IEEABR still having high success rate and lowest end-to-end delay.

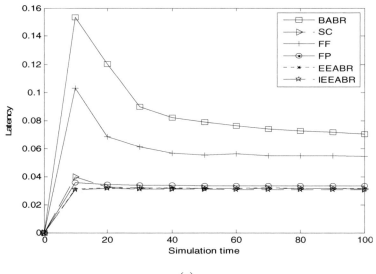

(a)

Fig. 1. Performance evaluation in static scenario among six (6) Ant-Based routing protocols: (a) Latency (b) Success rates (c) Energy consumption (d) Energy efficiency (e) Energy consumption for different network's densities

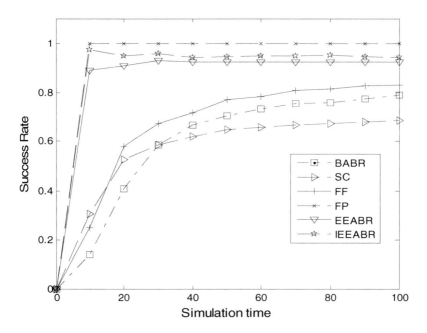

(b)

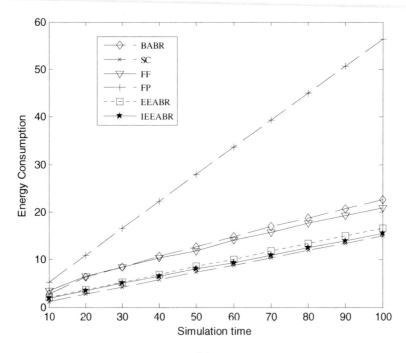

(c)

Fig. 1. (*Continued*)

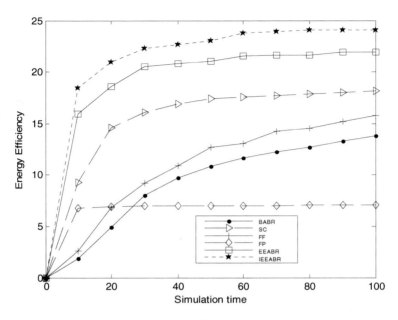

(d)

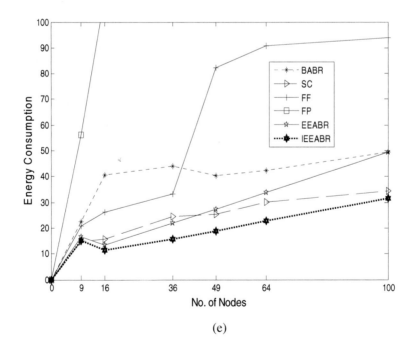

(e)

Fig. 1. (*Continued*)

Dynamic (Target tracking)

In the dynamic scenario, all sources are fixed while sink keeps changing position, and centre of the circle is randomly selected at the start of the experiment.

Success rate: Fig 2.a shows the success rate of the protocols in the dynamic scenario, where the sink keeps on changing position, which is sometimes known as the target tracking. The success rate of any protocol is the ability of the protocols to deliver successfully to the sink the packets generated at each node in the network. Though, FP still outperforms our proposed protocol in the dynamic scenario which is due to its tradeoff between high success rate and high energy consumption. Our proposed algorithm (IEEABR) not only having high success rate, but also, have the lowest energy consumption and more energy efficient. SC having the poorest delivering rate in static, now outperform BABR still shows itself in the poor nature of it delivery packets to the sink in the target tracking scenario, with about 20% difference. While, IEEABR outperforms its predecessor with 60% of packet delivered, which is quite a large difference in performance in terms of quality of service. The poor performance of the basic ant routing is the flooding of ants without consideration of energy of paths, in which some nodes of the paths might not be able to deliver the packets given to them for onward delivery.

Energy consumption: Limited available energy which is the major problem of wireless and visual sensor networks has to be look upon critically when designing an efficient protocol. Fig 2.b shows the energy consumption of protocols for 9 nodes in a grid network. While Fig 2.d is the energy consumption of protocols for different densities of the network for the variation from 9, 16, 36, 64, and 100 nodes. As it can be seen in fig 2.b, SC consumes more 72.65% energy as compared to IEEABR, which shows a high performance in the static scenario, where it assumes that it knows the location of the sink using a form of sensing level or otherwise GPS to detect the position of the sink during the initial routing process. Also IEEABR shows a great improvement on EEABR with percentage difference of 10.6%. As can be seen in fig 2.d, the percentage difference between IEEABR and SC when the network grows to 49 nodes is 60% which is a high performance difference. IEEABR with its predecessor at that point is 29.66%. Hence outperform all the protocols in term of low energy consumption. FP still performs worst in the tracking scenario, where almost all the nodes went down due to high energy consumption, consuming 812.7J in the network of 100 nodes where as IEEABR consumes 27.82J. The difference in the energy consumption is not comparable, even though it has the highest delivery ratio and lowest end-to-end delay in packet delivery. The high improvement of IEEABR is due to reduced flooding of ants in the network, and proper initialization of the routing table, while giving preference to the sink selection among the neighbors.

Energy efficiency: Energy efficiency which is a function of energy consumption and the success rate, tells how well a protocol performs in both quality of service and network life time. As a network is expected to perform optimally while also performing for a long period of time without the performance degradation, Fig 2.c

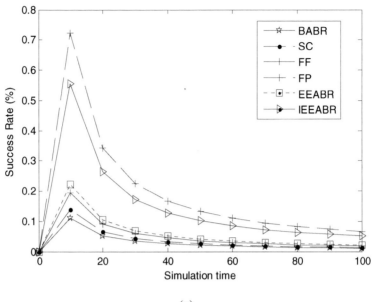

(a)

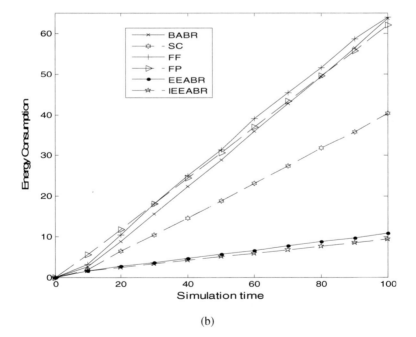

(b)

Fig. 2. Performance evaluation in dynamic scenario among six (6) Ant-Based routing protocols: (a) Success rates (b) Energy consumption (c) Energy efficiency (d) Energy consumption for different network's densities

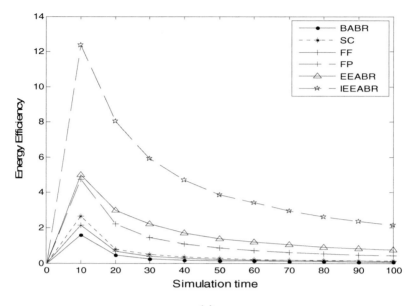

(c)

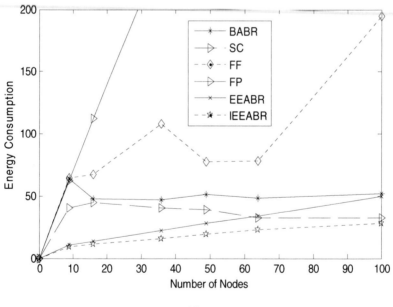

(d)

Fig. 2. (*Continued*)

shows the energy efficiency of the protocols. It is clearly seen that, IEEABR not only having high success rate, low energy consumption, it's the most energy efficient among the protocols under consideration. The percentage difference in the dynamic scenario between IEEABR and EEABR is 64.22% and 93.2% for SC which is most costly in its algorithm implementation. FP having the highest success rate in the low density network has the poorest result in term of energy efficiency. Though, IEEABR and EEABR are energy aware protocols, and IEEABR still having high success rate and lowest end-to-end delay.

5 Conclusions

As the advancement in technology growth has led to the designs of sensors capable of sensing and producing images, the characteristics of visual sensor networks strictly depends on the size of packets, energy consumption, bandwidth, success rate with low latency. In this work, packet were transmitted at a constant bit rate of 250kbps which is more than transmitting three (3) frames of size 320x240 (75kb). In this article, we have shown and proven beyond reasonable doubt that the proposed algorithm IEEABR perform quite well in all the metrics used for evaluation purpose, while also showing reasonable differences between itself and its predecessor. EEABR has 31% and 29.66% higher than IEEABR in term of energy consumption of nodes in the network for static and dynamic scenario respectively. Even SC which assumes that all sensor nodes have sensor to get the location of the sink did not do well as compared to IEEABR, despite the cost to be incurred in purchasing the GPS and attached to each sensor nodes before the implementation of the algorithm. The routing process uses special ant (forward ant) for best path searching and backward ant for the path update, which helps in high efficient packet handling. With the high success rate, low energy consumption, low latency, and high bandwidth, this then means that our proposed algorithm will surely do well in the real application of Images routing as in VSNs with low cost sensors.

In future, we intends to tune our algorithm to reactive protocol where the duty cycles of the participating nodes will be taken into consideration in the routing process to see its performance, and also prioritize the packets of some tasks above those of others so as to convey with minimum delay, packets of important events in the sensor networks by simply assigning low and high priority packets to the ants. This could help in Multimedia application so that cost of setting up multiple sensor networks will be drastically reduced to minima. We also want to compare it with other swarm intelligent protocols like the Beesensor [20-21] and classical routing protocols to ascertain its performance.

References

1. Baras, J., Mehta, H.: PERA: A Probabilistic Emergent Routing Algorithm for Mobile Ad hoc Networks. In: WiOpt 2003 Sophia-Antipolis, France (2003)
2. Katz, R.H., Kahn, J.M., Pister, K.S.J.: Mobile networking for smart dust. In: Proceedings of the 5th Annual ACM/IEEE International Conference on Mobile Computing and Networking (MobiCom 1999), Seattle, Washington, pp. 271–278 (1999)

3. Min, R., Bhardwaj, M., Cho, S., Shih, E., Sinha, A., Wang, A., Chandrakasan, A.: Low Power Wireless Sensor Networks. In: Proceedings of International Conference on VLSI Design, Bangalore, India, pp. 221–226 (2001)
4. Rabaey, J.M., Ammer, M.J., Silver, J.L.D., Patel, D., Roundy, S.: PicoRadio Supports Ad Hoc Ultra Low Power Wireless Networking. IEEE Computer 33(7), 42–48 (2000)
5. Sohrabi, K., Gao, J., Ailawadhi, V., Pottie, G.J.: Protocols for Self-Organization of a Wireless Sensor Network. IEEE Personal Communications 7(5), 16–27 (2000)
6. Obraczka, K., Manduchi, R., Garcia-Luna-Aveces, J.J.: Managing the information flow in visual sensor networks. In: The 5th International Symposium on Wireless Personal Multimedia Communications, pp. 1177–1181 (2002)
7. Soro, S., Heinzelman, W.: A Survey of Visual Sensor Networks, Advances in Multimedia, Article ID 640386, 21 pages (2009)
8. Akdere, M., Cetintemel, U., Crispell, D., Jannotti, J., Mao, J., Taubin, G.: SHORT PAPER: Data-Centric Visual Sensor Networks for 3D Sensing Data-Directed Localization. In: Networks
9. Cobo, L., Quintero, A., Pierre, S.: Ant-based routing for wireless multimedia sensor networks using multiple QoS metrics. Computer Networks 54, 2991–3010 (2010)
10. Saleem, M., Di Caro, G., Farooq, M.: Swarm intelligence based routing protocol for wireless sensor networks: Survey and future directions. Information Sciences (2010)
11. Çelik, F., Zengin, A., Tuncel, S.: A survey on swarm intelligence based routing protocols in wireless sensor networks. International Journal of the Physical Sciences 5, 2118–2126 (2010)
12. Akkaya, K., Younis, M.: A Survey on Routing Protocols for Wireless Sensor Networks. Ad Hoc Networks (Elsevier) 3(3), 325–349 (2005)
13. White, T., Pagurek, B., Oppacher, F.: Connection Management using Adaptive Mobile Agents. In: Proceeding of International Conference on Parallel Distributed Processing Techniques and Applications, pp. 802–809. CSREA Press (1998)
14. Dorigo, M., Di Caro, G.: AntNet: Distributed Stigmergetic Control for Communications Networks. Journal of Artificial Intelligence Research 9, 317–365 (1998)
15. Zhang, Y., Kuhn, L.D., Fromherz, M.P.J.: Improvements on Ant Routing for Sensor Networks. In: Dorigo, M., Birattari, M., Blum, C., Gambardella, L.M., Mondada, F., Stützle, T. (eds.) ANTS 2004. LNCS, vol. 3172, pp. 154–165. Springer, Heidelberg (2004)
16. Camilo, T.C., Carreto, S.J.S., Boavida, F.: An Energy-Efficient Ant Based Routing Algorithm for Wireless Sensor Networks. In: Dorigo, M., Gambardella, L.M., Birattari, M., Martinoli, A., Poli, R., Stützle, T. (eds.) ANTS 2006. LNCS, vol. 4150, pp. 49–59. Springer, Heidelberg (2006)
17. Kalpakis, K., Dasgupta, K., Namjoshi, P.: Maximum Lifetime Data Gathering and Aggregation in Wireless Sensor Networks. In: Proceedings of IEEE International Conference on Networking, vol. 42(6) (2003)
18. Zhang, Y.: Routing modeling application simulation environment (RMASE), http://www2.parc.com/isl/groups/era/nest/Rmase/
19. Sztipanovits, J.: Probabilistic wireless network simulator (Prowler), http://www.isis.vanderbilt.edu/Projects/nest/prowler/
20. Saleem, M., Farooq, M.: Beesensor: A bee-inspired power aware routing algorithms. In: Rothlauf, F., Branke, J., Cagnoni, S., Corne, D.W., Drechsler, R., Jin, Y., Machado, P., Marchiori, E., Romero, J., Smith, G.D., Squillero, G. (eds.) EvoWorkshops 2005. LNCS, vol. 3449, pp. 136–146. Springer, Heidelberg (2005)
21. Saleem, M., Farooq, M.: A framework for empirical evaluation of nature inspired routing protocols for wireless sensor networks. In: Evolutionary Computation (CEC 2007), pp. 751–758. IEEE Congress (2007)

Music Information Retrieval Algorithm Using Time-Frequency Dictionaries

Soe Myat Thu

University of Computer Studies,Yangon
thuthu052228@gmail.com

Abstract. In this paper, retrieving the required information from acoustic music signal in an efficient way is considered. The system is to determine similarities among songs, particularly, a piece of input music signal compared with storage music song's signal into the database and then to retrieve the similar song. Representing the music signal having sparse nature is accomplished by Matching Pursuit with time-frequency dictionaries. In order to match a candidate segment with the query segment, the music signal similarity measure is performed by Spatial Pyramid Matching. Evaluation results on music retrieval system illustrate that our music search system is better retrieval quality than such previous approaches.

Keywords: Content-based music information retrieval ,Matching Pursuit, Spatial Pyramid Matching.

1 Introduction

Music searching and browsing from audio signals is an interesting topic that receives a lot of attention these days. These feature sets are designed to reflect different aspects of music such as timbre, harmony, melody and rhythm. Individual sets of audio content and social context features have been shown to be useful for various MIR tasks such as classification, similarity, recommendation. Among them, similarity is crucial for the effectiveness of searching music information and the music segmentation. The generation of MIR (roughly 1995-2005), saw the introduction of the sophisticated features involving higher level time and frequency domain features such as beat histograms, Mel-frequency cepstral coefficients (MFCCs) and chromagrams. In addition, researchers began using more sophisticated statistics to aggregate the values of each feature within a song, and using newer machine learning techniques.

Various representations have been proposed for musical signals features. The time-domain representation (waveform) and frequency-domain (STFT or spectrogram) representation are the very basic and most widely used. Logan and Saloman present an audio content-based method of estimating the timbral similarity of two pieces of music that has been successfully applied to playlist generation, artist identification and genre classification of music. The signature is formed by the clustering, with the K-means algorithm, of Mel-frequency Cepstral Coefficients (MFCCs) calculated for short frames of the audio signal [1]. Another content-based method of similarity

A. Abd Manaf et al. (Eds.): ICIEIS 2011, Part II, CCIS 252, pp. 265–274, 2011.
© Springer-Verlag Berlin Heidelberg 2011

estimation, also based on the calculation of MFCCs from the audio signal, is presented by Aucouturier and Patchet. A mixture of Gaussian distributions is trained on the MFCC vectors from each song and are compared by sampling the distributions (generating random points according to one distribution and estimating their likelihood based on the other distribution) in order to estimate the timbral similarity of two pieces [2]. B. Logan and A. Salomon's technique forms a signature for each song based on K-means clustering of spectral features. For each song, this compute a signature based on K-means clustering of frames of MFCCs with audio sampled at 16kHz and divide this signal into frames of 25.6ms overlapped by 10ms [3]. D.Turnbull, G. L.E. Pampalk and M. Goto develop a set of difference features that indicate when there are changes in perceptual aspects (e.g., timbre, harmony, melody, rhythm) of the music. By combining these features and formulating the problem as a supervised learning problem using a publicly available data set of 100 copyright-cleared pop/rock songs [4]. M. Goto describe a method for obtaining a list of chorus (refrain) sections in compact-disc recordings of popular music and also tested on 100 songs of the popular-music database "RWC" Music Database [5]. Music used to show repetition and similarities on different levels, starting from consecutive bars to larger parts like chorus and verse. Some authors have tried to take this into account and proposed methods operating on several temporal levels. Jehan constructed several hierarchically related similarity matrices [6]. Finally, this defines a true musical boundary as a transition between 'intro', 'verse', 'chorus', bridge / solo', and 'outro' segments. For all metrics, performance is averaged over the 100 songs in the data set [7] .

This paper presents a content-based approach to determine similar song from a database and retrieve a whole music song according to the input query. Because of the challenge of matching a candidate segment with the query segment, the system could significantly improve similarity measure using Spatial Pyramid Matching. And the retrieval time could considerably improve using Matching Pursuit (MP) Method. Our particular approach to choose music song also makes it possible automatic retrieval using matching pursuit feature sets, for example for using the browsing system rapidly through a list of possible song of interest returned by a search engine. By guiding us to the most significant parts of a music song, it also allows the development of fast and efficient method for searching very large collections based purely on the audio content of the song, sidestepping the computational complexity of existing content-based search methods. The rest of this paper is organized as follows. In Section 2, the system is introduced for our music information retrieval algorithm. The feature extraction technique and similarity matrix from the musical audio signals are addressed in Section 2.1 and Section 2.2. Then, the system is represented music signal decomposition for music features with a dictionary and pattern similarity discovery with pyramid kernel level. Experimental setup is provided in Section 3 followed by the Conclusion in Section 4.

2   Music Information Retrieval System

A block diagram of the system can be seen in Figure 1. This new system creates matching pursuit features from a query input music signal (5-10 seconds) using matching pursuit method. Music signal structural features of input music query are represented as a dictionary with most prominent atoms that match their time-frequency signatures. Metadata database contained music signal structural features sets of very large collections music. Pyramid match kernel measures similarity achieved from a partial matching between two feature sets. A whole music is achieved to determine similarity between input music query features sets and all music features sets contained in the metadata database.

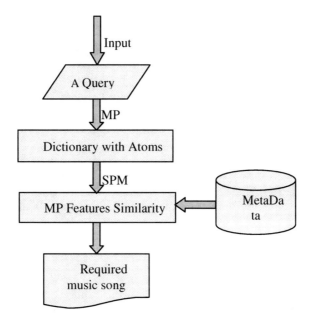

Fig. 1. Overview of our music information retrieval system

The optimal description of the music song from the meta database is found in respect to the faster and more similar function defined in Spatial Pyramid Matching method.

2.1 Matching Pursuit Features Extraction

Matching Pursuit is part of a class of signal analysis algorithms known as Atomic Decompositions. These algorithms consider a signal as a linear combination of known elementary pieces of signal, called atoms, chosen within a dictionary.

MP aims at finding sparse decompositions of signals over redundant bases of elementary waveforms [8].

2.1.1 Dictionary Approximation

Matching pursuit decomposes music signal into a linear expansion of waveforms that are selected from a redundant dictionary of functions. Wavelet transforms should be designed as follow: **Dictionary:** A dictionary contains a collection of blocks plus the signal on which they operate. It can search across all the blocks (i.e., all the scales and all the bases) for the atom which brings the most energy to the analyzed signal. **Book:** A book is a collection of atoms. Summing all the atoms in a book gives a signal. **Atoms:** An elementary piece of signal. An atom is organized by its Gabor atoms.

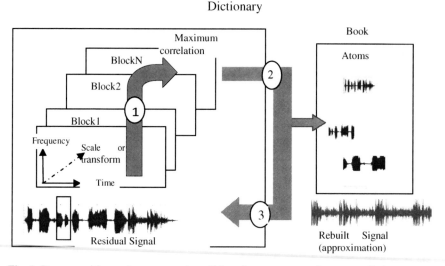

Fig. 2. Decomposition and reconstruction of time-frequency waveforms as a dictionary

In Figure 2, Music signal decomposes into the blocks, and several blocks corresponding to various scales or various transforms can be concurrently applied to the same signal, thus providing multi-scales or multi-basis analysis. Then this update the correlation by applying the relevant correlation computation algorithm to the analyzed signal, and search the maximum correlation in the same loop. The atoms are created by corresponding to the maximum correlation with the signal and store this atom in the book. The created atom is substracted from the analyzed signal thus obtaining a residual signal, and re-iterate the analysis on this residual [9].

Using Matching Pursuit method is price of efficiency and convergence. Time compression is quite excellent by extracting prominent atoms (features). In order to achieve the required information in our system, the algorithm search the most strongly correlated with the original signal x for each iteration m. It has the maximum inner product $\hat{w}_m$ with the signal. This MP algorithm uses the following steps:

1. initialization:

$$m = 0, x_m = x_0 = x; \tag{1}$$

2. computation of the correlations between the signal and every atom in dictionary D, using inner products :

$$\forall_w \epsilon D: \quad Corr(x_m, w) = |< x_m, w >| \tag{2}$$

3. search of the most correlated atom, by searching for the maximum inner product:

$$\widehat{w}_m = \underset{w \in D}{argmaxCorr}(x_m, w)$$

(3)

4. subtraction of the corresponding weighted atom

$\infty_m \widehat{w}_m$ from the signal :

$$x_{m+1} = x_m - \infty_m \widehat{w}_m$$

(4)

$$where \ \propto_m = < x_m, \widehat{w}_m >;$$

5. If the desired level of accuracy is reached, in terms of the number of extracted atoms or in terms of the energy ratio between the original signal and the current residual x_{m+1}, stop; otherwise, re-iterate the pursuit over the residual: $m \leftarrow m+1$ and go to step 2.

Music song signal analysis of our system is desirable to obtain sparse representations that are able to reflect the signal structures. The functions used for MP in our algorithm are Gabor function, i.e. Gaussian-windowed sinusoids. The Gabor function is evaluated at a range of frequencies covering the available spectrum, scaled in length (trading time resolution for frequency resolution), and translated in time. Each of the resulting functions is called an atom, and the set of atoms is a dictionary which covers a range of time-frequency localization properties. The Gabor function in our new search model is defined as

$$g_{s,u,\omega,\vartheta}(t) = K_{s,u,\omega,\vartheta} \left(\frac{t-u}{s}\right) \cos[2\pi\omega(t-u)\theta]$$

(5)

where $\gamma = (s, u, \omega, \theta)$ denotes the parameters to the Gabor function, with s, u, ω, θ corresponding to an atom's position in scale, time, frequency and phase, respectively. We focus on a dictionary by choosing 1500 gabor atoms of length 16384 sample points. The advantages of gabor dictionary representation is characterized the signal

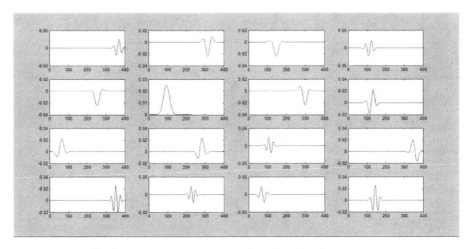

Fig. 3. Decomposition of signal using MP with 16 gabor atoms

time and frequency domain by resulting a few reconstruction error (signal to noise ratio is 10.99). The Gabor dictionary was implemented with the parameters of atoms chosen from dyadic sequences of integers [10].

Flexible decompositions play an important role to represent signal components whose localizations in time and frequency vary widely. Signal components must be expanded into waveforms which are called time-frequency atoms. In figure 3, it is the decomposition of signal using Matching Pursuit method. These waveforms are called time-frequency atoms which are an example of sixteen Gabor atoms from a whole song.

A music song is reconstructed using Gabor dictionary by the number of 150000 atoms in Figure 4. In (a) and (b) original song signal is decomposed into MP features using matching pursuit method and the best atoms are selected to reconstruct a music song without distortion. In (c) the residual song signal after song reconstruction. Decay signal after song reconstruction in (d) is represented.

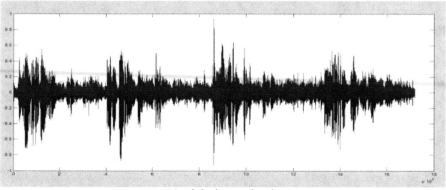

(a) original song signal

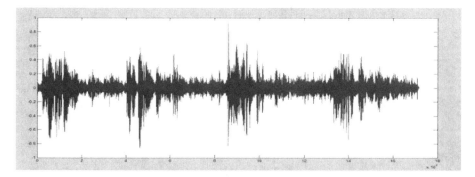

(b) reconstructed song signal

Fig. 4. (a) original signal (b) Reconstruction of a music song using Gabor dictionary with MP features by the number of 1500 atoms, (c) residual song signal and (d) reconstructed song error

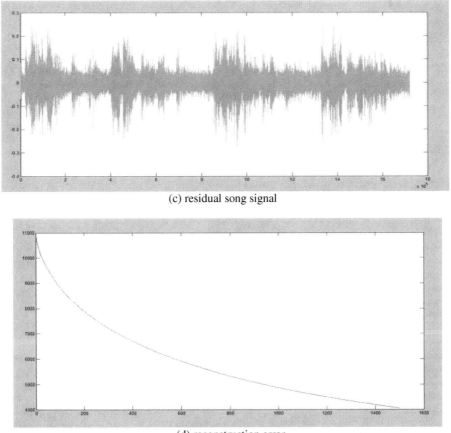

(c) residual song signal

(d) reconstruction error

Fig. 4. (*Continued*)

2.2 SPM Based Similarity Using Matching Pursuit Features

Spatial Pyramid Matching is to find an approximate correspondence features between two features sets step by step level. At each level of resolution, SPM works by placing a sequence of increasingly coarser grids over the features.

A pyramid matching pattern kernel allows for multi-resolution matching of two collections of features in a high-dimensional appearance space, however it discards all spatial information. Another problem is the quality of the approximation to the optimal partial match provided by the pyramid kernel degrades linearly with the dimension of the feature space. In our system, the approximate matching pattern discovery (SPM) is constructed the pyramid level and then the number of matches at each level is given by histogram intersection function. In determining SPM, SPM is used step by step level to improve matching musical data space and taking a weighted sum of the number of matches. At any fixed resolution, two feature points are said to match if they fall into the same cell of the grid. For matching pattern discovery, our system used histogram intersection function. Let X and Y are two features sets and construct a sequence of grids at each resolution. Each level has 2^l cells along each dimension(d), for a total of $D=2^{dl}$ cells. The histogram intersection function is as follows:

$$\mathcal{I}(H_X^l, H_Y^l) = \sum_{i=1}^{D} \min\left(H_X^l(i), H_Y^l(i)\right) \tag{6}$$

In the following, it will be abbreviated

$$\mathcal{I}(H_X^l, H_Y^l) \text{ to } \mathcal{I}^l.$$

To achieve more definitely pattern matching, our system modified step by step level pyramid kernel function. The number of matches found at level 'l' also includes all the matches found at the finer level l+1. Therefore, the number of new matches found at level l is given $\mathcal{I}^l - \mathcal{I}^{l+1}$ for l=0,.......L-1. The weight associated with level l is set to $\frac{1}{2^{L-l}}$, which is inversely proportional to cell width at that level. The definition of a matching pyramid kernel is:

$$K^L(X,Y) = \mathcal{I}^L + \sum_{l=0}^{L-1} \frac{l}{2^{L-l}}(\mathcal{I}^l - \mathcal{I}^{l+1}) \tag{7}\,[11]$$

A pyramid matching determines a partial correspondence by matching feature points once they fall into the same histogram bin as shown in Figure 4. In this example, two 1-D feature sets are used to form one histogram pyramid. Each row

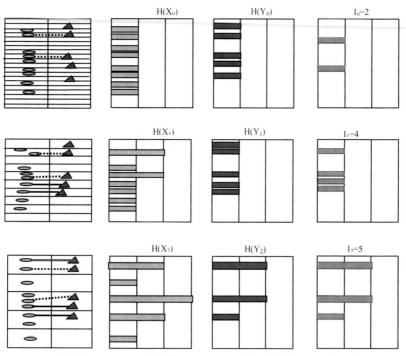

(a) Features sets   (b) Histogram pyramids   (c) Intersection points

Fig. 5. (a)Features sets, (b)Histogram pyramids and (c)Intersection points

corresponds to a pyramid level. In (a), the set X is on the left side, and the set Y is on the right. (Features Points are distributed along the vertical axis, and these same points are repeated at each level.) Bold dashed lines indicate a pair matched at this level, and bold black lines indicate a match already formed at a former resolution. In (b) multi-features histograms are shown, with bin counts along the horizontal axis. In (c) the intersection pyramid between the histograms in (b) are represented.

3 Experimental Setup

The performance of the new search system evaluates in simulations browsing the similar structure of a set popular music pieces. We performed to evaluate our system against based on Hierarchical Dirichlet Process (HDP). The HDP is a nonparametric Bayesian model and compute timbral similarity between recorded songs. Like the Gaussian Mixture Model (GMM), it represents each song as a mixture of some number of multivariate Gaussian distributions. This dataset consists of 121 songs from South by Southwest (SXSW) Dataset [12].

Our system has a ability to test on a collection of tracks including music genres in the database such as punk, hip-hop, jazz, metal, rock, country songs, etc. Our dataset contain 200 songs from SXSW dataset and other popular music pieces. These songs were varying lengths (3-5 minutes long) and downsampled to 22050 Hz sampling rate, mono channel. All songs were trained on the same sets of features vectors for each song consisted of 150000 MP features. Features were calculated from a rectangular window length 16384 sample points with 50% overlap. Input music pieces (5-10 seconds) segment and a whole music song into the database makes up for training and testing. For the performance evaluation, our system tested with R-Precision (RP), Average Precision (AP), and the Area Under the ROC Curve (AUC) which are standard metrics of music retrieval quality. In our optimized Matlab implementation, this reduce comparison time to retrieve a song. Evaluation results for our MP based algorithm are given as Table 1.This results are calculated over 10-fold cross-validation folds.

Table 1. Mean R-Precision(RP), mean Average Precision (AP), and mean Area Under ROC Curve (AUC) for HDP based algorithm and our MP based algorithm on the large SXSW dataset

	HDP	MP based algorithm
RP	0.3495	**0.3741**
AP	0.3995	**0.4145**
AUC	0.7002	**0.7286**

Table 2. Three measures of retrieval quality for HDP based algorithm and our MP based algorithm on the smaller dataset

	HDP	MP based algorithm
RP	0.6000	**0.6519**
AP	0.7154	**0.8000**
AUC	0.8983	**0.9552**

3.1 Testing on Addition Data

The results in table 2 show that the time-frequency dictionaries based algorithm does well to new songs. We use the MP trained on a smaller set consisting of 79 songs by artists not in the training set. The songs came from the SXSW artist showcase collection and other popular music, compare the HDP based algorithm for retrieval quality.

4 Conclusion

In music information retrieval, music searching and browsing particular music songs in an efficient manner is still demanding. We demonstrate new search system for assessing the similarity between songs. The system uses matching pursuit and spatial pyramid matching for determining significant features of music pieces and retrieving music songs in efficient way. Retrieving similar music pieces from a database is completed by matching the MP features space step by step level using spatial pyramid matching. Better speed and accuracy on large collection of musical songs are achieved upon the whole architecture of the system.

References

[1] Levy, M., Sandler, M., Casey, M.: Extraction of high-Level Musical Structure from Audio Data its Application to Thumbnail Generation. EPSRC grant GR/S84750/01
[2] Aucouturier, J.-J., Pachet, F.: Music similarity measures: What's the use? In: Proceedings of ISMIR 2002 Third International Conference on Music Information Retrieval (September 2002)
[3] Logan, B., Salomon, A.: A Content-Based Music Similarity Function, Cambridge, Massachusetts 02142 USA
[4] Turnbull, D., Lanckriet, G., Pampalk, E., Goto, M.: A Supervised Approach for Detecting Boundaries in Music. Austrian Computer Society, OCG (2007)
[5] Goto, M.: A Chorus-Section Detecting Method for Musical Audio Signals. In: ICASSP Proceedings, pp. V-437–440 (April 2003)
[6] Jehan, T.: Hierarchical multi-class self similarities. In: Proc. of 2005 IEEE Workshop on Applications of Signal Processing to Audio and Acoustics, New Platz, New York, USA, pp. 311–314 (October 2005)
[7] Turnbull, D., Pampalk, G.L.E., Goto, M.: A Supervised Approch For Detection Boundaries in Music using Difference Features and Boosting. Austrian Computer Society, OCG (2007)
[8] Mallat, S.G., Zhang, Z.: Matching Pursuits With Time-Frequency Dictionaries. IEEE Transactions on Signal Processing 41(12) (December 1993)
[9] Krstulovie, S., Gribonval, R.: The Matching Pursuit Tool Kit
[10] Chu, S., Narayanan, S., Jay Kuo, C.-C.: Environmental Sound Recognition using MP-Based Features. University of Southern California, Los Angeles, CA 90089-2564
[11] Lazebnik, S., Schmid, C.: Spatial Pyramid Matching
[12] Hoffman, M., Blei, D., Cook, P.: Content-Based Musical Similarity Computation Using The Hierarchical Dirichlet Process. In: ISMIR –session 3a Content-Based Retrieval, Categorization and Similarity 1 (2008)

Numerical Methods for Fuzzy Initial Value Problems under Different Types of Interpretation: A Comparison Study

Muhammad Zaini Ahmad[1,*] and Mohammad Khatim Hasan[2]

[1] Institute of Engineering Mathematics,
Universiti Malaysia Perlis,
02000 Kuala Perlis, Perlis, Malaysia
`mzaini@unimap.edu.my`
[2] School of Information Technology,
Faculty of Information Science and Technology,
Universiti Kebangsaan Malaysia,
43600 UKM Bangi, Selangor, Malaysia
`mkhatim@ftsm.ukm.my`

Abstract. In this paper, we present the solution of fuzzy initial value problem of the form $X'(t) = f(t, X(t))$, $X(t_0) = X_0$, where X_0 is a symmetric triangular fuzzy interval. In the first part, we review the existing analytical methods for solving such problem under different types of interpretation. We then provide detailed numerical procedures based on the different interpretations given in the first part. Finally, we give a property and establish some results on relationship between the existing numerical methods under different types of interpretation.

Keywords: fuzzy initial value problem, symmetric triangular fuzzy interval, analytical methods, numerical methods, relationship.

1 Introduction

A common approach in modelling real world problems is ordinary differential equations. This approach requires precise information about the problem under investigation. In many cases, this information will often not be known precisely. This is obvious when determining initial values, parameter values, or functional relationships. In order to handle such situations, the use of fuzzy sets may be seen as an effective tool for a better understanding of the studied phenomena. It is therefore not surprising that there is a vast literature dealing with fuzzy differential equations [9–11, 14, 17, 19, 22, 27–30].

In the literature, there are several approaches to study fuzzy differential equations. The first and the most popular one is Hukuhara derivative [16, 25]. However, this approach suffers from certain disadvantages since the solution of a fuzzy differential equation becomes fuzzier and fuzzier as independent variable

---

* Corresponding author.

A. Abd Manaf et al. (Eds.): ICIEIS 2011, Part II, CCIS 252, pp. 275–288, 2011.
© Springer-Verlag Berlin Heidelberg 2011

increases. According to Diamond [13], this approach does not reproduce the rich and varied behaviour of ordinary differential equations. Therefore, it is not suitable for modelling. In order to overcome this problem, Hüllermeier [17] has interpreted a fuzzy differential equation as a set of differential inclusions, i.e expressing the solution of a fuzzy differential equation as level setwise. However, in general, the solution is not convex on the time domain [13].

The alternative approach has been proposed by Buckley and Feuring [10], who fuzzified the solution of ordinary differential equations with fuzzy initial values using Zadeh's extension principle [31]. A further development has been studied by Mizukoshi et al. [22]. However, this approach seems to be somewhat less general and does not have a fuzzy character in the formulation of fuzzy differential equations. In order to overcome many problems existing in studying fuzzy differential equations, Bede and Gal [9] have introduced another concept of derivatives called the generalised Hukuhara derivative. Under this interpretation, the solution of a fuzzy differential equation may have less fuzzier as independent variable increases, depending on the choice of the fuzzy derivatives. However, under this interpretation the solution of a fuzzy differential equation is not unique. It has two solution locally.

Developing an accurate numerical method is one of the important parts in studying fuzzy differential equations. It will help scientists and engineers to approximate the solution of non-linear problems. In the literature, there has been a growing interest in developing numerical methods for fuzzy differential equations. All the ideas are based on extending the existing classical numerical methods to the fuzzy case. This process yields fuzzy Euler method [5, 7, 18, 21, 23], fuzzy Taylor method [1], fuzzy Runge-Kutta method [2, 4, 24] and many more. Efficient computational algorithms developed in [6, 8] can be incorporated in order to guarantee the convexity of fuzzy solution on the time domain. In this paper, we study the relationship between the several varieties of fuzzy Euler method for solving fuzzy differential equations.

This paper is organised in the following sequence. In Section 2, we recall some basic definitions and the theoretical background needed in this paper. In Section 3, we review some interpretations of fuzzy initial value problems. We then provide several varieties of fuzzy Euler method for fuzzy initial value problems based on the different interpretations given in Section 3. Under monotonicity condition, we give some relationships between them in Section 5. Some numerical examples are also given in this section. Finally in Section 5, we give some conclusions.

2   Preliminaries

In this section, we give some basic definitions and results that are needed throughout this paper.

2.1   Fuzzy Intervals

The basic definition of fuzzy interval is given in [32].

Definition 1. *A fuzzy interval is a function $U : \mathbb{R} \rightarrow [0,1]$ satisfying the following properties:*

(i) *U is normal: there exists $x_0 \in \mathbb{R}$ such that $U(x_0) = 1$;*
(ii) *U is convex: for all $x, y \in \mathbb{R}$ and $0 \leq \lambda \leq 1$, it holds that*

$$U(\lambda x + (1 - \lambda)y) \geq \min\left(U(x), U(y)\right);$$

(iii) *U is upper semi-continuous: for any $x_0 \in \mathbb{R}$, it holds that*

$$U(x_0) \geq \lim_{x \rightarrow x_0^{\pm}} U(x);$$

(iv) *$[U]^0 = \overline{\{x \in \mathbb{R} \mid U(x) > 0\}}$ is a compact subset of $\mathbb{R}$.*

A fuzzy interval can also be presented in parametric form as follows [21].

Definition 2. *A fuzzy interval in parametric form is a pair (u_1^α, u_2^α) of functions u_1^α and u_2^α for $\alpha \in [0,1]$, satisfying the following properties:*

(i) *u_1^α is a bounded increasing left continuous function of α over [0,1];*
(ii) *u_2^α is a bounded decreasing right continuous function of α over [0,1];*
(iii) *$u_1^\alpha \leq u_2^\alpha$ for $\alpha \in [0,1]$.*

If there is a $\alpha \in [0,1]$ such that $u_1^\alpha \geq u_2^\alpha$, then the order pair (u_1^α, u_2^α) is not a valid level set.

Definition 3. *Let U be a fuzzy interval in $\mathbb{R}$. The α-cuts of U, denoted $[U]^\alpha$, $\alpha \in [0,1]$, is*

$$[U]^\alpha = \{x \in \mathbb{R} \mid U(x) \geq \alpha\}.$$

For a fuzzy interval U, its α-cuts are closed intervals in $\mathbb{R}$. Let denote them by

$$[U]^\alpha = [u_1^\alpha, u_2^\alpha].$$

Definition 4. *Let U be a fuzzy interval in $\mathbb{R}$. The support of U, denoted $supp(U)$, is*

$$supp(U) = \{x \in \mathbb{R} \mid U(x) > 0\}.$$

Definition 5. *If U is a symmetric triangular fuzzy interval with support $[a, c]$, then the α-cuts of U is*

$$[A]^\alpha = \left[a + \alpha\left(\frac{c - a}{2}\right), b - \alpha\left(\frac{c - a}{2}\right)\right].$$

In this paper, the set of all symmetric triangular fuzzy intervals is denoted by $\mathcal{F}(\mathbb{R})$.

2.2   The Extension Principle

In [31], Zadeh proposed the so-called extension principle which becomes an important tool in fuzzy set theory and its applications. The principal idea of Zadeh's extension principle is that each function $f : \mathbb{R} \to \mathbb{R}$ induces another function $f : \mathcal{F}(\mathbb{R}) \to \mathcal{F}(\mathbb{R})$ mapping a fuzzy interval U to a fuzzy interval $f(U)$ defined by

$$f(U)(y) = \begin{cases} \sup\limits_{x \in f^{-1}(y)} U(x) & \text{, if } y \in \text{range}(f), \\ 0 & \text{, if } y \notin \text{range}(f). \end{cases}$$

In particular, if f is injective, it holds that

$$f(U)(y) = \begin{cases} U(f^{-1}(y)) & \text{, if } y \in \text{range}(f), \\ 0 & \text{, if } y \notin \text{range}(f). \end{cases}$$

Furthermore, in [26] if $f : \mathbb{R} \to \mathbb{R}$ is a real continuous function, then $f : \mathcal{F}(\mathbb{R}) \to \mathcal{F}(\mathbb{R})$ is well-defined function and

$$[f(U)]^\alpha = f([U]^\alpha), \quad \forall \alpha \in [0, 1], \quad U \in \mathcal{F}(\mathbb{R}),$$

where $f([U]^\alpha) = \{f(x) \mid x \in [U]^\alpha\}$. Consequently, if U is a fuzzy interval with the closure of its support is $[U]^0 - [u_1, u_2]$ and f is a real continuous function, then we have that

$$[f(U)]^0 = \left[\min_{x \in [u_1, u_2]} f(x), \max_{x \in [u_1, u_2]} f(x) \right].$$

2.3   Fuzzy Derivatives

In order to study fuzzy differential equations, we need some results on fuzzy derivatives. First, let us recall the definition of the Hukuhara difference [25].

Definition 6. *Let $X, Y \in \mathcal{F}(\mathbb{R})$. If there exists $Z \in \mathcal{F}(\mathbb{R})$ such that $Z = Y + Z$, then Z is called Hukuhara difference of X and Y and it is denoted by $X \ominus Y$.*

In this paper, the sign "$\ominus$" always stands for Hukuhara difference and also note that $X \ominus Y \neq X + (-1)Y$.

Definition 7. *[15] A function $X : (a, b) \to \mathcal{F}(\mathbb{R})$ is called a continuous fuzzy function if for every $t_0 \in (a, b)$ and every $\epsilon > 0$, there exists $\delta > 0$ such that, if $|t - t_0| < \delta$ then $D(X(t), X(t_0)) < \epsilon$.*

Next, we consider the following definition of generalised Hukuhara derivative for fuzzy functions. It was introduced by Bede and Gal [9] and later investigated by Chalco-Cano and Román-Flores [11].

Definition 8. *Let $X : (a, b) \to \mathcal{F}(\mathbb{R})$ and $t_0 \in (a, b)$. We say that X is differentiable at t_0, if there exists $X'(t_0) \in \mathcal{F}(\mathbb{R})$ such that*

(I) *for all $h > 0$ sufficiently close to 0, the Hukuhara differences $X(t_0 + h) \ominus X(t_0)$ and $X(t_0) \ominus X(t_0 - h)$ exist and (in metric D)*

$$\lim_{h \to 0^+} \frac{X(t_0 + h) \ominus X(t_0)}{h} = \lim_{h \to 0^+} \frac{X(t_0) \ominus X(t_0 - h)}{h} = X'(t_0),$$

or

(II) *for all $h > 0$ sufficiently close to 0, the Hukuhara differences $X(t_0) \ominus X(t_0 + h)$ and $X(t_0 - h) \ominus X(t_0)$ exist and (in metric D)*

$$\lim_{h \to 0^+} \frac{X(t_0) \ominus X(t_0 + h)}{-h} = \lim_{h \to 0^+} \frac{X(t_0 - h) \ominus X(t_0)}{-h} = X'(t_0).$$

If X is a fuzzy function and its derivative is defined under generalised Hukuhara derivative, then we have the following results.

Theorem 1. *[11] Let $X : (a, b) \to \mathcal{F}(\mathbb{R})$ and denote $[X(t)]^\alpha = [x_1^\alpha(t), x_2^\alpha(t)]$ for each $\alpha \in [0, 1]$.*

(i) *If X is differentiable in the first form (I), then $x_1^\alpha(t)$ and $x_2^\alpha(t)$ are differentiable functions and we have*

$$[X'(t)]^\alpha = [x_1^{\alpha\prime}(t), x_2^{\alpha\prime}(t)].$$

(ii) *If X is differentiable in the second form (II), then $x_1^\alpha(t)$ and $x_2^\alpha(t)$ are differentiable functions and we have*

$$[X'(t)]^\alpha = [x_2^{\alpha\prime}(t), x_1^{\alpha\prime}(t)].$$

In this paper, we assume that if X is differentiable in the first form (I), then it is not differentiable in the second form (II) and vice versa.

3   Fuzzy Initial Value Problems

We begin by considering the following non-fuzzy initial value problem:

$$\begin{cases} x'(t) = f(t, x(t)), & t \in [t_0, T], \\ x(t_0) = x_0, \end{cases} \tag{1}$$

where $f : [t_0, T] \times \mathbb{R} \to \mathbb{R}$ is a real-valued function defined on $[t_0, T]$ with $T > 0$ and $x_0 \in \mathbb{R}$. Supposing that the initial value in (1) is uncertain and replaced by a fuzzy interval, then we have the following fuzzy initial value problem:

$$\begin{cases} X'(t) = f(t, X(t)), & t \in [t_0, T], \\ X(t_0) = X_0, \end{cases} \tag{2}$$

where $f : [t_0, T] \times \mathcal{F}(\mathbb{R}) \to \mathcal{F}(\mathbb{R})$ is a fuzzy-valued function defined on $[t_0, T]$ with $T > 0$ and $X_0 \in \mathcal{F}(\mathbb{R})$.

In order to study the problem (2), we need to address the following questions: what is the interpretation of (2) and what does a solution of (2) mean? In the literature, there are three possibilities for representing the solution of (2).

3.1 Interpretation Based on Fuzzy Derivative

If we consider $X'(t)$ is the fuzzy derivative in the first form (I), then from Theorem 1 (i), we have the following procedures for solving (2):

(i) Solve the following system of ordinary differential equations:

$$\begin{cases} x_1^{\alpha\prime}(t) = f_\alpha(t, x_1^\alpha(t), x_2^\alpha(t)), & x_1^\alpha(t_0) = x_{0,1}^\alpha, \\ x_2^{\alpha\prime}(t) = g_\alpha(t, x_1^\alpha(t), x_2^\alpha(t)), & x_2^\alpha(t_0) = x_{0,2}^\alpha, \end{cases} \tag{3}$$

for $x_1^\alpha(t)$ and $x_2^\alpha(t)$.

(ii) Ensure that $[x_1^\alpha(t), x_2^\alpha(t)]$ and $[x_1^{\alpha\prime}(t), x_2^{\alpha\prime}(t)]$ are valid level sets.
(iii) Using the Representation Theorem [3], pile up the levels $[x_1^\alpha(t), x_2^\alpha(t)]$ to a fuzzy solution $X(t)$.

Now, if we consider $X'(t)$ is the fuzzy derivative in the second form (II), then from Theorem 1 (ii), we have the following procedures for solving (2):

(i) Solve the following system of ordinary differential equations:

$$\begin{cases} x_1^{\alpha\prime}(t) = g_\alpha(t, x_1^\alpha(t), x_2^\alpha(t)), & x_1^\alpha(t_0) = x_{0,1}^\alpha, \\ x_2^{\alpha\prime}(t) = f_\alpha(t, x_1^\alpha(t), x_2^\alpha(t)), & x_2^\alpha(t_0) = x_{0,2}^\alpha, \end{cases} \tag{4}$$

for $x_1^\alpha(t)$ and $x_2^\alpha(t)$.

(ii) Ensure that $[x_1^\alpha(t), x_2^\alpha(t)]$ and $[x_2^{\alpha\prime}(t), x_1^{\alpha\prime}(t)]$ are valid level sets.
(iii) Using the Representation Theorem [3], pile up the levels $[x_1^\alpha(t), x_2^\alpha(t)]$ to a fuzzy solution $X(t)$.

These procedures can be found in [11, 20].

3.2 Interpretation Based on Differential Inclusions

According to Hüllermeier [17], the fuzzy initial value problem in (2) can be interpreted as a set of differential inclusions as follow:

$$\begin{cases} x_\alpha'(t) = f(t, x_\alpha(t)), & t \in [t_0, T], \\ x_\alpha(t_0) = [X_0]^\alpha, \end{cases} \tag{5}$$

where $f : [t_0, T] \times \mathbb{R} \to \mathcal{F}(\mathbb{R})$ is a fuzzy-valued function defined on $[t_0, T]$ with $T > 0$ and $X_0 \in \mathcal{F}(\mathbb{R})$. For every $\alpha \in [0, 1]$, we say that $x_\alpha : [t_0, T] \to \mathbb{R}$ is the α-solution of (5) if it is absolutely continuous and satisfies (5) almost everywhere on $[t_0, T]$ with $T > 0$. Let M_α be the set of α-solution of (5), and define the attainable set as

$$\mathcal{A}_\alpha(t) = \{x_\alpha(t) \mid x_\alpha(\cdot) \in M_\alpha\},$$

then $\mathcal{A}_\alpha(t)$ is the α-cuts of fuzzy attainable set $\mathcal{A}(t)$. Therefore, the fuzzy attainable set is the solution of (2).

3.3   Interpretation Based on Zadeh's Extension Principle

In order to find the solution of (1) derived from (2), we refer to [12]. Let U be an open set in $\mathbb{R}$ such that there is a unique solution $x(\cdot, x_0)$ of (1) in the interval $[t_0, T]$ with $x_0 \in U$ and for all $t \in [t_0, T]$. Then $x(t, \cdot)$ is continuous on U and the operator:

$$L_t : U \to \mathbb{R},$$

given by $L_t(x_0) = x(t, x_0)$, is the unique solution of (1) and continuous with respect to x_0. So, applying the extension principle to the solution L_t, we obtain

$$\widehat{L}_t : \mathcal{F}(U) \to \mathcal{F}(\mathbb{R}),$$

which is the unique solution to the problem (2) for all $t \in [t_0, T]$.

4   Numerical Methods for Fuzzy Initial Value Problems

First, we recall Taylor's Theorem to derive the classical Euler method. Suppose that $x(t)$, the unique solution of (1) have two continuous derivatives on the interval $[t_0, T]$, so that for each $i = 0, 1, 2, ..., N-1$,

$$x(t_{i+1}) = x(t_i) + (t_{i+1} - t_i)x'(t_i) + \frac{(t_{i+1} - t_i)^2}{2}x''(\xi_i) \tag{6}$$

for some numbers $\xi_i \in (t_i, t_{i+1})$. By setting $h = t_{i+1} - t_i$, we have that

$$x(t_{i+1}) = x(t_i) + hx'(t_i) + \frac{h^2}{2}x''(\xi_i) \tag{7}$$

and, since $x(t)$ satisfies the problem (1), we have

$$x(t_{i+1}) = x(t_i) + hf(t_i, x(t_i)) + \frac{h^2}{2}x''(\xi_i) \tag{8}$$

By truncating the remainder term and denoting $x_i \approx x(t_i)$, then we have the following Euler method for the problem (1):

$$x_{i+1} = x_i + hf(t_i, x_i), \tag{9}$$

for each $i = 0, 1, 2, ..., N-1$.

In order to extend the classical Euler method (9) in fuzzy setting, we divided it according to the following interpretations.

4.1   Euler Method Based on Fuzzy Derivative

Let $[X(t_i)]^\alpha = [x_1^\alpha(t_i), x_2^\alpha(t_i)]$ and $[X_i]^\alpha = [x_{i,1}^\alpha, x_{i,2}^\alpha]$ be the exact and approximate solutions of (2), respectively. The fuzzy Euler method associated with fuzzy derivatives in the first form (I) and in the second form (II) are given as follows, respectively [23]:

$$\begin{cases} x_{i+1,1}^\alpha = x_{i,1}^\alpha + h\min\left\{f(h,t_i,x) \mid x \in [x_{i,1}^\alpha, x_{i,2}^\alpha]\right\}, \\ x_{i+1,2}^\alpha = x_{i,2}^\alpha + h\max\left\{f(h,t_i,x) \mid x \in [x_{i,1}^\alpha, x_{i,2}^\alpha]\right\}, \end{cases} \tag{10}$$

and

$$\begin{cases} x_{i+1,1}^\alpha = x_{i,1}^\alpha + h\max\left\{f(h,t_i,x) \mid x \in [x_{i,1}^\alpha, x_{i,2}^\alpha]\right\}, \\ x_{i+1,2}^\alpha = x_{i,2}^\alpha + h\min\left\{f(h,t_i,x) \mid x \in [x_{i,1}^\alpha, x_{i,2}^\alpha]\right\}. \end{cases} \tag{11}$$

4.2 Euler Method Based on Differential Inclusions

In order to approximate the fuzzy attainable set $\mathcal{A}(t_i)$, Hüllermeier [17] has proposed the following Euler method:

$$X_\alpha(t_{i+1}) = \bigcup_{x \in X_\alpha(t_i)} x + hf(t_i, x), \alpha \in [0,1], \tag{12}$$

where $X_\alpha(t_i)$ are the α-cuts of fuzzy attainable set $X(t_i)$. In this case, $X(t_i) \approx \mathcal{A}(t_i)$.

4.3 Euler Method Based on Zadeh's Extension Principle

In order to extend the classical Euler method (9) based on Zadeh's extension principle, Ahmad and Hassan [7] have proposed the following. First, let consider the following situation:

$$M(h,t,x) = x + hf(t,x). \tag{13}$$

If x is replaced by a fuzzy interval, then from the extension principle, we have

$$M(h,t,X)(z) = \begin{cases} \sup_{x \in M^{-1}(h,t,z)} X(x) & \text{, if } z \in \text{range}(M), \\ 0 & \text{, if } z \notin \text{range}(M). \end{cases} \tag{14}$$

Let $[X]^\alpha = [x_1^\alpha, x_2^\alpha]$ be the α-cuts of X for all $\alpha \in [0,1]$, then (14) can be computed as follows:

$$M(h,t,[X]^\alpha) = [\min\left\{M(h,t,x) \mid x \in [x_1^\alpha, x_2^\alpha]\right\}, \max\left\{M(h,t,x) \mid x \in [x_1^\alpha, x_2^\alpha]\right\}]. \tag{15}$$

By using this idea, the authors extended the classical Euler method (9) in fuzzy setting as follows:

$$\begin{cases} x_{i+1,1}^\alpha = \min\left\{(x + hf(t,x)) \mid x \in [x_{i,1}^\alpha, x_{i,2}^\alpha]\right\}, \\ x_{i+1,2}^\alpha = \max\left\{(x + hf(t,x)) \mid x \in [x_{i,1}^\alpha, x_{i,2}^\alpha]\right\}. \end{cases} \tag{16}$$

Up to this point, we have the following result.

Proposition 1. *If f is monotone with respect to the second argument and X_0 is a symmetric triangular fuzzy interval, then for all $t_i \in [t_0, T]$, $i = 1, 2, ..., N$, the numerical methods presented in this section will also generate symmetric triangular fuzzy interval.*

Proof. Let consider f is monotone increasing and $[X(t_i)]^\alpha = [x_1^\alpha(t_i), x_2^\alpha(t_i)]$. Then we have $f(t, x_1^\alpha(t_i)) \leq f(t, x_2^\alpha(t_i))$ and

$$f(t, [X(t_i)]^\alpha) = [f(t, x_1^\alpha(t_i)), f(t, x_2^\alpha(t_i))].$$

Since f is monotone increasing, the function values at the endpoints of the α-cuts are the correct endpoints of the output, which finally generate symmetric triangular fuzzy interval. This holds for all $t_i \in [t_0, T]$, $i = 1, 2, ..., N$. A similar explanation can be used for monotone decreasing function.

5   Relationship

In this section, we will give some results on relationship between the several varieties of fuzzy Euler method under different types of interpretation.

Proposition 2. *If f is monotone with respect to the second argument, then the approximate solution generated from fuzzy Euler method under fuzzy derivative in the second form (II) is subset of the approximate solution generated from fuzzy Euler method under fuzzy derivative in the first form (I).*

Proof. If f is monotone (increasing or decreasing), then fuzzy Euler method under fuzzy derivative in the second form (II) will generate approximation that has decreasing length of its support as t increases. This is clear from Definition 8 (II) that $\text{supp}(X_{i+1})$ should be smaller than $\text{supp}(X_i)$ for $i = 0, 1, ..., N-1$. In contrary, if we use fuzzy Euler method under fuzzy derivative in the first form (I), the approximate solution has increasing length of its support as t increases. This means that $\text{supp}(X_{i+1})$ is wider than $\text{supp}(X_i)$ for $i = 0, 1, ..., N-1$, which agrees with Definition 8 (I). This leads to the conclusion that the approximate solution generated from fuzzy Euler method under fuzzy derivative in the second form (II) is subset of fuzzy Euler method under fuzzy derivative in the first form (I).

Proposition 3. *If f is increasing with respect to the second argument, then the approximate solution generated from fuzzy Euler method under fuzzy derivative in the first form (I) is identical with the approximate solution generated from fuzzy Euler method under differential inclusions.*

Proof. From Eqs. (10) and (12), the proof is obvious.

Proposition 4. *If f is decreasing with respect to the second argument, then the approximate solution generated from fuzzy Euler method under fuzzy derivative in the second form (II) is identical with the approximate solution generated from fuzzy Euler method under differential inclusions.*

Proof. From Eqs. (11) and (12), the proof is obvious.

Proposition 5. *If f is monotone with respect to the second argument, then the approximate solution generated from fuzzy Euler method under differential inclusions is identical with the approximate solution generated from fuzzy Euler method under Zadeh's extension principle.*

Proof. From Eqs. (12) and (16), the proof is obvious.

Proposition 6. *If f is increasing with respect to the second argument, then the approximate solution generated from fuzzy Euler method under fuzzy derivative in the first form (I) is identical with the approximate solution generated from fuzzy Euler method under Zadeh's extension principle.*

Proof. The proof follows immediately from Propositions 3 and 5.

Proposition 7. *If f is decreasing with respect to the second argument, then the approximate solution generated from fuzzy Euler method under fuzzy derivative in the second form (II) is identical with the approximate solution generated from fuzzy Euler method under Zadeh's extension principle.*

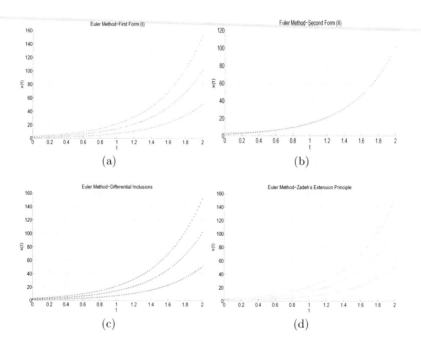

Fig. 1. The approximate solution of (17) using (a) fuzzy Euler method under fuzzy derivative in the first form (I), (b) fuzzy Euler method under fuzzy derivative in the second form (II), (c) fuzzy Euler method under differential inclusions and (d) fuzzy Euler method under Zadeh's extension principle

Proof. It follows immediately from Propositions 4 and 5.

In what follows, we illustrate these propositions on the following examples.

Example 1. Consider the following fuzzy initial value problem:

$$\begin{cases} X'(t) = 2X(t)\,, & t \in [0,2]\,, \\ X(0) = (1,2,3)\,, \end{cases} \tag{17}$$

Using fuzzy Euler methods presented in Section 4, the results are plotted in Fig. 1. From the results, we can see that the approximate solution obtained by using fuzzy Euler method under fuzzy derivative in the second form (II) is subset of the approximate solution obtained by using fuzzy Euler method under fuzzy derivative in the first form (I) (see Figs. 1(a),1(b)). This agrees with Proposition 2. Moreover, since f is increasing with respect to the second argument, then the approximate solutions obtained by using fuzzy Euler method under fuzzy derivative in the first form (I), fuzzy Euler method under differential inclusions and fuzzy Euler method under Zadeh's extension principle are equivalent, which agree with Propositions 3, 5 and 6 (see Figs. 1(a),1(c),1(d)).

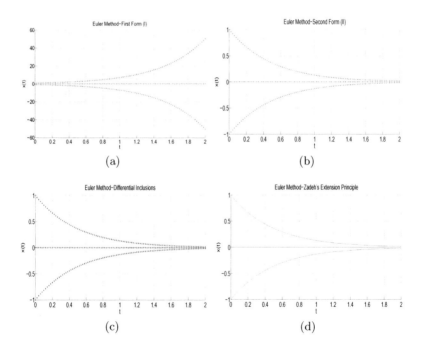

Fig. 2. The approximate solution of (18) using (a) fuzzy Euler method under fuzzy derivative in the first form (I), (b) fuzzy Euler method under fuzzy derivative in the second form (II), (c) fuzzy Euler method under differential inclusions and (d) fuzzy Euler method under Zadeh's extension principle

Example 2. Consider the following fuzzy initial value problem:

$$\begin{cases} X'(t) = -2X(t), & t \in [0, 2], \\ X(0) = (-1, 0, 1), \end{cases} \qquad (18)$$

In this example, again we can see that the approximate solution obtained by using fuzzy Euler method under fuzzy derivative in the second form (II) is subset of the approximate solution obtained by using fuzzy Euler method under fuzzy derivative in the first form (I) (see Figs. 2(a),2(b)). Hence, Proposition 2 holds. In addition, since f is decreasing with respect to the second argument, then the approximate solutions obtained by using fuzzy Euler method under fuzzy derivative in the second form (II), fuzzy Euler method under differential inclusions and fuzzy Euler method under Zadeh's extension principle are also equivalent (see Figs. 2(a),2(c),2(d)). Therefore, Propositions 4, 5 and 7 hold true.

6   Conclusions

We have studied some existing analytical and numerical methods for fuzzy initial value problems under different types of interpretation. Some relations among numerical methods considered in this paper have been established. Under monotonicity condition, we have shown that the considered numerical methods produce the same approximation solution. In future research, we are going to establish some results under non-monotonicity condition.

Acknowledgments. This research was co-funded by the Ministry of Higher Education of Malaysia (MOHE) and partially supported by Universiti Malaysia Perlis (UniMAP) under the programme "Skim Latihan Akademik IPTA".

References

1. Abbasbandy, S., Allahviranloo, T.: Numerical solutions of fuzzy differential equations by Taylor method. Computational Methods in Applied Mathematics 2, 113–124 (2002)
2. Abbasbandy, S., Allahviranloo, T.: Numerical solution of fuzzy differential equation by Runge-Kutta method. Nonlinear Studies 11, 117–129 (2004)
3. Agarwal, R.P., O'Regan, D., Lakshmikantham, V.: Viability theory and fuzzy differential equations. Fuzzy Sets and Systems 151, 563–580 (2005)
4. Ahmad, M.Z., De Baets, B.: A predator-prey model with fuzzy initial populations. In: IFSA/EUSFLAT Conf. 2009, pp. 1311–1314 (2009)
5. Ahmad, M.Z., Hasan, M.K.: A new approach to incorporate uncertainty into Euler method. Applied Mathematical Sciences 4, 2509–2520 (2010)
6. Ahmad, M.Z., Hasan, M.K.: Incorporating optimisation technique into Zadeh's extension principle for computing non-monotone functions with fuzzy variable. Sains Malaysiana 40, 643–650 (2011)

7. Ahmad, M.Z., Hasan, M.K.: A new fuzzy version of Euler's method for solving differential equations with fuzzy initial values. Sains Malaysiana 40, 651–657 (2011)
8. Ahmad, M.Z., Hasan, M.K., De Baets, B.: A new method for computing continuous functions with fuzzy variable. Journal of Applied Sciences 11, 1143–1149 (2011)
9. Bede, B., Gal, S.G.: Generalizations of the differentiability of fuzzy-number-valued functions with applications to fuzzy differential equations. Fuzzy Sets and Systems 151, 581–599 (2005)
10. Buckley, J.J., Feuring, T.: Fuzzy differential equations. Fuzzy Sets and Systems 110, 43–54 (2000)
11. Chalco-Cano, Y., Román-Flores, H.: On new solutions of fuzzy differential equations. Chaos, Solitons & Fractals 38, 112–119 (2008)
12. Chalco-Cano, Y., Román-Flores, H.: Comparison between some approaches to solve fuzzy differential equations. Fuzzy Sets and Systems 160, 1517–1527 (2009)
13. Diamond, P.: Stability and periodicity in fuzzy differential equations. IEEE Transactions on Fuzzy Systems 8, 583–590 (2000)
14. Ding, Z., Ma, M., Kandel, A.: Existence of the solutions of fuzzy differential equations with parameters. Information Sciences 99, 205–217 (1997)
15. Dubois, D., Prade, H.: Fuzzy Sets and Systems: Theory and Applications. Academic Press, New York (1980)
16. Goetschel, R., Voxman, W.: Elementary fuzzy calculus. Fuzzy Sets and Systems 18, 31–43 (1986)
17. Hüllermeier, E.: An approach to modelling and simulation of uncertain dynamical systems. Int. J. Uncertainty Fuzziness Knowledge-Based Systems 5, 117–137 (1997)
18. Hüllermeier, E.: Numerical methods for fuzzy initial value problems. Int. J. Uncertainty Fuzziness Knowledge-Based Systems 7, 439–461 (1999)
19. Kaleva, O.: Fuzzy differential equations. Fuzzy Sets and Systems 24, 301–317 (1987)
20. Kaleva, O.: A note on fuzzy differential equations. Nonlinear Analysis 64, 895–900 (2006)
21. Ma, M., Friedman, M., Kandel, A.: Numerical solution of fuzzy differential equations. Fuzzy Sets and Systems 105, 133–138 (1999)
22. Mizukoshi, M.T., Barros, L.C., Chalco-Cano, Y., Romn-Flores, H., Bassanezi, R.C.: Fuzzy differential equations and the extension principle. Information Sciences 177, 3627–3635 (2007)
23. Nieto, J.J., Khastan, A., Ivaz, K.: Numerical solution of fuzzy differential equations under generalized differentiability. Nonlinear Analysis: Hybrid Systems 3, 700–707 (2009)
24. Palligkinis, S.C., Papageorgiou, G., Famelis, I.T.: Runge-Kutta methods for fuzzy differential equations. Applied Mathematics and Computation 209, 97–105 (2008)
25. Puri, M.L., Ralescu, D.A.: Differentials of fuzzy functions. J. Math. Anal. Appl. 91, 552–558 (1983)
26. Román-Flores, H., Barros, L., Bassanezi, R.: A note on Zadeh's extension principle. Fuzzy Sets and Systems 117, 327–331 (2001)
27. Song, S., Wu, C.: Existence and uniqueness of solutions to the Cauchy problem of fuzzy differential equations. Fuzzy Sets and Systems 110, 55–67 (2000)
28. Vorobiev, D., Seikkala, S.: Towards the theory of fuzzy differential equations. Fuzzy Sets and Systems 125, 231–237 (2002)

29. Wu, C., Song, S.: Existence theorem to the Cauchy problem of fuzzy differential equations under compactness-type conditions. Information Sciences 108, 123–134 (1998)
30. Wu, C., Song, S., Lee, E.S.: Approximate solutions, existence and uniqueness of the Cauchy problem of fuzzy differential equations. Journal of Mathematical Analysis and Applications 202, 629–644 (1996)
31. Zadeh, L.A.: Fuzzy sets. Information and Control 8, 338–353 (1965)
32. Zimmermann, H.J.: Fuzzy Set Theory and Its Applications. Kluwer Academic Publishers, Dordrecht (1991)

Assessing the Suitability of MMORPGs as Educational Games Using HCI Evaluation Methods

Qin En Looi and Swee Lan See

Institute for Infocomm Research, A*STAR, Singapore,
1 Fusionopolis Way, #21-01 Connexis (South), Singapore 138632
{stuqel,slsee}@i2r.a-star.edu.sg

Abstract. Massive multiplayer online role playing games (MMORPGs) possess an untapped potential in game-based learning. They provide platforms which have been proven to be engaging for educators to incorporate educational elements into game play. In order to assess the suitability of MMORPGs in specific educational settings, we introduce the video-diary method, which evaluates human-computer interaction between the students and the game. Through the video-diary method, we can better assess the suitability of each MMORPG in meeting the curriculum objectives, as well as the engagement between gamer and game. We also review five popular MMORPGs: MapleStory, World of Warcraft, Second Life, Counter-Strike and Runescape for their suitability as educational games, suggesting specific subjects which can be taught because they are particularly suited to each MMORPG's game play.

Keywords: game-based learning, human computer interaction, massive multiplayer online role-playing games, evaluation methods, education pedagogy.

1 Introduction

The pervasiveness and effectiveness of computer games as classroom teaching aids has been speculated by many education technology researchers in recent years. There have been works such as [1, 2, 3] which identified and analyzed the characteristics of specific computer games which make them suitable for educational purposes. Such works postulate that learning in a non-traditional environment enhances the learning experience [4, 5] because of the fun and entertainment available. However, developers always face the challenge of building successful educational games to meet the curriculum's needs.

A more resource-friendly alternative would be to modify existing games available for e-learning so that games do not have to be developed from scratch [6]. By re-purposing existing games, more effort can be devoted to development of educational content instead of the game engine. In this paper, we consider the use of Massive Multiplayer Online Role-Playing Games (MMORPGs) in education.

As MMORPGs are developed for entertainment purposes with little education purpose that matches school curriculum, there is a need to assess how relevant and suitable each MMORPG is to meet different curriculum objectives and classroom

A. Abd Manaf et al. (Eds.): ICIEIS 2011, Part II, CCIS 252, pp. 289–298, 2011.
© Springer-Verlag Berlin Heidelberg 2011

settings. An effective generic assessment tool is required to assess the suitability of MMORPGs in education so that educators with different curriculum objectives can independently assess each game and decide which is most appropriate for use in the classroom.

We propose an amalgamation of two human-computer interaction (HCI) evaluation methods in this paper to assess the suitability of MMORPGS in education. By establishing proper HCI user interface studies, educators and game developers can use these methods to assess the suitability of the games and modify the platforms accordingly to achieve maximum learning effectiveness by meeting the curriculum objectives.

We will first introduce our HCI evaluation method which combines and improves on two existing usability evaluation methods, followed by an analytical evaluation of five MMORPGs of different genres: MapleStory, World of Warcraft, Second Life, Counter-Strike and Runescape for their suitability. These popular games were selected because of their popularity amongst the student population worldwide who can identify with these games, hence are more inclined to play the games if introduced into the classroom. Also, upon completion of in-game educational tasks, students will receive rewards which benefit their game character(s) and can enjoy for non-educational, entertainment purposes, thereby incentivizing gaming in education.

2 The Video-Diary Method

In order to assess the suitability of the MMORPGs as educational games to meet the curriculum objectives, we propose the video-diary method. This method not only assesses interaction between the game and the gamer as demonstrated in [7], but also incorporates assessment of the learning effectiveness; i.e. whether the student has learnt from the gaming experience.

The video-diary method was originally introduced in 1973 to evaluate managerial work [8]. In 2010, this method was modified to evaluate HCI in social games [7]. This video-diary method was different from the past HCI evaluation methods as it focused on the user rather than the game platform, thus adopting a user-centric approach. It was then found to be extremely effective in revealing valuable insights about the HCI and user engagement in these games, from the gamers' perspectives.

Conducted on the social game—Maplestory in this previous study, this video-diary method revealed that user-user communication and in-game social activities proved to be the most attractive factors.

Unlike other evaluation methods which focus on users' responses towards in-game activities, the diary component of the method requests users to log their rationale for carrying out certain activities, thereby revealing deeper insights towards how the gamers feel and think when engaged in game play.

Students are supposed to record down their in-game activities, as well as the rationale for carrying out these activities. Learning assessment can also be incorporated into the diary logsheets to keep track of the student's hourly progress to assess if the game is aiding the student to learn better and whether it is an effective teaching aid.

A sample of the diary, in the form of a logsheet is shown in Table 1.

Table 1. Extract from Diary Logsheet based on Previous Study

Hour	In-Game Activity	Comments
1	Character Job	Cleric
	Character Level	Lvl 40
	Training Area	Thailand
	Quest	Welcoming Ritual (Thailand)
	Interaction with other Players	Partied with 'Koduckie'

Whilst the students are gaming and recording down their in-game activities, they are also under video observation. This video observation captures physical and verbal responses of the students based on what was happening in the game, as well as the in-game activities. This not only allows educators to monitor the students' in game activities, but also reveals further insights as to how the students portray the game, whether they are interested or bored by it. This video observation is very valuable as the subtle motions and exclamations made by the student will not be recorded down on the logsheets usually.

Based on the first-person perspective (diary logsheet) and third-person perspective (video observation), teachers and game developers can accurately pinpoint the facets that engage the students and help them learn better; thus modifying the game such that the attractive elements are maintained whilst more educational content is included for maximal learning effectiveness.

3   Evaluation Criteria

Whilst it is relatively easy to assess the learning outcomes of the gaming experience by evaluating the quality of answers in response to questions posed in the diary logsheet, it is more challenging to evaluate user engagement based on results from the video-diary method. There is a gap between obtaining both first and third person perspectives and deriving whether user engagement has been sustained. Thus, a set of criteria needs to be established so that the video-diary method results can be benchmarked and assessed for effective user engagement.

The evaluation criteria have not been tested together with the video-diary method, and are developed based on a hypothetical situation. The criteria require the researcher, educator or game developer to ask a few questions, and derive the answers based on the video observation and logsheets:

1. Does the student show any sign of boredom or lack of interest during game play?
2. Is the student able to sustain long periods of game play (e.g. 5 hours)?
3. Does the student prefer to do non-learning related activities rather than stick to the learning tasks assigned?
4. Is the student able to complete the tasks individually, or does he/she need to work together as a group to finish the assignment?

The questions are varied; some of which are direct and the answers can clearly tell is engagement has been sustained (Questions 1 and 2), others are in-direct, whereby the engagement level has to be deduced by the researcher (Questions 3 and 4).

We propose that the following questions be answered based on a scale, from 1 (a strongly positive answer) to 5 (a strongly negative answer). Based on what is observed and deduced from the video and the logsheet (diary), the results from both perspectives are combined to assess the answers based on the scale.

It is highly likely for both perspectives to correlate; if no-correlation exists; i.e. what the logsheet reads and the video observation displays contrasts starkly, the results for the specific subject should be ignored.

Based on the scale above, it is then evident whether the students have been effectively engaged in the course of game-play.

Other than the questions proposed above to be included as criteria for the researchers, similar questions will be posed to the student after the gaming experience. Questions that mirror the aforementioned include:

1. Did you feel bored at any course of the game-play? If yes, please explain which aspects. If no, please explain why.
2. Did you think that the extended period of gaming was tiring and un-enjoyable? Explain.

Based on these answers, students will provide simple "Yes/No" answers followed by explanations. No rating scales are involved.

The combination of the two insights will then provide further backing for the overall results. It will then be irrefutable with regard to the success in effectively engaging students in educational games.

The feedback sought from the researchers and students are then compiled and aspects of the game, which are to be improved, are identified and improved on.

Now that we have understood how to assess the suitability of MMORPGs as educational games by using the video-diary evaluation method, we will conduct an analytic evaluation of several MMORPGs to assess their suitability for use in the classroom.

4   Maplestory: A Side Scrolling Game

MapleStory is a 2D side-scrolling MMORPG whose game-play centers on adventure quests and dueling with monsters. Gamers can either complete quests or duel with monsters individually, or as a group of up to six human characters. With over six hundred available quests of varying pre-requisites, nature and objectives, gamers seek to accomplish the goals in order to advance their character level and gain more in-game wealth.

MapleStory is highly popular with reported statistics of over 92 million users worldwide in 2009. In view the popularity of the game, educators and game developers can collaborate with MapleStory to develop educational quests or mini-games for their students to complete using their existing MapleStory accounts.

Quests in MapleStory are particularly suited towards the teaching of humanities subjects such as geography and history. The explorative natures of these quests allow students to embark on a self-learning process, and through the completion of various tasks and objectives, students will be able to learn effectively from the venture-based learning. The side-scrolling nature of MapleStory makes it suited for humanities subjects because students can better understand the sense of continuity between the flow of events (history) and visualize how the concepts learnt correlate to depicted reality (geography).

5 World of Warcraft: A Strategy Game

World of Warcraft is a 3D real-time strategy role-playing game where gamers control a character for exploration, combat, quests and interaction. Game play is highly varied, and gamers can either battle amongst other human gamers or fight with non-playing characters. As more combats occur, the character gains a wider set of skills and greater wealth.

World of Warcraft is widely recognized as the most popular MMORPG as of October 2010, with a gamer subscription of 12 million. As the Guinness World Record Holder for the most popular MMORPG, its introduction into the education landscape would bring about unprecedented transformation, and the vast potential of the game as teaching aids has been largely untapped on. Since most game play occurs on servers, game developers and educators can set up education servers where game content is slightly modified to complement teaching in the classroom rather than for entertainment purposes only.

There are two types of server platforms in World of Warcraft—Player versus Player (PvP) and Player versus Environment (PvE). Essentially, the gamer chooses to play with other gamers on PvP servers and artificial intelligence on PvE servers. A new category of servers for educational purposes can be developed, where gamers can control the same character they use on PvP and PvE servers, but instead of combating monsters and completing quests, they accomplish educational tasks. One of the potential subjects which can be taught using World of Warcraft is chemistry. In the game, various elements are required to cast magic spells to accomplish quests and combat monsters. These elements are usually gained from exploration of the game environment. On the educational servers however, chemistry knowledge can be incorporated into the game play, where gamers search for chemical elements and compounds in order to attain certain skills and cast spells. In order to make game play even more attractive, game developers can create special spells which only can be 'learnt' by the game character upon completion of the educational tasks, and these special spells can be used on PvP and PvE servers, giving gamers an added advantage over other gamers who do not engage in educational tasks. Hence this encourages students to accomplish the educational tasks in the game and learn the important concepts whilst having fun simultaneously.

6 Second Life: A Reality-Simulation Game

Second Life is a 3D virtual world MMORPG which is a virtual world where gamers are able to literally lead another life on the virtual platform. Each gamer has his/her own character, and they can explore, meet other characters, participate in group social activities and trade with one another. Second Life offers a flexible and open platform for characters to build their own 3D objects and using the scripting language provided by Linden Lab, the game developer, functionality can be added to these objects.

Second Life has been recognized as a highly potential game for use in education. It has already been implemented in a few education curricula worldwide, and various reputed organizations such as NASA (USA) and the National Physical Laboratory (UK) use Second Life for varied purposes. Similarly, an earlier study has shown that universities in the United Kingdom are adopting Second Life for learning activities with varying degrees of involvement [9].

Hence, educators can follow suit and develop their own educational content using existing scripts and platforms made available. Linden Lab provides tutorials and guides for educators who are interested in using Second Life in the classroom. In order to improve on existing infrastructure available, we strongly encourage the development of more intuitive platforms where educators devote less time and effort to create the educational tasks in the game. The lack of intuitiveness and difficulty of learning scripting was identified as the main barrier for educators who wanted to incorporate information-communication technologies in the classroom as indicated by previous studies [10]. Hence, since the foundations for use of Second Life in the classroom has been set and made available, the next step would be to make scripting and development more intuitive and easy to learn in order to encourage educators to incorporate Second Life into classroom teaching.

7   Counterstrike: A First-Person Shooter Game

Counter-Strike is a 3D tactical first-person shooter video game. Each gamer plays the role of a soldier who is part of a team, and two teams pit against each other to accomplish an objective or eliminate the opponent team. Based on the contributions made by each gamer, points are awarded and new weapons can be purchased using these points.

Though first-person shooter games have limited applicability in the classroom because it is challenging to create educational content and ensure that students learn from exploring and shooting, we suggest that Counter-Strike can be used to teach a specific subject—Physics.

Various topics in Physics such as rectilinear motion, kinematics and energy can be taught using Counter-Strike as students use Physics concepts to gain new skills or weapons, or even improve their chances for in-game victories. The physical intense nature of game play offers a plethora of opportunities for Physics concepts to be incorporated into the game to aid the students in understanding and applying.

Though Counter-Strike is has limited flexibility for us in educational settings because of the nature of game play, where the main in-game activity is to shoot, further research into this genre of games might possibly reveal other subjects which might be suitable for educational use.

8   Runescape: An Adventure Game

Runescape is a 3D fantasy graphical browser Java game where game play takes place in a medieval fantasy realm divided into kingdoms, regions and cities. Gamers select and control an in-game character, and there is no linear storyline for them to follow.

Gamers enjoy the freedom of setting their own goals and objectives, and usually have a variety of ways to go about accomplishing these goals.

Runescape has high potential for use in the classroom because of its open-ended nature where gamers are given the autonomy to accomplish their own goals and objectives. Educators can establish fixed objectives in the game, and students can choose how to go about achieving the objectives. The flexibility offered is important especially when the education landscape and student profile is transforming; that students now prefer to have their own way when completing tasks and activities instead of having to follow a set of guidelines linearly. Students would better appreciate Runescape as an educational game, thereby increasing learning effectiveness.

The high degree of autonomy accorded to students means Runescape is a generic game which can be used in the education of various subjects, from sciences to humanities to linguistics. Using the realm available, additional regions or cities can be established to suit various specific educational purposes and optimal outcomes would be achieved by encouraging students to explore beyond the educational regions and utilize the entire fantasy realm to achieve their objective in the most efficient and meaningful way

9   Using Multiple MMORPGs in the Classroom

In order to increase the effectiveness of implementing MMORPGs in the classroom, we suggest that educators offer a variety of popular MMORPGs for students to choose from and complete the educational in-game tasks on their preferred MMORPG.

As discussed earlier, most of the games were highly reliant on the popularity of the games amongst the student population, and those who were playing the MMORPGs before educational tasks were introduced would be more inclined to complete the educational tasks if they are introduced on the same MMORPG instead of another MMORPG. In essence, a student Warcraft gamer would be less inclined to complete a game task on MapleStory than if it were on the Warcraft platform. Gamers want a sense of continuity and to feel that their motivation for learning and completing the educational tasks would reap benefits for their entertainment purposes (e.g. upon completion of the educational tasks in Warcraft, a student's character level increases and becomes more 'powerful', hence incentivizing the game play). In addition, familiarity with the game environment would be an attractive factor because students experience a sense of identity and nostalgia when gaming, and are not totally foreign to the game platform, thereby shortening the learning curve and benefitting from game play efficiently.

Although this is slightly challenging especially when the notion of MMORPGs in education is first introduced because the educational elements in each MMORPG is unique to each curriculum, we believe that with the gradual widespread adoption of MMORPGs in education, there will be adequate resources for exchange amongst different curriculum, and modifying the games would be more efficient and resource-friendly. Educators can then implement the same educational content and tasks on a variety of MMORPG platforms and allow students to choose their MMORPG of choice, providing a sense of continuity and thus motivating the students to complete the educational tasks well.

We propose game developers to leave game-specific content open-ended and allow educators to create their own content to suit various purposes. In previous educational games, communication between developers and educators pose challenges, and either side were unsure of what was required, resulting in the inability to effectively create engaging games which suit the educators' specific needs. By developing game 'templates' and training educators with fundamental skills required to create their customized game activities, we will overcome challenges faced in previous educational game development and be able to introduce multiple MMORPGs in the classroom for students to have a range of choices to select from.

10 Challenges of Using MMORPGs in the Classroom

If MMORPGs are to be used for educational purposes, adequate learning opportunities must be made available. However, with the need to achieve a balance between user engagement from game entertainment and the availability of learning opportunities for students to learn, educators and game developers face a dilemma— to provide substantial content for learning at the risk of losing the students' interest or to increase the entertainment value of the tasks but compromise their educational value. Each aspect is pivotal towards building a successful game, and cannot be undermined [11].

Another challenge faced is the understanding that MMORPGs were developed not for educational purposes, but for entertainment purposes. As a result, there is a high possibility that students may be distracted from the learning activities in the game and engage in non-learning related activities instead. The autonomy and independence each student receives when games are introduced in the classroom makes it challenging for educators to supervise and exert influence, hence there is a need for future work in this aspect to assure educators that the use of MMORPGs in the classroom would be for educational purposes dominantly.

11 Conclusions

Although there has been much discussion over the potential of computer game transforming the pedagogical outlook, educational games are still unable to effectively pervade into education systems. Used mostly in experimental settings for research purposes, these educational games are unable to reach out into the actual classroom to complement mainstream classroom teaching.

In this paper, we have proposed the use of MMORPGs as educational games because MMORPGs offer an available platform for game developers and educators to work from, removing the need to start from scratch and experience difficulties in game development. Furthermore, the popularity of MMORPGs today proves that the game framework is robust and engaging to the younger generation, and hence would appeal to students.

In order to assess the suitability of MMORPGs for specific educational uses, we have proposed the video-diary method, which evaluates human-computer interaction between the gamer and the game. Through this method, not only are we able to assess if the level of engagement is affected because of the inclusion of educational content, but also if learning outcomes have been achieved. The video-diary method has shown to be useful in revealing detailed insights about engagement and human-computer interaction, and would provide educators with valuable information with regard to the effectiveness of the game in achieving the specific curriculum objectives.

We have reviewed five potential MMORPGs—MapleStory, World of Warcraft, Second Life, Counter-Strike and Runescape for their applicability and suitability in the classroom, as well as propose various subjects which are particularly suited for each game. One of the suggested ways to maximize the effectiveness of MMORPG in games is the combination of multiple MMORPGs for students to choose from, so that they will enjoy a sense of continuity and will be incentivized to accomplish the game tasks and achieve the learning objectives.

With the gradual acceptance of MMORPGs for use in classrooms and the video-diary method which assesses the effectiveness of these games, we believe that students' learning effectiveness would improve, leading to a more engaging and entertaining, but nevertheless productive learning experience

Acknowledgments. The authors would like to express our sincere gratitude to the staff members of Hwa Chong Institution and the Institute for Infocomm Research who have rendered assistance in many aspects.

References

1. Aldrich, C.: Learning by Doing: A Comprehensive Guide to Simulations, Computer Games, and Pedagogy in e-Learning and Other Educational Experiences. Pfeiffer, San Francisco (2005)
2. McFarlane, A., Sparrowhawk, A., Heald, Y.: Report on the educational use of games. Teachers Evaluating Educational Multimedia (TEEM), Cambridge (2002)
3. Mitchell, A., Savill-Smith, C.: The Use of Computer and Videogames for Learning: A Review of the Literature. Learning and Skills Development Agency, Trowbridge (2004)
4. Garris, R., Ahlers, R., Driskell, J.E.: Games, Motivation and Learning: A Research and Practice Model, Simulation & Gaming (2002)
5. Malone, T.W., Lepper, M.R.: Making learning fun: A taxonomy of intrinsic motivations for learning. In: Snow, R.E., Farr, M.J. (eds.) Aptitude, Learning and Instruction III: Cognitive and Affective Process Analysis, pp. 223–253. Lawrence Erlbaum, Hillsdale (1987)
6. Burgos, D., Tattersall, C., Koper, R.: Re-purposing existing generic games and simulations for e-learning. In: Sigala, M., et al. (eds.) Computers in Human Behavior, pp. 2656–2667. Elsevier, Amsterdam (2011)
7. Looi, Q.E., See, S.L.: Social Games—Analysing Human Computer Interaction Using a Video-Diary Method. In: The 2nd International Conference on Computer Engineering and Technology Proceedings, pp. 509–512. IEEE, New York (2010)

8. Mintzberg, H.: The Nature of Managerial Work. Harper Collins Publishers, New York (1973)
9. Kirriemuir, J.: Snapshots of Second Life use in UK. Eduserv Foundation, UK (2007), http://www.eduserv.org.uk/foundation/studies/slsnapshots (accessed on February 28, 2011)
10. Stefanova, E., Boytchev, P., Nikolova, N., Kovatcheva, E., Sendova, E.: Embracing and enhancing ideas as a strategy for ICT education. In: Research, Reflections and Innovations in Integrating ICT in Education, Formatex, Badajoz, Spain, vol. 1, pp. 206–211 (2009)
11. Looi, Q.E., See, S.L.: Effectively Engaging Students in Educational Games by Deploying HCI Evaluation Methods. In: Proceedings of the World Congress on Engineering and Computer Science 2010. Lecture Notes in Engineering and Computer Science, San Francisco, USA, pp. 272–275 (2010)

A Bottom-Up Algorithm for Solving Query-Answering Problems

Kiyoshi Akama[1] and Ekawit Nantajeewarawat[2]

[1] Information Initiative Center,
Hokkaido University, Hokkaido, Japan
akama@iic.hokudai.ac.jp
[2] Computer Science Program,
Sirindhorn International Institute of Technology,
Thammasat University, Pathumthani, Thailand
ekawit@siit.tu.ac.th

Abstract. Meaning-preserving Skolemization is essential for development of a correct and efficient method of solving query-answering problems. It requires global existential quantifications of function variables, which in turn require an extension of the space of first-order formulas. This paper proposes a bottom-up algorithm for computing a set of models that sufficiently represents the set of all models of a given clause set in the extended formula space. This algorithm provides a correct method for solving query-answering problems that include unrestricted use of universal and existential quantifications in problem representation.

Keywords: Query-answering problems, automated reasoning, bottom-up computation, meaning-preserving Skolemization.

1 Introduction

A *proof problem* is a pair $\langle K_1, K_2 \rangle$, where K_1 and K_2 are logical formulas. It is a yes-no question, i.e., the answer to a proof problem $\langle K_1, K_2 \rangle$ is "yes" if K_1 logically entails K_2, and the answer is "no" otherwise. Satisfiability checking provides a basis for solving proof problems: a formula K_1 logically entails a formula K_2 iff $K_1 \wedge \neg K_2$ is unsatisfiable [3]. Bottom-up computation can be used for checking whether $K_1 \wedge \neg K_2$ is unsatisfiable as follows: First, $K_1 \wedge \neg K_2$ is converted into a conjunctive normal form, which can be regarded as a set of clauses. Such conversion involves removal of existential quantifications by Skolemization, i.e., by replacement of an existentially quantified variable with a Skolem term. Next, a bottom-up computing algorithm is employed for constructing a model of the resulting clause set. If the construction fails, i.e., no model can be found, $K_1 \wedge \neg K_2$ is unsatisfiable.

The objective of this paper is to propose a bottom-up algorithm for solving a different class of problems, i.e., query-answering problems. A *query-answering problems* (*QA problems*) is a pair $\langle K, q \rangle$, where K is a logical formula and q is an atomic formula (atom). The answer to a QA problem $\langle K, q \rangle$ is the set of all

A. Abd Manaf et al. (Eds.): ICIEIS 2011, Part II, CCIS 252, pp. 299–313, 2011.
© Springer-Verlag Berlin Heidelberg 2011

ground instances of q that are logically entailed by K. This set can be equivalently defined as the intersection of all models of K and the set of all ground instances of q. By analogy with proof problems, we can adopt the following three computation phases for finding the answer to a QA problem $\langle K, q \rangle$: (i) convert K into a set Cs of clauses using Skolemization, (ii) use bottom-up computation to construct all models of Cs, and (iii) find the intersection of the obtained models and the set of all ground instances of q.

It is not obvious, however, how to establish an effective method for solving QA problems using the above three-phase bottom-up scheme. The following fundamental issues need to be addressed:

1. How to preserve the logical meaning of a formula in a Skolemization process? Although Skolemization always yields a satisfiability-preserving transformation step, it does not preserve the logical meaning of a source formula [3]. In order to obtain meaning-preserving Skolemization, an extended formula space that allows existential quantifications of function variables is required.

2. How to compute models of an extended clause set? A clause set in the extended space contains existentially quantified global function variables. How to compute a model of such an extended clause set has not been discussed in the literature.

3. How to bridge the gap between the set of computed models and the set of all models of an extended clause set? The set of computed models may be included by, but not equal to, the set of all models of a given clause set. A theoretical basis for ensuring that computed models can sufficiently represent all models of an extended clause set is required.

A solution to the first problem has been provided by our recent work [1], in which a theory for extending a space of logical formulas by incorporation of function variables was developed and how meaning-preserving Skolemization could be achieved in the obtained extended space was shown. A procedure for converting a logical formula into a set of extended clauses on the extended space was also given in [1]. This paper addresses the second and the third problems. A new bottom-up procedure for computing models of an extended clause set is presented. The concept of a representative set of a given collection of sets is introduced. An algorithm for solving a QA problem is devised based on computing a representative set of the set of all models of an extended clause set.

The rest of the paper is organized as follows: Section 2 formalizes a class of QA problems and outlines a general scheme for solving them based on equivalent transformation. Section 3 explains the necessity of meaning-preserving Skolemization and defines an extended clause space. After introducing the notion of a representative set, Section 4 defines a representative set of the collection of all models of an extended clause set. Section 5 presents our bottom-up algorithm for solving QA problems. Section 6 illustrates how the algorithm works. Section 7 describes fundamental differences between this work and previously existing theories. Section 8 concludes the paper.

2   Query-Answering Problems and Solutions Based on Equivalent Transformation

To begin with, a query-answering problem is defined. It is followed by a general solution scheme based on equivalent transformation.

2.1   Query-Answering (QA) Problems

A *query-answering problem* (*QA problem*) is a pair $\langle K, q \rangle$, where K is a logical formula and q is an atomic formula (atom). The *answer* to a QA problem $\langle K, q \rangle$, denoted by $ans(K, q)$, is defined by

$$ans(K, q) = \{q' \mid (q' \text{ is a ground instance of } q) \,\&\, (K \models q')\},$$

i.e., the set of all ground instances of q that follow logically from K. When K consists of only definite clauses, problems in this class are problems that have been discussed in logic programming [5]. In the class of QA problems discussed in [9], K is a conjunction of axioms and assertions in Description Logics [2]. Recently, QA problems have gained wide attention, owing partly to emerging applications in systems involving integration between formal ontological background knowledge [8] and instance-level rule-oriented components, e.g., interaction between Description Logics and Horn rules [4,6] in the Semantic Web's ontology-based rule layer.

2.2   Solving QA Problems by Equivalent Transformation

Using the set of all models of K, denoted by $Models(K)$, the answer to a QA problem $\langle K, q \rangle$ can be equivalently represented as

$$ans(K, q) = \left(\bigcap Models(K) \right) \cap rep(q),$$

where $\bigcap Models(K)$ is the intersection of all models of K and $rep(q)$ is the set of all ground instances of q.

Calculating $\bigcap Models(K)$ directly may require high computational cost. To reduce the cost, K is transformed into a simplified formula K' such that all models of K is preserved and $(\bigcap Models(K')) \cap rep(q)$ can be determined at a low cost. Obviously, if $Models(K) = Models(K')$, then $ans(K, q) = ans(K', q)$.

3   Meaning-Preserving Conversion into an Extended Clause Space

3.1   Need for Meaning-Preserving Skolemization

To solve a QA problem $\langle K, q \rangle$ by equivalent transformation, the logical formula K is usually converted into a conjunctive normal form that has the same logical meaning as K. The conversion involves removal of existential quantifications by

Skolemization, i.e., by replacement of an existentially quantified variable with a Skolem term determined by a relevant part of a formula prenex. Classical Skolemization, however, does not preserve the logical meaning of a formula—the formula resulting from Skolemization is equisatisfiable with, but not necessarily equivalent to, the original one [3]. Only the satisfiability property of a formula is preserved.

In [1], we developed a theory for extending the space of first-order logical formulas and showed how meaning-preserving Skolemization can be achieved in an obtained extended space. The basic idea of meaning-preserving Skolemization is to use existentially quantified function variables instead of usual Skolem functions. Function variables and extended conjunctive normal forms are introduced below.

3.2   Function Constants, Function Variables, and *func*-Atoms

A usual function symbol in first-order logic denotes an unevaluated function; it is used for constructing a syntactically new term from existing terms (possibly recursively) without evaluating those existing terms. A different class of functions is used in the extended space. A function in this class is an actual mathematical function; it takes ground terms as input, and associates with them an output ground term. The input ground terms are evaluated for determining the output. We called a function in this class a *function constant*. Variables of a new type, called *function variables*, are introduced; each of them can be instantiated into a function constant or a function variable, but not into a usual term.

In order to clearly separate function constants and function variables from usual function symbols and usual terms, a new built-in predicate *func* is introduced. Given any n-ary function constant or n-ary function variable $\bar{f}$, an expression

$$func(\bar{f}, t_1, \ldots, t_n, t_{n+1}),$$

where the t_i are usual terms, is considered as an atom of a new type, called a *func-atom*. When $\bar{f}$ is a function constant and the t_i are all ground, the truth value of this atom is evaluated as follows: it is true iff $\bar{f}(t_1, \ldots, t_n) = t_{n+1}$.

3.3   The Extended Clause Space (ECLS)

A procedure for converting a logical formula into an equivalent formula in an extended conjunctive normal form, called an existentially quantified conjunctive normal form (ECNF), is given in [1]. To define an ECNF, an extended clause is introduced.

Extended Clauses. An *extended clause* C is an extended formula of the form

$$\forall v_1, \ldots, \forall v_m : (a_1 \vee \cdots \vee a_n \vee \neg b_1 \vee \cdots \vee \neg b_p \vee \neg \mathbf{f}_1 \vee \cdots \vee \neg \mathbf{f}_q),$$

where $v_1, \ldots, v_m$ are usual variables, each of $a_1, \ldots, a_n, b_1, \ldots, b_p$ is a usual atom or a constraint atom, and $\mathbf{f}_1, \ldots, \mathbf{f}_q$ are *func*-atoms. It is often written simply as

$$a_1, \ldots, a_n \leftarrow b_1, \ldots b_p, \mathbf{f}_1, \ldots, \mathbf{f}_q.$$

The sets $\{a_1, \ldots, a_n\}$ and $\{b_1, \ldots b_p, \mathbf{f}_1, \ldots, \mathbf{f}_q\}$ are called the *left-hand side* and the *right-hand side*, respectively, of the extended clause C, denoted by $lhs(C)$ and $rhs(C)$, respectively. When $n = 1$, C is called an *extended definite clause*, the only atom in $lhs(C)$ is called the *head* of C, denoted by $head(C)$, and the set $rhs(C)$ is also called the *body* of C, denoted by $body(C)$. All usual variables in an extended clause are universally quantified and their scope is restricted to the clause itself. When no confusion is caused, an extended clause and an extended definite clause will also be called a *clause* and a *definite clause*, respectively.

Existentially Quantified Conjunctive Normal Forms (ECNFs). A formula α in an *existentially quantified conjunctive normal form* (*ECNF*) is defined as an extended formula of the form

$$\exists v_{h1}, \ldots, \exists v_{hm} : (C_1 \wedge \cdots \wedge C_n),$$

where $v_{h1}, \ldots, v_{hm}$ are function variables and $C_1, \ldots, C_n$ are extended clauses. The ECNF α above is often identified with the set $\{C_1, \ldots, C_n\}$, with implicit existential quantifications of function variables and implicit clause conjunction. Function variables in such a clause set are all existentially quantified and their scope covers all clauses in the set.

The Extended Clause Space (ECLS). The set of all ECNFs is referred to as the *extended clause space* (*ECLS*). By the above identification of an ECNF with a clause set, we often regard an element of ECLS as a set of (extended) clauses.

With occurrences of function variables, clauses contained in a clause set in the ECLS space are connected through shared function variables. By instantiating all function variables into function constants, the ECLS space becomes a space of usual clause sets, where clauses in each clause set are totally separated (i.e., no clause shares a usual variable with another clause).[1]

3.4   Meaning-Preserving Transformation in the Space ECLS

Given a QA problem $\langle K, q \rangle$, the formula K is converted into a clause set Cs in the ECLS space. The clause set Cs may be further transformed equivalently in this space into another clause set Cs' for problem simplification. Unfolding and other transformation rules may be used. The answer to the resulting problem $\langle Cs', q \rangle$ is

$$ans(Cs', q) = (\bigcap Models(Cs')) \cap rep(q).$$

A method of computing $\bigcap Models(Cs')$ in the space ECLS is therefore required.

---

[1] Clauses in the usual conjunctive normal form are also totally separated, i.e., usual variables occurring in one clause are considered to be different from those occurring in another clause.

4   A Representative Set for Solving QA Problems

Next, the notion of a representative set of a collection of sets is introduced (Section 4.1). The intersection of a given collection of sets can be determined in terms of the intersection of sets in its representative set (Theorem 1). Given a clause set Cs in the ECLS space, a set collection, $\mathrm{MM}(Cs)$, is defined (Section 4.2), with an important property being that $\mathrm{MM}(Cs)$ is a representative set of the set of all models of Cs (Theorem 2). Consequently, the answer to a QA problem concerning Cs can be computed through $\mathrm{MM}(Cs)$.

4.1   Representative Sets

A representative set is defined below:

Definition 1. Let G be a set and $M_1, M_2 \subseteq pow(G)$. M_1 is a *representative set* of M_2 iff the following conditions are satisfied:

1. $M_1 \subseteq M_2$.
2. For any $m_2 \in M_2$, there exists $m_1 \in M_1$ such that $m_2 \supseteq m_1$.   □

Theorem 1 below provides a basis for computing the intersection of the set of all models of a clause set using its representative set.

Theorem 1. *Let G be a set and $M_1, M_2 \subseteq pow(G)$ such that M_1 is a representative set of M_2. Then*

$$\bigcap M_1 = \bigcap M_2.$$

Proof. By Condition 1 of Definition 1, it is obvious that $\bigcap M_1 \supseteq \bigcap M_2$. We show that $\bigcap M_1 \subseteq \bigcap M_2$ as follows: Suppose that $g \in \bigcap M_1$. Then for any $m_1 \in M_1$, g belongs to m_1. It follows from Condition 2 of Definition 1 that for any $m_2 \in M_2$, g also belongs to m_2. So $g \in \bigcap M_2$.   □

4.2   A Representative Set for All Models of a Clause Set in ECLS

It is assumed that: (i) for any constraint atom a, $not(a)$ is a constraint atom; (ii) for any constraint atom a and any substitution θ, $not(a)\theta = not(a\theta)$; and (iii) for any ground constraint atom a, a is true iff $not(a)$ is not true.

Let Cs be a clause set in the ECLS space. We define a set collection $\mathrm{MM}(Cs)$ as follows:

1. First, we define $\mathrm{MVRHS}(Cs)$ by

$$\mathrm{MVRHS}(Cs) = \{\mathrm{MVRHS}(C) \mid C \in Cs\},$$

   where for any clause C, $\mathrm{MVRHS}(C)$ is the clause obtained from C as follows: For each constraint atom c in $lhs(C)$, remove c from $lhs(C)$ and add $not(c)$ to $rhs(C)$.
2. Next, we define $\mathrm{GINST}(Cs)$ as follows:

(a) Let $\mathbf{S}_1$ be the set of function-variable-free clause sets obtained from MVRHS(Cs) as follows:

$$\mathbf{S}_1 = \{\text{MVRHS}(Cs)\sigma \mid \sigma \text{ is a ground substitution for}$$
$$\text{all function variables occurring in MVRHS}(Cs)\}.$$

(b) Let $\mathbf{S}_2$ be the set of variable-free clause sets obtained from $\mathbf{S}_1$ by replacing each clause set Cs' in $\mathbf{S}_1$ with the clause set

$$\{C'\theta \mid (C' \in Cs') \ \& \ (\theta \text{ is a ground substitution for all usual variables}$$
$$\text{occurring in } C')\}.$$

(c) Let GINST(Cs) be the set of clause sets obtained from $\mathbf{S}_2$ by replacing each clause set Cs' in $\mathbf{S}_2$ with the clause set

$$\{\text{RMCON}(C') \mid (C' \in Cs') \ \& \ (\text{each constraint atom in } rhs(C') \text{ is true})\},$$

where for any clause C'', RMCON(C'') is the clause obtained from C'' by removing all constraint atoms from it.

3. Assume that Cs' is a clause set in GINST(Cs). We can construct from Cs', a set of definite clauses as follows: For each clause $C' \in Cs'$,
   (a) if $lhs(C') = \emptyset$, then construct a definite clause the head of which is $\perp$ and the body of which is $rhs(C')$;
   (b) if $lhs(C') \neq \emptyset$, then
       - select one arbitrary atom a from $lhs(C')$, and
       - construct a definite clause the head of which is a and the body of which is $rhs(C')$.
   Let DC(Cs') be the set of all definite-clause sets possibly constructed from Cs' in the above way.

4. We define a set DC(GINST(Cs)) of definite-clause sets by

$$\text{DC(GINST}(Cs)) = \bigcup \{\text{DC}(Cs') \mid Cs' \in \text{GINST}(Cs)\}.$$

5. For any definite-clause set D in DC(GINST(Cs)), we define the meaning of D, denoted by $\mathcal{M}(D)$, as follows:
   (a) Let a mapping T_D on the power set of the set of all ground atoms be defined by: for any set G of ground atoms,

$$T_D(G) = \{head(C) \mid (C \in D) \ \& \ (body(C) \subseteq G)\}.$$

   (b) $\mathcal{M}(D)$ is then defined as the set $\bigcup_{n=1}^{\infty} T_D^n(\emptyset)$, where $T_D^1(\emptyset) = T_D(\emptyset)$ and $T_D^n(\emptyset) = T_D(T_D^{n-1}(\emptyset))$ for each $n > 1$.

6. Then we define a set MM(Cs) of ground-atom sets by

$$\text{MM}(Cs) = \{\mathcal{M}(D) \mid (D \in \text{DC(GINST}(Cs))) \ \& \ (\perp \notin \mathcal{M}(D))\}.$$

With Theorem 1, the next theorem shows that $\bigcap \text{MM}(Cs) = \bigcap Models(Cs)$; as a result, the answer to a QA problem concerning Cs can be obtained through MM(Cs).

Theorem 2. $\mathrm{MM}(Cs)$ *is a representative set of* $\mathrm{Models}(Cs)$.

Proof. Each clause set in $\mathrm{GINST}(Cs)$ is obtained from $\mathrm{MVRHS}(Cs)$ by instantiation of function variables, instantiation of usual variables, and removal of true constraints. As a result, for any set G of ground atoms, G is a model of Cs iff G is a model of some clause set in $\mathrm{GINST}(Cs)$. Now suppose that $G \in \mathrm{MM}(Cs)$. Then there exists some clause set $Cs' \in \mathrm{GINST}(Cs)$ such that (i) G is the minimal model of the positive part of Cs', (ii) G does not satisfy the right-hand side of any negative clause in Cs', and (iii) G is a model of Cs'. Thus G is a model of Cs. Next, suppose that M is a model of Cs. Then M is a model of some clause set $Cs'' \in \mathrm{GINST}(Cs)$. Let M' be the minimal model of the positive part of Cs''. Then $M' \subseteq M$. Since M satisfies all negative clauses in Cs'', M' also satisfies all negative clauses in Cs''. Hence M' belongs to $\mathrm{MM}(Cs)$.   □

5   An Algorithm for Solving QA Problems

This section presents an algorithm for computing $\bigcap \mathrm{MM}(Cs)$ for any given clause set Cs in the ECLS space with no occurrence of usual function symbols.

5.1   Notations

The following notations are used:

- Given a clause set Cs in the ECLS space, let $\widehat{\mathrm{MVRHS}}(Cs)$ be the clause set obtained from $\mathrm{MVRHS}(Cs)$ by replacing each occurrence of the predicate *func* with the predicate *userfunc*.
- Given a function variable v_h such that $arity(v_h) = k$, a set T of ground terms, and a mapping $f : T^k \to T$, let

$$\mathrm{UF}(v_h, T, f) = \{(userfunc(v_h, t_1, \ldots, t_k, f(t_1, \ldots, t_k)) \leftarrow) \mid \langle t_1, \ldots, t_k \rangle \in T^k\}.$$

- Let Cs be a clause set in the ECLS space. Assume that $\{v_{h1}, \ldots, v_{hn}\}$ is the set of all function variables that occur in Cs. For any set T of ground terms, let

$$\begin{aligned}
\mathrm{GEN}(Cs, T) = \{&\widehat{\mathrm{MVRHS}}(Cs) \cup \mathrm{UF}(v_{h1}, T, f_1) \cup \cdots \cup \mathrm{UF}(v_{hn}, T, f_n) \mid \\
&(arity(v_{h1}) = k_1) \ \& \ \cdots \ \& \ (arity(v_{hn}) = k_n) \ \& \\
&(f_1 : T^{k_1} \to T) \ \& \ \cdots \ \& \ (f_n : T^{k_n} \to T)\}.
\end{aligned}$$

5.2   A Bottom-Up Algorithm for Computing $\bigcap \mathrm{MM}(Cs)$

Let a clause set Cs in the ECLS space be given. Assume that no usual function appears in a usual term, i.e., a usual term is either a usual variable or a constant. To compute $\bigcap \mathrm{MM}(Cs)$, we first initialize MM as the set of all ground usual atoms and then successively modify MM by performing the following steps until it can be no longer changed:

A1. Let **T** be the set of all ground terms that appear in Cs.
A2. Let $\mathbf{S} = \text{GEN}(Cs, \mathbf{T})$.
A3. Select $Cs' \in \mathbf{S}$.
A4. Compute $\mathbf{M}(Cs')$ using Steps B1–B3 below.
A5. If $\mathbf{M}(Cs') \neq \emptyset$, then modify MM by $MM := MM \cap (\bigcap \mathbf{M}(Cs'))$.
A6. Modify **S** by $\mathbf{S} := \mathbf{S} - \{Cs'\}$.
A7. If $\mathbf{S} \neq \emptyset$, then go to Step A3.
A8. If $\mathbf{S} = \emptyset$, then:
  1. Add a new ground term to **T**.
  2. Go to Step A2.

To compute $\mathbf{M}(Cs')$ at Step A4, perform the following steps:

B1. Let $\mathbf{M}(Cs') = \{\emptyset\}$.
B2. If there exists a clause $C \in Cs'$, a set $m \in \mathbf{M}(Cs')$, and a ground substitution θ for all usual variables occurring in C such that
  – all constraint atoms in $rhs(C\theta)$ are true,
  – all usual atoms in $rhs(C\theta)$ belong to m, and
  – no atom in $lhs(C\theta)$ belongs to m,

  then:
  1. If $lhs(C) = \emptyset$, then modify $\mathbf{M}(Cs')$ by $\mathbf{M}(Cs') := \mathbf{M}(Cs') - \{m\}$.
  2. If $lhs(C) \neq \emptyset$, then modify $M_{Cs'}$ by

  $$\mathbf{M}(Cs') := (\mathbf{M}(Cs') - \{m\}) \cup \{\{m \cup \{a\}\} \mid a \in lhs(C\theta)\}.$$

  3. Go to Step B2.
B3. Return $\mathbf{M}(Cs')$ to Step A4.

When the set MM cannot be further changed by Steps A2-A8, the algorithm converges with MM being the output.

6   Examples

Three examples illustrating application of the presented bottom-up computation algorithm are given below. It is assumed that a usual variable as well as a function variable begins with an asterisk.

Example 1. Consider a QA problem $prb_1 = \langle Cs, p(*x) \rangle$, where Cs consists of the following clauses, where neq stands for "not equal":

C_1 : $p(*x) \leftarrow q(*x)$
C_2: $q(*x) \leftarrow func(*h, *x)$
C_3: $r(*x) \leftarrow func(*h, *x)$
C_4: $s(*x) \leftarrow r(*x)$
C_5: $\leftarrow r(*x), neq(*x, A), neq(*x, B), neq(*x, C)$
C_6: $\leftarrow r(B)$
C_7: $\leftarrow s(C)$

Assume that p-, q-, r-, and s-atoms are usual atoms and neq-atoms are constraint atoms. $\widehat{\mathrm{MVRHS}}(Cs)$ is the same as Cs except that the predicate $func$ is replaced with $userfunc$. The algorithm works as follows:

- Initially, MM is the set of all ground atoms and $\mathbf{T} = \{A, B, C\}$.
- $\mathbf{S} = \mathrm{GEN}(Cs, \mathbf{T}) = \{Cs'_1, Cs'_2, Cs'_3\}$, where
  - $Cs'_1 = \widehat{\mathrm{MVRHS}}(Cs) \cup \{(func(*h, A) \leftarrow)\}$,
  - $Cs'_2 = \widehat{\mathrm{MVRHS}}(Cs) \cup \{(func(*h, B) \leftarrow)\}$,
  - $Cs'_3 = \widehat{\mathrm{MVRHS}}(Cs) \cup \{(func(*h, C) \leftarrow)\}$.
- Select Cs'_1 from $\mathbf{S}$ and compute $\mathbf{M}(Cs'_1) = \{\{p(A), q(A), r(A), s(A)\}\}$. MM is changed into $\{p(A), q(A), r(A), s(A)\}$.
- Select Cs'_2 from $\mathbf{S}$ and compute $\mathbf{M}(Cs'_1) = \emptyset$. MM is not changed.
- Select Cs'_3 from $\mathbf{S}$ and compute $\mathbf{M}(Cs'_1) = \emptyset$. MM is not changed.
- By the clause C_5, addition of any new ground term to $\mathbf{T}$ never yields a new clause set Cs' in $\mathrm{GEN}(Cs, \mathbf{T})$ such that $\mathbf{M}(Cs')$ is nonempty. So MM is never changed further and the algorithm converges.

The computed answer to the problem prb_1 is then the set $MM \cap rep(p(*x)) = \{p(A)\}$. □

Example 2. Next, consider a QA problem $prb_2 = \langle Cs, p(*x) \rangle$, where Cs consists of the following clauses:

$C_1 :\ p(*x), q(*x) \leftarrow r(*x), func(*h, *x)$
$C_2:\ r(1) \leftarrow$
$C_3:\ r(2) \leftarrow$
$C_4:\ \leftarrow p(1)$

Assume that p-, q-, and r-atoms are all usual atoms. Again, $\widehat{\mathrm{MVRHS}}(Cs)$ is the same as Cs except that the predicate $func$ is replaced with $userfunc$. The algorithm works as follows:

- Initially, MM is the set of all ground atoms and $\mathbf{T} = \{1, 2\}$.
- $\mathbf{S} = \mathrm{GEN}(Cs, \mathbf{T}) = \{Cs'_1, Cs'_2\}$, where
  - $Cs'_1 = \widehat{\mathrm{MVRHS}}(Cs) \cup \{(userfunc(*h, 1) \leftarrow)\}$,
  - $Cs'_2 = \widehat{\mathrm{MVRHS}}(Cs) \cup \{(userfunc(*h, 2) \leftarrow)\}$.
- Select Cs'_1 from $\mathbf{S}$ and compute $\mathbf{M}(Cs'_1) = \{\{r(1), r(2), q(1)\}\}$. MM is changed into $\{r(1), r(2), q(1)\}$.
- Select Cs'_2 from $\mathbf{S}$ and compute $\mathbf{M}(Cs'_2) = \{\{r(1), r(2), p(2)\}, \{r(1), r(2), q(2)\}\}$. MM is changed into $\{r(1), r(2)\}$.
- Adding a new ground term to $\mathbf{T}$ never results in a new clause set Cs' in $\mathrm{GEN}(Cs, \mathbf{T})$ such that $\mathbf{M}(Cs')$ is nonempty. MM can thus be no longer changed and the algorithm converges.

The computed answer to the problem prb_2 is the set $MM \cap rep(p(*x)) = \emptyset$. □

$$D1: \quad \geq 2 \; hasChild \sqsubseteq TaxCut$$

$$D2: \quad Man \sqcap Woman \sqsubseteq \bot$$

$$D3: \quad \exists motherOf.\top \sqsubseteq Woman$$

$$D4: \quad Peter : \exists hasChild.(\exists motherOf.\top)$$

$$D5: \quad hasChild(Peter, Paul)$$

$$D6: \quad Paul : Man$$

Fig. 1. Representation in Description Logics

$$F1: \quad \forall *x, *y, *z : ((hasChild(*x, *y) \wedge hasChild(*x, *z) \wedge neq(*y, *z))$$
$$\rightarrow TaxCut(*x))$$

$$F2: \quad \neg \exists *x : (Man(*x) \wedge Woman(*x))$$

$$F3: \quad \forall *x, *y : (motherOf(*x, *y) \rightarrow Woman(*x))$$

$$F4: \quad \exists *x : (hasChild(Peter, *x) \wedge (\exists *y : motherOf(*x, *y)))$$

$$F5: \quad hasChild(Peter, Paul)$$

$$F6: \quad Man(Paul)$$

Fig. 2. Representation in first-order logic

Example 3. The "Tax-cut" problem given in [6] is taken as another illustrative QA problem. This problem is to find all persons who can have discounted tax, with the knowledge that:

1. Any person who has two children or more can get discounted tax.
2. Men and women are disjoint.
3. A person's mother is always a woman.
4. Peter has a child, who is someone's mother.
5. Peter has a child named Paul.
6. Paul is a man.

These six statements are represented in Description Logics [2] using the axioms and assertions in Fig. 1, which can be represented in first-order logic as the formulas $F1$–$F6$ in Fig. 2. Fig. 3 shows the clauses $C1$–$C7$ obtained from these formulas using the conversion algorithm given in [1], where $*h1$ and $*h2$ are function variables.

The "Tax-cut" problem is then formulated as a QA problem $prb_3 = \langle Cs, TaxCut(*x) \rangle$, where Cs consists of the clauses $C1$–$C7$ in Fig. 3. The clause set $\widehat{\text{MVRHS}}(Cs)$ is the same as Cs except that the predicate *func* is replaced with *userfunc*. The bottom-up computation algorithm works as follows:

- Initially, MM is the set of all ground atoms and $\mathbf{T} = \{Peter, Paul\}$.
- $\mathbf{S} = \text{GEN}(Cs, \mathbf{T})$ consists of 2^3 clause sets.[2] These 8 clause sets can be divided into 3 groups:

---

[2] For the 0-ary function variable $*h1$, there are 2 choices of ground terms, i.e., *Peter* or *Paul*. For the unary function variable $*h2$, there are 2^2 possible functions from $\{Peter, Paul\}$ to itself.

$C1:$ $TaxCut(*x) \leftarrow hasChild(*x, *y), hasChild(*x, *z), neq(*y, *z)$

$C2:$ $\leftarrow Man(*x), Woman(*x)$

$C3:$ $Woman(*x) \leftarrow motherOf(*x, *y)$

$C4:$ $hasChild(Peter, *x) \leftarrow func(*h1, *x)$

$C5:$ $motherOf(*x, *y) \leftarrow func(*h1, *x), func(*h2, *x, *y)$

$C6:$ $hasChild(Peter, Paul) \leftarrow$

$C7:$ $Man(Paul) \leftarrow$

Fig. 3. Representation as a set of extended clauses

1. Group G1a consists of clause sets that contain
   - $userfunc(*h1, Peter) \leftarrow$,
   - $userfunc(*h2, Peter, Peter) \leftarrow$.

   2 clause sets belong to this group. For each clause set Cs' in this group, $\mathbf{M}(Cs') = \{M_{G1a}\}$, where

   $$M_{G1a} = \{hasChild(Peter, Paul), Man(Paul),$$
   $$hasChild(Peter, Peter), motherOf(Peter, Peter),$$
   $$Woman(Peter), TaxCut(Peter)\}.$$

2. Group G1b consists of clause sets that contain
   - $userfunc(*h1, Peter) \leftarrow$,
   - $userfunc(*h2, Peter, Paul) \leftarrow$.

   2 clause sets belong to this group. For each clause set Cs' in this group, $\mathbf{M}(Cs') = \{M_{G1b}\}$, where

   $$M_{G1b} = M_{G1a} - \{motherOf(Peter, Peter)\} \cup \{motherOf(Peter, Paul)\}.$$

3. Group G1c consists of clause sets containing $(userfunc(*h1, Paul) \leftarrow)$. There are 4 clause sets in this group. For each clause set Cs' in this group, $\mathbf{M}(Cs') = \emptyset$.

- After using all clauses in the above 3 groups, MM is modified by making intersection with M_{G1a} and M_{G1b}, i.e.,

   $$MM = \{hasChild(Peter, Paul), Man(Paul), hasChild(Peter, Peter),$$
   $$Woman(Peter), TaxCut(Peter)\}.$$

- Next, a new ground term c_1 is added to $\mathbf{T}$, i.e., $\mathbf{T} = \{Peter, Paul, c_1\}$.
- $\mathbf{S} = \text{GEN}(Cs, \mathbf{T})$ consists of 3^4 clause sets.[3] These 81 clause sets can be divided into 7 groups:

   1. Group G2a consists of clause sets that contain
      - $userfunc(*h1, Peter) \leftarrow$,
      - $userfunc(*h2, Peter, Peter) \leftarrow$.

---

[3] For $*h1$, there are 3 choices of ground terms, i.e., $Peter$, $Paul$, or c_1. For $*h2$, there are 3^3 possible functions from $\{Peter, Paul, c_1\}$ to itself.

9 clause sets belong to this group. For any clause set Cs' in this group, $\mathbf{M}(Cs') = \{M_{G1a}\}$.

2. Group G2b consists of clause sets that contain

   - $userfunc(*h1, Peter) \leftarrow$,
   - $userfunc(*h2, Peter, Paul) \leftarrow$.

   9 clause sets belong to this group. For any clause set Cs' in this group, $\mathbf{M}(Cs') = \{M_{G1b}\}$.

3. Group G2c consists of clause sets that contain

   - $userfunc(*h1, Peter) \leftarrow$,
   - $userfunc(*h2, Peter, c_1) \leftarrow$.

   9 clause sets belong to this group. For each clause set Cs' in this group, $\mathbf{M}(Cs') = \{M_{G2c}\}$, where

   $$M_{G2c} = M_{G1a} - \{motherOf(Peter, Peter)\} \cup \{motherOf(Peter, c_1)\}.$$

4. Group G2d consists of clause sets containing $(userfunc(*h1, Paul) \leftarrow)$. There are 27 clause sets in this group. For each clause set Cs' in this group, $\mathbf{M}(Cs') = \emptyset$.

5. Group G2e consists of clause sets that contain

   - $userfunc(*h1, c_1) \leftarrow$,
   - $userfunc(*h2, c_1, Peter) \leftarrow$.

   9 clause sets belong to this group. For each clause set Cs' in this group, $\mathbf{M}(Cs') = \{M_{G2e}\}$, where

   $$M_{G2e} = \{hasChild(Peter, Paul), Man(Paul),$$
   $$hasChild(Peter, c_1), motherOf(c_1, Peter),$$
   $$Woman(c_1), TaxCut(Peter)\}.$$

6. Group G2f consists of clause sets that contain

   - $userfunc(*h1, c_1) \leftarrow$,
   - $userfunc(*h2, c_1, Paul) \leftarrow$.

   9 clause sets belong to this group. For each clause set Cs' in this group, $\mathbf{M}(Cs') = \{M_{G2f}\}$, where

   $$M_{G2f} = M_{G2e} - \{motherOf(c_1, Peter)\} \cup \{motherOf(c_1, Paul)\}.$$

7. Group G2g consists of clause sets that contain

   - $userfunc(*h1, c_1) \leftarrow$,
   - $userfunc(*h2, c_1, c_1) \leftarrow$.

   9 clause sets belong to this group. For each clause set Cs' in this group, $\mathbf{M}(Cs') = \{M_{G2g}\}$, where

   $$M_{G2g} = M_{G2e} - \{motherOf(c_1, Peter)\} \cup \{motherOf(c_1, c_1)\}.$$

- After using all clauses in the above 7 groups, MM is modified by making intersection with M_{G2c}, M_{G2e}, M_{G2f}, and M_{G2g}, i.e.,

$$MM = \{hasChild(Peter, Paul), Man(Paul), TaxCut(Peter)\}.$$

- Augmenting **T** with any new ground term never changes MM further and the algorithm converges.

The obtained answer is the set $MM \cap rep(TaxCut(*x)) = \{TaxCut(Peter)\}$.   □

7   Fundamental Differences from Existing Theories

This work differs from existing theories for solving QA problems, e.g., [5,6,9], in the following fundamental main points:

1. *Use of meaning-preserving Skolemization:* Existing theories do not use meaning-preserving Skolemization. They use usual Skolemization, which preserves the satisfiability but not the meaning of a logical formula [3]. A model of a given formula is not necessarily a model of the formula obtained from it by usual Skolemization. Without meaning-preserving Skolemization, the range of possible processing methods is restricted, making it difficult to devise an effective solution for dealing with QA problems.
2. *Bottom-up computation with existentially quantified function variables:* Since usual Skolemization results in clauses with usual terms, previously existing theories do not use function variables. Resolution is used for usual proof methods [3,5,7], which deal with usual clauses without function variables. The use of function variables presents a new challenge to bottom-up computation. A fundamental distinction between our proposed algorithm and usual bottom-up proof methods is that our algorithm deals with instantiations of function variables whose scope covers an entire clause set, while the usual methods consider only instantiations of usual variables within an individual clause.
3. *A theory of representative sets:* Our theory makes clear the correctness of bottom-up computation for solving QA problems. The concept of a representative set is proposed. Given a clause set Cs with globally existentially quantified function variables, a representative set, denoted by $\mathbb{MM}(Cs)$, of the set of all models of Cs is defined. An algorithm for computing $\bigcap \mathbb{MM}(Cs)$ for a clause set Cs in this class is proposed. Through a representative set, the answer to a QA problem can be determined.

8   Concluding Remarks

Conventional Skolemization imposes restrictions on solving QA problems in the first-order domain. Adoption of meaning-preserving Skolemization is essential for establishment of a correct and efficient solver of QA problems. Meaning-preserving Skolemization introduces the concept of a function variable, which is outside of scope of the first-order logic. The use of function variables poses new challenges. This paper has proposed a correct bottom-up algorithm in the extended space with function variables, based on an insightful understanding of the extended space. It will provide a basis for construction of more general and more efficient QA-problem solvers.

Acknowledgments. The work was partly supported by the collaborative research program 2010, Information Initiative Center, Hokkaido University.

References

1. Akama, K., Nantajeewarawat, E.: Meaning-Preserving Skolemization. In: 2011 International Conference on Knowledge Engineering and Ontology Development, Paris, France (in press, 2011)
2. Baader, F., Calvanese, D., McGuinness, D.L., Nardi, D., Patel-Schneider, P.F.: The Description Logic Handbook, 2nd edn. Cambridge University Press (2007)
3. Chang, C.-L., Lee, R.C.-T.: Symbolic Logic and Mechanical Theorem Proving. Academic Press (1973)
4. Horrocks, I., Patel-schneider, P.F., Bechhofer, S., Tsarkov, D.: OWL Rules: A Proposal and Prototype Implementation. Journal of Web Semantics 3, 23–40 (2005)
5. Lloyd, J.W.: Foundations of Logic Programming, 2nd edn. Springer, Heidelberg (1987)
6. Motik, B., Sattler, U., Studer, R.: Query Answering for OWL-DL with Rules. Journal of Web Semantics 3, 41–60 (2005)
7. Robinson, J.A.: A Machine-Oriented Logic Based on the Resolution Principle. Journal of the ACM 12, 23–41 (1965)
8. Staab, S., Studer, R.: Handbook on Ontologies. Springer, Heidelberg (2004)
9. Tessaris, S.: Questions and Answers: Reasoning and Querying in Description Logic. PhD Thesis, Department of Computer Science, The University of Manchester, UK (2001)

Identification of Appropriate Database Relations through Attributes Extracted from Natural Language Queries

Mohammad Moinul Hoque and S.M. Abdullah Al-Mamun

Ahsanullah University of Science and Technology, Dhaka, Bangladesh
{moinul,almamun}@aust.edu

Abstract. This paper presents a novel approach for recognizing database relations from a Natural Language Query (NLQ). Various significant phrases, which are extracted from NLQs for mapping to database details, have been used to isolate database relations with a goal to make available the actual information asked for by database users. A few novel algorithms have been incorporated to carry out this work. Moreover, application of common database operations like 'natural join' carried out when information comes from more than one database relation have been thoroughly investigated to be able to respond accurately to an NLQ. Correctness of the 'join' operation is determined by applying a number of algorithms which ensure the criteria of the operation even if the NLQ does not have enough information to isolate proper database relations. Besides, supervised learning techniques have been used to improve the process of recognizing relations. Some heavy duty database systems were used for experimental verification of the proposed methodology and the outcome of the experiments clearly shows that our proposed method can identify appropriate database relations through attributes extracted from NLQs to databases.

Keywords: Natural Language Query, SQL, database relation, natural join.

1 Introduction

Analyzing a Natural Language Query (NLQ) for retrieving proper information from a database system has always remained a difficult task. In order to form an SQL (Structured Query Language) statement that various database management systems deal with for generating a response from a given database system we need to investigate an NLQ rigorously and find useful information that may be proved to be sufficient enough for the purpose. A number of recent works describe the process of inspecting an NLQ in terms of domain specific database systems [1-2] and mapping those information to database details with some novel algorithms. To face the multifaceted problem of ambiguity present in natural language texts, usual NLQ processing limits its scope within finding key words or their synonyms in the queries [3]. Others like Microsoft English Query, much talked about propose extensive use of English grammar. Authors in paper [1-2] rather opted to go for an approach that emphasizes structural analysis of queries. They emphasized on the facts that most common queries addressed to databases have a comparatively small number of strictly formulated structures. These structures can be outlined by marking the boundaries or

A. Abd Manaf et al. (Eds.): ICIEIS 2011, Part II, CCIS 252, pp. 314–328, 2011.

delimiters of phrases significant for formulating expressions in a form that is widely used, like SQL and it gives, we think, the fragrance of some sort of generality. Although the earlier works in this field claimed to be portable [4], those were, as correctly observed in [3], basically not so natural language oriented but mostly check-box based. Later works claimed achieving reliability [5], but at the cost of scope of functionality. Recent works claim of no generality at all [6-7]. Developing natural language based shared terminology for effective interaction with information repositories is a quite old research trend, [8], that survives vigorously till our days, [9-10]. This paper is a continuation of the works presented in [1-2] and proposes a novel approach to extract databases relations from the recognized attributes in any database systems of complex nature. Extracted database relations along with the determined join conditions are supposed to be used for generating commonly executable queries.

2   Organization of the Paper

The paper has 6 sections followed by references. Section 4-5 contains the core material, while others bear the introductory and concluding remarks. In Section 3, the scope of the current paper is discussed in the form of a brief review of its immediate predecessor [1-2]. Section 4 discusses various novel algorithms that are proposed in this paper for identifying relations from a database system through recognized attributes. Some supervised learning techniques that have been adopted for increasing efficiency of recognizing relations are discussed here. Section 5 presents the experimental setup and investigation results that verify the usefulness of the methodology proposed in section 4.

3   Marking Significant Phrases for Understanding NLQs to Databases

The idea of isolating significant phrases in NLQs to databases and then mapping them down to database details, that is to say, understanding NLQs, is presented thoroughly in [1]. It has been verified in that work with a good number of examples from different domains. The authors arrived at the fact that it is indeed possible to filter quite easily the very needful for formulating an SQL like query from a common NLQ. In particular, they had in their disposal different phrases like Attribute Phrases, Attribute Value Phrases (AVPs), Object Identifying Phrases and Aggregate Function Phrases. Their investigation revealed that, in most of the common queries to databases, these phrases can be isolated by analyzing the syntactic structures of the queries. It was observed that the number of syntactic structures outlining phrase boundaries is remarkably small. They used strict formalisms like finite automata and Moore machines for efficiently dealing with numerous syntactic structures. Thus they had two sets of machines for recognizing quite a big number of instances of NLQs. And those sets were reasonably small, that is to say, of very efficiently manageable cardinality.

The procedure involved there [1] comes out to be a simple one once the setup is established with a number of tools. First of all, a preprocessor removes insignificant words taking special care to potential phrase delimiters. Disambiguation of delimiters is performed following that, if required. At this point, the possible phrases are ready to be pressed out. And once the skeleton or structure shows up, the set of finite automata promptly recognizes it and the Moor machines then generate the candidate phrases. The process is depicted using the NLQ, Q_s given below.

Q_s: What are the names, basic salaries and designations of the employees who are from the accounts department and whose gross salary is over 15000?

The Preprocessed NLQ stands at: 'What names, basic salaries and designations of employees who accounts department and gross salary > 15000?'

First of all, the delimiter structure is extracted from the Q_s which is as follows:

What , and of who and

A DFA, DFAi accepts the above delimiter structure as shown in Fig.1 and a rule Ri is found for the corresponding DFAi.

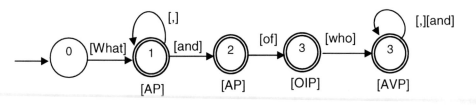

Fig. 1. DFA$_i$ `accepting the query, Q_s

$R_i \rightarrow$ What AP, AP and AP of OIP who AVP and AVP

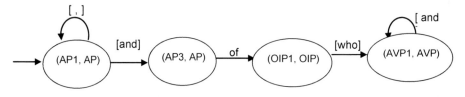

Fig. 2. Moore Machine that generates PS of Q_s

Where 'AP' stands for Attribute Phrase and 'OIP' stands for Object Identifying Phrase. Then the relevant Moore machine classifies using a predefined set, the phrases isolated from the query as shown in Fig.2.

The Attribute Phrases, Object Identifying Phrases and Aggregate function Phrases were classified more easily than Attribute Value Phrases (AVPs). In contrast to the former ones, the AVPs did not surface out by mere analysis of synonyms. AVPs were found to have diverse representations that made the search very costly. An AVP could be represented by just a typical value on one hand and, on the other, by a lengthy phrase where the attribute value lied at one end of the phrase while the attribute marker at the opposite end. In [2], the authors restricted their work to more simple queries and proposed to deal with more complex ones using heuristics, soft computing techniques. In paper [1], the authors presented a more general approach to recognize attribute value phrases in natural language queries to relational databases. Intensive use of parsing with formal grammars and exact matching of tokens were assumed to be replaced by localization of useful phrases and mapping them to database elements. A few heuristic rules have been proposed there. The heuristic rules and some techniques of inexact string matching have been incorporated to the algorithms to recognize attributes from the attribute value phrases.

4   Relation Identification

Once all the significant phrases have been extracted from an NLQ, we try to recognize valid database relations or tables from where the actual data will be retreived. We have the following common assumptions about relations and attributes: Primary keys are distinct and, except the foreign keys, all other attributes in relations are also distinct. We propose a novel **Relation Identifier (RI)** algorithm which identifies a valid set of relations from the attributes recognized in APs and AVPs through some strictly formulated maneuvers. **RI** utilizes some procedures proposed and discussed in the subsequent sections. Once we have the valid set of attributes recognized from various relations, **RI** tries to identify the relation or relations in the following way. Consider that we have the following recognized attributes involving APs and AVPs from an NLQ: x1, x2, x3, x4, and x5: Attribute x1 is common in both A and B relations; Attribute x2 is in relation C; x3 is in relation D; x4 is in relation A and attribute x5 is in both the relations A and D. If an attribute is common in two or more tables, it means that this attribute is a primary key in one relation and foreign key in other relations. Now, the algorithm detects the relation(s) in the following way. First of all it sorts in ascending order the recognized attributes in terms of the number of relations they are commonly in. In this case, the sorted list looks like:

$$x2 :\{C\}; x3 :\{D\}; x4 :\{A\}, x1 :\{A, B\} : x5 \{A, D\}$$

The order of x2, x3 and x4 is not important as they all have the same number of relations they belong to. Now, the algorithm creates a new set of relation(s) REL which is initially empty by intersecting it with the set of relations of the attributes one after another and updating it. If the result of an intersection between the set REL and any other set of relations is NULL, then all new attributes of the set are included in the REL. If the intersection result is not NULL, then the set REL remains unchanged. Let's check the procedure with the above example:

Step 1: REL = { };
REL ∪ $x2$ = { }; REL = REL ∪ $x2$; REL ={C};

Step 2: REL ∪ $x3$ = { }; REL = REL ∪ $x3$; REL ={C, D};

Step 3: REL ∪ $x4$ = { }; REL = REL ∪ $x4$; REL ={C, D, A};

Step 4: REL ∪ $x1$ = {A}; set REL remains unchanged.

Step 5: REL ∪ $x5$ = {A, D}; set REL remains unchanged.

Finally, we get the relation set REL ={C, D, A}. So, To answer the query involving the attributes $x_1, x_2, x_3, x_4,$ and x_5, we need to fetch information from the relations C, D and A. The various steps of the *Relation Identifier (RI)* algorithm is shown in Algorithm 1.

Algorithm 1. Relation Identifier (RI) algorithm

Begin Procedure
Initialize the REL set to NULL
For all recognized attribute x_i from APs and AVPs
Create a set X_i containing the relations in which the attribute x_i is a member
End For
Sort the Sets Xi according to cardinality IXiI in ascending order
For all X_i
Intersect REL and X_i
If the Result of the intersection is NULL then
REL = REL $\cup$ X_i
Else If the Result of the intersection is not NULL then
Set REL remains unchanged
End for
Set REL contains the name of the desired relations
Return REL

4.1 Fetching Information from Only One Relation

It is quite possible that a user of the database system will throw an NLQ where all the necessary data can be retrieved only from a single table. To illustrate this, let us consider the following schema. Here, primary keys and foreign keys in the relations are marked in bold and italic faces respectively.

> department = (**Deptno**, DeptName, EstdDate, Detail) ;
> student = (**ID**, name, gender, CGPA, address, religion, *Deptno*) ;
> course = (**Crsno**, crsname, credit)
> result = (*ID, Crsno, examtype, semester, marks, grade*)

The processing of the following NLQ by the *Relation Identifier (RI)* algorithm in the light of the above Schema looks like the following. : 'Show the id, name and address of the students whose CGPA is over 3.0'.

> Isolated and recognized attributes : ID, name, address and CGPA
> Once ordered the attributes, we get the following sets: name= {student};
> address= {student}; CGPA= {student}; ID = {student, result}.

Applying *RI algorithm*, we get the relation set REL = {student}. So, to answer the query involving the attributes *ID, name, address, CGPA,* we need to fetch information only from the relation 'student'. This is a very common situation where Relation identifier recognizes only one relation to fetch information from.

4.2 Fetching Information from More Than One Relation

If we take the NLQ: 'Find the name of those students who have scored A+ in the course number CSE101', we find the isolated and recognized attributes : name , grade, Crsno , ID, Once ordered the attributes, we get the following sets: name= {student}; grade= {result}; Crsno = {result, course}; ID = {student, result} and the *RI algorithm* returns the final relation set REL ={student, result}. When the number of relations detected is more than one, the best way we can fetch information from those relations is by joining them.

4.3 Testing the JOIN Compatibility

In case multiple relations are selected for information generation, a Natural Join operation is required . It must be mentioned that, in an SQL statement involving join operation between two tables, the join operation can only be performed if there is at least one common attribute between them. Then we call these relations to be join compatible. Otherwise, the join operation cannot be performed between them. In the case of a join operation between *n* numbers of tables there must be at least *n-1* join condition or more.

For example, in the above schema, we can see that a join operation cannot be performed between the result and department table because, there is no common attribute between these two tables. Similarly, no join operation can be performed between student and course table. But it is possible to join department, student and result table. Because there is one common attribute between department and student tables and also between result and student tables. It is very common that the user of an NLQ may place a query involving attributes where we need to perform a join operation, but there is not enough information in the NLQ to perform the join operation.

In order to test Join compatibility of these relations, we present an idea of storing the connectivity information of the relations as an undirected connected graph in a two dimensional adjacency data structure. The above schema can be stored as a graph shown below (Fig. 3). The corresponding graph can be labeled with numbers as shown in figure for storage purpose (Fig.4)

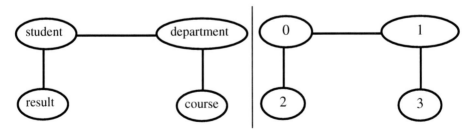

Fig. 3. Connectivity diagram of the schema   **Fig. 4.** Labeled Connectivity diagram of the schema

To check the join compatibility among {student, department, result} relations, we create a graph using these relations taken from the connectivity diagram. We then check whether the graph formed is connected or not using the standard algorithm known as number of connected component test.

A connected graph formed represents that the relations are join compatible. For the above example, the Join compatibility test is shown below in Fig. 5

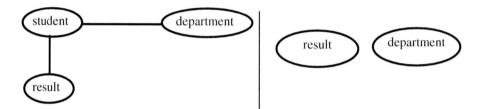

Fig. 5. Join compatibility test among student department and result relations

Fig. 6. Disconnected Components test between result and department relations

An NLQ in the following form : 'Show the roll and department name of those who have scored A+ in the course number CSE101' may generate the set of relations such as REL = {department, result}, which are not join compatible as the graph formed shows two disconnected components. The join compatibility test is shown below in Fig. 6.

4.4 Fixing Join Incompatible Relations Using the FixJoin Algorithm

It may be still possible to join incompatible relations by converting the disconnected graph into a connected one using some other relations. For doing this, we present a novel **FixJoin** algorithm to make join incompatible relations join compatible.

The **FixJoin** algorithm tries to add one or more relations with the set of final relations to make a join incompatible set join compatible. It is very easy for someone who knows the database system very well to think of such relations that can be added so that the join operation can be performed. For example, when we want to join the result and department table, we can decide that this join operation can be performed if the relation student is added to the join operation. So, the graph looks like the one after adding student relation is shown in fig 7.

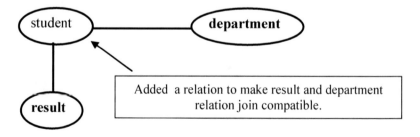

Fig. 7. Turning relations join compatible

Now, it is quite possible that such join operation could be performed by adding various relations other than the student relation. For example, if we look at the connectivity diagram shown in figure 8.

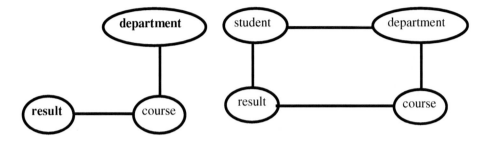

Fig. 8. Alternative ways to turn result and department relations join compatible

We can see that, the join operation between the relation result and departments could also be made possible by adding the course relation instead of the student relation. Now, as a database designer, we can decide whether this join operation should be done using course or student relations by analyzing the information contained in those relations. It may be more relevant to take the student relation instead of the course relation. To realize such situation, the *FixJoin* algorithm proposes to add some weights to the edges of the graph. These weights are added in such a way that when finding other relations to make these two relations join compatible, the **Fixjoin** considers one of the relations as a source and the other as a destination and finds the shortest path using the **Dijkstra's shortest path algorithm** between these two relations in the connectivity diagram considering the weights assigned on the edges of the graph. While finding the shortest path, the *FixJoin* algorithm adds all such relations that falls on the shortest path between department and result. Taking all such relations along with the source and destination guarantees passing the join compatibility test.

Let us take a deep look at how the *FixJoin* algorithm works for the connectivity graph shown in Fig. 9.

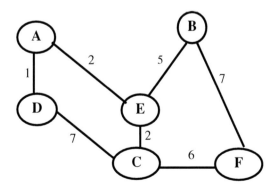

Fig. 9. A sample weighted graph for an arbitrary database schema

Here, we want to join the relations A, B, C. The graph is weighted randomly for the illustration process only. The E-R or the relational diagram can be weighted accordingly by the database designer.

The weighted graph shown above can be stored as an adjacency matrix as follows (Fig. 10). Now, from the above diagram we see here that the relations A, B, C are not join compatible as they form a disconnected graph as shown in Fig 11.

	A	B	C	D	E	F
A	0	0	0	1	2	0
B	0	0	0	0	5	7
C	0	0	0	7	2	6
D	1	0	7	0	0	0
E	2	5	2	0	0	0
F	0	7	6	0	0	0

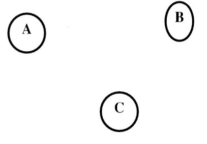

Fig. 10. Adjacency matrix for the graph in fig 9

Fig. 11. Disconnected components test between A, B, C relations

FixJoin finds shortest path from each of the nodes to all other nodes. Here the shortest path from A to C is A E C ;   A to B is A E B ; C to A is C E A; C to B is C B; B to A is B E A; B to C is B C.

Now, all the distinct nodes on all such paths are taken, which are A E B C here. We can see that the graph that forms between A E B C is a connected graph (Fig. 12), and is join compatible. So, to join the relations A, B, C we need to actually join A, E, C, B.

The *FixJoin* algorithm ensures that a response for the user's NLQ can always be generated regardless of whether or not the user provides enough information in the NLQ. In algorithm 2, we present the *FixJoin* algorithm.

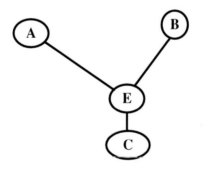

Fig. 12. Join Compatibility test between A, B, C relations

Initial weights assigned to the edges of the graph were leant empirically to get accurate paths that the **FixJoin** algorithm returns. We have used supervised learning (active learning approach) to analyze the relations recognized from various NLQs given to the system from various users and adjusted the weights on the edges according to the responses gathered from our system.

Algorithm 2. The FixJoin algorithm

Begin Procedure *FixJoin* **(relation set REL)**
> Initialize the Final Relation Set R to Empty
> For every two relations Rel_i and Rel_j from the set of all relations to join
>> Find a shortest path between Rel_i and Rel_j using Dijkstra's shortest path algorithm
>> Include all the relations that lie on the path from Rel_i to Rel_j in the Final Relation Set R.
> End for
> The resulting set of relations R is join compatible
> Return Final Relation Set R

End Procedure

4.5   The Voting Function

While finding the relation or relations from where information has to be fetched, the *RI algorithm* may suggests some redundant or un-necessary relations. For example let us take the following example to analyze such situations: 'What is the grade of the student bearing roll 4002 in CSE101 course?'

The RI algorithm suggests the final set of relation REL= {student, result}. if we observe carefully, we can see that this NLQ could be answered only from the result table alone which could reduce a lot of computational time. But here, a join operation is suggested and thus it increases the computational time. To avoid such anomaly, we propose a voting based algorithm *FixByVote* where every attribute involved in the query generation process will cast a vote for only those selected relations in which they are a part of the foreign key. In case, an attribute belongs to only a single relation, then that attribute votes for the relation it belongs to. For example, here the attribute 'grade' will vote for the result relation as it is a part of the foreign key in this relation, the attribute ID will vote for the result relation as the attribute ID is a foreign key in this relation. The attribute ID doesn't vote for the student relation as it is a part of the primary key in this table. The attribute Crsno will vote for the result relation as Crsno is a foreign key is this relation. The attribute Crsno doesn't vote for the course relation as it is a part of the primary key in this table. After all the attributes complete their voting, we can see that, the result table gets 3 votes where as the student table scores 0 vote and gets eliminated by the voting algorithm to reduce the unnecessary joining overhead.

A problem that may be encountered because of the Voting function is as follows. The FixJoin algorithm may take one or more relations to make a join compatible set of relations while those may be dropped by FixByVote algorithm considering them as unnecessary. This leaves us with a final set of relations that are join incompatible. In this case, we apply the *FixJoin* algorithm again. The FixByVote algorithm is not applied afterwards to avoid the system falling into a loop and getting stagnated.

Algorithm 3. The FixByVote algorithm

> **Procedure FixByVote**
> A ← Recognized attribute set ; R ← Recognized relation set
> For All element *attr$_i$* of set A
>   For All *relation$_i$* of Set R
>   If *attr$_i$* is a subset of the Foreign keys of *relation$_i$* or *attr$_i$* *belongs to*
>   *the relation$_i$ only.*
>   Cast a vote for *relation$_i$*
>   End if
>   End for
> End for
> Eliminate all those *relation$_i$* From *R* such that *vote(relation$_j$)* is EMPTY
> Return *R*

4.6 Major Steps of Relation Identification

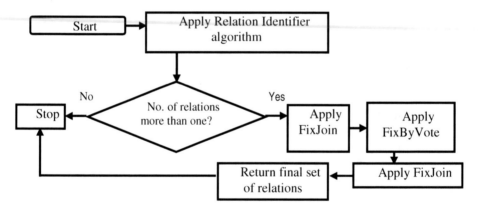

Fig. 13. The flow diagram of relations identifications process

5 Experimental Verification

Experimental encounters of the proposed methodology were designed keeping in front three of a very much common type but heavy duty database systems. The first one was the Result Processing System (RPS) of the University we work at and the other two, Air Travel Information System (ATIS) and Employee Information Management System (EIMS), had typical design and data that many can think of at ease. The database systems selected had the properties as shown in table 1.

Table 1. Experimental Data set in RPS, EIMS and ATIS

System	Number of relations	Number of distinct attributes
RPS	8	30
ATIS	6	19
EIMS	14	36

We have verified our proposed algorithms over these three different databases and tested our system using different levels of queries in terms of complexity. The main purpose of the proposed algorithms was to identify valid set of relations from the learned knowledge from where a response can be generated. Performance of the Relation Identifier algorithm was analyzed in terms of accuracy of the identified relations. Using a valid relational or E-R model guarantees that our proposed algorithm always finds a valid set of relations containing one or more relations from the learned knowledge base and they are join compatible incase the number of relations are more than one.

5.1 Accuracy of the Relation Identified by the RI Algorithm

We have used over 500 Natural Language Queries in RPS and over 300 queries in ATIS and EIMS to test the accuracy of the Relation Identification algorithm. The outcome is shown in table 2 and the graph of the result is shown in fig 14. The rate of accuracy is shown in Table 3 and in fig. 15. From Table 1 and 2, we see that, once the relational model was represented in connected graph with weights on edges and maintained the graph in adjacency matrix structure, the Relation Identification algorithm discovered around 80% relations correctly in RPS and 85.5% and 76.9% in ATIS and EIMS respectively. In some NLQs, multiple shortest paths were found initially. In that case, we used supervised learning method to analyze the relations recognized and if required, the weights on the edges were adjusted to drop a shortest path. We needed to continue the weight adjustment up to 10 iterations and after that, the accuracy went up to 93.5% in ATIS as shown in Table 3 and in fig 15. In other system, we also had a significant improvement which was over 90% .

Table 2. Performance analysis of RI algorithm

System	Number of NLQs	Valid relations recognized (without weight adjustment)	Valid relations recognized (with weight adjustment)
RPS	500	400	455
ATIS	305	260	285
EIMS	325	250	299

Table 3. Performance analysis of RI algorithms in terms of accuracy

System	Rate of accuracy (Without Weight Adjustment)	Rate of accuracy (With Weight Adjustment) (10 iteration)
RPS	80%	91%
ATIS	85.2%	93.44%
EIMS	76.9%	92%

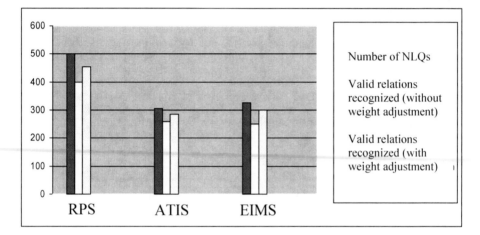

Fig. 14. Performance of RI algorithm

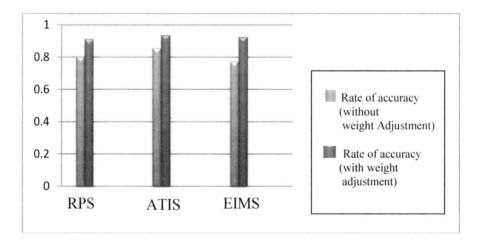

Fig. 15. Performance of RI in terms of accuracy with weight adjustment (10 iterations)

6 Conclusion and Future Works

The objective of the present work was to identify database relations from natural language queries posed to a domain specific database system of complex natures. The matters we wanted to highlight most in this paper include the possibility of tracking down a natural language query to database details, more specifically, the database relations along with the requirement of joining them with a significant precision. The ultimate goal is to be able to formulate optimal SQL query. Coming out of the practice of considering simple database systems consisting of only one relation, our system was designed based on three easily comprehensible database systems of multiple relations and numerous distinct attributes. We proposed a number of novel algorithms to identify database relations from learned attributes in some well defined steps. In this process, we also handled various database constraints like join operations and deployed a few algorithms to handle database join operations with insufficient information extracted from the natural language queries.

Our future plan consists of investigations related to synthesis of optimal queries involving the database details extracted from natural language queries. It seems very much tractable and interesting to get a SQL like query in view of the category and quality of information we have been able to extract so far. We are optimistic about the success of our efforts in this line.

References

1. Hoque, M.M., Al-Mamun, S.M.A.: Recognition of Attribute Value Phrases in Natural Language Queries to Databases. In: Proceedings of 3rd International Conference on Data Management (Innovations and Advances in Data Management), Ghaziabad, India, pp. 1–14 (March 2010)
2. Hoque, M.M., Mahbub, M.S., Al-Mamun, S.M.A.: Isolating significant phrases in common natural language queries to databases. In: Proceedings of 11th International Conference on Computer and Information Technology, Khulna, Bangladesh, pp. 554–559 (December 2008)
3. Dittenbach, M., Merkl, D., Berger, H.: A Natural Language Query Interface for Tourism Information. In: Proceedings of 10th International Conference on Information Technologies in Tourism (ENTER 2003), Helsinki, Finland, January 29-31, pp. 152–162 (2003)
4. Jerrold Kaplan, S.: Designing a Portable Natural Language Database Query System. ACM Transactions on Database Systems (TODS) 9, 1–19 (1984)
5. Popescu, A.-M., Etzioni, O., Kautz, H.: Towards a Theory of Natural Language Interfaces to Databases. In: Proceedings of the 8th International Conference on Intelligent User Interfaces, Miami, Florida, USA, pp. 149–157 (2003)
6. Owda, M., Bandar, Z., Crockett, K.: Conversation-Based Natural Language Interface to Relational Databases. In: Proceedings of ACM International Conferences on Web Intelligence and Intelligent Agent Technology Workshop, pp. 363–367 (2007)
7. Küçüktunç, O., Güdükbay, U., Ulusoy, Ö.: A Natural Language-Based Interface for Querying a Video Database. IEEE Multimedia 14(1), 83–89 (2007)
8. Kaplan, S.J.: Designing a Portable Natural Language Database Query System. ACM Transactions on Database Systems (TODS) 9, 1–19 (1984)

M. Moinul Hoque and S.M.A. Al-Mamun

9. Cimiano, P., Haase, P., Heizzmann, J.: Porting Natural Language Interfaces Between Domains: an experimental user study with the ORAKEL system. In: Proceedings of 12th International Conference on Intelligent User Interfaces, Honolulu, Hawaii, USA, pp. 180–189 (2007)
10. Li, Y., Chaudhuri, I., Yang, H., Singh, S., Jagadish, H.V.: DaNaLIX: a domain-adaptive natural language interface for querying XML. In: Proceedings of the 2007 ACM SIGMOD International Conference on Management of Data, Beijing, China, pp. 1165–1168 (2007)

Using Neural Networks to Detect Errors in Coding Exams

Jacek Stańdo

Technical University of Lodz, Center of Mathematics, ul. Al. Politechniki 11 Łódź, Poland
jacek.stando@p.lodz.pl

Abstract. The system of external evaluation has been in use in Poland for over 10 years now. The paper presents and thoroughly describes the algorithm used and discusses the efficiently of the applied method. Chapter 1 of the paper introduces the details of the system of external examinations in Poland and presents the basic concepts of RBF networks. Chapter 2 describes the structure of the examination and Chapter 3 deals with the problem and its solution.

Keywords: Neural networks, network RBF, exam, error coding.

1 Introduction

1.1 System of External Evaluation

The new system of external evaluation in Poland, which has been brought in gradually since 2002, makes it possible to diagnose the achievements as well as shortcomings of students' education in order to evaluate the efficiency of teaching and to compare objectively current certificates and diplomas irrespective of the place where they have been issued.
The parts of the external examination system are:

- The Competence Test in the sixth class of primary school.
- The Lower Secondary School (Gymnasium) Examination conducted in the third class of lower secondary school.
- The Matura Exam for graduates of general secondary schools, specialized secondary schools, technical secondary schools, supplementary secondary schools or post-secondary schools.
- The Examination confirming Vocational Qualifications (vocational examination) for graduates of: vocational schools, technical schools and supplementary technical schools.

The rules of external evaluation are described in detail in The Ordinance of the Minister of National Education. External evaluation is conducted at the end of a particular stage of education given all the requirements to realize the educational assignments described in the Core Curriculum.

The achievement standards signed by the Minister of National Education are the basis for conducting the tests and examinations.

A. Abd Manaf et al. (Eds.): ICIEIS 2011, Part II, CCIS 252, pp. 329–336, 2011.

The establishment of uniform and clearly stated attainment standards have a direct influence on the fairness and standardization of the external evaluation. Furthermore, those standards are relevant to move the main interest of the assessment from knowledge to skills and abilities obtained at a particular stage of education.

The Central Examination Board (www.cke.edu.pl) is a public education institution based in Warsaw. It was established on 1st January 1999 by the Minister of National Education on the strength of the Act on the System of Education, whose aim was to evaluate the educational achievements of students, to monitor the quality of the educational influence of school and to make all the certificates comparable regardless of the place where they have been issued. The responsibilities of the Central Examination Board are as follows:

- Preparing questions, tasks and exam sets for conducting the tests and examinations
- Preparing and presenting syllabuses containing a description of the scope of the tests and examinations, sample questions, tasks, tests, and criteria for evaluation.
  Analyzing the results of the tests and examinations and reporting them to the Minister of Education in the form of an annual report of students achievements at a given educational stage.

The examination at the end of The Lower Secondary School is obligatory, which means that every pupil must sit for it at the end of school.

The examination measures mastery of knowledge and skills specified in the current examination standards in all schools in Poland. The examination consists of three parts:

- The first one covers the knowledge and skills in the humanities: the Polish language, history, social studies, visual arts and music.
- The second one covers the knowledge and skills in mathematics and natural sciences: mathematics, biology, geography, chemistry, physics and astronomy
- The third one covers the knowledge and skills of a foreign language.

Each student taking the exam receives a set of tasks on paper along with an answer sheet. Specially prepared and trained examiners review and score the students' examinations. The answer sheets on which the answers are given to closed tasks (marked by students) and the results obtained by carrying out open tasks (written by examiners), are finally fed into electronic readers.

1.2 RBF Network

The design of a supervised neural network may be pursued in a variety of different ways. Radial basis functions were first introduced in the solution of the real multivariate interpolation problem. It is now one of the main fields of research in numerical analysis.

The construction of a radial-basis function (RBF) network in its most basic form involves three entirely different layers. The input layer is made up of source nodes (sensory units). The second layer is a hidden layer of high enough dimension, which serves a different purpose from that in a multilayer perceptron. The output layer supplies the response of the network to the activation patterns applied to the input layer.

The transformation from the input space to the hidden-unit space is nonlinear, whereas the transformation from the hidden-unit space to the output space is linear. From the output space we get:

$$F(x) = \sum_i w_i \varphi(\|x - c_i\|) \tag{1}$$

Where$(\| \ldots \|)$ is, for the most part, Euclidean norm, w_i are weights,$\varphi(\|x - c\|)$ are radial basis functions the values of which vary in a radial way around the centre c. A mathematical justification for this rationale maybe traced back to an early paper by Cover [1].

Learning is viewed as a problem of hyper surface reconstruction, given a set of data points that may be sparse. According to this viewpoint, the hyper surface reconstruction or approximation problem belongs to a generic class of problems called inverse problems, which may be well-posed or ill-posed. The problem of reconstructing the mapping F from domain X to a range Y is said to be well posed if three conditions are satisfied [9]: existence, uniqueness, continuity. If these conditions are not satisfied, the inverse problem is said to be ill-posed. Learning, viewed as a hyper surface reconstruction problem, is an ill-posed inverse problem. To make the learning problem well posed so that generalization to new data is feasible, some form of priori information about the input-output mapping is needed [3]. That is why we apply the regularization approach.

In early sixties Tikhonov put forward a new method called regularization for solving ill-posed problems. In context of approximation problems, the basic idea of regularization is to stabilize the solution by means of some auxiliary nonnegative functional that embeds priori information, e.g., smoothness constraints on the input-output mapping (i.e., solution to the approximation problem), and thereby convert an ill-posed problem into a well-posed one [5,7].

To be specific, let the set of input-output data available for approximation is described by:

Input signal:$x_i \in R^P$, $i = 1,2,3,..N$ and desired response: $d_i \in R$, $i = 1,2,3,..N$. Let the approximating function be denote by $F(x_i) = d_i$, where we have omitted the weight vector w of the network from the argument of the function F According to Tikhonov regularization theory, the function F is determined by minimizing a cost function:

$$E(F) = \frac{1}{2}\sum_{i=1}^{N}\left(d_i - F(x_i)\right)^2 + \frac{1}{2} \propto \|PF\|^2 \tag{2}$$

It involves two terms: standard error term and regularization terms. The P is a linear (pseudo) differential operator. Priori information about the form of solution is embedded in the operator P-we refer to P as a stabilizer in the sense that it stabilize the solution F, making it smooth and therefore continuous. The $\propto$ is a positive real number called the regularization parameter. There are several methods of choosing the regularization parameter [4]. In this paper we use U-curve criterion [2], [8].

2   Construction Exam and Coding

The second part of the Lower Secondary School (Gymnasium) Examination, which covers the knowledge and skills in mathematics and natural sciences: mathematics, biology, geography, chemistry, physics and astronomy, consists of 25 closed tasks and about 10 open tasks. Closed tasks are coded by students on the specially-tailored answer sheet presented in Fig. 1 (left side of the sheet). Similarly, the other encodes a test.

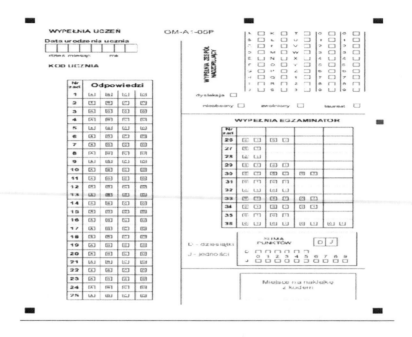

Fig. 1. Answer sheets

All the open tasks (right side of the answer sweet) are read and coded by external examiners. The answer sheet is then separated from the whole examination paper and input into the special readers for further processing. Student's ID number is coded in the top right corner of the answer sheet. Similar coding procedures apply to Matura examination and all other national examinations. Below there is a list of sample examination tasks from various mock exams.

The following three exercises show you how to perform virtual experiments by checking the appropriate knowledge and skills of the student.

The vessel is filled with the substance: water from precipitation (fig. 2). The exercise consisted of color indication on how the paper is stained (Litmus). The grading system: 1 point for the correct answer.

On the floating boat there are two forces: buoyancy and gravity. By using the mouse to move, the student has a chance to indicate the respective forces. The task of the pupil is to put them in the right place (fig. 3). The grading system: 1 point for applying forces to the location (the centre of the boat), 1 point for the correct direction of buoyancy and gravity, 1 point for balancing the forces. See [6].

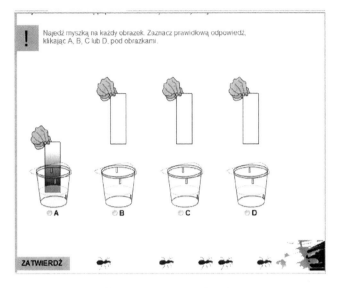

Fig. 2. E-exam- question 30

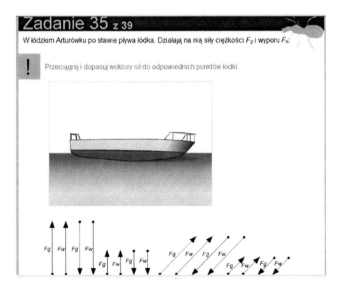

Fig. 3. E-exam- question 35

The exercise illustrated in figure 4 had arranged a system of equations and solve.

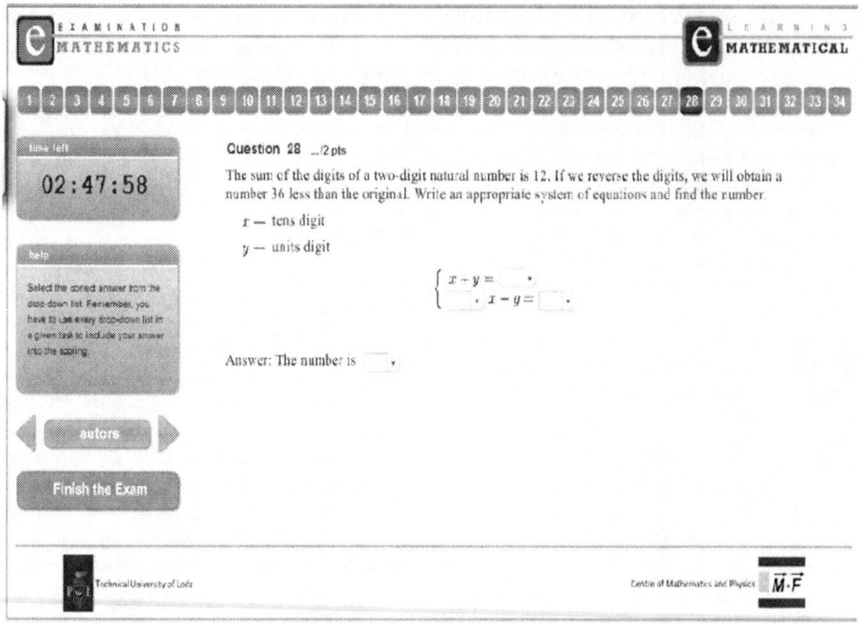

Fig. 4. E-mature 2011- projection Mathematical Emergency E-Services

3 Problem

After introducing the system of external examinations there appeared comments that students cheat during the exams trying to communicate in order to share the solutions to certain closed tasks. In order to find the solution to this problem the Central Examination Board introduced different versions of the same exam papers. The difference between the exam papers was subtle, they all contained the same tasks but the order, in which correct and incorrect answers to closed tasks were presented to students, was shuffled in order to make cheating more difficult. Content of tasks was not usually changed in order to maintain the same standards and enable comparability of the results. Unfortunately two years ago an error appeared during the coding session of the exams. The system was not able to track which student was writing which version of the exam paper. The problem was solved by applying statistical methods, which gave the efficiency results at the level of 90%.

3.1 The Proposed Solution with the Use of Neural Networks

The aim of this paper is to present a solution to the problem decoding method using a neural networks. Test conducted on the basis of e-exam in which 2020 students attended. The examination was conducted in 2008, 2011 (projection Mathematical Emergency E-Services - was the initiator and coordinator [6]).

Method

1. Random selection of 30 exam papers to work as the testing set/ validation set was carried out x^k, for $k = 1,2,3, \ldots 30$.
2. Vector x^k consisting of 32 variables worked as the input data was – results based on the open tasks x_i^k, $k = 1,2,3, \ldots 30$, $i = 1,2,3, \ldots 32$, where $x_i^k = 1$ or $x_i^k = 0$.
3. The output data consisted of the results achieved from closed task y_k, $k = 1,2,3, \ldots 30$.
4. To validate the process a modified RBF [8] neural network was applied in the Matlab software.
5. The calculation of the points from the closed tasks was done with the help of neural networks $sd(i)$, for $i = 31,32,33, \ldots 2020$.
6. The overall calculation of the points scored in each closed task by the student was performed z_l^i, for $i = 31,32,33, \ldots 2020$, $l = 1,2,3,4$.
7. Attribution of the set with the smallest error :

$$min\left(\left|sd(i) - z_1^i\right|, \left|sd(i) - z_2^i\right|, \left|sd(i) - z_3^i\right|, \left|sd(i) - z_4^i\right|\right)$$

Results

Number of training data: 30.
Number of testing date 1990
Efficiency:98%

The figure 5 shows (sorted) a graph of the difference between real value closed tasks *rv* and simulation data closed tasks *sd*, (i-student number) .

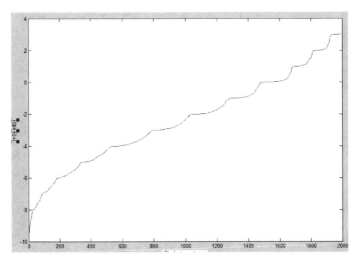

Fig. 5. Plot rv(i)-sd(i)

It occurred that 2% of students have been appointed a different set of exam tasks. However the difference in the amount of points was only 3.

4 Conclusion

The presented results proved that the problem with coding during the examination, which occurred two years ago, could have been successfully solved with the use of neural networks of RBF type, see [9].In the future this method can be used for example to detect cheating in schools, as well as to detect errors in coding which have not been researched, yet.

References

1. Cover, T.: Geometrical and statistical properties of systems of linear inequalities with applications in pattern recognition. IEEE Trans. Electronic Computers 14, 326–334 (1965)
2. Krawczyk-Stańdo, D., Rudnicki, M.: Regularization parameter in discrete ill-posed problems-the use of the U-curve. International Journal of Applied Mathematics and Computer Science 17(2), 101–108 (2007)
3. Poggio, T., Girosi, F.: Network for approximation and learning. Proceedings of the IEEE (78), 1481–1497 (1990)
4. Hansen, P.C., O'Leary, D.P.: The use of L-curve in the regularization of discrete ill-posed problems. SIAM J. Sci. Comput. 14, 1487–1503 (1993)
5. Tikhonov, A.N., Arsenin, V.Y.: Solutions of ill-posed problems. Winston-Wiley, New York (1977)
6. Stańdo, J.: First electronic examination for mathematics and sciences held in Poland - exercises and evaluation. In: Abd Manaf, A., et al. (eds.) ICIEIS 2011, Part II. CCIS, vol. 252, pp. 329–336. Springer, Heidelberg (2011)
7. Krawczyk-Stańdo, D., Rudnicki, M., Stańdo, J.: Modern regularization techniques for inverse modeling: a comparative study. Journal of Applied Computer Science (2011)
8. Krawczyk-Stańdo, D., Rudnicki, M., Stańdo, J.: Radial neural network learning using U-curve approach. Polish Journal of Environmental Studies 17(2A) (2008)
9. Stańdo, J.: Zastosowanie sztucznych sieci neuronowych do wyznaczania przelicznika między maturą rozszerzona a podstawową z matematyki, Prace monograficzne z Dydaktyki matematyki, Tom 1 (2008)

GPS Based Tracking Framework for Walking Pedestrian

Teddy Mantoro, Media A. Ayu, and Amir Borovac

Integ Lab, Kulliyah of Information and Communication Technology,
International Islamic University Malaysia, Kuala Lumput, Malaysia
teddy@iium.edu.my

Abstract. This paper discusses the problems in GPS based tracking system for walking pedestrian; these include the connectivity, map size and accuracy problems. These are the important factors affecting functionality of the GPS tracking system itself. The aim of this work is on how to setup an optimal connectivity, reducing map size of user location and to measure the acceptance of the location accuracy. To do this, a framework for tracking system using Global Positioning System (GPS) for positioning, General Packet Radio System (GPRS) and Short Message Service (SMS) for data transmission and Google Maps for displaying the location have been proposed. As a proof of concept, the prototype for the clients has been developed in various platforms including windows mobile (HTC), android (Samsung), iOS (iPhone) and Java Blackberry.

Keywords: Mobile Walking Pedestrian, Mobile Map, Tracking, GPS, GSM.

1 Introduction

GPS-enabled monitoring and tracking devices (and living beings that carry such devices) have been in widespread use over the last few years [1],[2]. Effective tracking and immediate locating of mobile users of the system, processing of obtained user information and managing that information are the core aspects of services to be provided by the proposed framework. Locating user by retrieving GPS data and converting it into information, channeled through user's request from its mobile device, is well defined process in our framework. However, such procedure relies on many factors such as age of the user, availability of the network as backbone of the communication, availability of GPS satellite signal, and such. In this paper we propose a framework that tries to minimize effects of such uncontrolled factors, and ensures the basic purpose of the system, which is tracking.

Many researchers identify landmarks as the most effective way of navigation, especially with elder people [3]. Crowded environment, especially for the walking pedestrian, is being the target of the system developed in this study to assist mobile user for tracking and/or monitoring purpose. In the environment where the structure looks alike, users sometime need a good navigation reference. Map can be considered to be the best indicator of user's location which leads to user navigation.

This paper discusses the problems in GPS based tracking system for walking pedestrian; these include the connectivity, map size and accuracy. These are the important factors affecting functionality of the GPS tracking system itself.

A. Abd Manaf et al. (Eds.): ICIEIS 2011, Part II, CCIS 252, pp. 337–348, 2011.
© Springer-Verlag Berlin Heidelberg 2011

The aim of this paper is to solve the common problems in tracking system especially on how to setup the connectivity, reducing map size of user location and to measure the acceptance of the location accuracy. To reach those objectives, this paper introduces a framework for tracking system using GPS for positioning, GPRS and SMS for data transmission and Google Maps for displaying location. As proof of concept, the prototype for the clients has been developed in various platforms which include windows mobile (HTC), android (Samsung), iOS (iPhone) and Java Blackberry. The server can also handle a special tracking device for eldery such as GT300.

This paper is structured as follows: Section 2 provides the background information regarding GPS, GPRS and Google Maps; Section 3 discusses the features and services for tracking user location. In Section 4, the framework of GPS Based Tracking is briefly described. Section 5 presents the prototype of GPS based tracking system which has been developed in several smart phones. Then Section 6 discusses the important factors affecting functionality of the tracking system i.e. connectivity, map size and accuracy. Finally, Section 7 concludes the paper.

2 Background

A GPS Technology

Global Positioning System (GPS) is a system composed of a network of 24 satellites, which are originally used in military services, and later allowed for commercial use. The satellites periodically emit radio signal of short pulses to GPS receivers. A GPS receiver receives the signal from at least three satellites to calculate distance and uses a triangulation technique to compute its two-dimension (latitude and longitude) position or at least four satellites to compute its three-dimension (latitude, longitude, and altitude) position. Once a location is computed, it can calculate an average speed and direction of traveling. Therefore, GPS is a key technology for giving device its position [4].

B GPRS Technology

General Packet Radio Service (GPRS) is an enhancement of GSM networks to support packet switched data services such as email and web browser in addition to existing GSM data services such as Short Message Service (SMS) and Circuit Switched Data (CSD) for fax transmission. GPRS operates on the existing GSM network infrastructure by utilising available time slots during each frame transmission. Thus, it does not overload the existing GSM network traffic and can efficiently provide data services. The GPRS can transfer data at the maximum rate of 115.2 kbps (with the eight available slots of each frame).

Due to a very large coverage area of GSM networks around the world, GPRS becomes the largest data service network available and always-on; thus, it is most suitable for a real-time tracking management system [5].

C   Google Maps JavaScript API

Google Maps is a Google service offering powerful, user-friendly mapping technology and local business information -- including business locations, contact information, and driving directions. The Google Maps Javascript API is a free service that enables the costumers to embed Google Maps in their own web pages. Currently, the version 3 of this API is especially designed to be faster and more applicable to mobile devices, as well as traditional desktop browser applications [6].

3   User Location Services

Our system which based on the proposed framework described in the next section is basically a location based service (LBS). Virrantaus et al. defines LBSs as information services accessible with mobile devices through the mobile network and utilizing the ability to make use of the location of the mobile device [7]. The definition suggests that LBS relates closely with location service as it adds value to the data available through the location service (LCS). Location service usually answers the 'where am I' question [8].

Location services to be provided by our system include the followings:

- Determining user's location
- Tracking user's location
- Informing the user of his/her location
- Informing other users, related to the user, of user's location
- Displaying user's location on Google Maps
- Informing appropriate institutions when the user is in the need of assistance.

Based on those location services, we propose a framework to provide a reliable service for tracking user location outdoor, in a manner that tries to minimize the problem of connectivity, map size and accuracy problems that might occur in the system.

4   GPS Based Tracking Framework

The framework, as depicted in Figure 1, is equipped with three types of servers, i.e. main sever, update server and sms server. Main server is the gateway for the clients to track their users, and it is located in the main centre operation. Update servers can be put in different locations/cities, and the SMS server is set up using GSM modem.

There are two main components of the framework, as shown in Figure 1. They include client application and server application. Client or the user is in possession of a mobile device (Smart Phone, PDA) with GPS sensor. Application residing on user's mobile device is constantly querying GPS sensor for data, and it is communicating the obtained data to the server application through the communication channel (satellite). The communication channel, depending on the settings of the client application, can be SMS, Wi-Fi link or GPRS connection. Wi-Fi is preferred than GPRS in sending update user location to update-server; whereas updating location to update-server is preferred than to SMS server. This level of preferance is based on cost consideration purpose.

Server is equipped with both subscriber identity module (SIM) card and internet link. Data retrieved from client is stored in a database by the server application.

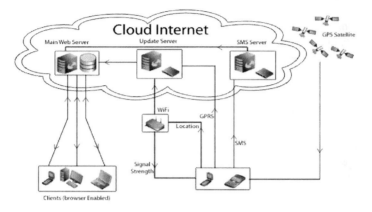

Fig. 1. GPS Tracking System Framework for Pedestrian

The frequency of location update is defined by the client application. By default, the values of 52 meters for distance-based update, and 1 minutes for time-based update, are used as being most suitable for crowds with majority of old pedestrians [3]. In this design, the GPS tracking system can monitor the speed of the mobile user. As the walking pedestrian is the target user of this study, the threshold of the speed for tracking purpose is set to 15 km per hour.

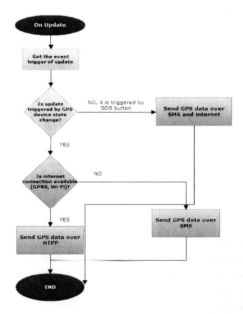

Fig. 2. Process Flow of GPS Update Data Functionality

Another client application is the one resides on the web that is accessible by user's peers who are having permission to access the system to track the user in order to know his/her whereabouts. This service is only available to the peers with eligible access through internet connection.

Figure 2 presents the process flow of GPS update data functions. Once the client (smart phones) get the event trigger for update from the GPS enabled devices, it will check the availability of the connection. If GPRS is on then it will send the data to the server directly through GPRS using HTTP protocol otherwise it will send the data using the SMS. In relation to this, Figure 7 presents the SMS Update Algorithm.

5   GPS Based Tracking Prototype

The development of GPS tracking prototype is a proof of concept of the framework presented in Section 4. The most important thing in this prototype is the functionally to do location update from several clients to the server. Process of location update based on stored settings is done automatically without user's assistance. System leaves the user with option to update the location manually, upon clicking a button, which takes the current data from the GPS sensor and sends it to the server.

Android (Samsung)   Windows Mobile (HTC)   iOS (iPhone)

Fig. 3. Snapshot of Client Applications, SOS Button Interface

The purpose of manual update is the implementation of panic situation when user wants to inform the system about his/her problem, being it health related, or being lost. When such scenario occurs, client application will utilize all available communication channels (Wi-Fi, GPRS and/or SMS). Such emergency situation requires special response, and such requests from the user are processed appropriately. Button used to invoke this scenario is marked as SOS button (Figure 3).

The Location updates can be classified into three different methods; which are the manual updating via user request, together with both of the automatically updating methods which are the time and distance basis. The users request updates are done every time they reach the designated points. Figure 4 shows the algorithm to calculate the time-based updating method and Figure 5 shows the algorithm to calculate the distance-based updating method.

```
if (checkBox2.Checked)
{
    DateTime tempTime = DateTime.Now;
    status2.Text += prevDate.AddMinutes((double)userTime) + " " +
tempTime + " " + userTime + "\r\n";
if (prevDate.AddMinutes((double)userTime) <= tempTime)
{

    prevDate = tempTime;
    mode = 2;
if (updateServer)
{
sendMessage(msg = constructMessage(position.Latitude,
position.Longitude, tempTime.ToString()));
    status2.Text += msg + " Message sent";
    }
    }
str += "The previous time is " + prevDate +
"\r\nThe time now is " + tempTime + "\r\n";
}
```

Fig. 4. Algorithm to calculate time-based updating

The server is to provide afore mentioned services in Section 4. To achieve those, the minimum server requirement includes web server, database server and GSM modem server. Whenever the user updates the location, the server will receive the GPS data sent from the client. The data is stored in a database, thus maintaining the history of user's locations. If the user sends request to the server containing GPS data along with SOS tag, server will store user's location and respond to the user's SOS request by notifying eligible parties, such as Rescue team, Police or family.

The User can view his/her location which is displayed using Google Maps. The map is displayed on client application, but it is retrieved via web from the server. In the absence of internet connectivity, map cannot be viewed. Depending on the relations to the other users, the user can view their location as well. This feature can be used if family members are performing an adventure or backpacking, and they are interested in the whereabouts of their friends or relatives.

The server provides global tracking overview, which enables the administrators of the system to view all the users of the system. It is implemented on web server by utilizing Google Maps to display the users. User data used by Google Maps interface is supplied as web service in JSON (JavaScript Object Notation) interchange format. A function using PHP will collect the data from the database and provide it in JSON format which is well structured and fast enough. Javascript, which is the main platform for Google Maps, renders JSON data into Javascript object, which is the very reason JSON is preferred over XML. Administrator of the system can query the map interface for user information by typing in the name or id of the user.

```
if (checkBox1.Checked) //if meters is chosed
{
string temp;
d = compareCoordinates(position.Latitude, position.Longitude);
temp = Convert.ToString(d);
if (d > (userDistance / 1000.0))
{
        prevLat = position.Latitude;
        prevLon = position.Longitude;
        mode = 1;
if (updateServer){
        sendMessage(msg = constructMessage(position.Latitude,
        position.Longitude,
        temp));
        status2.Text += msg + " Message sent";
        }
}
str += "The distance now is " + temp +
"\r\nThe distance specified is " +
Convert.ToString((userDistance / 1000.0)).Substring(0, 4) + "\r\n";
}
```

Fig. 5. Algorithms to calculate the distance-based updating

Connectivity between client and server is one of the main issues of this framework, and it tackles reliability aspect of it. Client initiates the connection in order to send GPS data through communication channel. In case of unavailability of Wi-Fi or GPRS connection, the client uses SMS to send GPS data.

Blackberry   **Android (Samsung)**   **iOS (iPhone)**

Fig. 6. Setting of Connectivity and Location Update of Mobile Clients

With the absence of internet connection, the client application is not able to display the mobile map interface, as it cannot establish TCP connection to the server, and

SMS cannot be used to establish such communication. Therefore user could be left unaware of his location, but nonetheless the rest of the system is capable of locating the user, so the panic situation can be resolved as well.

Another feature of the system that relies on internet connectivity is peer map interface, which provides the user with information on the whereabouts of related user's - peers. Relation role between users is defined in a relational database. To attain the list of peers, which is used to query mobile map interface, the user sends request to the web server. In the absence of internet connection, user is unable to attain the list, thus unable to display mobile map interface.

Upon retrieval of the list of the peers, user can query the mobile map interface by selecting a peer from the list, therefore triggering the display of the map with requested peer mapped on it.

In this prototype, for the purpose of user tracking and connectivity, the users can choose how they want to be tracked, including the intensity of automatic tracking based on time and distance or based on user request. The setting for the connectivities are also availabe (Figure 6) in all client platforms, including to set up the sms gateway, Wi-Fi or GPRS. For novice users, an automatic setting has also been prepared.

6   Result and Discussion

In the development and testing of the tracking system for pedestrian, there are three important factors affecting the system's functionality i.e. connectivity, map size and accuracy.

```
smsMessage smsMessage = new SmsMessage();
smsMessage.Body = data;
smsMessage.To.Add(new Recipient(SMSGatewayNumber));
smsMessage.RequestDeliveryReport = false;
smsMessage.Send();
status2.Text += "Data Sent to: " + SMSGatewayNumber + "\r\n";
status2.Text += "Data Sent is: " + data + "\r\n";
```

Fig. 7. SMS Update Algorithm

First, internet connectivity is the major factor, as it represents a bridge between server and client when the user is in need of guidance and information. As the system is modularized and all the services are distinctive in functional aspect, if one of the basic functionality modules fails, tracking will remain operable. In case of internet connection (GPRS) unavailability, tracking process still goes on by utilizing SMS for the location update purposed. Figure 7 shows the SMS algorithm for sending the GPS data through a SMS Gateway (GSM modem). Even if the internet connection is available, user might opt out due to the cost of internet traffic.

Second, mobile map interface provides images from Google Maps Static service in JPEG format, and though the size of one such image is quite small, when engaged in serious interaction with map interface (i.e. map tracking animation) it could take up a lot of traffic. In test performed on local ground, it was found out that the size of images tends to change slightly (Figure 8). It varied for few kilobytes with average size of 19,013 bytes.

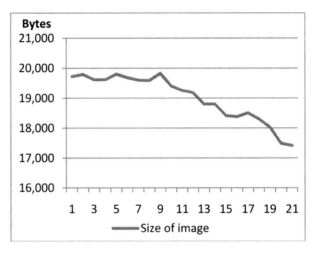

Fig. 8. The Changing of Map Image Size (Byte x Second)

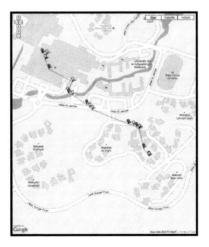

Fig. 9. Three different types of user location tracking image: based on time, distance and user request

In Figure 9, GPS user locations used for measurement of sizes of map images are displayed as sequence of markers laid out on a map. The markers are based on three different types of user location tracking image, i.e. time, distance and user request.

Each image, used for size measurement, is produced by setting each marker at the center of the map, therefore slightly moving the map. This is a good representation of a path a pedestrian might take during her/his travel. Therefore, it can be concluded that closeness of locations produce map images with similar size, and no sudden changes in sizes are observed. Taking into consideration average size of map image obtained in the test, and time based update of 1 minute, in 6 hours a client device would produce a traffic of 6.5 MB on image transport alone.

Third, the accuracy of the client devices are also an important factor, especially for fulfilling user satisfaction in such tracking device. Figure 10 presents the evaluation result in term of the accuracy of three devices, i.e. iPhone 4 (iOS4), Samsung Nexus S (Android) and GT300 special tracking device in measuring the longitude. The latitute and altitute for this testing has shown similar results. The testing shows that in a reasonable outdoor environment (open space, no cloud) when the devices can read minimal 4 satellites data, the level of accuracy in average of those three devices are acceptable. However, it should be noted that the position accuracy can be significantly improved if the devices are operated in the hot start tracking mode, in which it makes the frequency position determined based on its previous positions. In this case, Gauss-Markov model and Markov Chain model are used for the user motion and user mobility purpose [4],[9] in the outdoor. For indoor environment reference [10] can be used for further reading.

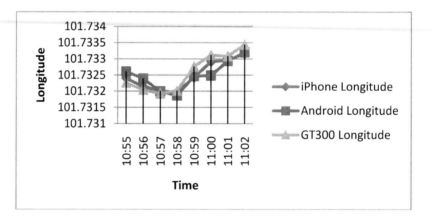

Fig. 10. The accuracy of the tracking devices using iPhone (iOS), Samsung (Android) and GT300

Gauss-Markov model permits adaptation of randomness of the mobility pattern by using a parameter that weights the random part of model against the deterministic part. Markov chains are stochastic process that is represented by a set of possible state with different transition probabilities. The chain can either evolve by changing state of stay in the same state, depending on the probability associated with the state transitions. The user motion and user mobility accuracy can be tracked based on a Markov chain where the Cartesian coordinates are treated independently, and for each location tracking only three possible states are considered, i.e.: (i) the coordinate value decrease by one unit, (ii) static or maintains its value, (iii) increase by one value [9].

7 Conclusion

This paper proposed a framework for tracking walking pedestrian. The framework is based on GPS location determination and Google Maps interface. It uses client/server approach with various technologies such as GPRS, SMS, Ajax and JSON to ensure stability and functionality of the system.

The connectivity, map size and accuracy are the common problems in GPS based tracking system. To solve that, the optimal connectivity, reducing map size of user location and measuring the acceptance of the location accuracy have been proposed. As a proof of concept, the prototypes to track the clients has been developed in various platforms including windows mobile (HTC), android (Samsung), iOS (iPhone) and Java Blackberry, as well as for a special tracking device such as GT300.

Location accuracy including user motion and user mobility has been discussed in this paper. In relation to those user mobility, future works can be enhanced to the study of crowed as the spatial distribution of moving users to facilitate the swift response to the emergency in public pedestrian domain. The fractal features can be used to describe the degree of users gathering. Brown motion [11] which describes the random movement of particles suspended in a fluid, can be used as a basis in studying human moving activity.

Further, most of the time people travel only over distances, between home and office, and occasionally take longer trips [12]. Thus, Levy-flight, which is a type of random walk with fat-tailed displacements and waiting-time distributions can be used for human travel pattern study. Hence, in this case Levy-flight is preferable to model human moving activity rather than Brown motion [13].

References

1. Álvarez, J.A., Ortega, J.A., González, L., Cuberos, F.J.: Where do we go? OnTheWay: A prediction system for spatial locations. In: ICUC 2006: Proceedings of the 1st International Conference on Ubiquitous Computing, pp. 46–53 (2006)
2. Chadil, N., Russameesawang, A., Keeratiwintakorn, P.: Real-time Tracking Management System Using GPS, GPRS and Google earth. In: Proceedings of the 5th International Conference on Electrical Engineering/Electronics, Computer, Telecommunications and Information Technology, vol. 1, pp. 14–17 (2008)
3. Knoblauch, R.L., Pietrucha, M.T., Nitzburg, M.: Field studies of Pedestrian Walking Speed and Start-Up Time, Transportation Research Record, vol. 1538, pp. 27–38. Springer, Heidelberg (1996)
4. Kaplan, D.: Understanding GPS: Principles and Applications. Artech House Publishers (1996) ISBN 0890067937
5. Bates, R.J.: GPRS: General Packet Radio Service, 1st edn. McGraw-Hill Professional (2001) ISBN 0071381880
6. Google, Inc., The Google Maps Javascript API V3,
   http://code.google.com/apis/maps/documentation/javascript/
   (last accessed on November 16, 2010)
7. Virrantaus, K., Markkula, J., Garmash, A., Terziyan, Y.V.: Developing GIS-Supported Location- Based Services. In: Proceedings of WGIS 2001 – First International Workshop on Web Geographical Information Systems, Kyoto, Japan, pp. 423–432 (2001)

8. Wang, S., Min, J., Yi, B.K.: Location Based Services for Mobiles: Technologies and Standards. In: IEEE International Conference on Communication (ICC) 2008, Beijing, China (2008)

9. Figueires, J., Frattasi, S.: Mobile Position and Tracking: From Conventional to Cooperative Techniques. Wiley (2010)

10. Mantoro, T., Johnson, C.: User Mobility Model in an Active Office. In: Aarts, E., Collier, R.W., van Loenen, E., de Ruyter, B. (eds.) EUSAI 2003. LNCS, vol. 2875, pp. 42–55. Springer, Heidelberg (2003)

11. Brockmann, D., Hufnagel, L., Geisel, T.: The Scaling Laws of Human Travel. Nature 439(7075), 462–465 (2006)

12. Mantega, R.N., Stanley, H.E.: Stochastic process with ultraslow convergence to Gaussian: the truncated Levy flight. Phys. Rev. Letters 73, 2946–2949 (1994)

13. Liao, Z., Yang, S., Liang, J.: Detection of Abnormal Crowd Distribution. In: IEEE/ACM International Conference on Cyber, Physical and Social Computing, pp. 600–604 (2010)

BBQE: Multi-language String Search Approach for Blackberry Environment

Teddy Mantoro, Media A. Ayu, and Merdin Macic

Integ Lab, Kulliyah of Information and Communication Technology,
International Islamic University Malaysia, Kuala Lumpur, Malaysia
`teddy@iium.edu.my`

Abstract. Mobile application development seems in popularity in a very fast pace. The reason for this is that pervasive computing and applications related to it, share small, inexpensive and robust networked processing devices distributed at all scales throughout everyday life. This paper discussed on how wireless networks affect the performance of a multi-language string search client-server based application for a Blackberry device in comparison to a standalone application. As a case study, five Al-Quran translations are used as proof of concept that string-search can be implemented in an efficient and fast search manner in several databases. The performance comparison between standalone and client-server application is presented including the discussion of the BBQE prototype.

Keywords: multi-language text search, client-server, wireless network, search techniques, mobile applications.

1 Introduction

Mobile applications which are used for performing searches in smaller databases are usually standalone applications, meaning that all the processing is done at the application which resides on the device itself. However, there are many applications which are based on the client-server model. Some data is collected at the client side and sent to the server in order to perform certain operations on the small device and return the results which were processed at the server to the client side. For a comparison purpose both approaches will be discussed and explained throughout this paper. However, many researchers put a lot of effort into examining how people use technology to aid in religious practices [1], which in this study the translation of Al Quran in 5 different languages will be used.

Performance comparison of two approaches, standalone and client-server approaches of the Quran application will be measured under the same circumstances and environment. For instance, the same searching method is used in both situations, one at the server side in the client-server approach and another in the standalone application on the Blackberry device itself. The main target of this study is to present and prove which performance between the two approaches is more effective in terms of speed and time consumption.

However, we should note that the performance of client-server approach depends on the connection the client and server use in order to communicate to each other. In

A. Abd Manaf et al. (Eds.): ICIEIS 2011, Part II, CCIS 252, pp. 349–359, 2011.

this study, a wireless connection is used and the influence of that connection to the performance of the application will also be taken into consideration.

The remainder of the paper is organized as follows. Section 2 briefly explains how our low-cost experimental setup of the approaches used has been done. Section 3 reviews some string search algorithms available. Section 4 describes the string search approach used in our work. Then, Section 5 shows and discusses our experimental results. Finally, Section 6 presents our concluding remarks.

2 Low-Cost Experimental Setup

The Qur'an search application which is based on a client-server model is comprised of a client, which resides on a Blackberry device and sends the search phrases to the server and receives the processed information afterwards. The server listens to incoming connections from the client(s) and uses the TCP protocol. It can handle multiple client connections.

The main task of the server is to perform a search of the search phrase received from the client in one of the five databases available. The five databases contain the text of the holy Qur'an in five different languages. The sizes of the five files are different hence the performance of the search in terms of speed or time will also be affected depending on the file size for a certain string-search.

The following figure depicts the client-server approach and explains how the experiment works.

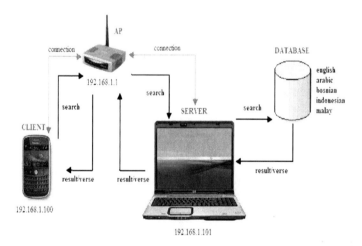

Fig. 1. Low Cost Experiment Set-up

Figure 1 shows that both, the client (Blackberry Bold 9700) and the server (HP laptop) are connected to a common access point (PCI access point). The Blackberry device is equipped with Marvell Tavor PXA930 CPU, 624 MHz which is the fastest one available in the time of experiment and 128 MB RAM.

The access point with an IP address has only one function and that is to provide a connection through which the client and server can then connect to each other and exchange data. The client (Blackberry) connects to the access point and gets an IP address. The server application listens on port 1555. The client application initiates a connection while creating a socket with ip-address:port-no [2],[3].

3 String-Search Algorithm

Searching for a string in a body of text is not an easy task. Computer scientists have been dealing with this problem area up till today. Several algorithms have been introduced for string searching including brute force algorithm, Karp-Rabin algorithm [13], Knuth-Morris-Pratt (KMP) algorithm [14] and Boyer-Moore algorithm [5]. These four searching algorithms are the ones that are reviewed as part of our consideration in deciding which one is going to be adapted to solve our particular searching problem.

Brute force algorithm or naïve algorithm is the simplest algorithm in string searching since it compares the pattern to the targeted text, one single character at a time, until the matched ones are found. Figure 2 shows the pseudo-code of this algorithm. The matching process is done from left to right. The expected complexity of this algorithm is O (nm) [15],[16].

```
do
   if (text letter == pattern text)
      compare next letter of pattern to next
      letter of text
   else
      move pattern down the text by one letter
while (entire pattern found or end of text)
```

Fig. 2. Brute force algorithm pseudo-code

The Karp-Rabin algorithm is a string searching algorithm that uses hashing technique. It calculates a hash value of the pattern, and for each subsequence portion of the target that aligned with the pattern. If their hash values are similar, then the algorithm will compare every single character of the pre-matching target whether it is matched with the pattern. Or in other words, brute force is applied only when a hash value match is found [13],[15]. Most of the time the complexity of the algorithm is O (m+n), but in unlikely worst case it can reach O (mn) [15].

The Knuth-Morris-Pratt algorithm or famously the KMP algorithm is a string searching algorithm which performs the searching comparison from left to right. Its basic idea is to perform searching by keeping tracks of information gained from previous comparisons [14]. The complexity of the KMP algorithm is generally O (n+m) but on worst case performance it may runs near O (mn) in time complexity [15].

The Boyer-Moore Algorithm basic idea is different from the previous ones reviewed. It believes that more information is gained by matching the pattern from the right than from the left [5]. This algorithm is considered as an efficient string searching algorithm, because it does not need to check every single character of the string being searched. It tends to examine only a fraction of the characters in the text string [6],[7]. Suppose that the pattern is of length p. The algorithm starts by comparing the last character of the pattern against t_p, which is the p-th character of the text/target. If there is a mismatch, the algorithm will determine the rightmost occurrence of t_p in the pattern and shift accordingly. For instance, if t_p does not appear in the pattern at all, then we can shift by m-4 and so forth. In general the algorithm gets faster when the key being search for becomes longer, because the potential shifts (i.e. skips of characters) are longer [15],[17]. The Boyer-Moore searching algorithm gets complexity of O (n/m) for a text of length n and a pattern of length m. This is obviously faster and requires less response time, compares to the brute force search which is known to have the complexity of O(nm).

```
1    j ← 0
2    while (j ≤ n - m)
3    do i ← m - 1
4       while (i ≥ 0) and x[i] = y[i + j]
5            do i ← i - 1
6       if (i < 0) then return j
7            j ← j +match(0, y[i + j])
8       else    j ← j + max(match(i, y[i + j]),
                occur[y[i + j]] - m+ i + 1)
```

The occurrence shift is defined as follows. For $a \in \Sigma$:

$$occur[a] = \begin{cases} \min\{i \mid 1 \leq i \leq m-1 \text{ and } x[m-1-i]=a\} & \text{if } a \text{ appears in } x, \\ m & \text{otherwise.} \end{cases}$$

Fig. 3. The Boyer–Moore algorithm pseudo code

4   Multi-language String-Search

Our searching problem is actually to search within five databases of languages of the Quran translations. In our research work, for the string search, a normal sequential search or known as brute force algorithm was considered at first but has proven to be very slow when tested in the standalone version. However, when used in the client-server approach the response time was not affected by the sequential search in comparison to other searches performed under the same circumstances. Other searches like binary search for example would not help much in this situation since the data was not sorted alphabetically or in any other special order which would let us benefit of using the binary search [4]. Therefore, the Boyer-Moore pattern matching algorithm was used in our searching problem. Other consideration actually is given to increase the speed and reduce the response time by creating an index file for the database files and perform a binary search on that index file. This method is obviously more effective but it demands index files for all five languages in database. The index files would be created for all words in the database to improve the search performance to O(log n) and the binary search can be implemented in the sorted index file [8]. The lastly mentioned method was not implemented yet and might be considered for future enhancements.

Regarding the search efficiency, it is important to mention that a normal substring search was used using the "indexOf()" Java method [9], which implements the Boyer-Moore algorithm. The algorithm finds the first occurrence of a substring in a string and returns the index of the substring found. Hence, the results primarily did not intend to find because it searched for substrings and not whole words. For instance, if the search used word "the", it would get verses which contain then, there, their, theory etc. In order to be more precise a search for whole words can be implemented in such a way that it checks the character before the search word and the character after it. In that case it would match only whole words, no substrings within a word. This approach depends on the end users, whether they want to find a substring or rather a full word regardless of the prefixes or suffixes. However, this approach appears to be more useful since it will find the basic word and sometimes depending on the structure or form of the word it will retrieve results where prefixes or suffixes are added. This has a special value in the Arabic version of the search since the root of the word plays an important role in finding other words in the Arabic language.

It is also important to mention that the database consists of five files each of them in a different language (English, Arabic, Indonesian, Malay and Bosnian) and each of them having a different size. The file size of course affects the performance since

Fig. 4. The sample of Screen Shots of BBQE in Arabic

some files are even two times bigger than the others. The following is the five different Quran translations size: English translation file is 920 Kbyte, Arabic translation 734 Kbyte, the Indonesian translation file is 1145 Kbyte, Malay translation 1466 Kbyte and the Bosnian translation file 765 Kbyte. Based on the file size we would expect that the response time for a search in the Malay file will be greater than the one in the Bosnian for instance. However the main focus of this study is the comparison between the two approaches, the client server and the standalone approach under same circumstances. Hence, the difference of the file size will not make a significant difference if it applied using the same approach.

An application called Blackberry Quran Explorer (BBQE) has been developed as an implementation of the multi-language string search technique explained earlier. The technique is based on Boyer-Moore string search algorithm. The BBQE application has been made to be freely available for the community to use. The Figure 4 and 5 are examples of some screen shots from the BBQE.

Manual book (installation and un-installation) and video tutorial for BBQuranExplorer is available online on our Research Group Website: (http://kict.iium.edu.my/integ/downloads.php.)

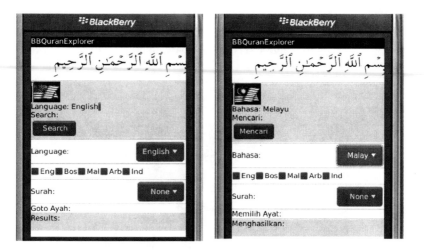

Fig. 5. The sample of Screen Shots of BBQE in English and Malay

5   Performance Comparison of Multi-language String Search

In the client-server approach, the whole application's performance depends on the wireless connection in the first place. If the connection is consider not good (weak) the performance of the whole application will suffer. Therefore, most of the tryouts performed on the application were when the signal was quite strong, or in this case up to -54 dB. When the signal is very weak (signal strength > 90 db) the performance of the whole application and the client side needs around 1.5 seconds to get the data from the server. This is the worst case scenario and happens when the signal is very week and the string has more than 500 characters. Figure 6 shows the application performance for client-server version. However, in the standalone version this is achieved in a response time of only a few milliseconds.

In some cases, when the devices connect and the search is performed for the first time it happens to be slower than the following few times. This is because of the connection establishment which sometimes proves to create problems considering that it is a wireless connection. This is related to the retrieval of a certain string itself.

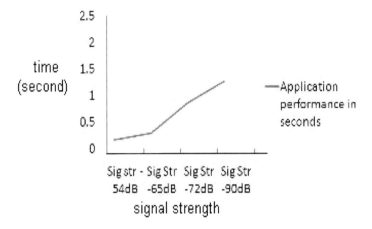

Fig. 6. Application Performance for Client/Server Version

The results for the searching itself on the server side have also shown some variations depending on changes implemented regarding the search. Some search methods proved to affect the speed and response time in the standalone version tremendously whereas in the client-server version was affected only slightly under the same circumstances. For instance when performing a search in the client-server approach using the linear search on the Arabic file and using the Boyer-Moore algorithm on that same file, the difference proves to be a few milliseconds or negligible.

Table 1. The Comparison between Client-Server and Standalone String Search in Bosnian language

String Search	Matches	Time Client Server	Time Stand alone
vrlo	24	172	1248
vrlo visoko	12	156	1293
Allah je	174	140	1295
na pravi put	104	141	1255
ono	1195	140	1242

However, when these two search methods is compared in the standalone version the difference is huge and affects the performance of the whole application tremendously. It takes up to 20 seconds to perform the linear search on the Arabic file in the standalone version which is an unacceptable response time compared to the approximately 100 milliseconds in the client-server approach. Moreover, the Boyer-Moore search algorithm takes only around 700 milliseconds in the standalone version. The reason for this is the processing power of the server which is remarkably stronger than the processing power of the Blackberry device. Table 1 clearly shows that the response time for the search in the client server approach is significantly less than the one in the standalone approach in Bosnian language and this is also similarly happen in Arab, Indonesia, Malay and English languages.

Measuring the performance of the standalone versions for five tryouts, using different words (different length). Still in Figure 7 and 8, the results show that the length of the word (search word) does not influence the performance. The only difference in the performance is between the languages since some of the files are bigger than others (e.g Arabic 760kb, Malay 1430kb).

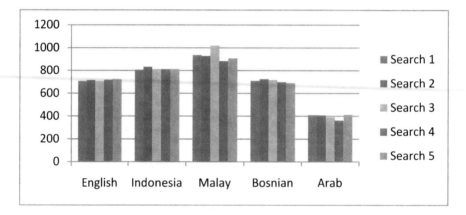

Fig. 7. Five String Search Performance Comparison in 5 Translations in the Holy Quran

The Comparison of string search between Client-Server and Standalone shows that in the normal connection the Client-Server has much in Bosnian language

The size of the application plays an important role as well. The size of the standalone application is almost 6 MB, whereas the size of the client application is about 800 KB. Hence, the standalone version requires about 5 seconds for the application to start. When for the client side of the client-server version, it needs only a few milliseconds.

The experiments conducted show that the application performance can suffer in speed because it's based on a client-server model which running on a wireless network connection. The worst case scenario is only about 1.5 seconds for a weak signal strength connection. The searching speed makes the client-server version even better as the response time for the standalone version about a second less.

However, there are still ways to improve the performance without having to change much on the approach itself. For instance, the searching approach could be enhanced in such a way that a special database could be created which would contain the top search phrases and their respective appearances in the databases. In other words, a search would have to be performed and the results stored to create an index for every search word. That index (database file) would contain the search phrase and the verses or lines where they appear. Then the string search process just has to perform a binary search on the index file and send the index to the client.

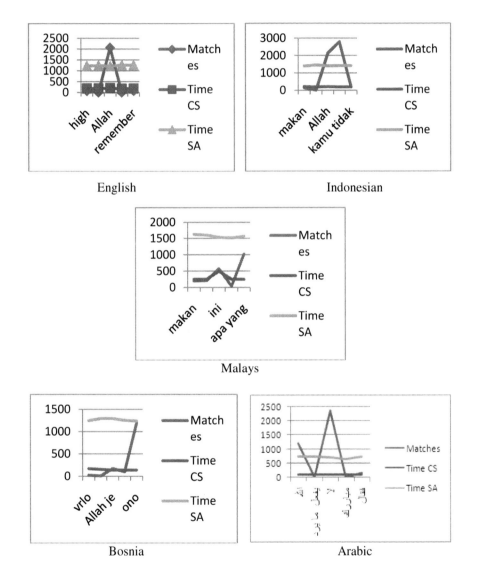

Fig. 8. The Time Comparison between Client-Server (CS) and Standalone (SA) String Search and Words Matches in 5 Translations of the Holy Quran

The same approach could be used for the standalone approach. This approach would need some time to create a program which would then create the index file but it would improve the performance of the application in terms of speed immensely or O(log n) performed on the index file which would be significantly smaller than the actual files [10].

The efficiency or the correctness of the search can also be improved. Instead of searching for a substring it would be more efficient to search for whole words or phrases. In this case, character by character matching would have to be performed whilst checking the characters before and after the search phrase. It would require more time for searching but it would not significantly influence the performance of the application in terms of speed or time.

On the other hand, the correctness of the search would be enhanced to the maximum. If the search phrase is a whole sentence or contains more than three words, it makes no difference, but if the search phrase is only one word than the correctness of the search using the substring search will not be quite satisfying if we intend to get the exact word only. Delimiters (eg. ; , - ' etc.) should be omitted during the searching process in order to get an exact match. The benefit of this application is that people can search and explore the Quran at any time and very quickly and that is actually of paramount importance [11],[12].

8   Conclusion

Our study shows that technique which based on the Boyer-Moore string search algorithm has outperformed the brute force one in multi-language string search problem. This paper also shows that client server approach performs better in the searching process compares to the standalone approach in the context of our mobile application. These results demonstrate that wireless networks do not restrict the usage of mobile application except if there is no network connection at all. It means that wireless networks do not affect the performance in any significant way.

Moreover, there are different types of wireless networks available, 802.11 wireless networks are even more limited than other wireless networks compare to CDMA or GSM or GPRS. Hence, the availability and performance might even be better using other than IEEE 802.11 (Wi-Fi).

References

1. Design and Religion: New Forms of Faith (special issue). I.D. Magazine (March/April 2006)
2. Pop, E., Barbos, M.: Mobile Communications Client Server System for Stock Exchange e-Services Access (2009)
3. Wagner, E.D.: Enabling mobile learning. EDUCASE, 41–52 (May/June 2005)
4. Shani, G., Meek, C., Paek, T., Thiesson, B., Venolia, G.: Searching Large Indexes on Tiny Devices: Optimizing Binary Search with Character Pinning (2009)
5. Boyer, R., Moore, S.: A Fast String Searching Algorithm. Communication of the ACM 20(10), 762–772 (1977)

6. Crochemore, M., Lecroq, T.: A fast implementation of the Boyer-Moore string matching algorithm (2008)
7. Bell, T., Powell, M., Mukherjee, A., Adjeroh, D.: Searching BTW compressed text with the Boyer-Moore algorithm and binary search (2001)
8. Sedgewick, R.: Algorithms, pp. 175–177. Addison-Wesley (1983)
9. Green, R.: Boyer-Moore: Java Glossary,
   `http://mindprod.com/jgloss/boyer.html` (accessed in July 2011)
10. NA, Koran Index, `http://www.submission.org/quran/koran-index.html` (acceseed on December 9, 2010)
11. Woodruff, A., Augustin, S., Foucault, B.E.: Sabbath Day Home Automation: 'It's like mixing technology and religion'. In: Proc. CHI 2007, pp. 527–536. ACM (2007)
12. Cao, Y., Tin, T., McGreal, R., Ally, M., Coffey, S.: The Athabasca University mobile library project: increasing the boundaries of anytime and anywhere learning for students. In: The International Conference on Communications and Mobile Computing (IWCMC), Vancouver, British Columbia, Canada (2006)
13. Karp, R.M., Rabin, M.O.: Efficient Randomized Pattern-Matching Algorithms. IBM Journal of Research and Development 31(2), 249–260 (1987)
14. Knuth, D.E., Morris Jr., J.H., Pratt, V.R.: Fast Pattern Matching in Strings. SIAM Journal on Computing 6(1), 323–350 (1977)
15. Lovis, C., Baud, R.H.: Fast Exact String Pattern-Matching Algorithm Adapted to the Characteristics of Medical Language. Journal of American Medical Information Association 7, 378–391 (2000)
16. Mohammed, A., Saleh, O., Abdeen, R.A.: Occurrences Algorithm for String Searching Based on Brute Force Algorithm. Journal of Computer Science 2(1), 82–85 (2006)
17. Wu, S., Manber, U.: A Fast Algorithm for Multi-pattern Searching. Technical Report (1994), `http://webglimpse.net/pubs/TR94-17.pdf` (accessed in June 2011)

Bottleneck Monitoring and Resource Allocation of Aerospace Sheet Metal Shop

Hsien-Ming Chang, Chikong Huang, and Chau-Chen Torng

Institute of Industrial Engineering and Management,
National Yunlin University of Science & Technology,
123, Section 3, University Road, Touliu, Yunlin, Taiwan 640, R.O.C.
g9321809@yuntech.edu.tw

Abstract. Aerospace industry is a value-added and technology integrated industry. Sheet metal parts are important portion of aerostructures. The sheet metal production line combines five different routing types together. This study introduces an indicator to identify and monitor bottleneck among work centers, then develops an algorithm to reallocate the resources of sheet metal shop. It helps to construct a balance production line and satisfy the dynamic demand of aerospace market.

Keywords: Bottleneck, Resource Allocation, Sheet Metal Shop.

1 Introduction

Aerospace industry is a value-added and technology integrated industry. In addition, it is a technique-intensive, capital-intensive, and labor-intensive industry. It also integrates the mechanical, electronic, material, chemical and information technology.

The characteristics of aerospace industry can be described as following:

1. Long life cycle.
2. Quality system certification.
3. High precision and lightweight.
4. Various part number, few quantity requirement [1-3].

Sheet metal parts are important portion of aero-structures. There are thousands of different sheet metal parts in one aircraft. The attribute of sheet metal production line combines different processes of parts together. According to the contour and function requirement, the aircraft sheet metal part includes five major processes as follows:

1. Stretch forming: Double curvature fuselage skin, wing skin, leading edge …etc.
2. Hydro forming: Bulkhead, rib, frames …etc.
3. Brake bending: Angle, support, bracket …etc.
4. Roll forming: Single curvature skin.
5. Drop hammering: Parts with complex contour, e.g. inlet duct.

Because of low quantity requirement of each part number; it is hard to achieve the economic quantity of automatic production. Therefore, introducing group technology and fabricating the parts by part family are suitable ways in aerospace industry.

A. Abd Manaf et al. (Eds.): ICIEIS 2011, Part II, CCIS 252, pp. 360–374, 2011.
© Springer-Verlag Berlin Heidelberg 2011

Characters of sheet metal production line of aircraft can be described as follows:

1. Quality of form block is key successful factor of parts.
2. Requirement of each part number is about several hundred pieces of parts.
3. Form block set-up time is much longer than forming time [4, 5, 6].

In comparison with the R & D, production and marketing, the profit of production is the least one among those three functions. Because of the profit-limited and complexity of production process, so integrate and allocate the production resources dynamically can increase the competitive advantages of enterprise.

2   Literature Review

2.1   Bottleneck

Bottleneck may happen in many different kinds of field, such as production, transportation, service...etc. The bottleneck will become the constraint of the system and the overall performance will be limited.

Cox et al. [7] define the protective capacity as a given amount of extra capacity at non-constraints above the system constraint's capacity, use to protect against fluctuations.

Ferdinando et al. [8] proposed local search method is based on a Tabu search technique and on the shifting bottleneck procedure used to generate the initial solution and to refine the next-current solutions.

I.G. Drobouchevitch et al. [9] present Heuristic Algorithm to solve strongly NP-hard problem for two-stage Job shop scheduling problem with a bottleneck machine.

Jinliang Cheng et al. [10] propose a heuristic algorithm being based on a shifting bottleneck approach which decomposes the parallel machine flow shop problem into m parallel-machine scheduling problems to be solved one by one.

Prakash G. Awatea et al. [11] apply Heuristic formulation to study optimizing loading policies at a bottleneck facility in an assembly line with random rejects.

Ramiro Varela et al. [12] use genetic algorithm to develop a knowledge-based evolutionary strategy for scheduling problems with bottlenecks.

Abraham P. Punnen [13] use Heuristic algorithm to solve bottleneck assignment problem under categorization.

In the behavior of multi-lane freeway traffic, upstream is an oversaturated off-ramp. Use the Variable capacity, can change the freeway discharge flow significantly without a change in the off-ramp flow when the percent of exiting vehicles changes [14].

Carlos F. Daganzo et al. [15] presents a numerical method to model kinematics wave (KW) traffic streams containing slow vehicles. The slow vehicles are modeled discretely as moving boundaries that can affect the traffic stream.

Boris S. Kerner [16] used numerical method to solve the problems of spatiotemporal congested traffic patterns at highway bottlenecks.

The above study uses many methods to solve or monitor the bottleneck, such as simulation, Tabu search method, heuristic algorithm, numerical method...etc. Because of shifting bottleneck will happen in the dynamic production system and hard to find it. This paper will create an indicator to monitor the bottleneck.

2.2   Resource Allocation

The resources allocation is important to customer-oriented enterprise. Reduce lead time and quick response to the demand of customer can increase the competitive advantage of the firms.

G. Allen Pugh [17] uses Fuzzy logic and simulation as a tool to investigate resources allocation in a manufacturing environment. Results indicate a fuzzy controller to be a feasible alternative.

K.K. Lai et al. [18] develop a methodology of fuzzy evaluation and fuzzy optimization for multiple-objective systems.

Hong Zhang et al. [19] integrates discrete-event simulation (DES) with a heuristic algorithm is developed to optimize dynamic resource allocation for construction scheduling. This heuristic algorithm is based on the objective of minimizing project duration and would consider activating multiple activities at the same time based on limited quantities of resources.

Anabela P. Tereso et al. [20] present an approach to resource allocation under stochastic conditions for multi-modal activity networks. Optimization is via dynamic programming, which proves to be demanding computationally.

Zne-Jung Lee et al. [21] use a hybrid search algorithm with heuristics for resource allocation problem encountered in practice is proposed.

Ricardo M. Bastosa et al. [22] introduce an autonomic solution based in a multi-agent model for resource allocation in a manufacturing environment. This model considers the temporal and synchronism aspects involved in the allocation process.

Vivek F. Farias et al. [23] use Approximation algorithms for dynamic resource allocation; they consider a problem of allocating limited quantities of M types of resources among N independent activities that evolve over T epochs.

The above study uses many methods to solve resources allocation problem, such as fuzzy, simulation, dynamic programming, heuristic algorithm...etc. This paper will develop a heuristic algorithm to solve the resources allocation of aerospace sheet metal shop.

2.3   Theory of Constraints

Theory of Constraint (TOC) represents an application of general systems theory for optimizing production. It uses the most constrained of the firm's activities to guide production and process improvement decisions. Firms adopting the TOC indicate that it has aided in reducing lead-time, cycle time, and inventory, while improving productivity and quality [24].

The theory of constraints was developed by Goldratt as a process of continuous improvement. The primary focus of the TOC is managing bottleneck activities that restrict the firm's performance. Any system must have at least one constraint. The TOC consists of a set of focusing procedures for identifying a bottleneck and managing the production system with respect to this constraint, while resources are expended to relieve this limitation on the system. When a bottleneck is relieved, the firm moves to a higher level of goal attainment and one or more new bottlenecks will be encountered. The cycle of managing the firm with respect to the new bottleneck(s) is repeated, leading to successive improvements in the firm's operations and performance [25].

The TOC is implemented through the global operational measurements of throughput, the rate at which the system generates money through sales; inventory, all money the system invests in purchasing items the system intends to sell; and operating expenses, all money the system spends turning inventory into throughput [26].

Theory of Constraint applies in many different fields, such as production, supply chain management, project management...etc. In this paper, we use concept of Theory of Constraint to develop a heuristic algorithm to solve the resources allocation of aerospace sheet metal shop.

3   Modeling

3.1   Problem Description

Due to the investment of aerospace industry is high and the pay back period is long, the type of aircraft production belongs to make-to-order system. Quality, cost and delivery on schedule are the basic principle of production line management. The uncertain factor of production control describe as follows:

1.   Air on ground.
2.   Configuration change related to fly safety.
3.   Shortages of row material.
4.   Quality issue during production.
5.   Machine/facility breakdown.
6.   Poor supply chain management.

Due to the above uncertain factors occur, the management level will face following problems:

Capacity and load of shop floor and raw material can not be handled precisely.

Bottlenecks occur in shop floor and products can not meet master production schedule.

Emergent demand of customer can not be satisfied immediately.

The operators who belong to bottlenecks complain too much overtime work.

The customers complain the service level decreased.

There are five forming process constructed by 14-work centers in sheet metal production line. Process flows of sheet metal parts are complex in aerospace industry. Bottleneck of capacity will cause interaction effects between work centers in both the upstream and downstream. If any work center becomes the bottleneck, it will delay the schedule of part fabrication and aircraft assembly. If the product could not delivery on schedule, company will lose credit and cause penalty.

3.2   Precedence Diagram

Consider the construction of work center: Some are depend on forming machines, e.g. stretch forming, hydro forming, rolling, brake bending...etc.   Some depend on manpower, e.g. straightening, bench work...etc.

Consider the characteristics of work center: Some are common resource of difference routing types, e.g. heat treatment, bench work...etc. Some work centers just serve for specific routing type, e.g. Stretch forming, rolling, joggling. The detail routing types for five major types are shown as Table 1. The associated precedence diagram is shown as Figure 1.

Table 1. Detail Routing of Sheet Metal Parts

Routing type ID.	Routing Type	Detail Process
1.	Brake Bending Parts	First Cut(F)→NC Routing(NC)→ Brake Bending(SB)→Straightening(S)→Bench Work(B)→QC Inspection(Q)
2.	Hydro Forming Parts	First Cut(F)→NC Routing(NC)→ Hydro Forming(SH)→Straightening(S)→Bench Work(B)→QC Inspection(Q)
3.	Joggling Parts	First Cut(F)→Joggling (SJ)→Hand Routing(R)→Bench Work(B)→QC Inspection(Q)
4.	Rolling Parts	First Cut(F)→Rolling(SR)→Hand Routing(R)→Bench Work(B)→QC Inspection(Q)
5.	Stretch Forming Parts	First Cut(F)→Stretch Forming(SS)→Hand Routing(R)→Bench Work(B)→QC Inspection(Q)

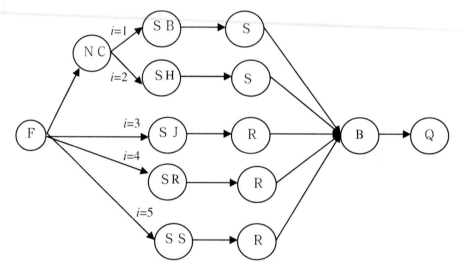

Fig. 1. Precedence Diagram of Sheet Metal Parts

Where:

i : Routing type identification number. i =1~5
(1: Brake bending parts, 2: Hydro forming parts, 3: Joggling parts, 4: Rolling parts, 5: Stretch forming parts)
ij : Identification number in the *jth* work center of routing type i.

3.3   Measurement Indicators

Define the measurement indicators as the baseline to evaluate the bottleneck among those work centers. The evaluation and measurement indicators are shown as following:

Load-Capacity Ratio (R_{ij}): The ratio of total load and total capacity of each work center in sheet metal shop, shown as Equation (1). If the Load-Capacity Ratio of specific work center is higher than others, it would become the bottleneck of all routing types.

$$R_{ij} = \frac{L_{ij}}{S_{ij}} \tag{1}$$

Where:

R_{ij}: Load-Capacity Ratio
L_{ij}: Load of the work center *ij*. (Unit: hour/month)
S_{ij}: Capacity of work center *ij*. (Unit: hour/month)

4   Algorithm and Case Study

4.1   Algorithm

Heuristic Algorithm describes as follows and flow chart show as figure 2.

Step 1: Confirm the Production Rate (d_k) of component in every project.

where:

d_k: Production Rate of component in project k. (unit: ship-set)
k : Project identification number. $k = 1 \sim n$.

Step 2: Calculate monthly demand (D_i) of detail parts in each routing type, shown as Equation (2).

$$\left[D_i \right]_{5 \times 1} = \left[C_{ik} \right]_{5 \times 5} \left[d_k \right]_{5 \times 1} \tag{2}$$

where:

D_i : Demand of detail parts in process *i*. (unit: piece/month)
C_{ik} : parts required   of routing type *i*   per shipset in project k.(unit: piece/shipset).

Step 3: Determine monthly load (L_{ij}) of detail parts in each work center, shown as Equation (3).

$$L_{ij} = D_i \cdot T_{ij} \tag{3}$$

where:

L_{ij} : Load of the work center *ij*.(unit: hour/month)
T_{ij} : unit working hour in the *jth* work center of routing type *i*.(unit: hour/piece).

Step 4: Identify the resources (manpower/machine) allocation (Q_{ij}) in each work center.

Step 5: Determine monthly capacity (S_{ij}) of detail parts in each work center, shown as Equation (4).

$$S_{ij} = h \cdot Q_{ij}$$ (4)

where:

Q_{ij}: Number/quantity of resources (manpower/machine) in the work center ij.(Unit: quantity)
h: Total working hour per month.(Unit: hour)
Sij: Capacity of work center ij. (Unit: hour/month).

Step 6: Calculate the Load-Capacity Ratio (R_{ij}) in each work center, shown as Equation (1).

Load-Capacity Ratio (R_{ij}): The ratio of total load and total capacity of each work center in sheet metal shop, shown as equation (1). If the Load-Capacity Ratio of specific work center is higher than others, it would become the bottleneck of all routing types.

$$R_{ij} = \frac{L_{ij}}{S_{ij}}$$ (1)

where:

R_{ij}: Load-Capacity Ratio
L_{ij}: Load of the work center ij. (Unit: hour/month)
S_{ij}: Capacity of work center ij. (Unit: hour/month)

Step 7: Find and record the maximum Load-Capacity Ratio (Max. R_{ij}) among these work centers. If Max. R_{ij} is less than lower limit (l), then there has no bottleneck in the system and go to step 11.

Step 8: If Max. R_{ij} is less than upper limit (u) and greater than lower limit (l), and then the bottleneck can be managed by overtime work. Arrange the overtime manpower and go to step 4.

Step 9: If Max. R_{ij} is greater than upper limit (u) and the bottleneck resource is machine and manpower, then working hour of bottleneck machine add one shift and move one unit of alternative manpower from the work center of Min. R_{ij} to the bottleneck Max. R_{ij}, and then goes to step 4.

If Max. R_{ij} is greater than u and the bottleneck resource is manpower, and then moves one unit of alternative manpower from the work center of Min. R_{ij} to the bottleneck Max. R_{ij}, then goes to step 4.

Step 10: Observe the trend of Load-Capacity Ratio (Max. R_{ij}) converge during above iterations and use linear programming to verify the resource satisfy the demand.

Step 11: End of the iteration.

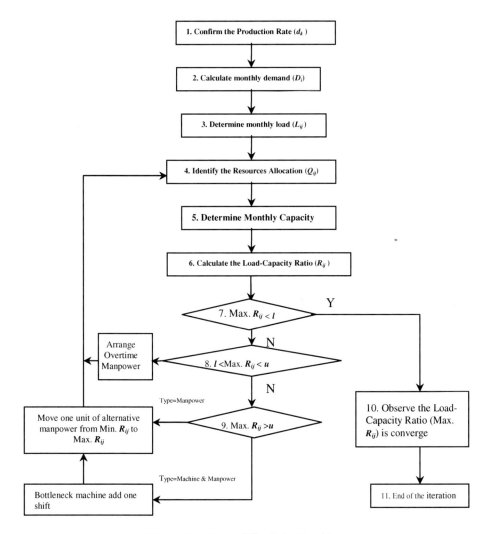

Fig. 2. Flow Chart of Heuristic Algorithm

4.2   Case Study

Heuristic Algorithm:

Step 1: Confirm the Production Rate (d_k) of component in every project.

The sheet metal shop of aircraft factory has to provide sheet metal parts to assembly line and build the components. The finished components will deliver to tier one aircraft manufacturing companies, such as Airbus and Boeing, to do final assembly and final test.

Project A, B, C, D and E belong to 5 different components, which required by 5 different tier-one aircraft manufacturing companies. The production rate is shown as Table 2.

Table 2. The production rate of different project.

Project	A($k=1$)	B($k=2$)	C($k=3$)	D($k=4$)	E($k=5$)
Production Rate (dk)	4	5	3	2	5

Step 2: Calculate monthly demand (D_i) of detail parts in each routing type, shown as Equation (2).

$$[D_i]_{5\times1} = [C_{ik}]_{5\times5}[d_k]_{5\times1}$$
(2)

Consider the aircraft delivery quantity (shipset), parts required of routing i per shipset in specific project (piece/shipset) and schedule of each project. Determine the monthly requirement throughput of each routing (piece/month), shown as Table 3.

Table 3. Monthly requirement throughput of each routing type

Project	Routing type	SB ($i=1$)	SH ($i=2$)	SJ ($i=3$)	SR ($i=4$)	SS ($i=5$)	TOTAL
A	Part/Ship set	633	1,146	74	79	101	8,132
($k=1$)	Production Rate	4	4	4	4	4	
B	Part/Ship set	1,274	1,122	182	67	81	13,630
($k=2$)	Production Rate	5	5	5	5	5	
C	Part/Ship set	178	348	10	158	18	2,136
($k=3$)	Production Rate	3	3	3	3	3	
D	Part/Ship set	168	889	43	56	15	2,342
($k=4$)	Production Rate	2	2	2	2	2	
E	Part/Ship set	559	1,057	69	75	96	11,136
($k=5$)	Production Rate	6	6	6	6	6	
Total (D_i)		13,126	19,358	1,736	1,687	1,469	37,376
Percentage (%)		35.12%	51.79%	4.64%	4.51%	3.93%	100.00%

Base on the result of Table 4 and explain as follows:

The monthly production rates of project A, B, C, D and E is 4/5/3/2/6 ship set respectively, and the total requirement quantity is 37,376 EA/month at least.

The proportion of each routing type describes as follows:

Brake bending part is 35.12%; hydro forming part is51.79%; joggling part is 4.64%, rolling part is 4.51%; and stretch-forming part is 3.93%.

Step 3: Determine monthly load (L_{ij}) of detail parts in each work center, shown as Equation (3).

$$L_{ij} = D_i \cdot T_{ij}$$
(3)

Consider the monthly requirement throughput of each routing and average unit working hour (hour/piece). Determine the monthly load (L_{ij}) of detail parts in each work center (hour/month), shown as Table 4.

Step 4: Identify the resources (manpower/machine) allocation (Q_{ij}) in each work center. The original resources (manpower/machine) allocation (Q_{ij}) in each work center shows as Table 5.

Table 4. Monthly requirement throughput of each routing type

Routing Type	Stage	Forming (j=1)	Straighten (j=2)	Routing (j=3)	Bench Work(j=4)	Total
	Part Required	Hr/EA	Hr/EA	Hr/EA	Hr/EA	Hr/EA
	(EA)	Load	Load	Load	Load	Load
SB	13,126	0.05	0.12	0.02	0.05	0.24
(i=1)	(D1)	656.3	1575.12	262.52	656.3	3150.24
SH	19,358	0.08	0.2	0.03	0.06	0.37
(i=2)	(D2)	1548.64	3871.6	580.74	1161.48	7162.46
SR	1,736	0.5	0.2	0.18	0.12	1
(i=3)	(D3)	868	347.2	312.48	208.32	1736
SJ	1,687	0.3	0.2	0.15	0.14	0.79
(i=4)	(D4)	506.1	337.4	253.05	236.18	1332.73
SS	1,469	0.5	0.3	0.2	0.18	1.18
(i=5)	(D5)	734.5	440.7	293.8	264.42	1733.42

Table 5. The original resources allocation

Routing Type	Forming (j=1)	Straighten (j=2)	Routing (j=3)	Bench Work(j=4)	Total
SB(i=1)	3	4	1	2	10
SH(i=2)	6	15	3	4	28
SR(i=3)	3	2	6	3	14
SJ(i=4)	3	5	3	3	14
SS(i=5)	4	3	5	2	14

Step 5: Determine monthly capacity (S_{ij}) of detail parts in each work center, shown as Equation (4).

$$S_{ij} = h \cdot Q_{ij} \tag{4}$$

Consider the quantity of resources (manpower/machine) and total working hour per month. Determine the monthly capacity of work center ij. (hour/month), shown as Table 6.

Step 6: Calculate the Load-Capacity Ratio (R_{ij}) in each work center, shown as Equation (1).

$$R_{ij} = \frac{L_{ij}}{S_{ij}} \tag{1}$$

Consider the load (hour/month) and capacity of each work center (hour/month). Determine the Load-Capacity Ratio (R_{ij}), shown as Table 7. The maximum ratio of load and capacity of each work center is 2.401($ij=12$) and the minimum ratio is 0.318($ij=33$). The difference of maximum and the minimum ratio is 2.804.

Table 6. The original resources allocation

Routing	Stage	Forming (j=1)	Straighten (j=2)	Routing (j=3)	Bench Work(j=4)	Total
SB	Resource	3	4	1	2	10
(i=1)	Capacity	492	656	164	328	1640
SH	Resource	6	15	3	4	28
(i=2)	Capacity	984	2460	492	656	4592
SR	Resource	3	2	6	3	14
(i=3)	Capacity	492	328	984	492	2296
SJ	Resource	3	5	3	3	14
(i=4)	Capacity	492	820	492	492	2296
SS	Resource	4	3	5	2	14
(i=5)	Capacity	656	492	820	328	2296

Table 7. Load-Capacity Ratio (R_{ij}) of each work center-1

Routing Type	Stage	Forming (j=1)	Straighten (j=2)	Routing (j=3)	Bench Work(j=4)
SB (i=1)	Load	656.3	1575.12	262.52	656.3
	Capacity	492	656	164	328
	Ratio	1.334	2.401	1.601	2.001
SH (i=2)	Load	1548.64	3871.6	580.74	1161.48
	Capacity	984	2460	492	656
	Ratio	1.574	1.574	1.180	1.771
SR (i=3)	Load	868	347.2	312.48	208.32
	Capacity	492	328	984	492
	Ratio	1.764	1.059	0.318	0.423
SJ (i=4)	Load	506.1	337.4	253.05	236.18
	Capacity	492	820	492	492
	Ratio	1.029	0.411	0.514	0.480
SS (i=5)	Load	734.5	440.7	293.8	264.42
	Capacity	656	492	820	328
	Ratio	1.120	0.896	0.358	0.806

Repeat Step 7-9:

Iteration 2:

Consider the load (hour/month) and capacity of each work center (hour/month). Determine the Load-Capacity Ratio (R_{ij}). The maximum ratio of load and capacity of each work center is 2.001($ij=14$) and the minimum ratio is 0.358($ij=53$). The difference of maximum and the minimum ratio is 1.643.

Iteration 3:

Consider the load (hour/month) and capacity of each work center (hour/month). Determine the Load-Capacity Ratio (R_{ij}). The maximum ratio of load and capacity of each work center is 1.711($ij=24$) and the minimum ratio is 0.411($ij=42$). The difference of maximum and the minimum ratio is 1.359.

Iteration 9:

Consider the load (hour/month) and capacity of each work center (hour/month). Determine the Load-Capacity Ratio (R_{ij}). The maximum ratio of load and capacity of each work center is 1.440($ij=44$) and the minimum ratio is 0.669($ij=43$). The difference of maximum and the minimum ratio is 0.669.

Step 10: Observe the trend of Load-Capacity Ratio (Max. R_{ij}) is converged during above iterations.

The Load-Capacity Ratio of each task center converges to the level which can cover by the overtime work after 9 iterations, shown as Table 8.

Table 8. The maximum/minimum Load-Capacity Ratio of 9 iterations

Iteration	1	2	3	4	5	6	7	8	9
Maximum	2.401	2.001	1.771	1.764	1.601	1.574	1.574	1.475	1.440
Minimum	0.318	0.358	0.411	0.423	0.480	0.514	0.720	0.771	0.771
Max-Min.	2.083	1.643	1.360	1.341	1.121	1.060	0.854	0.704	0.669

Step 11: End of the iteration.

4.3 Data Analysis

Apply the difference of Load-Capacity Ratio of each work centers as the evaluation indicators. Analyze the data which are collected from 9 iterations.

Two cases (beginning and the end of iteration) are described as follows:

1. **The beginning iteration:** The maximum ratio of load and capacity of each work center is 2.401($ij=12$) and the minimum ratio is 0.318($ij=33$).

The difference of maximum and the minimum ratio is 2.804, shown as Figure 3.

2. **The end iteration:** T he maximum ratio of load and capacity of each work center is 1.440($ij=44$) and the minimum ratio is 0.669($ij=43$). The difference of maximum and the minimum ratio is 0.669, shown as Figure 4.

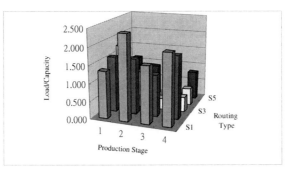

Fig. 3. The difference of maximum/minimum ratio at the beginning of iterations

3. From the beginning to the end of iteration, the difference of maximum and the minimum ratio is reduced from 2.804 to 0.669.

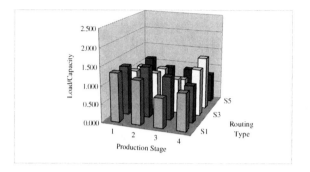

Fig. 4. The difference of the maximum/minimum ratio at the end of iterations

4. The trend of maximum ratio is reduced and toward to 1.00 after each iteration. The trend of minimum ratio increase and toward to1.00 after each iteration, shown as Figure 5.

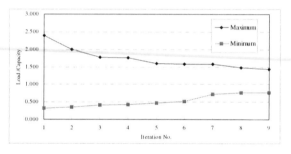

Fig. 5. The trends of the maximum/minimum ratio

5. The trend of trends of the difference of maximum and minimum ratio converges to certain level (0.669) after 9 iterations, shown as Figure 6.

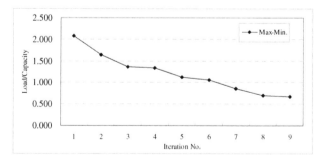

Fig. 6. The trends of the difference of maximum/minimum ratio

5   Conclusion

According to precedence diagram of sheet metal fabrication process, the model and approach can be constructed. The heuristic algorithm is then used to process the real-world case. After the iteration processes, we analysis the Load-Capacity Ratio of each work center which collected by 9 iteration.

From the model construction process, this study provides the following suggestion:

The ratio of load and capacity can be a bottleneck indicator of each work center. If the Load-Capacity Ratio of specific work center is higher than others, it would become the bottleneck of all routings.

From the model construction process, this study provides the following suggestions:

1. The beginning iteration: The maximum ratio of load and capacity of each work center is 2.401(ij=12) and the minimum ratio is 0.318(ij=33). The difference of maximum and the minimum ratio is 2.804.
2. The end iteration: The maximum ratio of load and capacity of each work center is 1.440(ij=44) and the minimum ratio is 0.669(ij=43). The difference of maximum and the minimum ratio is 0.669.
3. From the beginning to the end of iteration, the difference of maximum and the minimum ratio is reduced from 2.804 to 0.669.
4. The trend of maximum ratio is reduced and toward to 1.00 after each iteration. The trend of minimum ratio is increased and toward to 1.00 after each iteration.
5. The trends of the difference of maximum and minimum ratio converge to certain level (0.669) after 9 iterations.

References

1. Driscoll, J., Thilakawardana: The definition of assembly line balancing difficulty and evaluation of balance solution quality. Robotics and Computer Integrated Manufacturing 17, 81–86 (2001)
2. Watanabe, T., Hashimoto, Y., Nishikawa, I., Tokumaru, H.: Line balancing using a genetic evolution model. Control Engineering Practice 3(1), 69–76 (1995)
3. Rubinovite, J., Levitin, G.: Genetic algorithm for assembly line balancing. International Journal of Production Economics 41, 343–354 (1995)
4. Esrock, Y.P.: The impact of reduced setup time. Production & Inventory Management 26(4), 94–101 (1985)
5. Trevino, J., Hurley, B.J., Friedrich, W.: A mathematical model for the economic justification of setup time reduction. International Journal of Production Research 31, 191–202 (1993)
6. Kabir, M.A., Tabucanon, M.T.: Batch-model assembly line balancing: A multi-attribute decision-making approach. International Journal of Production Economics 41, 193–201 (1995)
7. Cox III, J.F., Blockstone Jr., J.H., Spencer, M.S.: APICS Dictionary, 8th edn. American Production and Inventory Control Society, Falls Church (1995)
8. Pezzella, F., Merelli, E.: A tabu search method guided by shifting bottleneck for the job shop scheduling problem. European Journal of Operational Research 120, 297–310 (2000)

9. Droubouchevitch, I.G., Strusevich, V.A.: European Journal of Operational Research 123, 229–240 (2000)
10. Cheng, J., Karuno, Y., Kise, H.: A shifting bottleneck approach which decomposes the parallelmachine flowshop problem. Journal of the Operations Research Society of Japan 44(2), 140–156 (2001)
11. Awatea, P.G., Moorkanat, J., Rangaraj, N.: Optimizing loading policies at a bottleneck facility in an assembly line with random rejects. International Journal of Production Economics 84, 319–334 (2003)
12. Varela, R., Vela, C.R., Puente, J., Gomez, A.: A knowledge-based evolutionary strategy for scheduling problems with bottlenecks. European Journal of Operational Research 145, 57–71 (2003)
13. Punnen, A.P.: On bottleneck assignment problems under categorization. Computers & Operations Research 31, 151–154 (2004)
14. Munoz, J.C., Daganzo, C.F.: The bottleneck mechanism of a freeway diverge. Transportation Research Part A 36, 483–505 (2002)
15. Daganzo, C.F., Laval, J.A.: Moving bottlenecks: A numerical method that converges in flows. Transportation Research Part B 39, 855–863 (2005)
16. Kerner, B.S.: Control of spatiotemporal congested traffic patterns at highway bottlenecks. Physica A 355, 565–601 (2005)
17. Allen Pugh, G.: Fuzzy allocation of manufacturing resources. Computers Industrial Engineering 33(1-2), 101–104 (1997)
18. Lai, K.K., Li, L.: A dynamic approach to multiple-objective resource allocation problem. European Journal of Operational Research 117, 293–309 (1999)
19. Zhang, H., Li, H.: Simulation-based optimization for dynamic resource allocation. Automation in Construction 13, 409–420 (2004)
20. Tereso, A.P., Aralujo, M.M.T., Elmaghraby, S.E.: Adaptive resource allocation in multimodal activity networks. Int. J. Production Economics 92, 1–10 (2004)
21. Lee, Z.-J., Lee, C.-Y.: A hybrid search algorithm with heuristics for resource allocation problem. Information Sciences 173, 155–167 (2005)
22. Bastosa, R.M., de Oliveira, F.M., de Oliveira, J.P.M.: Autonomic computing approach for resource allocation. Expert Systems with Applications 28, 9–19 (2005)
23. Farias, V.F., Van Roy, B.: Approximation algorithms for dynamic resource allocation. Operations Research Letters 34, 180–190 (2006)
24. Jayson, S.: Goldratt & Fox, Revolutionizing the factory floor. Management Accounting 68(11), 18–22 (1987)
25. Goldratt, E.: What Is This Thing Called Theory of Constraints and How Should It Be Implemented? North River Press, Croton-on-Hudson (1990)
26. Goldratt, E., Fox, R.: The Race. North River Press, Croton-on-Hudson (1986); Rand, G.K.: Critical chain: the theory of constraints applied to project management. International Journal of Project Management 18, 173–177 (2000)

Arabic Spoken Language Identification System (ASLIS): A Proposed System to Identifying Modern Standard Arabic (MSA) and Egyptian Dialect

Areej Alshutayri and Hassanin Albarhamtoshy

King Abdulaziz University, Jeddah, Saudi Arabia
aalshetary@kau.edu.sa

Abstract. There are millions of people in the world speak many languages. To communicate with each other it is necessary to know the language which we use. To do this operation we use language identification system.

In general, Automatic Speech Recognition for English and other languages has been the subject of most researches in the last forty years. Arabic language research has been growing very slowly in comparison to English language research. The Arabic language has many different dialects; they must be identified before Automatic Speech Recognition can take place.

This paper describes the design and implementation of a new spoken language identification system: Arabic Spoken Language Identification (ASLIS) . It focuses only on two major dialects: Modern Standard Arabic (MSA) and Egyptian. It presents a spoken Arabic identifier using Hidden Markov Models (HMMs), and it is developed using the portable Hidden Markov Model Toolkit (HTK).

Keywords: Arabic Spoken Language Identification - Modern Standard Arabic - Hidden Markov Models - Hidden Markov Model Toolkit - Automatic Language Identification - Classical Arabic.

1 Introduction

Due to the many languages of the world's population, we need to know the language spoken by the speaker. To do this operation we use language identification system.

Automatic Language Identification (LID) is the task of identifying the language of a spoken utterance. There are several important applications of automatic language identification. For instance, such a system could be used as a preprocessor to identify the language spoken before the translation takes place. The telephone companies will be better equipped to handle foreign language calls if an automatic language identification system can be used to route the call to an operator fluent at that language. Also, rapid language identification and translation can even save lives.

Arabic language research has been growing very slowly in comparison to English language research. This slow growth is mainly due to a lack of modern studies on the acoustic-phonetic nature of the Arabic language and to the inherent difficulties in speech recognition. Additionally, there is no standardized database of Modern Standard Arabic (MSA) language in general.

A. Abd Manaf et al. (Eds.): ICIEIS 2011, Part II, CCIS 252, pp. 375–385, 2011.

To build a system of automatic identification on the language of speaker, we use Hidden Markov Models (HMMs). HMMs have become very famous method to build speech recognition system. It is set of hidden states and probabilities for transition from one of the states to another.

Following is an explanation of the HMMs and the differences between MSA and Egyptian dialect.

1.1 Automatic Language Identification

Automatic Language Identification (LID) is the task of identifying the language of a spoken utterance. "Automatic", because the decision is performed by a machine. As the global economic community expands, there is an increasing need for automatic spoken language identification services, it could be used to provide interactive telephone assistance, when a caller to language line does not speak any English language, identification system might be used to route an incoming telephone call to a fluent human switchboard operator in the corresponding language [1]. Everybody can imagine the multi-lingual system for example, in the airport or rail station for information, checking into hotel, making travel arrangements and so on. All this can be difficult for non-native speakers.

Languages differ in the inventory of phonological units which is used to produce words, the frequency of occurrence of these units, and the order of the occurrence in words [1].

Most language Identification systems operate in two phases: training and recognition. During the training phase, the typical system is presented with examples of speech from a variety of languages. Fundamental characteristics of the training speech then can be used during the second phase of language identification: recognition. During recognition, a new utterance is compared to each of the language-dependent models [2].

Each language has characteristics which are different form language to other. We need to examine the sentence as a whole to determine the acoustic signature of the language, the unique characteristics that make one language sound distinct from another [1].

1.2 Hidden Markov Model

A Hidden Markov Model (HMM) is a statistical model in which the system being modeled assumed to be a Markov process with unobserved state.

In a regular Markov model, the state is directly visible to the observer, and therefore the state transition probabilities are the only parameters. In a hidden Markov model, the state is not directly visible, but output which is dependent on the state is visible. Each state has a probability distribution over the possible output tokens. Therefore the sequence of generated tokens by an HMM gives some information about the sequence of states [3].

There are several different ways to classify data using HMM. If we have several HMMs trained for different words and we have sequence of phonemes as result, then for each HMM we compute the probability of matching the particular sequence of phonemes (output) with the current HMM. The HMM that has the highest probability is considered as the most likely word. To do this task, we should train the HMMs for every word [4].

To bis a freely available Hidden Markov Model Toolkit from Cambridge University. HTK is a state-of-the-art tool in the speech recognition community. HTK is a toolkit for building Hidden Markov Models (HMMs). HMMs can be used to model any time series. However, HTK is primarily designed for building HMM-based speech processing tools, in particular recognisers. Thus, much of the infrastructure support in HTK is dedicated to this task [5].

In the recognition process there are two major processing stages involved. Firstly, the HTK training tools are used to estimate the parameters of a set of HMMs using training utterances and their associated transcriptions. Secondly, unknown utterances are transcribed using the HTK recognition tools.

1.3 Arabic Language and Its Dialects

Arabic is one of the oldest languages in the world. It is the fifth widely used language nowadays.

The bulk of classical Islamic literature was written in Classical Arabic (CA), and the Holy Qur'an was revealed to Prophet Mohammed, peace be upon him, in the Classical Arabic language.

The Arabic language has multiple variants, including Modern Standard Arabic (MSA), the formal written standard language of the media, culture and education, and the informal spoken dialects that are the preferred method of communication in daily life. MSA is primarily written not spoken [6]. Modern Standard Arabic (MSA) is the mother (spoken) tongue for more than 338 million people living in the Arab world, which includes countries such as Saudi Arabia, Oman, Jordan, Syria, Lebanon and Egypt [7].

Modern Standard Arabic is syntactically, morphologically and phonologically based on Classical Arabic but it lacks the extreme formality of Classical Arabic. The researches on Arabic language are mainly concentrated on MSA which is considered the standard dialect of all Arabic speaking nations [7, 8].

Modern Standard Arabic has basically 34 phonemes of which six are basic vowels, and 28 are consonant. This phonemes contain two distinctive classes which are named pharyngeal and emphatic phonemes. Arabic language has three long, three short vowels and two diphthongs (/ay/ and /aw/). The allowed syllables in Arabic language are: CV, CVC, and CVCC where V indicates a (long or short) vowel while C indicates a consonant. Arabic utterances can only start with a consonant [8].

The Arabic dialects are the true native language forms. They are generally restricted in use for informal daily communication. They are not taught in schools or even standardized. Dialects are primarily spoken, not written.

They are the result of the interaction between different ancient dialects of Classical Arabic and other languages that existed in neighbored and/or colonized what is today called the Arab world. For example, Algerian Arabic has a lot of influences from Berber as well as French due to the French occupation[6, 9].

Arabic dialects are loosely related to Classical Arabic. They differ substantially from MSA and each other in terms of phonology, morphology, lexical choice and syntax [6, 9]. Arabic dialects can be divided based on geography into [6]:

- Gulf Arabic includes the dialects of Kuwait, Saudi Arabia, United Arab Emirates, Bahrain, Qatar and Oman. Iraqi Arabic is sometimes included.
- Levantine Arabic includes the dialects of Lebanon, Syria, Jordan, Palestine and Israel.
- Egyptian Arabic covers the dialects of the Nile valley: Egypt and Sudan.
- North African Arabic (Maghrebi Arabic) covers the dialects of Morocco, Algeria, Tunisia and Mauritania. Libya is sometimes included.
- Yemenite Arabic is often considered its own class.
- Maltese Arabic is not always considered an Arabic dialect. It is the only Arabic variant that is considered a separate language and is written with Latin script.

Egyptian Arabic is spoken by about 80 million people in Egypt. It is perhaps the most widely understood throughout the Arab world due to the popularity of Egyptian filmmaking, TV production and the great number of Egyptian teachers and professors who were instrumental in setting up the education systems of various countries in the Arabian Peninsula. Consequently, the Egyptian dialect is frequently taught in many American and European schools due to its popularity and because it, like MSA, can be understood in most of the Arab world.

Arabic dialects vary phonologically from standard Arabic and each other. Some of the common variations include the following, table 1.

Table 1. Differences between MSA and Egyptian Dialect

MSA Consonant	MSA Example	Egyptian Consonant	Egyptian Example
Qaaf (/q/)	The MSA word /tariq/	**Qaaf** (/q/) is realized as a glottal stop (/ʔ/)	/tariʔ/
Jiim (/dʒ/)	The word 'beautiful' is /dʒamil/	**Jiim** (/dʒ/) is realized as (/g/)	/gamil/
Thaa (/θ/)	The word 'three' is pronounced /θalaθa/ The word 'then' is pronounced /θuma/	**Thaa** (/θ/) is pronounced as (/t/) or (/s/)	/talata/ /suma/
Dhaal (/ð/)	The word 'this' is pronounced /haða/ The word 'that' is pronounced /ðalik/	**Dhaal** (/ð/) is pronounced as (/d/) or (/z/)	/da/ /zalik/
Dhaad (/dˤ/)	The word 'police officer' is /dˤabit/ The word 'hit' is /yadˤrubu/ The word 'fog' is /dˤbab/	**Dhaad** (/dˤ/) is pronounced as (/d/) or (/z/)	/zabit/ /yadrub/ /zbab/
Dhaa (/ðˤ/)	The word 'appear' is /ðˤhar /	**Dhaa** (/ðˤ/) is pronounced as (/z/)	/zhar/

2   Related Work

A speaker-independent natural Arabic speech recognition system is presented by .Elshafei et al. [10]. Data was collected by recording the audio files from several TV news channels. A total of 249 news stories, summing up to 5.4 hours of speech, were recorded and split into 4572 files with an average file length of 4.5 seconds. The length of wave files range from 0.8 seconds to 15.6 seconds.

The system was trained on 4.3 hours of the 5.4 hours of Arabic broadcast news corpus and tested on the remaining 1.1 hours. The phonetic dictionary contains 23,841 definitions corresponding to about 14232 words. The percent of the correctly recognized words was 92.84%. The Word Error Rate came to 9.0%.

Nofal et al. [11] research presented Arabic/English language identification system for short duration, telephone quality, speech utterances based on speaker identification, vowel spotting, and Continuous Hidden Markov Models (HMMs). The effect of vowel spotting on both speaker identification and language identification accuracy is also studied. Three different designs and implementations of this system are introduced in this study, the first one is based on speaker identification, the second is based on speaker identification using a language dependent vowel spotter while the third one is based on speaker identification using a language independent vowel spotter. Training set consists of 10 utterances from 10 speakers and the test set consists of 10 utterances from 10 speakers. The test speakers are different than the training speakers.

The same set of test speakers and test utterances from both languages were used to test the three systems.

Tests were conducted for many N-best speakers where N ranges from 1 to 10. The result of the basic Language Identification (LID) system which doesn't use a vowel spotter shows 100% language identification accuracy for the Arabic test utterances for all N values.

Results of the LID system with a language dependent vowel spotter shows 80% language identification for the Arabic test utterances for all N values. Results of the LID system with a language independent vowel spotter shows 60% language identification accuracy for the Arabic test utterances with N=1 and N=10.

3   Arabic Spoken Language Identification System (ASLIS)

The task of this identification system is to classify the input speech as either MSA or Egyptian dialect. It consists of two phases: training and testing. The speech signal is processed in the signal processing module that extracts feature vectors for the decoder.

Acoustic models include the representation of knowledge about acoustics, phonetics, microphone and environment variability, gender and dialect differences among speakers [12].

Language models refer to a system's knowledge of what constitutes a possible word, what words are likely to appear together, and in what sequence.

The decoder uses both acoustic and language models to generate the word sequence that has the maximum posterior probability for the input feature vectors [12].

Figure1 shows the block diagram of a Spoken Arabic Language identification and the following subsections illustrate the operations of the proposed ASLIS.

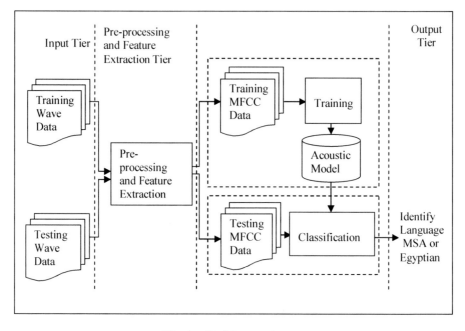

Fig. 1. ASLIS Block Diagram

3.1 Pre-processing and Feature Extraction

The functionality of pre-processing stage is to prepare the input signal to Feature Extraction stage. In the Pre-processing stage a speech waveform transforms into a sequence of parameter vectors.

Feature Extraction is a fundamental part of any speech recognition or identification system. The functionality of feature extraction stage is to extract feature vector for each frame which was calculated from pre-processing stage.

To do Pre-processing and Feature Extraction job, the speech recognition tools was used, but it cannot process directly on speech waveforms. These have to be represented in a more compact and efficient way. This step is called acoustical analysis.

- The signal is segmented into successive frames whose length is 25ms, overlapping with each other.
- Each frame is multiplied by a windowing function (e.g. Hamming function).
- A vector of acoustical coefficients is extracted from each windowed frame.

3.1.1 Mel-Frequency Cepstral Coefficients (MFCC)

MFCC is the most popular feature in speech identification systems. It is based on that the human ear's critical bandwidths vary with frequency. Filters spaced linearly at low frequencies and logarithmically at high frequencies which have been used to capture the phonetically important characteristics of speech. This is expressed in the mel-frequency scale, which is a linear frequency spacing below 1000 Hz and a logarithmic spacing above 1000 Hz.

3.1.2 Additional Features

In the speech recognition and language identification field, different speech features have been used such as spectral features or prosodic ones. The effort to select suitable features containing relevant information for speech recognition brought researchers after thorough analysis of process of human hearing to parameterization techniques based on mel-frequency cepstral (MFCC). An experience with speech recognition showed that it is beneficial to use also delta and delta-delta coefficients which decrease the word error rate. Even though the original set of features of the MFCC is more or less correlated then after addition of delta and delta-delta features the information redundancy of elements in feature vectors increases. Since in this system we are concerned with the spectral features such as MFCC features, we add different features related to the MFCC such as time derivatives. The first order regression coefficients of the MFCC feature vector called Delta is included. Also, the second order regression coefficients, called Delta-Delta, is included [7].

3.2 Training and Classification Processes

Before starting the training process, the HMM parameters must be properly initialised with training data in order to allow a fast and precise convergence of the training algorithm. The training stage creates flat start monophones which is based on HMM training to define a prototype model. It will scan a set of training data files, compute the global mean and variance and set all of given HMM to have the same mean and variance. Then re-estimate the flat start monophones by using the embedded re-estimation tool. In classification stage the system will classify the testing data into MSA or Egyptian Dialect. This classification doing by using HTK recognition tool. The re-estimated HMMs have to be tested on the test corpus.

The monophone acoustic models are built using 5-state continuous HMMs without state-skipping, with a mixture of 12 Gaussians per state. We extract standard Mel Frequency Cepstral Coefficients (MFCC) features from 25 ms frames, with a frame shift of 10 ms. Each feature vector is 39, is computed from the length of the parameterised static vector (MFCC_0 = 13, 12 cepstral features plus energy) plus the delta coefficients (+13) plus the acceleration coefficients (+13).

3.3 Data Preparation

The first stage of any recognizer development research is data preparation. Speech data is needed for both training and testing. In general, there is a lack of Arabic language databases in general, not only for Modern Standard Arabic (MSA) but also for other dialects of Arabic. Most databases in existence for either MSA speech recognition or Arabic Dialect identification were created solely for private research. Therefore, we created database for our work by recording TV Broadcast News and Talk shows programs containing both the Egyptian and MSA dialects. Unfortunately, these recordings often contain background noises such echoes and background music. The overall condition of these recorded databases is poor compared to that of a standard speech database. The speech corpus of this work consists of MSA and

Egyptian dialect. The database used in training and testing the system for each dialect is a combination of twenty-five speakers, sixteen males and nine females. The speech of ten male speakers and five female speakers are used for training, and the speech of six male speakers and four female speakers are used for testing. The speech for training from each speaker is one minute long. The speech for testing from each speaker is 30 second long. See table 2.

Table 2. MSA and Egyptian Database

	Training		Testing	
	Male	**Female**	**Male**	**Female**
MSA	10	5	6	4
Egyptian	10	5	6	4

3.4   Implementation of ASLIS by Using HTK Toolkit and MATLAB

ASLIS was programmed by using HTK Toolkit and MATLAB program. ASLIS used MATLAB to create a user interface and to enable the user to enter audio file and see the result on the screen, see figure 2.

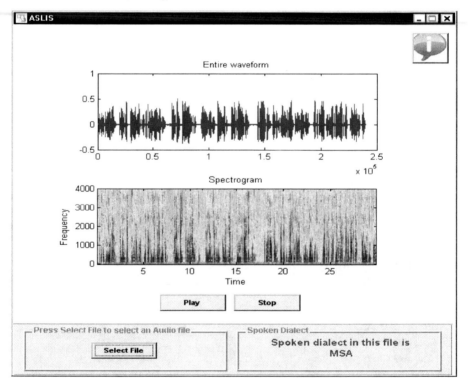

Fig. 2. Result of audio wave file (MSA Dialect)

4 Results and Discussion

This section presents the results of the identification process. Table 3 shows the testing results. It should be mentioned that no detailed or word-level labelling was done for this database; speech is labelled according to the corresponding dialect data. For instance, an Egyptian speech file is labelled with the letter "E" while a MSA speech file is labelled with "M".

Three training ways:

- **Training with MSA files (speakers):** The system could identify all MSA testing files and nothing of EGYPTIAN files.
- **Training with Egyptian files:** The system could identify all EGYPTIAN testing files and nothing from MSA files.
- **Training with both MSA and EGYPTIAN files:** The system could identify all 10 testing files of MSA and nine files from 10 testing files of EGYPTIAN dialect.

Table 4 shows the result of testing by using 30 seconds from the training database with the same speaker and speech.

Table 5 show the result of testing by using 30 seconds from the training database with the same speaker and different speech.

Table 3. Testing with Testing Database

Testing with	Training with		
	MSA	**Egyptian**	**MSA & Egyptian**
MSA	100%	0%	100%
Egyptian	0%	100%	90%

Table 4. Testing with part of Training Database (Same speaker and speech)

Testing with	Training with
	MSA & Egyptian
MSA	100%
Egyptian	100%

Table 5. Testing with part of Training Database (Same speaker with different speech)

Testing	Training with
with	**MSA & Egyptian**
MSA	100%
Egyptian	90%

In this system, we have found that the most distinguishable dialect is MSA with accuracy equals to 100%. Egyptian dialect is the second with accuracy equals to 90%. We have obtained a total accuracy of 95% in this classification task when we were given 30s-duration utterances.

In order to come up with the ultimate number of training files to be used for the MSA and EGYPTIAN dialects, accuracy tests were carried out by using different number of training files. Figure 3 shows the results of using 5, 10, and 15 training files. The last result was close to 95% accuracy; therefore, 15 training files were chosen when accuracy tests were conducted.

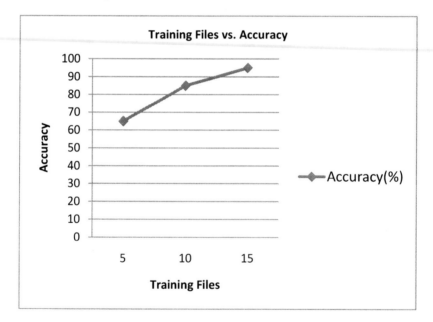

Fig. 3. The relationship between number of training files and accuracy

5   Conclusion

This paper presents a system that automatically identifies the MSA and Egyptian dialect using the HMM which was developed by using HTK Toolkit. HTK is an integrated suite of software tools for building and manipulating continuous density Hidden Markov Models HHMs.

Due to the limited availability of Arabic speech databases, it was necessary to create new data to build ASLIS for two dialects: MSA and EGYPTIAN. This database which contains 50 speakers for all dialect, 15 speakers from each dialect is used in training process, and 10 speakers from each dialect are used for the testing process.

A new model has been presented in this work based on the features of Arabic dialects; namely, a model that recognizes the similarities and differences between each dialect. The model utilized in this work was the Hidden Markov Model. The MFCC + Delta + Delta-Delta features performed best reaching an identification score. The accuracy of ASLIS system is about 95%.

References

1. Muthusamy, Y.K., Barnard, E., Cole, R.A.: Reviewing Automatic Language Identification. IEEE Signal Processing Magazine 11(4), 33–41 (1994)
2. Zissman, M.A.: Comparison of Four Approaches to Automatic Language Identification of Telephone Speech. IEEE Transactions on Speech and Audio Processing 4(1), 31 (1996)
3. Abdulla, W.H., Kasabov, N.K.: The Concepts of Hidden Markov Model in Speech Recognition, Department of Information Science, University of Otago, New Zealand (1999)
4. Rabiner, L.R.: A Tutorial on Hidden Markov Models and Selected Applications in Speech Recognition. Proceedings of the IEEE 77(2), 257–286 (1989)
5. Steve Young, G.E., Gales, M., Hain, T., Kershaw, D., Liu, X., Moore, G., Odell, J., Ollason, D., Povey, D., Valtchev, V., Woodland, P.: The HTK Book Version 3.4. Cambridge University Engineering Department (2006)
6. Biadsy, F., Hirschberg, J., Habash, N.: Spoken Arabic Dialect Identification Using Phonotactic Modeling, pp. 53–61. Association for Computational Linguistics (2009)
7. Alorifi, F.: Automatic Identification of Arabic Dialects Using Hidden Markov Models, Pittsburgh (2008)
8. Alotaibi, Y.: Comparative Study of ANN and HMM to Arabic Digits Recognition Systems. JKAU: Eng. Sci. 19(1), 43–60 (2008)
9. Diab, M., Habash, N.: Arabic Dialect Processing Tutorial. In: Proceedings of the Human Language Technology Conference of the North American Association for Computational Linguistics, pp. 5–6 (2007)
10. Elshafei, M., Al-Muhtaseb, H., Al-Ghamdi, M.: Speaker-Independent Natural Arabic Speech Recognition System. In: The International Conference on Intelligent Systems (2008)
11. Nofal, M., Abdel-Reheem, E., El Henawy, H.: Arabic/English Automatic Spoken Language Identification. In: 1999 IEEE Pacific Rim Conference on Communications, Computers and Signal Processing (1999)
12. Huang, X., Acero, A., Hon, H.-W.: Spoken Language Processing: A Guide to Theory, Algorithm, and System Development. Prentice Hall PTR (2001)

Fuzzy Based Approach for Complaint Management

Razulaimi Razali and Jafreezal Jaafar

Computer & Information Sciences Department,
Universiti Teknologi PETRONAS,
Tronoh, Perak, Malaysia
razul@pahang.uitm.edu.my, jafreez@petronas.com.my

Abstract. Complaint management is about the management of feedback from customers in a form of the complaint. The complaint handling process involved high level of uncertainties and imprecision. Hence, type-2 fuzzy sets are a suitable approach to handle this kind of information. The purpose of this paper was to present the proposed solution on the complaint handling process using the type-2 fuzzy sets approach. Literature on type-2 fuzzy and complaint management domain has been done to confirm there were gaps that can be fulfilled with new knowledge. As a result, reliable complaint management ranking technique was identified. This method has the potential to overcome time-consuming and inefficiency issues in the complaint handling process. The study on implementing this method will be continued to identify proper parameters and complaint specifications that will be used in the propose method. Therefore, simulations and testing will be performed to prove the proposed method has a reliable and optimum solution to handle a complaint handling process.

Keywords: Multi criteria, complaint management, type-2 fuzzy, fuzzy ranking.

1 Introduction

Complaint is related to human behaviour in expressing their dissatisfactory in a unique method [1]. Informally, a complaint can be categorized as information. This kind of information has a lot of potential, which is useful to the organizations. Especially for those organizations that provide services and looking forward to having an effective method to improve their services. In information technology perspective, this kind of information can be managed properly, and valuable information can be extracted for organizations benefit. For that reason, reliable information systems need to be used [2]. The process of ranking and identifying the complaints is based on matching the customer's complaint against the complaint's criteria (area, type of service, type of facility, level of satisfaction, level of impact and time frame, etc.). This process is usually conducted by experts from respective departments. Main problem within this process is that there is no systematic and consistent way for specifying the complaint's criteria and the matching process.

The complaint handling process involved uncertainties and imprecision. Customer's complaint consists of wording and perceptions that cause a high level of

A. Abd Manaf et al. (Eds.): ICIEIS 2011, Part II, CCIS 252, pp. 386–400, 2011.

uncertainties. The task of formulating complaint's criteria and identifying customer's complaint is the responsibility of respective departments. This usually involves a group of people that have expertise related to the complaint domain associated with the customer's complaint. A collective opinion will be derived from the experts to use as a based for group decision making process. Each expert produced their own opinions and preferences based on their roles, knowledge and experience related to their departments and job scope. The differences of the opinions and preferences of the experts cause a high level of uncertainties when specifying complaint's criteria and identifying complaint's solutions. Due to that when the number of expert increases, level of uncertainties also increases. Typically, these uncertainties are being addressed through departments meeting and discussion sessions. This exercise can be both time consuming and difficulty to coordinate for different departments and divisions. The difference opinions of each expert also make it difficult to achieve agreement among the group. Normally, the final decision may not always reflect the opinions of all experts in a consistent and objective way.

The group decision making process always involves uncertainties. These uncertainties can be modelled by using the type-2 fuzzy sets. Fuzzy models are the mathematical representation of the characteristics of the process, which uses the principles of fuzzy logic [3]. Fuzzy set originally introduced by Zadeh in 1965. Fuzzy set also known as type-1 fuzzy set [4-5]. Type-1 fuzzy sets have been successfully used in many applications. Unfortunately, the type-1 fuzzy sets still have limited capabilities related to directly handle data uncertainties [5]. In 1975 Zadeh [4-5] presented type-2 fuzzy set. Type-2 fuzzy sets could be called a "fuzzy fuzzy set" where the fuzzy degree of membership is a type-1 fuzzy sets [5]. Type-2 fuzzy sets very useful to use in situations where lots of uncertainties and imprecision are present [5-6].

2 Literature Review

Research on ranking methodology that uses the interval type-1 fuzzy sets approach has been done by many researchers. They are kept on developing the most effective ranking method that efficiently used and mostly focus on the multiple attributes group decision problem. Several test cases are being used to perform the simulation and testing for the designing process. Wang and Kerre [7] introduced the ordering indices in the first and second class. Based on more than 35 indices some ways to formulate the ranking orders among fuzzy quantities are suggested. Then they proposed some axioms, which serve as the reasonable properties to figure out the rationality of an ordering procedure. H. Noguchi *et al.* [8] proposed a new ordering to solve the weights of ranks by considering feasible solutions' region of the constraint. Later, a method for ranking the sequences of fuzzy values is proposed. The proposed method assigns a preference degree to each ranked sequence. It gives information regarding which sequence could be classified as the most-preferred sequence and which sequences as alternatives [9].

To this extent the proposed ranking methodologies are based on type-1 fuzzy sets. The next proposed ranking methodology is based on type-2 fuzzy sets. The first type-2 fuzzy based ranking methodology is introduced by H. B. Mitchell. He proposed a type-2 fuzzy rank and a type-2 rank uncertainty for each intuitionistic fuzzy number. The proposed method adopted a statistical viewpoint and interpret each type-2 fuzzy number as an ensemble of ordinary fuzzy numbers [10]. Later, Wu and Mendel [11] improved this method and proposed a new ranking method for interval type-2 fuzzy sets. This new ranking method is being compared with others ranking methods based on real survey data. This test is performed to identify the most suitable ranking method that can be used in the computing with words paradigm. Gu and ZhangIn [12] developed the Web Shopping Expert, a new type-2 fuzzy online decision support system order to handle the uncertainty problem. The proposed web system used a fast interval type-2 fuzzy method to directly use all rules with type-1 fuzzy sets to perform type-2 fuzzy reasoning efficiently.

Z. Shang-Ming et al. [13] presented two novel indices for type-2 fuzzy rule ranking to identify the most influential fuzzy rules in designing type-2 fuzzy logic systems, and named them the R-value and the c-value of fuzzy rules. F. Doctor et al. [14] introduced a novel approach for ranking job applicants by employing type-2 fuzzy sets for handling the uncertainties in group decisions in a panel of experts. Li-Wei and C. Shyi-Ming [15] presented a new method for handling fuzzy multiple attributes hierarchical group decision-making problems based on the ranking values of interval type-2 fuzzy sets. Chen and Lee [16] proposed a new method to handle fuzzy multiple attributes group decision-making problems based on the ranking values and the arithmetic operations of interval type-2 fuzzy sets. Dongrui and Mendel [17] introduced two fuzzy extensions of the OWA, ordered fuzzy weighted averages for type-1 fuzzy sets and ordered linguistic weighted averages for interval type-2 fuzzy sets, as wells as procedures for computing them. Shyi-Ming and Li-Wei [18] presented a new method for handling fuzzy multiple criteria hierarchical group decision-making problems based on arithmetic operations and fuzzy preference relations of interval type-2 fuzzy sets.

As regards to complaint handling Jarrar et al. [19] presented an ontology-based approach for managing and maintaining multilingual online customer complaints. Veronica and Tamayo [2] proposed a simple yet comprehensive customer complaint management system (CCMS) which includes tools and concepts from total quality management (TQM) and quality function deployment (QFD). Zirtiloglu and Yolum [20] developed an ontology-based complaints management system to manage complaints. In the proposed system they developed a complaints ontology with which the complaints of the citizens can be expressed. Coussement and Poel [21] introduced a methodology to improve complaint handling strategies through an automatic email-classification system that distinguishes complaints from non-complaints. Kopparapu [22] developed a natural English enabled mobile interface which can be used to lodge complaints. The proposed system enables and assists citizens to lodge compliant and seek redressal through their mobile phone in natural language. Galitsky et al. [23] presented a novel approach for modelling and classifying complaint scenarios associated with customer-company dialogues. Such dialogues are formalized as labelled graphs, in which both company and customer interact through communicative actions, providing arguments that support their points.

Pyon, *et al.* [24] proposed a web-based decision support system for business process management employing customer complaints, namely Voice of the Customer (VOC). The presented system is handling data for service improvement. It involves VOC conversion for data enrichment and includes analysis of summarization, exception and comparison. Trappey *et al.* [1] presented a new framework of the complaint handling system for a Japanese restaurant chain. The operations between the headquarter and branches are studied to show the benefits of the proposed complaint handling process. Y. Park and S. Lee [25] presented a framework for extracting customer opinions from websites and transforming them into product specification data. Razali *et al.* [26] developed new complaint management system known as *e-Aduan.* The proposed system allows both customers and management has access to the system to send a complaint and retrieve information.

In summary, work in the field of type-2 fuzzy based ranking method has been focused more on industrial applications compared to service applications. Furthermore, the work on complaint handling that involves a lot of uncertainties has been focused on other approaches except type-2 fuzzy approach. Whereas, cases that involve with high levels of uncertainties are proper to be handled with type-2 fuzzy approach. Hence, this paper proposes type-2 fuzzy based ranking method to handle the complaint handling process. Through further simulation and testing, it can prove that the approach can automate the complaint handling efficiently and less time consuming. Therefore, a new complaint handling framework also needs to design to let the complete method work properly and fulfils all the requirements and constraints. The study is based on a case study of the complaint management model that implemented in Universiti Teknologi MARA (UiTM) Pahang [26]. Process flow of the model is being investigated to implement the propose method.

3 Complaint Management Model (Case Study)

Previously, a complaint management model was being developed by the researcher and implemented in UiTM Pahang. The model is used as a platform for the customers to give a feedback regarding facilities and services that being provided by UiTM Pahang. Basically, there are two main components on the implementation of the model. The main components are the complaint management system and the working flow process. The complaint management system is the platform that is used to capturing and processing the data. Second component, the working flow process highlights the roles of the staff towards the system. Fig. 1 shows the working flow process of the complaint management system. The process is starting with receiving a complaint from the customer. Next step, the complaint needs to be processed and there are two things need to be identified. First, need to identify the department that will be responsible on the complaint. Second, need to identify the source of the problem. Once the complaint process is completed, the next step is the respective department or unit needs to investigate, take immediate action and produce reports based on the complaint. Then, the process needs to be updated into the system and lastly, need to update the complaint status. Even though all the data is being updated into the system but the process is still being performed manually especially on the step on processing the complaint process.

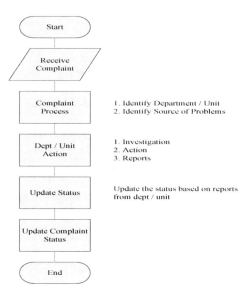

Fig. 1. Complaint management working flow process [26]

This manual process is time consuming, inefficient and not always consistent. Regardless of this issue, the propose method could improve the current process. The propose method is concentrating on improving the second step (complaint process) as shown in Fig. 2. Implementing the propose method could identify the complaint automatically and rank the complaint based on the level of important. With that, the respective department can take action based on the identified rank.

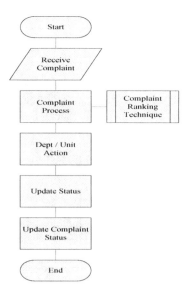

Fig. 2. Complaint management working flow process with propose method

4   The Proposed Method

This section proposes a methodology that will be used to perform the research. Basically, the model is based on [14]. The model is being modified to suit the process that involves in the complaint handling process. Steps that involve in the methodology will be described.

4.1   A Review of Mendel Interval Type-2 Fuzzy Sets

Membership Functions (MFs) of type-2 fuzzy sets are themselves fuzzy [27]. This made type-2 fuzzy sets are able to model the uncertainties. Imagine blurring the type-1 MF depicted in Fig. 3 by shifting the points on the triangle either to the left or to the right and not necessarily by the same amounts. Then, at a specific value of x, say x', there no longer is a single value for the MF (u'); instead, the MF takes on values wherever the vertical line intersects the blurred area shaded in grey [14, 28]. Those values need not all be weighted the same; hence, we can assign an amplitude distribution to all of those points. Doing this for all $x \in X$, we create a three-dimensional MF—a type-2 MF—that characterizes a type-2 fuzzy sets [28]. When this third dimension amplitude distribution is equal to $1 \forall u \in J_x \subseteq [0,1]$, and, if this is true for $\forall x \in X$, we have the case of interval type-2 MF which characterizes the interval type-2 fuzzy sets [14, 28].

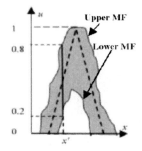

Fig. 3. A type-2 MF formed by blurring the type-1 MF drawn in dashed line [14]

The shaded area in grey in Fig. 3 is termed the Footprint Of Uncertainty (FOU) which is bounded by two type-1 MFs which are the upper MF ($\bar{\mu}_{\tilde{A}}(x)$) and the lower MF ($\underline{\mu}_{\tilde{A}}(x)$) [14, 28]. An interval type-2 fuzzy sets $\tilde{A}$ is written as:

$$\tilde{A} = \int_{x \in X} \left[\int_{u \in \left[\underline{\mu}_{\tilde{A}}(x), \bar{\mu}_{\tilde{A}}(x) \right]} \frac{1}{u} \right] / x \tag{1}$$

The new third-dimension of the type-2 fuzzy sets and the FOU provide additional degrees of freedom that can make it possible to directly model and handle uncertainties [28]. These additional degrees of freedom enable type-2 fuzzy sets to handle the uncertainties that can arise in group decision making it to better model the collective group opinion [14].

4.2 Type-2 Fuzzy Group Decision Modelling & Complaint Ranking Technique

A set of complaint's characteristics that associated with complaint domain is being used to define each complaint. These characteristics comprise of area, type of service, type of facility, level of satisfaction, level of impact and time frame from which complaint specification for the complaint will be created. The complaint characteristics may be derived from complaint management system database, complaint taxonomy or could be specific to the complaint areas defined within the organization. There are four steps of operation that involve in the type-2 fuzzy group decision modelling approach for ranking the complaints as shown in Fig. 4.

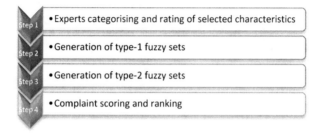

Step 1 • Experts categorising and rating of selected characteristics

Step 2 • Generation of type-1 fuzzy sets

Step 3 • Generation of type-2 fuzzy sets

Step 4 • Complaint scoring and ranking

Fig. 4. A flow diagram showing the main steps of type-2 fuzzy complaint ranking model. Modified from [14].

Step 1: Categorizing and Rating of Selected Characteristics

Step 1 starts with a selection panel of R experts. Each expert denote as E_k where $k=1$ to R. L is the set of complaints specific characteristics which contains N characteristics c_i where $i=1$ to N. From the set L each expert E_k is asked to select her/his choices of the characteristics for the three requirements categories ('*High*', '*Moderate*' and '*Low*') in the categorizing scheme. Each category formally denote as C_j where $j=1$ to 3 is the index for the categories: ('*High*', '*Moderate*' and '*Low*' respectively. The expert selects Q_{jk} unique characteristics c_{mjk} (from the set L) for each category C_{jk} where $0 < Q_{jk} < N$ and $m=1$ to Q_{jk}. The expert numerically rates the importance of each selected characteristic c_{mjk} using a predefined rating scale. The importance rating for each characteristic c_{mjk} is denoted as r_{mjk}. Most complaint area also have a '*Minimum*' or '***must have***' set of characteristics without which complaint will be ignored. This is fixed for the complaint domain and defined in advance.

We denote this as a subset Minimum characteristics $L_{(minimum)}$ of L comprising of U characteristics c_p where $1 < p < U$. The importance ratings for the characteristics in $L_{(minimum)}$ can also be set by each expert where the importance ratings of each '*Minimum*' required characteristic c_p is denoted as r_{pk}.

From the process described above each expert E_k produces a completed complaint specification that categories and rates the importance of their preferences on the '*Minimum*', '*High*', '*Moderate*' and '*Low*' characteristics. Fig. 5 describes the process flow for step 1.

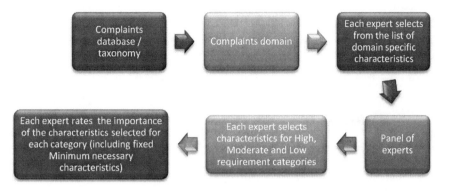

Fig. 5. Flow diagram showing the process for categorizing and rating an expert's selected characteristics

Step 2: Generation of Type-1 Fuzzy Sets

In step 2 the categorized and rated characteristics for each expert E_k are used to generate the parameters for type-1 MFs that represent the fuzzy sets associated with the linguistic labels '*Normal*', '*Serious*' and '*Critical*' based on the expert's preferences. More formally A_s^k is a type-1 fuzzy sets associated with a linguistic label s where $s=1$ to 3 is the index for the labels: '*Normal*', '*Serious*' and '*Critical*' respectively for each expert E_k. In our system the shapes of the type-1 MFs for each type-1 fuzzy sets are based on left shoulder (for '*Normal*' complaint), non-symmetric triangular (for '*Serious*' complaint), and right shoulder (for '*Critical*' complaint) MFs respectively as shown in Fig. 6 where M is the maximum range of the MFs. The parameters $[a_{MF}, b_{MF}]$ denote the left and right defining points of the support of a MF, as shown in Fig. 6. In the case of the non-symmetric triangular type-1 membership function (for '*Serious*' complaint) the point for the MF equalling to 1 is denoted as e (see Fig. 6b). The parameters $[a_{MF_{(s)}}^k, b_{MF_{(s)}}^k]$ and $e_{(2)}^k$ for each type-1 MF are derived directly from the categorized and rated requirement characteristics supplied by each expert E_k and are calculated as follows:

For Left shoulder MF:

$$a_{MF_{(1)}}^k = \sum_{p=1}^{U} r_{pk} \tag{2}$$

$$b_{MF_{(1)}}^k = \sum_{m=1}^{Q_{1k}} r_{m1k} \tag{3}$$

For the Triangular MF:

$$a_{MF_{(2)}}^k = a_{MF_{(1)}}^k \tag{4}$$

$$b_{MF_{(2)}}^k = b_{MF_{(1)}}^k + \sum_{m=1}^{Q_{2k}} r_{m2k} \tag{5}$$

$$e_{(2)}^k = b_{MF_{(1)}}^k \tag{6}$$

For the Right shoulder MF:

$$a^k_{MF(3)} = b^k_{MF(1)} \tag{7}$$

$$b^k_{MF(3)} = b^k_{MF(2)} \tag{8}$$

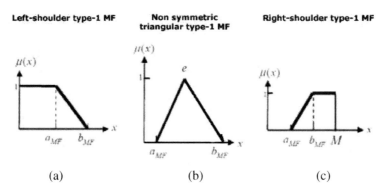

Fig. 6. (a) Left shoulder type-1 MF. (b) Non symmetric triangular type-1 MF. (c) Right shoulder type-1 MF [14, 29].

Based on Equations (2), (3), (4), (5), (6), (7) and (8) the generated type-1 fuzzy sets for an expert E_k will conform with the required guidelines in CMS where complaint will receive a maximum membership in the type-1 fuzzy sets for '*Serious*' if it contains all the '*High*' rated characteristics and will only receive a maximum membership in the type-1 fuzzy sets for '*Critical*' if it contains the combination of all the '*High*' and '*Moderate*' plus some '*Low*' characteristics. It should be noted that having the combination of all the '*High*' characteristics and some of the '*Moderate*' characteristics will lead to being on the boundary between the '*Serious*' and '*Critical*' sets.

Step 3: Generation of Type-2 Fuzzy Sets

The type-1 fuzzy sets that are generated for each expert E_k in step 2 are aggregated to create the FOU's for type-2 fuzzy sets. Using the Representation Theorem [27], each interval type-2 fuzzy set $\tilde{A}_s$ is computed as:

$$\widetilde{A_s} = \cup^R_{k=1} A^k_s \tag{9}$$

Where A^k_s is referred to as the kth embedded type-1 fuzzy set and $\cup$ is the union operation [29]. The process of generating $\tilde{A}_s$ is based on approximating the upper MF $\left(\bar{\mu}_{\tilde{A}_s}(x)\right)$ and the lower MF $\left(\underline{\mu}_{\tilde{A}_s}(x)\right)$ of $\tilde{A}_s$. This will depend on shape of the embedded type-1 fuzzy sets and the FOU model which is to be generated for $\tilde{A}_s$. The propose system use interior FOU models (shown in Fig. 7a) for approximating the upper and lower MF parameters from all the embedded non-symmetric triangular type-1 MFs (thus representing the '*Serious*' category). The resulting interior interval type-2 fuzzy set is described by parameters: $\underline{a}_{MF}$, $\underline{c}_{MF}$, $\overline{c}_{MF}$, $\overline{b}_{MF}$ denoting a trapezoidal upper MF and the parameters: $\overline{a}_{MF}$, $\underline{b}_{MF}$ for a non-symmetric triangular lower MF, with an intersection point (d, μ_d) [29], as shown in Fig. 7a. Shoulder FOU models are used for approximating all the left and right shoulder embedded type-1 MFs. The resulting left and right shoulder interval type-2 fuzzy sets are described by the parameters: $\underline{a}_{MF}$, $\underline{b}_{MF}$, $\overline{a}_{MF}$ and $\overline{b}_{MF}$ to represent the upper and the lower shoulder MFs [29], as shown in Fig. 7b and 7c respectively. The procedures for calculating these parameters are now described as follows:

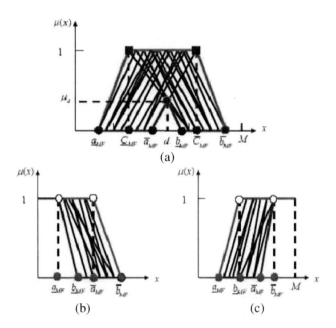

(a)

(b)   (c)

Fig. 7. (a) An interior type-2 MF embedding the different type-1 triangle MFs. (b) A left shoulder type-2 MF embedding different left shoulder type-1 MFs. (c) A right shoulder type-2 MF embedding different right shoulder type-1 MFs [14, 29].

1) *FOU models for interior FOUs:* Given the parameters for the symmetric triangular type-1 MFs generated for each of the k experts $\left[a^k_{MF_{(2)}}, b^k_{MF_{(2)}} \right]$ and $e^k_{(2)}$ the procedure for approximating the FOU model for interior FOUs is as follows [29]:

For the upper MF $\overline{\mu}_{\tilde{A}_{(2)}}(x)$ we need to follow the following steps:

(1) For $\mu(x) = 0$, find $\underline{a}_{MF}$ to be equal to the minimum $a^{min}_{MF_{(2)}}$ of all left-end points $a^k_{MF_{(2)}}$ and $\overline{b}_{MF}$ to be equal to the maximum $b^{max}_{MF_{(2)}}$ of all right-end points $b^k_{MF_{(2)}}$ [29].

(2) For $\mu(x) = 0$, find $\underline{c}_{MF}$ to be equal to the minimum $e^{min}_{(2)}$ of the centres $e^k_{(2)}$ and $\overline{c}_{MF}$ to be equal to, maximum $e^{max}_{(2)}$ of the centres $e^k_{(2)}$.

(3) Approximate the upper MF $\overline{\mu}_{\tilde{A}_{(2)}}(x)$ by connecting the following points with straight lines: $\underline{a}_{MF}$, $\underline{c}_{MF}$, $\overline{c}_{MF}$ and $\overline{b}_{MF}$. The result is a trapezoidal upper MF as depicted in Fig. 7a.

The steps to approximate the lower MF $\underline{\mu}_{\tilde{A}_{(2)}}(x)$ are as follows:

(1) For $\mu(x) = 0$, find $\underline{a}_{MF}$ to be equal to the maximum $a_{MF_{(2)}}^{max}$ of all left-end points $a_{MF_{(2)}}^k$ and $\overline{b}_{MF}$ to be equal to the minimum $b_{MF_{(2)}}^{min}$ of all right-end points $b_{MF_{(2)}}^k$ [29].

(2) Compute the intersection point (d, μ_d) by the following equations [29]:

$$d = \frac{\underline{b}_{MF}(\overline{c}_{MF} - \overline{a}_{MF}) + \overline{a}_{MF}(\underline{b}_{MF} - \underline{c}_{MF})}{(\overline{c}_{MF} - \overline{a}_{MF}) + (\underline{b}_{MF} - \underline{c}_{MF})} \tag{10}$$

$$\mu_d = (\underline{b}_{MF} - d)/(\underline{b}_{MF} - \underline{c}_{MF}) \tag{11}$$

(3) Approximate the lower $\overline{\mu}_{\tilde{A}_{(2)}}(x)$ by connecting the following points with straight lines: $\overline{a}_{MF}$, d, and $\underline{b}_{MF}$. The results is a triangle lower MF as shown in Fig. 7a.

2) *FOU models for shoulder FOUs:* Given the parameters $\left[a_{MF_{(1)}}^k, b_{MF_{(1)}}^k\right]$ and $\left[a_{MF_{(3)}}^k, b_{MF_{(3)}}^k\right]$ for the respective left and right shoulder type-1 MFs generated for each of the k experts, the following is the procedure to approximate the FOU model for left-shoulder FOUs [29].

(1) For $\mu(x) = 0$, find $\overline{b}_{MF}$ to be equal to the maximum $b_{MF_{(1)}}^{max}$ of all end points $b_{MF_{(1)}}^k$ [29].

(2) For $\mu(x) = 1$, find $\overline{a}_{MF}$ to be equal to the maximum $a_{MF_{(1)}}^{max}$ of all end points $a_{MF_{(1)}}^k$ [29].

(3) Approximate the upper MF $\overline{\mu}_{\tilde{A}_{(1)}}(x)$ by connecting the following points with straight lines: $(0:1)$, $(\overline{a}_{MF}, 1)$ and $(\overline{b}_{MF}, 0)$. The results is a left shoulder upper MF as depicted in Fig. 7b.

The steps to approximate the lower MF $\underline{\mu}_{\tilde{A}_{(1)}}(x)$ are as follows:

(1) For $\mu(x) = 0$, find $\underline{b}_{MF}$ to be equal to the minimum $b_{MF_{(1)}}^{min}$ of all end points $b_{MF_{(1)}}^k$ [29].

(2) For $\mu(x) = 1$, find $\underline{a}_{MF}$ to be equal to the minimum $a_{MF_{(1)}}^{min}$ of all end points $a_{MF_{(1)}}^k$ [29].

(3) Approximate the lower $\underline{\mu}_{\tilde{A}_{(1)}}(x)$ by connecting the following points with straight lines: $(0:1)$, $(\underline{a}_{MF}, 1)$ and $(\underline{b}_{MF}, 0)$. The results is a left shoulder lower MF as shown in Fig. 7b.

The procedure for approximating a FOU model for right-shoulder FOUs is similar to the one for left-shoulder FOUs. The upper MF $\overline{\mu}_{\tilde{A}_{(3)}}(x)$ is approximated as follows:

For $\mu(x) = 0$, $\underline{a}_{MF} = a_{MF_{(3)}}^{min}$ and for $(x) = 1$, $\underline{b}_{MF} = b_{MF_{(3)}}^{min}$. Therefore the resulting right shoulder upper MF $\overline{\mu}_{\tilde{A}_{(3)}}(x)$ is approximated by connecting the following points with straight lines: $(\overline{a}_{MF}, 0)$, $(\overline{b}_{MF}, 1)$, and $(M, 1)$, depicted in Fig. 7c. The lower $\overline{\mu}_{\tilde{A}_{(3)}}(x)$ is approximated as follow: For $\mu(x) = 0$, $\overline{a}_{MF} = a_{MF_{(3)}}^{max}$ and for $(x) = 1$, $\overline{b}_{MF} = b_{MF_{(3)}}^{max}$. Therefore the resulting right shoulder lower MF $\underline{\mu}_{\tilde{A}_{(3)}}(x)$ is approximated by connecting the following points with straight lines: $(\overline{a}_{MF}, 0)$, $(\overline{b}_{MF}, 1)$, and $(M, 1)$ as shown in Fig. 7c.

Step 4: Complaint Scoring and Ranking

The process of ranking complaint is based on comparing the complaint characteristics extracted from the complaint with the rated and categorised characteristics defines by each expert. Complaint characteristics can be extracted from CMS using language processing and information extraction techniques. The extracted complaint characteristics are then scored using a scoring method (depicted in Fig. 8) which will describe in the following paragraphs.

A complaint can be formally defined as a set of W complaints characteristics c_h where $h=1$ to W. Each complaint characteristic c_h is compared to the characteristics c_{mjk} which have been selected by each expert E_k to see if there is a match $(c_h == c_{mjk})$. Each matching complaint characteristic is denoted as c_x where $c_x = c_h = c_{mjk}$ and $x=1$ to W_x where W_x is the number of matching characteristics. For each matching complaint characteristic c_x (belonging originally to characteristics m in category j), the average rating score among all the experts who selected it, is calculated as follows:

$$AVr_x = \frac{\sum_{k=1}^{V} r_{mjk}}{V} \tag{12}$$

Where V is the number of experts that selected and rated c_x. Not all the experts may categorise c_x with the same requirements category. The requirement category that AVr_x will be assigned to is therefore chosen as the most frequently occurring category C_j which the V experts had selected for categorizing c_x. For each requirements category C_j, the assigned average rating scores AVr_{xj} are aggregated to produce a total category score Cs_j which is weighted using predefined weighting factor w_j based on the significance that is given to the C_j category in the selection process. The final score for a complaint is then calculated as follows:

$$FRs = \sum_{j=1}^{3}(Cs_j w_j) \tag{13}$$

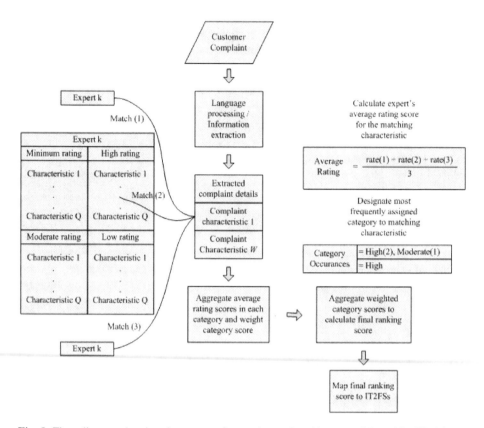

Fig. 8. Flow diagram showing the process for scoring and ranking complaints. Modified from [14].

The final ranking score *FRs* will be mapped to each type-2 fuzzy set $\tilde{A}_s$ to determine the membership degree of the complaint to each type-2 fuzzy set. The membership degree is calculated as the centre of gravity of the interval membership of $\tilde{A}_s$ at x as follows [30]:

$$\mu_{\tilde{A}_s}^{cg}(x) = f_x^{cg}(\tilde{A}_s) = \frac{1}{2}\left[\overline{\mu}_{\tilde{A}_s}(x) + \underline{\mu}_{\tilde{A}_s}(x)\right] \tag{14}$$

Where $x = FRs$.

The type-2 fuzzy set with the highest interval membership is selected for ranking the complaint as follows:

$$\mu_{\tilde{A}_s^{q*}}^{cg}(x) \geq \mu_{\tilde{A}_s^q}^{cg}(x) \tag{15}$$

Where $q* \in \{1, \dots 3\}$.

The type-2 fuzzy sets provide a methodology for representing the ranking decision for the complaint in terms of linguistic labels which are easily understandable by the human user. The scoring scheme provides a transparent break down of how each complaint characteristic in the complaint is categorised and rated by the selection panel of experts. This can be used to provide justification for the system selection and ranking decision.

5 Conclusion

Prior research related to type-2 fuzzy based ranking method and complaint management, specifically on the automated complaint handling and complaint handling framework are reviewed. From the reviewed a ranking method based on type-2 fuzzy to handle complaint handling issues is being introduced. To the researcher's knowledge, this is the first research that exploits complaint handling process using type-2 fuzzy approach. The development of this approach to handle complaint handling issues will give positive impact, specifically to improve the complaint handling effectiveness and less time consuming. Further research work is to do a simulation and testing to prove the reliability of the propose method.

References

1. Trappey, A.J.C., et al.: A framework of customer complaint handling system. In: 2010 7th International Conference on Service Systems and Service Management (ICSSSM), pp. 1–6 (2010)
2. Veronica Gonzalez, B., Francisco Tamayo, E.: TQM and QFD: exploiting a customer complaint management system. International Journal of Quality & Reliability Management 22, 30–37 (2005)
3. Dereli, T., et al.: Industrial applications of type-2 fuzzy sets and systems: A concise review. Computers in Industry (2010) (in press, corrected proof)
4. Zadeh, L.A.: The concept of a linguistic variable and its application to approximate reasoning–I. Information Sciences 8, 199–249 (1975)
5. Mendel, J.M.: Type-2 fuzzy sets and systems: an overview. IEEE Computational Intelligence Magazine 2, 20–29 (2007)
6. Castillo, O., et al.: Type-2 Fuzzy Logic: Theory and Applications. In: IEEE International Conference on Granular Computing, GRC 2007, pp. 145–145 (2007)
7. Wang, X., Kerre, E.E.: Reasonable properties for the ordering of fuzzy quantities (I). Fuzzy Sets and Systems 118, 375–385 (2001)
8. Noguchi, H., Ogawa, M., Ishii, H.: The appropriate total ranking method using DEA for multiple categorized purposes. Journal of Computational and Applied Mathematics 146, 155–166 (2002)
9. Lee, S., Lee, K.H., Lee, D.: Ranking the sequences of fuzzy values. Information Sciences 160, 41–52 (2004)
10. Mitchell, H.B.: Ranking type-2 fuzzy numbers. IEEE Transactions on Fuzzy Systems 14, 287–294 (2006)
11. Wu, D., Mendel, J.M.: A comparative study of ranking methods, similarity measures and uncertainty measures for interval type-2 fuzzy sets. Information Sciences 179, 1169–1192 (2009)
12. Gu, L., Zhang, Y.: Web shopping expert using new interval type-2 fuzzy reasoning. Soft Computing - A Fusion of Foundations, Methodologies and Applications 11, 741–751 (2007)

13. Shang-Ming, Z., et al.: New Type-2 Rule Ranking Indices for Designing Parsimonious Interval Type-2 Fuzzy Logic Systems. In: IEEE International Fuzzy Systems Conference, FUZZ-IEEE 2007, pp. 1–6 (2007)
14. Doctor, F., et al.: A type-2 fuzzy based system for handling the uncertainties in group decisions for ranking job applicants within Human Resources systems. In: IEEE International Conference on Fuzzy Systems, FUZZ-IEEE 2008 (IEEE World Congress on Computational Intelligence), pp. 481–488 (2008)
15. Li-Wei, L., Shyi-Ming, C.: Fuzzy multiple attributes hierarchical group decision-making based on the ranking values of interval type-2 fuzzy sets. In: 2008 International Conference on Machine Learning and Cybernetics, pp. 3266–3271 (2008)
16. Chen, S.-M., Lee, L.-W.: Fuzzy multiple attributes group decision-making based on the ranking values and the arithmetic operations of interval type-2 fuzzy sets. Expert Systems with Applications 37, 824–833 (2010)
17. Dongrui, W., Mendel, J.M.: Ordered fuzzy weighted averages and ordered linguistic weighted averages. In: 2010 IEEE International Conference on Fuzzy Systems (FUZZ), pp. 1–7 (2010)
18. Shyi-Ming, C., Li-Wei, L.: Fuzzy Multiple Criteria Hierarchical Group Decision-Making Based on Interval Type-2 Fuzzy Sets. IEEE Transactions on Systems, Man and Cybernetics, Part A: Systems and Humans 40, 1120–1128 (2010)
19. Jarrar, M., Verlinden, R., Meersman, R.: Ontology-Based Customer Complaint Management. In: Chung, S. (ed.) OTM-WS 2003. LNCS, vol. 2889, pp. 594–606. Springer, Heidelberg (2003)
20. Zirtiloglu, H., Yolum, P.: Ranking semantic information for e-government: complaints management. In: Proceedings of the First International Workshop on Ontology-supported Business Intelligence, pp. 1–7. ACM, Karlsruhe (2008)
21. Coussement, K., Van den Poel, D.: Improving customer complaint management by automatic email classification using linguistic style features as predictors. Decision Support Systems 44, 870–882 (2008)
22. Kopparapu, S.K.: Natural language mobile interface to register citizen complaints. In: TENCON 2008 - 2008 IEEE Region 10 Conference, pp. 1–6 (2008)
23. Galitsky, B.A., González, M.P., Chesñevar, C.I.: A novel approach for classifying customer complaints through graphs similarities in argumentative dialogues. Decision Support Systems 46, 717–729 (2009)
24. Pyon, C.U., Woo, J.Y., Park, S.C.: Service improvement by business process management using customer complaints in financial service industry. Expert Systems with Applications (2010) (in press, corrected proof)
25. Park, Y., Lee, S.: How to design and utilize online customer center to support new product concept generation. Expert Systems with Applications 38, 10638–10647 (2011)
26. Razali, R., Halim, K.N.A., Jusoff, K.: Quality Improvement of Services in Universiti Teknologi Mara Pahang from a Management Perspective. Management Science and Engineering 5, 71–80 (2011)
27. Mendel, J.M., John, R.I.B.: Type-2 fuzzy sets made simple. IEEE Transactions on Fuzzy Systems 10, 117–127 (2002)
28. Mendel, J.M., John, R.I., Liu, F.: Interval Type-2 Fuzzy Logic Systems Made Simple. IEEE Transactions on Fuzzy Systems 14, 808–821 (2006)
29. Feilong, L., Mendel, J.M.: An Interval Approach to Fuzzistics for Interval Type-2 Fuzzy Sets. In: IEEE International Fuzzy Systems Conference FUZZ-IEEE 2007, pp. 1–6 (2007)
30. Mendel, J.M.: Uncertain Rule-Based Fuzzy Logic Systems: Introduction and New Directions. Prentice-Hall, Upper Saddle River (2001)

Optimization of the Commutator Motor Using the Genetic Algorithm with the Gradient Modified Selection Operator (GAGMSO)

Grzegorz Kusztelak[1] and Marek Rudnicki[2]

[1] Centre of Mathematics and Physics, Technical University of Lodz,
Al. Politechniki 11, 90-924 Lodz, Poland
grzegorz.kusztelak@p.lodz.pl
[2] Institute of Computer Science, Technical University of Lodz,
Wolczanska 215, 93-005 Lodz, Poland
marek.rudnicki@p.lodz.pl

Abstract. The problem of commutator motors optimal design with given properties is a very complex task of nonlinear constrained optimization. The range of decision variables, the number of constraints and confusing properties regarding the design make the process of optimization a challenge regardless of the method. The paper presents a genetic algorithm with the gradient modified selection operator. This algorithm was used to optimize the performance of a commutator motor. We present the results which are also compared with those obtained using other methods. The comparison confirmed the effectiveness of the introduction of approximate gradient information to the selection operator in the genetic algorithm.

Keywords: Optimization, electrical machines, genetic algorithms, selection operator, gradient.

1 Introduction

The issue of optimal design of commutator motors with a given characteristic is an extremely complex task of constraint optimization. Apart from having to comply with spotting constraints on decision variables, for reasons of the plausibility of construction, are required to meet many of the confounding constraints. The number of decision variables, the multitude of constraints and confusing properties of the objective function make the process of optimization a big challenge for not only deterministic but also probabilistic methods. There are few methods in the literature serving as the solution to the optimization problem presented above:

– PROJKRYT [3], [4] - involves discrete stimulation of changes in several decision-making parameters and allows you to select the best design according to one or more independent criteria. Changes in the decision-making parameters are controlled by the user selecting the decision-making areas, in which one expects to find the optimum solution. This method, however, required from the user not only the vast experience but also extensive knowledge in the field of the problem.

A. Abd Manaf et al. (Eds.): ICIEIS 2011, Part II, CCIS 252, pp. 401–406, 2011.

- PROJMAT [5], [6] - enables precise searching (without rounding and standardization) of decision-making space defined by the decision-making parameters and their limitations. Starting from any point (project) its closest local minimum can be found. The full search of decision-making space requires repeated mobilization of optimization procedure starting from different, distant starting points. The system was implemented in Matlab and uses a gradient optimization tools available in the Optimization Toolbox.

- Simulated annealing (SA) [7] is a method that simulates one of the processes used in metallurgy. When a piece of metal particles are arranged in a random manner, the metal is brittle and fragile. Annealing process leads to the ordering of the material structure.

- Genetic Algorithms (GA) are ways of solving problems by mimicking the same processes mother nature uses. They use the same combination of selection, recombination and mutation in order to customize the solution to the problem.

- Vector Evaluated Genetic Algorithm (VEGA) [8] and the Niched Pareto Genetic Algorithm (NPGA) [9] are modifications of classical genetic algorithm dedicated to a multiobjective optimization. VEGA is based on the division of population into subpopulations (with the same size), each of which is responsible for one criterion. The selection procedure takes place independently for each criterion, but crossover is done by borders of sub-population. NPGA combines tournament selection and the concept of Pareto-dominance.

The detailed analysis helps identify the advantages and disadvantages of each of given approaches to the basic problem.

2 Intention

Authors' intention was to "reconcile" the deterministic with nondeterministic approach. In order to do that the genetic algorithm (nondeterministic method) was used and gradient modification selection operator was proposed (deterministic factor).

3 Used Methodology

3.1 Objective Function

Optimization of the commutator motor is reduced to optimize the objective function:

$$\min_{\mathbf{x} \in D} f(\mathbf{x}), \quad D = \{\mathbf{x} : \mathbf{g}_i(\mathbf{x}) \le 0, i = 1,2,\ldots m\} \tag{1}$$

where $f(\mathbf{x})$ denotes the objective function, $\mathbf{x}$ - vector of decision-making or design parameters (variables) , D - the feasible region, $g(\mathbf{x})$ – constraint function, m - total number of constraints.

There are considered 10 decision variables and 46 simple, confounding and technological constraints.

The approach presented below the engine design has been described by the function:

$$F : R^{10} \to R^3, \quad F(x) = [K_t, W_M, \eta] \qquad (2)$$

where:

- K_t - the cost of active materials;
- W_M - torque per unit cost;
- η - motor efficiency.

K_t, W_M, η are the criteria, because of which make the optimization, but of course we are striving for minimizing K_t and maximizing W_M and η. In order to standardize the type of optimization (minimization) we consider the converse of the W_M and η:

$$G = \left[K_t, \frac{1}{W_M}, \frac{1}{\eta} \right] \qquad (3)$$

In addition, we introduce values normalization

$$H = \left[\frac{G_1}{\|G\|}, \frac{G_2}{\|G\|}, \frac{G_3}{\|G\|} \right] \qquad (4)$$

where $\| . \|$ denotes the Euclidean norm.

Most optimization methods can be used only for the one-dimensional functions, so using the method of weighted sum we transform the multiobjective optimization problem to the one-dimensional optimization problem. Additionally, to meet the demand constraints a penalty term is being introduced. Then, the optimization of the function may be presented in the following form:

$$f(\mathbf{x}) = \left(\omega_1 H_1(x) + \omega_2 H_2(x) + \omega_3 H_3(x) \right) + p(x) \qquad (5)$$

where:

- $p(\mathbf{x}) = \sum_{i=1}^{26} h_i^2(x)$ - penalty function;

- $h_i(x) = \begin{cases} 0 & \text{if } g_i(x) \le 0 \\ 1 + g_i(x) & \text{otherwise} \end{cases}$.

To focus the attention we assume that all the criteria are equally important for us:

$$\omega_1 = \omega_2 = \omega_3 = \frac{1}{3} \qquad (6)$$

3.2 Genetic Algorithm with a Gradient Modified Selection Operator

Idea. We know that if the function g is differentiable at the point P_0 and reaches a local extreme in that point, the gradient of the function at a point P_0

$$\nabla g(P_0) = \left[\frac{\partial g}{\partial x_1}(P_0), \frac{\partial g}{\partial x_2}(P_0), \dots, \frac{\partial g}{\partial x_n}(P_0) \right] \tag{7}$$

is a zero vector

$$\nabla g(P_0) = [0, 0, \dots, 0]. \tag{8}$$

This gave rise to the idea of promoting (on the selection stage) individuals for which approximate gradient is close to zero vector. More precisely: the norm of the gradient approximation is as small as possible.

The question of optimization, however, is a global optimization problem, so selection pressure should be increased (in the view of the authors) for individuals, which together with the approximate value of the gradient norm is close to zero and the value of the objective function is as small as possible (minimizing).

Of course, we consider only the gradient for differentiable functions. However, the partial derivatives at a fixed point, we can approximate in differential quotient for a very small increment of the argument. The differential quotient is determined not only for differentiable functions. The function has to have particular values in the consideration points.

To sum up: The proposed modification method of selection operator is based on the idea of increasing the selection pressure for the fittest individuals for which at the same time the norm approximations of the objective function gradient is near zero.

The description of the algorithm. To implement the idea described above, follow these steps:

1. The values of the fitness function of all individuals multiplied by the scaling factor sf ($sf \in (0; 1)$).In this way we get, "reserve" adaptation equal to

$$sf \cdot \sum_{i=1}^{N} f(v_i).$$

2. From all the individuals belonging to the current population, we choose p percent of the largest fitness value.

3. For individuals selected in the step 2 we calculate the approximate objective function gradient and select some of them with mean values of the gradient near zero (more precisely, the q percentage in the whole population, where $q \leq p$).

4. For individuals that were selected in steps 2 and 3 (so those who at the same time belong to the p percent of the fittest individuals and q percentage of the norm closest to zero) we divide "reserve " of the fitness obtained in step 1. The division of "reserve" is inversely proportional to the value of the approximate gradient of the objective function.

The above description means that the method is triparametric – and depends on: sf, p, q.

4 Obtained Results

The main focus here constitutes the optimization engine to electric tools, power of 1200 W, 18000 rpm. The algorithms were actuated 100 times. The following table includes the best results obtained using each of given methods.

Table 1. The best results obtained using each of considered methods after 100 actuations

Method	K_t	W_M	η	$p(x)$
PROJMAT	11,4054	52,8482	0,6803	7,000
SADET	10,357	58,3325	0,7014	8,253
SA	11,8257	51,8765	0,6924	9,143
GA	11,6190	52,1726	0,6821	6,298
GAGMSO	10,1061	60,0088	0,7012	5,348
VEGA [10]	5,4643	109,9	0,6664	149,915
NPGA [10]	4,6096	130,1	0,6500	113,325

where:

- PROJMAT - deterministic method used in the PROJMAT system;
- SADET - simulated annealing starting at the same point as PROJMAT;
- SA - simulated annealing started at a random point;
- GA - genetic algorithm with proportional selection;
- GAGMSO - a genetic algorithm with the modified gradient selection operator;
- VEGA - Vector Evaluated Genetic Algorithm;
- NPGA - Niched Pareto Genetic Algorithm;
- $p(\mathbf{x})$ - the value of the penalty function.

In the considered methods only typical parameter values were used. Using a modified gradient operator selection (GAGMSO) we have adopted: $sf = 0.8$, $p = 10\%$, $q = 5\%$ respectively. The other parameters remain unchanged to ensure the comparability with the standard GA selection operator.

5 Conclusions

As seen above, NPGA and VEGA allowed to obtain a commutator motor design with a very low cost, high torque per unit cost and reasonable efficiency. Unfortunately, this involves a very large violation of the constraints which makes the practical usefulness of the results obtained by NPGA and VEGA negligible.

The smallest violation of the constraints and very good value of all the criteria (the best, if you do not take into account the results of the VEGA and NPGA) gave a genetic algorithm with the gradient modified selection operator (GAGMSO). Similar results because of the value of criteria, gave simulated annealing, but in a variant of the starting point close to the optimum. In addition, for the simulated annealing the sum of violated confounding constraints was greater than that of the GAGMSO. This confirms the effectiveness of introduction of the approximate gradient information to the selection operator.

References

1. Michalewicz, Z.: Genetic Algorithms + Data Structures = Evolution Programs, 3rd edn. Springer, Heidelberg (1996)
2. Kusztelak, G., Stańdo, J., Rudnicki, M.: Difference Selection Operator in GA, pp. 223–231. Academic Publishing House EXIT, Warsaw (2008)
3. Puternicki, P.: Multiobjective analysis of small commutator motors. Proceedings of Electrotechnical Institute, nr 192 (1997) (in polish)
4. Puternicki, P.: Software of Projkryt system to design and multiobjective optimization of small commutator motors. Proceedings of Electrotechnical Institute, nr 194 (1997) (in polish)
5. Puternicki, P., Rudnicki, M.: Mathematical metod of multiobjective optimization of small commutator motors. Proceedings of Electrotechnical Institute, nr 204 (2000) (in polish)
6. Puternicki, P., Rudnicki, M.: Optimal design methodologies with application to small commutator motors. COMPEL: International Journal for Computation and Mathematics in Electrical and Electronic Engineering 19(2), 639–645 (2000)
7. Metropolis, N., Rosenbluth, A., Rosenbluth, M., Teller, A., Teller, E.: Equation of State Calculations by Fast Computing Machines. Journal of Chemical Physics 21, 1087–1092 (1953)
8. Schaffer, J.D.: Multiple Objective Optimization with Vector Evaluated Genetic Algorithms, PhD thesis, Vanderbilt University (1984)
9. Horn, J., Nafpliotis, N.: Multiobjective Optimization Using the Niched Pareto Genetic Algorithm, Technical Report 93005, Illinois Genetic Algorithms Laboratory (1993)
10. Rudnicki, M., Segovia, J., Koszuk, J., Isasi, P.: Multiobjective and Multiconstrained Optimization of Small Commutator Motors. In: Evolutionary Methods for Design Optimization and Control with Applications to Industrial Problems, Athens, Greece, pp. 373–378 (2001)
11. Puternicki, P., Rudnicki, M.: Optimal design methodologies with application to small commutator motors. In: Proceedings of the International Symposium on Electromagnetic Fields in Electrical Engineering, Pavia, Italy, pp. 397–400

Optimizing Distributed Cooperative Sensing Performance Using Swarm Intelligence

Rozeha A. Rashid, Yacub S. Baguda, N. Fisal, M. Adib Sarijari,
S.K.S. Yusof, S.H.S. Ariffin, N.M.A. Latiff, and Alias Mohd

Faculty of Electrical Engineering, Universiti Teknologi Malaysia,
Johor, Malaysia
{rozeha,adib_sairi,sheila,sharifah,kamilah,
muazzah,alias}@fke.utm.my, baguda@gmail.com

Abstract. Cognitive radio (CR) technology offers attractive solution to overcome spectrum scarcity problem and improve spectrum utilization. Opportunistic spectrum access concept adopted by a CR network allows unlicensed or cognitive users (CUs) to access a frequency band that is not in use by the licensed or primary users (PUs). In enabling such spectrum-aware communication protocol, spectrum sensing becomes the fundamental requirement to exploit the unused spectrum and effectively protect the quality of service (QoS) of PUs. An increase in sensing time results in a higher detection probability (P_d) and lower false alarm probability (P_f), which leads to better protection of the primary users from harmful interference in addition to improved utilization of the available unused spectrum. However, this will reduce the amount of time for data transmission and hence, affects the achievable throughput of CUs. In this paper, this sensing-throughput tradeoff is addressed in terms of distributed approach of cooperative channel sensing. In order to find the optimal sensing time that maximizes the throughput of an OSA based CR network, the decision fusion scheme of OR rule are subjected to particle swarm optimization (PSO). The results show that a lower sensing time is achieved under PSO based cooperative sensing. The maximum achievable normalized throughput also increases with the increase of sensing terminals under optimal fusion scheme compared to normal fusion technique.

Keywords: Cognitive Radio, Spectrum sensing, Probability of detection, Probability of false alarm, Throughput, Sensing time, Particle swarm optimization.

1 Introduction

The growing demand for larger amount of spectrum to satisfy the required Quality of Service (QoS) for emerging wireless services has led to current spectrum scarcity problem. However, several spectrum occupancy measurements [1-3] show an inefficient spectrum usage as the workload in different spectrum bands varies significantly where some bands are overcrowded while other portions are moderately or sparsely utilized. Cognitive radio (CR) is a new wireless communication paradigm

A. Abd Manaf et al. (Eds.): ICIEIS 2011, Part II, CCIS 252, pp. 407–420, 2011.
© Springer-Verlag Berlin Heidelberg 2011

to enhance utilization of limited spectral resources by adopting the concept of Opportunistic Spectrum Access (OSA). OSA allows secondary or cognitive users (CUs) to sense the idle periods of primary users (PUs), opportunistically access such spectrum holes and thus improves spectral efficiency. However, CUs need to be sufficiently agile to vacate the space (time, frequency or spatial) once PUs are detected as not to cause harmful interference [4][5]. Hence, spectrum sensing is an important aspect of OSA based CR network.

There are two probabilities that are of interest in spectrum sensing. First is the probability of correctly detecting the PU when it is active. Another is the probability of false alarm which is a wrong detection of PU when it is inactive. A longer sensing time gives a higher probability of detection that increases PU protection, and reduces probability of false alarm, thus enhances spectrum usability for CUs. However, in a conventional frame structure consisting of a sensing and data transmission timeslots respectively, a longer sensing time leads to lower transmission time. Consequently, this will decrease the achievable throughput of CUs. In addition, stand-alone sensing technologies such as energy detection, matched filter and feature detection often suffer from noise uncertainty, fading and shadowing [6]. They can also experience low sensing probabilities at specific geographical locations, and thus, increase the interference on PUs.

A natural solution to cope with the problems above is nodes' cooperation. This approach is found to be robust to possible unbalance of the channel qualities of different CUs [7]. Cooperative communication technology can considerably improve the sensing efficiency and reliability by facilitating the sharing of sensing load between network nodes. In addition, it solves the latency and power consumption problems that occur in large-scale spectrum sensing [7]. The probabilities of detection and false alarm are also improved [6]. Cooperative sensing can be classified into centralized or distributed approach. In centralized sensing, information from different CUs is fused at a base station or fusion center to reach a global decision of PU's activity. This scheme is complex as it requires a backbone infrastructure and effective information sharing algorithm [6]. In contrast, even though CUs share sensing information among each other in distributed approach, they make their own decisions. Hence, no backbone infrastructure is needed.

Many research works on cooperative sensing are on improving the sensing performance metrics of probability of detection, P_d, and probability of false alarm, P_f. Authors in [6] proposes a decision fusion scheme based on weighting factor in distributed sensing to reduce the probabilities of false alarm and miss-detection. However, no relation to achievable throughput of CUs is made. In [8], the performance of cooperative sensing is optimized using constant detection rate (CDR) where P_d is fixed and P_f is optimized (minimized) and constant false alarm rate (CFAR) where P_f is fixed and P_d is optimized (maximized). The analysis is carried out in terms of cooperating number of users to get the optimum performance. Again, there is no consideration for achievable throughput of CUs. Studies in [9] and [10] address the sensing-throughput tradeoff but only in the perspective of a stand-alone CU. The work in [11] addresses the sensing-throughput tradeoff in terms of maximizing achievable throughput for CUs under the constraint that PUs are sufficiently protected for distributed cooperative sensing using Majority-rule decision fusion. In this paper, the fundamental tradeoff between sensing time and achievable throughput of the CU in distributed approach cooperative sensing is also studied. Based on energy detection scheme, we investigate the peformance of decision fusion scheme OR rule that are subjected to particle swarm optimization (PSO) with the objectives of minimizing sensing time to maximize the achievable throughput for CUs for a given frame duration.

The rest of the paper is organized as follows. Section II presents the performance metrics and system parameters of channel sensing. The problem formulation regarding the sensing-throughput tradeoff and OR-rule decision fusion for cooperative sensing are also included. The PSO algorithm and the objectives of the optimization problem are introduced in Section III while Section IV gives the results and discussion. The conclusion of this paper is outlined in Section V.

2 Channel Sensing

In the following, a brief review of sensing hypotheses, the energy detection scheme and its relation to the sensing performance metrics of probabilities of detection and false alarm are provided. The formulation of sensing-throughput tradeoff, channel efficiency and OR-rule cooperative sensing are also presented for the purpose of addressing the optimization problem.

2.1 Sensing Hypotheses

The sensed signal, $X[n]$ of CU will have two hypotheses as follows:

$$H_0: X[n] = W[n] \qquad \text{if PU is absent}$$
$$H_1: X[n] = W[n] + S[n] \qquad \text{if PU is present} \qquad (1)$$

where $n = 1, ..., N$; N is the number of samples. The noise $W[n]$ is assumed to be additive white Gaussian (AWGN) with zero mean and variance σ_w^2. $S[n]$ is the PU's signal and is assumed to be a random Gaussian process with zero mean and variance σ_x^2.

A block diagram of an energy detector is given in Figure 1. The output of the energy detector, Y, which serves as decision statistic, is described by [12]:

$$Y = \frac{1}{N} \sum_{n=1}^{N} (X[n])^2 \qquad (2)$$

Comparing with a threshold, γ, and based on optimal decision yielded by the likelihood ratio Neyman-Pearson hypothesis testing [12], P_d and P_f can now be defined as the probabilities that the CU's sensing algorithm detects a PU under H_0 and H_1, respectively.

$$P_f = P(Y > \gamma \,/\, H_0)$$
$$P_d = P(Y > \gamma \,/\, H_1) \qquad (3)$$

Since we are interested in low SNR regime, where signal-to-noise ratio (*SNR*) is taken as $\frac{\sigma_x^2}{\sigma_w^2}$, large number of samples should be used. Thus, we can use central limit theorem to approximate the decision statistic as Gaussian. Then

$$P_f = Q\left(\frac{\gamma - N\sigma_w^2}{\sqrt{2N\sigma_w^4}}\right) \tag{4}$$

$$P_d = Q\left(\frac{\gamma - N(\sigma_w^2 + \sigma_x^2)}{\sqrt{2N(\sigma_w^2 + \sigma_x^2)^2}}\right) \tag{5}$$

where $Q(.)$ is the complementary distribution function of the standard Gaussian. Combining eq. (4) and (5), P_d is derived to be;

$$P_f = Q\left((Q^{-1}(P_d)(1 + SNR) + SNR\sqrt{N/2}\right) \tag{6}$$

Thus the number of samples needed for PU detection is

$$N = 2\left[\frac{Q^{-1}(P_f) - Q^{-1}(P_d)}{SNR} - Q^{-1}(P_d)\right]^2 \tag{7}$$

Using the sampling time, τ of the system used, sensing time T_s is derived as shown in (8);

$$T_s = \tau N \tag{8}$$

It can be seen that as the number of samples needed for PU detection increases, the sensing time becomes longer. In addition, there will be an increase in P_d and a decrease in P_f, respectively. It is desirable to have a high P_d for better PU protection. Meanwhile, a low P_f is favorable for a better opportunistic access and higher achievable throughput for CU. However, a longer sensing time will reduce the amount of time for data transmission in a frame and hence, results in a lower achievable throughput for CU. Since these two magnitudes pose a trade-off, an optimal sensing time needs to be determined such that throughput for CU can be maximized and a certain Quality of Service (QoS) is attained by PU.

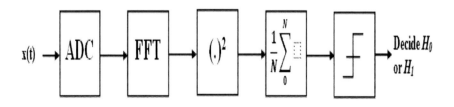

Fig. 1. Block diagram of an energy detector

2.2 Sensing-Throughput Tradeoff

In this work, we consider CU to operate in a frame-by frame basis. The frame structure with duration T_f is shown in Figure 2. The structure consists of sensing slot with duration T_s and transmission slot with time T_t. The sensing task is executed at the beginning of the frame to assess the status of a channel whether it is active or idle. If the channel is idle, CU will transmit to its intended receiver in the remaining duration of a frame. At the end of the frame, if PU is detected, CU's data transmission will be ceased to protect the PU from harmful interference. Otherwise, CU will access the frequency band again in the next frame. The process is repeated. Obviously, the relationship is as given below;

$$T_f = T_t + T_s \qquad (9)$$

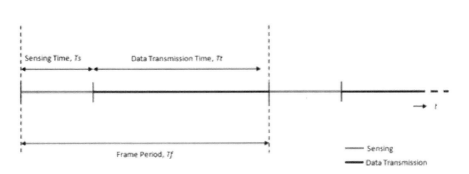

Fig. 2. Frame Structure for CU System

The utilization of licensed channel by PU follows a Markov chain process of exponential ON/OFF states. During the ON period, generated packets of PU is transmitted immediately on the channel.

Two scenarios where the CU can operate in the licensed channel is reported in [9]. First scenario is when the PU is absent and no false alarm is generated by CU. The achievable throughput is then given by;

$$R_0(T_s) = \frac{T_f - T_s}{T_f}\left(1 - P_f\right)C_0 \qquad (10)$$

In the second scenario, CU doest not detect the PU although it is active. Therefore, the achievable throughput is represented as;

$$R_1(T_s) = \frac{T_f - T_s}{T_f}\left(1 - P_d\right)C_1 \qquad (11)$$

where C_0 and C_1 denote the throughput of CU operating in the absence of PU and the throughput of CU operating the presence of PU, respectively. If we define SNR_{cu} as the received signal-to-noise ratio of the CU's transmission at the CU receiver and

SNR_{pu} as the signal-to-noise ratio of PU received at the same receiver, then $C_0 = log_2(1 + SNR_{cu})$ and $C_1 = log_2\left(1 + \frac{SNR_{cu}}{SNR_{pu}}\right)$. In the case of only one transmission in the CR network, we will have $C_0 > C_1$.

The average achievable throughput of a CU system with the frame structure of Figure 2 can be expressed as [11];

$$R(T_s) = P(H_1)R_1(T_s) + P(H_0)R_0(T_s) \tag{12}$$

where $P(H_1)$ is the probability of PU being active in the sensed channel and $P(H_0) = 1 - P(H_1)$.

The challenge of sensing-throughput tradeoff is to find an optimal sensing time that leads to maximized transmission time, and therefore, higher throughput for the CU. The optimization problem can be described mathematically as;

$$\max_{T_s} \quad R(T_s) = P(H_1)R_1(T_s) + P(H_0)R_0(T_s) \tag{13}$$

$$\text{s.t} \quad P_d \geq \overline{P_d} \tag{14}$$

where $\overline{P_d}$ is the target probability of detection for PU to be sufficiently protected. In this work, $\overline{P_d}$ is set at 98% based on the statistical distribution of locally captured data.

By assuming $P(H_1)$ is small (<0.2) [11] and taking note of the condition of $C_0 > C_1$, the second term of the optimization problem will dominate and simplifies the equation to become

$$\max_{T_s} \quad R(T_s) = P(H_0)\frac{T_f - T_s}{T_f}(1 - P_f)C_0 \tag{15}$$

under similar contraint for the target probability of detection.

The relationship of sensing time and achievable throughput for CU can further be defined for energy detection scheme. Choosing $P_d = \overline{P_d}$, the achievable throughput for CU system is given by

$$\tilde{R}(T_s) = C_0 P(H_0)\left(1 - \frac{T_s}{T_f}\right)\left(1 - Q\left(\alpha + \sqrt{\frac{T_s}{\tau}}SNR\right)\right) \tag{16}$$

where $\alpha = \sqrt{2SNR + 1}Q^{-1}(\overline{P_d})$. It can be seen obviously in (16) that the achievable thoughput of the CU system is a function of sensing time T_s.

Channel efficiency is measured by the product of spectrum opportunity and normalized transmission time and described as given as follows [13];

$$ChEff = (1 - P_f)\left(1 - \frac{T_s}{T_f}\right) \tag{17}$$

2.3 Distributed Cooperative Sensing

As mentioned, a stand-alone CU often suffers from noise uncertainty, fading, shadowing and hidden node problems. Multiple CUs can be coordinated to perform spectrum sensing cooperatively and the sensing information exchanged between neighbors is expected to have a better chance of detecting PU compared to individual sensing.

In a cooperative spectrum sensing system using OR-rule, the PU is considered to be present if any of the CUs detects the presence of the primary user. Assuming that there are M identical and independent CUs in the cooperative spectrum sensing system, the cooperative probability of detection Q_d and probability of false alarm Q_f using OR-rule are given by [7]:

$$Q_d = 1 - \prod_{i=1}^{M}(1 - P_{d,i}) \tag{18}$$

$$Q_f = 1 - \prod_{i=1}^{M}(1 - P_{f,i}) \tag{19}$$

where P_d and P_f are respectively the probability of detection and probability of false alarm of a stand-alone cognitive radio.

In this work, distributed approach of cooperative sensing is used. Each CU independently senses the environment for the presence of PU. Each CU then becomes like a data fusion center and derives its own cooperative decision based on OR rule. An example of the distributed spectrum sensing architecture is shown in Figure 3. There are several assumptions considered [6]:

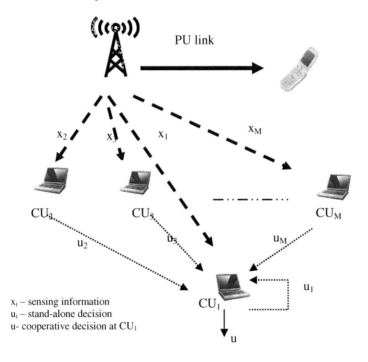

Fig. 3. Distributed Spectrum Sensing Architecture

- Energy detection is used as stand-alone spectrum sensing in a distributed system as it has low computational and implementation complexities and requires no knowledge on PU's features such as modulation and frame format. CUs
- CUs are synchronized and they sense PU in the same spectrum segements
- All exchanged information among CUs recaches its destination succesfully and noiselessly
- The exchanging process does not cause any interference to channel environment.

3 Optimizing Distributed Sensing Performance

Particle swarm optimization (PSO) is a population based and stochastic optimization approach designed primarily to mimic the social behaviour of school of fish or flock of birds [14][15][16]. This social behaviour has been used in solving more complex optimization problems in a more sophisticated and efficient manner. The particles are grouped into swarm and each particle is a potential solution to the optimization problem. Each particle within a neighbourhood moves toward the best optimal solution in the neighbourhood depending on its past experience and neighbours as well. This clearly shows the unique behaviour PSO in which it cooperatively takes decision to achieved optimal solution. In a nutshell, it has been referred as symbiotic cooperative algorithm [17]. It is very obvious that the performance of each particle is determined by the fitness function. PSO has been applicable to other fields but not much work has been done related to spectrum sensing in cognitive radio networks. The key success to the deployment of PSO in many optimization problems is due to the fact that it is very simple, high convergence and searching capability [18][19].

PSO is primarily governed by two fundamental equations representing the velocity and position of the particle at any particular time. After each iteration, the particle position and velocity is updated until the termination condition has been reached. The termination condition can be based on the number of iteration and achievable output required. Once the required number of iterations or predetermined output has been achieved, the searching process is terminated automatically. For a particle with n dimension can be represented by vector $X = (x_1, x_2 \ldots \ldots \ldots x_n)$. The position of the particcles at time t can be mathematically expressed as P= $(p_1, p_2 \ldots \ldots \ldots p_n)$ while the corresponding velocity of the particles is represented as $V = (v_1, v_2 \ldots \ldots \ldots v_n)$. In general, the velocity and position of the particles at $t+1$ can be mathematically represented using equation (20) and (21) respectively

$$v(t+1) = \omega v(t) + \varphi_1 \big(P_l + x(t)\big) + \varphi_2 \Big(P_g + x(t)\Big) \tag{20}$$

$$x(t+1) = x(t) + v(t+1) \tag{21}$$

Equation (20) describes the velocity of the particles at time $t+1$. ω is the inertia weight which keeps track of the previous velocity history on the current velocity of each particles. It balances the trade-off between the local and global exploration of the swarm. $v(t)$ ensures that the particles are on the right flight direction and it prevents the particle from sudden change in direction. $\varphi_1(P_l \ x(t))$ computes the performance of the particle relative to the past performance. In a nutshell, it draws the particles to their best known position. $\varphi_2(P_g \ x(t))$ measures the performance of particle relative to its neighbours.

   Both the cognitive and social components depend greatly on φ_1 and φ_2 respectively. It is very important to note that the global best (P_g) determines the best possible solution for the entire swarm. The global best used star structure which converges faster [16], but can be trapped in local minima. The position can be computed using (21) whenever the velocity is determined. These special and unique features of PSO have been used in this work to select the minimal sensing time required in order to achieve high throughput. The detrimental impact of reducing the sensing time on other parameters is considered in our optimization problem. The flow chart for the PSO based optimal sensing algorithm for distributed cooperative sensing is given in Figure 4.

   The objective of this work is to reduce sensing time and subsequently increase the throughput as result of using the required optimal sensing time needed at any particular time depending on the probability of false alarm for a distributed sensing. Given the frame duration T_f is set at 100 ms and $f(x)$ represents the sensing time as the objective function, an optimal normalized achievable throughput, $\widetilde{R_n}(T_s)$, can thus be derived using (22);

Minimize $f(x) = 100 - \left(\dfrac{100 * \widetilde{R_n}(T_s)}{1 - P_f} \right)$

Minimize

$$f(x) = 100 - \frac{100 \left(1 - \frac{T_s}{T_f}\right)\left(1 - Q\left(\alpha + \sqrt{\frac{T_s}{\tau}} SNR\right)\right)}{1 - P_f} \tag{22}$$

$$Objective \ function = \arg\min f(x)$$
$$Subject \ to: \ \ 0 \leq T_s \leq T_f$$
$$0 \leq P_f \leq 1$$
$$0 \leq \widetilde{R_n}(T_s) \leq 1$$

The impact of the derived optimal sensing time on channel efficiency of the distributed cooperative system is also studied.

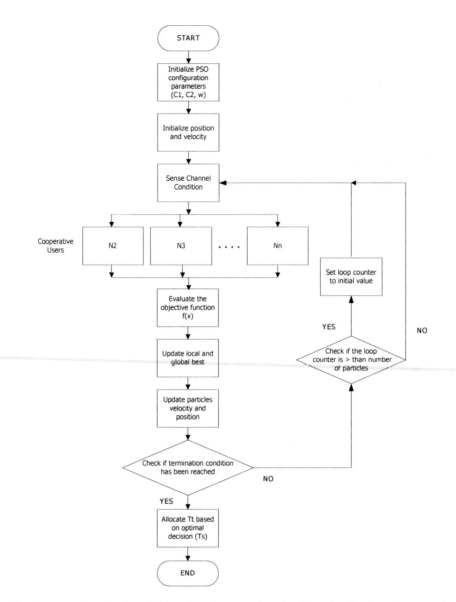

Fig. 4. Flow chart for the PSO-based optimal sensing algorithm for distributed cooperative sensing

4   Results and Discussion

The scenario for optimal sensing is simulated in MATLAB and the following settings of Table 1 have been used for the experimentation:

Table 1. Parameter setting

Parameters	Value
Number of particles	30
Number of iteration/users	30
Learning factors φ_1 & φ_2	1
Inertia weight ω	1
Sensing time	10 mS
Data transmission time	90 mS
Frame time	100mS
Target P_d	0.98
SNR	-30 dB

As mentioned in previous section, to give PU its desired level of protection, P_d is fixed at 0.98. In addition, the primary goal is to minimize sensing time and at the same time achieve high throughput. The trade-off between sensing time and throughput is then achieved through PSO scheme. This approach has been able to counter the problem of achieving high throughput for CUs and at the the same time protecting the PU as well. In order to verify the efficiency of the developed scheme, we used exponential function to generate the traffic which varies exponentially with time for each CU. As can be seen from (22), the probability of false alarm is related to data transmission and frame duration time. This has allowed us to optimally minimized the required time to sense for the presence of PU within certain constraints of probability of false alarm, frame duration and data transmission time, in a distributed cooperative sensing scenario based on OR rule decision fusion.

As observed from Figure 5, it is reported in previous work that a stand-alone CU system achieves an optimal sensing time of 2 ms under PSO [20]. This is a reduction of 80% from the original setting of 10 ms or 10% of the frame duration, as given in Table 1. Decision fusion subjected to PSO seems to further reduce the optimal sensing time to 1 ms. The decrease in sensing time contributes significantly to lower energy spent on sensing for distributed CU system with PSO. Furthermore, this finding tallies with the result in [11] where sensing time is significantly reduced when cooperative sensing is deployed.

The performance of decision fusion subjected to PSO in terms of normalized achievable throughput is shown in Figure 6. The maximum achievable normalized throughput increases with the increase of sensing terminals under optimal fusion scheme compared to normal fusion technique.

The trend is similarly displayed for the performance of channel efficiency for the optimized and normal OR-rule as can be seen in Figure 7. The channel efficiency is significantly improved by introducing PSO scheme in its decision fusion scheme. The improvement is also linearly related to the number of cooperating users.

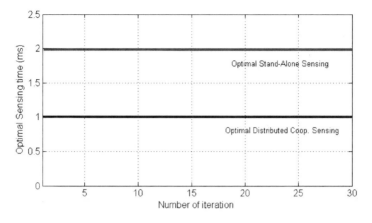

Fig. 5. Comparison of optimal sensing time derived for stand-alone and distributed cooperative sensing

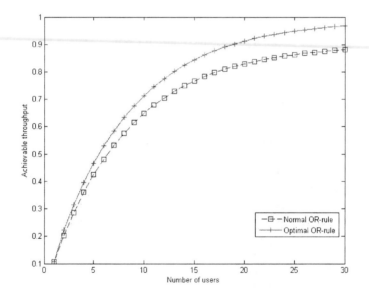

Fig. 6. Normalized achievable throughput for optimal and normal OR decision fusion

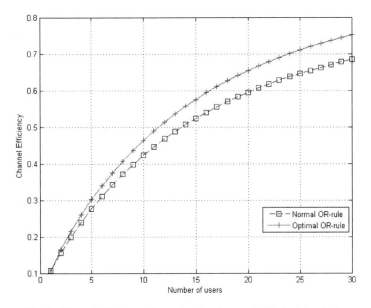

Fig. 7. Channel efficiency for optimal and normal OR decision fusion

5 Conclusion

The issue of sensing-throughput tradeoff in cooperative sensing scenario is studied. It is seen that optimal sensing time is reduced when distributed channel sensing is applied. Using energy detection, the proposed scheme of PSO based OR-rule decision fusion gives encouraging results. The maximum achievable normalized throughput increases with the increase of sensing terminals. Channel efficiency also reflects the same trend as it improves with the increasing number of cooperating users. In addition, optimized OR-rule gives a better performance in terms of both achievable throughput and channel efficiency compared to the normal OR fused technique.

Future works will include implementing PSO approach into an SDR platform and extend the strategy to AND rule based cooperative sensing.

Acknowledgment. The authors wish to express their gratitude to Ministry of Higher Education (MOHE), Malaysia and Research Management Center (RMC), Universiti Teknologi Malaysia for the financial support of this project under GUP research grant no: Q.J130000.7107.03J81.

References

1. McHenry, M.A., Tenhula, P.A., McCloskey, D., Roberson, D.A., Hood, C.S.: Chicago spectrum occupancy measurements & analysis and a long-term studies proposal. In: 1st International Workshop on Technology And Policy For Accessing Spectrum, Boston, Massachusetts, August 05 (2006)

2. Cabric, D., Mishra, S.M., Brodersen, R.W.: Implementation Issues in Spectrum Sensing for Cognitive Radios. In: Asilomar Conference on Signals, Systems, and Computers, vol. 1, pp. 772–776 (November 2004)
3. Akyildiz, F., Lee, W.-Y., Vuran, M.C., Mohanty, S.: Next Generation Dynamic Spectrum Access Cognitive Radio Wireless Networks: A Survey. Computer Networks 50, 2127–2159 (2006)
4. Rashid, R.A., Fisal, N.: Issues of Spectrum Sensing in Cognitive Radio based System. In: 3rd South East Asia Technical Universities Consortium (SEATUC) 2009, Johor, Malaysia, February 25-26 (2009)
5. Hamid, M.: Dynamic Spectrum Access in Cognitive Radio Networks: Aspects of Mac Layer Sensing. Master Thesis, Blekinge Institute of Technology, Ronneby, Sweden (December 2008)
6. Duong, N.D., et al.: A Novel Architecture for Distributed Spectrum Sensing for Cognitive Radio Applications. In: TENCON 209, Singapore, November 23-26 (2009)
7. Rashid, R.A., Aripin, N.M., Fisal, N., Ariffin, S.H.S., Yusof, S.K.S.: Integration of Cooperative Sensing and Transmission: Performance Evaluation of Cooperation Strategies in Cognitive Radio. IEEE Vehicular Technology Magazine 5(3), 46–53 (2010)
8. Peh, E., Liang, Y.-C.: Optimization for Cooperative Sensing in Cognitive Radio Network. In: WCNC 2007, Hong Kong, March 11-15 (2007)
9. Pei, Y., Hoang, A.T., Liang, Y.-C.: Sensing-Throughput Tradeoff in Cognitive Radio Networks: How Frequently Should Spectrum Sensing be Carried Out? In: IEEE 18th International Symposium on Personal, Indoor and Mobile Radio Communications, PIMRC 2007, Athens, September 3-7, pp. 1–5 (2007)
10. Stotas, S., Nallanathan, A.: Overcoming the Sensing-Throughput Tradeoff in Cognitive Radio Networks. In: IEEE ICC 2010 (2010)
11. Liang, Y.-C., Zeng, Y., Peh, E.C.Y., Hoang, A.T.: Sensingthroughput tradeoff for cognitive radio networks. IEEE Trans. Wireless Commun. 7(4), 1326–1337 (2008)
12. Poor, H.V.: An Introduction to signal detection and estimation, 2nd edn. Springer, New York (1994)
13. Gong, S., Wang, P., Liu, W., Yuan, W.: Maximize Secondary User Throughput via Optimal Sensing in Multi-channel Cognitive Radio Networks. In: GLOBECOM 2010, Miami, Florida, USA, December 6-10 (2010)
14. Kennedy, J., Eberhart, R.C.: Particle swarm optimization. In: Proc. IEEE International Conference on Neural Networks, Australia (1995)
15. Kennedy, J., Eberhart, R.C.: Swarm Intelligence. Morgan Kauffman Publishers, California (2001)
16. Løvberg, M., Krink, T.: Extending Particle Swarm Optimisers with Self-Organized Criticality. In: Proceedings of the IEEE Congress on Evolutionary Computation (2002)
17. Engelbrecht, A.P.: Computational Intelligence. Wiley, England (2007)
18. Mendis, C., Guru, S.M., Halgamuge, S., Fernando, S.: Optimized Sink node Path using Particle Swarm Optimization. In: 20th International Conference on Advanced Information Networking and Applications. IEEE Computer Society (2006)
19. Gheitanchi, S., Ali, F., Stipidis, E.: Particle swarm optimization for Resource Allocation in OFDMA. IEEE (2007)
20. Rashid, R.A., Baguda, Y.S., Fisal, N., Adib Sarijari, M., Yusof, S.K.S., Ariffin, S.H.S.: Optimizing Achievable Throughput for Cognitive Radio Network Using Swarm Intelligence. In: APCC 2011, Kota Kinabalu, Sabah, Malaysia, November 10-12 (in press, 2011)

Weighted RED (WTRED) Strategy for TCP Congestion Control

Nabhan Hamadneh, David Murray, Michael Dixon, and Peter Cole

Murdoch University, School of IT,
Murdoch, WA, Australia
{n.hamadneh,d.murray,m.dixon,p.cole}@murdoch.edu.au

Abstract. This work presents the Weighted Random Early Detection (WTRED) strategy for congestion handling in TCP networks. The strategy dynamically adjusts RED's maximum threshold, minimum threshold and weight parameters to increase network performance. This work describes RED and FRED implementations and highlights their disadvantages. Using the NS-2 simulator, we compare WTRED with these classic congestion control strategies. The simulation results demonstrate the shortcomings of RED and FRED. The results also show that WTRED achieves greater link utilization and throughput than RED and FRED.

Keywords: TCP Congestion, RED, AQM, WTRED.

1 Introduction

Transmission Control Protocol (TCP) is a set of rules that govern end-to-end data delivery in modern networks [1] [2] [3]. When demand exceeds the available capacity, congestion occurs, resulting in large delays and packet losses [4] [5]. Data flows in the internet are chaotic and self-similar [31], hence, queue management and scheduling mechanisms are required at routers.

Real time traffic, including voice and video, has become increasingly important, necessitating the development of new TCP congestion control strategies. Tail Drop (TD) was one of the earliest strategies, applied by TCP networks, to solve congestion. Random Drop (RD) and Early Random Drop (ERD) [6] were proposed to overcome some of TD's drawbacks. Random Early Detection (RED) [7] was proposed in 1993 to solve the shortcomings of previous congestion control strategies; particularly TD. Following the publication and adoption of RED, variants have been designed to enhance its performance. This study, describes the characteristics, advantages and disadvantages of TD, RED and FRED. We propose a novel RED variant to improve network performance using a dynamic weight parameter.

This paper is organized as follows: Section 2 describes the background of congestion and the traditional solutions to this problem. Section 3 describes the Random Early Detection (RED) strategy. Refined Random Early detection

A. Abd Manaf et al. (Eds.): ICIEIS 2011, Part II, CCIS 252, pp. 421–434, 2011.
© Springer-Verlag Berlin Heidelberg 2011

(FRED) is detailed in section 4. Section 5 proposes the new weighted RED (WTRED) strategy. Simulation and discussion is presented in section 6; and section 7 concludes the study.

2   Background

Current congestion control algorithms are expected to prevent unsatisfactory performance. The performance of these strategies is evaluated against the following goals [8]: i. high bandwidth utilization, ii. fairness iii. reduced jitter iv. high responsiveness. v. Fairness and compatibility with widely used protocols. Network performance involves four main parameters, which are: throughput, link utilization, packet loss and average delay. The design of a new congestion control strategy is subject to enhance one or more of these parameters.

The Tail Drop (TD) strategy uses a First In First Out (FIFO) queue management approach to control congestion. When the queue size reaches the buffer limit, packets are dropped in the order they arrive. This approach causes four problems that reduce network performance:

☐ **Full Queue [9]:** This problem occurs when a gateway continually sends full queue signals to sources for an extended period of time. In Fig. 1, a buffer of size 64 packets is full throughout the majority of the network operation time. In addition to the long delays associated with large queues, TD will penalize some connections by inequitably dropping packets. This will cause unfair resource allocation, which is illustrated in Fig. 2. In this figure, connection 2's window size is always lower than the other connections.

☐ **Lock Out [9]:** This problem occurs when TD allows a few connections to monopolize the whole buffer space. In Fig. 2, connection 4 receives more link bandwidth than the other connections in the network.

☐ **Global Synchronization [6]:** This problem occurs when all TCP senders reduce their sending rate simultaneously, reducing the network throughput

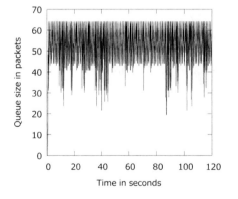
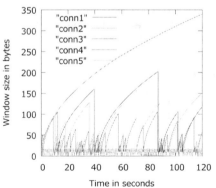

Fig. 1. Full queue problem of TD strategy   **Fig. 2.** Lock out problem of TD strategy

[10] [11]. Fig. 3 shows TD algorithm causing global synchronization. Fig. 4 shows 5 seconds of global synchronization for the same scenario between time 20s to 25s.

☐ **Bias against bursty traffic [12]:** The nature of TCP transactions often result in data packets being sent and received in groups. When the source receives acknowledgments of packet delivery from the destination node, it increases the number of packets to be sent in the next group. The maximum number of packets allowed in transit is the congestion window size *cwnd*. In network steady state, the congestion window size is increased. When the network becomes congested, the congestion window size is decreased. Due to the bursty nature of many transactions, dropping packets in the order that they arrived is unfair because it is likely that the majority of packets being dropped, may be from the same source. This will unfairly decrease the sending rate of that source whilst it needs more bandwidth to send this bursty traffic. Resulting in low network throughput.

Another strategy, Early Random Drop (ERD), begins packet drops at a rate derived from the current network congestion level. For example, if the queue size exceeds a certain threshold, then every arriving packet will be dropped with prefixed drop probability. The following code, illustrates the algorithm of this strategy:

Early Random Drop (ERD)'s Algorithm, see [6] for more details

```
if (queue_length > drop_level ) then
if get.random( ) < drop_probablity then
drop(packet)
```

Relating to some ERD suggestions, Random Early Detection (RED) was developed to maintain adjustable threshold and drop probability. RED solves the problems associated with the traditional congestion control strategies.

3   Random Early Detection (RED)

Random Early Detection (RED) maintains six main parameters[1]. For every packet arrival, the average queue size is estimated using Eq. (1). If the average is greater than the maximum threshold, then all arriving packets will be dropped with probability 1. If the average is less than the minimum threshold, then no packets are to be dropped. If the average is in between the minimum and

---

[1] Many of RED's features were originally proposed in prior work [6]. The random early packet drop, dynamic drop level and dynamic drop probability were derived from work by Hashem [6]. RED also uses the uniform distribution for drop probability by [6]. The average queue size and weight parameter were originally proposed by Ramakrishnan et al [14].

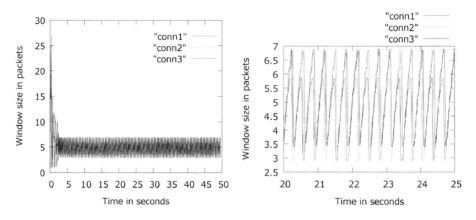

Fig. 3. TD global synchronization   **Fig. 4.** TD global synchronization (x 50 zoom in)

maximum thresholds, then RED calculates the immediate drop probability p_b by Eq. (2). RED then calculates the accumulative drop probability p_a using Eq. (3). As a final step, it drops packets with the accumulative drop probability.

$$avg = (1 - w_q) * avg + w_q * q \tag{1}$$

$$p_b = max_p(\frac{avg - min_{th}}{max_{th} - min_{th}}) \tag{2}$$

$$p_a = p_b(\frac{1}{1 - count * p_b}) \tag{3}$$

Where:

avg : *Average queue size*
w_q : *Weight parameter, $0 \leq w_q \leq 1$*
q : *Current queue size*
p_b : *Immediately marking probability*
max_p : *Maximum value of p_b*
min_{th} : *Minimum threshold*
max_{th} : *Maximum threshold*
p_a : *Accumulative drop probability*
$count$: *Number of arrived packets since the last dropped one*

RED solves the problems associated with traditional congestion control strategies, such as TD. Fig. 5 depicts the weighted average and the actual queue sizes for the same scenario used in Fig. 1; in this instance RED rather than TD is used. Fig. 5 shows that RED has no biases against bursty traffic. While the average queue size is nearly 17 packets, a few bursts, between size 17 and 26, are allowed.

The weighted average defines the level of congestion to start packet dropping. In Fig. 5, avg is always less than 13 packets and this helps the gateway detect congestion before the buffer overflows. By reducing the actual and average queue sizes, RED lowers queuing delays, prevents the full queue problem and provides fair resource allocation.

RED also solves lock out and global synchronization problems. Fig. 6 shows the congestion window size for RED. It is the same network used to plot Fig. 2 with TD. It is clear from Fig. 6, that the connections receive fair resource allocation. Lock out problems are also eliminated. The global synchronization, caused by TD, is also solved. This is evidenced in Fig. 7.

Despite the strong design of RED, drawbacks have been revealed in a number of studies. Parameter measurement and the recommended values have been subject to change over time [16]. A new RED-based strategy, ARED, was developed. ARED dynamically adjusts the max_p parameter depending on the values of avg, max_{th} and min_{th} [17]. Blue-RED is another strategy that dynamically adjusts the drop probability of RED p_a to increase network performance [18]. Other strategies suggest dynamic thresholds for RED, such as RED-DT [19] and PDT-RED [20]. Diffusion Early Marking (DEM) [22] is a RED based strategy designed to avoid global synchronization. In order to avoid excessive congestion marking, DEM has been designed to optimize the distribution of packet marking. For further details in newly designed congestion control strategies, see [23].

Parameter setting in new RED-based strategies is dynamic. Some studies suggest optimal values for the weight parameter w_q. BF-RED [21], proposes different weight parameters for different flows to ensure fair bandwidth allocation. Also, RT-RED adjusts RED's parameters based on the ratio between the actual queue size and the average queue size. RED performance evaluations in real networks are further investigated in [24] [25] [26].

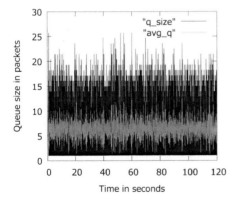

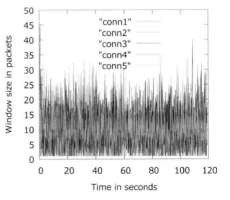

Fig. 5. Average and actual queue sizes on a RED gateway

Fig. 6. Congestion window size on a RED gateway

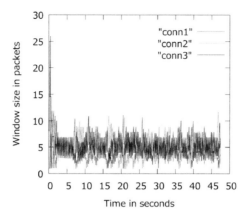

Fig. 7. Congestion window size on a RED gateway without global synchronization

Table 1. The maximum drop probability for FRED's sub-phases

Sub-Phase	1	2	3	4	5	6
max_p	max_p	$2max_p$	$4max_p$	$6max_p$	$8max_p$	$10max_p$

4   FRED

Refined Random Early Detection (FRED) [27] is a modification of RED that uses a dynamic weight w_q and max_p to control congestion. It divides the area between the maximum threshold and minimum threshold into six sub-phases. As the average increases from the minimum threshold to the maximum threshold, the max_p is increased. A different value is assigned for the different sub-phases illustrated in Table 1.

In addition to a dynamic max_p parameter, FRED maintains a dynamic weight parameter w_q. It, also, makes use of a third threshold, called the warn threshold. The weight parameter is adjusted whenever the actual queue size exceeds the warn threshold. FRED normally assigns half of the buffer size to this value. After the actual queue size exceeds the warn threshold, it has to go through another six sub-phases, but this time, with different weight parameters for each sub-phase. The weight values for these sub-phases are illustrated in Table 2. In order to apply the weight parameter sub-phases, the actual queue size must be greater than the average queue size.

Table 2. The weight parameter for FRED's sub-phases

Sub-Phase	1	2	3	4	5	6
w_q	w_q	$4w_q$	$8w_q$	$12w_q$	$16w_q$	$20w_q$

RED calculates the average queue size for every packet arrival. FRED extends RED by additionally calculating the average queue size for every packet departure.

5   WTRED Design Guidelines

Before outlining the WTRED algorithm we highlight some of the parameter and implementation issues with RED and FRED.

5.1   RED's Parameters

RED maintains a set of parameters to prevent congestion. Improper parameter configuration increases the oscillations in the average queue size and data packet loss [28]. Thus, RED suffers from heavy oscillations in the average queue size, which reduces the network stability. Some RED variants provide Auto parametrization for RED [29], however, parameter configuration is problematic. The following section outlines the main parameters of RED:

Average queue size: Rather than using the actual queue to reflect congestion in gateways, RED uses an Exponentially Weighted Moving Average (EWMA) to reflect historic queue dynamics. This EWMA helps gateways distinguish between transient and permanent congestion. It also avoids global synchronization and bias against bursty traffic [7]. RED uses Eq. (1) to calculate the EWMA of the queue size.

Minimum threshold: The first dropping level of RED. When the average queue size is lower than this threshold, no packets will be dropped. *Higher minimum thresholds increase throughput and link utilization* [7].

Current drop probability: The immediate drop probability in Eq. (2) which is used to calculate the accumulative drop probability in Eq. (3). As shown in Eq. (2), the current drop probability p_b is a function of the maximum drop probability max_p. Consequently, the accumulative drop probability p_a is a function of max_p. *A higher max_p will result in a higher drop rate.* In Sec. 6.3, we show how this can cause problems with FRED's implementation.

Accumulative drop probability: This parameter is a value between zero and one. When the average queue size exceeds the minimum threshold, a packet is chosen randomly from the queue. If the probability is less than the drop probability then the packet is dropped. The calculation of this parameter is illustrated in Eq. (3).

Maximum drop probability: This parameter reflects the maximum drop rate of RED. For example, if the maximum drop probability is 0.1, the gateway cannot drop more than one packet out of ten which is calculated using the formula 1 out of $1/max_p$.

Weight parameter: This parameter is used to calculate the EWMA queue size in Eq. (1). It reflects the sensitivity of the average to the actual changes in the queue size. It takes values from zero to one. *Setting the weight parameter* *to larger values means that fewer packets are required to increase the average from A to B.* For instance: if a RED gateway with a weight parameter of 0.001 needs 60 packet arrivals to increase the average queue size from 6 to 10, then the same gateway with 0.003 weight parameter will need fewer packets (40) to increase the average from 6 to 10.

Maximum threshold: As the average queue size increases from the minimum threshold toward the maximum threshold, the drop rate is increased slowly. As the average queue sizes hits the maximum threshold, the drop probability turns to one and every arriving packet has to be dropped. This keeps the actual queue size between the minimum and the maximum threshold. In RED, the values of the minimum and the maximum threshold are assigned depending on *the desirable actual average of the queue size.* Our strategy, WTRED, uses different criteria to configure these parameters. This is further detailed in Sec. 5.2.

5.2   WTRED Proposal

The maximum and minimum thresholds in RED divide the buffer into three main areas. The area between 0 and the minimum threshold, the area between the minimum threshold and maximum threshold and the area between the maximum threshold and buffer limit. In FRED, they call these areas green, yellow and red respectively. When the average queue size is in the green area, all traffic is allowed with no drops. In the yellow area some of the traffic will be dropped. In the red area no traffic is allowed and all incoming packets will be dropped.

In RED, the maximum and minimum thresholds are dependent from the actual buffer size and they are preset before network operation time. Also, the weight parameter is a prefixed parameter. The default values of the maximum threshold, minimum threshold and the weight parameter in RED are 5, 15 and 0.002 respectively. It has been suggested that the maximum threshold should be set to twice the minimum threshold [7].

In FRED, the green area is divided into six equal areas with different maximum drop probabilities. Also, the area between the warn threshold and the buffer limit is divided into another six equal areas, each area with a different weight parameter. *The mechanism proposed in this study ,WTRED,* uses different weight parameters for each area in RED. Furthermore, WTRED also adjusts the maximum and minimum thresholds based on the actual buffer size.

Fig. 8 to Fig 11 illustrate the network performance for the topology depicted in Fig. 13. NS-2 was used to examine the four network performance parameters with weight parameters in the range 0.001 to 0.1. The results suggest that RED works most efficiently when the weight parameter is between 0.001 and 0.003. To be more specific, two performance parameters are improved: throughput and link utilization. Loss rate will be at an acceptable level but the delays will increase. These results agree with the original parameter recommendations for RED [7] that suggest a weight parameter of 0.002.

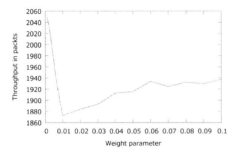

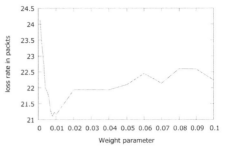

Fig. 8. Throughput for a range of weight parameters from 0.001 - 0.1

Fig. 9. Loss rate for a range of weight parameters from 0.001 - 0.1

The new *parameter configuration in WTRED* is to assign the weights 0.003, 0.002 and 0.001 to the green, yellow and red areas respectively. Also, the minimum threshold will be set at 40% of the buffer size and the maximum threshold will be 70% of the buffer size. This high minimum threshold will guarantee higher network throughput and link utilization. For the average to respond quickly to the changes in the green area we assign the value 0.003 to the weight parameter. In case that persistent traffic bursts accumulate the queue size, the average will be increased faster to hit the minimum threshold and initiate congestion recovery.

When the average reaches the yellow area, RED starts dropping packets. In this area there is no need to have higher value for the weight parameter. Hence, WTRED assigns the value 0.002 to the weight parameter. Another reason to use a lower weight parameter in this area is to maintain reasonable time before the average hits the maximum threshold. When the maximum threshold is reached, the drop probability will be 1.0 and every arriving packet will be dropped. Setting the weight parameter to 0.002 in this area is better than using high values for the maximum drop probability. High max_p values lead to shorter time to reach the maximum threshold which will reduce the link utilization.

When the average queue size exceeds the maximum threshold and enters the red area, RED will drop every packet arriving at the gateway. FRED uses higher weight parameters to increase the sensitivity to the changes in the actual queue size. In this case, the actual queue size and the average queue size will closely follow each other and FRED's behavior may approach the TD strategy, dropping packets based on the actual queue size. Fig. 12 illustrates the WTRED algorithm.

6 Simulation and Discussion

Our strategy, WTRED, is simulated using the NS-2 simulator. WTRED, RED and FRED are compared against the four network performance parameters which are: throughput, link utilization, average delay and packet loss. The network topology in Fig. 13 is used to run 11 different scenarios with different weight parameters and buffer sizes. Table 3, illustrates the weight and buffer size for each scenario used in this simulator.

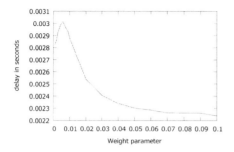

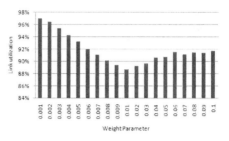

Fig. 10. Delays for a range of weight parameters from 0.001 - 0.1

Fig. 11. Link utilization for a range of weight parameters from 0.001-0.1

Table 3. Buffer sizes for FRED's sub-phases

w_q	0.001	0.0015	0.002	0.0025	0.003	0.0035	0.004	0.0045	0.005	0.0055	0.006
Buffer (packet)	40	50	60	70	80	90	100	110	120	130	140

6.1 Network Topology

We use the NS2 simulator [27] to define five FTP sources. A duplex link with 10Mb/s bandwidth connects each source with the gateway. Connection delays are uniformly distributed between 1ms and 5ms. Another duplex link with 10Mb/s bandwidth and 5ms delay connects the gateway with a TCP sink. The packet size is 552 bytes and the TCP variant is Reno. Fig. 13 illustrates the simulation network topology.

6.2 Simulation Results

RED [7] suggests that, in order to filter out transient congestion at the gateway, the weight (w_q) must be assigned small values. Low weights mean that

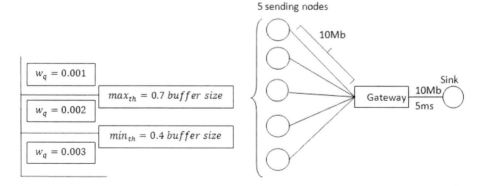

Fig. 12. WTRED algorithm

Fig. 13. Simulation network topology

the EWMA will respond slowly to actual queue size changes. This reduces the gateway's ability to detect the initial stages of congestion. The maximum and minimum threshold values are restricted by the desired average queue size. Also, the difference between the maximum threshold and the minimum threshold must be sufficiently large to avoid global synchronization. Small differences between maximum threshold and minimum threshold allow the average queue size to oscillate up to the maximum threshold.

Fig. 14 to Fig. 17 depict the throughput, packet losses, average delay and link utilization respectively. Fig. 14 shows that WTRED achieved the highest throughput among the three strategies. FRED generates very poor throughput due to the high weight parameters and maximum drop probability. This also increases the loss rate as shown in Fig. 15. FRED also has the lowest delays among the three strategies as in Fig. 16. This comes at the price of very poor throughput, Fig. 14 and link utilization, Fig. 17.

The figures demonstrate that WTRED outperforms RED and FRED. WTRED improves throughput and link utilization while maintaining acceptable delays and loss rates.

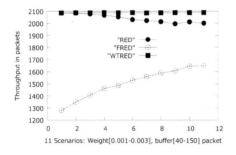

Fig. 14. Network throughput for RED, FRED and WTRED

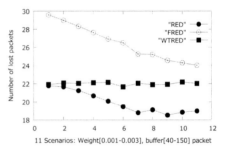

Fig. 15. Packet loss rate for RED, FRED and WTRED

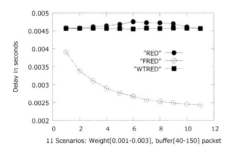

Fig. 16. Average delay for RED, FRED and WTRED

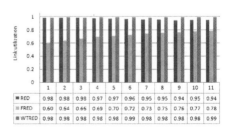

Fig. 17. Link utilization for RED, FRED and WTRED

6.3   Issues with RED's and FRED's Implementations

Research has shown that parameter setting in RED is sensitive and problematic [9]. FRED proposed a new parameter configuration for RED in an effort to increase network performance. Unfortunately, FRED has numerous drawbacks.

FRED uses a very high max_p value. In some phases this value is ten times the initial value in RED. Given the same queue conditions, sometimes FRED will drop ten times as many packets as RED. The maximum threshold in this case is actually reduced, resulting in a lower average queue size and lower average delay. Although FRED lowers delays, its overall performance is poor due to lower throughput, link utilization and higher loss rates, as demonstrated in section 6.2.

The suggested exponent value of the weight parameter using the normalized notation is -3. For example, the default value for w_q in RED is 0.002. When the actual queue size exceeds the warn threshold, FRED starts to increase the weight parameter. In Table 2, sub-phase 6, FRED multiplies the weight parameter by 20. In this case, w_q is not just doubled, it is also shifted one decimal point.

TD does not maintain an EWMA. RED maintains the average between the minimum and maximum thresholds while allowing transient bursts of traffic [7]. Higher weights mean that the average queue size will closely follow the actual queue size. In case of bursty traffic overwhelming the gateway for an extended period, FRED will behave like a TD algorithm.

7   Conclusion

Random Early Detection (RED) uses parameters, such as: maximum threshold, minimum threshold, weight and maximum drop probability to control congestion in TCP networks. Some RED variants use different parameter settings to enhance RED's implementation. FRED dynamically adjusts the maximum drop probability and the weight parameter to increase network performance. This study highlights some of RED's and FRED's drawbacks and proposes the Weighted RED (WTRED) strategy to overcome these shortcomings.

WTRED uses a dynamic weight parameter and new maximum threshold and minimum threshold. NS-2 simulations show that FRED reduces loss rates and delays; but this comes at the cost of dramatically reduced throughput and link utilization. Comparatively, RED generates higher throughput and higher link utilization with acceptable delays and losses. WTRED provides the highest throughput and link utilization. The packet loss rate is slightly higher than RED, but the benefit of these slightly higher losses is a lower average delay. Overall, the results suggest that WTRED provides a better balance of throughput, loss, delay and network utilization.

References

1. Postel, J.: Transaction Control Protocol. DDN Network Information Center. RFC-793 (1981)
2. Stevens, W.R.: TCP/IP illustrated, vol. 1. Addision Wesley Company (1994)

3. Thompson, K., Miller, G.J., Wilder, R.: Wide Area Internet Traffic Patterns and Characteristics. IEEE Network 11, 10–23 (1997)
4. Ranjan, P., Abed, E.H., La, R.J.: Nonlinear Instabilities in TCP-RED. In: Proc. IEEE INFOCOMM, New York (2002)
5. La, R.J., Ranjan, P., Abed, E.H.: Nonlinearity of TCP and Instability with RED. In: Proc. SPIE ITCom, Boston, MA (2002)
6. Hashem, E.S.: Analysis of Random Drop for Gateway Congestion Control. Massachusetts Institute of Technology (1989)
7. Floyd, S., Jacobson, V.: Random early detection gateways for congestion avoidance. IEEE/ACM Trans Netw. 1, 397–413 (1993)
8. Head, E.C., Head, S.: A Survey on Congestion Control. Global Journal of Computer Science and Technology 9(5)(Ver 2.0), 82–87 (2010)
9. Ryu, S., Rump, C., Qiao, C.: Advances in Internet Congestion Control. IEEE Communications Surveys and Tutorials 5 (2003)
10. Shenker, S., Zhang, L., Clark, D.D.: Some Observations on The Dynamics of a Congestion Control Algorithm. ACM Computer Communication Review, 30–93 (1990)
11. Zhang, L., Shenker, S., Clark, D.D.: Observations on The Dynamics of a Congestion Control Algorithm: The Effects of Two Way Traffic. In: Proc. of ACM SIGCOMM 1991, Zurich, Switzerland, pp. 133–148 (1991)
12. Floyd, S., Jacobson, V.: On Traffic Phase Effects in Packet Switched Gateways. Internetworking Research and Experience 3, 115–156 (1992)
13. Mankin, A., Ramakrishnan, K.K.: Gateway Congestion Control Survey. IETF Performance and Congestion Control Working Group. RFC 1254, p. 21 (1991)
14. Ramakrishnan, K.K., Jain, R.: A Binary Feedback Scheme for Congestion Avoidance in Computer Networks. ACM Transactions on Computer Systems 8, 158–181 (1990)
15. Pingali, S., Tipper, D., Hammond, J.: The Performance of Adaptive Window Flow Controls in a Dynamic Load Environment, pp. 55–62 (1990)
16. Lin, D., Morris, R.: Dynamics of Random Early Detection. In: ACM SIGCOMM 1997, Cannes, France, pp. 127–137 (1997)
17. Feng, W., Kandlur, D., Saha, D., Shin, K.: A Self-Configuring RED Gateway. In: Proceedings of INFOCOM 1999, pp. 1320–1328 (1999)
18. Feng, W.: BLUE: A New Class of Active Queue Management Algorithms. University of Michigan (1999)
19. Vukadinovic, L., Trajkovic, L.: RED With Dynamic Thresholds For Improved Fairness. In: ACM Symposium on Appied Computing (2004)
20. Sun, L., Wang, L.: A Novel RED Scheme with Preferential Dynamic Threshold Deployment. Presented at the International Conference on Computational Intelligence Security Workshops (2007)
21. Jie, Y., Jun, L., Zhenming, L.: BF-RED: A Novel Algorithm for Improving Bandwidth Fairness of RED. In: Proceedings of the 2006 IEEE International Conference, ICNSC 2006, Ft. Lauderdale, FL, pp. 1001–1005 (2006)
22. Barrera, I.D., Arce, G.R., Bohacek, S.: Statistical approach for congestion control in gateway routers. Computer Networks 55(3), 572–582 (2011)
23. Welzl, M., Eddy, W.: Congestion Control in the RFC Series, IRTF, RFC-5783 (2010)
24. May, M., Bolot, J., Diot, C., Lyles, B.: Reasons Not to Deploy RED. In: IEEE/IFIP IWQoS, London, UK, pp. 260–262 (1999)
25. Christiansen, M.: Tuning RED for Web Traffic. IEEE/ACM Trans. Netw. 9, 249–264 (2001)

26. Le, L., Aikat, J., Jeffay, K., Smith, F.D.: The Effect of Active Queue Management on Web Performance. In: Proc. of SIGCOMM 2003, Karlsruhe, Germany, pp. 265–276 (2003)
27. Wang, H., Shin, K.: Refined Design of Random Early Detection Gatewways. Presented at the Global Telecommunication Conference-Globcom 1999 (1999)
28. Liu, F., Guan, Z.H., Wang, H.O.: Controlling bifurcations and chaos in TCPUD-PRED. Real World Applications 11(3), 1491–1501 (2010)
29. Wu, C., Yang, S.H.: The mechanism of adapting RED parameters to TCP traffic. Computer Communications 32(13-14), 1525–1530 (2009)
30. McCanne, S., Floyd, S.: NS-LBNL Network Simulator, http://www.nrg.ee.lbl.gov/ns
31. Pei, L.J., Mu, X.W., Wang, R.M., Yang, J.P.: Dynamics of the Internet TCPRED congestion control system. Real World Applications 12(2), 947–955 (2011)

A Holistic Survey of IT Governance in Thai Universities through IT Executive Perspectives

Kallaya Jairak and Prasong Praneetpolgrang

Doctor of Philosophy Program in Information Technology,
Information Science Institute, Sripatum University, Bangkok, Thailand 10900
ajkallaya@gmail.com, prasong.pr@spu.ac.th

Abstract. IT Governance (ITG) has increasingly become an important role of university governance. Recent research has focused on the finding of effective approaches for improving ITG in the university. Similar to the focal point of Thai universities, IT executives need the progressive direction for ITG. Consequently, the objective of this research is to explore the various aspects of ITG in Thai universities by surveying. The questionnaires were distributed to 117 IT executives from 117 universities and the response rate was 50.4%. In summary, the results reveal that ITG in Thai universities were in the initial stage and IT executives were not familiar with the ITG principles. The other problems and obstacles in ITG implementation were also criticized in this research. In addition, the realized gap for using ITG performance measurement by comparing between public and private universities were also reviewed and discussed in this paper.

Keywords: IT governance, IT governance performance measurement, IT governance obstacles, Thai universities.

1 Introduction

IT Governance (ITG) has been identified as a vital issue in the successful of IT business strategic alignment. In [1], Weill and Ross performed the international survey by asking 256 commercial and non-commercial organizations from 23 countries, covering America, Europe and Asia Pacific. They found a strong relationship between corporate performance and ITG implementation. Furthermore, their finding also revealed that the organizations which performed ITG could generate profit up to 20% compared with non-ITG. Other studies have also addressed the important of ITG in several industries, including banking, health care, and public sectors [2, 3, 4]. However, there is a limited amount of research concerning the ITG practices in university.

In university, the staffs use IT to support learning activities, research, and management. Then, they need an effective strategy for controlling, governing and managing IT. In a recent study, Creasey [5] discovered a positive relation between effective of ITG and organizational performance in higher education. Therefore, ITG also plays a vital role in university.

A. Abd Manaf et al. (Eds.): ICIEIS 2011, Part II, CCIS 252, pp. 435–447, 2011.
© Springer-Verlag Berlin Heidelberg 2011

In Thailand, there are very few studies on ITG for Thai universities. Consequently, our research aims to explore a various aspects of ITG in Thai universities. The research questions in this study are: what is the status of ITG in Thai universities, what is the ITG performance measure which the IT executives give respect, how frequency they use it, and what are the obstacles in ITG implementation.

The rest of this paper is organized as follows. First, in section 2, we provide the basic concepts and theoretical background of ITG. In section 3, we describe the measurement development and data collection that performed in this research. Then, the data analysis and results are presented in section 4, which consists of four subsections: 1) Overview of governing IT in Thai universities, 2) ITG awareness, 3) ITG performance measurement, and 4) Obstacles of ITG implementation in Thai universities. Section 5 provides a brief conclusion. And lastly, the final section provides a discussion of research limitation and key directions for future research.

2   Theoretical and Concept Background of IT Governance

In the following subsections, previous studies related to the definition of ITG, background of Thai university governance, and measurement of ITG performance, are reviewed and discussed.

2.1 The Definition of IT Governance

After reviewing research on IT Governance (ITG), we have found that the approximate definition of ITG was described by Loh and Venkatrama in 1992, and Henderson and Venkatrama in 1993. They identified the meaning of ITG from the mechanism of using IT in full capacity. At that time, the word ITG was not remarkable until the year 1997 when Sambamurthy and Zmud in 1999 mentioned the word "IS Governance Framework". After that in academic article, this definition has been adapted to "IT Governance frameworks" [6]. Recently, many organizations and some researchers have defined various meaning of ITG for examples:

IT Governance Institute (ITGI): IT governance is an integral part of enterprise governance and consists of the leadership and organizational structures and processes that ensure that the organization's IT sustains and extends the organization's strategies and objectives [7].

Weill and Ross: IT Governance is specifying the decision rights and accountability frameworks to encourage desirable behavior in the use of IT [1].

Grembergen: IT Governance is the organizational capacity exercised by the board, executive management and IT management to control the formulation and implementation of IT strategy and in this way ensuring the fusion of business and IT [8].

IT Governance definitions given above have been mentioned in many research. Briefly, ITG means controlling IT appropriate with business management process, strategy and goals of organization. All executive departments co-operate and make decision for specific efficiency and usefulness procedure. These definitions underline that ITG tasks are strategic alignment, value delivery, risk management, performance management and resource management [9].

2.2 Thai University Governance

Thai universities are governed by Office of the Higher Education Commission (OHEC) [10] and Office for National Education Standards and Quality Assessment (ONESQA) [11]. The role of OHEC is to maintain internal quality assurance [12] and ONESQA response to the external evaluation of quality assurance among all universities in Thailand [13]. Both organizations aim to create quality assurance system and mechanism to control, audit, and assess operations of institutions to comply with each institution's policies [12]. After the national education act was performed by OHEC and ONESQA, they announced Thailand university ranking for the first time in 2006 [14]. Based on OHEC and ONESQA approaches, we have found many indicators for governing university but there is still a lack of indicators for governing IT in university. Moreover, ITG indicators were not mentioned in ICT master plan for education that was announced by Ministry of Education [15].

2.3 Measurement of IT Governance Performance

Evaluation of the ITG performance has become an important issue for many organizations. The study in [16] proposed an idea for evaluating ITG performance by applying from the Balanced Scorecard (BSC) approach, which has been introduced by Kaplan and Norton in 1996 [17]. This approach consists of four perspectives: 1) Corporate contribution perspective, to present IT ability organization from the executive attitude; 2) Customer orientation perspective, to present IT ability from user; 3) Operational excellence perspective, to present IT process ability from IT management; and 4) Future orientation perspective, to present in point of preparation challenge in the future. These 4 perspectives are cause-effect relationships, which also illustrates the objectives of the measuring related to ITG scorecard perspective [18]. In 2005, Abu-Musa applied ITGBSC to investigate ITG performance in Saudi Arabia by surveying 500 organizations. 121 of them (24.5%) participated in this study and the results revealed that ITG performance can be measured properly by using ITGBSC [19].

3 Research Methodology

This research aims to explore the current stage and various perspectives on ITG in Thai universities. We have developed a questionnaire for gathering data from IT executives. The questionnaire consists of four parts. The first part asks about demographic information of the participants. The second part asks about current stage of ITG and awareness in their university. The third part explores the importance level and frequency of use in ITG performance measurement. Lastly, the fourth part asks about obstacles in ITG implementation.

3.1 Measurement Development

We have developed the survey measurement items from recent studies. The questionnaire consists of 4 parts. The first part of the questionnaire aims to collect demographic information. The questionnaire items in the second part are related to the followings ITG perspectives: 1) the current state of governing IT, 2) understanding in ITG principle, 3) the current state of ITG framework that use in Thai universities, and 4) ITG awareness. ITG frameworks for IT executive to consider are COBIT, ITIL, CMM/CMMI, COSO, ISO/IEC 38500, ISO/IEC 20000, ISO/IEC 27001 and Val IT.

In the third part, all 23 items are adapted from ITG Balanced Scorecard Model (ITGBSC) as introduced in [16]. The model consists of 4 categories, which are 1) Corporate contribution, 2) Future orientation, 3) Customer orientation, and 4) Operational excellence. This part aims to capture the current stage of using ITG performance indicators.

Finally, the fourth part is the questions about obstacles in ITG implementation, which may happen when university implement ITG framework in the future. Each item has been reviewed from the research that related to obstacles of ITG implementation. All items have been measured by using a negative word questions on a five-point Likert scale ranging from 1-lowest to 5-highest, the items of this part are shown in Table 1.

Table 1. Sources of literature for ITG obstacles

Items	Sources of literature
Lack of Clear ITG Principles	
Lack of clear ITG principles	[20][21][22]
Lack of IT management support	[20][23]
Lack of senior management support	[21]
Inadequate Support for Financial Resources	
Budget limitations for support ITG initiatives	[20][24]
Inadequate Stakeholder Involvement	
Difficulties in obtaining sufficient business involvement in ITG initiatives	[20][25]
Resistance to change	[22][25]
Resistance to acceptance of standard/policy	[20][25]
Inadequate Organizational Cultures	
Culture	[22]
Lack of Communication	
IT/Business lacks close relationships	[23][22]
Lack of Clear ITG framework and Tool	
Lack of method for selecting the ITG framework	[26]
Existing ITG frameworks are not appropriate with university	[27]

3.2 Data Collection

The questionnaires were sent to 117 public and private universities in Thailand. From the 59 responses received, 42 (71.2%) are public universities and 17 (28.8%) are private universities. Most of the respondents are IT directors (78%) and they have strong influence in IT budgeting, IT project planning, and IT strategic planning. Most of them (62.7%) have more than 5 years of experiences in IT management. Table 2 shows demographic information of the respondents.

Table 2. Demographic details (number of respondents = 59)

Subject	List	Frequency	Percentage (%)
Type of University	Public University	42	71.2
	Private University	17	28.8
Roles of the Respondents	Chief Information Officer (CIO)	9	15.3
	IT Director	46	78.0
	IT Project Manager	3	5.2
	IT Audit	1	1.7
Work Experience (yrs)	< 1	1	1.7
	1-3	12	20.3
	4-5	9	15.3
	> 5	37	62.7

4 Data Analysis and Results

This section presents data analysis and research results. Descriptive statistics have been used for data analysis. The comparison of ITG performance measurements perspective between public and private universities is also described in this section. The analysis is divided into 4 parts as follows.

4.1 Overview of Governing IT in Thai Universities

Table 3 shows that 32.2% of universities allocated about 1-5% from overall budget for IT. Most (76.3%) of respondents believed that the IT budget is not enough. More than a half of IT executives (54.2%), who govern IT in university, agreed that the stakeholders should understand the relationship between IT strategy and university strategy. Minority of IT executives (1%) stated that IT projects which have planned in each year misalignment with university strategy. Although, the respondents have stated that most of IT projects are well aligned with university strategy, there are still no explicit tools to confirm these results. 59.4% of respondents stated that they rarely emphasize the co-meeting for IT planning between IT and other departments. In addition, almost IT executives (78%) did not clear about ITG principles. This obstacle is the main factor that impact to ITG implementation [23].

Table 3. Governing IT and ITG understanding in Thai universities

Subject	List	Frequency	Percentage (%)
Budget (From the total university budget)	< 1%	5	8.5
	1- 5%	19	32.2
	5.01-10%	11	18.6
	> 10%	9	15.3
	Don't know	15	25.4
IT budget	Not enough	45	76.3
	Enough	14	23.7
Stakeholders should understand IT strategy and university strategy	Disagree	1	1.7
	Agree	32	54.2
	Strongly agree	26	44.1
Alignment between IT project and university strategy	Misalignment	1	1.7
	Some IT Project are aligned	23	39.0
	Mostly align	24	40.7
	All project are aligned	11	18.6
Co-meeting between IT and other departments	Never	8	13.6
	Sometime	27	45.8
	Always	24	40.6
Understanding ITG principles	Not at all	6	10.2
	Have heard but don't know	17	28.8
	Somewhat understand	23	39.0
	Fully understand	13	22.0

Currently, there are many frameworks that have different characteristics and each framework has its own standards. IT executives need to have a base understanding of ITG frameworks for appropriate selection and implementation in their university. Table 4 presents the cognitive levels of ITG frameworks that evaluated from IT executive self-assessment. The results show that the most well-known ITG framework is ITIL (40.7%), the second is COBIT and CMM/CMMI that obtained the same rate (32.2%), and the third is ISO/IEC 27001 (30.5%). Furthermore, most of IT executives are expertise in CMM/CMMI (10.2%). It is noteworthy that the respondents were not familiar with Val IT framework. This study also did not find any Val IT expert in Thai universities.

Table 4. The cognitive levels of IT executives in ITG frameworks

IT Governance Framework	Not at All	Have Head But Don't Know	Well-Know	Expert
		(%)		
COBIT	28.8	37.3	32.2	1.7
ITIL	35.6	18.6	40.7	5.1
CMM / CMMI	35.6	22.0	32.2	10.2
COSO	50.8	22.0	25.4	1.7
ISO/IEC 38500	50.8	33.9	13.6	1.7
ISO/IEC 20000	45.8	33.9	18.6	1.7
ISO/IEC 27001	44.1	22.0	30.5	3.4
Val IT	69.0	20.7	10.3	0.0

4.2 IT Governance Awareness

Table 5 illustrates the IT executive awareness in ITG. The results show that more than half of the IT executives have integrated ITG concept in IT master plan. 70% of them have specified ITG concept in mission (23.7%), project or activity (22.0%), strategy (16.9%), and vision (10.2%) respectively. Remarkable that 27.1% of respondents have not specified ITG concept in IT master plan. For ITG planning perspective, the results demonstrate that more than a half of respondents (59.2%) did not implement ITG frameworks in their university. More than 90% of IT executives pointed out that ITG is necessary and important. Furthermore, 90% of them agreed that ITG frameworks should be developed along with the context of university.

Table 5. ITG awareness of IT executives in Thai universities

Subject	List	Frequency	Percentage (%)
The section of IT Master Plan that integrated with ITG	Strategy	10	16.9
	Vision	6	10.2
	Project /Activity	13	22.0
	Mission	14	23.7
	Not specified	16	27.1
ITG Planning	No plan	3	5.1
	No plan but interesting	23	38.9
	Have plan but not implemented yet	9	15.2
	During implement	20	33.8
	Already implement	4	6.8
The need and important of ITG	Disagree	3	5.1
	Agree	23	39.0
	Strongly agree	33	55.9
Development ITG in the context of university	Disagree	1	1.7
	Agree	45	77.3
	Strongly agree	13	22.0

According to the results in Table 5, almost half of IT executives (49%) have established ITG plan in their university. Consequently, Table 6 presents an overview of ITG frameworks that university decided to use in their ITG plan. The IT executives have selected the following ITG frameworks that most embedded in ITG plan and also actual implementation from COBIT, ITIL, ISO/IEC 27001, COSO respectively. However, ISO/IEC 38500 and Val IT are only the two frameworks that are not mentioned in actual implementation within Thai universities.

Table 6. The stage of ITG frameworks implementation

IT Governance Framework	Do not have ITG Plan	Have Planned But Not Implemented Yet	During Implement or Already Implement
	(%)		
COBIT	69.5	22.0	8.5
ITIL	69.5	20.3	10.2
CMM / CMMI	74.6	22.0	3.4
COSO	72.9	23.7	3.4
ISO/IEC 38500	81.4	18.6	0.0
ISO/IEC 20000	76.3	22.0	1.7
ISO/IEC 27001	72.2	22.0	6.8
Val IT	84.7	15.3	0.0

4.3 IT Governance Performance Measurement

The results in Table 7 are divided into 2 parts. Part one is an importance of performance measures that the respondents can choose one of the following options: 1) VI = "Very Important", 2) I = "Important", and 3) NI = "Not Important". Part two is a using frequency that the respondents can also select one of the following: 1) AU = "Always Used", 2) SU = "Sometime Used", and 3) NU= "Never Used".

Corporate contribution: The results show that the vast majority of the respondents (>90%) believed that all indexes under this category should be stated in "Important" and "Very Important". However, less than half of the respondents (between 29.3 to 44.8%) stated that the following indexes are "Always Used": (1.1) aligning IT with business objectives, (1.2) delivering value, (1.3) managing costs, (1.4) managing risks and (1.5) achieving inter-organization. While half of respondents (between 46.6 to 50.0%) reported that those indicators are "Sometime Used". Furthermore, a few of them (between 8.6 to 19.0%) confirmed that it had never been measured within their university.

Future orientation: This category is related to building the foundation for future delivery of IT value within the university. The results reveal that (2.1) attracting and retaining people with key competencies is the most important performance measurement under this category. However, the statistics reveal that only 31% of respondents rated as "Always Used" for this indicator. For other indicators, the majority of respondents rated the following indicators as "Important": (2.3) building a climate of empowerment and responsibility (51.7%), (2.4) measuring/rewarding individual and team performance (65.5%), and (2.5) capturing knowledge to improve performance (58.6%).

Customer orientation: The results reveal that most of the respondents considered (3.1) customer satisfaction (50.0%), (3.3) delivering good service (60.3%), and (3.4) developing good service (62.1%) are "Very Important". While 62.1% of the respondents rated the (3.2) demonstrating competitive costs as "Important". For frequency of use in this category, the indicators are mostly addressed in "Sometime Used" except for (3.1) customer satisfaction that is stated in "Always Used".

Operational excellence: This category is one of the perspectives from performance measure in ITG Balanced Scorecard. Our study has found that many of respondents generally stated that the following indexes are "Important": (4.1) maturity internal IT process (67.2%), (4.2) managing operational service performance (60.3%), (4.3) achieving economies of scale (70.7%), (4.6) understanding business unit strategies (55.2%), (4.7) proposing and validating for enabling solutions (75.9%), (4.8) understanding the emerging technologies (62.1%), and (4.9) developing organization architecture (63.3%). Furthermore, for frequency of use, respondents rated as "Sometime Used" in this category.

Table 7. Comparative between importance and frequency of use in ITG performance measures

IT Governance Performance Measures	Importance of Performance Measures			Frequency of Use Performance Measures		
	VI (%)	I (%)	NI (%)	AU (%)	SU (%)	NU (%)
1. Corporate Contribution						
1.1 Align IT with Business Objectives	43.1	51.7	5.2	31.0	50.0	19.0
1.2 Deliver Value	46.6	50.0	3.4	34.5	50.0	15.5
1.3 Manager Costs	37.9	56.9	5.2	29.3	48.3	22.4
1.4 Manage Risks	44.8	51.7	3.4	41.4	44.8	13.8
1.5 Achieve Inter-Organization	51.7	44.8	3.4	44.8	46.6	8.6
2. Future Orientation						
2.1 Attract and Retain People with Key Competencies	65.5	34.5	0.0	31.0	58.6	10.3
2.2 Focus on Professional Learning and Development	58.6	41.4	0.0	36.2	51.7	12.1
2.3 Build a Climate of Empowerment and Responsibility	48.3	51.7	0.0	32.8	53.4	13.8
2.4 Measure/Reward Individual and Team Performance	34.5	65.5	0.0	29.3	56.9	13.8
2.5 Capture Knowledge to Improve Performance	39.7	58.6	1.7	25.9	60.3	13.8
3. Customer Orientation						
3.1 Customer Satisfaction	50.0	50.0	0.0	55.2	39.7	5.2
3.2 Demonstrate Competitive Costs	25.9	62.1	12.1	17.2	53.4	29.3
3.3 Delivery Good Service	60.3	39.7	0.0	37.9	51.7	10.3
3.4 Develop Good Service	62.1	37.9	0.0	34.5	55.2	10.3

Table 7. (*Continued*)

4. Operational Excellence						
4.1 Mature Internal IT Processes	31.0	67.2	1.7	22.4	62.1	15.5
4.2 Manager Operational Service Performance	37.9	60.3	1.7	29.3	53.4	17.2
4.3 Achieve Economies of Scale	24.1	70.7	5.2	13.8	53.4	32.8
4.4 Build Standard, Reliable Technology Platforms	50.0	50.0	0.0	25.9	51.7	22.4
4.5 Deliver Successful IT Projects	53.4	46.6	0.0	36.2	53.4	10.3
4.6 Understand Business Unit Strategies	44.8	55.2	0.0	31.0	58.6	10.3
4.7 Propose and Validate Enabling Solutions	37.9	62.1	0.0	19.0	62.1	19.0
4.8 Understand Emerging Technologies	37.9	62.1	0.0	17.2	63.8	19.0
4.9 Develop Organization Architecture	37.9	63.3	1.7	17.2	60.3	22.4

Fig. 1 illustrates the gap between important of ITG performance measure and frequency of using ITG performance measure by comparing between "Very Importance" and "Always Used" in public and private universities. In public group, all indicators that rated as "Very Important" but not rated as "Always Used" are as follows: 2.1, 3.3, 3.4, and 4.4. However, 1.4 and 4.7 are two indicators that have no gap between these conflicts. We also have found the significant gap of indicators in private group that IT executives rated as "Very Important" but not rated as "Always Used" are as follows: 1.1, 1.5, 2.1, 2.2, 2.3, 3.3, 3.4, 4.4, 4.5, and 4.9. According to above results, we can conclude that the public university group has more alignment between important of performance measure and frequency of using performance measure than private university group.

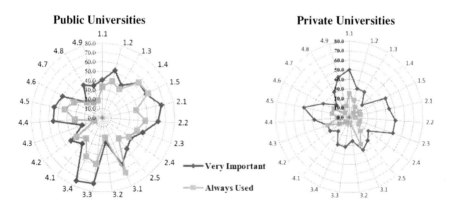

Fig. 1. A Comparison of performance measurement between "Very Important" items and "Always Used" items

4.4 Obstacles of ITG Implementation in Thai Universities

In this section, IT executives criticized many obstacles which influence to implementation of ITG in their university. According to Fig. 2, we have found that lack of clear ITG principles, budget limitation and lack of method for selecting the ITG framework are the major obstacles for ITG implementation. The obstacle with higher score represents a major priority that should be discussed in order to mitigate the impediment of ITG adoption in Thai universities.

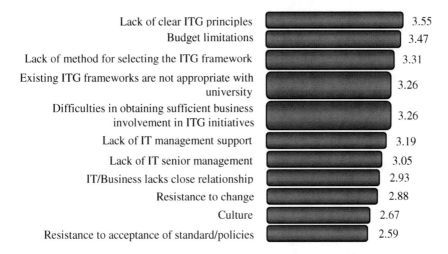

Lack of clear ITG principles	3.55
Budget limitations	3.47
Lack of method for selecting the ITG framework	3.31
Existing ITG frameworks are not appropriate with university	3.26
Difficulties in obtaining sufficient business involvement in ITG initiatives	3.26
Lack of IT management support	3.19
Lack of IT senior management	3.05
IT/Business lacks close relationship	2.93
Resistance to change	2.88
Culture	2.67
Resistance to acceptance of standard/policies	2.59

Fig. 2. The obstacles of ITG implementation in Thai universities

5 Conclusion

The objective of this research is to explore the various aspects of ITG in Thai universities by surveying from IT executives. The research questions in this study are: what is the status of ITG in Thai universities, what is the ITG performance measure which the IT executives give respect, how frequency they use it, and what are the obstacles in ITG implementation.

About half (50.4%) of the respondents have been participated in this survey. We have found that ITG status in Thai universities is in the initial stage and not all IT projects can be aligned with university strategy. Although, there are many ITG performance measurements that IT executives criticize very importance, many indicators are not used in association with this weight. This means there are still many gaps that need to be translated into ITG practice. Thai universities still have many obstacles in ITG implementation that consist of: 1) almost IT executives are not clear in ITG principle, 2) limited budget for starting ITG, 3) lack of comprehension in ITG framework concepts, and 4) ITG frameworks are not appropriate with their university context. Our results also show that IT executives have only sometime co-meeting for IT project planning. Furthermore, IT executives also suggest that Thai universities should have to develop their own ITG framework that can be accepted from stakeholders.

Even though, ITG improvement in universities has many obstacles, it can be solved and improved by co-operation from stakeholders. Even if this research is still a primary survey, it can be an important starting point to extend ITG research for Thai universities.

6 Limitation and Future Research

ITG research in Thai universities is in an initial stage, it primarily focuses on analyzing information concerning among Thai universities. Since the application of ITG in Thailand is relatively new, many of them have limited experience in ITG performance measurement. Therefore, survey questions especially in part 3 have not been completely for measuring ITG performance.

This study has identified that existing ITG frameworks are not appropriate for universities and lack of method for ITG framework selection. Further research therefore needs to explore effective approaches to suggest Thai universities address the suitable ITG frameworks.

References

1. Weill, P., Ross, J.W.: IT governance: How top performers manage IT decision rights for superior results. Harvard Business School Press, Boston (2004)
2. Lemus, S.M., Pino, F.J., Velthius, M.P.: Towards a Model for Information Technology Governance applicable to the Banking Sector. In: 5th Iberian Conference on Information Systems and Technologies, pp. 1–6. Santiago de Compostela (2010)
3. Wilkin, C.L., Riddett, J.: IT governance challenges in a large not-for-profit healthcare organization: The role of intranets. Electronic Commerce Research 9(4), 351–374 (2009)
4. Nfuka, E.N., Rusu, L., Johannesson, P., Mutagahywa, B.: The State of IT Governance in Organizations from the Public Sector in a Developing Country. In: 42nd Hawaii International Conference on System Sciences, Big Island, Hawaii, pp. 1–12 (2009)
5. Creasey, W.: The Influences of Information Technology Organizational Performance in Higher Education. Doctoral Dissertation, the Faculty of the Department of Educational Leadership, East Carolina University (2008)
6. Brown, A., Grant, G.: Framing the Frameworks: A Review of IT Governance Research. Communication of the AIS 15, 696–712 (2005)
7. IT Governance Institute,
   http://www.itgi.org/template_ITGIa166.html?
   Section=About_IT_Governance1&Template=/ContentManagement/
   HTMLDisplay.cfm&ContentID=19657
8. Grembergen, W.V.: IT Governance and its Mechanisms. In: 38th Annual Hawaii International Conference on System Science (2005)
9. Burtscher, C., Manwani, S., Remenyi, D.: Towards A Conceptual Map of IT Governance: A Review of Current Academic and Practitioner Thinking. In: UK Academy for Information Systems Conference (2009)
10. Office of the Higher Education Commission (OHEC),
    http://www.inter.mua.go.th/main2/index.php
11. Office for National Education Standards and Quality Assessment (ONESQA),
    http://www.onesqa.or.th/en/home/index.php

12. Manual for Internal Quality Assurance for Higher Education Institution,
    `http://www.mua.go.th/users/bhes/bhes2/QA_Training/`
    `manual_eng/manual_qa_13_03_51.pdf`
13. Manual for External Quality Assurance for University,
    `http://www.onesqa.or.th/th/profile/`
    `index.php?SystemMenuID=1&SystemModuleKey=185`
14. Thai Top Ranked Universities,
    `http://www.sut.ac.th/Engineering/metal/articles/Uranking.html`
15. Ministry of Education Thailand,
    `http://www.moe.go.th/moe/th/news/detail.php?NewsID=815&Key=news19`
16. Grembergen, W.V., De Haes, S.: Measuring and Improving IT Governance Through the Balanced Scorecard. Information Systems Control Journal 2 (2005)
17. Grembergen, W.V., De Haes, S.: Enterprise Governance of Information Technology: Achieving Strategic Alignment and Value. Springer Science+Business Media LLC (2009)
18. Grembergen, W.V., De Haes, S.: Implementing Information Technology Governance: Models, Practices and Cases. IGI Publishing, Hershey (2008)
19. Abu-Musa, A.A.: Exploring Information Technology Governance (ITG) in Developing Countries: An Empirical Study. The International Journal of Digital Accounting Research 7(13), 71–117 (2007)
20. Lee, C.H., Lee, J.H., Park, J.S., Jeong, K.Y.: A Study of the Causal Relationship between IT Governance Inhibitors and Its Success in Korea Enterprises. In: 41st Annual Hawaii International Conference on System Sciences (2008)
21. Weill, P., Ross, J.W.: IT Governance on One Page. Technical report. MIT Sloan School of Management, Cambridge, USA (2006)
22. Bhattacharjya, J., Chang, V.: Adoption and Implementation of IT Governance: Cases from Australian Higher Education. In: 17th Australasian Conference on Information Systems, Adelaide, South Australia (2006)
23. Luftman, J.N., Papp, R., Brier, T.: Enablers and Inhibitors of Business-IT Alignment. Communications of the Association for Information Systems 1, 1–33 (1999)
24. Guldentops, E., Grembergen, W.V., De Haes, S.: Control and Governance Maturity Survey: Establishing a Reference Benchmark and a Self-Assessment Tool. Information Systems Control Journal 6, 32–35 (2002)
25. ISACA.: New Thought Leadership on IT Governance in Practice: Insight from leading CIOs,
    `http://www.isaca.org/About-ISACA/Press-room/`
    `News-Releases/2007/Pages/New-Thought-Leadership-on-IT-`
    `Governance-in-Practice-Insight-From-Leading-CIOs.aspx`
26. Fasanghari, M., NasserEslani, F., Naghavi, M.: IT Governance Standard Selection Based on Two Phase Clustering Method. In: 4th IEEE International Conference on Networked Computing and Advanced Information Management, Korea (2008)
27. Fernández, A., Llorens, F.: An IT Governance Framework for Universities in Spain. Research Report, Universidad de correos 99, 03080 Alicante Apain (2009)

The Development of a New Capability Maturity Model for Assessing Trust in B2C e-Commerce Services

Rath Jairak and Prasong Praneetpolgrang

Doctor of Philosophy Program in Information Technology,
Information Science Institute, Sripatum University, Bangkok, Thailand 10900
rathjairak@gmail.com, prasong.pr@spu.ac.th

Abstract. Trust has been identified as a vital key for e-Commerce business success. Therefore, trust issues should be embedded along with e-Commerce development process. This research aims to propose a new approach for assessing both trust and quality improvement in e-Commerce services. This proposed model is called Trust Capability Maturity Model (TCMM). TCMM is established based on the following concepts: 1) trust formation process, 2) ISO 9126 standard, 3) SERVQUAL, and 4) Delone and Mclean's IS success model. The benefits of using TCMM are twofold: one, customers can measure the level of trust by creating their own vendor profile; two, B2C vendors can construct their own trust development programs. This model consists of 55 initial criteria for five maturity levels. B2C vendors can develop their trust capability from one stage to another by achieving the performance tasks in each maturity level. Future research will focus on the empirical validation of TCMM framework.

Keywords: Trust capability maturity model, e-Commerce services, Quality improvement, Trust attributes.

1 Introduction

Nowadays, service activities play a crucial role in driving economic growth. The service functions are complicated and associated with business activities in everyday life such as banking, communications, transport and health care. Service providers, which aim to succeed in providing a high quality of services, require interdisciplinary knowledge to walk through [1]. In traditional economy, business cycle has been focused on supply-side approach that aims to deliver products with high quality standards. Unlike traditional cycle, business services are shifting from supply-side strategy to demand-driven strategy. Customer satisfaction is a key to drive revenue in demand-driven business [2]. The phenomenon of demand-side effect is widespread in the world of business services and this is not an exception for e-Commerce services. It is widely accepted that effective e-Commerce application alone cannot bring consumer trust and gain competitive advantage in this business [3, 4, 5].

Preferable services in e-Commerce have moved beyond the scope of system and industry standards, doing e-Commerce business is more associated with customer experience and perception management. The proper way to respond to this clue is to reach the balance between operational efficiency and customer satisfaction.

A. Abd Manaf et al. (Eds.): ICIEIS 2011, Part II, CCIS 252, pp. 448–462, 2011.
© Springer-Verlag Berlin Heidelberg 2011

If customers perceive a website as the best destination for delivering high quality of products and services, they will put their trust and do not hesitate to come back to the same website. Thus, the concept of quality improvement for gaining customer trust is very important in e-Commerce services.

Both Capability Maturity Model (CMM) and Capability Maturity Model Integration (CMMI) are widely accepted as a powerful tool for process improvement in the software and related industries. In fact, the process for each business has its own nature. Therefore, the guidance in both CMM and CMMI do not map one to one with all types of business [6]. It means that when we aim to expand the concept of CMM and CMMI to other business areas, we should apply for a new maturity model that compromise in other specific areas. In a Business-to-Customer (B2C) model, business owners build their website to provide customers with products and services online. A prime example of B2C website is Amazon.com. Both small and large firms around the world can start B2C website with a minimum budget but it is hard to gain trust from their customers. Trust is mentioned as a prerequisite for e-Commerce interaction and also acts as a vital key to success in this business [4, 7].

As we mentioned early, e-Commerce business is not only concerned with software operation but also with trusted support in service activities. Following this aspect, this paper aims to propose a new maturity model for assessing trust in e-Commerce services. The proposed model is developed from the following concepts: 1) trust formation process, 2) ISO 9126 standard, 3) SERVQUAL, and 4) Delone and Mclean's IS success model. This emerging maturity model is flexible enough to accommodate both customers and online vendors. Customers can use our proposed model to measure the level of trust in online vendors, and B2C vendors can specify their own development of trust from initial assessment tool.

The rest of this paper is organized as follows. Section 2, we review recent research on topics related to trust building process and quality improvement in e-Commerce services. In section 3, we identify the key components in Trust Capability Maturity Model (TCMM) and briefly describe how to implement TCMM framework. In the last section, we summarize this work and point out key directions for future research.

2   Literature Review

In this section, we review related research and focus on the important issues that support for the development of TCMM in the context of B2C e-Commerce services.

2.1 Maturity Models for Process Improvement

The Capability Maturity Model (CMM) [8] has been accepted as a practical model for product and process improvement in software industry. The principle of CMM is applicable not only to software development process, but also to other process improvement areas such as workforce performance [9], e-Learning capability [10], and data governance [11]. The original CMM and other examples of maturity models are described in Table 1.

Table 1. The examples of maturity models for process improvement

Maturity Model	Target	Description
Capability Maturity Model (CMM) [8]	Focus on software process improvement.	*Five Levels :* 1. **Initial:** still ad-hoc and lack of disiplined procedures in workflow project. 2. **Repeatable:** software project is stable and earlier success can be repeated. 3. **Defined:** standard software process is well defined and documented. 4. **Managed:** standard process can be predicted by quantitative measurement. 5. **Optimized:** continuous process improvement to prevent the occurrence of defects.
People Capability Maturity Model (P-CMM) [9]	Focus on human capital development.	*Five Levels :* 1. **Initial:** lack of workforce management. 2. **Managed:** manager is responsible for workforce management. 3. **Defined:** workforce strategy is aligned with business strategy. 4. **Predictable:** applied quantitative control. 5. **Optimizing:** continuous improvements at both the individual and workgroup levels.
e-Learning Maturity Model (eMM) [10]	Focus on e-Learning capability improvement.	*Five Levels :* 1. **Initial:** ad-hoc processes. 2. **Planned:** clear objectives for e-Learning. 3. **Defined:** defined process for development. 4. **Managed:** ensuring the quality of both the e-Learning resources and student learning outcomes. 5. **Optimizing:** continual improvement.
Data Governance Maturity Level [11]	Focus on data governance development.	*Five Levels :* 1. **Initial:** no policy setting and environment for data management is unstable. 2. **Managed:** defined data governance programs. 3. **Defined:** established standard process for data governance. 4. **Quantitatively Managed:** defined a set of metrics to monitor the data governance performance. 5. **Optimizing:** established policy enforcement for data governance programs.

CMM is an initiative to establish a continuous improvement programs in various target areas. The maturity model based on CMM concept is described by separating the evolutionary stages into 5 levels. The details for each level will vary depending on the context of development goals, as described in Table 1. Generic details for each maturity level can be summarized briefly as follows. At level 1, the exact configuration does not exist in the workflow process. At level 2, the procedures are established to qualify for the process improvement programs. At level 3, the standards for process improvement have been defined. At level 4, the standard processes can be specified by the quantitative measurement. Lastly, at level 5, the continuous improvement programs have been established. Under this generic setting, we can extend maturity idea to other development areas more expediently.

When considering process improvement in e-Commerce services, trust issues should be embedded in e-Commerce development process due to the fact that customers may perceive risk even when they use a system that has already been secured [12]. While some customers are looking for more efficient e-Commerce websites, many also want to meet the trusted websites that they can rely on. If website managers can understand customers' trust formation process in e-Commerce services, they will also develop a trusted process in their website.

2.2 Trust Formation Process in e-Commerce Services

It is widely agreed that lack of trust in online vendors is the important barrier to obstruct internet users to exchange personal information or money online [13, 14]. Trust is a prerequisite for e-Commerce interaction and also acts as a key to success in this business [4, 7]. Trust can be formed through customer experiences and perceptions of website quality [14, 15]. In e-Commerce environments, the business transaction can be divided into three phases: 1) information phase, 2) agreement phase, and 3) settlement phase [16], as shown in Fig. 1.

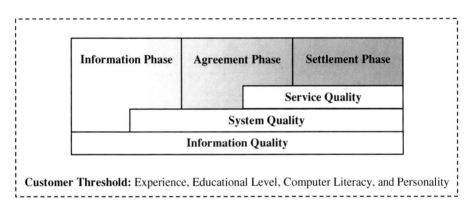

Fig. 1. Trust formation model in e-Commerce services

Information Phase. In this phase, customers have no purchasing experience with a target website, trust formation is perceived from information quality, design quality, website reputation, and company background [16, 17, 18, 19]. Customers begin to evaluate the website from information quality such as accuracy, completeness, and up-to-date information. After consideration of all available information, customers will continue to evaluate other vital components including accessibility, usability, privacy, and security [18, 20]. If customers perceive that the website can operate well, they will consider move to the next phase.

Agreement Phase. This phase is also called as negotiation phase [16]. In this phase, customers have already made their decision to purchase and the expectations will rise after payment and shipping details are confirmed. The system quality is a major requirement in agreement phase, especially for security in the transaction process [21]. The customers expect that their personal information and business transaction are protected, as well as orders are delivered on time as promised.

Settlement Phase. In the last phase, customers determine the quality of physical or virtual products that have already been delivered and they will decide whether or not to repurchase new items from the same website. The possibility of repurchase is due to the following vendor competencies: 1) the ability to deliver products and services as promised, 2) the willingness to help customers and provide prompt services, 3) the ability to inspire customer confidence, and 4) the ability to customize for personal needs [19]. Thus, the quality of services is the key to success in this phase.

In addition, factors that affect online purchasing intention depend not only on website quality, but also on customer threshold that shown in Fig. 1 [14, 15]. Trust is built gradually through personal allowance threshold during the initial relationship. After forming initial trust, customers become more familiar with online shopping process and the value of the website is perceived from the quality outcomes [17, 19].

2.3 Quality Aspects in e-Commerce Services

A purchasing process in e-Commerce stores generally has the same structure. The process begins with user login, followed by adding preferred items in a virtual basket. And lastly, the process ends with payment and delivery method selection. A sequence of actions in e-Commerce application is described in Fig. 2.

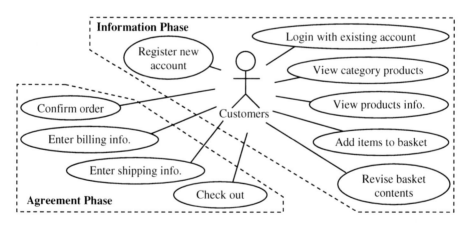

Fig. 2. Use case diagram for e-Commerce application [22]

According to Fig. 2, the workflow process in e-Commerce application has support for information and agreement phase but that does not cover all activities in the settlement phase. Because the nature of settlement phase is more associated with off-line interaction such as after-sales services, guarantee claims and help desk [16]. This argument is concurrent with the concept of measuring e-Commerce success in [21, 23]. The success of e-Commerce services can be achieved not only from the performance of application, but also from the perceived quality of after-sales services [17, 24]. Thus, the major aspects of quality in the context of e-Commerce are information quality, system quality, and service quality.

Information Quality. The role of information is intended to present high quality content for describing the details of products and services and also to provide support for decision making process [18, 20]. The most common dimensions for information quality are accuracy, currency, relevance, completeness, and understandability [25]. Table 2 provides a summary of the proposed dimensions for information quality.

Table 2. Dimensions of information quality

Dimensions	Description / Measure	Sources
Accuracy	Correctness and precision of information	[19, 21, 23, 25, 26]
Currency	Information is up-to-date and available on time	[19, 21, 23, 25, 26]
Relevance	Concurrent with the interests of consumer	[20, 21, 23, 25]
Completeness	Sufficient information for customer to make informed purchasing decision	[20, 21, 23, 25, 26]
Understandability	Easy to understand and present in a proper format	[19, 21, 25, 26]

System Quality. Based on software quality which is defined in ISO 9126 standard [27] and recent studies in [19, 28], we have found that functionality, usability, and reliability are emphasized as three main key dimensions to describe system quality aspect. According to ISO 9126, security and privacy are identified as a subdimension in functionality [27, 29]. However, protection of personal information and business transaction is very vital issue in e-Commerce business and should be excluded for consideration as the separate dimension [21, 26]. Furthermore, we extend adaptablity and multimedia capability to complete for all dimensions in system quality [20, 26, 30]. The proposed dimensions for system quality are summarized in Table 3.

Table 3. Dimensions of system quality

Dimensions	Description / Measure	Sources
Functionality	Capability of software to maintain suitability and accuracy in interactive functions	[19, 27, 28, 29]
Usability	Capability of software to maintain end-user interaction	[19, 25, 27, 28, 29]
Reliability	Dependability of software operation	[19, 25, 27, 28]
Adaptability	Changing demands for personalization	[20, 21, 23, 25, 26]
Security and Privacy	Protection of personal information and business transaction	[21, 26, 27, 29]
Multimedia Capability	Proper use of multimedia features	[20, 26, 30]

Service Quality. The service quality measurement scale (SERVQUAL) has been widely used within various industries over the past 20 years [31]. This traditional scale can also be extended to describe the quality of services in e-Commerce [24, 25, 26]. The SERVQUAL instrument consists of 22 items on five dimensions including tangible, reliability, responsiveness, assurance, and empathy [32]. Under e-Commerce context, tangible can be addressed through website interaction [30, 33], which is already included in the system quality. Thus, the proposed dimensions for service quality are described in four dimensions as shown in Table 4.

Table 4. Dimensions of service quality

Dimensions	Description / Measure	Sources
Reliability	The ability of online vendor to deliver products and services on time as promised	[19, 31, 32, 33]
Responsiveness	The willingness of online vendor to help customers and provide prompt services	[19, 31, 32, 33]
Assurance	The ability of employees to build customers confidence	[19, 31, 32, 33]
Empathy	The ability of online vendor to provide personalized services to the customers	[19, 31, 32, 33]

2.4 Trust Attributes in e-Commerce Website

Trust attributes in e-Commerce context are defined as a set of attributes that establish trust relationships between customers and online vendors, which is the combination of application-based factors (information and system quality) and services-based factor (service quality) [34, 35]. Trust attributes should be associated with consumer trust and can be observed within the website [34]. After considering the relevant research on e-Commerce measurement model, we have found that there are many assessment tools and guidelines that can be used to assess the capability of online vendors [23, 27, 28, 31, 34, 36, 38, 39].

B2C online vendors can use the ISO 9126 standard as a guideline to evaluate their e-Commerce application, but this guideline does not provide assessment methods for offline interaction in the settlement phase. To bridge this gap, online vendors can apply SERVQUAL to measure their capability for improving the quality of services · (reliability, responsiveness, assurance, and empathy). However, we believe that the use of two different approaches to evaluate interrelated issues is not proper discipline for the assessment process. Another way to measure the quality of online vendors is to utilize Delone and Mclean's IS success model [23].

Recent research in [19, 23, 24, 25, 26] has shown that Delone and Mclean's IS success model is congruous with all aspects of trust building process in e-Commerce services. Following the Delone and Mclean framework, this study proposes a practical idea for measuring the stages of trust development with identify from trust attributes in the quality aspects (information quality, system quality, and service quality). Trust attributes are the key elements to identify trusted process in e-Commerce services. The evidences for approval of trust attributes in each quality dimension are described in Table 5 through 7.

Table 5. Trust attributes for information quality

Dimensions	Evidences for approval of trust attributes
Accuracy	I1: Ensure that the company profile contained in the website is similar to information provided in the trusted third-party websites such as Alexa.com, Whois.com, and NetworkSolution.com. The approval for accuracy consists of three items [34, 36] which are as follows: I1-1: Physical address I1-2: Telephone and fax number I1-3: E-mail address *Remark: The accuracy of information can also be embedded in other parts of the trust attributes. Therefore, we only emphasize the information that is necessary to determine the accuracy of online vendor profile.*
Currency	I2: Ensure that information provided on the website is kept up-to-date [25, 26, 29]. The approval is considered from two criteria as follows: I2-1: Update latest information. (Example scenario: update at least once every two days.) [25, 37] I2-2: Products and services available on the website are kept up-to-date. (Example scenario: update at lease 10 items that are appropriate for current market trends.)
Completeness	I3: Ensure that information available on the website is adequate for potential buyers [20, 25]. The criteria for approving completeness are as follows: I3-1: Provide purchase policies including purchase cancellation policy, return policy, shipping policy, and payment policy [34, 36, 37]. I3-2: Provide sufficient information to make a purchase decision (e.g., complete description, image availability, promotion campaign, product comparison) [28, 36, 37]. I3-3: Display expert and customer reviews for each products or services on the website [29, 36, 37]. I3-4: Offer campaigns for testing products or services.
Understand ability	I4: Ensure that information available on the website is easy to understand and present in a proper format [25, 26]. The criteria for approving understandability are listed as follows: I4-1: Webpage should be clean and clear with text and graphics [37, 38]. I4-2: Provide layout that is consistent in every pages on the website [37, 38, 39]. I4-3: Provide a site map for entire view on the website [29, 36, 39]. I4-4: Use concise and grammatically correct sentences to describe the products or services information [39]. I4-5: Text links or buttons should be clearly written and understandable [39]. I4-6: Provide FAQ and help features [29, 36].
Relevance	I5: Provide information that useful for purchasing decision and concurrent with the interests of consumer [25]. The criteria for approving relevance are as follows: I5-1: Allow customers to share their shopping experiences [16, 37]. I5-2: Provide a proper mechanism for helping customers to find trusted reviews in the open community [16, 29, 34, 37]. I5-3: Provide a proper mechanism for price comparison [36, 37]. I5-4: Provide personal-customized content such as custom search and personal product recommendation [37]. I5-5: Support for multiple language [29, 36].

Table 6. Trust attributes for system quality

Dimensions	Evidences for approval of trust attributes
Functionality	S1: Identify the capability of e-Commerce application to maintain suitability and accuracy in interactive functions [33]. The criteria for approving functionality are listed as follows: S1-1: Require only information that is meaningful for user registration [16, 38]. S1-2: Provide capability to manage customer's account [36]. S1-3: Provide capability to add, delete, edit, and recalculate the quantity of items [28, 36]. S1-4: Recalculate with precision after adding, modifying, and deleting items [28]. S1-5: Provide capability to save items for later use [28]. S1-6: Provide capability to present the inventory information [36].
Usability	S2: Identify the capability of software to maintain end-user interaction [28]. The criteria for approving usability are identified as follows: S2-1: Allow to browse the website without logging in [37]. S2-2: Shopping cart icon/lable is easy to recognize [28]. S2-3: Provide shopping cart help and FAQ for visitors [28]. S2-4: Provide effective navigation structure. (Example scenario: users can locate specific information that they need in 3 clicks [36].) S2-5: Provide effective searching mechanism. (Example scenario: more than 90% of the target products can be found.) S2-6: Provide support for both quick search and advanced search [29].
Reliability	S3: Ensure that the operation of e-commerce application is dependable [25, 28]. The criteria for approving reliability are as follows: S3-1: e-Commerce application is always available. (Provide 99% uptime during the test scenarios.) [28, 39] S3-2: Testing for broken/invalid links. (Provide 99% error free rate during the test scenarios.) [16, 28]
Adaptability	S4: Identify the capability of changing demands for personalization. The criteria for approving adaptability are depicted as follows: S4-1: Provide quick purchase programs (1-click or similar) [36]. S4-2: Provide cross selling recommendation programs [16, 29]. S4-3: Provide personal-customized mechanism. (Example scenario: members can ask for specific products or services that match their personal characteristic.) [16, 37]
Security and Privacy	S5: Identify the capability of personal information and business transaction. The criteria for approving security and privacy are listed as follows: S5-1: Offer reliable security features for business transaction (such as Secure Sockets Layer (SSL), digital certificates, etc.) [16, 34]. S5-2: Ensure that all seal information is authorized from a trusted third-party [34]. S5-3: Offer security protection for personal information. S5-4: Provide multiple payment mechanisms [16, 29].
Multimedia Capability	S6: Identify the capability of proper use of multimedia features. The criteria for approving multimedia capability are identified as follows: S6-1: Provide proper multimedia presentation (check for audio and video) [29, 30]. S6-2: Provide multimedia content associated with products or services.

Table 7. Trust attributes for service quality

Dimensions	Evidences for approval of trust attributes
Reliability	SE1: Enable the ability to deliver products and services on time as promised The approval for service reliability consists of four criteria which are as follows: SE1-1: Provide order tracking system [16, 37]. SE1-2: Provide FAQ and help for order tracking system. SE1-3: Provide the guarantee for products or services. SE1-4: Establish a physical location to return the products.
Responsiveness	SE2: Enable the ability to help customers and provide prompt services. The approval is considered from three criteria as follows: SE2-1: Provide customer service (e.g., call center, live chat) [38]. SE2-2: Offer the ability to speak to a live person if there is a problem [24]. SE2-3: The feedback response times must be adequate to the medium used [16].
Assurance	SE3: Enable the ability to build customer confidence. The criteria for approving assurance are as follows: SE3-1: Deliver effective customer service. (Example scenario: Send request for asking some questions via call center, live chat, or e-mail and consider for the return answers.) SE3-2: Provide support unit with respect to solving problems related to products and services [37]. SE3-3: Provide global reach capability.
Empathy	SE4: Enable the ability to provide personalized services to the customers. The criteria for approving empathy are as follows: SE4-1: Offer special products or services to the valued customers. SE4-2: Offer special products or services for customer's special times.

3   Trust Capability Maturity Model

In the previous section, we have reviewed the important concepts that are identified as the key elements for constructing Trust Capability Maturity Model (TCMM). TCMM consists of the following components: 1) internal structure, 2) maturity levels, and 3) assessment tool. In this section, we describe the components in TCMM framework and provide the initial guideline for assessing trust in B2C e-Commerce services.

3.1   Internal Structure of the Trust Capability Maturity Levels

The key process areas are used to address the achievement of process improvement in CMM framework. Based on this approach, we employ the performance tasks as the key for determining the capability of trust development in TCMM. The performance tasks that address trust building process are approved by the trust criteria. We separate the approval process for trust criteria into twofold: 1) the achievement goals that identify trust criteria by the checklist and 2) the achievement goals that identify trust criteria by the scenario. The internal structure in each level is depicted in Fig. 3.

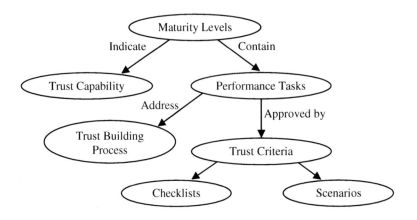

Fig. 3. The TCMM structure

3.2 Trust Capability Maturity Levels

Building upon the same principles as CMM, the operational framework of TCMM is composed by five hierarchical levels as shown in Fig. 4. The progress of continuous improvement program is starting from level 2 and the characteristics at each level can be expressed as follows.

Trust Maturity Level 1 (Initial) is the preliminary stage and trust cannot be defined. Online vendors are not interested in trust issues. Their website seems unprofessional and not suitable in the long run.

Trust Maturity Level 2 (Definition) is the primary stage for building trust in e-Commerce services. At TCMM level 2, customers can form initial trust. The approvals of initial trust in online vendors are derived from the following list: 1) accuracy of vendor profile, 2) clean and clear presentation, 3) up-to-date information, and 4) clear purchasing policy.

Trust Maturity Level 3 (Standard) is the intermediate stage of trust development in e-Commerce services. The activities at this level are focused on setting the standards for e-Commerce application. The performance tasks for the standard level are identified as follows: 1) acceptable security and privacy standards, 2) reliable system, 3) maintainable user accounts, and 4) maintainable information flow and user interaction.

Trust Maturity Level 4 (Manage and Control) is the design stage for customer centric, customers can manage and control for access the best quality of services. The requirements for this level are defined as follows: 1) customers can monitor and control for their purchasing activities, 2) the information provided on the website is supported for purchase decision, and 3) the manager provide the comprehensive strategy for employee training and customer focus.

Trust Maturity Level 5 (Optimization) is the continuous improvement stage. At the final level, the vendors should ensure that their practice meets the following criteria: 1) maintain trust by keeping track of valued customers, and 2) establish the strategy that can achieve sustainable growth and global reach.

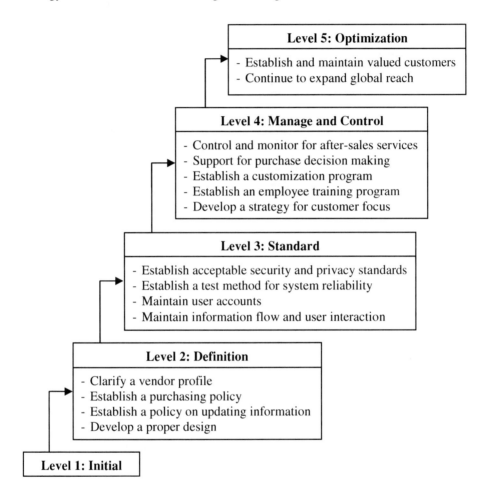

Fig. 4. Trust capability maturity levels

3.3 TCMM Assessment Tool

TCMM assessment tool is established based on TCMM framework to support both self-assessment for online vendors and creating trusted vendors profile for customers. The 55 initial criteria are developed by using trust attributes as the key components to clarify the level of trust in B2C online vendors. After considering the settlement criteria as shown in Table 5 through 7, we have decided to define categories for initial trust criteria in each maturity level as depicted in Fig. 5.

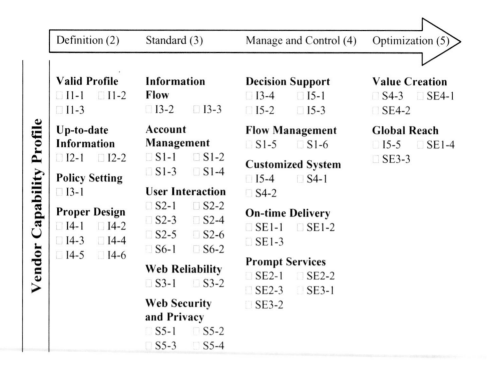

Fig. 5. TCMM Assessment Tool

B2C vendors can evaluate their trust capability level by identify the evidences for approving the trust attributes as specified in Table 5 through 7. If the vendors plan to step from one level to another, they should pass all categories in each level that described in Fig. 5. For example, if the vendors aim to pass the category of valid profile in level 2, they should ensure that the subcategories from I1-1 to I1-3 are satisfied with the setting details that provided in Table 5. According to this method, B2C vendors can create their own capability checklists and develop improvement programs to satisfy the specific details for subcategories in each level.

4   Conclusions and Future Research

In this paper, we propose TCMM that can be used for assessing both trust and quality improvement in e-Commerce services. Based on TCMM guidance, customers can identify the level of trust in online vendors and B2C vendors can construct their own trust development programs from this framework. The TCMM consists of the three components as follows: 1) internal structure, 2) maturity levels, and 3) assessment tool. The internal structure in TCMM is designed according to customers' trust building process. Therefore, B2C vendors can develop their capability in accordance with the process of trust. The way to move from one maturity level to another is accessed by achieving the performance tasks in each maturity level. The main objective of each level is to gradually build customer trust, step by step, following from building initial trust, setting standards for e-Commerce application, setting customer centric strategy, and developing sustainable improvement programs.

Future research will focus on the empirical validation of TCMM framework. By applying TCMM in practice, the validation method can be achieved by comparing the results from TCMM evaluation with customer satisfaction scores. We expect that online vendors with higher maturity level also achieve higher satisfaction scores.

References

1. IfM, IBM.: Succeeding through service innovation: A service perspective for education, research, business and government. White paper, University of Cambridge Institute for Manufacturing (2008)
2. Rust, R.T., Kannan, P.K., Ramachandran, A.D.: E-Service: The Revenue Expansion Path to E-Commerce Profitability. Advances in Computers 64, 159–193 (2005)
3. Gefen, D., Karahanna, E., Straub, D.W.: Trust and TAM in Online Shopping: An Integrated Model. MIS Quarterly 27(1), 51–90 (2003)
4. Reichheld, F.F., Schefter, P.: E-Loyalty: Your Secret Weapon on the Web. Harvard Business Review 78(4), 105–113 (2000)
5. Ren, Z., Hassan, T.M.: Trust in e-Commerce. In: e-Business in Construction. Wiley-Blackwell, Oxford, UK (2009)
6. CMMI Product Team.: CMMI for Development, Version 1.3. Technical report, Software Engineering Institute (2010)
7. Jairak, R., Praneetpolgrang, P., Mekhabunchakij, K.: An Empirical Investigation of e-Trust in e-Business for Instructors and Undergraduate Students. In: RIIT 2009, pp. 72–78 (2009)
8. Paulk, M.C., Curtis, B., Chrissis, M.B., Weber, C.V.: The Capability Maturity Model for Software. Technical report, Software Engineering Institute (1993)
9. Curtis, B., Hefley, W.E., Miller, S.A.: People CMM: A Framework for Human Capital Management, 2nd edn. Addison-Wesley, Boston (2010)
10. Marshall, S., Mitchell, G.: An E-Learning Maturity Model? In: Proceedings of the 19th Annual Conference of the Australian Society for Computers in Learning in Tertiary Education, Auckland, New Zealand (2002)
11. Soares, S.: The IBM Data Governance Unified Process: Driving Business Value with IBM Software and Best Practices. MC Press Online, LCC Ketchum (2010)
12. Salam, A., Iyer, L., Palvia, P., Singh, R.: Trust in E-Commerce. Commun. ACM 48(2), 72–77 (2005)
13. Hoffman, D.L., Novak, T.P., Peralta, M.: Building Consumer Trust Online. Commun. ACM 42(4), 80–85 (1999)
14. Othman, N.Z., Hussin, A.R.C., Rakhmadi, A.: Trust Mechanisms: An Integrated Approach for E-Commerce Website Development Process. In: ITSim 2008, vol. 1, pp. 1–8 (2008)
15. Beldad, A., De Jong, M., Steehouder, M.: How shall I trust the faceless and the intangible? A literature review on the antecedents of online trust. Computers in Human Behavior 26(5), 857–869 (2010)
16. Schubert, P., Selz, D.: Measuring the effectiveness of e-commerce Web sites. In: E-commerce & V-business: Business Models for Global Success. Butterworth-Heinemann, Oxford (2001)
17. Kim, H.W., Xu, Y., Koh, J.: A Comparison of Online Trust Building Factors between Potential Customers and Repeat Customers. Journal of the Association for Information Systems 5(10), 392–420 (2004)
18. Chen, Y.H., Barnes, S.: Initial trust and online buyer behaviour. Industrial Management and Data Systems 107(1), 21–36 (2007)

19. Sulong, S., Aziz, A., Wongsim, M.: Modelling the Quality Aspects of Internet Commerce with Customers' Shopping Experiences. In: ICCET 2010, vol. 7, pp. 425–429 (2010)
20. McKinney, V., Yoon, K., Zahedi, F.M.: The Measurement of Web-Customer Satisfaction: An Expectation and Disconfirmation Approach. Information Systems Research 13(3), 296–315 (2002)
21. Delone, W.H., Mclean, E.R.: Measuring e-Commerce Success: Applying the DeLone & McLean Information Systems Success Model. International Journal of Electronic Commerce 9(1), 31–47 (2004)
22. Jacqueline, J.: Metrics in E-Commerce: Function Point Analysis and Component-Based Software Measurements. In: IT Measurement: Practical Advice from Experts. Addison-Wesley Professional, Boston (2002)
23. Delone, W.H., McLean, E.R.: The DeLone and McLean model of information systems success: A ten-year update. Journal of Management Information Systems 19(4), 9–30 (2003)
24. Chiu, C., Chang, C., Cheng, H., Fang, Y.: Determinants of customer repurchase intention in online shopping. Online Information Review 33(4), 761–784 (2009)
25. Chen, C.W.D., Cheng, C.Y.J.: Understanding consumer intention in online shopping: a respecification and validation of the DeLone and McLean model. Behaviour & Information Technology 28(4), 335–345 (2009)
26. Ahn, T., Ryu, S., Han, I.: The impact of Web quality and playfulness on user acceptance of online retailing. Information & Management 44(3), 263–275 (2007)
27. ISO/IEC 9126-1.: Software Engineering – Product Quality – Part 1: Quality Model. International Organization for Standardization (2001)
28. Olsina, L., Papa, F., Molina, H.: How to Measure and Evaluate Web Applications in a Consistent Way. In: Springer HCIS book Web Engineering: Modeling and Implementing Web Applications, pp. 385–420. Springer, Heidelberg (2008)
29. Stefani, A., Xenos, M.: E-commerce system quality assessment using a model based on ISO 9126 and Belief Networks. Software Quality Journal 16(1), 107–129 (2008)
30. Cao, M., Zhang, Q., Seydel, J.: B2C e-commerce web site quality: an empirical examination. Industrial Management & Data Systems 105(5), 645–661 (2005)
31. Ladhari, R.: A review of twenty years of SERVQUAL research. International Journal of Quality and Service Sciences 1(2), 172–198 (2009)
32. Parasuraman, A., Zeithaml, V.A., Berry, L.L.: SERVQUAL: A Multiple-Item Scale for Measuring Consumer Perceptions of Service Quality. Journal of retailing 64(1), 12–40 (1988)
33. Zhou, T., Lu, Y., Wang, B.: The Relative Importance of Website Design Quality and Service Quality in Determining Consumers' Online Repurchase Behavior. Information Systems Management 26(4), 327–337 (2009)
34. Macaulay, L., Keeling, K., Hussin, A.: The Importance Ranking of Trust Attributes in e-Commerce Website. In: 11th Pacific-Asia Conference on Information Systems (2007)
35. Bandara, K.Y., Wang, M.X., Pahl, C.: Context Modeling and Constraints Binding in Web Service Business Processes. In: CASTA 2009, pp. 29–32 (2009)
36. Olsina, L., Rossi, G.: Measuring Web Application Quality with WebQEM. IEEE Multimedia 9(4), 20–29 (2002)
37. Chiou, W.C., Lin, C.C., Perng, C.: A strategic framework for website evaluation based on a review of the literature from 1995–2006. Information & Management 47(5-6), 282–290 (2010)
38. Fang, X., Salvendy, G.: Customer-Centered Rules for Design of E-Commerce Web Sites. Commun. ACM 46(12), 332–336 (2003)
39. Lam, W.: Testing E-Commerce Systems: A Practical Guide. IT Professional 3(2), 19–27 (2001)

Web Design Considerations for Realizing Functions in Content Management Systems

Ahmad Shoara[1], Kambiz Badie[2], and Maryam Tayefeh Mahmoudi[2]

[1] Management group,
Farabi Inistitue of higher education,
East 100 Str., 631, Mehrshahr, Karaj, Iran
Ahmad.Shoara@gmail.com
[2] Knowledge Management & E-organizations Group,
IT Research Faculty,
Research Institute for ICT (ITRC), Iran
{K_Badie,mahmodi}@itrc.ac.ir

Abstract. In today's competitive world for companies and institutions, providing correct and instant information using the global internet network for successful managers is critical. Considering the high importance of websites in various economic, educational, social, cultural and political areas, senior managers of companies or institutions are willing to monitor their content personally. On the other hand, attracting and retaining the user or customer is also important. One of the systems that can save resources and, because of its dynamic features, is user-friendly and can attract and maintain users, is content management system (CMS) which- using a simple, dynamic and professional environment- provides facilities to users and administrators enabling them to easily manage their website. In this paper, after studying and comparing some of these systems and their crucial factors, strengths and weaknesses, we use e-mail questionnaires to collect CMS users' opinions on some components of CMS. Next, we discuss the proposed structure and the software factors which must be considered in the design and construction of these systems.

Keywords: CMS, Software considerations, Developer, Module, Component.

1 Introduction

Considering the importance of taking advantage of free text content management systems publicly, in all working groups, including educational, political, cultural, and economic ones; and considering the fact that these systems help content managers use databases and edit, publish and manage data without programming, the present paper discusses this area of research. This study begins with the introduction and expression of features, capabilities, strengths and weaknesses of selected systems, namely, Joomla, Drupal, Wordpress, Taypo 3, MODx, e107, DotNetNuke, Xoops and Plone. Next, a comparison of the structural factors of a content management system is done and the findings and considerations about two software companies, Ideal Ware [1] and Water & Stone [2], are studied.

A. Abd Manaf et al. (Eds.): ICIEIS 2011, Part II, CCIS 252, pp. 463–478, 2011.
© Springer-Verlag Berlin Heidelberg 2011

This information alongside the information collected from questionnaires administered to the three groups of content managers- beginner content managers, professional managers and developers- who were randomly chosen from among Iranian university students and academic personnel, is used to achieve factors of a software framework for content systems. As no research has been conducted so far and there is no comprehensive standard in this area, we try to check several possible factors and conduct the survey based on the resulting information.

2   Statement of the Problem

Along with the latest advances in the science of dynamic management, individuals or organizations have to make informed and useful innovations. On the other hand, in the present world, the role and importance of information is continuously increasing and has Global Internet network as the most important information providing tool and the richest resource of information with an increasing and extensive content. With the increased production of Internet information, timely publication and availability are important factors, because the news lifetime varies from several minutes to several days or more.

Today, Websites have facilitated access to news and information and the use of archive information. On the other hand, vast publication of educational eBooks and pamphlets shows the role and position of electronic products in this area. But the production and supply of electronic content is one side of the coin, the other being information management which is one of the main concerns of many executives of small and large databases. To make progress in today's progressive world, management is heavily dependent on information.

No manager can advance his organization or institute without information. It is generally believed that information is power and anyone who has information is powerful. It is an important required resource for the development of other resources. Another important aspect in this area is publishing and making available this information to the users.

In this research, effort has been done to introduce a general structure of a system that can display both sides of the coin as stated above. In recent years, content management software are provided and used in different categories and with different titles such as general content management system (CMS), comprehensive content management system (Portal), personal blogs, sales management systems (E-Commerce), groups and associations management systems (Forum/Groupware), Knowledge Content Management System[1], Document Management System[2], E-Learning Management System[3], Learning Content Management System[4], etc[3].

In this study, taking a look at general content management system (CMS), we discuss various features of web based free content management systems (free text)

---

[1] KCMS
[2] DMS
[3] ELMS
[4] LCMS

and provide a structure for software considerations in web design which is necessary for realizing functions defined in a content management system.

Content management systems have many capabilities and let users store and retrieve information quickly at a high level of efficiency and effectiveness of the business [4]. A Content Management System represents an integrated approach for storing and organizing data types including, notes, data, reports, content and digital assets. Content Management System is specifically a tool used to optimize data collection and organization and improve using and updating information and materials [5]. In addition, ability to manage the database structure and insert new pages in the appropriate place makes navigating within the space possible for users [6].

The main components of a CMS include, (1) Content Production Management, (2) User Management, (3) Services Management, (4) User level management, (5) Content Beauty and Efficiency Management. Web content management systems support design, production, web, multimedia or publishing articles with different objectives [7]. Using CMS instead of the old methods of static pages has many economic benefits such as:

- Saving time when creating and updating web pages;
- Higher consistency and strength;

- Advanced navigation [8];
- More flexibility;

- Non-centralized site control;
- Higher website safety;

- Reduced repetitive data entry; and
- Dramatic reduction of maintenance costs.

In fact, Lado and Zhang (1998) [9] state that content management can be promoted by using special tools for knowledge collection and data analysis. This tool can simply be added to customize them for users. Also Yan & Lewis (1999) [10], believed that this tool increase access to new knowledge and network and individual participation. Based on the literature review on sources of knowledge, they provide a better theory compared to that of Adamides (2006) [11].

3   The Proposed Structure

After investigating various types of content management systems including Joomla, Drupal, Word Press, MODx, Plone, dot net nuke, xoops, Typo 3 and e107 and comparing factors and benefits of each, a general structure is suggested for providing software considerations necessary for providing a content management system in figure:

As stated, the target population in this study includes three groups of content management system users. So the reasons for justification of this structure are expressed based on these three user groups. The first category of reasons belongs to

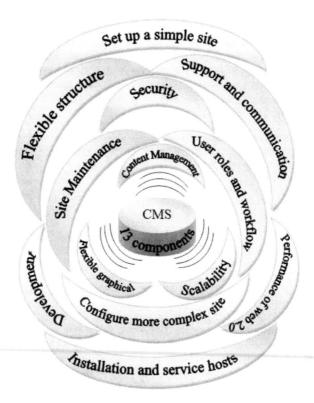

Fig. 1. General structure

those who want to use content management systems and are only regular users and consumers of such systems and see no reason for changing the default versions. The second category includes justified reasons on the part of people who intend to use, extend and customize these systems. The third category belongs to people who intend to build and create appropriate add-ons necessary for themselves and the content management community, that you can see in figure2, figiure3 and figure4.

3-1: Justified Reasons for Novice Administrators

The most important concerns for users in creating and establishing a suitable site for users who are entering the world of internet communication include: providing an appropriate host from a good server, choosing a domain name suitable for the topic and designing a website with good graphic design which is also light and user-friendly and has high security. It should also provide sections suitable for different subjects and should have the ability to update and extend.

Content management systems are developed for solving this problem. These systems are easily downloaded, and once installed on the server, provide users with the ability to edit, delete and add content easily. Content management systems, not only make website design easier, but also they do not need learning HTML, or PHP on the part of users.These users are offered some suggestions:

1 – Select a system whose installation is very simple and can guide you in the use of default options such as themes, language, creation of accounts and initial settings.

2 – A system can help you move closer to your goals, provided its management section is strong and simple, so that you can easily find what you expect and you can implement the basic settings.

3 – Choose a system that is highly flexible in structure and graphics appearance. Easy-to-use graphic features and possibility to make changes in color and design of templates with supports needed by the system play an important role in attracting visitors (customers) and in keeping them interested.

4 – You need special care to make the overall structure of your system flexible. Flexibility can make management face the challenge of lack of technical information. Therefore, choose a system that defines different levels of access to facilities and supports the desired number of pages and different languages.

5 – Use systems that utilize Web 2 technology and support it. Using RSS Feeds, supporting a variety of comments, supporting blogs, rapid downloads and . . . , are the results of this technology.

6 – Install a system with high security in its structure. No doubt, no content manager likes its website's information being stolen or altered.

7 – The system should provide the ability to create a backup of the entire site. It should also provide you with the updated versions of your chosen content management system in the future.

8 – Select a system which has help files, or provides you with printed or electronic books or a website to support you in this area.

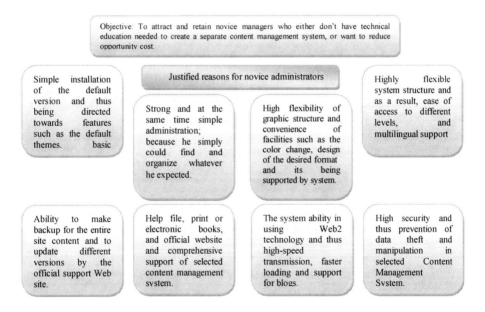

Fig. 2. Justified reasons for novice administrators

3-2: Justified Reason for Professional Content Managers

In this part, some important proposals and recommendations for this group of people are provided. These individuals should note that, besides recommendations described in the previous section, they should take into account the following recommendations in order to enrich their chosen content management system:

1 - Ease of changing the default version into a more complex version can be one important factor affecting your choice. This is made possible only using modules and add-ons provided by the website supporting your chosen Content Management System. Certainly, any system that has your desired add-ons and is easy to use and update would be the best.

2 - Content managers who want to develop their own web sites are recommended to take their selected system's extensibility into account. The system's degree of flexibility in customization, support for programming languages and for add-ons and the ability to integrate with other systems are factors that will help you in this area.

3 - Regarding scalability, in addition to the storage system and the ability to accept newly installed tools, the minimum hardware requirements and software extensions also should be taken into account. Making the system unique will be possible only if we use add-on facilities available to the system.

4 - Finally, these managers are suggested to enhance web site performance and customer satisfaction by taking advantage of add-ons that, in addition to having the ability to share content with other sites (link exchange) and to create a working alliance with them, help content management systems optimize and prepare for search engines.

Objective: To attract and retain professional convention managers who want to professionalize much his site and add new features and content to fill their own content management system.

Justified reason for professional content managers

The ability to add some plugins, for sharing content with other sites as well as the ability to create business alliances with other systems.	Amount of storage systems and capabilities being matched with new tools installed according to the minimum hardware and software.
Easily change the default version to sophisticated version, with using modules and additives that can be updated.	Selected systems that using Web2.0 technology and its followers quickly transfer, faster downloads and support blogs, etc.
Backup the entire contents of the site and updating different versions, supported by the official site.	High security and lack of data theft and manipulation Selected Content Management System.
Help file, print or electronic books, and sometimes informal support comprehensive Web content management system selected.	Strong administration and on the other hand simply because he simply could be expected whatever the setting must be found.
High flexible system structure and ease of access to the followers of different levels, multiple language support	High flexible system structure and ease of access to the followers of different levels, multiple language support
Amount of extensibility selected system, amount of flexibility to customize the system and supported programming languages, etc.	High flexibility of graphic structure and convenience facilities such as the following, color, design and support the desired format of his system.

Fig. 3. Justified reason for professional content managers

3-3: Justified Reasons for System Developers

The final part in this section, includes our recommendations for developers. As was stated, content management systems are systems that make three actions possible: creating, managing and grading information. Considering these three main factors the following suggestions are offered:

1 – Create a system usable for all groups of users (novice, semi-professional, professional). Separate versions can also be considered for each group. For example, for novice users, a light, beautiful, user-friendly version with convenient host facilities can be offered which includes user installation manual.

2 – Note that systems that, in addition to their easy installation and comprehensive default version, provide the possibility to create an account and to find the default theme and use them in the content format can experience general acceptance. System's simple and understandable organizational structure has a great role in its user friendliness.

3 – As one way to attract the audience is through using charts, tables, pictures (motion and non-motion) and audio files, facilities should be provided to help content managers use these capabilities in order to produce, develop and even edit user-friendly content.

4 – Developers who want to attract audience (customers) at first glance are recommended to provide systems or facilities that, in addition to having a dynamic appearance and providing selection possibility, make changing or replacing the user's or content managers' desired themes easy. The higher the graphic flexibility, the more audience will be attracted.

5 - As flexible structure is one of the success secrets for any system or organization, it is suggested that a system or facility be provided that support multiple pages, different levels of access, automated content representation based on access level, different kinds of unusual content (and using modules to remove them) and automated content representation based on system's regulations. Multi-language support, ease of sharing content with related sites, support for linking several URL address and strong internal search engines should also be present in the system structure.

6 – They should use the "new internet generation" or Web 2 to get rid of information challenges. Wikis, podcasts and RSS are all concepts and technologies affecting Web 2. Since the main characteristic of this new generation is its focus on the user, it can be a way to make internet more interactive. Supporting blogs and their inter-relationships and providing for comments, discussion forums and social networking as well as publishing RSS feeds are essential in making these systems more interactive.

7 – Create a system that has the ability to expand and to integrate with other systems. Certainly, useful, up-to-date add-ons play an important role in increasing the popularity of systems. This role is so vital that users who do not use these systems mention lack of add-ons as a reason for so doing. On the other hand, the ability to integrate with other systems is also important. You might find it interesting that in the second half of 2009, Joomla developers started a new project called Joopal. It is nothing but a combination of two powerful content management systems, i.e, Joomla and Drupal. It combines the power of Joomla with Drupal configurability.

8 – Systems that support high traffic and high data volume are successful. Developers are recommended to create a system that can support high levels of traffic and also have a high caching rate. This will be possible by developers or modules that are created with this purpose.

9 – Because the purpose is audience satisfaction and creation of a safe environment for internet interactions, it is recommended that developers set factors like maintaining a safe environment, protecting privacy, updating security section and reducing vulnerability as their top priorities.

10 – Support and maintenance of systems after creating and delivering them to the audience (the customer) can improve the quality of human interactive communication and customer satisfaction. Therefore, it is recommended that developers keep in touch with customers to maintain and keep them satisfied. Changes in systems, updates, new features and new add-ons should be announced to users.

11 – Finally, developers are recommended to provide facilities that enable content managers to backup existing files and to restore them from backup easily when necessary. They should provide facilities for content managers to simply identify files and materials that have lower number of visitors.

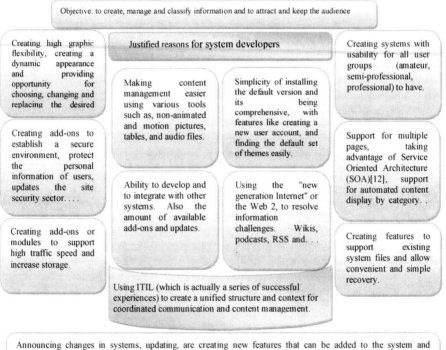

Objective: to create, manage and classify information and to attract and keep the audience

Justified reasons for system developers

Creating high graphic flexibility, creating a dynamic appearance and providing opportunity for choosing, changing and replacing the desired

Creating add-ons to establish a secure environment, protect the personal information of users, updates the site security sector....

Creating add-ons or modules to support high traffic speed and increase storage.

Making content management easier using various tools such as, non-animated and motion pictures, tables, and audio files.

Ability to develop and to integrate with other systems. Also the amount of available add-ons and updates.

Simplicity of installing the default version and its being comprehensive, with features like creating a new user account, and finding the default set of themes easily.

Using the "new generation Internet" or the Web 2, to resolve information challenges. Wikis, podcasts, RSS and...

Using ITIL (which is actually a series of successful experiences) to create a unified structure and context for coordinated communication and content management.

Creating systems with usability for all user groups (amateur, semi-professional, professional) to have.

Support for multiple pages, taking advantage of Service Oriented Architecture (SOA)[12], support for automated content display by category. .

Creating features to support existing system files and allow convenient and simple recovery.

Announcing changes in systems, updating, are creating new features that can be added to the system and communicating with the audience, not only elevates their trust in the system, but also warn you about weaknesses, strengths, threats and opportunities. Also using the Help Desk can be very important.

Fig. 4. Justified reasons for system developers

Note: This strategy is possible only when your developed system either has a strong and complete core or possesses facilities and features which can make the core rich and complete. For example, regarding the website of Xoops Persian[5], in an article under the title of "Why xoops was not chosen as the best content management system of the year?", states that the weak core of previous versions of xoops is one of the key factors affecting this failure.

4   Method of Research

For the purpose of this study, we investigated the factors present in nine selected content management systems and chose their positive points taking into account executive proposals for all three categories of users in question. The sample was selected from content managers and developers of selected content management systems. The study population comprised a number of university students and professors from Shiraz, Tehran, and Khaje Nasir Tusi universities and Farabi Institute of Higher Education. A questionnaire was developed and used for data collection to examine factors in the proposed framework (88 factors in the form of 13 components as shown in Figure 6). Finally, the results are discussed based on SPSS analysis and the hypotheses are tested using t-test, correlations and the chi-square goodness of fit test.

4-1: Research Methodology

This study is practical in terms of purpose, in-depth in terms of study intensiveness [13] and descriptive analytical and co relational in terms of methods [14].

4-2: Population

A statistical population is the largest group of organisms in a given time in which we are interested for study purposes. They have at least one common trait [15]. Our study population in this study includes three groups of content managers.

4-3: Sampling

To choose our study sample from the study population, simple random sampling method was used. In this method, n units are chosen from a community with N units, so that every (N / n) member of the population has an equal and independent chance of being selected [16]. This sampling method is used when the selection is done from an infinite population. In this study, because the target population is too large, to make it smaller, first 40 of the content managers were identified and then they were reduced to 14 who belong to one of these groups: novice content managers (beginner), professional content managers and developers of content management systems. They answered to the final questionnaire in electronic form.

4-4: Measurement and Data Collection Instrument

Data can be collected in different ways, in different places and from various sources. Methods of data collection in scientific-technical areas include readings, experiment,

---

[5] See more, http://www.xoops.ir/index.php

observation, questionnaires and interviews [17]. However, from a more specific point of view, data collection methods can include telephone interviews, face to face interviews, computer (internet) interviews, in-person questionnaire, people or events observed with or without audio or video recording, and various motivational techniques like extraversion tests [18].

In the present study we used library research, internet content, and resources available to complete the literature review. For the field study, library and Internet research were used alongside questionnaires. The questionnaire was developed according to our studies and literature review and also research done by Ideal Ware and Water & Stone in 2009 and was distributed among the honorable experts. Questionnaires consist of 88 questions, in which the researchers have tried to include most factors in a general structure of the content management system, in 13 overall sections.

4-5: Analysis of Results and Confirmation of the Structure

In this part, the results of the study are addressed in order to know whether, in reality, there is a significant relationship between structural proposals achieved from three categories of users in this study.

4-5-1: Descriptive Analysis
In this section, the researchers report and describe statistics obtained from the results of the study.

Table 1. Gender frequency of the sample content managers

--------	relative frequency	relative frequency (percentage)	Cumulative frequency
Male	2	14.30	14.30
Female	12	85.70	100.00
Total	14	100.0	

Table 2. Age frequency of the sample

---------------	relative frequency	relative frequency (percentage)	Cumulative frequency
Under 25	2	14.30	14.30
25-34	12	85.70	100.00
Total	14	100.0	

Table 3. Frequency distribution of sample acquaintance rate

--------------	relative frequency	relative frequency (percentage)	Cumulative frequency
Medium	11	78.6	78.6
High	2	14.3	92.2
Very high	1	7.1	100
Total	14	100	

Table 4. Distribution of the best factor for using content management systems by the sample

-------------------	relative frequency	relative frequency (percentage)	Cumulative frequency
No need for programming	5	35.7	35.7
Better content management	9	64.3	100
total	14	100	

Table 5. Frequency distribution of the most effective factor for the samples' rejecting content management systems

-----------------	relative frequency	relative frequency (percentage)	Cumulative frequency
Lack of trust	2	14.3	57.1
Complexity	4	28.6	42.9
The difficulty of solving problems	2	14.3	57.1
Unavailability of add-ons	6	42.9	100
Total	14	100	

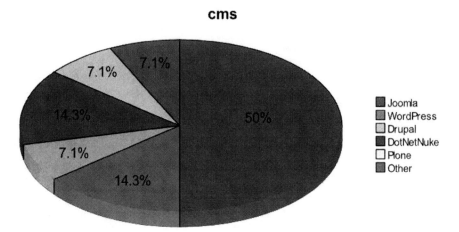

Fig. 5. A pie chart of the extent to which the selected content management systems were used by the sample

4-5-2: Inferential Analysis
In this section the researchers discuss inferential statistics.

Testing Research Hypotheses
Using data and information obtained research hypotheses are tested. It should be noted that the hypotheses are tested based on values of degrees of freedom, T statistics and P-Value. In all hypotheses, H_0 is lack of positive and significant relationship between variables and H_1 is positive and significant relationship between variables. Now, testing each hypothesis is discussed.

Hypothesis 1: Software considerations in web design have a positive role in attracting and keeping the users to fulfill the functions defined for novice managers in a content management system.

In testing hypothesis 1, considering all factors related to beginner managers and putting them in one group, as can be seen in Table 6, and considering the correlation coefficient between presenting the structure and its impact on novice managers and the fact that P-Value is zero; the statistic T value is also significant.

Table 6. Testing the first research hypotheses

The first hypothesis	Spearman correlation coefficient	test criterion	t	P-Value	The result of test
Impact of the structure on the novice managers	0.4	$\mu = 3$	6.09	00.00	Hypothesis supported

Hypothesis 2: Software considerations in web design have a positive role in attracting and keeping the users to fulfill the functions defined for professional managers in a content management system.

In testing hypothesis 2, considering all factors related to professional managers and putting them in one group, as can be seen in Table 7, and considering the correlation coefficient between presenting the structure and its impact on novice managers and the fact that P-Value is zero, the statistic T value is also significant.

Table 7. Testing the second research hypotheses

The second hypothesis	Spearman correlation coefficient	test criterion	t	P-Value	The result of test
Impact of the structure on the professional managers	0.7	$\mu = 3$	7.26	00.00	Hypothesis supported

Hypothesis 3: Software considerations in web design have a positive role in attracting and keeping the users to fulfill the functions defined for developers of content management systems.

In testing hypothesis 3, considering all factors related to developers and putting them in one group, as can be seen in Table 8, and considering the correlation coefficient between presenting the structure and its impact on developers and the fact that P-Value is zero, the statistic T value is also significant.

Table 8. Testing the third research hypotheses

The third hypothesis	Spearman correlation coefficient	test criterion	t	P-Value	The result of test
Impact of the structure on developers	0.4	$\mu = 3$	5.45	00.00	Hypothesis supported

Hypothesis 4: providing a structure that has software considerations in web design necessary to fulfill the functions defined for a content management system, has a positive role in attracting and keeping the users.

As can be seen in Table 9, and considering the fact that P-Value is zero, the statistic T value is also significant.

Table 9. Testing the fourth research hypotheses

The fourth hypothesis	test criterion	t	P-Value	The result of test
Impact of the structure	$\mu = 3$	6.75	00.00	Hypothesis supported

Chi-square Goodness of Fit Test

In this section, after testing hypothesis using t-test, another test called the chi-square goodness of fit test is used to support the entire structure and confirm tests of hypotheses above. As can be seen in Table 10, in this test, H_0 indicates that variables are unimportant and H_1 indicates that variables are important.

Table 10. Chi square test results

Chi square	571.4
Degree of freedom	1
P - Value	0.033

As can be seen in the table above, Chi square test result equals 0.033. So, as was stated, considering that in this test, H_0 indicates that variables are unimportant and H_1 indicates that variables are important, the null hypothesis is rejected and the importance and impact of the subject can be seen here.

5   Conclusion

This study investigated the 13 proposed components which include: easy installation and host services, easy creation of a simple website, communication/support power, ease of learning to configure a more complex site, ease of using the content management section, graphic flexibility, flexibility in structure, user roles and workflow, site maintenance, Web 2.0 performance, expansion (stretching) and combination (merging), scalability and security. These components were selected through a process of investigating the factors present in nine selected content management systems and choosing their positive points. The sample was divided into three groups of novice managers, professional managers, and developers. The purpose was to propose a framework for improving, attracting and satisfying these three groups of users. It should be noted that this strategy is possible only when your developed system either has a strong and complete core or possesses facilities and features which can make the core rich and complete. For example, regarding the website of Xoops Persian[6], in an article under the title of "Why xoops was not chosen as the best content management system of the year?", states that the weak core of previous versions of xoops is one of the key factors affecting this failure.

Little research has been conducted about content management systems and about providing a structure for their software considerations. Therefore, to make better use of these systems in order to achieve their goals, researchers should study more content management systems to provide software considerations necessary for web design. These considerations are necessary to fulfill the functions defined in a content management system. They can also study content management systems in terms of their applications in order to provide these considerations. In addition, researchers and technical developers can work on creating and building the structure of content management systems, whose 13-fold components can be seen in Figure 6. In fact, the creation and implementation of this structure are proposed in this part.

---

[6] See more, `http://www.xoops.ir/index.php`

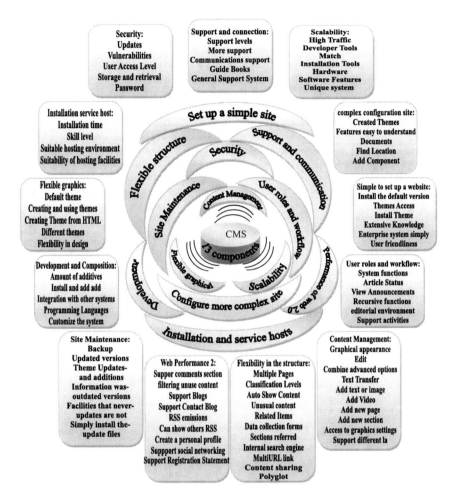

Fig. 6. The suggested framework and factors of its 13 components

References

1. Team, I. s.: Comparing Open Source Content Management Systems. From Idealware, Helping Nonprofits Make Smart Software Decisions (March 01, 2009), http://www.idealware.org/reports/2010-os-cms (retrieved April 15, 2009)
2. Shreves(The lead analyst on this report), R (n. d.), open-source cms market share report. Retrieved 01 15, from Waterandstone - A full service digital agency (2010), http://www.waterandstone.com/sites/default/files/2010OSCMSReport.pdf
3. Zarei, J.: Important parameters in choosing content management software. Tahlilgaran Asre Etelaat Magezine (25) (2011)

4. Bianco, F., Michelino, F.: The role of content management systems in publishing firms. International Journal of Information Management 30, 117–124 (2010)
5. Smith, H.A., Mckeen, J.D.: Developments in practice VIII: Enterprise content management. Communications of the Association for Information Systems 11, 647–659 (2003)
6. Sate, A.: The cognitive content management system. Rah Avard Magezine, Ghom (2001)
7. Venkatraman, N.: IT-enabled business transformation: From automation to business scope redefinition. Sloan Management Review 35, 73–87 (1994)
8. Lado, A.A., Zhang, M.J.: Expert systems, knowledge development and utilization, and sustained competitive advantage: A resource-based model. Journal of Management 24(4), 489–509 (1998)
9. Yan, A., Lewis, M.R.: The migration of organizational functions to the work unit level buffering, spanning, bringing up boundaries. Human Relations 52(1), 25–47 (1999)
10. Nielsen, J.: Alertbox: Is navigation Useful?, January 9th, 2000, last consulted January 19 (2009), http://www.useit.com/alertbox/20000109.html
11. Castro-Leon, E., Chang, M., He, J.: Scaling Down SOA to Small Businesses. In: Proceedings of the IEEE International Conference on Service-Oriented Computing and Applications, SOCA 2007 (2007)
12. Adamides, E.D., Karacapilidis, N.: Information technology support for the knowledge and social processes of innovation management. Technovation 26, 50–59 (2006)
13. Saro Khani, B.: Research methods in social sciences, vol. 1. Humanities and Cultural Studies, Tehran (2000)
14. Hafeznia, M.R.: Introduction to Research in the Humanities. Samt, Tehran (2003)
15. Khaki, G.R.: Research Method in Management. Azad Eslamaic University, Tehran (2003)
16. Amidi, A.: Sampling methods. Payam e Noor, Tehran (2003)
17. Rohani Rankoohi, S.M.T.: Presentation style: Scientific – Technical. Jelveh, Tehran (2005)
18. Sekaran, O.: Research methods in management. Translators, Saebi, M. & Shirazi, M. State Management Training Center, Tehran (2001)
19. Olmos et al., Emerging Web Browsing Alternatives. In: Trant, J., Bearman, D. (eds): Museums and the Web 2009: Proceedings. Toronto: Archives & Museum Informatics. Published March 31, 2009. Consulted February 1, 2011 (2009), http://www.archimuse.com/mw2009/papers/olmos/olmos.html
20. Wikipedia: Personalization (definition), page was last modified on 22 January 2009. Last consulted January 22 (2009), http://en.wikipedia.org/wiki/Personalization

A Suggested E-Government Framework for Assessing Organizational E-Readiness in Developing Countries

Ibrahim A. Alghamdi, Robert Goodwin, and Giselle Rampersad

School of Computer Science, Engineering and Mathematics, Flinders University
GPO Box 2100, Adelaide SA 5042, Australia
{Algh0044,robert.goodwin,giselle.rampersad}@flinders.edu.au

Abstract. Information and Communication Technologies (ICTs) have been presented in the government sector all over the world last two decades in an effort to accomplish better operational efficiency and effectiveness. This study focuses on the main internal factors in the assessment of e-government organizational readiness in developing countries and how do they lead to successful e-government adoption. Consequently, this study contributes an integrated e-government framework for assessing the e-readiness of government organizations. Most assessment models are more appropriate for the assessment of the overall growth of e-government in each country; they are not focusing on the difficulties that exist in the internal factors affecting transformation of a government organization caused by ICT diffusion. Most of these modules disregard the vision of external stakeholders and employees, although they represent the basis in the success of any e-government project. The suggested e-government framework consists of seven dimensions of e-readiness assessment for government organizations including e-government organizational strategy, user access, e-government program, portal architecture, business process, ICT infrastructure, and human resource. This article extended the previous work particularly in the literature review and the processes dimension. This article is significant to management in assessing organizational e-readiness to improve the effectiveness of e-government initiatives. The next step of this study is to test the relations of these factors in an emerging e-government environment using a case study on an government organization as an essential step in the process of testing the framework suggested.

Keywords: e-government, organizational adoption, organizational strategy, e-readiness.

1 Introduction

An e-government defined as *"the use by government agencies of information technologies (such as Wide Area Networks, the Internet, and mobile computing) that have the ability to transform relations with citizens, businesses, and other arms of government. These technologies can serve a variety of different ends: better delivery of government services to citizens, improved interactions with business and industry, citizen empowerment through access to information, or more efficient government management. The resulting benefits can be less corruption, increased transparency, greater convenience, revenue growth, and/or cost reductions"*. [1].

A. Abd Manaf et al. (Eds.): ICIEIS 2011, Part II, CCIS 252, pp. 479–498, 2011.
© Springer-Verlag Berlin Heidelberg 2011

This article will attempt to answer the question: What are the main internal factors in the assessment of government organizational e-readiness in developing countries and how do they lead to successful organizational e-government readiness?

Each factors of e-government needs leadership, cross-coordination and knowledge, all integrated with an e-government organizational strategy to accomplish the vision and goals [2, 3]. The need of an e-government framework for assessing the ICT readiness in public sectors is critical in developing effective e-government policies and strategies [4]. While there are many e-readiness assessment tools, there is a need for fixed guidelines on how these tools can be shaped as frameworks in implementing assessment in particular e-government contexts [4]. The design of e-government readiness assessment frameworks requires comprehensible measurement of the assessment design that determines internal factors clearly derived from information needs [4-6].

With the new generations of ICT, this article suggests that organizational ICT strategy use in depth to be directed to cover more dimensions than simply integration issues and supportive factors of formal government primarily provided by technology. This article considers the national e-government program as one of the main factors from the government organization agencies prospective such as availability, compatibility and security.

In addition, the key aim of this article is that the comprehensive framework for assessing the e-readiness of public agencies for e-government stages require to capture the future use of ICT applications with the external users not only citizens, other governmental agencies and businesses, but also employees, and other group when performing the core activities in government. This paper focusing not on the Internet only but on other important delivery channels such as ATMs, PCs, fixed-line and mobile phones (WAP), and kiosks in public places. Furthermore, this article covers important applications need to be considered in government organizations to transform to e-government. The proposed comprehensive framework that could help further progress of the e-government is labeled the Business Process Re-engineering (BPR) model.

This article provides an integrated framework for assessing organizational e-readiness of e-government that integrates pertinent components in a developing country public sector. The framework assesses e-government organizational e-readiness through seven dimensions: user access, e-government program, Portal Architecture, business processes, ICT infrastructure and human resources, and e-government strategy which influences the other factors.

2   Theories in Support of E-Readiness

From an academic viewpoint, the e-government adoption that have came out with the development and diffusion of ICT and known as a most important provider to economic, social and environmental development in developed countries [7-11]. The e-government researchers have investigated the potential impacts of ICT and management issues, information systems ICT transfer, culture and country-specific factors in e-government development, and diffusion in developing countries [12-15].

However, more research is required on organizational issues impacting on e-government effectiveness. The literature has a predominant focus on technological issues such as Portal Architecture and infrastructure such as portals, security and authentication, web standards [16]; interoperability [17]; metadata, open source software, domain policy, connectivity [18]; procurement practices, project design [19, 20]; and implementation issues [21-23]. Extant research predominantly focuses on issues of functionality [17, 22] and the technical aspects [24, 25] of ICT in an e-service delivery context. However, there is a considerable gap between what can be done by using ICTs and what has been achieved in reality [26, 27]. E-government initiatives are frequently unsuccessful because of one of the following: the technical system is never implemented; the technology is discarded after implementation; key goals are not achieved (relating to cost, implementation timeframes, and capability) and/or they result in considerable unpredicted outcomes [28]. While some studies focus on the success and failure rates of e-government, more than one-third of e-government initiatives are overall failures (e.g. the failure of decision support systems in East Africa); an additional, half can be viewed as limited failures (e.g. the limited or partial failure of management information systems in Eastern Europe); and approximately one seventh are successes [29].

The maturity model developed by Layne and Lee in 2001 has been quoted by different researchers and is one of few studies within e-government where one can classify a association of functionality of IT applications and users access. This maturity model has been extended by Kim Andersen and Helle Henriksen in 2006 for e-government stages in order to upgrade the utilize of IT applications with the external users such as citizens, businesses, and other governmental agencies while accessing the governmental organization's applications. But, both studies focus on the Internet only but not on other important delivery channels such as such as, ATMs, PCs, fixed-line and mobile phones (WAP), and kiosks in public places. These studies do not cover users such as employees and other groups, also do not civer other important factors such organizational ICT strategy and national e-government program in depth.

Also, Kim Andersen in 2010 extended e-government and Public Sector Process Rebuilding by providing an input to rebuild and improve the processes in which the public sector perform activities and interact with the citizens, companies, and the formal elected decision-makers. It is essential to succeed in implementing e-government to stress serious capability challenges inhibiting the digital transformation using activity and customer centric applications [30].

The current e-readiness models not succeed to sufficiently identify organizational factors. for example, information access within organizations is often disregarded [31]. Measures of physical ICT infrastructure and education are popular factors in e-readiness assessments tools. Extant tools provided unsuitable parameters and factors in assessing the comprehensive e-readiness of organizations and were matched by policy and economic environment surroundings [32]. Stephen et al. (2006) suggest that a new e-readiness integrated tool is needed that highlights information access and also co-locates the different segments of organizational, ICT, human resources, and external readiness.

In addition to ignoring organizational issues, existing tools do not place sufficient emphasis on e-government considerations. Studies of e-government framework assessment point out that some e-readiness tools do not comprise e-government in their assessments [33]. These tools mainly evaluate e-services and accessibility, support and usage of ICT [33]. E-readiness assessment tools are inadequate in considering factors relating to e-government, such as culture and technology acceptance of public officials [13], excellence of ICT infrastructure in government organizations, strategies, national e-government program architecture. There is insufficient research linking e-readiness and e-government implementation in a nation [34]. A concentration on the mainly specific issues to e-government when endeavouring to measure it is highly recommended [35].

While the literature recognizes the significance of e-readiness in organizations [36], empirical work remains limited. E-government literature focuses on technical capabilities and relations and their consequences on e-services [36, 37]. However, e-government literature largely ignores e-government organisational strategy, and national e-government program model connected to relative factors. Since e-government is a relatively new research area, organizational ICT architecture and adoption strategy have not been widely discussed in the literature. Some studies have discussed the factors of e-government, such as [38], [29], and [39]. However, these studies did not concentrate on the component of e-government organizational strategy and national e-government program model and its relationship to the e-readiness, organizational architecture, business process and Information systems, ICT infrastructure and human resource factors. Research is required that presents an integrated architecture framework for e-government adoption that can help organization and ICT managers in assessing the e- readiness for a government organization.

3 Conceptual Framework Development of E-Readiness Assessment for Government Organizations

This study suggests that e-government organizational ICT strategy and national e-government program should be regarded equally as important components of the e-readiness assessment. The study also suggests that the e-readiness tools should clearly reflect this fact in their frameworks in addition to ICT, business considerations and important applications, users and regulatory factors.

Due to the relationship between strategy and other dimensions, the study argues that all six dimensions: user's access, e-government program, organizational architecture, business processes and information systems, ICT infrastructure, and human resources, are influenced by e-government strategy dimension in view of the fact that this strategy consists of major features that lead to key changes in the declared six dimensions.

The suggested framework has been created based on previous studies on information systems e-government success, and e-readiness. As illustrated in Figure 1, it integrates seven dimensions of e-government organizations. First, it explains organizational ICT strategy as a major factor in reaching a successful e-government adoption in Section 3.1. Section 3.2 clarifies the high demand for e-service delivery channels in the public sector. Section 3.3 describes the three major components of the e-government program which should be connected to the government agencies.

Section 3.4 explains Portal Architecture roles to advance the success of e-government organization portals. Section 3.5 focuses on business processes, knowledge management, change management, and ICT applications. Section 3.6 describes technologies that should be prepared before e-services can be offered consistently and efficiently to the citizens. Finally, Section 3.7 explains the important factors of human resources in the success of e-government.

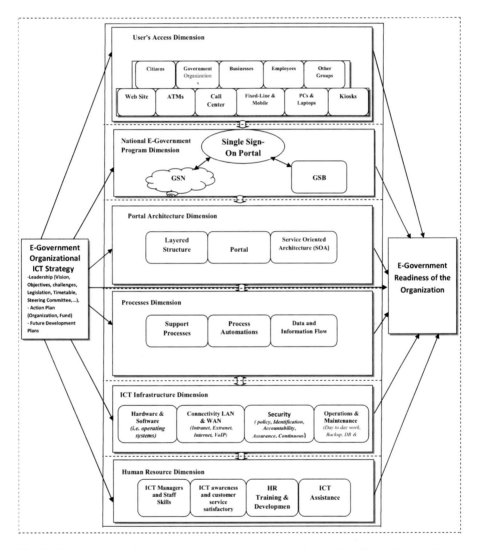

Fig. 1. E-government framework for assessing organizational E-readiness in developing countries

3.1 Strategy

The e-government strategy is *"the all-of-government approach to transforming how agencies use technology to deliver services, provide information, and interact with people, as they work to achieve the outcomes sought by government"* [40].

A lack of consensus exists within the literature about the importance of strategy for e-government adoption. Some studies on e-readiness assessment tools stress that ICT strategy is fundamental for e-government adoption to be succeed [2, 5, 41] studies reveal that IT strategy does not have a strong impact on e-government readiness [33]. However, these studies and e-readiness assessment tools consider the strategy as a national e-government strategy not as a government organizational ICT strategy.

E-government strategy should identify a number of visions and goals to validate its cost and to verify the degree to which these are accomplished [1]. Strategy should identify possible challenges, technological, economic, and political [1]. An e-government strategy should be aligned with the organization's business and information systems strategy. Also, e-government strategy should be compatible with the strategy of e-government national program [42]. In addition, both [33] and [2] develop a framework for e-readiness assessment model. One of their categories is a strategy. The strategy construct in both models includes leadership and action plans. Strategy should apply an action plan that includes: organization (accountability, structure, resource allocation, IT policies and procedures) [33]. It offers the suitable strategy to assist all programs in a aligning the goal, framework, capacity, and risks identified by the whole organization.

Furthermore, action plans should consider funding sources, and recognize various e-government stakeholders in order to verify their responsibilities and the significance to be achieved [33].

When e-government strategy applied properly in organizations, strategy can promote e-government productivity in the public sector. This article suggests that strategy can influence e-government organizational e-readiness drivers including e-government user access, e-government program, processes, ICT infrastructure, and human resources. Each of the mentioned dimensions is described in the following sections below.

3.2 User's Access

Service delivery refers to the process of providing government services through e-government portals [43]. Accessibility refers to the ease of attaining information and services offered through an e-government portal [44]. E-government services accessibility through various channels offers range of reach and enlarge adopt of an e-government portal [45].

ICT has emerged as an intermediary in assisting successful communication between stakeholders [12]. While extant research predominantly focuses on functionality factors and e-services delivery prospect [46, 47], little attention has been placed on factors such as usability, accessibility and the availability of public e-services from an e-government user's perspective [48]. E-government needs to be driven by user demand, not only by cost reduction goals. These user requirements includes time savings, increased convenience and accessibility [1, 42], has been affected by the need to provide e-government users with more extensive and effective channels for interacting with government using web-based systems [49]. Service delivery refers to the process of providing government services through e-government portals [43]. Moreover, accessibility refers to the ease of attaining information and services offered through an e-government portal [44].

Access channels are important for e-government and refer to the means by which users can obtain different government services [38]. Users can be citizens, employees, government sector, private sector, and other groups or communities [38]. Access channels comprise online and offline channels of delivery through which products, services and information are utilized, accessed and communicated by various technologies such as Internet, ATMs, PCs, fixed-line and mobile phones (WAP), and kiosks in public places [38, 50].

3.3 National E-Government Program

3.3.1 What Is National E-Government Program?

This dimension is regarding integrating digital data of different organizations into a single-sign on of e-government website portal. E-government program intends to deliver interoperability and integration of services among all government organizations (G2G), between government organizations and customers (G2C), between government organizations and business organization (G2B), and between government organizations and their employees (G2E) [42].

E-government program attempts to accomplish superior efficiency in government performance, in the course of raising the performance of services and transactions for users from various sectors of society with ease and professionalism [51]. E-services could include services such as rate paying, licensing or information queries [51]. Experts describe the portal as "a service transformation program" because it serves as an umbrella for all government departments, authorities and administrations. The e-government program can lead to increased government efficiency and effectiveness in delivering suitable services to various sectors of customers through multiple delivery channels [52]. The national e-government program can be designed to achieve objectives including raising the public sector's productivity and efficiency; providing better and more easy-to-use services for individual and business customers; increasing return on investment (ROI); and providing the required information in a timely and highly accurate fashion [27, 42].

There are three levels of e-government portal complication which are information distributing and linking of existing web sites, single organization transactions, and transactions involving integration of multiple organizations [53]. From a portal management viewpoint, it is essential to offer stable and Single-Sign On (SSO) interface to ease and enlarge user access and control, for instance using authorized e-services, search capabilities, and instant messaging. In addition, having compatible systems for linking affective tool such as Government Service Bus (GSB) which should be available on e-government portal to register, dynamically identify and categorize users/organizations, and providing the organization the ability to access specific applications and information to meet the particular requirements of organization. Security is another key element of this dimension, through connecting to a secure network such as Government Secure Network (GSN) which should be available as well by e-government portal, the organizations will achieve protected transactions. The framework proposed in this study comprises three factors to help in assessing the organizational portal readiness that linked to the e-government national portal, from which: SSO, GSB, and GSN more details provided in the three below sections.

3.3.2 Single-Sign-On Portal (SSO)

A website portal is a multi-functional information systems which provides a single point of access to relevant services via the Web-enabled interface [54]. The SSO portal enables login to multi-portals and applications [55]. Accounts created in one portal can be shared and used to login to other portals [24, 56]. Users will not need to remember multiple accounts to access different portals or applications [55]. Most governments in developed and developing countries have established web portals to offer electronic service delivery to their citizens [24, 56].

Portals are single-point web browser interfaces applied to encourage the collection, exchange and diffusion of information [57]. Moreover, a national portal, along with other regional portals, establishes an interface between citizens, government departments, businesses, and employees. Organizations should develop SSO portals that require knowledge of specific organizations to result in efficient e-government projects, and to lead to effective integration of different governmental agencies [55].

3.3.3 Government Service Bus (GSB)

Government Service Bus (GSB) should be the middle platform of integration and services for government e-services and transactions, and should offer frequent services such as identity management, e-Payment and core data exchange through e-government national portal [42]. The new generation of integration called Enterprise Service Bus (ESB) launches ready-made integration codes using open standard, messaging, and freely joined Service Oriented Architecture (SOA) rules [58]. Organizations should apply the solution which required for as a quick win phase, enabling the provision of e-services from different governmental agencies to use a common infrastructure for integration, sharing of data and the use of centralized shared services through the GSB.

3.3.4 Government Secure Network (GSN)

The Government Secure Network (GSN) is important in providing a communications network specifically for electronic government transactions. Thus, it links government agencies to the e-Government Data Centre, which should be established at the highest technical specifications and security for use in hosting the gate of the national electronic services, and the host site for the e-government program [42]. The GSN facilitates the e-government program to becoming a key connection point among government organizations in a security and a cost effective manner. Organization communications should be characterized by a high degree of efficiency and reliability to provide very high transfer speeds and should provide security in the transfer of data through the use of the latest techniques of data transfer protocols to be able to connect to other agencies through GSN.

3.4 Portal Architecture

Portal architecture refers to the fundamental technological architecture of an e-government portal [43]. In Portal architecture, stability and scalability are critical for successfully implementing an e-government portal. A government organization's portal must be ready and capable to offer access to all government back-end services from delivery channels; to meet diverse back-office needs; to cater for varying levels of technology; to handle digital authorization; and to manage increased degrees of traffic [59].

However, implementing e-government projects is problematic for many authorities because these projects frequently fail to advance e-service value and quality [45]. E-government portals allow governments to extend services to citizens, other government agencies, businesses and employees integrated as a single unit [60]. Despite high possible advantages, few e-government organizational portals can be considered as successful [61].

Technical architecture is an important technical indicator that refers to the technical structure and orientation. To implement e-enablement projects, several technical structure requirements are demanded; for software development, hardware structure and standards, services orientation and design. There are several factors to help in assessing the technical architecture readiness, from which: availability of portal, layered structure, and Service Oriented Architecture (SOA) as described in next sections [62].

3.4.1 Availability of Portal

Availability refers to the types, levels, and number of services provided through an government public sector portal [43]. A portal can offer many services that are consistent with principles of customer centric portal design, for example services are triggered from portal using shared IT support services such as payment, security, DMS [63]. A [64] study suggests that five types of services can be provided through e-government portals including emerging, enhanced, interactive, transactional, and integrated services. Portal availability is an essential aspect for e-government services. The portal existence effects readiness perception.

3.4.2 Layered Structure

Layered structures are commonly used in architectural design. They permit classification into vertical hierarchy and reduction of package combination [65].

Presentation Control Mediator Entity Foundation (PCMEF) aims to minimize dependency and object intercommunication (Maciaszek, 2004). PCMEF acquires stimulation from previous design patterns such as Data Mapper, MVC, Observer, Chain of Responsibility and Mediator [65]. PCMEF is a layered architectural framework which is comprised of four layers: presentation, control, domain and foundation [65]. These layers reflect the portal design, which can be assess the readiness of the portal performance through the: operating systems, communication standards used, and infrastructure accessibility.

This study s PCMEF framework to assess layered structure which has the three layers: presentation layer (including existing portal solution), middle layer/layer domain (including sepal-rated logic of business and support application), and back-office/foundation layer (including data bases, ECM, ERP, Web services, etc..).

3.4.3 Service Oriented Architecture (SOA)

A Service Oriented Architecture (SOA) approach to e-governance supports IT with service delivery objectives and allows different government agencies to reprocess developed assets [62, 66]. It is useful to offer flexible SOA solutions as this can be beneficial for governing, integrating, deploying, securing, and managing services, irrespective of the platforms on which they were created [62, 66].

SOA diminishes the dependency on back-end applications and reduces the requirement to write code every time there is a change in policy because it can deal with different platforms, and can establish new software that advances the direct collaboration of e-government users irrespective of the delivery model [62, 66]. Furthermore, internal and various external interfaces between applications and/or databases follow principles of service orientation [62].

3.5 Processes

Business and information process systems includes the collaborative meeting between the business management and ICT management to define, agree, and communicate the vision, goals, objectives, action, requirements, and governance in understanding the incorporated modification of the business through the ICT supported information systems [26].

However, the current e-readiness tools are inadequate in effectively addressing the issue of information access [31]. Therefore, the proposed framework focuses on three important factors of business processes including support processes, process automations and data and information flow.

3.5.1 Support Processes

Reforming e-government processes can play an important role supporting government internal work processes to advance efficiency [57]. Reengineering government work processes using ICT is fundamental to increasing accuracy by providing integrated reporting systems of central and local governments also to advancing efficiency by sharing information both within and between agencies [57].

One of the important tools utilized to accomplish business process innovation is Business Process Reengineering (BPR) [57]. BPR includes redesigning the work flow within or between department for enhancing process affectively and efficiency such as to reduce inefficiency in the work process [57]. In addition, BPR in e-governance includes significant analysis and thorough re-engineering of workflows and processes in the organization [66]. BPR can help to achieve high level of process performance and service delivery that to the government employees and citizens [66]. Moreover, state that a BPR project initiates to resolve barriers of the decision making process and to advance the process in the cabinet secretary office [55].

The main stages in BPR methodology are: Map existing processes; Define end-state; Gap analysis;Redesign of workflow and processes. Adoption of BPR in e-governance helps to Lower cost; Increase revenue; Enhance effectiveness, efficiency, and re-usability; and increase customer satisfaction [57, 66].

The impact of e-government is maximum in the field of services quality and government processes.

3.5.2 Process Automations

Every business process should be performed with significant use of ICT; most processes should be fully automated, i.e., after initial data input all operation should be performed by applications.

ICT applications refer to logical systems that manage the data objects in the data architecture and that support the business functions in the business architecture [67]. ICT application offers a design for each application system to be implemented and deployed [67]. This provides integration between application systems and the core business processes of the organization [67]. ICT applications can be used to improve user's trust, knowledge sharing and information processing for interacting within and between organizations [68]. ICT applications integrate front-end e-government layer applications, for example online transaction interfaces in the government portal with back-end actions for instance, presented databases and data warehouses [38].

E-government component has two categories: front-office and back-office [57]. The front-office category involves online service delivery to citizens, businesses and employees, via the Internet or other multiple access channels [57]. The back-office category contains internal government management and information sharing both within and between government agencies. Government-to-Citizens (G2C) and Government-to-Business (G2B) services are classified as front-office, and Government-to-Government (G2G) and Government-to-Employees (G2E) as back-office [57].

This article summarizes previous studies view of effective e-government delivery, this requires the following ICT applications as shows in Table 1.

Table 1. Processes - Applications and systems

Application/Systems	Description	References
Core Business Applications	Applications that are specifically used by one government organization.	[52]
Enterprise Resource Planning (ERP)	Integrated and draw directly from live databases linked to the systems such as HR, Payroll, Finance, Procurement, etc..	[42, 69]
Enterprise Application Integration (EAI)	Systems have emerged to overcome some of the limitations of ERP, through facilitating integration through the use of technologies that allow corporate IS subsystems to communicate with one another. In the context of using enterprise technologies to integrate ERP with other organizational business systems (because ERP systems is a difficult, costly, and risky).	[70] [69]
Web services	Standards-based and suited to build common infrastructure to reduce the barriers of business integrations, hence, enable e-government systems to collaborate with each other of infrastructure.	[71, 72]
Electronic Data Interchange (EDI)	Designed to exchange documents between organizations.	[73, 74]
Customer Relationship Management (CRM)	An integrated approach to managing relationships by focusing on customer retention and relationship development. CRM has evolved from advances in information technology and organizational change in customer-centric processes.	[75] [76]
Geographic Information Systems (GIS)	A digital tool to help in the storing, analysis, mapping, and illustration of large amounts of diverse electronic data.	[77]
Enterprise Content Management (ECM)	The technologies, tools, and methods used to capture, manage, store, preserve, and deliver content across an enterprise. This is a broad definition that covers a wide range of technological categories such as Electronic Document Management (EDM), Business Process Management (BPM) and business process.	[78] [79]
Database Management System (DBMS)	A necessity for any course in database systems or file organization. DBMS offers "a hands-on approach" to relational database systems, with a highlighting on practical topics such as indexing methods, SQL, and database design.	[80, 81]
Data Warehousing	A collection of data from multiple sources, integrated into a data store and widened by outline information such as aggregate views.	[82] [83]

In addition, after reviewing literature, ICT applications in government organizations can be classified into three categories:

- Common Applications used by all government organizations such as HR systems, financial systems, and ECM.

- Applications that are used by many government organizations such as recruitment applications.
- Applications that are used by one government organization such as a core business application.

3.5.3 Data and Information Flow

Major share of data entry should take place by database query, i.e., for example citizen ID should be used to avoid data entry by calling historic correspondence; most customers are should be notified by e-mail, internet or mobile besides traditional ways [42].

3.6 ICT Infrastructure

The dimension of ICT infrastructure has been a key issue for many researchers. Several studies identify the organization's ICT infrastructure and focuses technology components [2, 84]. However, the ICT infrastructure concept is more complicated. In addition, ICT design relies on the service oriented architecture model implemented with web-services.

Having a successful e-government strategy that requires that government organizations establish a suitable IT infrastructure to support information systems and applications [53]. Many developing countries suffer from implementing ICT projects, and are not able to install the suitable ICT infrastructure for e-government deployment. The digital divide between richer countries and developing ones is large with high-income economies [85].

Based on previous studies, ICT infrastructure includes a group of shared, physical ICT resources that offer a foundation to facilitate existing and future business applications. These resources include: (1) hardware and software (e.g., operating systems); (2) connectivity; (3) security; and (4) operations.

3.6.1 Hardware and Software

E-government ICT infrastructure possibly will include some technologies with a network infrastructure at its origin; containing web servers, application servers, storage devices, PCs, printers, scanners, routers, switches, firewalls, hardware and operating systems, and data and application development tools [67, 86]. The storage, acquisition, and data exchange must be provided through these technologies in order to allow date access internally or externally to the organization. Moreover, these technologies particularly servers work through professional network technology and internet connectivity that advance communication and information transmission within and between organizations online [38].

3.6.2 Connectivity

Connectivity offers necessary technologies, such as Local Area Network (LAN) and Wide Area Network (WAN). LANs *"allow integration with current hardware resources such as PCs, laptops, and mobile phones straightforward and without complications which supporting the organization existing IT provision"* [38]. Also, LANs support the provision of user-friendly and innovative online services involving the transmission of data of various formats such as text, graphics, audio and video ([38]. WAN is a communications network that makes use of existing technology to connect local computer networks into a larger working network that may cover both national and international locations [67, 86]. This is in contrast to LAN which provides communication within a restricted geographic area.

The aim of these technologies is to support and integrate the operations of business processes and information systems dimension across organizations by providing the necessary standards and protocols all the way through ICT network and communication infrastructure solutions such as the intranet, extranet, Internet, and VOIP.

3.6.3 Security

This dimension must integrate a high level of security solutions and technologies such as Public Key Infrastructure (PKI), firewall, biometrics, digital signature and certificate, and sophisticated encryption technique, which secure e-government interoperation, government electronic transactions, and delivery systems to guarantee protection and prevent fraud and other vulnerabilities at all levels of the government ICT infrastructure [38].

One of the most important aspects of the security plan is its set of security objectives [87]. There are five objectives of computer network security including (1) a security policy: an explicit and well-defined security policy imposed by the system is essential; (2) identification: the objects have to be individually identified: identification is essential so that objects access can be examined; (3) accountability: all tasks that influence the security system must maintain complete and secure records, for instance, actions include identifying new users to the system, assigning or updating the security level of elements, and denying access attempts; (4) assurance: the computing system must contain techniques that enforce security, and it must be able to assess these effectiveness of the techniques and (5) continuous protection: the techniques that implement security must be protected against unauthorized access or change [87].

3.6.4   Operations and Maintenance

The operations set of processes provides the day-to-day work needed to monitor and maintain a continuous ICT infrastructure and operating systems [88]. They explain a number of the jobs associated with the processes are job scheduling, data management (including backup and recovery management), enterprise command centre, physical database administration and proactive hardware maintenance. Furthermore, the increased demand in recent years for continuous operation of applications and database in the presence of disasters [89]. Disaster Recovery (DR) solution is fundamental to ensure continuous operation through a remote backup of applications, database and communication, even in the incidence of widespread failures [89].

3.7 Human Resources

Identifying the roles and responsibilities of employees are essential to accomplish the organisation's vision [90]. There are important factors should be considered to succeed e-government such as ICT managers and staff skills, ICT awareness and customer service satisfactory, training and development and ICT assistance [33].

Governance or management from technology perspective defined as a good management at different levels [91]. ICT management specifies the decision making authority and accountability to encourage desirable behaviors in the use of ICT. Over 75% of businesses today have ineffective or nonexistent ICT management [92]. For ICT to move forward rapidly in the business-driven environment, ICT management must change radically and swiftly to maximize the business value of IT [92]. Most enterprises should "blow up" their existing governance models and start over from scratch" [93]. In order to achieve a certain level of service delivery agreement by e-government, it is important to set and identify the roles of leadership and management. That could be done taking into consideration some guidelines that would help in this regard such as identify a Service Manager with end-to-end responsibility for service delivery and identify a Service Level agreement, the time, quality and cost, evaluation and customer service satisfactory [94].

Technical support can play a significant role for supporting three issues [88]. First, it assists with design and planning by given that technical assessments, both in the form of Proof of Concept (POC) and pilot tests of new technologies. Second, it helps the RFI (Request for Information) and RFP (Request for Price) processes. Technical Support takes actions as a relationship with dealers on technical issues. Third, it is responsible for creating and maintaining the technical library and the technical knowledge base for the organization.

A major challenge of an e-government initiative is the lack of ICT skills in the public sector. This is a particular problem in developing countries [95]. In addition, there are number of constructs need to be considered such as user satisfaction, impact on employees, skills (Adaptation to change, Use of technology, Integration, Customer service) and HR training and development [33].

Human resources factors which contributes towards an organisation's e-government goals include suitably qualified ICT mangers and staff within the public organisations and technical e-government experience; ICT awareness and customer service satisfactory; training and support system which maintains the currency of personnel skills sets in keeping with e-government developments; ICT assistance; such as help desks (that meet customer needs) is should be available during hours within their organisations.

4   Conclusion

In order to provide key stakeholders with a framework that could be applied in performing regular assessment of e-government readiness it is essential to identify limitations and provide proper solutions. This article reviewed previous appraisal models of e-government readiness, focusing on their limitations. This article proposed an integrated framework for assessing readiness of e-government organizations. Unlike the previous e-government literature that focuses predominantly on internal organization factors and employs generic e-readiness tools, this study contributes an organizational perspective for assessing e-readiness that incorporates relevant factors to an e-government context. The suggested e-government framework consist of seven factors of e-readiness assessment for government organizations including strategy, user access, national e-government program, portal architecture, processes, infrastructure, and people.

This article provides helpful suggestions to e-government decision makers, ICT mangers, ICT specialists and suppliers in the public sector by providing insights geared towards improving business decision-making, and expanding competitive advantage from effective e-government services. Agencies assigned responsibility for assessing e-readiness may refer to this framework as a useful resource during the e-government project. The suggested framework for assessing e-government readiness will diminish complexity related to unsuccessful e-government strategies in the government sector through understanding the significant e-government factors mentioned in the suggested framework.

This article addresses the challenges and opportunities for developing a successful e-government, and discussing different factors for achieving the success for e-government projects and the role of ICT to lead organizations self assessments.

Even though this framework is supportive more research is necessary. The conceptual framework provided in this study paves the way for future quantitative empirical research through a case study to test the framework. Nevertheless, this study is an important conceptual step in identifying relevant factors from an organizational perspective for assessing e-readiness in an e-government context.

References

1. World Bank, E-Ready for What? E-Readiness in Developing Countries: Current Status and Prospects toward the Millennium Development Goals, I.f.D. Program, Editor: USA (2005)
2. Bakry, S.H.: Development of e-Government: A STOPE view. International Journal of Network Management 14(4), 339–350 (2004)
3. Caldow, J.: The Quest for Electronic Government: A Defining Vision, The Institute for Electronic Government, IBM Corporation (1991)
4. ACM, ACM International Workshop on Vehicular Ad Hoc Networks. In: Proceedings of the... ACM International Workshop on Vehicular Inter-Networking. ACM Press, New York (2008)
5. APEC, e-Commerce Readiness Assessment Initiative, APEC (2008)
6. CID, Readiness for the Networked World: A Guide for Developing Countries. The GeoSinc Facilitation Center, The Harvard University Center for International Development (2002)
7. Cohen, G.: Technology Transfer: Strategic Management in Developing Countries. Sage Publications, New Delhi (2004)
8. Dutton, W.H.: Information and Communication Technologies: Visions and Realities. Oxford University Press (1996)
9. Kahen, G.: Building a Framework for Successful Information Technology Transfer to Developing Countries: Requirements and Effective Integration to a Viable IT Transfer. International Journal of Computer Applications in Technologies 6(1), 1–8 (1996)
10. Snellen, I.: Is "Informatisation" after 20 years still a "corpus alienum" in Public Administration?' in Information Polity. The International Journal of Government and Democracy in the Information Age 12(4), 201–206 (2007)
11. Taylor, J.: Rediscovering the grand narratives of the information polity: Reflections on the achievement and potential of the EGPA Study Group on ICT in Public Administration. Information Polity The International Journal of Government and Democracy in the Information Age 12(4), 213–218 (2007)

12. Abdalla, K.A.: Stakeholder Perceptions of Issues for Successful Information Technology Transfer in a Developing Country: A Case Study of the United Arab Emirates. Department of Information Systems Faculty of Business, The University of Southern Queensland: Toowoomba, Australia (2006)
13. Alshihi, H.: Critical factors in the Adoption and Diffusion of e-government initiative in Oman. Victoria University, Melbourne (2005)
14. Baark, E., Heeks, R.: Donor-funded information technology transfer projects: evaluating the life-cycle approach in four Chinese science and technology projects. Information Technology for Development 8, 185–197 (1999)
15. Rahman, H.: E-Government Readiness: from the Design Table to the Grass Roots. ACM 978-1-59593-822 -0/07/12 (2007)
16. Moon, M.J.: The evolution of e-government among municipalities: rhetoric or reality? Public Administration Review 26(4), 424–434 (2002)
17. Millard, J.: European e-Government (2005-2007),
    http://www.epractice.eu/files/download/awards/
    ResearchReport2007.pdf
18. Reddick, C.G.: Citizen Interaction with E-government: From the Streets to Servers? Government Information Quarterly 22(1), 38–57 (2005)
19. Gil-Garcia, J.R., Pardo, T.A.: E-government success factors: Mapping practical tools to theoretical foundations. Government Information Quarterly (2005)
20. Martin, B., Bryne, T.: Implementing e-Gov: widening the lens. The Electronic Journal of E-Government 1(1), 11–22 (2003)
21. Heeks, R.: e-Government as a Carrier of Context. Journal of Public Policy 25(1), 51–74 (2005)
22. Layne, K., Lee, J.: Developing fully functional E-government: A four stage model. Government Information Quarterly 18(2), 122–136 (2001)
23. O'Neill, R.: E-government: Transformation of Public Governanace in New Zealand? Victoria University of Wellington, New Zealand (2009)
24. Chen, H.: Issue Digital Government: technologies and practices. Decision Support Systems 34, 223–227 (2002)
25. Safai-Amin, M.: Information technologies: challenges and opportunities for local governments. Journal of Government Information 27, 471–479 (2002)
26. OECD, E-Government Project: Key Issues and Findings. Public Governance and Territorial Development Directorate, Public Management Committee (2002)
27. OECD, e-Government Studies: The E-Government Imperative, OECD Publishing (2003)
28. Heeks, R.: Implementing and Managing E-Government: An International Text. Sage Publishers (2005)
29. Heeks, R.: Most eGovernment-for-Development Projects Fail: How Can Risks be Reduced?, http://unpan1.un.org/intradoc/groups/public/
    documents/NISPAcee/UNPAN015488.pdf
30. Andersen, K.V.: E-government and Public Sector Process Rebuilding: Dilettantes, Wheel Barrows, and Diamonds Springer; 1st ed. Softcover of orig. ed. 2004 edition, November 4 (2010)
31. Stephen, M., Mutula, Pieter, v.B.: An evaluation of e-readiness assessment tools with respect to information access: Towards an integrated information rich tool. International Journal of Information Management 26(3), 212–223 (2006)
32. Rizk, N.: E-readiness assessment of small and medium enterprises in Egypt: A micro study, http://www.luc.edu/orgs/meea/volume6/Rizk.pdf

33. Azab, N.A., Kamel, S., Dafoulas, G.: A Suggested Framework for Assessing Electronic Government Readiness in Egypt. Electronic Journal of e-Government 7(1), 11–28 (2009)
34. Altman, C.: Converging Technologies: The Future of the Global Information Society. First Committee Chair Report to the UN General Assembly UNISCA (2002)
35. Jansen, A.: Assessing e-Government Progress – Why and What, Department of e-Government Studies: University of Oslo (2005)
36. Andersen, K.V., Henriksen, H.Z.: The First Leg of E-Government Research: Domains and Application Areas 1998 – 2003. International Journal of Electronic Government Research 1(4), 26–44 (2005)
37. Norris, D.F., Lloyd, B.A.: The Scholarly Literature on E-Government: Characterising a Nascent Field. International Journal of Electronic Government Research 2(4), 40–56 (2006)
38. Ebrahim, Z., Irani, Z.: E-government adoption: Architecture and Barriers. Business Process Management Journal 11(5), 589–611 (2005)
39. Richard, L.F.: Office of Information Technology E-Government Services, N.J.S. Legislature, O.o.L. Services, and O.o.t.S. Auditor, Editors (2001)
40. State Services Commission, Enabling transformation a strategy for e-government: Wellington, New Zealand. pp. 1-36 (2006)
41. APEC. e-Readiness Assessment Guid,
    http://www.apdip.net/documents/evaluation/
    e-readiness/geosinc01042002.pdf
42. Yesser, Supporting plans and methodologies (a) E-Readiness assessment methodology for government organizations, E-government Program, Ministry Communications and Information Technology (MCIT) Riyadh, Saudi Arabia (2005)
43. Maheshwari, B., et al.: E-Government Portal Effectiveness: Managerial Considerations for Design and Development, Computer Society of India (2009)
44. Criado, J.I., Ramilo, M.C.: E-Government in practice: an analysis of website orientation to citizens in Spanish municipalities. International Journal of Public Sector Management 18(3), 191–218 (2003)
45. Accenture, Leadership in Customer Service: New Expectations, New Experiences, The Government Executive Series (2005)
46. Becker, S.A., Nowak, L.L.: Automated support for older adult accessibility of e-government web sites. Digital Government Society of North America 130, 1–4 (2003)
47. Carter, L., Belanger, F.: The utilization of e-government services: citizen trust, innovation and acceptance factors. Information Systems Journal 15(1), 5–25 (2005)
48. Alsobhi, F.M., Weerakkody, V.: CurrentT State of E-services in Saudi Arabia: The Case of Intermediaries in Facilitiing Government Services in Madinah City. In: European and Mediterranean Conference on Information Systems. Crown Plaza Hotel, Izmir (2009)
49. Brannen, A.: E-Government in California: Providing Services to Citizens through the Internet. Journal of State Government 74(2) (2001)
50. IDA, Multi-channel delivery of eGovernment services. In: Interchange of Data between Administrations (2004)
51. Almarabeh, T., Abuali, A.: A General Framework for E-Government: Definition Maturity Challenges, Opportunities, and Success. European Journal of Scientific Research 39(1), 29 42 (2010)
52. AlMansoori, R.: Abu Dhabi e-Government Program,
    http://www.abudhabi.ae/egovPoolPortal_WAR/
53. IBM. Creating an Infrastructure for eGovernment: Enabling Government Innovation

54. Forman, M., Thompson, D.: National e-Government Portals. The Tip of the Iceberg, or Tools for Citizen-Centric Transformation of Government, http://www.egov.vic.gov.au/trends-and-issues/ e-government/national-e-government-portals.html
55. Sharifi, H., Zarei, B.: An adaptive approach for implementing e-government I.R. Iran. Journal of Government Information 30(1) (2004)
56. Lee, S.M., Tan, X., Trimi, S.: Current practices of leading e-government countries. Communications of the ACM 84(10), 99–104 (2005)
57. Lee, Y.N.: E-Government Application, http://www.unapcict.org/academy
58. Chappell, D.A.: Enterprise Service Bus. O'Reilly Media, Inc., USA (2004)
59. Accenture, eGovernment Leadership: High Performance, Maximum Value, The Government Executive Series (2004)
60. Stauffacher, G.: E-Government as and Instrument of Public Management Reform. In: E-Government Conference, 2nd edn., pp. 22–24 (2002)
61. Norris, D.F., Moon, M.J.: Advancing E-Government at the Grassroots: Tortoise or Hare? Public Administration Review 65(1), 64–75 (2005)
62. Oracle. Oracle portal, http://education.oracle.com/pls/ web_prod-plq-dad/db_pages.getCourseDesc?dc=D68842GC20
63. Bretschneider, S., Gant, J., Ahn, M.: A General Model of E-Government service Adoption: Empirical Exploration. In: Public Management Research Conference. Georgetown Public Policy Institute, Washington, DC (2003)
64. UNDPEPA/ASPA. Benchmarking e-government: A global perspective, http://www.itpolicy.gov.il/topics_egov/docs/benchmarking.pdf
65. Maciaszek, L.A.: International Conference on Enterprise Information Systems, Porto, Portugal (2004)
66. Behara, G., Varre, V., Rao, M.: Service Oriented Architecture for E-Governance, BPTrends (2009)
67. Macasio, J.: ICT Services Management Practitioner's Not E-enterprise Architecture, http://www.scribd.com/doc/24641260/ ENTERPRISE-ARCHITECTURE-PRACTITIONER-S-NOTE-draft-release
68. Moodley, S.: The challenge of e-business for the South African apparel sector. Technovation 23(7), 557–570 (2003)
69. Sharif, A.M., Irani, Z., Love, P.E.D.: Integrating ERP using EAI: a model for post hoc evaluation. European Journal of Information Systems 14, 162–174 (2005)
70. Themistocleous, M., Irani, Z.e.a.: Enterprise application integration: an emerging technology for integrating ERP and supply chains. In: European Conference on Information Systems, Gdansk (2002)
71. Samtani, G., Sadhwani, D.: Web Services and Application Frameworks (.NET and J2EE): Tect Ltd. (2002)
72. Huang, W., D'Ambra, J., Vikrant, B.: Key Factors Influencing the Adoption of E-Government in Australian Public Sectors. In: 8th Americas Conference on Information Systems, Dallas, USA (2002)
73. Meena, R.S.: Environmental-informatics—A solution for long term environmental research. Global Journal of Enterprise Information System 1(2) (2009)
74. Chesher, M., Kaura, R., et al.: Electronic Business & Commerce. Springer, London (2003)
75. Chen, I.J., Popovich, K.: Understanding customer relationship management (CRM): People, process and technology. Business Process Management Journal 9(5), 672–688 (2003)

76. Pan, S.-L., Tan, C.-W., Lim, E.T.K.: Customer relationship management (CRM) in e-government: a relational perspective. Decision Support Systems 42(1) (2006)
77. Rifai, H.S., et al.: A Geographic Information System (GIS) User Interface for Delineating Wellhead Protection Areas 31(3), 480–488 (2005)
78. IBM and PTC, Enterprise Content Management: Challenges and Considerations XML Publisher Journal (2) (2010)
79. Blair, B.T.: An Enterprise Content Management Primer. The Information Management Journal (2004)
80. Ramakrishnan, R., Gehrke, J.: Database Management System, 2nd edn (1999) ISBN: 0072322063
81. Seres, A.: Three Database Management Systems (DBMS) compared. Open Source Science Journal 2(4), 65–82 (2010)
82. Bazerman, M.: In Announcing IACM 2010 23rd Annual Conference Abstracting eJournal. Social Science Electronic Publishing, Inc. (2010)
83. Mumick, I.S., Quass, D., Mumick, B.S.: Maintenance of Data Cubes and Summary Tables in a Warehouse. In: Proc. ACM SIGMOD Int. Conf. on Management, pp. 100–111 (1997)
84. Center for International Development - Harvard University and IBM, Readiness for the Networked World: A Guide for Developing Countries (CID) and IBM (2007)
85. World Bank, Information and Communications for Development 2006: Global Trends and Policies. World Bank Publications (2006)
86. IBM. ICT Infrastructure, http://www.ibm.com
87. Pfleeger, C.P., Pfleeger, S.L.: Security in Computing, 3rd edn. Prentice Hall, NJ (2003)
88. Patrizio, D.N., et al.: ICT Infrastructure - the Regional Dimension. Benchmarking the Information Society: e-Europe Indicators for European Regions, BISER (2004)
89. Garcia-Molina, H., Polyzois, C.A.: Thirty-Fifth IEEE Computer Society International Conference, San Francisco, CA, USA (2002)
90. Macasio, J.: Open Practitioner Notes: Information Systems Strategic Planning Basics, http://www.scribd.com/doc/24641437/INFORMATION-SYSTEM-STRATEGIC-PLANNING-PRACTITIONER-S-NOTE-draft-version
91. Katib, H.: Science and Technology in Jordan, Towards Sustainable Policies (Policies, Strategies, Financing and Governance). The Seventh Jordanian Science Week, Jordan (2001)
92. Al-Omari, A., Al-Omari, H.: E-Government Readiness Assessment Model. Journal of Computer Science 2(11), 841–845 (2006)
93. Dallas, S.: IT Governance in the Business-Driven Environment. Gartner IT EXPo: Orlando Florida, USA (2002)
94. Gartner Group, Gartner Group Report to The Jordanian Ministry of Information & Communication Technology (MoICT), M.o.I.C.T (MoICT), Editor, Gartner Group: Amman (2002)
95. United Nations, UN E-Government Survey 2008 From E-Government to Connected Governance, Department of Economic and Social Affairs. Administration and Development Management, United Nations Online Network in Public Administration and Finance (UNPAN), Division for Public. United Nations Publications, USA (2008)

Recovery of Memory Based on Page Replacement Algorithms

Ahmad Rashidah, Chin Lay Gan, and Mohd Yunus Rubiah

Centre for Diploma Programmes,
Multimedia University,
Melaka, Malaysia
{rashidah.ahmad,gan.chin.lay,rubiah.yunus}@mmu.edu.my

Abstract. In the Main Memory Database (MMDB), the primary copy of the database resides in volatile main memory. This makes the MMDB more vulnerable to failures compared to Disk Resident Database (DRDB). A backup copy of the database is maintained in secondary storage for recovery purposes. Recovery activities like logging, check pointing and reloading are used to restore the database to a consistent state after system failure. In this paper, a recovery scheme using two page replacement algorithms for MMDB was implemented. The performance of the recovery mechanism as a function of the number of pages and size of pages was measured. From the results, the recovery time increase almost linearly with the increase in the size of the memory and that the number of pages in the memory affects the recovery. The simulation results show that the Least Recently Used (LRU) algorithm will have the least recovery time compared to First-in First-out (FIFO) algorithm. These techniques can be utilized for replacement of the lost memory to improve the recovery time and can be further enhanced to other areas of web caching.

Keywords: page replacement algorithm, memory recovery, Least Recently Used (LRU), First-in First-out (FIFO), Main Memory Database (MMDB).

1 Introduction

A failure is an event at which the system does not perform according to specifications. Some failures are caused by hardware faults (e.g., a power failure or disk failure), software faults (e.g., bugs in programs or invalid data) or human errors (e.g., the operator mounts a wrong tape on a drive, or a user does something unintentional). A failure occurs when an erroneous state of the system is processed by algorithms of the system. The term error is in this context used for that part of the state which is "incorrect." An error is thus a piece of information which can cause a failure. In order to cope with failures, additional components and abnormal algorithms can be added to a system. These components and algorithms attempt to ensure that occurrences of erroneous states do not result in later system failures. Ideally they remove these errors and restore them to "correct" states from which normal processing can continue. These additional components and abnormal algorithms, called recovery techniques [12], are the subject of this research paper.

A. Abd Manaf et al. (Eds.): ICIEIS 2011, Part II, CCIS 252, pp. 499–511, 2011.

There are many kinds of failures and therefore many kinds of recovery. There is always a limit to the kind of recovery that can be provided. If a failure not only corrupts the ordinary data, but also the recovery data, i.e. redundant data maintained to make recovery possible, complete recovery may be impossible [12]. Recovery mechanism will only cope with certain failures. It may not cope with failures, for example, that are rare, that have not been thought of, that have no effects, or that would be too expensive to recover from. For example, a head crash on disk may destroy not only the data but also the recovery data. It would therefore be preferable to maintain the recovery data on a separate device. However, there are other failures which may affect the separate device as well; for example, failures in the machinery that writes the recovery data to that storage device.

2   Review of Literature

2.1   Virtual Memory

Virtual memory or virtual memory addressing is a technique of memory management that allows processes to execute not entirely in the memory by means of automatic storage allocation upon request [1] [3]. It is a hardware that makes a computer appear to have more physical memory than it actually does. This is accomplished by swapping unused resources out of physical memory and replacing them with those required to execute the current operation.

Virtual memory addressing is typically used in paged memory systems [5]. This in turn is often combined with memory swapping, whereby memory pages stored in primary storage are written to secondary storage, thus freeing faster primary storage for other processes to use [1]. If the page referenced by the virtual address is not currently in main memory, a page fault occurs, triggering an operating system handler that swaps in the page. Some other page might be swapped out to make room. Data is transferred from secondary to primary storage as and when necessary and the data replaced is written back to the secondary storage [3] according to a predetermined replacement algorithm.

Each process typically has its own separate virtual address space with its own mappings and protections [4]. A program generated address or "logical address" consisting of a logical page number plus the location within that page must be interpreted or "mapped" onto an actual (physical) main memory address by the operating system using an address translation function or mapper.

If the page is present in the main memory, the mapper substitutes the physical page frame number for the logical number. If the mapper detects that the page requested is not present in main memory, a fault occurs and the page must be read into a frame in main memory from secondary storage using the page replacement policies. In this case, the page replacement algorithm influences the memory recovery.

2.2   Page Replacement

Generally page replacement is to determine which page in the main memory to remove or overwrite. As more users (or active processes) reside in a system, the more allocated memory tends to become. With paging, this means that all of the page frames tend to be in use most of the time. When the page need to be loaded into a memory, probably because it has been referenced by a running process, the operating system must make room for it.

The operating system must decide which existing page to replace. A page fault occurs whenever the page referenced is not in the main memory, i.e. when a valid page entry cannot be found in the address translator (which include in main memory page tables in the Translation Look-aside Buffers (TLB) method). When this occurs, the required page must be located in the secondary memory using the secondary memory pages table, and a page in the main memory must be identified for removal if there is no free space in the main memory. When the page fault occurs, the operating system loads the faulted page from disk into a page frame of the memory.

At some point, the process has use the entire page frame. When this happens, the operating system must replace a page for each page faulted in free page frame. The goal of the replacement algorithm is to reduce the fault rate by selecting the best victim page to remove. When a process is fault and memory is full, some page must be swapped out. The replacement algorithms for the policy are a useful property known as the stack property.

2.3 Page Replacement Algorithms

Page replacement algorithms are also known as page replacement policies. The primary objective is to select a page replacement strategy that yields the smallest page fault rate. Below are several page replacement algorithms.

Least Recently Used (LRU). The LRU algorithm replaces the page which has not been accessed for the longest time. It performs very well, but it is difficult to implement. This seemingly good algorithm is not very efficient, since it's expensive to store count for every page table referenced [2].

First-in First-out (FIFO). The FIFO algorithm is extremely simple. It removes the page with the earliest creation time. This can be implemented using a list. New pages are inserted at the head of the list, and the page at the tail is swapped out [2]. Another implementation is to use a ring (usually referred to as "clock"). Every time a page has to be replaced, the page the pointer points at is swapped out and at the same place the new page is swapped in. After this, the pointer moves to the next page [6].

Second Chance. The Second Chance algorithm is very similar to FIFO. However, it interferes with the accessing process. Every page has, in addition to its "dirty bit", a "referenced bit" (r-bit). Every time a page is accessed, the r-bit is set. The replacement process works like FIFO, except that when a page's r-bit is set, instead of replacing it, the r-bit is unset, the page is moved to the list's tail (or the pointer moves to the next page) and the next page is examined. Second Chance algorithm performs better than FIFO, but it is far from optimal.

Least Frequently Used (LFU). The LFU algorithm is another classic replacement algorithm. It replaces the block that is least frequently used. The motivation for this algorithm is that some blocks are accessed more frequently than others so that the reference counts can be used as an estimate of the probability of a block being referenced. The "aged" LFU usually performs better than the original LFU because the former gives different weight to the recent references and very old references.

2.4 Page Replacement Algorithm Process

When a page fault occurs, the operating system has to choose a page to remove from memory to make room for the page that has to be brought in. If the page to be removed has been modified while in memory, it must be rewritten to the disk to bring the disk copy up to date. If the page has not been changed (e.g., it contains program text), the disk copy is already up to date, so no rewrite is needed. The page to be read in just overwrites the page being evicted.

While it would be possible to pick a random page to evict at each page fault, system performance is much better if a page that is not heavily used is chosen. If a heavily used page is removed, it will probably have to be brought back in quickly, resulting in extra overhead. Much work has been done on the subject of page replacement algorithms, both theoretical and experimental. It is worth noting that the problem of page replacement occurs in other areas of computer design as well [6].

For example, most computers have one or more memory caches consisting of recently used 32-byte or 64-byte memory blocks. When the cache is full, some block has to be chosen for removal. This problem is precisely the same as page replacement except on a shorter time scale (it has to be done in a few nanoseconds, not milliseconds as with page replacement) [6]. The reasons for the shorter time scale is that cache block misses are satisfied from main memory, which has no sought time and no rotational latency.

A second example is in a Web server. The server can keep a certain number of heavily used Web pages in its memory cache. However, when the memory cache is full and a new page is referenced, a decision has to be made as to which Web page to evict. The considerations are similar to pages of virtual memory, except for the fact that the Web pages are never modified in the cache, so there is always a fresh copy on disk. In a virtual memory system, pages in main memory may be either clean or dirty.

3   Research Objectives

The objective of this research is to develop a simulation system and adapt the existing page replacement algorithms into the different area of memory recovery. The page replacement algorithms used are LRU and FIFO. With this, the objective is divided into two:

- To develop a simulation system and adapt the existing LRU and FIFO page replacement algorithms into different areas for memory recovery.

- To evaluate the best performance page replacement algorithms for memory recovery.

4   Scope of Research

The scope of this research is limited to the following:

- Recovery of lost memory based on LRU and FIFO page replacement algorithms.

- Evaluate the performance of memory recovery based on page replacement algorithms.

5   Research Methodology

The performance evaluation technique used to study the proposed method is simulation. The simulator, which uses the C++ programming language, is used to simulate the implementation of page replacement and the simulation was developed where all the parameters interact like a real system.

5.1   Simulation Model

The simulation model, as shown in figure 1 is based on a process used to simulate the performance of two page replacement algorithms. The simulated model involves applications, a memory and a processor. The applications or in this case pages requested is generated randomly. The size for each page generated is between 6400 bits to 64 Kbit. The size of memory simulated in this simulation is between 8 MB to 32 MB with the fixed amount of pages generated for each simulation tested.

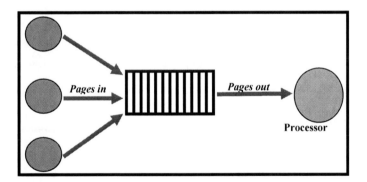

Fig. 1. Simulation Model

The simulated model will simultaneously process the requested pages. If the pages requested are not in the memory, the system crashed, the requested pages will find the place to reside into the memory using two different page replacement algorithms (LRU and FIFO). For LRU, the pages will find the least time the pages in memory used by the processor to shift out from the memory. By using the FIFO algorithm, the first pages inserted into the memory will be shift out to replace with the requested pages.

5.2 Performance Metrics

Two performance metrics have been selected as a method of evaluating the model. These metrics are commonly used in the performance study of memory recovery. The simulation was designed to capture these performance metrics.

Delay. Delay is defined as the time taken for searching an appropriate memory allocation for the requested pages by using two different page replacement algorithms (LRU and FIFO) to perform the searching after crash memory occurred.

Recovery time. Recovery time is defined as the time taken of requested page, inserted plus the delay time for searching a suitable memory allocation after crash memory occurred. The less delay time to recover the memory the better best algorithm scheme used in the simulation.

$$\text{Recovery Time} = \text{Time Page In} + \text{Delay Time} \tag{1}$$

For the purpose of the simulation, pages generated carries size in the range of 6400 bits to 64 Kbit. This size is generated randomly for each page. The size of these documents is used to calculate the byte hit when the document hit either in local cache, proxy cache, or index file. The byte hit increases every time the document is found in the cache. Figure 2 shows the process for searching the suitable memory location to shift out the data before inserting the requested pages.

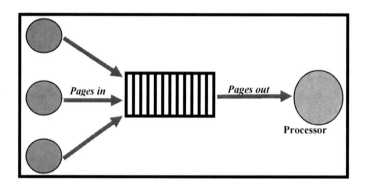

Fig. 2. Simulation Process

5.3 Page Replacement Algorithms

This section gives a very short overview of the page replacement algorithms which will be simulated in this research.

FIFO. FIFO algorithm is one of the low-overhead paging algorithms. The operating system maintains a list of all pages currently in memory, with the page at the head of the list the oldest one and the page at the tail the most recent arrival. On a page fault, the page at the head is removed and the new page added to the tail of the list [6].

LRU. A good approximation to the optimal algorithm is based on the observation that pages that have been heavily used in the last few instructions will probably be heavily used again in the next few. Conversely, pages that have not been used for ages will probably remain unused for a long time. This idea suggests a realizable algorithm. When a page fault occurs, throw out the page that has been unused for the longest time [6].

Although LRU is theoretically realizable, it is not cheap. To fully implement LRU, it is necessary to maintain a linked list of all pages in memory, with the most recently used page at the front and the least recently used page at the rear. The difficulty is that the list must be updated on every memory reference. Finding a page in the list, deleting it, and then moving it to the front is a very time consuming operation, even in hardware (assuming that such hardware could be built).

However, there are other ways to implement LRU with special hardware. Let us consider the simplest way first. This method requires equipping the hardware with a 64-bit counter that is automatically incremented after each instruction. Furthermore, each page table entry must also have a field large enough to contain the counter. After each memory reference, the current value of the counter is stored in the page table entry for the page just referenced. When a page fault occurs, the operating system examines all the counters in the page table to find the lowest one. That page is the least recently used.

5.4 Simulation Assumptions

The assumptions made before design and implementing the simulation system for this research are:

First Assumption. During the implementation of the two page replacement algorithms (FIFO and LRU), first assumptions has been made to make sure this simulation run smoothly and research objective achieved. A fixed memory size 8 MB, the numbers of pages inserted into the memory exceed to 100K pages and the pages size within range of 6400 bits to 64 Kbit were chosen to run into this program and to evaluate the recovery time and delay time. It might be shown in the graph the influences between the various sizes of pages versus the numbers of pages inserted into the memory.

Second Assumption. During the implementation to evaluate the performance and influences between the sizes of memory versus the size of pages, memory size used are from the range of 8MB – 32MB, fixed numbers of pages inserted into the memory, which is 100K pages and the pages size within range of 6400 bit to 64 Kbit was setup to run the algorithms and to evaluate the recovery and delay time.

6 Design and Implementation

6.1 Simulation Model Design and Process Flow

Figure 3 shows an overall picture for the simulation process. The memory will be fully inserted with the data; in this case it is referring to pages. The page will be inserted one by one using FIFO and LRU. After the memory has been fully inserted by the data, in order to complete and to evaluate the performance for the replacement algorithms, one crash mechanism was created to this program by performing deletion mechanism for several data in the memory.

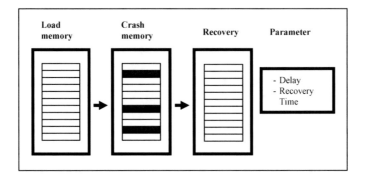

Fig. 3. Process flow for simulation model

6.2 FIFO

Arrival times for every page inserted into the memory are the important value to perform the FIFO algorithm. The time will be captured using a piece of code below:

$$\text{event\_time[next\_apps][next\_event]} = \text{clock} + \text{logx}; \qquad (2)$$

$$\text{logx} = - \log(\text{x/rand\_size})/\text{arrival\_rate};$$

Figure 4 illustrates the simulation process for FIFO algorithm after a memory crashes. When the processor requests a page, and the page is currently not in the memory, then FIFO algorithm will start a task by searching the earliest arrival time for all the pages in the memory. The selected page will be removed out from the memory. The entire pages are shifted to fill the blank space at the in front of the memory. The page requested by a processor will be inserting at the end of the memory after all the pages are shifted.

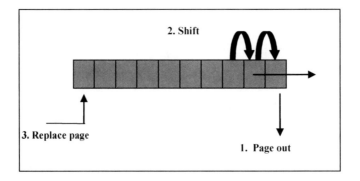

Fig. 4. FIFO Simulation Process

6.3 LRU

The number of times the page used in the memory is the key value to perform LRU algorithm. Figure 5 illustrates the simulation process for LRU algorithm after a crashed memory.

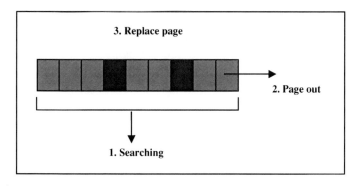

Fig. 5. LRU Simulation Process

When the processor requests a page, and the page is currently not in the memory, then LRU algorithm will start a task by searching the page with the longest time not been used in the memory. The selected page will be removed out from the memory. The page requested by a processor will be inserting at the end of the memory after all the pages shifted. The code used is as shown below:

$$rand\_loc=rand()\%MAX\_C\_SIZE; \qquad (3)$$

$$arr\_time[rand\_loc]=clock;$$

$$src\_bff[rand\_loc]=next\_source;$$

7 Results and Discussions

This section discussed in detail the result for each graph plotted based on page size 6400 bits to 64 Kbit. Graph showed that the page size influences the memory recovery time and increase linearly for all two algorithms tested which are FIFO and LRU.

7.1 Number of Pages vs. Page (6400bits – 64000bits)

The page size was run using two algorithms and the performance are recorded and plotted. Figure 6 shows the result for execution time for a page size 6400 bit.

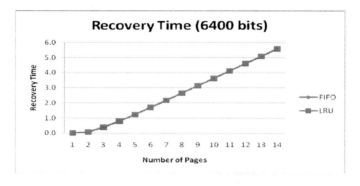

Fig. 6. Page Size – 6400 bits

Figure 7 graph plotted the result for execution time for a page size of 16 Kbit.

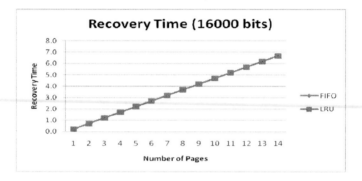

Fig. 7. Page Size – 16Kbit

Figure 8 graph plotted the result for execution time for a page size 32 Kbit.

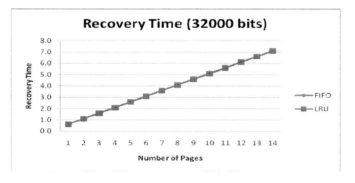

Fig. 8. Page Size – 32Kbit

Figure 9 graph plotted the result for execution time for a page size 64 Kbit.

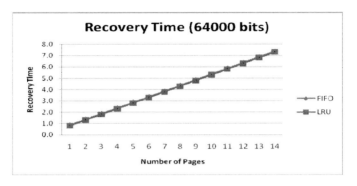

Fig. 9. Page Size – 64Kbit

7.2   Comparison of Results for Pages Size Range 6400bit to 64Kbit

Results showed that LRU and FIFO have very little differences of time for memory recovery.

7.3   Memory Size (8MB) vs. Page Size

The fixed page size was run using all two algorithms and the performances are recorded based on the three different size of the memory. Figure 10 graph plotted the result for execution time for a page size of 8 MB.

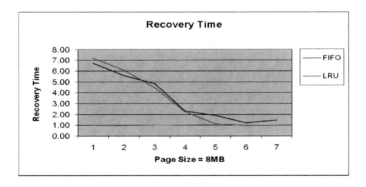

Fig. 10. Page Size – 8MB

Figure 11 graph plotted the result for execution time for a page size 16 MB.

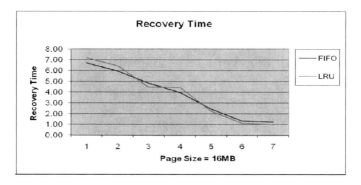

Fig. 11. Page Size – 16MB

Figure 12 plotted the result for execution time for a page size 32 MB.

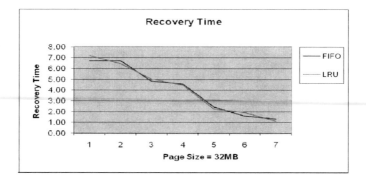

Fig. 12. Page Size – 32MB

Comparison of Results for Page Size 8Mb to 32MB

Result simulation for 8 MB, 16 Mb and 32 Mb memory size shown in the graphs. As the page size and number of pages increases, it significantly decreases the recovery time.

8   Conclusion

The results indicate the influence of number of pages and page size as compared to the size of memory on the recovery time. Furthermore, the number of pages and the size of pages is a crucial factor that affects the behavior of pages reload and recovery for page replacement algorithms. If this number is not selected carefully; the recovery of system cannot be achieve in time and memory cannot be recovered after memory crashed and thus will lead to a worse overall of system performance.

The simulation results obtained confirm the superiority goes to Least Recently Used page replacement approaches in memory recovery performance.

References

1. Hennessy, J.L., Patterson, D.A.: Computer Architecture, A Quantitative Approach, ISBN 1-55860-724-2
2. Wiemann, F.: Simulation of Page Replacement Algorithms
3. The Memory Management Reference Beginner's Guide Overview,
   l.http://www.memorymanagement.org/articles/begin.html
4. Gopalakrishnan, S., Patil, S.: Study of Memory Management Schemes in Windows / WindowsNT / MAC OS/ Linux. Computer Science Department. State University of NewYork at Binghamton. Binghamton, NY 13902-6000 (OS Term Paper Fall 2000)
5. Virtual Memory, http://en.wikipedia.org/wiki/Virtual_memory
6. Tanenbaum, A.S.: Modern Operating System, 2nd edn. Prentice Hall (2001) ISBN-10: 0-13-031358-0
7. Le, L.G., Huang, J., Dunham, M.H., Lin, J.-L., Peltier, A.C.: Survey of Recovery in Main Memory Databases. Engineering Intelligent Systems 4/3, 177–184 (1996)
8. Wang, Y., Kumar, V.: Performance Comparison of Main Memory Database Recovery Algorithms
9. Bahannon, P., Rastogi, R., Sheshadri, S., Shudarshan, S.: Detection and Recovery Techniques for Database Corruption
10. Korupolu, M.R., Dahlin, M.: Coordinated placement and replacement for large-scale distributed caches. In: Proceedings of the 1999 IEEE Workshop on Internet Applications, pp. 62–71 (1999)
11. Rezaei, M., Kavi, K.M.: A New Implementation Technique for Memory Management. Preprint from the Proceedings of the 2000 SoutheastCon, Nashville, TN (April 2000)
12. Verhofstad, J.S.M.: Recovery Technique for Database Systems, vol. 10(2) (June 1978)

Intention to Use E-Government Services in Malaysia: Perspective of Individual Users

Uchenna Cyril Eze[1], Mei Huey Goh[2], Heng Yaw Ling[2] and Chai Har Lee[2]

[1] School of Business, Monash University, Jalan Lagoon Selatan,
46150 Bandar Sunway, Selangor, Malaysia
uc_chinwe@hotmail.com
[2] Multimedia University, Jalan Ayer Keroh Lama,
75450 Bukit Beruang, Melaka, Malaysia
{linghengyaw,chaiharlee}@gmail.com

Abstract. The growing need for convenience in the manner people conduct their activities in the 21st century, has popularized the notion of Internet-enabled government services. Various governments now offer key services through the Internet, but what is still unclear, is the key to a successful e-government platform. In this study, therefore, an extended Technology Acceptance Model (TAM) was used to underpin the development of a conceptual framework used to examine the influence of six independent variables (perceived ease of use, perceived usefulness, security, Internet infrastructure, reliability and convenience) on the dependent variable, the intention to use e-government services in Malaysia. The 230 valid responses in this study were the bases of the analysis, and the data analysis included correlation and regression analyses. The findings revealed that four of the six hypotheses were significant. Research and practice contributions of this study were highlighted including limitations of study and agenda for future research.

Keywords: Intention to use e-government, extended TAM, security, Internet, Malaysia.

1   Introduction

Internet has become part of our daily life because of its critical place in business and social settings. Pascual [24] indicated that Information and Communications Technologies (ICTs) were growing rapidly and were essential functions that direct the daily life of people such as reforming our work and altering the business rules. The adoption and practice of ICT has bigger impact on the most entities relying on the Internet, which is used by many sectors such as commercial sectors (e-commerce, online banking), education sectors including online tuition or for working from home. Many sectors, therefore, rely on Internet for key activities, and they all strive to be the first to embrace the improvements in the innovation. This had led to an increase the online services such as online purchase, online auction, online banking, and many others [8].

A. Abd Manaf et al. (Eds.): ICIEIS 2011, Part II, CCIS 252, pp. 512–526, 2011.
© Springer-Verlag Berlin Heidelberg 2011

Pascual [24] revealed that with the advancement of ICT, individuals were living in faster communication environment that enables seamless connection with everyone globally. The rapid pace of Internet development has also driven the use active use of new technologies for government services delivery in some countries. Thus, Malaysian government is adopting Internet systems in transforming the government services to serve their citizens better. Government are now able to transform the traditional method to online services with new and advanced technology. Azab et al. [3] noted that electronic government (e-government) was going to be a worldwide trend, which will continuously attract the awareness of government to improve service provision with the potential to attract various entities including, students, employees, politicians, policy makers' economists, and other businessperson as well.

Despite the aforementioned, e-government in Malaysia is still in its infancy and additional studies have been advised to determine the factors that affect the intention to use e-government services. In fact, there are still many governments that appear unready to deploy e-government infrastructure for better online public service provision [19]. They might have planned to do so, but may be either slow to execute the plan or they may have weak political structure, management, and type of leadership that may be considered unsupportive for required changes to enable e-government services. One of the common issues with e-government implementation is the apparent lack of understanding of approaches and frameworks for effective e-government services.

Devadoss et al. [7] indicated that factors influencing how citizens react and view e-government include time, reliability and ease of use of e-government services. E-government is relatively new in Malaysia as there are still high numbers of individuals who seem to be more comfortable to use the traditional approach in dealing with the government compared to e-government system. Based on the foregoing and the recognition that there are limited studies in Malaysia in the subject area, particularly, among working adults, additional studies are imperative to examine Malaysians' perspective on the willingness to use this system. Hence, this research aims to determine the key factors that affect individuals' intention to use e-government services.

1.1 Development of E-Government in Malaysia

There are several international bodies conducting e-government studies such as, United Nations Public Administration Network (UNPAN), Brookings Institution, Waseda University, Accenture and World Economic Forum. In this study, due to the availability of information, we will discuss the study conducted by Waseda University and UNPAN only. Waseda University World e-government ranking was first conducted in year 2005, the objective of the ranking is to conduct a research on the status and development of e-government in the world, and to rank the surveyed countries based on the various criteria for an ideal e-government. On 14 January 2011, the Waseda University Institute of e-government has released the 2011 Waseda University World e-government Ranking. Five countries were analysed as compared to only 40 countries last year. The ranking are decided based on seven major indicators covers management optimisation, required interface-functioning applications, national portal, e-government promotion, CIO in Government, network preparedness and e-participation [32]. Table 1 indicates that Malaysia's ranking was in declining trend, Malaysia was listed in top 10 in year 2005 when this research first conducted. However, with the increasing number of countries involved, Malaysia ranking has decreased dramatically.

Table 1. Malaysia's E-Government Ranking in Waseda University World E-Government Ranking (Year 2005 to Year 2011)

Year	Ranking	Number of countries involved
2005	9	23
2006	14	32
2007	15	32
2008	18	34
2009	22	34
2010	24	40
2011	24	50

Source: Waseda University World E-Government Ranking Report

UNPAN conducted a global e-government readiness survey to assess the level of willingness and readiness of governments around the world to improve the quality and accessibility of basic social services provided to people with the advancement of ICT to sustain human development. This survey was first conducted in 2003, followed by year 2004, 2005, 2008, and 2010. This survey involved more countries as compared to survey conducted by Waseda University. However, the purposes of both surveys are varied. As shown in Table 2, in year 2010, Malaysia ranking has increased to higher position as compared to previous years.

Table 2. Malaysia's E-Government Ranking in United Nations E-Government Readiness Survey (Year 2005 to Year 2010)

Year	Ranking	Number of countries involved
2005	43	191
2006	N/A	N/A
2007	N/A	N/A
2008	34	192
2009	N/A	N/A
2010	32	192

Source: United Nations E-Government Survey 2005 - 2010

According to the UNPAN e-government survey 2010 report [31], the most highly ranked e-government development nations among Asia are Republic of Korea, Singapore and Bahrain. Malaysia was placed 6th with index value of 0.6101. The index value was above world average index, 0.4406.

Table 3. Asia Top 10 E-Government Development Ranking for Year 2010

Rank	Country	E-Government development index value
1	Republic of Korea	0.8785
2	Singapore	0.7476
3	Bahrain	0.7363
4	Japan	0.7152
5	Israel	0.6552
6	Malaysia	0.6101
7	Cyprus	0.5705
8	Kazakhstan	0.5578
9	United Arab Emirates	0.5349
10	Kuwait	0.5290
	World Average	0.4406

Source: United Nations E-Government Survey 2010

Malaysia launched the programme of Multimedia Super Corridor (MSC) in the year 1996 to enable local citizens to use the Internet more often as well as to improve the demand for the Internet. Today, Malaysian government makes use of MSC to transform the traditional government services into online services, known as e-government. E-government is one of the seven flagship applications introduced by MSC. Under e-government flagships, seven pilot projects, i.e. Electronic Procurement (eP), Project Monitoring System (PMS), Electronic Services Delivery (eServices), Human Resource Management Information System (HRMIS), Generic Office Environment (GOE), E-Syariah and Electronic Labour Exchange (ELX) were identified. There were also other supporting projects under e-government flagships such as EG*Net, JobsMalaysia, etc. In addition, an official portal of the government of Malaysia had been created named myGovernment (www.malaysia.gov.my) to serve as the single gateway for Malaysian Government information and services. As shown in Table 4, total number of online services provided by myGovernment portal had increased by 8.9% in year 2010 as compared to year 2009.

Table 4. Summary of Services Provided in MyGovernment Portal (as of December 2010)

Services	Dec' 2009	Mar' 2010	June' 2010	Sept' 2010	Dec' 2010
Internal Online Services (Form service)	49	49	49	49	49
External Online Services (Hyperlink)	1070	1244	1401	1436	1447
Downloadable Form	3092	3208	3130	3085	3090

Source: myGoverment portal

E-government was later renamed as 1e-government because of national slogan of Malaysia called "1Malaysia". Malaysian Administrative Modernisation and Management Planning Unit (MAMPU) who administrated the e-government in Malaysia, defined e-government as "a multimedia networked paperless administration linking government agencies within Putrajaya with government centres around the country to facilitate a collaborative government environment and efficient service to business and citizens" [2]. On May 2009, MAMPU was involved in a program named modernising and reforming the public sector. MAMPU was then assigned to upgrade Putrajaya Campus Network (PCN) by implementing Intelligent Resilient Framework (IRF) to enhance network scalability and availability. Several new networks were introduced to support high bandwidth services including Multiple Protocol Label Switching (MPLS), IPv6, network security, network port virtualisation and high availability virtual core switching. This upgrading will also help MAMPU to save on energy costs as the new equipment uses lesser power than previous generation equipment [17].

Since 2005, Multimedia Development Corporation (MDeC) had conducted Malaysia Government Portals and Websites Assessment (MGPWA), a yearly assessment to serve as a guide to enhance online services delivered by Malaysia Government via portals and web sites. These portals and web sites were evaluated against the preset criteria and rate accordingly from 1 to 5-star rating. With this ranking, the agencies can therefore strategise approaches to enhance web services and target to improve their ranking from year to year. MGPWA 2010 assessment indicated that 61.57% of the portals and web sites obtained 3-star and above, this figure shown an increase of 12.22% as compared to year 2009. The findings also revealed that myGovernment portal was found need to be more streamlined. This portal has to continuous update their URLs on myGovernment as there were still 91 inaccessible portals/web sites [18].

Despite e-government is still new for local citizens, but MAMPU will continuous their effort in implement the best service to public and they held the conference once a year to review previous performance, identified any possible improvement, and announce new services created. It was also trying to raise the awareness of public on e-government and to modernize the governmental administration where the traditional approach is by now not suitable in this new century. E-government implementation in Malaysia is consider relatively new for most people. This happen because government still using the traditional method to address public. Therefore, government recently was in aggressive effort to strive the services through online. For instance, there is 1e-government introduced in year 2010 regard to the national slogan "1Malaysia". On 3 November 2010, government had also launched Malaysia Corporate Identity Number (MyCoID) gateway system to simplify the process of new businesses registration. With this service, people can now simultaneously register with five government agencies online and complete the process within a day compared to 11 days previously [28]. Ruslan et al. [27] also pointed out that e-government issue is still relatively new among local citizens, so the research in e-government in Malaysia is still limited in number. Hence, this research aim to examine factors affects Malaysian working adults' intentions to use e-government services.

2   Conceptual Framework and Hypotheses Development

Figure 1 presents the conceptual framework for this paper and illustrates the independent and the dependent variables. This framework was developed based on prior research and underpinned in the Technology Acceptance Model (TAM) with additional variables. Six hypotheses were developed based on the framework, which are discussed in the next section.

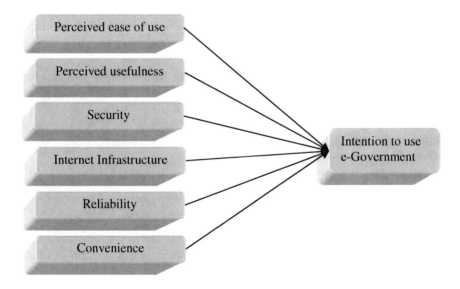

Fig. 1. Conceptual Framework

2.1   Perceived Ease of Use

Prior research found ease of use to have positive relationship with to the intention to use e-government in research done by Ooh et al. [22]. It will be difficult for the public to use the government web portal if there is no guidance from government to teach potential users or a manual on how to use the service online. A complex e-government system would frustrate users and could create unwilling among users towards the system. This might subsequently affect the intended government's mission to deliver a better service to the public. E-government is an online service, and the public will use it independently for searching and for exploring, therefore, it should be simple and easy to use. This analysis leads to hypothesis 1:

Hypothesis 1: Perceived ease of use will positively affect intention to use e-government services.

2.2 Perceived Usefulness

Ooh et al. [22] indicated that perceived usefulness is significant positively influence the intention to use e-government. Many other researchers support this. Pardhasaradhi and Ahmed [23] described that IT was a useful way for governments to transform public service. They believed IT could perform the task faster, including saving cost, time and performing the activity more effectively. Alawadhi and Morris' [1] findings indicate that the rate of using e-government service will increase if citizens noticed that the services are useful. The public will use the service only if the service can benefit them. Li [16] pointed out that information in the government web portal should be useful and services should be helpful. In normal circumstances, people log on to the web site with a purpose, such as, they want to search for the information or to obtain certain information. A web portal that is perceived to be useful will attract the public interest to use it. One of the successful web portals is e-bay, which is used for online business and electronic commerce. Besides, when the web portal is perceived to be useful, the public may recommend it to their friends and family to encourage more usage. Words of mouth can be one of the best and least costly advertisement tools. Colesca and Dobrica [5], and Kumar et al. [14] suggested that perceived usefulness for a particular system would enhance their job performance. They also defined perceived usefulness as system utility to the user. Hence, the next hypothesis:

Hypothesis 2: Perceived usefulness will positively affect intention to use e-government services.

2.3 High Security

Security is considered the most critical path of an e-government initiative as it concerns mainly citizens of a country [34]. E-government will require several networks of systems to connect government agencies. People are usually concerned about the security of online services, especially their confidential information. For example, people are afraid to lose their credit card information when they purchase products online; this is because others could use their private information without permission. Unscrupulous individuals could use such information to apply for bank loan. West [33], in his paper, indicated that most website owners are concerned about the privacy and security statements and thus there are increasing number of sites that now provide security function to its users. Hence, the third hypothesis:

Hypothesis 3: High security will positively affect the intention to use e-government services.

2.4   Internet Infrastructure

Singapore government implemented PSi to execute the e-government service, which could develop, deploy, and operate e-services in an efficient and speedy manner [4]. Zarei et al. [34] indicted that the ICT infrastructure is a global connectivity and network infrastructure, which uses the advantage of new technologies to transform the old approach of government services into a modern of e-governmental administration. It helps the government to standardize the services in a more effective manner and to deliver better information and other services to users at a reduced cost. This leads to hypothesis:

Hypothesis 4: Internet infrastructure will positively affect the intention to use e-government services.

2.5   Reliability

Reliability refers to the trust of public on the use of e-government services [16]. This is because the public will only use the online service when they trust the website and are assured that the website provides the information they require. Since the e-government is created to provide adequate and efficient service to users, it would appears to be provide strong basis for trusted and reliable information dissemination to key stakeholders. It is equally important to ensure good quality of the e-government performance. This analysis leads to the fifth hypothesis:

Hypothesis 5: Reliability will positively affect the intention to use e-government services.

2.6   Convenience

Convenience is considered a key factor that affects the public's acceptance of e-government services. It is defined as anything that is intended to save time, energy, or frustration. It could also mean any system that saves or simplifies work; add to one's ease of comfort. Convenience in e-government context involves saving time and increasing service efficiency as compared to branch agencies. It can be conceptualized as relative advantage of adopt the new service channel [25]. Convenience, viewed as timesavings, can be accessed 24 hours with excellent service quality, is one of the most cited beneficial features of Internet banking [6]. Convenience plays an important role in enabling good public's perception towards e-government services. This factor could help users to save more time on any transaction with the government compared to the traditional method, which could involve the public visiting government agencies. Hence, the sixth hypothesis:

Hypothesis 6: Convenience will positively affect the intention to use e-government services.

Table 5. Variables definition and sources

Variable	Definition	Sources
Perceived ease of use	Online services are easy to learn and use, especially when support is provided.	Alawadhi and Morris [1]
Perceived usefulness	Perceived usefulness is the system utility to the user.	Kumar et al. [14]
Security	The protection of owns information and control of access to information in e-government, privacy, trustworthy and reliability.	Colesca and Dobrica [5]
Internet infrastructure	Internet infrastructure helps government in created and implements new services or enhances the former services when it is necessary.	Ndou [20]
Reliability	Reliability represents the degree of being capable to maintain the service and service quality.	Halaris [11]
Convenience	User can access the service without constraint of time and distance barriers.	Rotchanakitumnuai [26]

3 Research Method

Primary and secondary data were used in this study. The primary data derive from survey questionnaire. The survey questionnaire was developed based on prior research and the conceptual framework, it solicited background of participants and responses on the key construct of the research framework. These questionnaires were distributed to participants to complete and were collected for analysis. While secondary data is collected from existing sources such as journals, Internet, newspaper and articles. The secondary data will enhance our understanding of the fields of research better. We used a 5-point Likert-type scale for the questionnaire responses, where '1' represent "Strongly Disagree", "2" represent "disagree", "3" represent "neutral", "4" represent "agree" and '5' represent "Strongly Agree". The unit of analysis in this study was working adult, and the target population was respondents from Penang, Malacca and Kuala Lumpur. These cities were chosen because of their higher working population. Convenience sampling method was used in selecting the participants. Pilot study was also conducted to ensure the validity and reliability of the questionnaire [15]. A pre-designed questionnaire was pre-tested based on a small sample of 50 respondents to gather their responses and feedbacks. Corrective measures were then carried out to revise and restructure the identified items in the final survey questionnaire.

4   Data Analysis and Findings

Two hundred and fifty questionnaires were distributed and 230 valid responses were received. This indicates 92% response rate. We then used the 230 valid responses for data analysis. Statistical Package for Social Sciences (SPSS) was used to analyse the data. Pearson's correlation analysis and linear regression were used to evaluate the hypotheses outlined earlier in this paper.

4.1   Descriptive Analysis

Table 6 presents demographic profile of the respondents in this research.

Table 6. Respondents' Demographic Profile

	Frequency	Percent	Cumulative percent
Gender			
• Male	117	50.9	50.9
• Female	113	49.1	100.0
Age			
• 18 – 22	21	9.1	9.1
• 23 – 27	60	26.1	35.2
• 28 – 32	59	25.7	60.9
• 33 – 37	28	12.2	73.0
• 38 and above	62	27.0	100.0
Race			
• Malay	56	24.3	24.3
• Chinese	152	66.1	90.4
• Indian	16	7.0	97.4
• Others	6	2.6	100.0
Marital status			
• Single	122	53	53
• Married	108	47	100.0
Education level			
• SPM	33	14.3	14.3
• Diploma	55	23.9	38.3
• Degree	82	35.7	73.9
• MBA/PhD	41	17.8	91.7
• Others	19	8.3	100.0
Occupation			
• Clerical	56	24.3	24.3
• Managerial	36	15.7	40.0
• Sales	13	5.7	45.7
• Executive	111	48.3	93.9
• Self-employed	14	6.1	100.0

4.2 Mean and Reliability Analysis

The mean values for all the variables except security emerged above 3 points and above, which reveal that majority of the respondents are neutral or tend to agree with the statements on the variables. We have conducted Cronbach's Alpha to test the reliability of the data; value for Cronbach's Alpha of 0.7 or higher is considered acceptable [21]. The result in Table 7 indicate that Cronbach's Alpha value for all variables are greater than 0.70, therefore, we can conclude that the data on these variables are reliable and consistent with research standards.

Table 7. Variable Mean, Standard Deviation, and Reliability Values

	No. of Items	Mean	Std. Deviation	Cronbach's Alpha
Perceived Ease of Use	7	3.333	0.573	0.866
Perceived Usefulness	5	3.552	0.584	0.829
Security	6	2.954	0.731	0.890
Internet Infrastructure	4	3.235	0.637	0.789
Reliability	7	3.228	0.627	0.891
Convenience	6	3.491	0.738	0.904

4.3 Pearson Correlation Matrix

Results in Table 8 indicate the correlation matrix of the conceptual variables. A two-tail test at 0.01 significance level indicates that there are positive relationships among dependent variable and the independent variables.

Table 8. Pearson Correlation Coefficient Matrix

	PEOU	PU	SC	IF	E	C	DV
PEOU	1.000						
PU	0.600**	1.000					
SC	0.526**	0.448**	1.000				
IF	0.646**	0.587**	0.648**	1.000			
RE	0.628**	0.568**	0.614**	0.717**	1.000		
C	0.616**	0.575**	0.452**	0.628**	0.727**	1.000	
DV	0.649**	0.573**	0.635**	0.760**	0.763**	0.761**	1.000

**Correlation is significant at the 0.01 level (2-tailed).

4.4 Multiple Regression Analysis – Model Summary

From Table 9, R=0.866 and R^2 value = 0.750 shows that 75.0% of the variation in Y can be explained by all 6 predictors (or accounted for by) the variation in X.

Table 9. Multiple Regression Analysis (R and R^2)

Model	R	R^2	Adjusted R^2	Std. Error of Estimate	Durbin-Watson
1	0.866[a]	0.750	0.743	0.32469	2.136

4.5 Regression Coefficients

The results in Table 10 indicate that 4 of the 6 hypothesized relationships appeared significant at 0.05 significance level (<0.05). The variables that emerged insignificant are perceived ease of use and perceived usefulness. Table 10 also shows the analysis of coefficients for specific relationships hypothesized in this study. In the column of unstandardised coefficient, the β-value indicates positive or negative relationship between predictor (independent) variables and dependent variable. Based on the results, the most important variable is convenience with a Beta-value of 0.354 followed by internet infrastructure with a Beta-value of 0.265.

Table 10. Linear Regression Analysis

Model	Unstandardized Coefficients		Standardized Coefficients	T	Sig.	Collinearity Statistics	
	β	Std. Error	Beta			Tolerance	VIF
(Constant)	0.142	0.146		0.970	0.333		
PEOU	0.069	0.055	0.062	1.249	0.213	0.557	2.190
PU	0.006	0.050	0.005	0.114	0.910	0.538	1.859
SC	0.141	0.041	0.161	3.472	0.001	0.520	1.921
IF	0.266	0.056	0.265	4.732	0.000	0.659	2.789
RE	0.179	0.060	0.176	2.987	0.003	0.524	3.082
C	0.307	0.046	0.354	6.705	0.000	0.603	2.480

5 Discussion and Conclusions

The findings in this study provide specific knowledge on the factors that affect intention to use e-government, particularly, among working adults in Malaysia. Prior research by Schaupp and Carter [29] established that perceived ease of use and perceived usefulness will have positive influence on the intention to use e-government. In this study, however, the data failed to support these hypotheses, and were inconsistent with prior findings. This could be due to the context we discussed in this paper, including that this paper focused on working adults only. It will be interesting to know what findings emerge from future related research that focused on broader sections of the population. The remaining variables such as security, Internet infrastructure, reliability and convenience were all found to have positive influence on the participants' intention to use e-government services. In addition, as the regression coefficients indicate that some factors have stronger impacts compared to others. The findings on these factors are consistent with findings from prior research [12, 13, 20].

E-government plays a critical role in disseminating knowledge and connecting the public with the government and government agencies more efficiently. The system acts as a link to public services at any time and any place, and consequently minimizes time and distance constraints for the public. It also acts as a one-stop-centre to serve citizens located in disparate regions in Malaysia and overseas. The public can easily perform online transactions or submit digital documents on time even when they are overseas. E-government could reduce manual activities, thus avoiding clerical errors, and achieving a better productivity level with higher accuracy, though the efficiency and transparency of the e-government structure implemented [30]. Through the services provided on the Internet and government portals, citizens and businesses could now have the capacity to handle government processes without visiting several government agencies in different locations [8]. This highlights the key benefits of e-government in bridging the boundaries between governments and citizens.

As indicated earlier, this research has identified key factors that could contribute to intentions to use e-government. Malaysian government agencies could use the findings to enhance their service offerings by deploying more information and knowledge management systems with stronger capabilities. Malaysian government agencies should also incorporate new technologies in creating more online services in order to strive for a better online service. This can also attract more citizens to use their online services. However, government agencies should not only focus on the latest technology, but also identify obstacles that hamper the transformation of traditional government into e-government, particularly on the readiness of citizens to use online services [9, 10, 15]. The government should continue to motivate, through campaigns, citizens and other stakeholders to use online services. For instance, offering cash discount to citizens for online payment. In addition, government agencies should provide hassle-free portals or web sites so that users are comfortable with it and feel that the portals are reliable and secure, so that it is more likely users will buy-in into the concept in future. Overall, it is vital for Malaysian government agencies to enhance their online services by providing functional websites, and they should respond well to users' needs in order to strive for higher online participation rate from citizens. This, most likely, will increase the publics' intentions to experience and the e-government services in Malaysia. In addition, a well-implemented system could enable a higher global ranking, perhaps to be a notable leading e-government country the world.

Lastly, this paper focused on a small number of participants. Future research should cover a wider range of respondents to enable a more balanced perspective, and to enable a wider application of statistical tools such as Structural Equation Modelling (SEM).

References

1. Alawadhi, S., Morris, A.: Factors influencing the adoption of E-government services. Journal of Software 4(6), 584–590 (2009)
2. Aliah, N.: E-government Malaysia: way forward. In: Journal of Conference, Malaysian Administrative Modernisation and Management Planning Unit, pp. 1–47 (2009)

3. Azab, N.A., Kamel, S., Dafoulas, G.: A suggested framework for assessing electronic government readiness in Egypt. Electronic Journal of e-Government 7(1), 11–28 (2009)
4. Chan, C.M.L., Lau, Y., Pan, S.L.: E-government implementation: a macro analysis of Singapore's e-government initiatives. Journal of Government Information Quarterly 25(2), 239–255 (2008)
5. Colesca, S.E., Dobrica, L.: Adoption and use of e-government services: the case of Romania. Journal of Applied Research and Technology 6(3), 204–217 (2008)
6. Daniel, E.: Provision of electronic banking in the UK and the Republic of Ireland. International Journal of Bank Marketing 17(2), 72–82 (1999)
7. Devadoss, P.J., Pan, S.L., Huang, J.C.: Structural analysis of e-government initiatives: a case study of SCO. Journal of Decision Support Systems 34(3), 253–269 (2003)
8. Ebrahim, Z., Irani, Z.: E-government adoption: architecture and barriers. Journal of Business Process Management 11(5), 589–611 (2005)
9. Eze, U.C.: E-business deployment in Nigerian financial firms: an empirical analysis of key factors. International Journal of Electronic Business Research 4(2), 29–47 (2008)
10. Eze, U.C., Tan, K.S., Ismail, H., Poong, Y.S.: ISP's service quality and customer satisfaction in the southern region of Malaysia. In: The Proceedings of the Australasian Conference on Information Systems, Christchurch, New Zealand, pp. 290–299 (2008)
11. Halaris, C., Magoutas, B., Papadomichelaki, X., Mentzas, G.: Classification and synthesis of quality approaches in e-government services. Internet Research 17(4), 378–401 (2007)
12. Hesson, M., Hayder, A.H.: Online security evaluation process for new e-services. Journal of Business Process Management 13(2), 223–246 (2007)
13. Huang, J.H., Shyu, H.P.: E-government web site enhancement opportunities: a learning perspective. The Electronic Library 26(4), 545–560 (2008)
14. Kumar, V., Mukerji, B., Butt, I., Persaud, A.: Factors for successful e-government adoption: a conceptual framework. The Electronic Journal of e-Government 5(1), 63–76 (2007)
15. Lee, C.H., Eze, U.C., Ndubisi, N.O.: Analysing key determinants of online repurchase intentions. Asia Pacific Journal of Marketing and Logistics 23(2), 200–221 (2011)
16. Li, H.: Use of state government websites: a survey of Michigan citizens (2004), http://www.ippsr.msu.edu/Publications/AREGovernment.pdf (accessed January 28, 2011)
17. Low, C.: Malaysia govt to upgrade federal network (2009), http://www.futuregov.asia/articles/2009/may/15/ malaysia-govt-upgrade-federal-network/# (accessed February 1, 2011)
18. MGPWA (2010), http://www.mscmalaysia.my/codenavia/portals/msc/images/img/ government/partner_msc_malaysia/msc_malaysia_worldwide/ MGPWA_2010_Report.pdf
19. Montagna, J.M.: A framework for the assessment and analysis of electronic government proposals. Journal of Electronic Research and Application 4(3), 204–219 (2005)
20. Ndou, V.: E-government for developing countries: opportunities and challenges. Journal on Information Systems in Developing Countries 18(1), 1–24 (2004)
21. Nunnaly, J.C.: Psychometric theory. McGraw-Hill, New York (1978)
22. Ooh, K.L., Zailani, S., Ramayah, T., Fernando, Y.: Factors influencing intention to use e-government services among citizens in Malaysia. International Journal of Information Management 29(6), 458–475 (2009)
23. Pardhasaradhi, Y., Ahmed, S.: Efficiency of electronic public service delivery in India: public-private partnership as a critical factor. In: The 1st International Conference on Theory and Practice of Electronic Governance, pp. 357–369 (2007)
24. Pascual, P.J.: E-government. E-Asean task force UNDP-APDIP, 1–40 (2003)

25. Polatoglu, V.N., Ekin, S.: An empirical investigation of the Turkish consumers' acceptance of Internet banking services. International Journal of Bank Marketing 19(4), 156–165 (2001)
26. Rotchanakitumnuai, S.: Exploring the antecedents of electronic service acceptance: evidence from Internet securities trading. Journal of the Computer, the Internet and Management 13(3), 1–6 (2005)
27. Ruslan, R., Ummi, K.S., Noornina, D., Norazuwa, M.: An empirical study of the intention to use electronic government in Majlis Perbandaran Seberang Prai, Penang. Journal of ICT 4, 1–16 (2005)
28. Samy, F.A.: Business registration reduced to one day via online (2010), http://thestar.com.my/news/story.asp?sec=nation&file=/2010/11/4/nation/7359289 (accessed February 1, 2011)
29. Schaupp, L.C., Carter, L.: E-voting: from apathy to adoption. The Journal of Enterprise Information Management 18(5), 586–601 (2005)
30. Sharma, S.: Exploring best practices in public–private partnership (PPP) in e-government through select Asian case studies. The International Information & Library Review 39 (3-4), 203–210 (2007)
31. United Nations E-government Survey (2010), http://unpan1.un.org/intradoc/groups/public/documents/UN-DPADM/UNPAN038853.pdf
32. Waseda University World E-Government Ranking Report (2011), http://www.waseda.jp/eng/news10/110114_egov.html
33. West, D.M.: State and federal electronic government in the United States. Government Studies at Brookings (2008), http://www.brookings.edu/~media/Files/rc/reports/2008/0826_e government_west/0826_egovernment_west.pdf (accessed January 28, 2011)
34. Zarei, B., Ghapanchi, A.: Guidelines for government-to-government initiatives architecture in developing countries. Journal of Information Management 28(4), 277–284 (2008)

A Study towards Proposing GPS-Based Mobile Advertisement Service

Pantea Keikhosrokiani, Norlia Mustaffa, Muhammad Imran Sarwar,
Amin Kianpisheh, Faten Damanhoori, and Nasriah Zakaria

School of Computer Sciences,
Universiti Sains Malaysia, 11800, Penang, Malaysia
Pantea.keikhosrokiani@gmail.com,
{norlia,faten,nasriah}@cs.usm.my,
imrans@live.com.my, a.kianpisheh@gmail.com

Abstract. A GPS-based advertisement service is one which uses customer-location tracking to provide different location specific information to users via mobile devices, wherever they are and whenever it is needed. As the first step in this study, a preliminary online survey conducted to determine users' opinions and interests with regards to GPS-based advertisement systems. The results of the study led to the proposed new service called e-Brochure, which would send advertisement and promotion information for points of interest such as hotels, restaurants and all cultural sites of interests according to the user's current location.

Keywords: Global Positioning System (GPS), real-time and location-based services, advertisement and promotion, e-Brochure, Mobile-Commerce.

1 Introduction

Advertising is an essential and integral part of any business. Businesses need to attract customers' attention in order to communicate with them and persuade them to take part in business related activity; therefore, effective advertising can increase consumption of a company's products. These days, customers are bombarded by many different product choices and confusion often occurs. A system is needed that navigates the options for the customer, helping them choose according to their preferences. For Mobile Commerce (M-Commerce) based advertisement systems, information on hotels, restaurants, point of interests (e.g. shopping malls, public and private sector venues), and local media (radio, newspaper, and television) are all needed, as well as any relevant promotional marketing packages. Global Positioning System (GPS) technology is increasingly being used to enable customers to access services provided by modern advertising systems [1].

GPS was first used in military applications in the early 1960s, but by the 2000s its use has spread to civilian applications and services. The advantage of GPS is that its signals can be received anywhere in the world without any distortion and within one meter of precision [2]. Garmin [3] and TomTom [4] were among the first to develop applications for GPS enabled devices that offered a wide variety of services ranging

A. Abd Manaf et al. (Eds.): ICIEIS 2011, Part II, CCIS 252, pp. 527–544, 2011.
© Springer-Verlag Berlin Heidelberg 2011

from road navigation to weather and traffic update information ;interestingly, they also include non-road information of potential interest to travelers, such as food and lodging. Foursquare [5] combines location-based information with social networking, while Dunkin Donuts and Cold Stone Creamery used in-car GPS devices to inform drivers about special offers near their location; both of these, are good real world examples of using GPS as a marketing tool. Garmin and TomTom continue to enhance their software to effectively use GPS location co-ordinates in order to search geographical location and places of interest in their database [6].

Section 2 of this paper reviews related work on location-based services from a technological prospective in. Section 3 describes the preliminary study conducted to investigate the demographics of mobile GPS users and the services they would prefer to have. Section 4 presents a proposed solution called e-Brochure, which is a hybrid cellular network and GPS-based mobile advertisement service, followed by discussion and conclusion.

2 Related Work

M-Commerce and Location-Based Systems

Mobile commerce (generally referred to as M-Commerce) is the ability to conduct transactions using a mobile device. This generally makes business processes more efficient. With today's rapid technological advances, especially in mobile technology, people can communicate easily, anytime and from any place. In fact, M-Commerce will be more beneficial for new business services, if it is used for appropriate targeting of potential audiences/customers. These days, delivering real-time news about businesses to potential customers via modern advertisement systems is critical to improving the use of the M-Commerce. M-Commerce can join with location-based services to provide advertisement and promotion information directed at potential customer based on their current location [7].

Global Positioning System (GPS)

Before the development of GPS, captains and pilots would "steer by the stars" using devices such as sextants or octants for determining their position. Thus; GPS, which is the discovery of one's earthly position from space, is not an entirely fresh idea. Nowadays people can use GPS coordinates to determine their position; they can then combine it with map or GIS data to know their location. "Global" means anywhere on earth except inside buildings, underground, under very heavy tree canopy, around strong radio transmission, in urban canyons amongst tall buildings and near powerful radio transmitter antennas. "Positioning" indicates not only the user's location but also their movement, speed and direction [8]. Lastly, "system" means the GPS comprise a collection of interconnected components: earth, earth-orbiting satellites, ground-based stations, receivers and receiver manufacturers.

Earth, the first component of GPS, holds satellites in orbit with its mass. Satellites orbit the earth at four kilometers per second. Because the surface of the earth is dotted with buildings which are positioned metal or stone markers, it is possible to determine the position of any object based on the position of the monuments. The earth-orbiting satellite system, designed by the United States, consists of 24 to 32 solar-powered radio transmitters forming a satellite constellation, which orbits below the geostationary satellites used for communication, TV and telephone. The GPS satellites are each fitted with an atomic clock that keeps time accurately to within a few billionths of a second. Since satellites are influenced by the gravitational effects of the moon and sun and by solar wind, here are also ground-based stations at different places plus a master control station to monitor and control the GPS satellites. These stations include an antenna, electronics to receive the satellite signals, a microcomputer to process the position data, controls for user input and finally, a screen to display information. A GPS which has the ability to receive location data at a fixed station and broadcast that data to other roving GPS receivers is called "real-time differential GPS" [8].

Location-Based Service

Location-based services are those which can be accessed using a mobile network, and which effectively utilize the current location of the mobile device accordingly [9]. Location-based services are not new; their roots go back to the era when mobile devices were first used. Position-specific information can be person to person communication in the form of post-it notes and graffiti, while advertisement to local audiences can be in the form of posters or simplified graphic signs and navigational information [10]. Additionally, location-based services make possible two way communication and interaction. In this way, users will get information according to their needs and requirements. Location based services are a combination of information and telecommunication technologies including Web GIS, Mobile GIS, Mobile Internet, Spatial Database, Internet and mobile devices as shown in Fig. 1.

Generally location based services are composed of some components: a mobile device, a communication network, a positioning component, a service and application provider, and a data and content provider. Location-based services can be characterized as follows:

1) **Mobile User:** Person or device (like car navigational system) that communicates with and utilizes the location-based services.

2) **Mobile Activities:** Activities performed by the Mobile User, e.g. locating, navigating, searching, identifying, event checking etc.

3) **Information Model:** Defines the possible types of queries incorporating geographic based data and location information that can be used by the location service to promote or broadcast information on points of interest like hotels and restaurants.

4) **Search and Spatial Analysis:** Determines which algorithms are more suitable for real-time information queries to the internet. By going more deeply, we can integrate of data and information of different scales, quality, data types and prices.

5) **Graphic User Interface (GUI):** Present information in a pleasing and usable manner, and can display either user navigation instructions (how to get from one place to another) or location-based services (rates of nearby hotel for example, or visiting or visiting hours for a cultural site).

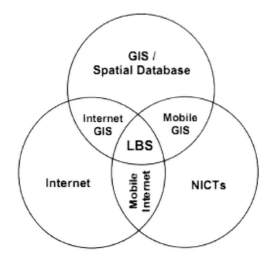

Fig. 1. Location-Based Services as an Intersection of Technologies [11]

6) **Visualization:** Visual representation of the information in the form of text, images, graphics, maps or lists.

7) **Technology:** Handles the transfer of information from the location-based service's server to the mobile user's device (examples include GPS, GIS, etc.).

Global Positioning System (GPS) and Location-Tracking

GPS uses triangulation to calculate the real-time location of its users and provide position and time data. A location-based service is a mixture of communication technology, satellite navigation and geo-information. Coordinates and navigational parameters are delivered to the user from three or four satellites to compute both two and three dimension positions. GPS is a core technology for location-tracking and is free of charge [12-13].

GPS uses a position location technique from wireless communication called "multilateration". Multilateration locates objects by sending a signal to multiple receivers at known location and calculating the differences in arrival times [14]. GPS calculates the distance between a satellite and GPS device; the satellites send a message with accurate orbit data and the exact time of sending; the receiver receives this information and computes the time differentials of these messages to calculate the location.

User location information is given in latitude and longitude coordinates [15]. These coordinates have broad effects on application-level as well as network-level software, which cater to new services such as advertisement, geographic messaging, resource discovery etc. Approaches to geographic routing through DARPA's GloMo program has been implemented which presents the geographical location by closed circles (centre point, radius) or polygons (point1, point2, point3... pointN-1, pointN) where each vertex is represented by geographical co-ordinates.

Geographic Information System (GIS) and Location-Tracking

GIS is an information system that deals with geographic data. Location-based services are a specific form of GIS which were born recently from the increasing sophistication of mobile devices. Although GIS and LBS have different roots, LBS can be considered a specialized form of GIS; the advent of GIS came a decade ago while LBS is still in its infancy and is evolving continuously in step with mobile technology and communication infrastructures. The origins of GIS lie in academic research in the 1960s which was commercialized during the 1980s. Well-known commercial GIS-based software packages ArcGIS [16] and Oracle Spatial [17] provide extensive functionality like handling of spatial data, efficient geographic data management systems, high quality visualization of geographic information, and more [9].

Several aspects of GIS functionality can be used in location based services, including geographic data collection and conversion, geographic data management, geographic data analysis and geographic data presentation. For instance, in the case of geographic data collection and conversions, GIS positioning techniques can be used to get the current position of a mobile object, thanks to the vast data available for projection and coordinate systems worldwide. Similarly, advanced GPS technology can give 3D model information by laser scanning. On the other hand, GIS data is made up nothing more than points, curves, polygons and volumes that can be represented in the form of graphs. Similarly, in the case of geographic data management, geographic databases are open and accessible to anyone around the world but are saved in a distributed manner, so it retrieval and processing of the data will take time [9].

In the case of geographic data presentation, location-based services can gain many advantages from GIS. Traditional visual representation uses 2D images but, over time, visualization has become more interactive, adding animation and 3D or 4D virtual models along with additional features that facilitate ease of use with respect to the user's interests. With recent technological advancements, it is possible now to have an interactive map with 3D functionality and proper visual animation on any mobile phone [18].

Apart from adding sophisticated GIS functionality in location-based services, serious consideration should also be given to mobile devices that have limited memory, low computational power, small screen size and lower battery life.

Reference [19] proposed a World Wide Media eXchange (WWMX) database which would indexes large collections of images and associated meta-data (e.g. timestamp, owner and most importantly location) with the help of the GIS community. Their main contribution was the development of a light-weight travelogue application built on top of WWMX to provide appropriate context maps with images of locations tagged by users. The image indexes are coordinated and precision indexed to quasi-rectangular regions with angled parameters represented by a square on a globe. The square is projected as a grid using equirectangular projection that sub-divides it into grids. In their paper, they apply GIS using latitude and longitude coordinates to the location tagging of images and define unique rectangular areas by center, latitude, longitude, wideth and height [19].

Technology Used for Location-Tracking

In location based services, communication technology plays an important role in terms of quality of service and convenience for the end user. Researchers have proposed and implemented different communication standards and infrastructure for location tracking and services. This section, elaborates on these proposals with respect to different communication standards that are evolving and improving over time. This section also analyzes and explains the positive aspects of communication protocol that can later be enhanced and modified in order to take advantage of these communication standards in location-based services.

WLAN (Wireless Local Area Network) and Location-Tracking

A Wireless Local Area Network, or WLAN, is a network that spans a limited distance using high frequency radio signals to send and receive data. WLANs can be used as location-tracking systems by applying the WLAN infrastructure to determine the location of the users' devices. A WLAN location-based system refers to mobile devices that rely on a relationship between the location of the device and signals transferred from WLAN access points. The RSS method, illustrated in Fig. 2, uses a WLAN positioning system and works with all mobile devices. RSS is the feature of choice in WLAN, using three or more reference nodes to approximate position in location in 2D or 3D [14].

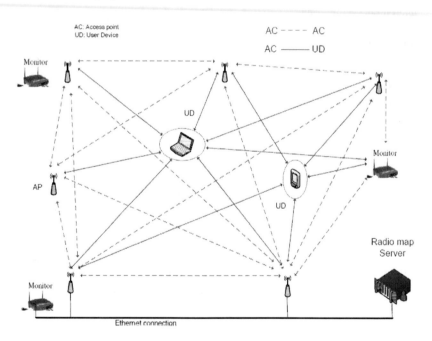

Fig. 2. Fingerprinting Method Using RSS in WLAN for Indoor Scenario [14]

One of the most important standards for wireless networks are WLAN is IEEE 802.11 in which the Wireless Positioning System (WPS) for location-tracking is been used where collections of visible access point IDs (BSSID) and similar strength (RSS) will be used as measurement of distance[20].

Location Tracking Using Hybrid Technologies (GPS and Wi-Fi)

Reference [21] proposed an autonomous and co-operative working model for cars that would collect and estimate the traffic jam statistics from source to the destination for each subject car by using an inter-vehicle communication systems. The proposed method gathers statistical traffic data using inter-vehicle communication (WiFi and GPS) in order to get the estimation for the arrival time to destination. In this method, different geographical regions are divided into areas and the system analyzes the estimated time taken by the car to pass from one point to another in that specific area. Information for the research method was gathered by using a mix of technologies: short communication network (IEEE 802.11/Wi-Fi) and GPS receiver. Their proposed method of traffic simulation employs IEEE802.11 and is implemented in NETSTREAM simulator and C++ [21]. They proposed segmentation model in which the geographical region is divided into square shape areas with incoming and outgoing link that is helpful for the estimation of the traffic information.

Cellular Network and GPS Location-Tracking

Reference [22] developed the InHand application for local and remote use which provides context and location-aware functionality for mobile devices through GPS. InHand location system provides real-time positioning and navigation through maps, tracking of client's movement in terms of location, daily schedule of client's visits and finally stores the gathered information in a proper manner. The application handles the communication between the mobile device and the server through both wireless (Wi-Fi) and cellular networks (GPRS/3G/3.5G). In InHand proposed architecture, the server has an administrative front end that uses web services and as well as SQL Server 2005 as a backend database repository [22].

3   Preliminary Study

In most cases users must install a Java-based software application on their mobile devices in order to access a GPS-based advertisement system. With e-Brochure, users who are looking for a hotel, restaurant, shopping mall or UNESCO site will receive advertisements and promotional messages based on their current location, and GPS will guide them to their requested choice. E-Brochure is a type of multimedia messaging service (MMS) which includes photographs, advertisements and promotional information for places of interest.

In order to understand the requirements of an effective GPS-based advertisement system, a preliminary study was conducted to get the opinions and interests of users' with regards to a real-time and location-based marketing system that would deliver preferred information on lodging, food or shopping based on the user's current location. The main purpose of this preliminary study was to investigate the proportion of cell phone users that also use GPS and how mobile users react to GPS.

Furthermore, the survey wished to understand user preferences for Points of Interests (POI) and to estimate what price mobile GPS user would be willing to pay for an m-commerce advertising service. In line with this intention, the study which is a very basic survey was conducted in Penang, Malaysia beginning on 26 October, 2010. It focused on people working in the industry and on university students who were cell phone users. The flow of the preliminary study is depicted in Fig. 3.

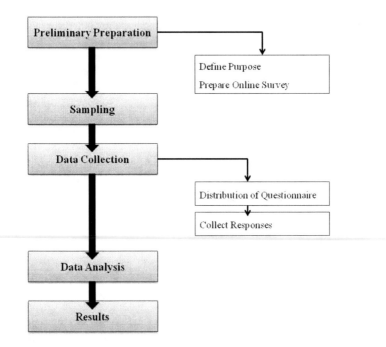

Fig. 3. Flow of Preliminary Study

Preliminary Preparation

Purpose of Preliminary Research

The goal of the preliminary study was to gauge user interest in a GPS-based advertisement system that would provide information about hotel, restaurant or shopping mall promotions according to the current location of the mobile user via short message service short message service (SMS) or multimedia message service (MMS). To do this, we prepared a survey. The results of the survey assisted us in designing the proposed e-Brochure service.

Design Online Survey

The desired respondents for our survey were cell phone users. The best and fastest way to approach them was to design the questionnaire and distribute/broadcast it online. After providing and designing the survey questionnaire online, we sent it to recipients via email. The link was sent to university students and professionals in all industry. On 26th October 2010 and the questionnaire remained online for two weeks. This online survey consisted of ten simple questions in four categories as shown in Table 1.

Table 1. Categories of Questions

Question	Category
1,2	Demographics
3,6	GPS User and MMS User
4,7,9,10	Preferred Service/Information through GPS and MMS
5,8	Reason for Rejecting GPS and MMS

   In order to determine our user group characteristics, the survey asked the age of the user (from below 20 to 60), their usage of the GPS features of their mobile device, the types of services they are interested in, whether they are using GPS features of their mobile device and if not why not, finally whether they are an MMS user or SMS user. The survey also asked the user about the type of information they would like receive such as food promotions, shopping promotions and sales, entertainment information, lifestyle coverage for both men and women, hotel information, UNESCO site reviews, technology news and promotions etc. To assess preferred medium, the survey asked whether the preferred SMS or MMS. Finally, the user was asked about the cost of the e-Brochure, specifically whether they would be willing to pay more or less RM 0.50. This information was designed to help us determine the market trends and interests of those who are using a GPS device and who would like to receive information on their favorite point of interests.

Select Representative Sample and Solicit Responses

First we needed to know the population of GPS users in Penang; of these, we then needed to identify those who use use their cell phone to receive SMS and MMS. For purposes of this preliminary study, respondents were selected randomly from university students and industry professionals. A total of 400 cell phone users in Penang, Malaysia who had e-mail addresses or Facebook accounts were selected. An invitation email along with a link to the survey website was sent to the subjects. Out of 400 surveys sent, 100 complete responses were received, which is 33.3% response rate.

Data Collection

After receiving the responses we filtered the sample based on the respondents who stated that they use GPS and GPS functionality in their daily life. After categorizing them by GPS usage, we further determined their points of interest (e.g., food, shopping, UNESCO sites etc.) and identified which were popular among the community.

Data Analysis

To analyze the data from our survey, we used SPSS (Statistical Package for the Social Sciences) version 15.0, which provides descriptive statistics such as frequencies, descriptive analysis and etc. Since this is a preliminary study we did not undertake advanced statistical analysis.   Given our requirements, we analyzed all the questionnaires to find the percentage of GPS users and the frequency of their preferred points of interests. We further calculated the frequency of users who preferred to have the e-Brochure cost or less than RM 0.50. Results of the analysis are presented in the next section.

Analysis of Results

Question 1 and 2 asked the ethnicity and age of the respondents; results are shown in Table 2. Of the 100 respondents 21% are Malay followed by Indian (12%), Chinese (21%) and other (46%). Other which accounts for 46% of the responses, probably consists of people from other countries who have come to study and work   in Malaysia, and believe that this service would be beneficial to them as they are not familiar with points of interests in Malaysia. In age, 2% of the respondents are below 20, 31% are 21-25 years old, 35% are 26-30 years old, 21% are 31-35 years old, 8% are 36-40, 2% are 41-45 years old and 1% are 46-50 years old. None were over 50 years old. These results show that young people (the age range 21-35 covers 87 of the sample) are more interested in using GPS-based services. These results show that there is an interest for GPS-based advertisement services and therefore there is feasibility in the proposed e-Brochure system.

Table 2. Demographic Data

Question	Item	Choices	Frequency	%
1	Ethnic Group	Malay	21	21
		Indian	12	12
		Chinese	21	21
		Others	46	46
2	Age	Below 20	2	2
		21-25	31	31
		26-30	35	35
		31-35	21	21
		36-40	8	8
		41-45	2	2
		46-50	1	1
		51-55	-	-
		56-60	-	-
		61-65	-	-
		Above 66	-	-

Table 3 shows results for whether the respondents are GPS and MMS users. Of the 100 respondents, 54% are GPS users and 54% are MMS users. The most important point which fulfills one of the objectives of this survey, is the substantial percentage of GPS users among cell phone users. Because the proposed e-Brochure service track the location of the users via GPS, and then send promotion and advertising information via MMS, this percentage of GPS is also the percentage of potential users of e-Brochure. For the same reason, it is important to understand the percentage of MMS users, since e-Brochure information will be sent via MMS.

Table 3. GPS User & MMS User

Question	Item	Choices	Frequency	%
3	Are you a GPS User?	Yes	54	54
		No	45	46
6	Are you a MMS User?	Yes		54
		No		45

For the e-Brochure service to be useful to end-users, identification of their preferred services is important. Responses to question 4 in Table 4 show that 43.6% of the respondents are interested in addresses, 52.7% in position, 85.5% in maps and 56.4% in places of interests such as hotels and restaurants. (Percentages total more that 100% since respondents could choose more than one preferred service.)

Table 4. Preferred Service/Information through GPS and MMS

Question	Item	Choices	Frequency	%
4	If Yes, what type of services?	Addresses	24	43.6
		Position	29	52.7
		Map	47	85.5
		Places of Interest (hotel, restaurant)	31	56.4
7	If yes, what type of information will you pay for?	Food Promotion	26	51
		Shopping Promotion	23	45.1
		Entertainment	20	39.2
		Lifestyle	14	27.5
		Hotel Information	20	39.2
		UNESCO Sight	34	66.7
		Technology Promotion	22	43.1
		Spa Promotion	6	11.8
		Monthly Event Update (PC Fair, STAR Edu Fair)	17	33.3
9	How much are you willing to pay for e-Brochure?	< RM 0.50	81	82.7
		> RM 0.50	17	17.3
10	Are you comfortable with receiving promotions and other information through messaging?	Yes	66	66
		No	34	34

Question 7 in Table 4 shows what types of promotion and advertising information users willing to pay for. Results show that 51% of respondents would pay for food promotions, 45.1% for shopping promotions, 39.2% for entertainment, 27.5% for lifestyle, 39.2% for hotel information, 66.7% for UNESCO sights, 43.1% for technology promotion, 11.8% for spa promotion and 33.3% for monthly event updates such as PC fair and so on. The results of question 9 are important in setting the price of the e-Brochure advertising service. Of the respondents, 82.7% would not pay more than RM 0.50. Finally, users' willingness to receive promotion and advertising messages as exposed in question 10 is important for the design of a GPS-based advertisement service. In this case, 66% percent of respondents indicate they would be comfortable receiving promotional and advertising messages.

Table 5. Reason of Rejecting GPS and MMS

Question	Item	Choices	Frequency	%
5	If No [to GPS use], why not?	Expensive	12	25
		Don't have a device	36	75
		Technology Illiterate	3	6.3
		Not reliable	5	10.4
8	If No [to MMS use], why not?	Expensive	18	37.5
		Don't Have MMS Enabled Mobile Phone	11	22.9
		I don't Like	10	20.8
		SMS is Preferred	22	45.8

The most important part of the survey was the percentage of GPS users: about 54% as shown in Table 3. These respondents were filtered and analysis conducted on the essential data that identifies the survey objectives that is GPS users' data. For this reason, questions related to GPS users (for instance, the reason for rejecting GPS and MMS) were not considered. Results from these questions are given in Table 5.

After filtering GPS users from all respondents, analysis was conducted on the questions pertinent to the main objectives of this survey as shown in Table 6. The first objective of this survey was to determine the percentage of GPS users. Therefore, we filtered the respondents that gave a positive answer to the question "Are you a GPS user?" The next objective was to identify GPS user's preferred services and POIs. Another objective was to investigate the percentage of MMS users within the GPS users and the amount of money they would be willing to pay. Finally, we needed to understand whether GPS/MMS users would be comfortable to receiving promotional and advertising messages to hotels, restaurants, UNESCO sites, etc. Fig. 4 shows all the survey items relevant to proposing our new GPS-based advertisement system (e-Brochure).

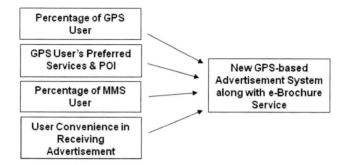

Fig. 4. Items Relevant to Proposed System

The main objective of this preliminary study was to find out the percentage of GPS users in Penang as illustrated in Table 3; therefore, we categorized respondents as GPS users and non-GPS users. From this, we could estimate the number of end users potentially interested in e-Brochure. According to Table 3, 54% of cell phone users also use GPS, meaning that 54% are likely to be interested. Next, we investigated their preferred services in order to identify the scope of e-Brochure. As shown in Table 6, 85.2% of the GPS users are interested in map services; therefore, we will include a map search option as a part of our software menu. We will send promotions and advertisements related to points of interest to users, which we will display on the map relative to their current location, and we will navigate their selected users to the destination POI.

As shown in Table 3, we also categorized respondents based on whether they preferred to use SMS or MMS, so we could determine how many users would able to receive POI information through SMS or MMS. According to our survey, a healthy number of GPS users (68%) prefer to use MMS. Accordingly, we will focus on providing our location-based advertising information through MMS.

In the survey, a list of POIs has been given to GPS users and they were asked to select their preferred POIs based on their interests. As illustrated in Table 6, the results were food promotion 54.3%, shopping promotion 42.9% entertainment 45.7%, life-style 22.9%, hotel information 40%, UNESCO sites 71.4%, technology promotion 48.6%, spa promotion 14.3% and monthly event updates 31.4%. A high percentage of users are interested in promotions for both hotels and restaurants, which matches the main focus of our research. UNESCO sites and food promotion garnered the highest percentages (71.4% for UNESCO sight and 54.3% for food promotion). On the other hands, the first thing that all travelers will look for is a hotel. Consequently, we will also focus on the hotel as a POI, despite its relatively low preference ranking.

Based on the results as presented in Table 6, we can reasonably conclude how much GPS users' are willing to pay for a location-based advertising service like e-Brochure. A majority of the respondents (76.9%) stated they would be willing to pay less than 50 cents; only 23.1% would pay more than 50 cents. Finally we have a better understanding of users' willingness to receive promotion and advertising messages. Table 6 shows that 75.9% of GPS users would agree to receive such messages. Consequently, we can feel comfortable about sending location based promotion and advertising information regarding hotels, restaurants and UNESCO sites to users.

Table 6. Summary of GPS Users' Data

Question No	Questions	Categories/Opinion	Frequency	%
3	Are you a GPS user?	Opinion (Yes/No)	Yes = 54	54
4	If Yes, what type of services?	Attributes (e.g. Hotel, Restaurant)		
		Address	24	44.4
		Position	29	53.7
		Map	46	85.2
		Place of Interest	31	57.4
6	Are You a MMS User?	Opinion		
		Yes	36	67.9
		No	17	32.1
7	If yes, what type of information will you pay for?	Categories (e.g.PC Fair, STAR Edu Fair)		
		Food Promotion	19	54.3
		Shopping Promotion	15	42.9
		Entertainment	16	45.7
		Lifestyle	8	22.9
		Hotel Information	14	40
		UNESCO Sight	25	71.4
		Technology Promotion	17	48.6
		Spa Promotion	5	14.3
		Monthly Event Update	11	31.4
9	How much are you willing to pay for e-brochure?	< RM 0.50	40	76.9
		> RM 0.50	12	23.1
10	Are you comfortable with receiving promotions and other information through message?	Opinion (Yes/No)		
		Yes	41	75.9
		No	13	24.1

4 Proposed e-Brochure Solution

Our proposed system is a hybrid cellular network and Global Positioning System (GPS) based mobile client system that tracks the location of mobile users to deliver to them accurate and detailed advertisement and promotion information about hotels, restaurants, and UNESCO sites.

Fig. 5 illustrates the architecture of our proposed system. We assume that the client has already installed e-Brochure on their Java-capable mobile phone. When the client opens the application, the device will request its current GPS location summary from the satellite and store it in the mobile device. The system will display the main menu screen to the mobile user so that they can select from the list of available POI categories (e.g., Hotels, Restaurants or UNESCO sites). After the user selects a POI category, the appropriate GPS co-ordinates are sent to the remote server through the Internet. On the other end of the system, the server receives the mobile client request that contains its current GPS co-ordinates along with the desired POI category.

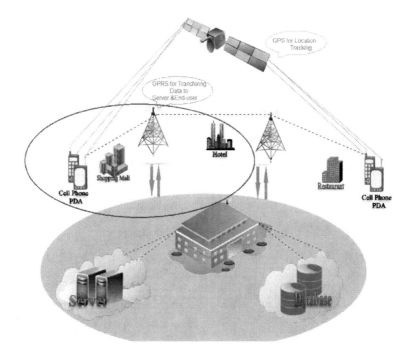

Fig. 5. Architecture of Proposed GPS-based Advertisement System [1]

The GPS co-ordinate processor sends the mobile user's current location to the database in order to get the appropriate location ID. The selected POI category is also sent to the database repository. The database component manager processes the information and searches for all items in the specified POI category based on the location ID. Message containing the list of the POIs is will be sent to the mobile user through the cellular network. On receiving the information, the mobile device displays the information on the screen. The flow diagram of the proposed system is shown in Fig. 6.

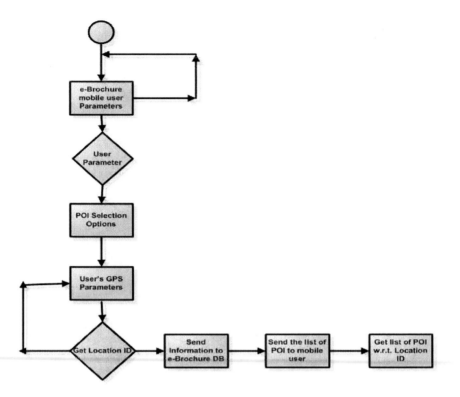

Fig. 6. Flow Diagram of e-Brochure

5 Discussion

Section 2 of this paper presented, a collection of related work in communication technology that is been used for location tracking of mobile users. After thorough investigation of previous works and after completing our preliminary study (survey), we were able to propose a new system for GPS-based advertisement services called e-Brochure. In M-Commerce, tracking the location of a mobile user is necessary in order to provide any location-based service – in this case, information on POI (hotels, restaurant, and UNESCO sites) that are geographically near the user's current location. Normally, location tracking is done by GPS or A-GPS (Assisted-Global Positioning System) via mobile device which provides the exact co-ordinates of the mobile user's location. The location co-ordinates can then be used by the system to search for appropriate POI that have been requested by the user through a wireless or cellular network. Therefore a modeling technique is needed that is able to accommodate and search for multiple POIs with accurate, efficient and robust manner, without delay, so that the mobile user does not need to wait for a response.

6 Conclusion

GPS-based technology can clearly be used as an advertisement tool. GPS, space-based satellite systems, and wireless positioning systems can determine a user's location and the distance from the user to a desired other location. By adding location-dependent information to position information, a modern advertising service can take advantage of both. Imagine a user is passing a particular street corner; he or she can immediately receive special advertisements or promotions pertaining to businesses on that route by using the e-Brochure service. Based on our preliminary study, there is a significant percentage of cell phone users who are using GPS and who would be interested in particular POI; therefore, it is likely that GPS-based advertisement systems will be the current trend for M-Commerce and that integration between GPS maps and GPS-based advertisement system will facilitate both end users and businesses in taking part in M-Commerce activities.

References

1. Keikhosrokiani, P.: E-Torch: Ellipse Model Framework for Location-Based and M-Commerce Advertising System. Dissertation for MSc IT vol. Master. Universiti Sains Malaysia (2011)
2. Getting, I.A.: Perspective/navigation-The Global Positioning System. IEEE Spectrum 30, 36–38, 43-47 (1993)
3. Garmin, http://www.garmin.com/garmin/cms/site/us
4. Samsung, Intel Products, AT&T Products, http://reviews.cnet.com/best-gps/
5. Foursquare, http://foursquare.com/
6. Cobanoglu, C., Ciccarelli, S., Nelson, R.R., Demicco, F.J.: Using Global Positioning Systems as a Marketing Tool: An Analysis of U.S. Consumers' Use and Perceptions. Journal of Hospitality Marketing & Management (2010)
7. Xu, Z., Yuan, Y.: What is the Influence of Context and Incentive on Mobile Commerce Adoption?—A Case study of a GPS-based Taxi Dispatching System. IEEE (2007)
8. Kennedy, M.: The global positioning system and GIS: an introduction. Taylor & Francis (2002)
9. Virrantaus, K., Markkula, J., Garmash, A., Terziyan, V.Y., Veijalainen, J., Katasonov, A., Tirri, H.: Developing GIS-Supported Location-Based Services. In: Web Information Systems Engineering, pp. 66–75 (2001)
10. Espinoza, F., Persson, P., Sandin, A., Nyström, H., Cacciatore, E., Bylund, M.: GeoNotes: Social and Navigational Aspects of Location-Based Information Systems (2001)
11. Brimicombe, A.J.: GIS - Where are the frontiers now? In: Proceedings GIS 2002, Bahrain (2002)
12. Wang, P., Zhao, Z., Xu, C., Wu, Z., Luo, Y.: Design and Implementation of the Low-Power tracking System Based on GPS-GPRS Module IEEE (2010)
13. Chadil, N., Russameesawang, A., Keeratiwintakorn, P.: Real-Time Tracking Management System Using GPS, GPRS and Google Earth. IEEE (2008)
14. Khalel, A.M.H.: Position Location Techniques in Wireless Communication Systems. In: Electrical Engineering Emphasis on Telecommunications, vol. Master, pp. 53. Blekinge Institute of Technology Karlskrona, Sweden (2010)
15. Imielinski, T., Navas, J.C.: GPS-Based Geographic Addressing, Routing, and Resource Discovery. Communications of the ACM 42, 86–92 (1999)
16. Esri, http://www.esri.com/software/arcgis
17. Oracle, http://otn.oracle.com/products/spatial

18. Kukkonen, J., Myllärinen, J., Nissinen, A., Voipio, M.: A dual approach for creating very large virtual models. In: International Symposium on Virtual and Augmented Architecture, VAA 2001 (2001)
19. Toyama, K., Logan, R., Roseway, A., Anandan, P.: Geographic location tags on digital images. In: 11th ACM International Conference on Multimedia, MM 2003, pp. 156–166 (2003)
20. Athanasiou, S., Georgantas, P., Gerakakis, G., Pfoser, D.: Utilizing Wireless Positioning as a Tracking Data Source. Springer, Heidelberg (2009)
21. Shibata, N., Terauchi, T., Kitani, T., Yasumoto, K., Ito, M., Higashino, T.: A Method for Sharing Traffic Jam Information using Inter-Vehicle Communication. IEEE (2006)
22. Neves, P.A.C.S., Ferreira, D.J.M., Esteves, D., Felix, D.R.M., Rodrigues, J.J.P.C.: InHand – Mobile Professional Context and Location Aware Tool. IEEE (2008)

A Framework for Direct Marketing with Business Intelligence: An Illustrative Case Study in Retailing

Adel Flici[1], Kevin Lü[1], and Andrew Fearne[2]

[1] Brunel University, London, United Kingdom
{Adel.Flici,Kevin.Lu}@brunel.ac.uk
[2] Kent Business School, University of Kent, United Kingdom
A.Fearne@kent.ac.uk

Abstract. Direct Marketing has become a key strategy for businesses to develop strong customer relationships, which is a marketing method that targets specific customers with personalised advertising and promotional campaigns. Business Intelligence tools, in turn, are effective tools for advanced data analysis and decision support. However, to utilise Business Intelligence tools in direct marketing is not a straightforward task since it requires expert knowledge of various functions provided by Business Intelligence as well as a good understanding about direct marketing practice. This study focuses on developing efficient and effective way of applying Business Intelligence tools for direct marketing processes. A formalised and structured Direct Marketing Process Framework (DMPF-BI) has been introduced using BI tools as an integrated system platform. To evaluate the framework, a sale promotion related data set of a well known UK supermarket has been used for assessments. It demonstrates the robustness and usefulness of our framework in the context of direct marketing in retailing.

Keywords: Direct marketing (DM), Business Intelligence (BI), Direct Marketing Process with Business Intelligence (DMP-BI).

1 Introduction

Retail markets operate in a highly competitive and volatile environment where consumers' purchasing behaviour is constantly changing and difficult to predict. In such competitive markets, direct marketing has become a key method to enhance promotion campaigns as well as develop strong customer relationships [7]. Traditional one-size-for-all general marketing techniques are no longer enough to develop effective marketing campaigns. Direct marketing methods are needed to increase marketing campaign responses and to lower costs. Unlike general marketing which is a product oriented strategy, direct marketing is a customer oriented method. It uses customers details commonly held in databases, to understand their needs [16]. This is achieved through a process which includes identifying customers' characteristics to recognise their market values, and predict their likelihood to respond to sales promotions [3][5].

A. Abd Manaf et al. (Eds.): ICIEIS 2011, Part II, CCIS 252, pp. 545–558, 2011.
© Springer-Verlag Berlin Heidelberg 2011

There are a number of studies focused on technical aspects of direct marketing, such as performance issues. For example, studies of [9] [11] [17] have proposed to improve data mining techniques and machine learning methods for more effective direct marketing. The main contributions of these studies are in general adding, merging or modifying algorithms to enhance the existing data mining methods for direct marketing purposes.

However, very little attention has been paid on formalising the process of applying data mining and advanced data analysis techniques to the direct marketing process, thus the non-analyst user can use such tools to resolve direct marketing issues. This process involves incorporating a collection of marketing concepts and business analytics principles which together form an entirely 'self-contained' choice for marketers. This makes it a rather challenging process to perform [16]. Moreover, the direct marketing process is commonly executed as several disconnected activities and operations in many organisations. It is also considered as an ad hoc process as it is usually executed in different ways depending on the process objectives. For example, the marketing strategy for a company focusing on a particular product is more likely to differ from those focusing on services. Meanwhile, the diversity of the parameters affecting the performance of the direct marketing process designed for a given situation makes it possible to have a number of different ways of executing a direct marketing process. Consequently, marketers are facing many challenges to undertake the direct marketing process effectively. The complexity of advanced analytics such as data mining makes marketers more reluctant to utilise the resulting models due to difficulty, poor comprehensibility, and trust issues [6][9][12].

In this study, we develop a framework of the Direct Marketing Process with Business Intelligence (DMP-BI). The framework utilises BI tools as an integrated system platform on which the direct marketing process can be executed. BI tools provide marketers/analysts with the abilities to produce more accurate and timely knowledge using techniques such as data mining, advanced analytics, and other decision support tools [8].

The empirical evaluation of the DMP-BI framework is conducted using a dataset of a major supermarket in the United Kingdom. This case study illustrates the effectiveness of the framework in executing the direct marketing process. It also demonstrates the framework ability to guide marketers/analysts through a structured path, which can reduce the uncertain factors commonly experienced in the direct marketing process. Finally, a case study demonstrates business intelligence tools are effective system platform to run the direct marketing process.

The remainder of the paper is organised as follows. Section 2 provides an overview of the direct marketing process, and discusses the main issues surrounding it. In Section 3, we present the DMP-BI framework with an explanation of the main stages and BI functions involved. Section 4 covers the case study approach used to evaluate the DMP-BI framework. Finally, a study conclusion is presented.

2 Direct Marketing Process Overview

The basic aim of any direct marketing process is to obtain a measurable response which will generate an immediate or eventual profit. There are two fundamentals in the direct marketing process: understanding customers and interacting with customers. This study concerns the first. On the one hand, the most creative or best offer may result in low response if an inappropriate group of customers is targeted. On the other hand, if a badly performed creative or poorly formulated offer is aimed at the right target group (i.e. a group that is interested in a product or service provided), it may depress consumer response, but not completely eliminate it. Thus, understanding customers' preferences and needs are more critical than an impressive creative or offer. This is because regardless of the promotion attractiveness, if the wrong group of customers is targeted, there will most probably be a low response.

This study focuses on analytical techniques in understanding customers' needs and requirements. The success of the direct marketing outcome relies heavily on the effective application of these activities. The following sub-sections provide direct marketing applications for understanding customers and issues related to direct marketing process.

2.1 Direct Marketing Applications

There are two main activities involved in understanding customers: Segmentation and Targeting [16]. These two activities are primarily aimed to achieve customer acquisition and retention. Firstly, customer segmentation is the process of identifying homogenous groups of consumers which have similar tastes, needs and preferences toward a company's products/services. Secondly, customer targeting consists of identifying customers who are most likely to respond to a particular campaign.

There are two principle analytical techniques used to perform direct marketing applications: 1) standard statistical techniques, and 2) data mining/machine leaning techniques. Statistical techniques can be powerful and have been used to build models of consumer responses. However, statistical techniques can only handle a limited amount of data and have limited explanatory ability. Data mining offers several distinctive benefits dealing with large data sets with more functions at a higher speed. Data mining techniques offer companies the capability to analyse large amounts of data and provide better explanatory [9].

In direct marketing discipline, data mining and machine learning techniques can perform several tasks which can be grouped into two main categories: classification and numerical prediction. Firstly, classification is the process of examining the features of a new object and allocates it to a class. For example, credit applicants can be classified as low, medium or high [2]. Secondly, numerical prediction involves predicting continuous (or ordered) values for a particular input. For example, the income of college graduates with 15 years' experience can be predicted, or the probability of how well a product may sell based on its price [12]. There are many techniques used to carry out classification and numerical prediction tasks. Table 1 presents the most common techniques used in the direct marketing field.

Table 1. Most common data mining and machine learning techniques for direct marketing applications. Adapted from [18]

Direct marketing models	Commonly used techniques	Direct marketing applications
Classification	Decision Trees, Automatic Clustering Detection, Neural Networks, k-nearest-neighbour, Support Vector Machines	To which segment does a customer belong? What characteristics define a segment? How can firms classify customers?
Numerical Prediction	Neural Networks, Naïve Bayesian, Decision Trees, Association Rules, Support Vector Machines, Automatic Clustering Detection	How can companies predict customer response to targeted offers? What is the effect of prices and promotions on the probability of purchase? How likely is a customer to respond on a given advertisement? How can firms predict customers' relationship duration?

2.2 Direct Marketing Process Issues

Previous research studies such as [9][11][17] on direct marketing in Information Systems context, are predominantly related to data mining. It is therefore important to examine process issues of direct marketing in relation to data mining. The process of choosing mining objectives and methods in direct marketing context is still unstructured and based mostly on judgment. According to [3], there are no studies performed on data mining which provide detailed guidelines on how to extract marketing intelligence for direct marketing. It can be explained that on the one hand there are many techniques that can be used; on the other hand, the process of extracting marketing intelligence can be difficult, time-consuming and many uncertain elements can be involved. Meanwhile, data mining techniques can be complex and difficult to use and manipulate. The high level of interaction and iteration between analysts and marketers can be a difficult task which involves collecting, analysing, and acting upon enterprise data in dynamic environments [14].

There are methodologies such as CRISP-DM[1] and KDD[2] developed for applying data mining for general purposes which can be used to execute the direct marketing process. However, these methodologies lack the detailed support required for direct marketing. Therefore, marketers/analysts face many difficulties to execute the

---

[1] CRISP-DM is a process model aimed at facilitating the management of small to large data mining projects.
[2] Knowledge Discovery in Databases (KDD) can be described as a non-trivial process that aims to identify valid, novel, useful and understandable patterns in data.

process, partly because the general nature of these methodologies increases the risk for marketers/analysts to deal with a lot of uncertainties.

The following sub-section discusses the process models that were specifically developed for the direct marketing process. It also presents these models limitations.

2.3 Existing Process Models in Direct Marketing

[16] proposed a process view of direct marketing to help marketers manage and execute it more effectively. However, this study did not propose a specific information system to support the model, arguing that it was a platform on which the process runs.

Another direct marketing process was proposed by [1]. This author also suggested the usage of recommender systems[3], arguing that they are the most developed matchmaking technologies. These systems can be used, for instance, to recommend products or services to consumers similar to the ones they preferred in the past. The main drawback of recommender systems is that it does not support the entire process model. The study suggested that there are no existing systems capable of supporting the whole process. Moreover, this study did not clearly show how recommender systems functions can support each stage and activity involved in the process model.

Furthermore, [10] provided a conceptual model for direct marketing, which links the use of database to the creation of customised and electronic media, in order to build interactive and integrated marketing communication. In this case, the model does not suggest an information system platform on which the process model can run.

Most existing direct marketing process models do not consider the information system which will be used to support the activities involved in the process. In the case where an information system is suggested, however, no detailed guidelines have been provided for the direct marketing process. As a result, users such as marketers and analysts have to identify the appropriate functions within a given system to execute a specific activity.

In order to overcome the limitations of existing work, this study proposes the usage of BI tools to support the activities involved in the direct marketing process. It aims to demonstrate that BI tools offer a complete set of capabilities which can effectively support the execution of any direct marketing process.

3 DMP-BI Framework

This section introduces the Direct Marketing Process with Business Intelligence (DMP-BI) framework. The following sub-sections present detailed description of the stages and functions that constitute the framework.

3.1 Process Models Used to Develop the DMP-BI Framework

A typical direct marketing process involves two major activities: data analysis, and direct marketing planning [3][16]. Data analysis in direct marketing is commonly

---

[3] Recommender systems use methods such as statistics, data mining, and machine learning to personalise recommendations, content, and services to users.

performed using data mining and predictive analytics (e.g. [5] [7]. Therefore, it was deemed appropriate to use CRISP-DM methodology (business analytics industry standard) to develop the DMP-BI framework. CRISP-DM is a process model aimed to facilitate the management of small to large data mining and predictive analytics projects in various industries (Chapman et al. 2000).

Four other direct marketing process models are used to develop the DMP-BI framework including *Personalisation Process* [1], *The Process of Personalisation, A Typical Direct Marketing Process* [16], and *A Systems Perspective of Direct Marketing Models* [3].

The overall structure of the DMP-BI framework is a synthesis of the above process models. It is composed of four stages: 1) Direct Marketing Objectives, 2) Data Preparation, 3) Data Modelling, and 4) Direct Marketing Planning. The first stage was derived from [16], which set 'direct marketing objectives' as the starting point of the process. The second stage and third stage are based on data mining methodologies, which were adapted for direct marketing by the following researchers: [13]. The final stage was adapted from the direct marketing process of [16].

3.2   BI Tools as an Integrated Information System Platform

While there are various specialized software tools which support individual steps of the direct marketing process, this study proposes the usage of Business Intelligence tools as an integrated system platform. The following are the three main reasons for selecting BI tools to support the DMP-BI framework.

Firstly, BI tools provide marketers/analysts with software applications, technologies, and analytical methodologies that help them produce accurate and timely marketing knowledge. Moreover, BI tools offer them the functionality, scalability, and reliability of modern database management systems [8]. This can allow organisations to efficiently store and manage data. As a result, marketers/analysts will have access to an organised collection of data rather than unstructured data commonly stored in different spreadsheets.

Secondly, BI tools are well integrated with transactional systems allowing a closed loop between operations and analysis. This provides an efficient access to data which can be analysed, and results can have a straight impact into marketing activities [14].

Thirdly, BI tools advanced analytics offer marketers/analysts a better understanding of their market dynamics and customers future behaviour. This is achieved using analytical models that provide marketers/analysts with great explanatory power to perform tasks such as prediction. In the last decade, BI has been particularly useful in marketing and financial sectors that operate in highly dynamic environments [17].

BI tools are used to support the DMP-BI framework from a system perspective. They provide a complete set of functions capable of supporting each stage involved in the DMP-BI framework. These functions can be summarised into six main functions: 1) Reporting, 2) Data Integration, 3) Visualisation techniques, 4) database management, 5) analytical techniques, and 6) dashboards & scorecards [4][13]. Figure 1 describes the DMP-BI framework graphically.

The following sub-sections provide detailed explanations on how each stage and BI functions of the DMP-BI framework are used to execute a direct marketing process.

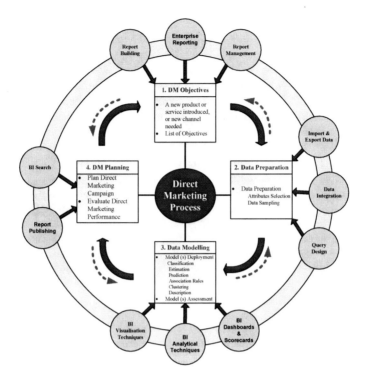

Fig. 1. Direct Marketing Process with Business Intelligence (DMP-BI) Framework

3.3 Direct Marketing Objectives

This stage is commonly initiated by an internal or external entity, i.e. a new product, or service, or channel which needs to be marketed [16]. The stage aims to define the objectives of the direct marketing process. While addressing the direct marketing objectives, marketers/analysts need to consider key questions such as what product/service will be offered, how they will be positioned/channelled, and what customers will be targeted.

After defining the process objectives, marketers/analysts are required to identify a suitable data source to achieve these objectives. There are numerous variables which can help marketers/analysts achieve direct marketing objectives. Transaction variables are commonly the most useful because they can reveal customers' behaviors [3].

The outcome of this stage is a list of objectives and a dataset to execute the direct marketing process. In this stage, BI reporting is used to report the objectives of the direct marketing process to share with departments that are concerned or for future record.

3.4 Data Preparation

The second stage of the framework requires marketers/analysts to prepare data for the data modelling stage. The direct marketing process often exposes marketers/analysts to a large amount of attributes and values within a dataset. This may result in a high number of possibilities to formulate from the attributes and values. Therefore, it is important to achieve attribute focus by selecting the most important ones [15].

This stage typically involves two key activities: attribute selection and data sampling. To begin with, attribute selection is choosing a set of attributes by removing attributes which are redundant or not relevant for the given objectives. Next is data sampling and entails choosing a small number of examples to deploy a direct marketing model (ibid). [13] stressed on the importance of conducting a sensitivity analysis to select the optimal amount of data to use for the data modelling phase. Direct marketing objectives are the best references to select the appropriate amount of data, hence achieve efficient data sampling.

Data preparation activities are commonly performed using BI database management functions such as data integration and query design. In fact, the BI database management platform offers all major capabilities to add, change, and manipulate dataset attributes. The primary purpose of data preparation is to provide a solid foundation on which data models can be deployed. The direct marketing models accuracy and reliability relies heavily on the integrity of the prepared data.

3.5 Data Modeling

Data modelling for direct marketing is commonly performed using data mining techniques (see Section 2.2). At this stage, advanced modelling is required in order to ensure a strong platform to search for interesting patterns and extract marketing intelligence. According to [2], direct marketing modelling using data mining can be classified into two main approaches: 1) directed data mining approach, and 2) undirected data mining approach. Firstly, directed data mining involves the tasks of classification, estimation, prediction, and profiling. The objective of directed data mining methods is to search and find patterns that explain a specific result. Secondly, undirected data mining entails the tasks of clustering, finding association rules, and description. The objective of undirected data mining is to determine whether or not the patterns identified are relevant.

There are no universally best data mining techniques and selecting a specific or combination of methods needs subjective judgments on the suitability of an approach. This stage proposes two approaches to facilitate marketers/analysts selection of data mining technique(s). The first approach is based on the direct marketing objectives. Marketers/analysts need to map the direct marketing objectives with one of the two categories provided in Table 1. After that, the data mining and machine learning methods that are suggested on the table are used to deploy the direct marketing models [18]. The second approach is mass modelling and entails using multiple or combination of data mining techniques. According to [10], mass modelling is a pragmatic method yielding good results in real-world marketing projects. In fact, the direct marketing process often requires a combination of data mining models to achieve the process objectives. For example, clustering can be used to perform customer segmentation for the initial classes of the data modelling. In this case, clustering only supports preliminary direct marketing analyses and prediction of customer's behaviour is the main purpose of the analyses.

After the model(s) deployment(s), marketers/analysts have to evaluate the accuracy of the results. Lift chart model can be used to estimate the accuracy of data mining models. This technique is a graphical model where the x-axis represents the percentage of data used for prediction and the y-axis represents the percentage of prediction correctness. A model is considered reliable if its accuracy is over 50% [13].

This stage final activity is to select the models to perform the analysis. It is rational to first use the most accurate model to perform the analysis. It is also suggested that if the most accurate model provides enough information to achieve the objectives, the other model(s) should not be considered for further analysis. Similarly, if the most accurate model does not fulfil the process objectives, the following most accurate model is subject to further analysis and so on until the process objectives are achieved.

BI analytical techniques are used to complete this stage. BI tools provide a variety of analytical techniques ranging from standard statistical techniques to more advanced data mining techniques. Model assessment is commonly performed using lift chart methods and most BI tools provide this capability. This stage can be quite tedious in terms of interpreting the model(s) results. However, it is a critical stage in the direct marketing process, because it is where patterns are identified. The following stage involves the planning of a direct marketing campaign using the model(s) results.

3.6 Direct Marketing Planning

Direct marketing model(s) analysis provides marketers/analysts with information which can help them develop customised products, services, channels, and communications for customers. For example, particular products can be marketed to customers with different colour preferences, discount coupons, and customised leaflets. Customers are then contacted through personal media (e.g. direct mail or post) in order to maximise the direct marketing impact. The outcome of the campaign responses is added to the marketing database [14]. It is common that companies have an end date to their promotions. Therefore, updating the marketing database should be performed after the deadline of the promotions has passed. Finally, the responses data can be used to evaluate the campaign impact. This will show whether the direct marketing campaign (e.g. targeting specific customers' segment) was effective [16]. Typically, it is done by reviewing the number of responses achieved.

There are cases where the direct marketing process lead to the discovery of more patterns than originally intended. This can result in formulating a new direct marketing process, in order to further investigate the patterns discovered. This is the reason the direct marketing process is iterative. BI search and reporting can be used in this stage to search for previous direct marketing or for documentation purposes.

4   Supermarket Promotions Case Study

The purpose of this case study is to evaluate the usage of DMP-BI in a retailing context. Specifically, it investigates supermarket sales promotions. This section begins with an overview of the transaction dataset used to illustrate the utility of the DMP-BI framework. It then describes the study proposition used to execute the direct marketing process. Finally, it evaluates the usage of the DMP-BI framework to execute the direct marketing process.

4.1 An Overview of the Transaction Dataset

This case study aims to evaluate the DMP-BI framework practicality and usefulness in executing a direct marketing process. This is achieved using a real transactional dataset provided by a major supermarket chain in the United Kingdom. The supermarket does not want to be identified, as promotion strategies and transactions are confidential. For convenience, the supermarket is referred to "Supermarket_1".

Supermarket_1 is committed to direct marketing practice which makes it an ideal case for this study. The dataset contains a broad range of information which could be used to investigate several consumer behaviours. However, a study proposition is adopted to execute the direct marketing process in a specific context. The following is the study proposition:

- Each region in the UK has different consumer purchasing behaviour and therefore requires a customised promotion campaign.

The DMP-BI framework is applied to the dataset to provide evidence for the study proposition. The aim is to prove that each region should have a specific promotion campaign. This study required to install a business intelligence tool to execute the direct marketing process with the DMP-BI framework. Microsoft SQL Server 2008 is a Business Intelligence tool which provides all the major business intelligence functions including data integration, reporting, and analysis. SQL Server 2008 was selected because it is one of the market leaders in the business intelligence industry.

Due to space limitations, it is not possible to provide a step by step illustration of the DMP-BI framework application to the dataset. Therefore, the following section provides an evaluation of the supermarket promotions case study findings.

4.2 Case Study Evaluation

This section evaluates the DMP-BI framework application in the sales promotion case study. Linking together several facts and events which occurred in the case study; three interrelated themes were drawn and will require in-depth evaluation.

The first theme is the suitability of the stages in the DMP-BI framework. Having used each stage to execute a real-world direct marketing process, it is necessary to evaluate and discuss their impact. This includes the suitability of the activities, guidance and recommendations provided by the DMP-BI framework. The first sub-section presents the evaluation of the DMP-BI stages.

The second theme is the applicability of the BI functions in the DMP-BI framework. This theme seeks to verify the usability of the BI functions within the DMP-BI framework. The case study required the usage of various BI functions to complete the direct marketing process. Therefore, the case study provides empirical information to evaluate and discuss whether the recommended BI functions in the DMP-BI framework were useful. The second sub-section assesses the BI function impact on the direct marketing process.

The third theme is the structure and organisation of the stages within the DMP-BI framework. This theme is concerned with evaluating whether the DMP-BI framework provided a systematic approach using the case study findings. The final sub-section examines the link between each stage in the DMP-BI framework.

The DMP-BI Stages. This sub-section investigates the impact of the activities provided in each DMP-BI stage. The aim of these activities is to facilitate the process of executing direct marketing process more effectively. Therefore, it is critical to verify whether these activities have provided the predicted benefits in executing the direct marketing process. The followings evaluate the impact of each stage on the direct marketing process execution.

Firstly, the "Direct Marketing Objectives" stage aims to provide a basis to execute the direct marketing process. It recommends three main activities for marketers/analysts to follow including *identify process initiator(s), consider key questions, and identify a suitable data source*. In this case, the latter activity was not required, because the dataset was already provided by Supermarket_1. The other two activities have been used. The first one requires marketers/analysts to identify the process initiator(s) (Is the process initiated internally or externally?). In this case, it was initiated by the study proposition, which is categorised as an external entity. This is because the study proposition is not related to a previous direct marketing process. The second activity recommends key questions that can assist marketers/analysts to formulate the direct marketing objectives. In this case, the process used two key questions: *"How price sensitive are customers?"*, and *"What customers would be most receptive to our offerings?"*. The outcome of this stage was as expected a list of objectives and a dataset to execute the process. The "Data Sampling" activity was not necessary in this stage, as all data is needed for analysis.

Secondly, the "Data Preparation" stage provides marketers/analysts with two key activities: 1) attribute selection, and 2) data sampling. The "Attribute Selection" activity aims to select the appropriate attributes to use for the data modelling stage. As recommended by the DMP-BI framework stage, the selection process was based on the "Direct Marketing Objectives" stage. This ensures data integrity in terms of redundancy and relevance towards the process objectives.

Thirdly, the "Data Modelling" stage involves five activities: 1) select a data mining approach, 2) model(s) deployment, 3) model(s) accuracy, 4) model(s) selection, and 5) model(s) analysis. In this case, all of the activities have been used to complete the stage. The stage began with selecting an appropriate data mining approach. Given the process objectives, directed data mining was selected, because the process was searching for specific results (see Section 3.5). Next, mass modelling was performed to complete the models deployment activity. It is important to clarify that marketers/analysts have the other option of using Table 1 to select data mining methods. However, in this case, it was more suitable to use the mass modelling approach. Selecting data mining techniques is highly subjective, and requires marketers/analysts to choose the best approach based on the specific process objectives. The "Model(s) Accuracy" activity was then calculated using the lift chart method. This allowed the identification of the most accurate model to use for analysis. The neural networks model was the most accurate, hence selected for analysis. However, the neural networks model's analysis did not reveal sufficient patterns to achieve the process objectives. In this case, the DMP-BI framework recommends marketers/analysts to use the next most accurate model and so on. Therefore, the decision tree and naïve bayes models were used for more in-depth analysis.

Finally, the "Direct Marketing Planning" stage recommends marketers/analysts to *check whether the process objectives are achieved, revise key patterns, and provide a direct marketing campaign or a list of suggestions.* In this case, all the objectives were achieved apart from identifying the promotions impact in each region. The "revise key patterns" activity was performed and a series of suggestions were provided for further analysis. Planning a direct marketing campaign was not feasible, because of the lack of access to the organisations' information such as budget allowance.

BI Functions. This sub-section examines the impact of BI functions in each stage of the DMP-BI framework. The aim of BI tools functions is to provide an integrated information system platform on which the process can be executed. Therefore, it is important to investigate whether Microsoft SQL Server 2008 business intelligence suite has provided all the required functions to execute the direct marketing process.

In the first stage, BI enterprise reporting is recommended for use in order to facilitate documentation sharing in organisations. However, this study was performed outside the organisation environment. Therefore, it was not required to share the direct marketing process documentation with other concerned departments.

The second stage used three database management functions namely *data import, data integration,* and *attribute selection.* These functions have all been recommended by the DMP-BI framework, and were available in the SQL Server 2008 BI suite.

The third stage involved deploying the data models. SQL Server 2008 BI tool provides the necessary data mining techniques to deploy the models. In this case, mass modelling was performed and the nine techniques available in SQL Server 2008 were used to deploy the models. After that, the lift chart accuracy technique was used to evaluate the performance of each model. This BI function allows the identification of the most accurate model.

The final stage included two BI functions: BI search and report publishing. These two functions were not used in this process, because it was not required to share results across the organisation, and it was not required to search for a new direct marketing process to execute.

The DMP-BI Structure. This sub-section evaluates the structure and organisation of the DMP-BI framework. In this case study, the stages have occurred in a systematic way, where each stage has caused the next stage to start. Also, each stage provided the relevant information for the next stage to be executed, except for the "Data Preparation" stage. In fact, the user had to navigate back from the "Data Modelling" stage to the "Data Preparation" stage. This is because of the incomplete models, which were deployed using the dataset without a field that uniquely identified each field. In addition, the SQL Server 2008 did not allow the use of a combination key as an alternative way to uniquely identify each transaction. This has led the user to navigate to the "Data Preparation" stage and perform the data integration activity. Overall, the sales promotion case study has illustrated that the DMP-BI structure is suitable to execute a direct marketing process.

6   Conclusion

Direct marketing is an emerging marketing method with great potential. This method aims to enhance organisations' marketing campaign responses which can ensure higher return on their investments. Accordingly, direct marketing has become an important discipline within the marketing research and business community. Most of research on direct marketing focuses on the technical aspects of data mining to improve analytical models accuracy. Yet these researches fail to consider the organisational and managerial issues related to the direct marketing process.

This study presented the DMP-BI framework which is intended to facilitate the direct marketing process. The framework was developed using direct marketing and business intelligence academic and industry literature. It is aimed to address the major issues surrounding direct marketing process including the complexity of its concepts and practices. The evaluation of the developed framework was performed using a case study approach. Specifically, a real world transaction dataset was used from a major supermarket chain in the UK. Using the framework and the dataset, a direct marketing process was executed. The case study illustrates that the DMP-BI framework can help marketers/analysts execute the direct marketing process. This is achieved by leading marketers/analysts through systematic stages with specific supporting BI functions. The valuation of the developed framework practicality and usefulness is clear. However, it is intended to further evaluate the developed framework in other industries, in order to generalise its application.

References

1. Adomavicius, G., Tuzhilin, A.: Personalization technologies: a process-oriented perspective. Commun. ACM 48(10), 83–90 (2005)
2. Berry, M.J.A., Linoff, G.S.: Data Mining techniques: For Marketing, Sales, and Customer Relationship Management, 2nd edn. Wiley Publishing, Inc., Indianapolis (2004)
3. Bose, I., Chen, X.: Quantitative models for direct marketing: A review from systems perspective. European Journal of Operational Research 195(1), 1–16 (2009)
4. Butler Group 2006, Business intelligence: a strategic approach to extending and standardising the use of BI, Butler Group, Hull (2006)
5. Changchien, S.W., Lee, C., Hsu, Y.: On-line personalized sales promotion in electronic commerce. Expert Systems with Applications 27(1), 35–52 (2004)
6. Chapman, P., Clinton, J., Kerber, R., Khabaza, T., Reinartz, T., Shearer, C., Wirth, R.: CRISP-DM 1.0: Step-by-step data mining guide (2000)
7. Chen, M., Chiu, A., Chang, H.: Mining changes in customer behavior in retail marketing. Expert Systems with Applications 28(4), 773–781 (2005)
8. Cody, W.F., Kreulen, J.T., Krishna, V., Spangler, W.S.: The integration of business intelligence and knowledge management. IBM Systems Journal 41(4), 697–713 (2000)
9. Cui, G., Wong, M.L., Lui, H.: Machine Learning for Direct Marketing Response Models: Bayesian Networks with Evolutionary Programming. Manage. Sci. 52(4), 597–612 (2006)
10. Gersten, W., Wirth, R., Arndt, D.: Predictive modeling in automotive direct marketing: tools, experiences and open issues. In: KDD 2000: Proceedings of the Sixth ACM SIGKDD International Conference on Knowledge Discovery and Data Mining, p. 398. ACM, New York (2000)
11. Ha, K., Cho, S., MacLachlan, D.: Response models based on bagging neural networks. Journal of Interactive Marketing 19(1), 17–30 (2005)
12. Han, J., Kamber, M.: Data Mining: Concepts and Techniques, 2nd edn. Morgan Kaufmann, San Francisco (2006)

13. Harinath, S., Quinn, S.R.: Analysis Services 2005 with MDX. Wiley Publishing, Inc. (2006)
14. Kohavi, R., Rothleder, N.J., Simoudis, E.: Emerging trends in business analytics. Communications of the ACM 45(8), 45–48 (2002)
15. Mitra, S., Pal, S.K., Mitra, P.: Data mining in soft computing framework: a survey. IEEE Transactions on Neural Networks 13(1), 3–14 (2002)
16. Tapp, A.: Principles of Direct and Database Marketing, 4th edn. Pearson Education Limited (2008)
17. Tettamanzi, A., Carlesi, M., Pannese, L., Santalmasi, M.: Business Intelligence for Strategic Marketing: Predictive Modelling of Customer Behaviour Using Fuzzy Logic and Evolutionary Algorithms (2007)
18. Murthi, B.P.S., Sarkar, S.: The Role of the Management Sciences in Research on Personalisation, vol. 49(10), pp. 1344–1362 (2003)

Intelligent Web Proxy Caching Approaches Based on Support Vector Machine

Waleed Ali[1,*], Siti Mariyam Shamsuddin[1], and Abdul Samed Ismail[2]

[1] Soft Computing Research Group,
Faculty of Computer Science and Information Systems,
Universiti Teknologi Malaysia, 81310 Johor, Malaysia
waleedalodini@gmail.com, mariyam@utm.my
[2] Department of Communication and Computer Systems,
Faculty of Computer Science and Information Systems,
Universiti Teknologi Malaysia, 81310 Johor, Malaysia
abdsamad@utm.my

Abstract. Web proxy caching is one of the most successful solutions for improving the performance of Web-based systems. In Web proxy caching, the popular web objects that are likely to be revisited in the near future are stored on the proxy server which plays the key roles between users and web sites in reducing the response time of user requests and saving the network bandwidth. However, the difficulty in determining the ideal web objects that will be revisited in the future is still a problem faced by existing conventional Web proxy caching techniques. In this paper, support vector machine (SVM) is used to enhance the performance of conventional web proxy caching such as Least-Recently-Used (LRU) and Greedy-Dual-Size-Frequency (GDSF). SVM is intelligently incorporated with conventional Web proxy caching techniques to form intelligent caching approaches called SVM_LRU and SVM_GDSF with better performance. Experimental results have revealed that the proposed SVM_LRU and SVM_GDSF improve significantly the performances of LRU and GDSF respectively across several proxy datasets.

Keywords: Web proxy caching, Cache replacement, Support vector machine.

1 Introduction

Web proxy caching plays a key role in improving the Web performance by keeping Web objects likely to be used in the future in the proxy server. Thus, the web proxy caching helps in reducing user perceived latency, lessening network bandwidth usage, and alleviating loads on the origin servers.

Since the apportioned space to the cache is limited, the space must be utilized judiciously. Therefore, an intelligent mechanism is required to manage the Web cache content efficiently. The cache replacement is the core or heart of the web caching; hence, the design of efficient cache replacement algorithms is crucial for caching mechanisms achievement [1-2]. The most common Web caching methods are not

---

* Corresponding author.

A. Abd Manaf et al. (Eds.): ICIEIS 2011, Part II, CCIS 252, pp. 559–572, 2011.

efficient enough and may suffer from a cache pollution problem since they consider just one factor and ignore other factors that have impact on the efficiency of Web proxy caching [1, 3-5]. The cache pollution means that a cache contains objects that are not frequently visited. This causes a reduction of the effective cache size and affects negatively on performance of the Web proxy caching. Many Web proxy caching policies attempted to combine some factors which can influence the performance of web proxy caching for making decision of caching. However, this is not an easy task because one factor in a particular environment may be more important in other environments [6]. So far, the difficulty in determining which ideal web objects will be re-visited is still a major challenge faced by the existing Web proxy caching techniques. In other words, which Web objects should be cached or replaced to make the best use of available cache space, improve hit rates, reduce network traffic, and alleviate loads on the original server [1, 7-8].

In Web proxy server, Web proxy logs file can be considered as complete and prior knowledge of future accesses. Availability of Web proxy logs files that can be exploited as training data is the main motivation for utilizing machine learning techniques in adopting intelligent Web caching approaches. The second motivation is, since Web environment changes and updates rapidly and continuously, an efficient and adaptive scheme is required in Web environment.

Recent studies have proposed exploiting machine learning techniques to cope with the above problem [1, 3, 5, 9-10]. Support vector machine (SVM) is popular supervised learning algorithm that performs classification more accurately and faster than other algorithms. SVM has a wide range of applications such as text classification, Web page classification and bioinformatics application [11-12]. Hence, SVM has been utilized in Web proxy caching contents classification in our previous work[7]. The results have revealed that SVM achieves much better accuracy and faster than others.

This study combines the most significant factors depending on SVM for predicting Web objects that can be re-visited later. In this paper, we present new approaches that depend on the capability of SVM to learn from Web proxy logs files and predict the classes of objects to be re-visited or not. More significantly, in this paper, the trained SVM classifier is incorporated effectively with traditional Web proxy caching algorithm to present novel intelligent web proxy caching approaches.

The remaining parts of this paper are organized as follows. Materials and methods of this study are presented in Section 2. Web proxy caching and the related works, including conventional and intelligent approaches, are discussed in Section 2.1 and Section 2.2. Section 2.3 describes support vector machine. The intelligent Web proxy caching approaches based on support vector machine are illustrated in Section 3. Section 4 elucidates implementation and performance evaluation. Finally, Section 5 concludes the paper and future works.

2   Material and Methods

2.1 Web Proxy Caching

Web caching is one of the most successful solutions for improving the performance of Web-based systems. In Web caching, the popular web objects that are likely to be used in the near future are stored on devices closer to the Web user such as, client's machine or proxy server. Thus, Web caching has three attractive advantages: Web caching decreases user perceived latency, reduces network bandwidth usage and reduces load on the origin servers.

Typically, the web cache is located in the browser, proxy server and/or origin server. The browser cache is located on the client machine. The user can notice the cache setting of any modern Web browser. At the origin server, web pages can be stored in a server-side cache for reducing the redundant computations and the server load.

The proxy cache is found in the proxy server which is located between the client machines and origin server. It works on the same principle of browser cache, but it has a much larger scale. Unlike the browser cache which deals with only a single user, the proxy server serves hundreds or thousands of users in the same way. When a request is received, the proxy server checks its cache. If the object is available, the proxy server sends the object to the client. If the object is not available, or it has expired, the proxy server will request the object from the origin server and send it to the client. The requested object will be stored in the proxy's local cache for future requests. The proxy caching is widely utilized by computer network administrators, technology providers, and businesses to reduce user delays and to reduce Internet congestion [4, 8, 13]. In this study, much emphasis will be focused on web proxy caching because it is still the most common caching strategy.

2.2 Related Works

2.2.1 Web Proxy Caching Algorithms

Most Web proxy servers are still based on traditional caching policies. These conventional policies are suitable in traditional caching like CPU caches and virtual memory systems, but they are not efficient in Web caching area. This is because they only consider one factor in caching decisions and ignore the other factors that have impact on the efficiency of the Web proxy caching [1, 3-5]. The simplest and most common cache management approach is Least-Recently-Used (LRU) algorithm, which removes the least recently accessed objects until there is sufficient space for the new objects. LRU is easy to implement and proficient for uniform size objects such as the memory cache. However, it does not perform well in Web caching since it does not consider the size or the download latency of objects[1]. Least-Frequently-Used (LFU) is another common web caching that replaces the object with the least number of accesses. LFU keeps more popular web objects and evicts rarely used ones. However, LFU suffers from the cache pollution in objects with the large reference accounts, which are never replaced even if they are not re-accessed again.

SIZE policy is one of the common web caching policies that replaces the largest object(s) from cache when space is needed for a new object. Thus, the cache can be polluted with small objects which are not accessed again. To alleviate the cache pollution, Cao and Irani (1997) [14] suggested Greedy-Dual-Size(GDS) policy as extension of the SIZE policy. The algorithm integrates several factors and assigns a key value or priority for each web object stored in the cache. When cache space becomes occupied and new object is required to be stored in cache, the object with the lowest key value is removed. When user requests an object g, GDS algorithm assigns key value $K(g)$ of object g as shown in Eq.(1):

$$K(g) = L + \frac{C(g)}{S(g)} \qquad (1)$$

where $C(g)$ is the cost of fetching object g from the server into the cache; $S(g)$ is the size of object g; and L is an aging factor. L starts at 0 and is updated to the key value of the last replaced object. The key value $K(g)$ of object g is updated using the new L value since the object g is accessed again. Thus, larger key values are assigned to objects that have been visited recently. If the cost is set 1, it becomes GDS(1), and when the cost is set to P=2+size/536, it becomes GDS(P).

Cao and Irani (1997)[14] proved that the GDS algorithm achieved better performance compared with some traditional caching algorithms. However, the GDS algorithm ignores the frequency of web object. Cherkasova(1998) [15] enhanced GDS algorithm by integrating the frequency factor into the key value $K(g)$ as shown in Eq.(2). The policy is called Greedy-Dual-Size-Frequency (GDSF).

$$K(g) = L + F(g) * \frac{C(g)}{S(g)} \qquad (2)$$

where $F(g)$ is frequency of the visits of g. Initially, when g is requested by user, $F(g)$ is initialized to 1. If g is in the cache, its frequency is increased by one. Similar to GDS, we have GDSF(1) and GDSF(P).

In fact, some few important features (characteristics) of Web objects that can influence the web proxy caching [6, 16-17] are: recency, frequency, size, cost of fetching the object, and access latency of object. Depending on these factors, the web proxy policies are classified into five categories [17]: Recency-based polices, Frequency-based polices, Size-based polices, Function-based polices and Randomized polices. Many Web cache replacement policies have been proposed for improving performance of web caching. However, it is difficult to have an omnipotent policy that performs well in all environments or for all time because the combination of the factors that can influence the web proxy cache is not an easy task[6]. Hence, there is a need for an effective and adaptive approach, which can incorporate these factors into web caching decision effectively. This is motivation in adopting intelligent techniques in solving Web caching problems.

2.2.2 Intelligent Web Proxy Caching Algorithms

Although there are many studies in Web caching, the research using learning machine techniques in Web caching is still fresh. Recent studies have shown that the intelligent approaches are more efficient and adaptive to Web caching environments compared to other approaches. More details about intelligent web caching approaches are illustrated in [18].

In our previous work ICWCS[9], the neuro-fuzzy system has been employed to predict Web objects that can be re-accessed later. Although the simulation results have proven that ICWCS helps in improving the performance in terms of hit ratio; the performance in terms of byte hit ratio is not good enough since ICWCS does not take into account the cost and size of the predicted objects in cache replacement process. Moreover, the training process requires a long time and extra computational overhead. In NNPCR [5] and NNPCR-2[3], ANN has been used for making cache replacement decision. An object is selected for replacement based on the rating returned by ANN. However, employment of ANN classifier in cache replacement decision is still not clear. Moreover, the performance of ANN relies on the optimal selection of the network topology and its parameters that are still a matter of trial and error; besides that, ANN learning process can be time consuming.

Sulaiman et al.(2008)[10] used particle swarm optimization (PSO) for improving neural network performance. ANN has also been used by Koskela et al.(2003) [1] who depends on syntactic features from HTML structure of the document and the HTTP responses of the server as inputs of ANN. However, this method ignored frequency factor in web cache replacement decision. On the other hand, it hinged on some factors that do not affect the performance of web caching.

From the previous studies, we can observe two approaches in intelligent web caching. An intelligent technique is employed in web caching individually or integrated with LRU Algorithm. Both approaches may predict Web objects that can be re-accessed later. However, they did not take into account the cost and size of the predicted objects in the cache replacement process. Secondly; some important features of object are ignored in the above mentioned approaches. Lastly, the training process requires long time and extra computational overhead.

This study takes into consideration the most significant factors in caching decision. Moreover, our study utilizes the most powerful classifier in predicting Web objects that can be re-visited later. In addition, we present new intelligent web proxy caching approaches, which depend on the capability of SVM to learn from Web proxy logs files and predict the classes of objects to be re-visited or not. The proposed approaches differ significantly about the intelligent existing web caching works. In our proposed approaches, the trained classifiers are integrated effectively with conventional web proxy caching to provide more effective proxy caching policies.

2.3 Support Vector Machine

Support vector machine (SVM) is one of the most robust and accurate methods in all well-known machine learning algorithms. SVM has been used successfully in a wide range of applications such as text classification, Web page classification and bioinformatics applications[11-12].

SVM is invented by Vapnik(1995) [19]. The primary idea of SVM is using a high dimension space to find a hyperplane to do binary division with two classes, positive and negative samples. The SVM attempts to place a liner boundary or hypeplane between the two different classes, and orient it in such a way that the margin is maximized. The nearest data points are used to define the margins and are known as support vectors (SV).

In training phase, the SVM is trained to find several support vectors that represent training data. These support vectors will be formed into a model by the SVM, representing a category. Consequently, the SVM will classify a given unknown data set depending on this model.

For many real-life problems, the data is a nonlinearly separable data. So, it is not easy to find a hyperplane to classify the data such as nonlinearly separable data. The nonlinearly separable data is classified with the same principle of the linear case. However, the input data is only transformed from the original space into higher dimensional space using a kernel function.

3   The Proposed Intelligent Web Proxy Caching Approaches

In Web proxy caching, if the requested object is not in the cache or not fresh, the requested object will be fetched into the cache buffer from the origin server. This is called a cache miss. If the requested object is in the cache and still fresh, the request will be served from the cache directly and this is called a cache hit.

When the cache buffer is full and a new web object is fetched from the server, the proposed intelligent caching approaches are used to identify unwanted web objects for replacement. In this section, we present intelligent web proxy caching approaches depending on integrating SVM with traditional Web caching to provide more effective caching policies. Two intelligent web proxy caching approaches are proposed and called SVM-GDSF and SVM-LRU.

3.1   SVM-GDSF

One advantage of GDSF policy is that it performs well in terms of the hit ratio. However, the byte hit ratio of GDSF policy is too low. Therefore, SVM classifier is integrated with GDSF for improving the performance in terms of the byte hit ratio of GDSF. The proposed intelligent proxy caching approach is called SVM-GDSF.

In SVM-GDSF, the trained SVM classifier is used to predict class of Web objects either objects may be re-visited later or not. Then, classification decision is integrated into cache replacement policy (GDSF) to give key value for each object in cache buffer as in Eq.(3). Consequently, the objects with lowest values are removed first to make sufficient space for incoming objects.

$$K(g) = L + F(g) * \frac{C(g)}{S(g)} + W(g) \tag{3}$$

where $W(g)$ represents the value of predicted class of object g, based on SVM classifier. $W(g)$ will be assigned to 1 if object g is classified by SVM as an object to be re-visited, otherwise $W(g)$ will be assigned to 0. This means that the key value of object g is determined not just by its past occurrence frequency, but also by the class predicted depending on the six factors that will mentioned in subsection 4.3. The rationale behind the proposed SVM-GDSF approach is to enhance the priority of those cached objects that may be revisited in the near future according to the SVM classifier, even if they are not accessed frequently enough. Fig. 1 explains the algorithm of the proposed SVM-GDSF.

In this study, SVM-GDSF is proposed for improving the performance of GDSF(1) since GDSF(1) is widely used in a real and simulation environment. Thus, the cost $C(g)$ is set to 1 in all polices: GDS, GDSF and SVM-GDSF.

```
Begin

Initialize L=0;
    For each web object g requested by user
    Begin
        If g in cache
        Begin
            Cache hit occurs
            Update information of g
            // update priority of g based on SVM
            W(g) = apply_SVM( common features)
```

$$K(g) = L + F(g) * \frac{C(g)}{S(g)} + W(g)$$

```
        End

        Else
        Begin
            Cache miss occurs
            While no enough space in cache buffer for g
            Begin
                L = min(k(q)), for all q in cache
                Evict q such that k(q)=L
            End
            Fetch g into cache from origin server.
        End
    End

End
```

Fig. 1. The intelligent proxy cache SVM-GDSF algorithm

3.2 SVM-LRU

LRU policy is the most common proxy caching policy among all the web proxy caching algorithms [3-5, 13]. However, LRU policy suffers from cold cache pollution, which means unpopular objects remain in the cache for a long time. In other words, in LRU, a new object is inserted at the top of the cache stack. If the object is not requested again, it will take some time to be moved down to the bottom of the stack before removing it from the cache. For reducing cache pollution in LRU, SVM classifier is combined with LRU to form a new algorithm called SVM-LRU.

The proposed SVM-LRU works as follows. When the Web object g is requested by user, SVM predicts the class of that object either be revisited again or not. If the object g is classified by SVM as object to be re-visited again, the object g will be placed on the top of the cache stack. Otherwise, the object g will be placed in the middle of the cache stack. Hence, SVM-LRU can efficiently remove the unwanted objects early to make space for the new Web objects. By using this mechanism, the cache pollution can be reduced and the available cache space can be utilized effectively. The algorithm for SVM-LRU is illustrated in Fig. 2.

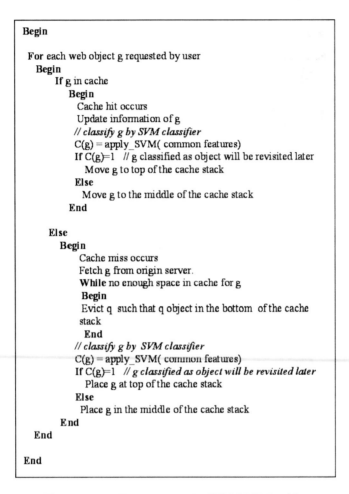

Begin

  For each web object g requested by user
    Begin
        If g in cache
          Begin
            Cache hit occurs
            Update information of g
            // classify g by SVM classifier
            C(g) = apply_SVM(common features)
            If C(g)=1 *// g classified as object will be revisited later*
              Move g to top of the cache stack
            Else
              Move g to the middle of the cache stack
          End

    Else
      Begin
            Cache miss occurs
            Fetch g from origin server.
            While no enough space in cache for g
            Begin
            Evict q such that q object in the bottom of the cache
            stack
            End
            // classify g by SVM classifier
            C(g) = apply_SVM(common features)
            If C(g)=1 *// g classified as object will be revisited later*
              Place g at top of the cache stack
            Else
              Place g in the middle of the cache stack
      End
  End

End

Fig. 2. The intelligent proxy cache SVM-LRU algorithm

4   Implementation and Performance Evaluation

4.1   Raw Data Collection

We have obtained data of the proxy logs files and traces of web objects requested in four proxy servers, called BO2, NY, SV and SD proxy server, which are located around the United States of the IRCache network for fifteen days[20]. The four proxy datasets were collected between 21st August and 4th September, 2010 except SD proxy dataset that were collected between 21st and 28th August, 2010. In this study, the proxy logs files of 21st August, 2010 were used in the training phase, while the proxy logs files of the following days were used in simulation and implementation phase to evaluate the proposed approaches. An access proxy logs entry usually consists of the following ten fields: Timestamp, Elapsed time, Client address, Log tag and HTTP code, Size, Request method, URL, User identification, Hierarchy data and hostname, and Content type.

4.2 Data Pre-processing

The data have undergone some pre-processing in order to become suitable for getting results reflecting the behavior of the algorithms. In this study, the data pre-processing involves that irrelevant requests are removed from the logs proxy files since some of the entries are either not valid or relevant. The data pre-processing is carried out as follows:

- **Parsing:** This involves identifying the boundaries between successive records in log file as well as the distinct fields within each record.
- **Filtering:** This includes elimination of irrelevant entries like: the uncacheable requests (i.e., queries with a question mark in the URLs and cgi-bin requests) and entries with unsuccessful HTTP status codes. We only consider successful entries with 200 as status codes.
- **Finalizing:** This involves removing unnecessary fields. Moreover, each unique URL is converted to a unique integer identifier for reducing time of simulation. Thus, the data are finalized into the final format that is amenable for experiment. The final format of our data consists of URL ID, timestamp, elapsed time, size and type of web object

4.3 Training Phase

In order to prepare the dataset of training, the desired features of web objects are extracted from trace and logs proxy files. Subsequently, these features are converted to the input/output dataset or training patterns required at the training phase. The training pattern takes the format:

$$< \; x_1 \,, \, x_2 \,, \, x_3 \,, \, x_4 \,, \, x_5 \,, \, x_6 \,, \, y \; >$$

where $x_1, ..., x_6$ represent the inputs and y represents target output of the requested object. Table 1 shows the inputs and their meanings for each training pattern. x_1 and x_3 are extracted based on sliding window as suggested by [21]. The sliding window of a request is the time before and after when the request was made. In other words, the sliding window should be around the mean time that an object generally stays in a cache. In this study, 30 minutes are used as the sliding window length (SWL) for all datasets. In a similar way to [22] , x_6 is classified into five categories: HTML with value 1, image with value 2, audio with value 3, video with value 4, application with value 5 and others with value 0. The value of y will be assigned to 1 if the object is re-requested again in the forward-looking sliding window. Otherwise, the target output will be assigned to 0.

Once the dataset is prepared and normalized, SVM is trained depending on the finalized dataset to classify the web objects into objects that will be re-visited or not. In SVM training, several kernel functions like polynomial, sigmoid and RBF can be used in SVM. However, in this study, RBF kernel is used since it can achieve a better performance compared to other kernel functions[23]. Depending on recommendations of Hsu et al.(2009) [23], SVM is trained as follows:

1) Prepare and normalize the dataset.
2) Consider the RBF kernel.
3) Use cross-validation to find the best parameters C (margin softness) and γ (RBF width).
4) Use the best parameters to train the whole training dataset.
5) Test.

Table 1. The inputs and their meanings

Input	Meaning
x_1	Recency of web object based on sliding window
x_2	Frequency of web object
x_3	Frequency of Web object based sliding window
x_4	Retrieval time of web object
x_5	Size of web object
x_6	Type of web object

SVM is trained using the libsvm library [24]. The generalization capability of SVM can be controlled through a few parameters like the term C and the kernel parameter like RBF width γ. To decide which values to choose for parameter C and γ, a grid search algorithm is implemented as suggested in [23]. We keep the parameters that obtain the best accuracy using a 10-fold cross validation on the training set. Then, a SVM model is trained depending on the optimal parameters to predict and classify the web objects whether the objects will be re-visited or not. After training, the trained classifiers can be saved in the files to be utilized in improving the performance of the conventional Web proxy caching policies.

4.4 Performance Evaluation and Discussion

We have modified the simulator WebTraff [25] to meet our proposed proxy caching approaches. WebTraff is a trace-driven simulator for evaluating different replacement policies such as LRU, LFU, GDS, FIFO, and RAND policies. The trained SVM classifier is integrated with WebTraff to simulate the proposed intelligent web proxy caching approaches. The WebTraff simulator receives the prepared logs proxy file as input and generates files containing performance measures as outputs. In addition, the maximum cache size should be determined in the simulator. Automatically, the simulator starts with a cache size of 1 Megabyte, and scales it up by a factor of two for each run until the maximum cache size is reached. The output of simulator shows cache size (in MB), hit ratio, and byte hit ratio for each cache size simulated.

In web proxy caching, Hit Ratio (HR) and Byte Hit Ratio (BHR) are two widely used metrics for evaluating the performance of Web proxy caching policies [1, 3, 5-6, 9]. HR is defined as the ratio of the number of requests served from the proxy cache and the total number of requests. BHR refers to the number of bytes served from the cache, divided by the total number of bytes served. In fact, the hit rate and byte-hit rate work in somewhat opposite ways. It is very difficult for one strategy to achieve the best performance for both metrics [3, 14].

In this section, the proposed approaches are compared to LRU, GD and GDSF policies that are the most common policies in squid software and form the basis of other web cache replacement algorithms [3].

Figs. 3 and 4 show HR and BHR of different policies for the four proxy datasets with varying cache sizes. As it can be seen, when the cache size increases, the HR and BHR boost as well for all algorithms. However, the percentage of increase is reduced when the cache size increases. When the cache size is close to the maximum size of cache, the performance becomes stable and close to maximum performance.

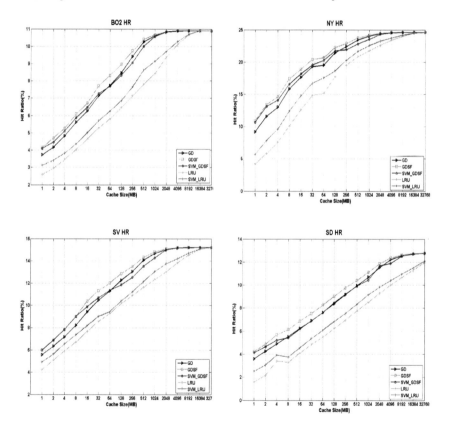

Fig. 3. Impact of cache size on HR for different proxy datasets

In terms of HR, the results in Fig. 3 clearly indicate SVM_LRU improve the performance in terms of HR for LRU in all proxy datasets. On the contrary, HR of GDSF_SVM is similar or slightly worse than HR of GDSF. This is because that GDSF tends to store the small object for increasing HR but at the expense of BHR.

From Fig. 3, it can be observed that GDSF achieves the best HR among all algorithms, while LRU achieves the worst HR among all algorithms.

In terms of BHR, Fig. 4 shows that BHR of LRU is better than BHR of GDS and GDSF in the four proxy datasets. This is expected since LRU policy removes the old objects regardless of their sizes. However, the results in Figs. 3 and 4 clearly indicate that SVM_LRU improves LRU performance in terms of HR and BHR in all proxy datasets with different cache sizes. This is mainly due to the capability of SVM_LRU in storing the preferred objects predicted by SVM classifier and removing the unwanted objects early. This resulted in lessening the pollution of the LRU cache. Consequently, the performance in terms of HR and BHR is improved in SVM_LRU. From Fig. 4, it can be observed that SVM_LRU achieves the best BHR among all algorithms, while GDS and GDSF attain the worst BHR among all algorithms.

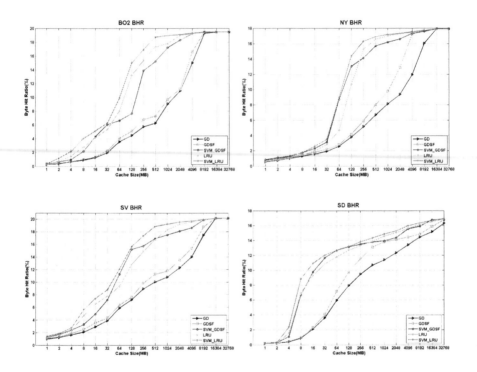

Fig. 4. Impact of cache size on BHR for different proxy datasets

Although GDS and GDSF have better performance in terms HR compared to LRU, it is not surprising that the BHR of GDS and GDSF are the worst among all algorithms (see Fig. 4). This is due to GDS and GDSF discriminate against large objects, allowing for small and recent objects to be cached. In the proposed SVM_GDSF approach, Fig. 4 shows that SVM_GDSF improves significantly BHR of GDSF and GDS respectively, especially with small cache. In SVM_GDSF, the value of the class predicted by SVM is added as extra weight to give more priority of those cached objects that may be revisited soon even if their sizes are large. That explained the significant improvement of BHR for GDS and GDSF. From Figs. 3 and 4, we can also observe that SVM_GDSF achieves HR close to the best HR achieved by GDSF, and SVM_GDSF achieves BHR close to the best BHR achieved by SVM_LRU. That means SVM_GDSF is able to make better balance between HR and BHR than other algorithms.

5   Conclusion and Future Works

This study has proposed intelligent Web proxy caching approaches called SVM_LRU and SVM_GDSF for improving performance of the conventional Web proxy caching algorithms. Initially, SVM learns from Web proxy logs file to predict the classes of objects to be re-visited or not. More significantly, the trained SVM is integrated effectively with conventional web proxy caching to provide more effective proxy caching policies. From the simulation results, we can conclude some remarks as follows. Firstly, GDSF achieved the best HR among all algorithms across the four proxy datasets. Secondly, SVM_LRU achieved the best BHR among all algorithms across the four proxy datasets. Lastly, SVM_GDSF achieved the best balance between HR and BHR among all algorithms across the four proxy datasets.

In the future, other intelligent classifiers can be utilized to improve the performance of traditional web caching policies. Moreover, clustering algorithms can be used for enhancing performance of web caching policies.

Acknowledgements. This work is supported by Universiti Teknologi Malaysia(UTM) under Research University Grant Category (VOT Q.J130000.7128.00H71). We would like to thank Research Management Centre (RMC), Universiti Teknologi Malaysia, for the research activities and Soft Computing Research Group (SCRG) for the support and incisive comments in making this study a success. Authors are also grateful for National Lab of Applied Network Research (NLANR) located in United States for providing us access to traces and proxy logs files.

References

1. Koskela, T., Heikkonen, J., Kaski, K.: Web cache optimization with nonlinear model using object features. Computer Networks 43(6), 805–817 (2003)
2. Chen, T.: Obtaining the optimal cache document replacement policy for the caching system of an EC website. European Journal of Operational Research 181(2), 828–841 (2007)
3. Romano, S., ElAarag, H.: A neural network proxy cache replacement strategy and its implementation in the Squid proxy server. Neural Computing & Applications 20(1), 59–78 (2011)
4. Kaya, C.C., Zhang, G., Tan, Y., Mookerjee, V.S.: An admission-control technique for delay reduction in proxy caching. Decision Support Systems 46(2), 594–603 (2009)
5. Cobb, J., ElAarag, H.: Web proxy cache replacement scheme based on back-propagation neural network. Journal of Systems and Software 81(9), 1539–1558 (2008)
6. Kin-Yeung, W.: Web cache replacement policies: a pragmatic approach. IEEE Network 20(1), 28–34 (2006)

7. Ali, W., Shamsuddin, S.M., Ismail, A.S.: Web proxy cache content classification based on support vector machine. Journal of Artificial Intelligence 4(1), 100–109 (2011)
8. Kumar, C., Norris, J.B.: A new approach for a proxy-level web caching mechanism. Decision Support Systems 46(1), 52–60 (2008)
9. Ali, W., Shamsuddin, S.M.: Intelligent client-side Web caching scheme based on least recently used algorithm and neuro-fuzzy system. In: Yu, W., He, H., Zhang, N. (eds.) ISNN 2009. LNCS, vol. 5552, pp. 70–79. Springer, Heidelberg (2009)
10. Sulaiman, S., Shamsuddin, S.M., Forkan, F., Abraham, A.: Intelligent Web caching using neurocomputing and particle swarm optimization algorithm. In: Second Asia International Conference on Modeling & Simulation, AICMS 2008 (2008)
11. Chen, R.-C., Hsieh, C.-H.: Web page classification based on a support vector machine using a weighted vote schema. Expert Systems with Applications 31(2), 427–435 (2006)
12. Liu, B.: Web Data Mining: Exploring Hyperlinks, Contents, and Usage Data. Springer, Heidelberg (2007)
13. Kumar, C.: Performance evaluation for implementations of a network of proxy caches. Decision Support Systems 46(2), 492–500 (2009)
14. Cao, P., Irani, S.: Cost-aware WWW proxy caching algorithms. In: Proceedings of the 1997 Usenix Symposium on Internet Technology and Systems, Monterey, CA (1997)
15. Cherkasova, L.: Improving WWW proxies performance with Greedy-Dual-Size-Frequency caching policy. In: HP Technical Report, Palo Alto (1998)
16. Vakali, A.: Evolutionary techniques for Web caching. Distrib. Parallel Databases 11(1), 93–116 (2002)
17. Podlipnig, S., Böszörmenyi, L.: A survey of Web cache replacement strategies. ACM Comput. Surv. 35(4), 374–398 (2003)
18. Ali, W., Shamsuddin, S.M., Ismail, A.S.: A survey of Web caching and prefetching. Int. J. Advance. Soft Comput. Appl. 3(1), 18–44 (2011)
19. Vapnik, V.: The nature of statistical learning theory. Springer, New York (1995)
20. NLANR, National Lab of Applied Network Research (NLANR). Sanitized access logs (2010), http://www.ircache.net/
21. ElAarag, H., Romano, S.: Improvement of the neural network proxy cache replacement strategy. In: Proceedings of the 2009 Spring Simulation Multiconference, pp. 1–8. Society for Computer Simulation International, San Diego (2009)
22. Foong, A.P., Yu-Hen, H., Heisey, D.M.: Logistic regression in an adaptive Web cache. IEEE Internet Computing 3(5), 27–36 (1999)
23. Hsu, C.W., Chang, C.C., Lin, C.J.: A practical guide to support vector classification (2009)
24. Chang, C.C., Lin, C.J.: LIBSVM: A library for support vector machines (2001), http://www.csie.ntu.edu.tw/~cjlin/libsvm
25. Markatchev, N., Williamson, C.: WebTraff: A GUI for Web proxy cache workload modeling and analysis. In: Proceedings of the 10th IEEE International Symposium on Modeling, Analysis, and Simulation of Computer and Telecommunications Systems, pp. 356–363. IEEE Computer Society (2002)

Maximizing the Early Abandon Effect
in Time-Series Similar Sequence Matching

Jeong-Gon Lee, Sang-Pil Kim, Bum-Soo Kim, and Yang-Sae Moon[*]

Department of Computer Science, Kangwon National University,
192-1, Hyoja2-Dong, Chunchon, Kangwon 200-701, Korea
{jglee,spkim,bskim,ysmoon}@kangwon.ac.kr

Abstract. In recent years, there have been many efforts on exploiting a large time-series database, and their major research topic is similar sequence matching that identifies data sequences similar to a query sequence. In this paper, we address the problem of maximizing the early abandon effect in computing the Euclidean distances for similar sequence matching. The early abandon improves the matching performance by stopping the computation process immediately after the intermediate distance exceeds a user-specified tolerance. We observe that the starting offset highly influences the early abandon effect, and we thus try to select the starting offset so as to maximize the early abandon effect. We first propose MaxOffset that uses the maximum entry of a query sequence as its starting offset. As an extension of MaxOffset, we then propose BiDirection that considers both directions of the maximum entry, i.e., left-side adjacent entries as well as right-side adjacent entries. The intuition behind these algorithms is that a large portion of the actual distance might be accumulated around maximum entries. We empirically showcase the superiority of the proposed algorithms.

Keywords: similar sequence matching, time-series databases, data mining, early abandon.

1   Introduction

Owing to advances in computing power and storage devices, there have been many research efforts on *similar sequence matching* to exploit large time-series databases [2, 6, 10, 16, 17]. In addition, there have been several recent attempts to apply these similar sequence matching techniques to practical applications such as handwritten recognition [15], image matching [13, 19], and biological sequence matching [14]. In general, computing the distance between time-series is the most importance performance factor in similar sequence matching. In this paper, we discuss how to efficiently compute the distance to achieve the higher matching performance.

The Euclidean distance [3, 4, 5] is one of the most popular similarity measures in similar sequence matching. Definition 1 shows how to compute the Euclidean distance between two sequences. We hereafter use *time-series* and *sequences* interchangeably.

---

[*] Corresponding author.

A. Abd Manaf et al. (Eds.): ICIEIS 2011, Part II, CCIS 252, pp. 573–583, 2011.
© Springer-Verlag Berlin Heidelberg 2011

Definition 1: Given two sequences $Q(=\{q_0,q_1,...,q_{n-1}\})$ and $S(=\{s_0,s_1,...,s_{n-1}\})$, their *Euclidean distance* $D(Q,S)$ is defined as Eq. (1).

$$D(Q,S) = \sqrt{\sum_{i=0}^{n-1}|q_i - s_i|^2} \tag{1}$$

In Eq. (1), the *starting offset* is 0 since the distance accumulation is started from the offset 0 (i.e., $i = 0$).

For a given query sequence of length n, the time complexity of computing the Euclidean distance to a data sequence of length n is $\Theta(n)$, which incurs a severe overhead for a large volume of time-series databases. To reduce this overhead, *early abandon* [12] is widely used. The early abandon is known to reduce unnecessary computations not only for the Euclidean distances but also the DTW distances [7, 10]. In this paper, we try to maximize the early abandon effect so as to achieve fast computation of the Euclidean distance and the higher matching performance[1].

The early abandon [12] is a simple but very efficient technique to improve the performance of distance computations. It stops the computation process immediately after the intermediate distance exceeds the given tolerance. That is, even though the complete distance is not obtained yet, the computation process is stopped if two sequences are decided to be non-similar. Fig. 1 shows an example of the early abandon effect. In Fig. 1, the accumulated distance exceeds the tolerance at offset 101, and thus, we can discard the rest of entries after offset 101 since the actual distance will definitely exceeds the tolerance.

To maximize the early abandon effect, we use different starting offsets for different query sequences by referring their characteristics. That is, instead of using 0 as the

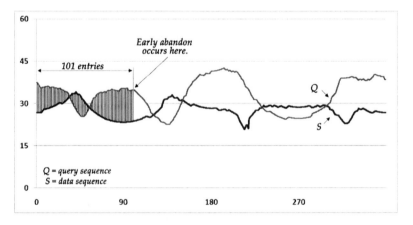

Fig. 1. An example of incurring the early abandon in computing the Euclidean distance

---

[1] Many research efforts [2, 6, 7, 16] on similar sequence matching use a multidimensional index to achieve the high performance. Even though using the index, however, we still need to compute the Euclidean distances for candidate sequences in the post-processing part. Thus, we can use the proposed approach for the post-processing part of existing work.

starting offset for all query sequences, for each query sequence, we try to select its appropriate staring offset that incurs large differences in between data and query sequences. To this end, we first propose the maximum offset-based algorithm, called **MaxOffset**, which uses the maximum entry of a query sequence as its staring offset. This approach is based on a simple intuition that, for a query sequence, a large portion of its actual distance from a data sequence might be accumulated around its maximum entry. As an advanced version of **MaxOffset**, we then propose the maximum offset-based bi-direction algorithm, called **BiDirection**, which moves the index (i.e., i in Eq. (1)) to both right and left directions to rapidly increase the intermediate distance. The purpose of **BiDirection** is to fully exploit left-side entries (as well as right-side entries) of the maximum entry. Experimental results show that the proposed algorithms outperform the traditional one by up to 62.4%.

The rest of this paper is organized as follows. Section 2 explains related work with the traditional algorithm. Sections 3 and 4 propose **MaxOffset** and **BiDirection**, respectively. Section 5 explains experimental results of the proposed and traditional algorithms. We finally summarize and conclude the paper in Section 6.

2   Related Work

A time-series is a sequence of real numbers representing values at specific time points [16]. Typical examples of time-series data include stock prices, exchange rates, sensor data, weather data, medical data, multimedia data, and trajectory data [18]. To efficiently and effectively use those time-series data, there have been many efforts on lower-dimensional transformations [6, 10], similar sequence matching [2, 7, 16], privacy preserving data mining [1, 9, 17], and time-series applications [13, 14, 15, 18]. Among these issues, in this paper we focus on similar sequence matching on a large time-series databases, which identifies data sequences similar to the given query sequence from the database [2, 6, 16].

As the similarity measure of similar sequence matching, Euclidean [6, 16], DTW(dynamic time warping) [7, 10], and LCSS(longest common subsequences) [8] distances are popularly used. Among these distances, in this paper we focus on the Euclidean distance (refer to Definition 1 for its formal description). In the Euclidean distance-based similar sequence matching, two sequences are identified to be similar if their Euclidean distance is less than or equal to the user-specified tolerance ε [6, 16]. That is, given two sequences Q and S, if $D(Q,S) \leq \varepsilon$, we say that Q and S are similar to each other. The Euclidean distance-based similar sequence matching has been studied in [2, 6, 15, 16]. These efforts have focused on using multidimensional indexes for the performance improvement, but they have not considered the early abandon effect. (For the other distance models except the Euclidean distance, readers are referred to [7, 10, 12]). Since the Euclidean distances are frequently computed in similar sequence matching, alleviating the overhead of computing the Euclidean distances is an important performance issue. Thus, we here focus on the early abandon effect in similar sequence matching since it is known to reduce unnecessary multiplications and additions in computing the Euclidean distances.

Fig. 2 shows the traditional distance computation algorithm, **ZeroOffset**, which exploits the early abandon effect in similar sequence matching. As shown in the figure, when computing the Euclidean distance between a query sequence Q and a data sequence S, it immediately stops the computation process if the intermediate square sum exceeds the given squared tolerance (Lines 3 and 4). The computation starts from the first entry, and thus, we can say that **ZeroOffset** uses 0 as its starting offset. In this paper, we differentiate this starting offset to incur the early abandon as early as possible.

Function **ZeroOffset**(query sequence Q, data sequence S, tolerance ε)

1. $sqdist := 0$;
2.   **for** $i := 0$ **to** $(n-1)$ **do**
3. $sqdist := sqdist + \left(q_i - s_i\right)^2$;
4.   **if** $(sqdist > \varepsilon^2)$ **then return** $\sqrt{sqdist}$;
5.   **end-for**
6.   **return** $\sqrt{sqdist}$;

Fig. 2. Traditional computation algorithm exploiting the early abandon effect

3   Maximum Offset-Based Algorithm

In computing the Euclidean distance, different starting offsets may cause different early abandon effects. In other words, if we can consider appropriate offsets first whose differences between query and data entries are large, the early abandon may occur at an early stage. In particular, for a large time-series database having a huge number of data sequences, if early abandon occurs very fast, the overall matching performance can be significantly improved by omitting many unnecessary computations. The starting offset of **ZeroOffset** is fixed as 0 for all data sequences; in contrast, in this paper we use a different starting offset for each data sequence so as to maximize its early abandon effect.

In this section we propose a new offset selection algorithm, named **MaxOffset**, which uses the offset of the maximum entry in a query sequence. **MaxOffset** is based on the simple intuition that there might be large differences around the maximum entry. That is, if query and data sequences are not similar, the maximum and its adjacent entries of the query sequence is likely to be far from those of the data sequence, and they contribute large differences to the intermediate distance. Example 1 shows the case of incurring the early abandon when using **MaxOffset**.

Example 1: Fig. 3 shows an example of computing the Euclidean distance starting from the maximum entry of query sequence Q. We use the same data and query sequences for Figs. 1 and 3, and the shaded areas represent the Euclidean distances. As the starting offset, we use an offset of the maximum entry in **MaxOffset** of Fig. 3 while we use 0 in **ZeroOffset** of Fig. 1. As shown in Fig. 3, the intermediate distance increases rapidly at the beginning part of the computation. According to our analysis, for the tolerance of 80, **ZeroOffset** considers 101 entries in Fig. 1 while **MaxOffset** does only 65 entries in Fig. 3. Thus, in this example we note that **MaxOffset** incurs the early abandon faster than **ZeroOffset**.   □

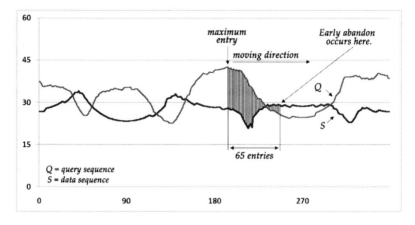

Fig. 3. An example of incurring the early abandon in **MaxOffset**

Fig. 4 shows **MaxOffset**, the proposed maximum offset-based algorithm. In Line 2, we first find the maximum entry of query sequence Q, and we then set its offset to the starting offset. The rest part of Lines 3 to 7 is the same as Lines 2 to 6 of **ZeroOffset,** which computes the Euclidean distance by exploiting the early abandon effect. We can use the minimum entry instead of the maximum entry, but we think their effects might be similar. Thus, we consider the maximum case only in this paper. The overhead of finding the maximum entry (Line 2) is negligible since we execute the process only once for all data sequences. That is, for each query sequence, we use the same starting offset for all data sequences, and thus, for a large time-series database, the overhead of Line 2 is negligible. **MaxOffset** of Fig. 4 can be seen as an advanced variant of **ZeroOffset** by simply changing the starting offset to cause many fast early abandons. We now extend **MaxOffset** to **BiDirection** in the following section.

4   Maximum Offset-Based Bi-Direction Algorithm

As shown in Fig. 4, **MaxOffset** increments the index ($= j+i$ in Fig. 4), i.e., moves the index to the right direction in computing the distance. Adjacent entries of time-series data, however, have a general characteristic having similar values [6, 16]. In this section we apply this characteristic to **MaxOffset** so as to much more increase the early abandon effect. The advanced approach also starts from the maximum entry, but it moves the index to both directions (i.e., right and left directions) in a toggle fashion while **MaxOffset** does it to the right direction only. Since we move the index to both directions, we call this approach **BiDirection**. The purpose of **BiDirection** is to fully exploit left-side entries (as well as right-side entries) of the maximum entry. Example 2 shows the case of incurring the early abandon when using **BiDirection**.

Function **MaxOffset**(query sequence Q, data sequence S, tolerance ε)

1. $sqdist := 0$;

2. $j :=$ an offset where q_j is the maximum entry in Q;

3.   **for** $i:=0$ **to** $(n-1)$ **do**

4. $sqdist := sqdist + \left(q_{(j+i)\%n} - s_{(j+i)\%n} \right)^2$;

5.   **if** $(sqdist > \varepsilon^2)$ **then return** $\sqrt{sqdist}$;

6.   **end-for**

7.   **return** $\sqrt{sqdist}$;

Fig. 4. Maximum offset-based algorithm starting from the maximum entry

Example 2: Fig. 5 shows an example of using **BiDirection** for the same time-series data of Figs. 1 and 3. As shown in Fig. 5, adjacent entries of the maximum entry have similar large values not only for the right side but also for the left side. Thus, considering both directions increases the intermediate distance much faster than considering the right direction only. The real experiment shows that, for the tolerance of 80, **BiDirection** computes only 32 entries. This is significant reduction comparing with 101 entries of **ZeroOffset** in Fig. 1 and 65 entries of **MaxOffset** in Fig. 3. Thus, in this example we note that **BiDirection** of considering both directions is much more efficient than **MaxOffset**.   □

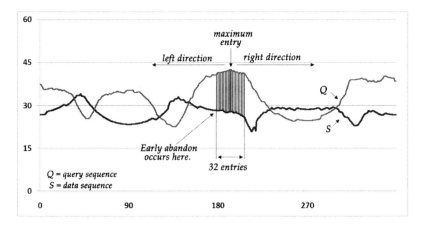

Fig. 5. An example of incurring the early abandon in **BiDirection**

Fig. 6 shows **BiDirection**, the proposed maximum offset-based bi-direction algorithm. Similarly with Fig. 4, Line 2, which finds the maximum entry of query sequence Q, is executed only once. In Lines 3 to 8, we compute the Euclidean distance in both directions and perform the early abandon if the intermediate distance exceeds the tolerance. More precisely, in Line 4 we compute the distance by considering right-side entries of the maximum entry, and in Line 5 we check whether the early abandon occurs or not; analogously, in Lines 6 and 7 we consider left-side entries in the same manner. This computation process continues in a toggle fashion (one for the right direction in Lines 4 and 5; another for the left direction in Lines 6 and 7) until the early abandon occurs or the real distance is obtained. As shown in Lines 4 and 6, we use the modular operator (%). This is because, to guarantee the correctness of computing the distance, we need to move the index in a circular way. That is, for the right direction, if the index (= $offset + i$) reaches to the end offset (= $n - 1$), we move it to the begin offset (= 0); similarly, for the left direction, if the index (= $offset - i - 1$) reaches to 0, we move it to $n - 1$. This guarantees the correctness of computing the Euclidean distance. Without loss of generality, we assume the length of query and data sequences is even in **BiDirection**. Also, if we use the minimum entry instead of the maximum entry as the starting offset, we can get the similar results, and we thus omit the case of using the minimum entry.

Function **BiDirection**(query sequence Q, data sequence S, tolerance ε)

1. $sqdist := 0;$

2. $j :=$ an offset where q_j is the maximum entry in Q;

3. **for** $i:=0$ **to** $\left(\dfrac{n}{2} - 1\right)$ **do**

4. $\quad sqdist := sqdist + \left(q_{(offset+i)\%n} - s_{(offset+i)\%n}\right)^2;$

5. $\quad$ **if** $(sqdist > \varepsilon^2)$ **then return** $\sqrt{sqdist}$;

6. $\quad sqdist := sqdist + \left(q_{(n+offset-i-1)\%n} - s_{(n+offset-i-1)\%n}\right)^2;$

7. $\quad$ **if** $(sqdist > \varepsilon^2)$ **then return** $\sqrt{sqdist}$;

8. **end-for**

9. **return** $\sqrt{sqdist}$;

Fig. 6. Bi-direction algorithm considering both directions from the maximum entry

5   Experimental Evaluation

In this section, we discuss the experimental results of three algorithms, **ZeroOffset**, **MaxOffset**, and **BiDirection**. In Section 5.1, we first present the experimental data and environment. In Section 5.2, we show and discuss the experimental results.

5.1   Experimental Data and Environment

In the experiment, we use five data sets: the first four data sets are obtained from [11], and the last one comes from [18]. The first data set contains the voltage measurement data, which consists of 1,000 time-series of length 100. We call it *VOLT_DATA*. The second one is the Wavelet data measured in NASA, which consists of 44 time-series of length 20,000. We call it *NASA_DATA*. The third one represents the traffic measurement of crossroads, which consists of 154 time-series of length 1,000.

We call it *CROSS_DATA*. The fourth one is the electrocardiogram (ECG) data, which consists of 44 time-series of length 1,000. We call it *ECG_DATA*. The fifth one is the image time-series data [18], which consists of 160 time-series of length 360. We call it *IMAGE_DATA*.

The hardware platform was SUN Ultra 25 workstation equipped with UltraSPARC IIIi CPU 1.34 GHz, 1.0 GB RAM, and an 80 GB hard disk. Its software platform was Solaris 10 operating system. We evaluate three matching algorithms: **ZeroOffset** of Fig. 2, **MaxOffset** of Fig. 4, and **BiDirection** of Fig. 6. For a given pair of query and data sequences, we measure the number of entries contributed to the distance computation. That is, we measure how many entries are used before the early abandon occurs. For each data set, we randomly select ten query sequences, compute their distances to all other data sequences, and use their average as the experimental result. We determine the tolerance ε as follows: we first measure the average Euclidean distance of the data set, divide the average distance by a specific number, and use the divided distance as the tolerance. This is because different data sets may have different distance ranges, and thus, the relative distances for each data set rather than the fixed distances for all data sets are suitable for the tolerances. We here use 2, 3, 4, and 5 as the specific number.

5.2 Experimental Results

Fig. 7 shows the average number of entries of three evaluation algorithms by varying the tolerance. Figs. 7(a), 7(b), and 7(c) represent the experimental results of VOLT_DATA, NASA_DATA, and ECG_DATA, respectively. Here we decrease the tolerance from ED/2 to ED/5, where ED means the average Euclidean distance of the data set. As shown in the figures, the number of entries decreases as the tolerance decreases. This is because the smaller tolerance incurs a large number of early abandons at an early stage. In Fig. 7(a) of VOLT_DATA, we note that our **MaxOffset** and **BiDirection** outperform **ZeroOffset**. This means that our maximum offset-based approach works well in incurring fast early abandons. In particular, **BiDirection** shows the best result by largely reducing the number of entries compared with **MaxOffset** as well as **ZeroOffset**. This is because considering right and left directions at the same time is much more effective than considering only one direction. Three data sets of Fig. 7 have a common characteristic that changes of adjacent entries are small, that is, values of adjacent entries are very similar to each other. Thus, many adjacent entries of the maximum entry have large values, and the proposed algorithms, which consider those large (adjacent) entries first, show the better performance than **ZeroOffset**.

Figs. 7(b) and 7(c) show the similar trend with Fig. 7(b). A notable point is that, compared with Fig. 7(a), performance differences are much larger in Figs. 7(b) and 7(c) than in Fig. 7(a). According to the analysis on data sets, this is because changes of adjacent values in NASA_DATA and ECG_DATA are much smaller than those of VOLT_DATA. That is, the smaller changes of adjacent entries cause the larger differences in between data and query sequences around the maximum entry, and this eventually incurs fast early abandons. Also in Figs. 7(b) and 7(c), **BiDirection** shows the best performance, and in particular, it improves the performance by up to 62.4% compared with **ZeroOffset** when the tolerance is ED/2.

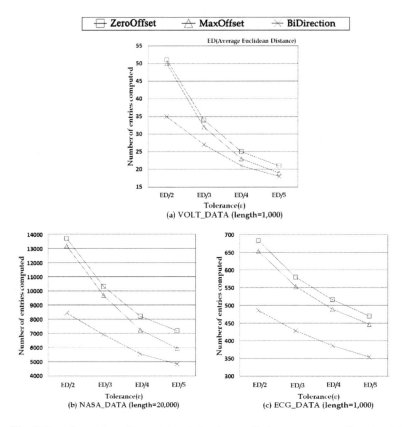

Fig. 7. Experimental results on data sets having small changes among adjacent entries

Fig. 8 shows the experimental results of CROSS_DATA and IMAGE_DATA. According to the analysis, the characteristic of these two data sets is different from that of three data sets in Fig. 7. That is, in these two data sets, changes of adjacent entries are large (i.e., NOT small), that is, values of adjacent entries are not similar to each other. As shown in Fig. 8, the decreasing trend is the same as in Fig. 7, that is, as the tolerance decreases, the number of entries decreases. Compared with Fig. 7, however, the difference between the proposed approach and **ZeroOffset** is not large. Especially, the difference between **MaxOffset** and **ZeroOffset** is negligible. This is because changes of adjacent entries are large in CROSS_DATA and IMAGE_DATA. In particular, we note that right-side entries of the maximum entry decrease very rapidly, and these right-side entries having relatively smaller values do not much contribute to the intermediate distance. On the other hand, **BiDirection** still shows the best performance. This is because it considers left-side entries of the maximum entry, whose values are larger than right-side entries.

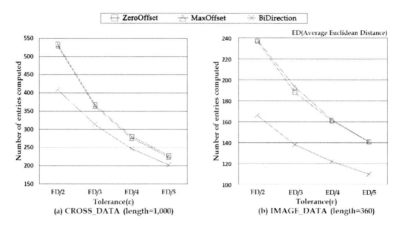

Fig. 8. Experimental results on data sets having large changes among adjacent entries

We can summarize the experimental results of Figs. 7 and 8 as follows. In general, the proposed **MaxOffset** and **BiDirection** show the better performance than **ZeroOffset**. In particular, **BiDirection** shows the best performance for all data sets. These performance differences, however, may vary largely depending on types of data sets. More precisely, the performance improvement of our approach is significant when adjacent entries are similar to each other, but it is not much significant when adjacent entries are not similar to each other. Based on this observation, we may develop an adaptable approach that considers changes of adjacent entries, and we leave this issue as a further study.

6   Conclusions

In this paper we tried to maximize the early abandon effect in the Euclidean distance-based similar sequence matching to improve the overall matching performance. That is, instead of using 0 for all query sequences, we used different starting offsets for different query sequences and exploited the early abandon at an early stage. To this end, we first proposed **MaxOffset** that used the maximum entry of a query sequence as its starting offset. As an extension of **MaxOffset**, we then proposed **BiDirection** that considered both right and left adjacent entries of the maximum entry. We finally empirically showcased the superiority of the proposed **MaxOffset** and **BiDirection** against the traditional **ZeroOffset**. According to these results, we believe that our maximum offset-based approach can be widely used in many similar sequence matching applications.

Acknowledgments. This work was supported by the National Research Foundation of Korea(NRF) grant funded by the Korea government(MEST) (No. 2011-0013235).

References

1. Aggarwal, C.C., Yu, P.S.: Privacy-preserving Data Mining: A Survey. In: Handbook of Database Security: Applications and Trends, pp. 431–460 (2007)

2. Agrawal, R., Faloutsos, C., Swami, A.: Efficient Similarity Search in Sequence Databases. In: Lomet, D.B. (ed.) FODO 1993. LNCS, vol. 730, pp. 69–84. Springer, Heidelberg (1993)

3. Boxer, L., Miller, R.: Efficient Computing of the Euclidean Distance Transform. Computer Vision and Image Understanding 80, 379–383 (2000)

4. Breu, H., Gil, J., Kirkpatrick, D., Werman, M.: Linear Time Euclidean Distance Transform Algorithms. IEEE Trans. on Pattern Analysis and Machine Intelligence 17(5), 529–533 (1995)

5. Chen, L.: Optimal Algorithm for Complete Euclidean Distance Transform. Chinese J. Computers 18(8), 611–616 (1995)

6. Faloutsos, C., Ranganathan, M., Manolopoulos, Y.: Fast Subsequence Matching in Time-Series Databases. In: Proc. of Int'l Conf. on Management of Data, ACM SIGMOD, Minneapolis, Minnesota, pp. 419–429 (May 1994)

7. Han, W.-S., Lee, J.-S., Moon, Y.-S., Hwang, S.-W., Yu, H.: A New Approach for Processing Ranked Subsequence Matching Based on Ranked Union. In: Proc. of Int'l Conf. on Management of Data, ACM SIGMOD, Athens, Greece, pp. 457–468 (June 2011)

8. Hunt, J.W., Szymanski, T.G.: A Fast Algorithm for Computing Longest Common Subsequences. Communications of ACM 20(5), 350–353 (1977)

9. Jiang, W., Murugesan, M., Clifton, C., Si, L.: Similar Document Detection with Limited Information Disclosure. In: Proc. of the 24th Int'l Conf. on Data Engineering, Cancun, Mexico, pp. 7–12 (April 2008)

10. Keogh, E.: Exact Indexing of Dynamic Time Warping. In: Proc. of the 28th Int'l Conf. on Very Large Data Bases, Hong Kong, pp. 406–417 (August 2002)

11. Keogh, E., Xi, X., Wei, L., Ratanamahatana, C.A.: The UCR Time Series Classification/Clustering Homepage (2006),
    http://www.cs.ucr.edu/~eamonn/time_series_data

12. Keogh, E., Wei, L., Xi, X., Vlachos, M., Lee, S.-H., Protopapas, P.: Supporting Exact Indexing of Arbitrarily Rotated Shapes and Periodic Time Series under Euclidean and Warping Distance Measures. The VLDB Journal 18(3), 611–630 (2009)

13. Kim, B.-S., Moon, Y.-S., Kim, J.: Noise Control Boundary Image Matching Using Time-Series Moving Average Transform. In: Proc. of the 19th Int'l Conf. on Database and Expert Systems Applications, Turin, Italy, pp. 362–375 (September 2008)

14. Lee, A.J.T., et al.: A Novel Filtration Method in Biological Sequence Databases. Pattern Recognition Letters 28(4), 447–458 (2007)

15. Loh, W.-K., Park, Y.-H., Yoon, Y.-I.: Fast Recognition of Asian Characters Based on Database Methodologies. In: Proc. of the 24th British Nat'l Conf. on Databases, Glasgow, UK, pp. 37–48 (July 2007)

16. Moon, Y.-S., Whang, K.-Y., Han, W.-S.: General Match: A Subsequence Matching Method in Time-Series Databases Based on Generalized Windows. In: Proc. of Int'l Conf. on Management of Data, ACM SIGMOD, Madison, Wisconsin, pp. 382–393 (June 2002)

17. Moon, Y.-S., Kim, H.-S., Kim, S.-P., Bertino, E.: Publishing Time-Series Data under Preservation of Privacy and Distance Orders. In: Proc. of the 21th Int'l Conf. on Database and Expert Systems Applications, Bilbao, Spain, pp. 17–31 (September 2010)

18. Moon, Y.-S., Kim, B.-S., Kim, M.-S., Whang, K.-Y.: Scaling-invariant Boundary Image Matching Using Time-series Matching Techniques. Data & Knowledge Engineering 69(10), 1022–1042 (2010)

19. Vlachos, M., Vagena, Z., Yu, P.S., Athitsos, V.: Rotation Invariant Indexing of Shapes and Line Drawings. In: Proc. of ACM Conf. on Information and Knowledge Management, Bremen, Germany, pp. 131–138 (October 2005)

Regression Using Partially Linearized Gaussian Fuzzy Data

Andreea Iluzia Iacob[1] and Costin-Ciprian Popescu[2]

[1] Department of Statistics and Econometrics,
The Bucharest Academy of Economic Studies,
Romania
aiacob@ase.ro
[2] Department of Mathematics,
The Bucharest Academy of Economic Studies,
Romania
ciprian.popescu@csie.ase.ro

Abstract. In this work is presented a regression model based on partially linearized Gaussian fuzzy numbers. First we define them and we study some properties compared to conventional Gaussian numbers. Second, these numbers are used in a general least squares procedure for fuzzy data. We also give a numerical example in which the applicability of the proposed method is tested.

Keywords: regression, least squares, fuzzy data, Gaussian fuzzy numbers, partially linearized Gaussian fuzzy numbers.

1 Introduction

The least squares method applied to fuzzy data is an important issue in the field of data mining. In the literature there are various approaches concerning this topic. In some studies are used particular types of fuzzy numbers, such as triangular [6]. In other studies with a wider applicability like [14] is used a general model containing fuzzy numbers, but still characterized by membership functions with certain properties. For example, we can mention: normality, continuity and a compact support (In particular, a triangular fuzzy number meets these requirements). Such a number can be uniquely characterized by its image in a Banach function space [5]. Thus, the distance between two numbers was defined using these images [14]. On the other hand, it should be noted that triangular or trapezoidal fuzzy numbers are used in many applications from Statistics, Economics or Informatics field [10,16,17]. One of the reasons is to simplify certain calculus. However, these numbers have some limitations, especially in certain situations of data modeling, when nonlinear type fuzzy numbers are required. A remarkable type of fuzzy number with various applications and characterized by a nonlinear membership function is the Gaussian number [9,11,13,15]. In order to apply the regression model discussed in [14], but also to use as much of the modeling ability of the Gaussian fuzzy numbers, we use a composite number. Therefore, in this paper are employed partially linearized Gaussian fuzzy numbers for the regression procedure mentioned above. Such a number is linearized only from a certain point using the tangent at that point to the

A. Abd Manaf et al. (Eds.): ICIEIS 2011, Part II, CCIS 252, pp. 584–595, 2011.

membership function graph. The procedure enables the use of an approximative Gaussian pattern in the fuzzy regression model and looks more naturally than other possible linearizations.

2 Partially Linearized Gaussian Fuzzy Numbers

2.1 Preliminary Concepts and Results

An asymmetrical Gaussian fuzzy number, $\mathrm{Gau}(m,\sigma_s,\sigma_d)$, is characterized by the membership function:

$$f_G(x) = \begin{cases} \exp\left(-\dfrac{(x-m)^2}{2\sigma_s^2}\right), & x < m \\[3mm] \exp\left(-\dfrac{(x-m)^2}{2\sigma_d^2}\right), & x \geq m. \end{cases} \tag{1}$$

If $\sigma_s = \sigma_d = \sigma$ we obtain a symmetrical Gaussian fuzzy number, $\mathrm{Gau}(m,\sigma)$, given by:

$$f_G(x) = \exp\left(-\frac{(x-m)^2}{2\sigma^2}\right), \ \forall x \in \mathbf{R}. \tag{2}$$

Example 1. Consider $\mathrm{Gau}(m,\sigma_s,\sigma_d)$ with $m = 12$, $\sigma_s = 3$, $\sigma_d = 6$. Its membership function is represented in Figure 1.

We define a partially linearized Gaussian fuzzy number $\mathrm{Gl}(m,\sigma_s,\sigma_d;a,b)$ by its membership function:

$$f_{Gl}(x) = \begin{cases} a\sigma_s^{-1}\sqrt{-2\ln a}\,(x-m)+a(1-2\ln a), & x \in \left[l-\dfrac{\sigma_s}{\sqrt{-2\ln a}},l\right] \\[3mm] \exp\left(-\dfrac{(x-m)^2}{2\sigma_s^2}\right), & x \in (l,m] \\[3mm] \exp\left(-\dfrac{(x-m)^2}{2\sigma_d^2}\right), & x \in (m,r] \\[3mm] -b\sigma_d^{-1}\sqrt{-2\ln b}\,(x-m)+b(1-2\ln b), & x \in \left(r,r+\dfrac{\sigma_d}{\sqrt{-2\ln b}}\right] \\[3mm] 0, & \text{otherwise} \end{cases} \tag{3}$$

where $a,b \in (0,1)$ are real parameters and

$$l = m - \sigma_s\sqrt{-2\ln a}, \quad r = m + \sigma_d\sqrt{-2\ln b}. \tag{4}$$

In particular, for $a = b$, we use the notation $\mathrm{Gl}(m,\sigma_s,\sigma_d;a)$.

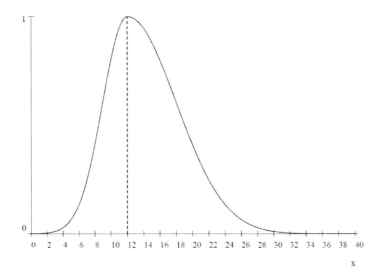

Fig. 1. Asymmetrical Gaussian fuzzy number

Remark. Consider the graph of $f_G(x)$, as the set:

$$\Gamma_G = \left\{ (x, f_G(x)) \in \mathbf{R}^2 \middle| x \in \mathbf{R} \right\}. \tag{5}$$

and the points $A\left(f_G^{-1}(a), a\right) \in \Gamma_G$, $B\left(f_G^{-1}(b), b\right) \in \Gamma_G$. The tangent to Γ_G in A has the slope equal to $a\sigma_s^{-1}\sqrt{-2\ln a}$. Further, we obtain the equation of the tangent to Γ_G in A as:

$$y = a\sigma_s^{-1}\sqrt{-2\ln a}\,(x - m) + a(1 - 2\ln a). \tag{6}$$

On the right side of the graph the calculus are similar. This explains the definition of $Gl(m, \sigma_s, \sigma_d; a, b)$.

Among the following will be discussed another form, equivalent to the definition of a number $Gl(m, \sigma_s, \sigma_d; a, b)$, needed in subsequent considerations. Some fuzzy numbers can be completely characterized in two ways: by membership function or by a special triplet [7,8,12]. Consider F the membership function of a general fuzzy number, $\tilde{F}$, with the following properties: F is upper semicontinuous; it exists a real number m, for which $F(m) = 1$; there are real numbers c_1, c_2 such that $F(x) = 0$ for all $x \notin [c_1, c_2]$, F is increasing on $[c_1, m]$ and decreasing on $[m, c_2]$. For such a number, there is a possibility of an alternative writing, in the form $\left\{ \left(\underline{F}(\gamma), \overline{F}(\gamma), \gamma \right) \middle| \gamma \in [0,1] \right\}$. It is determined using the γ-level sets. Some properties of the functions $\underline{F}(\gamma)$, $\overline{F}(\gamma)$ are given in [12] and also in [14]. A Gaussian number do not exactly meet all the requirements listed above, while one of the type $Gl(m, \sigma_s, \sigma_d; a, b)$, it fully meet.

Moreover, the latter one can be presented in the form $\left\{\left[\underline{f}_{Gl}(\gamma), \overline{f}_{Gl}(\gamma), \gamma\right] \middle| \gamma \in [0,1]\right\}$, where, after calculations, we obtain:

$$\underline{f}_{Gl}(\gamma) = \begin{cases} \dfrac{\sigma_s}{a\sqrt{-2\ln a}}\gamma + m - \sigma_s\sqrt{-2\ln a} - \dfrac{\sigma_s}{\sqrt{-2\ln a}}, \gamma \in [0,a] \\ m - \sigma_s\sqrt{-2\ln\gamma}, \gamma \in (a,1], \end{cases} \tag{7}$$

$$\overline{f}_{Gl}(\gamma) = \begin{cases} -\dfrac{\sigma_d}{b\sqrt{-2\ln b}}\gamma + m + \sigma_d\sqrt{-2\ln b} + \dfrac{\sigma_d}{\sqrt{-2\ln b}}, \gamma \in [0,b] \\ m + \sigma_d\sqrt{-2\ln\gamma}, \gamma \in (b,1]. \end{cases} \tag{8}$$

Example 2. Based on the previous example, we consider the following additional values: $a = 0.3$, $b = 0.2$. Thus, we can determine the number $Gl(12,3,6;0.3,0.2)$ (Fig. 2).

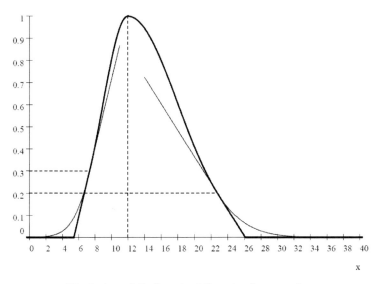

Fig. 2. A partially linearized Gaussian fuzzy number

For $i \in \{1,2\}$ we consider $Gl(m_i, \sigma_{si}, \sigma_{di}; a, b)$ given by $\left\{\left[\underline{f}_{Gl_i}(\gamma), \overline{f}_{Gl_i}(\gamma), \gamma\right] \middle| \gamma \in [0,1]\right\}$.

We use as a starting point the general considerations regarding the addition of two fuzzy numbers and multiplication by scalars given in [7,12,14]. For example, the sum of the numbers $\tilde{F}_1 \equiv \left\{\left[\underline{F}_1(\gamma), \overline{F}_1(\gamma), \gamma\right] \middle| \gamma \in [0,1]\right\}$ and $\tilde{F}_2 \equiv \left\{\left[\underline{F}_2(\gamma), \overline{F}_2(\gamma), \gamma\right] \middle| \gamma \in [0,1]\right\}$ is computed as follows:

$$\tilde{F}_1 + \tilde{F}_2 \equiv \left\{\left[\underline{F}_1(\gamma) + \underline{F}_2(\gamma), \overline{F}_1(\gamma) + \overline{F}_2(\gamma), \gamma\right] \middle| \gamma \in [0,1]\right\}. \tag{9}$$

Then it can be shown that:

$$
\begin{aligned}
\mathrm{Gl}\!\left(m_1,\sigma_{s1},\sigma_{d1};a,b\right)+\mathrm{Gl}\!\left(m_2,\sigma_{s2},\sigma_{d2};a,b\right)= \\
\mathrm{Gl}\!\left(m_1+m_2,\sigma_{s1}+\sigma_{s2},\sigma_{d1}+\sigma_{d2};a,b\right).
\end{aligned}
\tag{10}
$$

Moreover, as a generalization, for a natural number $n \geq 2$ and $i = \overline{1,n}$ one can write:

$$
\sum_{i=1}^{n}\mathrm{Gl}\!\left(m_i,\sigma_{si},\sigma_{di};a,b\right)=\mathrm{Gl}\!\left(\sum_{i=1}^{n}m_i,\sum_{i=1}^{n}\sigma_{si},\sum_{i=1}^{n}\sigma_{di};a,b\right).
\tag{11}
$$

In a similar way, using general theoretical considerations and making some calculations, it follows that if k is a real number, then:

$$
k\mathrm{Gl}\!\left(m,\sigma_s,\sigma_d;a,b\right)=\mathrm{Gl}\!\left(km,k\sigma_s,k\sigma_d;a,b\right),\ \text{for}\ k>0
\tag{12}
$$

and

$$
k\mathrm{Gl}\!\left(m,\sigma_s,\sigma_d;a,b\right)=\mathrm{Gl}\!\left(km,k\sigma_d,k\sigma_s;b,a\right),\ \text{for}\ k<0.
\tag{13}
$$

2.2 Possibilistic Mean and Variance

Possibilistic mean value (E) and possibilistic variance (Var) are significant numerical characteristics of a fuzzy number with multiple applications in optimization problems [2,3]. For a general number $\tilde{F}\equiv\left\{\left(\underline{F}(\gamma),\overline{F}(\gamma),\gamma\right)\middle|\gamma\in[0,1]\right\}$, the mean is given by:

$$
E_F=\frac{1}{2}\left(\frac{\int_0^1\gamma\underline{F}(\gamma)d\gamma}{\int_0^1\gamma d\gamma}+\frac{\int_0^1\gamma\overline{F}(\gamma)d\gamma}{\int_0^1\gamma d\gamma}\right)=\int_0^1\gamma\!\left(\underline{F}(\gamma)+\overline{F}(\gamma)\right)d\gamma.
\tag{14}
$$

Also, possibilistic variance is calculated as:

$$
\begin{aligned}
\mathrm{Var}_F &=\int_0^1\gamma\left[\left(\frac{\underline{F}(\gamma)+\overline{F}(\gamma)}{2}-\underline{F}(\gamma)\right)^2+\left(\frac{\underline{F}(\gamma)+\overline{F}(\gamma)}{2}-\overline{F}(\gamma)\right)^2\right]d\gamma= \\
&=\frac{1}{2}\int_0^1\gamma\!\left(\overline{F}(\gamma)-\underline{F}(\gamma)\right)^2 d\gamma.
\end{aligned}
\tag{15}
$$

The significance, importance and some theoretical consequences of such definitions are discussed in detail in [2]. Their applications are also numerous, especially in some fuzzy optimization problems in Financial Mathematics [1,3,10]. Customizing general definition, we get that for a number of type $\mathrm{Gl}\!\left(m,\sigma_s,\sigma_d;a,b\right)$, the possibilistic mean is:

$$E_{\mathrm{Gl}} = \int_0^1 \gamma \left(\underline{f}_{\mathrm{Gl}}(\gamma) + \overline{f}_{\mathrm{Gl}}(\gamma) \right) d\gamma . \tag{16}$$

After integration we obtain:

$$E_{\mathrm{Gl}} = m + \frac{1}{2} \left(b^2 \sigma_d \sqrt{-2\ln b} - a^2 \sigma_s \sqrt{-2\ln a} \right) + \frac{1}{6} \left(\frac{b^2 \sigma_d}{\sqrt{-2\ln b}} - \frac{a^2 \sigma_s}{\sqrt{-2\ln a}} \right) + \\ + \sigma_d I_d - \sigma_s I_s \tag{17}$$

where:

$$I_s = \int_a^1 \gamma \sqrt{-2\ln \gamma} \, d\gamma , \quad I_d = \int_b^1 \gamma \sqrt{-2\ln \gamma} \, d\gamma . \tag{18}$$

With the substitutions

$$-2\ln \gamma = \alpha \ \ (\text{for } I_s), \quad -2\ln \gamma = \beta \ \ (\text{for } I_d) \tag{19}$$

we get an equivalent form for the previous two integrals:

$$I_s = \frac{1}{2} \int_0^{-2\ln a} \alpha^{\frac{1}{2}} e^{-\alpha} d\alpha , \quad I_d = \frac{1}{2} \int_0^{-2\ln b} \beta^{\frac{1}{2}} e^{-\beta} d\beta . \tag{20}$$

In practice, I_s and I_d can be computed by some approximate integration method (for example, numerical integration can be realized using certain software packages). Remark that E_{Gl} can be also viewed as a function $E_{\mathrm{Gl}}(a,b)$. In this way we can write:

$$\lim_{\substack{a \to 0 \\ b \to 0}} E_{\mathrm{Gl}}(a,b) = m + \frac{1}{2} \left(\sigma_d \int_0^\infty \beta^{\frac{1}{2}} e^{-\beta} d\beta - \sigma_s \int_0^\infty \alpha^{\frac{1}{2}} e^{-\alpha} d\alpha \right) = m + (\sigma_d - \sigma_s) \frac{\sqrt{\pi}}{4} \tag{21}$$

which is the possibilistic mean for a number $\mathrm{Gau}(m, \sigma_s, \sigma_d)$. It can be concluded that the two mean values coincide at the limit. This is one of the reasons why we choose such a linearization. From this moment we will work with the numbers of subtype $\mathrm{Gl}(m, \sigma_s, \sigma_d; a)$, so we calculate variance for this case only. Further, if such a number is denoted by $\tilde{X}$ and $\tilde{X} \equiv \left\{ \left(\underline{X}(\gamma), \overline{X}(\gamma), \gamma \right) \middle| \gamma \in [0,1] \right\}$, we find the relationship:

$$\mathrm{Var}_X = \frac{1}{2} \int_0^1 \gamma \left(\overline{X}(\gamma) - \underline{X}(\gamma) \right)^2 d\gamma = \frac{(\sigma_s + \sigma_d)^2}{4} \int_0^{-2\ln a} \lambda e^{-\lambda} d\lambda + \\ + \frac{(\sigma_s + \sigma_d)^2}{2} \left(\frac{a^2}{3} - a^2 \ln a - \frac{a^2}{24\ln a} \right). \tag{22}$$

3 The Regression Model

We use the general metric on a fuzzy number space given in [14]. In this framework, the distance between the fuzzy numbers $\tilde{g}_1 = \mathrm{Gl}(m_1, \sigma_{s1}, \sigma_{d1}; a, b)$ and $\tilde{g}_2 = \mathrm{Gl}(m_2, \sigma_{s2}, \sigma_{d2}; a, b)$ becomes:

$$D^2(\tilde{g}_1, \tilde{g}_2) = \underline{D}^2(\tilde{g}_1, \tilde{g}_2) + \overline{D}^2(\tilde{g}_1, \tilde{g}_2) \tag{23}$$

where

$$\underline{D}^2(\tilde{g}_1, \tilde{g}_2) = \int_0^1 \left(\underline{f}_{\mathrm{Gl}_1}(\gamma) - \underline{f}_{\mathrm{Gl}_2}(\gamma) \right)^2 d\gamma, \; \overline{D}^2(\tilde{g}_1, \tilde{g}_2) = \int_0^1 \left(\overline{f}_{\mathrm{Gl}_1}(\gamma) - \overline{f}_{\mathrm{Gl}_2}(\gamma) \right)^2 d\gamma \tag{24}$$

and $\underline{f}_{\mathrm{Gl}_i}$, $\overline{f}_{\mathrm{Gl}_i}$ (for $i \in \{1,2\}$) are determined according to the formulas (7), (8). The generic regression relationship for n fuzzy data, $(\tilde{X}_i, \tilde{Y}_i)$, has the following form [14]:

$$\tilde{Y} = q + t\tilde{X} . \tag{25}$$

For this regression model, the real parameters q and t will be calculated according to an algorithm of the least squares type. The function that must be minimized is:

$$S(q,t) = \sum_{i=1}^n D^2\left(q + t\tilde{X}_i, \tilde{Y}_i\right). \tag{26}$$

For all $i = \overline{1, n}$, consider the input data of the type:

$$\tilde{X}_i = \mathrm{Gl}(m_i, \sigma_{si}, \sigma_{di}; a), \; \tilde{Y}_i = \mathrm{Gl}(n_i, \mu_{si}, \mu_{di}; a). \tag{27}$$

We have:

$$q + t\tilde{X}_i = \begin{cases} \mathrm{Gl}(q + tm_i, t\sigma_{si}, t\sigma_{di}; a), t > 0 \\ \mathrm{Gl}(q + tm_i, t\sigma_{di}, t\sigma_{si}; a), t < 0. \end{cases} \tag{28}$$

If $\left\{ \underline{f}_i(\gamma), \overline{f}_i(\gamma), \gamma \middle| \gamma \in [0,1] \right\}$, $\left\{ \underline{h}_i(\gamma), \overline{h}_i(\gamma), \gamma \middle| \gamma \in [0,1] \right\}$ are the parameterizations of $\tilde{X}_i$ and $\tilde{Y}_i$ respectively, then, according to [14], the normal equations are:

$$\begin{cases} 2nq + t\sum_{i=1}^n J_{1i} = \sum_{i=1}^n J_{2i} \\ q\sum_{i=1}^n J_{1i} + t\sum_{i=1}^n J_{3i} = \sum_{i=1}^n J_{4i} \end{cases} \tag{29}$$

where $J_{1i} = \int\limits_0^1 \left(\underline{f}_i(\gamma) + \overline{f}_i(\gamma) \right) d\gamma$, $J_{2i} = \int\limits_0^1 \left(\underline{h}_i(\gamma) + \overline{h}_i(\gamma) \right) d\gamma$, $J_{3i} = \int\limits_0^1 \left(\underline{f}_i^2(\gamma) + \overline{f}_i^2(\gamma) \right) d\gamma$

and

$$J_{4i} = \begin{cases} \int\limits_0^1 \left(\underline{f}_i(\gamma) \underline{h}_i(\gamma) + \overline{f}_i(\gamma) \overline{h}_i(\gamma) \right) d\gamma \text{ if } t > 0 \\ \int\limits_0^1 \left(\overline{f}_i(\gamma) \underline{h}_i(\gamma) + \underline{f}_i(\gamma) \overline{h}_i(\gamma) \right) d\gamma \text{ if } t < 0. \end{cases} \tag{30}$$

For the studied case, we have:

$$J_{1i} = \int\limits_0^a \left(\frac{\sigma_{si}}{a\sqrt{-2\ln a}} \gamma + m_i - \sigma_{si}\sqrt{-2\ln a} - \frac{\sigma_{si}}{\sqrt{-2\ln a}} \right) d\gamma +$$

$$+ \int\limits_0^a \left(-\frac{\sigma_{di}}{a\sqrt{-2\ln a}} \gamma + m_i + \sigma_{di}\sqrt{-2\ln a} + \frac{\sigma_{di}}{\sqrt{-2\ln a}} \right) d\gamma + \tag{31}$$

$$+ \int\limits_a^1 \left(m_i - \sigma_{si}\sqrt{-2\ln \gamma} \right) d\gamma + \int\limits_a^1 \left(m_i + \sigma_{di}\sqrt{-2\ln \gamma} \right) d\gamma .$$

After calculation, it results:

$$J_{1i} = 2m_i + \left(\sigma_{di} - \sigma_{si} \right) \left(a\sqrt{-2\ln a} + \frac{a}{2\sqrt{-2\ln a}} + K \right) \tag{32}$$

where

$$K = \int\limits_a^1 \sqrt{-2\ln \gamma}\, d\gamma \stackrel{-\ln \gamma = \theta}{=} \sqrt{2} \int\limits_0^{-\ln a} \theta^{\frac{1}{2}} e^{-\theta} d\theta . \tag{33}$$

In a similar way we obtain:

$$J_{2i} = 2n_i + \left(\mu_{di} - \mu_{si} \right) \left(a\sqrt{-2\ln a} + \frac{a}{2\sqrt{-2\ln a}} + K \right) . \tag{34}$$

Taking into account that

$$\int\limits_a^1 \ln \gamma\, d\gamma = a - a\ln a - 1 , \tag{35}$$

we can write:

$$J_{3i} = 2m_i^2 + \left(\sigma_{si}^2 + \sigma_{di}^2\right)\left(2 - a - \frac{a}{6\ln a}\right) +$$

$$+ \left(\sigma_{di} - \sigma_{si}\right)\left(2m_i a\sqrt{-2\ln a} + \frac{m_i a}{\sqrt{-2\ln a}} + 2m_i K\right). \tag{36}$$

For $t > 0$ the last integral, J_{4i}, can be computed as follows:

$$J_{4i} = 2m_i n_i + \left(\sigma_{si}\mu_{si} + \sigma_{di}\mu_{di}\right)\left(2 - a - \frac{a}{6\ln a}\right) +$$

$$+ \left(\sigma_{di} - \sigma_{si}\right)\left(n_i a\sqrt{-2\ln a} + \frac{n_i a}{2\sqrt{-2\ln a}} + m_i K\right) + \tag{37}$$

$$+ \left(\mu_{di} - \mu_{si}\right)\left(m_i a\sqrt{-2\ln a} + \frac{m_i a}{2\sqrt{-2\ln a}} + n_i K\right).$$

For the case $t < 0$ the calculus is performed similarly.

4 Numerical Example

To show the applicability of the model for numerical data, we give in the following, an example. Consider the data $\left(\tilde{X}_i, \tilde{Y}_i\right)$, $i = \overline{1,3}$, such as:

$$\tilde{X}_1 = \text{GI}(13,3,5;0.25), \quad \tilde{X}_2 = \text{GI}(20,2,2;0.25), \quad \tilde{X}_3 = \text{GI}(27,4,1;0.25),$$

$$\tilde{Y}_1 = \text{GI}(15,2,3;0.25), \quad \tilde{Y}_2 = \text{GI}(19,3,1;0.25), \quad \tilde{Y}_3 = \text{GI}(22,1,2;0.25). \tag{38}$$

From the beginning should be considered two possibilities: $t > 0$ or $t < 0$. If it is assumed that $t > 0$, we obtain the system (see (29) and the formulas that follows it):

$$\begin{cases} 6q + 118.79t = 112 \\ 118.79q + 2568.2t = 2356.9. \end{cases} \tag{39}$$

We obtain the solution:

$$q = 5.9025, \ t = 0.64471 > 0. \tag{40}$$

In the other case, $t < 0$, we have:

$$\begin{cases} 6q + 118.79t = 112 \\ 118.79q + 2568.2t = 2230.5 \end{cases} \tag{41}$$

from which we get:

$$q = 17.469, \ t = 0.060487 > 0. \tag{42}$$

The sign restriction is fulfilled only in the first case. So the solution is given in (40). According to [14], if both solutions meet the initial assumption on the signs, we must compare the results for sum $S(q,t)$ (see formula (26)) in the two cases. The solution is the pair $(q,t) \in \mathbf{R}^2$ leading to a lower value of the sum studied.

Some processes can be modeled by fuzzy numbers using methods such as Delphi [4,17]. A more direct approach is given in [10] and it is mainly based on variations in time of certain data studied. The latter brings together the viewpoint of the observer and some statistical data available. Must be said that the fuzzification process may be a separate study, this is actually a complex issue. However we will briefly illustrate one way of obtaining a fuzzy number of type discussed above. For example, if we study the performance of certain investments (e.g. part of a portfolio), we can use several approaches. In [10] is given a method of obtaining a trapezoidal fuzzy number, based on historical data. More specifically, certain statistic frequencies are used. A similar reasoning can be used for obtaining a partially linearized Gaussian number. The type of fuzzy number used is suggested, among others, by the trend of known concrete data.

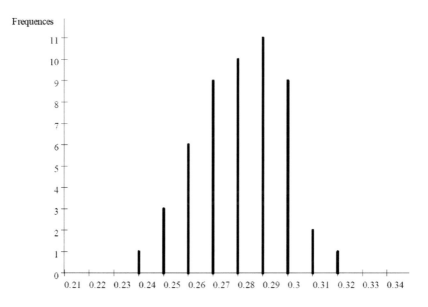

Fig. 3. Possible values of an investment return

Based on data from Figure 3, representing daily returns of an investment in a certain time period studied, we can build a fuzzy pattern. With the notation used in this paper, a possible representation of data considered is the partially linearized Gaussian number $Gl(0.29, 0.024814, 0.013699; 0.27273)$ (graphically represented in Fig. 4). It is clear that, for data distributed in a certain way, a number of type $Gl(m, \sigma_s, \sigma_d; a, b)$ (including the particular case: $a = b$) has the ability to more accurately preserve the specific pattern.

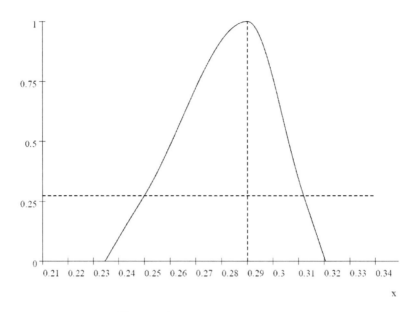

Fig. 4. A fuzzy pattern of daily returns

5   Conclusions

In this work we studied the issue of fuzzy least squares algorithm and its application in the case of partially linearized Gaussian fuzzy numbers. Regarding the concept of regression, we can say that the applications are numerous. They also relate to research areas for which data analysis is essential. Gaussian fuzzy numbers are appropriate for improving accuracy in terms of modeling certain processes. However, some regression models do not fit well with Gaussian numbers, one reason being their asymptotic spreads. In order to bring together the two issues, regression and approximate Gaussian fuzzification, in this paper we propose the application of partially linearized Gaussian fuzzy numbers. As discussed, at the limit, some characteristics (possibilistic mean, for example) of these numbers tend to those of the Gaussian type. In addition, the proposed numbers are used as data for a fuzzy regression model.

Acknowledgments. This work was supported by CNCSIS – UEFISCDI, project number PNII – IDEI code 1793/2008, financing contract no. 862/2009.

References

1. Appadoo, S.S., Bhatt, S.K., Bector, C.R.: Application of Possibility Theory to Investment Decisions. Fuzzy Optimization and Decision Making 7, 35–57 (2008)
2. Carlsson, C., Fullér, R.: On Possibilistic Mean Value and Variance of Fuzzy Numbers. Fuzzy Sets and Systems 122, 315–326 (2001)

3. Carlsson, C., Fullér, R.: A Fuzzy Approach to Real Option Valuation. Fuzzy Sets and Systems 139, 297–312 (2003)
4. Chang, P.T., Huang, L.C., Lin, H.J.: The Fuzzy Delphi Method via Fuzzy Statistics and Membership Function Fitting and an Application to the Human Resources. Fuzzy Sets and Systems 112, 511–520 (2000)
5. Cong Xin, W., Ming, M.: Embedding Problem of Fuzzy Number Space: Part I. Fuzzy Sets and Systems 44, 33–38 (1991)
6. Diamond, P.: Fuzzy Least Squares. Information Sciences 46, 141–157 (1988)
7. Dubois, D., Prade, H.: Operations on Fuzzy Numbers. International Journal of Systems Science 9, 612–626 (1978)
8. Dubois, D., Prade, H.: Fuzzy Sets and Systems: Theory and Applications. Mathematics in Science and Engineering 144 (1980)
9. Ebadat, A., Karimaghaee, P., Mahdiyar, H.: Application of Gradient-Based Control Methods in Efficient Oil Well Placement through Dynamic Fuzzy Neural Network Modeling. In: Ariwa, E., El-Qawasmeh, E. (eds.) DEIS 2011. CCIS, vol. 194, pp. 616–630. Springer, Heidelberg (2011)
10. Fang, Y., Lai, K.K., Wang, S.Y.: Portfolio Rebalancing Model with Transactions Costs Based on Fuzzy Decision Theory. European Journal of Operational Research 175, 879–893 (2006)
11. Garg, A., Singh, S.R.: Solving Fuzzy System of Equations Using Gaussian Membership Function. International Journal of Computational Cognition, 25–32 (2009)
12. Goetschel, R., Voxman, W.: Elementary Fuzzy Calculus. Fuzzy Sets and Systems 18, 31–43 (1986)
13. Hanss, M.: Applied Fuzzy Arithmetic. An Introduction with Engineering Applications. Springer, Heidelberg (2005)
14. Ming, M., Friedman, M., Kandel, A.: General Fuzzy Least Squares. Fuzzy Sets and Systems 88, 107–118 (1997)
15. Pacheco, M.A.C., Vellasco, M.M.B.R.: Intelligent Systems in Oil Field Development under Uncertainty. Springer, Heidelberg (2009)
16. Pushkar, S., Mishra, A.: IT Project Selection Model Using Real Option Optimization with Fuzzy Sets Approach. In: Ariwa, E., El-Qawasmeh, E. (eds.) DEIS 2011. CCIS, vol. 194, pp. 116–128. Springer, Heidelberg (2011)
17. Rebiasz, B.: Hybrid Method for Forecasting a Steel Mill's Sales. Journal of Business & Economic Research 5, 33–48 (2007)

AIFSA: A New Approach for Feature Selection and Weighting

Walid Fouad, Amr Badr, and Ibrahim Farag

Department of Computer Science,
Faculty of Computers and Information, Cairo University, Egypt
{w.fouad,amr.badr,i.farag}@fci-cu.edu.eg

Abstract. Feature selection is a typical search problem where each state in the search space represents a subset of features candidate for selection. Out of n features, 2n subsets can be constructed, hence, an exhaustive search of all subsets becomes infeasible when n is relatively large. Therefore, Feature selection is done by employing a heuristic search algorithm that tries to reach the optimal feature subset. Here, we propose a new wrapper feature selection and weighting algorithm called Artificial Immune Feature Selection Algorithm (AIFSA); the algorithm is based on the metaphors of the Clonal Selection Algorithm (CSA). AIFSA, by itself, is not a classification algorithm, rather it utilizes well-known classifiers to evaluate and promote candidate feature subset. Experiments were performed on textual datasets like WebKB and Syskill&Webert web page ratings. Experimental results showed AIFSA competitive performance over traditional well-known filter feature selection approaches as well as some wrapper approaches existing in literature.

Keywords: Data Mining, Text Classification, Artificial Immune Systems, Clonal Selection, Wrapper Feature Selection, Feature Weighting.

1 Introduction

Classification is a supervised learning task which aims to assigning one or more predefined class label to a given input object such as text document, image, speech...etc. The classification scenario is a multistep process of data gathering, feature selection/representation, training, and finally testing/validation. The key in most classification tasks is to identify suitable set of features and to form a good measurement of similarity associated with a strong matching process.

Feature selection methods can be divided into two main categories: filter and wrapper methods [1]. Filter methods - or simply filters - are one cycle processes; they use the full features set extracted from the training samples and select those features that are most relevant in terms of a well-known metric. These features are then fed to the learning algorithm along with the training samples to build the learning model. [2] presented an empirical study on twelve feature selection metrics used by filter methods. As they run once, filters are scalable and most suited for problems with very large number of features. Their main disadvantage is that they select relevant features without analyzing their impact on the employed learning algorithm.

A. Abd Manaf et al. (Eds.): ICIEIS 2011, Part II, CCIS 252, pp. 596–609, 2011.
© Springer-Verlag Berlin Heidelberg 2011

Wrapper methods - or simply wrappers - are iterative search methods that consider the learning algorithm bias; they require search space, operators, search technique, and evaluation function [1]. Wrappers use the employed learning algorithm to evaluate each feature subset relevancy until reaching the most relevant subset. Usually, relevancy is measured in terms of the learning algorithm performance. Wrappers, by this scheme, are tailored for the learning algorithm employed; if the algorithm is changed, the wrapper must run again to promote another feature subset suited for the new algorithm. A good wrapper is one that owns efficient heuristic search mechanism which enables it to explore the search space as quick as possible to reach the optimal subset.

Usually, wrappers give better results than filters as they consider the learning algorithm performance when evaluating feature subset relevance. However, they are computationally expensive in terms of time and cost. Filters are fast and cheap, but they may lead to suboptimal performance when the selected subset of features is not suitable for the biases of the utilized learning algorithm.

In the context of text classification, web classification has emerged as the process of assigning one or more predefined category label to a given web page. As surveyed by [3], several approaches to feature subset selection for web page classification have been proposed with different degrees of success. These approaches differ mainly in the source of selected features and may be categorized into:

Text-Only Approach: depends only on textual features extracted from the content of the web page [4].

Hypertext Approach: depends on both context as well as content features of web documents. Context features are extracted either from the document itself such as HTML tags or from neighboring documents such as anchortext [5][6][7].

Link Analysis Approach: employs web page URL features as they can be extracted without downloading the target page itself [8][9][10].

Neighborhood Category Approach: iteratively exploits the assigned class label of already classified neighboring web pages to determine the class label of the test page [11][12].

In this paper we propose a new wrapper method for feature subset selection and weighting called Artificial Immune Feature Selection Algorithm (*AIFSA*). Starting with the full set of features, *AIFSA* randomly generates an initial population of feature subsets. Classification accuracy of each subset is calculated to determine its affinity where high affinity subsets are cloned, randomly mutated, and then evaluated to determine their affinity. Merging is done by selecting high affinity subsets as the initial population of the next iteration while pruning low affinity ones. This process repeats iteratively until optimal feature subset is reached.

A distinctive characteristic of *AIFSA* is its inherent feature weighting mechanism where features weights are governed by their contribution to their subset affinity. Features weights are updated incrementally as they are selected for either replacement or mutation; during mutation, features with higher weights are given priority over those with lower weights for replacement while lower weights features are given priority over higher weights ones for mutation. By this scheme, *AIFSA* quickly asserts feature usefulness to its subset when it is selected for mutation and to other subsets when it is selected for replacement.

Through experiments, we utilized three main classifiers to train the algorithm: Naïve Bayes (*NB*), K-Nearest Neighbors (*kNN*), and Support Vector Machines (*SVM*). Experiments target classification of web pages of two web datasets: WebKB and Syskill&Webert web page ratings.

The paper is structured as follows: section 2 discusses related work to the problem of feature selection for web classification, section 3 introduces in details the design of the proposed algorithm, and finally, section 4 presents experimental results and conclusion.

2   Related Work

The problem of feature selection for classification is an attractive research problem. Several approaches were introduced in literature and all of them try to extract the most relevant feature subset that lead to optimal classification performance. No single approach proved its superiority over all others for all problems. In the field of web classification, filter and wrapper feature selection techniques were examined.

Here we explore similar approaches proposed and applied to the same datasets used in our experiments. A comparative study between these approaches and our proposed algorithm will be presented in section 4.

2.1   Syskill&Webert Experiments

The usage of Syskill&Webert web page ratings dataset was explored in [13] through using algorithms for learning and revising user profiles. The aim was to assist users to reach interesting web sites on a given topic. To identify interesting web pages, irrelevant features are firstly eliminated using stop-word list, then, the *k* most informative features are extracted using the expected Information Gain (*IG*) technique. Experiments were run using an *NB* classifier.

[14] used Syskill&Webert dataset in the evaluation of their proposed biologically-inspired classification algorithm. The algorithm was based on the metaphors of the human immune system and was applied to the problem of document classification. Features were extracted by converting all words into upper case, then, removing all words on the stop-word list, and finally, expected *IG* is calculated for each word and those with the highest scores were selected.

2.2   WebKB Experiments

[15] investigated the use of linguistic phrases as input features for the WebKB corpus. Experiments were performed using the leave-one-university-out cross-validation technique with two different learning algorithms: The *NB* classifier *RAINBOW* and the rule learning algorithm *RIPPER* [16].

[17] presented a new approach to learning hypertext classifiers that combines an *NB* statistical text learner with a FOIL relational rule learner. Experiments were performed on the WebKB dataset where the leave-one-university-out cross-validation scheme was employed, the bag-of-words representation was used, stop-words were

removed, and words were stemmed. Experimental results indicated that the proposed approach is more accurate than purely statistical or purely relational alternatives.

The use of features like web page text, hyperlinks, content of linked pages, and meta-data for web page classification was investigated in [18]. Experiments were performed using three learning algorithms: *NB*, *kNN*, and Quinlan's FOIL algorithm [19]. Experimental results showed that using web page content as the only source of features often yields suboptimal performance.

SVM classifiers were proposed by [20] to classify web pages by combining both their content and context features. Four types of features were investigated; text features were used as the baseline then different combinations of text, title, and hyperlink features were experimented. Experiments were performed on the WebKB dataset. The set-of-words representation was used and no feature selection was employed. All experiments used the leave-one-university-out cross-validation scheme to conduct training and evaluation. The results showed better performance of the proposed method than FOIL-PILFS method in terms of *F1* measure.

[21] proposed a variant of mutual information (*MI*) technique for feature selection that is called Weighted Average Pointwise Mutual Information (*WAPMI*). The approach also allowed determining the best feature subset size through maximizing an objective function. Experiments were performed on different corpora including the WebKB using multinomial *NB* classifier. The results showed competitive performance of the proposed approach over classical feature selection methods like *MI*, Chi-squared, and Bi-normal separation.

[22] introduced an approach for text classification that is based on Semantic Latent Indexing (*LSI*) with background knowledge. The approach depends on incorporating the sprinkling features into the original *LSI* and expanding the term-by-document matrix using background knowledge from unlabeled documents. Firstly, Sprinkling is performed by augmenting artificial features representing terms based on class labels in the term-by-document matrix. Thereafter, feature reduction is done by the common Singular Value Decomposition (*SVD*) technique. Experiments employed the *kNN* classifier on different datasets including the WebKB dataset using the top 1000 features with the highest *MI* gain.

3   Proposed Algorithm

AIFSA is a co-evolutionary algorithm which is designed for the purpose of feature selection and weighting for classification tasks. The algorithm is based on the metaphors of the Clonal Selection Algorithm (*CSA*). It belongs to the set of wrapper feature selection methods.

Proposed *AIFSA* was experimented with well-known classifiers such as *NB*, *kNN*, and *SVM* on two web page classification tasks. Experimental results were encouraging in terms of classification accuracy and *F1* measure values for each task.

3.1   AIFSA in Brief

Starting with the full set of features extracted from the training samples, *AIFSA* randomly generates an initial population of feature subsets of different sizes where each subset represents an antibody *AB*. Using classification accuracy as the main affinity measure, affinity of each *AB* is calculated such that high affinity *ABs* are cloned. The set of *AB* clones are mutated randomly by replacing one or more of their features with other features from the Full Features Vector (*FFV*). Mutation is governed by features weights as will be explained later. Mutated *ABs* are then evaluated to determine their affinities.

Antibody/Clone merging is done by selecting those subsets with the highest affinities as initial population of next iteration while pruning low affinity ones. This process repeats iteratively until 1) no improvement in the population affinity is achieved for specific number of iterations, or 2) maximum predefined number of iterations was performed, or 3) maximum predefined affinity threshold is reached. The best feature subset is constructed by selecting those features with highest weights among all features in the *FFV*.

A distinctive characteristic of the proposed algorithm is its inherent feature weighting mechanism where features weights are updated incrementally as they are selected for either replacement or mutation. Features weights are calculated based on two metrics: feature Useful Select Count (*USC*) and feature Useful Replace Count (*URC*). The *USC* of a feature is incremented when selecting it to replace another one increases its new subset affinity, while, the *URC* of a feature is incremented when replacing it with another one decreases its old subset affinity. By this scheme, features are weighted according to their contribution to their subset affinity.

Mutation is governed by features weights where: 1) higher weights features are given priority over lower weights ones for selection (replace other features), and 2) lower weights features are given priority over higher weights ones for mutation (replaced by other features).

3.2 AIFSA Anatomy

AIFSA learns to select the optimal subset of features through repetitive multi-step process as shown in Figure 1.

```
1. initialize a pool of antibodies randomly.
2. match each antibody with the antigen.
3. for each antibody
      i.    clonal selection & expansion
     ii.    hypermutation.
    iii.    Antibody/Clone merging.
     iv.    Weighting
      v.    Cell death.
```

Fig. 1. *AIFSA* is a repetitive multi-step process of clonal selection/expansion by affinity maturation, hypermutation, antibody/clone merging, weighting, and cell death

Repertoire Construction. *AIFSA* antibody Repertoire (*R*) is a pool of feature subsets with preconfigured size. Each subset represents an *AB*. The construction of *R* starts with selecting features randomly from the *FFV* and adding them to current *AB*. Generated *AB* is then added to *R* until reaching the preconfigured size.

Affinity Maturation. This is *AIFSA* main step where each *AB* in *R* is evaluated to determine its affinity (Aff_{AB}). Calculating Aff_{AB} is done by measuring classification accuracy of *AB* (ACC_{AB}) according to Equation 1. When comparing affinities of two *ABs* with same affinity, precedence is given to the one with the smaller length.

$$Aff_{AB} = ACC_{AB} \tag{1}$$

Clonal Selection & Expansion. At this step, Each *AB* in *R* is proliferated to generate a set of clones CL_{AB} that contain same features as *AB*. Proliferation rate of each *AB* is proportional to its affinity Aff_{AB} and is governed by preconfigured clonal probability (CL_{prop}) according to Equation 2.

$$CL_{AB} = CL_{prop} \times Aff_{AB} \times 100 \tag{2}$$

Hypermutation. The set of clones CL_{AB} generated from *AB* contain the same features as their parent. Hypermutation is the process of mutating these clones by replacing certain number of features by other ones from the *FFV*. The mutation process id guided by these rules: 1) mutation rate of each clone of CL_{AB} is inversely proportional to the affinity of *AB*, 2) features selected for replacing or being replaced are selected randomly, and 3) features marked as useless (as will be explained later) cannot be selected for replacing other ones.

The number of mutated features of each clone of CL_{AB} (MU_{CL}) is calculated according to Equation 3 where MU_{prop} is a preconfigured mutation probability value, Len_{CL} represents number of features in the clone, and MU_{ex} is a preconfigured value representing constant percentage of extra mutated features.

$$MU_{CL} = \left(100 \times MU_{prop} \times (1.0 - Aff_{AB}) + MU_{ex}\right) \times Len_{CL} \tag{3}$$

Antibody/Clone Merging. After performing hypermutation, affinity of each mutated clone (Aff_{CL}) is calculated as described before. Because resultant affinities could be larger than current repertoire affinities, merging of new mutated clones into current repertoire *R* is done by constructing new repertoire *R`* whose members are the union of antibodies currently in *R* and the newly mutated clones. Greedy selection is applied to select members with the highest affinities in *R`* to replace all members in *R* such that the total number of antibodies in *R* remains the same.

Feature Weighting. *AIFSA* has a distinctive mechanism for feature weighting by associating each feature in the *FFV* with a weight (W_f). Each feature *f* is associated with four counts (initially set to 0): Select Count (SC_f), Replace Count (RC_f), Useful Select Count (USC_f), and Useful Replace Count (URC_f). These counts are updated iteratively on two stages: 1) during mutation of a clone *CL* from CL_{AB}, if a feature *f1* in *CL* was replaced by feature *f2* from the *FFV* then *RC* of *f1* is incremented and *SC* of *f2* is incremented, and 2) after affinity maturation, if affinity of *CL* is greater than affinity of *AB* from which *CL* was cloned then the *USC* of all replacing features is incremented, otherwise, the *URC* of all replaced features is incremented. By the end of each iteration, all features weights are updated according to Equation 4.

$$W_f = \frac{\log(UTC_f)}{\log(TC_f)} \ where$$

$$UTC_f = USC_f + URC_f \ and \ TC_f = SC_f + RC_f$$

(4)

Feature Pruning. This step is performed in order to mark features as either useful or useless according to Equation 5. The aim is to ensure that during mutation: 1) priority is given to features with higher weights (useful) for replacing, and 2) priority is given to features with lower weights (useless) for being replaced. Thereby, useless features are pruned and cannot be selected for replacing other features while useful features are not replaced unless all useless features were already replaced.

$$useful(f) = \begin{cases} yes, & W_f \geq W_{min} \\ no, & W_f < W_{min} \end{cases} \quad \forall f \ such \ that \ TC_f > TC_{min}$$

(5)

Antibody Cell Death. This step is performed at the end of each iteration where all antibodies in *R* are checked to determine whether they will live for the next iteration or die and replaced by new ones. All antibodies whose affinity below preconfigured minimum affinity threshold (Aff_{min}) are removed from *R* and replaced by new antibodies generated randomly.

4   Experiments and Results

Conducted experiments are intended to prove the capability of the proposed algorithm to promote highly discriminative feature subset for the target class as compared with other feature subset selection approaches. In all experiments, three fifth of all input documents were selected randomly to represent the selection set while the remaining two fifth represent the evaluation set. During feature selection phase, the selection set is divided equally into selection training and selection test sets. During feature evaluation phase, the whole selection set is used for training and the evaluation set is used for testing. Table 1 lists *AIFSA* configuration parameters used during all experiments unless mentioned otherwise.

After training *AIFSA* for *N* iterations, two extra iterations are performed to assert the power of *AIFSA* feature weighting scheme. The first iteration is the Useless features removal iteration (*U*) where all repertoire feature subsets are shrank by removing useless features. The second iteration is the Optimization iteration (*O*) where all repertoire feature subsets are mutated by replacing features with minimum weights by maximum weighted ones. After each iteration, resultant subsets are reevaluated and average Accuracy (*Acc*) and *F1* measure are recorded.

Table 1. *AIFSA* configuration parameters used during experiments

Parameter	Value	Example
L_{min}	20	Min. antibody length
L_{max}	20	Max. antibody length
R_{size}	50	Antibody repertoire size
N	20	Number of iterations to run before halt
# of clones	3	Fixed number of clones for each antibody
Mu_{prop}	100%	Affinity inversely proportional mutation probability
Mu_{ex}	20%	Percentage of extra features to be mutated
Mu_{min}	2	Min. number of mutated features
Aff_{min}	0%	Min. affinity required for an antibody to live for next iteration
TC_{min}	5	Min. threshold a feature must reach to evaluate its usefulness
W_{min}	0.6	Min. feature weight required to mark it as useful

4.1 Classifiers

Three classifiers were employed during experiments: *NB*, *kNN*, and *SVM*. Implementation provided by RM^1 tool for the three classifiers was utilized. Laplace correction was used with the *NB* classifier to prevent high influence of zero probabilities. Euclidian distance similarity measure was employed with *kNN* where $k=3$, and finally, linear kernel functions were used with the *SVM* classifier.

4.2 Syskill&Webert Experiments

The Syskill&Webert web page ratings corpus contains HTML pages on four topics: *Bands*, *Goats*, *Sheep*, and *Biomedical*. Each web page is rated as `hot`, `medium`, or `cold` based on how interesting the page is. Thus, web pages can be classified as belonging to one of two classes: interesting (pages rated as `hot`), and not interesting (pages rated as `medium` or `cold`). Table 2 gives statistical summary of this dataset.

Table 2. Syskill&Webert dataset summary

Topic	Interesting	Not Interesting	Total
Bands	15	46	61
Biomedical	32	99	131
Goats	33	37	70
Sheep	14	51	65

Experiments were performed on the four topics. The problem was divided into four binary classification tasks where each task targets classification of web pages of certain topic as being interesting (*I*) or not interesting (*N*). In each task, target topic web pages were divided randomly into selection/evaluation subsets. The selection set was then divided into training/test subsets as summarized in Table 3. Features extracted from selection training subset were fed to *AIFSA* repertoire constructor where *AIFSA* was trained using the selection training/test subsets for promoting the optimal feature subset.

---

[1] Available at http://rapid-i.com

To assert the discriminative power of *AIFSA* promoted features, for each topic, a subset of the top 20 weighted features from each classifier were evaluated separately using the topic evaluation set. *Acc* and *F1* measure values obtained during experiments are presented in Table 4. Figure 2 shows *Acc* curve of the top 20 features where features were evaluated adding one by one.

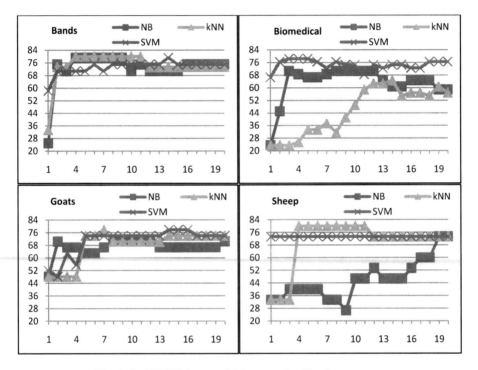

Fig. 2. Syskill&Webert top 20 features classification accuracy

Table 3. Training/Test subsets for Syskill&Webert dataset

Subset	Bands		Biomedical		Goats		Sheep	
	I	N	I	N	I	N	I	N
Selection training	5	14	12	36	12	14	6	19
Selection test	4	14	8	24	8	9	3	12
Evaluation training	9	28	20	60	20	23	9	31
Evaluation test	6	18	12	39	13	14	5	20
# of features	660		416		1190		557	

Table 4. Syskill&Webert top 20 features classification accuracy and F1 measure

Classifier	Bands		Biomedical		Goats		Sheep	
	Acc	F1	Acc	F1	Acc	F1	Acc	F1
NB	75.00	0.71	58.82	0.56	70.37	0.72	73.33	0.70
kNN	79.17	0.68	56.86	0.61	74.07	0.76	73.33	0.71
SVM	75.00	0.71	76.47	0.66	77.78	0.78	73.33	0.71

To compare the performance of *AIFSA* to other approaches on the Syskill&Webert corpus, a subset of the top 128 weighted features from each classifier were evaluated separately using each topic evaluation set. The results in Table 5 present *Acc* obtained from each classifier for each topic compared to the results obtained by the *Prof-NB* algorithm [13] and *Bio-IG* algorithm [14]. The results show that *Acc* obtained with the *Bands*, *Biomedical*, and *Goats* topics using *AIFSA* exceeds the other two approaches while the *Prof-NB* gave better results with the *Sheep* topic.

Table 5. Syskill&Webert top 128 features classification accuracy - Comparison

Topic	NB	kNN	SVM	Prof-NB	Bio-IG
Bands	75.00	70.83	79.17	74.38	69.00
Biomedical	76.47	74.51	76.47	73.33	69.00
Goats	74.07	62.96	59.26	71.67	68.00
Sheep	66.67	80.00	73.33	83.33	75.00

4.3 WebKB Experiments

The WebKB corpus contains HTML pages from computer science departments of four universities: *Coenell*, *Texas*, *Washington*, and *Wisconsin*. It was collected by the World Wide Knowledge Base project of the CMU text learning group. The corpus contains 8,282 web pages classified manually into seven categories: *Student*, *Faculty*, *Staff*, *Department*, *Course*, *Project*, and *Other*. Only 4,162 web pages were collected from the four universities while the remaining 4,120 were collected from other universities. Table 6 summarizes the four categories used during experiments.

Table 6. WebKB dataset summary

Category	Total	Cornell	Texas	Washington	Wisconsin	Misc
Course	930	44	38	77	85	686
Faculty	1124	34	46	31	42	971
Project	504	20	20	21	25	418
Student	1641	128	148	126	156	1083

During experiments, the leave-one-university-out cross-validation scheme was employed where, for each class, web pages from three universities were used to represent the selection set while the fourth university web pages were used to represent the evaluation set. During selection phase, each of the three universities web pages was divided randomly into selection train/test subsets. The classifier used selection training subset as training samples and selection test subset as testing samples.

To assert the quality of *AIFSA* promoted features, the top 20 weighted features obtained from each classifier were evaluated separately using the class evaluation set. Resultant *Acc* and *F1* measure values are presented in Table 7. Figure 3 shows *Acc* curve obtained from the top 20 features adding one by one.

Table 7. WebKB top 20 features classification accuracy and F1 measure

Classifier	Course		Faculty		Project		Student	
	Acc	F1	Acc	F1	Acc	F1	Acc	F1
NB	92.08	0.88	84.67	0.75	78.57	0.62	81.03	0.80
kNN	86.84	0.84	89.58	0.77	85.31	0.57	76.97	0.77
SVM	94.70	0.91	92.41	0.81	94.23	0.66	81.65	0.59

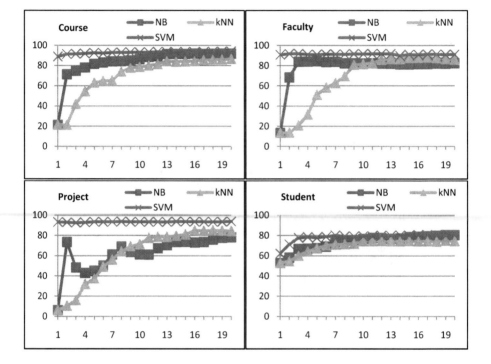

Fig. 3. WebKB top 20 features classification accuracy

Table 8 presents a comparison between *AIFSA* and other approaches using the same experimental setup on the WebKB corpus [9][17][20] . For each class, a subset of the top 20 weighted features from each classifier was evaluated separately using the class evaluation set.

F1 measure values show that *AIFSA* gave better results than [17] using the *NB* classifier for the four classes. Using *SVM* classifier, *AIFSA* results were better than both [9] and [20] for the *Course* and *Faculty* classes. For the *Project* class, *AIFSA* was better than [20] but not [9] while for the *Student* class, *AIFSA* was better than [9] but not [20].

Table 8. WebKB top 20 features F1 measure - Comparison

Method	Course	Faculty	Project	Student	Approach
AIFSA-NB	0.88	0.75	0.62	0.80	
AIFSA-kNN	0.84	0.77	0.57	0.77	AIFSA
AIFSA-SVM	0.91	0.81	0.66	0.59	
FOIL	0.53	0.41	0.20	0.52	Relational Rule Learner[17]
FOILPILFS	0.53	0.44	0.27	0.54	using NB
SVM(X)	0.58	0.56	0.14	0.69	
SVM(T)	0.63	0.63	0.16	0.71	Content/Context based
SVM(A)	0.62	0.67	0.31	0.72	classification using SVM [20]
SVM(TA)	0.68	0.66	0.33	0.73	
X+A+T+Ui	0.61	0.40	0.67	0.25	URL based classification [9]
X+A+T+Uf	0.61	0.41	0.67	0.25	using SVM

The overall predictive accuracy of *AIFSA* was compared to the results obtained in [15] which uses the *NB* classifier *RAINBOW* and the rule learning algorithm *RIPPER*. The results in Table 9 show *AIFSA* superiority over [15] with all classifiers.

Table 9. WebKB top 20 features overall predictive accuracy - Comparison

Method	WebKB	Approach
AIFSA-NB	84.09	
AIFSA-kNN	84.68	AIFSA
AIFSA-SVM	90.75	
Rainbow-Words	45.70	
Rainbow-Phrases	51.22	Linguistic phrases based
Rainbow-Words+Phrases	46.79	classification using NB
Ripper-Words	77.78	RAINBOW & RIPPER
Ripper-Phrases	74.51	[15]
Ripper-Words+Phrases	77.10	

5   Conclusion

In this paper, we introduced a proposal for a new algorithm for feature selection and weighting named *AIFSA*. The algorithm was inspired by the basic principles of clonal selection algorithms.

The performance of the algorithm was analyzed through classification experiments on two famous web corpuses: Syskill&Webert web page ratings and WebKB datasets. Empirical results showed that *AIFSA* could successfully promote features that are highly discriminative for classifying newly unseen samples.

The results proved *AIFSA* superiority over existing approaches on the same datasets. The results also proved robustness of *AIFSA* weighting scheme. This claim was based on two observations: 1) accuracy and *F1* measure curves were increasing by adding more features, and 2) the useless features removal and optimization iterations gave better results during learning.

The highly discriminative power of promoted features is ascribed to *AIFSA* robust weighting scheme which depends heavily on the degree of gain/harm, in terms of classification accuracy, introduced by adding/removing certain feature to/from an existing feature subset. This weighting scheme was very useful during hypermutation and feature pruning.

References

1. Kohavi, R., John, G.H.: Wrappers for feature subset selection. Artificial Intelligence, Special Issue on Relevance 97, 273–324 (1997)
2. Forman, G.: An extensive empirical study of feature selection metrics for text classification. Machine Learning Research 3, 1289–1305 (2003)
3. Qi, X., Davison, B.D.: Web Page Classification: Features and Algorithms. ACM Computing Surveys 41(2) (2009)
4. Singh, S.R., Murthy, H.A., Gonsalves, T.A.: Feature Selection for Text Classification Based on Gini Coefficient of Inequality. Journal of Machine Learning Research 10, 76–85 (2010)
5. Xhemali, D., Hinde, C.J., Stone, R.G.: Naïve Bayes vs. Decision Trees vs. Neural Networks in the classification of training web pages. International Journal of Computer Science Issues 4(1), 16–23 (2009)
6. Otsubo, M., Hung, B.Q., Hijikata, Y., Nishida, S.: Web Page Classification using Anchor-related Text Extracted by a DOM-based Method. Information and Media Technologies 5(1), 193–205 (2010)
7. Othman, M.S., Yusuf, L.M., Salim, J.: Features Discovery for Web Classification Using Support Vector Machine. In: 2010 International Conference on Intelligent Computing and Cognitive Informatics (ICICCI), Kuala Lumpur, pp. 36–40 (2010)
8. Baykan, E., Henzinger, M., Marian, L., Weber, I.: Purely URL-based topic classification. In: 18th International Conference on World Wide Web (WWW 2009), pp. 1109–1110 (2009)
9. Meshkizadeh, S., Rahmani, A.M.: Webpage Classification based on Compound of Using HTML Features & URL Features and Features of Sibling Pages. International Journal of Advancements in Computing Technology 2(4), 36–46 (2010)
10. Rajalakshmi, R., Aravindan, C.: Naive Bayes Approach for Website Classification. Communications in Computer and Information Science 147(2), 323–326 (2011)
11. Neville, J., Jensen, D.: Iterative classification in relational data. In: Workshop on Learning Statistical Models from Relational Data (AAAI 2000), pp. 13–20 (2000)
12. Slattery, S., Mitchell, T.M.: Discovering Test Set Regularities in Relational Domains. In: 17th International Conference on Machine Learning (ICML 2000), Stanford, CA, pp. 895–902 (2000)
13. Pazzani, M., Billsus, D.: Learning and revising user profiles: The identification of interesting web sites. Machine Learning 27(3), 313–331 (1997)
14. Twycross, J., Cayzer, S.: An immune-based approach to document classification. In: Intelligent Information Processing and Web Mining, Proceedings of the International IIS (IIPWM 2003), Zakopane, pp. 33–46 (2002)
15. Fürnkranz, J., Mitchell, T., Riloff, E.: A case study in using linguistic phrases for text categorization on the WWW. In: Working Notes of the AAAI/ICML Workshop on Learning for Text Categorization, pp. 5–12. AAAI Press (1998)
16. Cohen, W.W.: Fast effective rule induction. In: 12th International Conference on Machine Learning (ML 1995), Tahoe City, California, pp. 115–123 (1995)

17. Craven, M., Slattery, S.: Relational learning with statistical predicate invention: better models for hypertext. Machine Learning 43(1/2), 97–117 (2001)
18. Ghani, R., Slattery, S., Yang, Y.: Hypertext categorization using hyperlink patterns and meta data. In: 18th International Conference on Machine Learning (ICML 2001), Williamstown, pp. 115–178 (2001)
19. Quinlan, J.R.: Learning logical definitions from relations. Machine Learning 5(3), 239–266 (1990)
20. Sun, A., Lim, E.P., Ng, W.K.: Web classification using support vector machine. In: 4th ACM CIKM International Workshop on Web Information and Data Management (WIDM 2002), Virginia, pp. 96–99 (2002)
21. Schneider, K.M.: Weighted Average Pointwise Mutual Information for Feature Selection in Text Categorization. In: 9th European Conference on Principles and Practice of Knowledge Discovery in Databases, Porto, pp. 252–263 (2005)
22. Yang, H., King, I.: Sprinkled Latent Semantic Indexing for Text Classification with Background Knowledge. In: Köppen, M., Kasabov, N., Coghill, G. (eds.) ICONIP 2008. LNCS, vol. 5507, pp. 53–60. Springer, Heidelberg (2009)

A Preprocessing for Approximate String Matching

Kensuke Baba[1], Tetsuya Nakatoh[1], Yasuhiro Yamada[2], and Daisuke Ikeda[1]

[1] Kyushu University, Fukuoka, Japan
{baba@lib,nakatoh@cc,daisuke@inf}.kyushu-u.ac.jp
[2] Shimane University, Shimane, Japan
yamada@cis.shimane-u.ac.jp

Abstract. Approximate string matching is a basic and important concept in many applications of information retrieval. This paper proposes an algorithm for the problem of approximate string matching. The algorithm solves the match-count problem as a preprocessing. For input strings of each length n, the time complexities of the approximate string matching problem and the match-count problem are $O(n^2)$ and $O(n \log n)$, respectively. Therefore, the computation time of the algorithm is expected to be short when the scope of search is drastically restricted by the preprocessing. This paper makes clear the relation between the solutions of the two problems.

Keywords: algorithm, approximate string matching, FFT.

1 Introduction

Similarity on strings is one of the most important concepts in many applications of information retrieval. Especially for mining on a huge database such as homology search in biology, the process of pattern matching is required to be fast and flexible.

The aim of this paper is to speed up the process of approximate string matching [7]. Exact string matching is the problem to find the occurrences of a (short) string, called a "pattern", in another (long) string, called a "text". The problem of approximate string matching is defined to be the string matching problem which allows some errors with a threshold based on the edit distance [11]. The edit distance is the minimal number of the edit operations which transform one string to the other, where the permitted operations are "insertion", "deletion", and "replacement" of a character. The generalizations in the sense of weight [11] and local similarity [10] are the essence of some popular systems for sequence analysis in biology [9]. It is significant for many applications to speedup solving the approximate string matching problem.

An approach to the speedup is parallel computation which depends on the performance of a computer. If we assume a computational model which corresponds to a computer with a multi-core processor, a straightforward method is to part the text with overlaps, and then solve the problem for each parted text

A. Abd Manaf et al. (Eds.): ICIEIS 2011, Part II, CCIS 252, pp. 610–615, 2011.

separately. Another simple parallel computation is "wavefront" which computes the matrix for the dynamic programming approach. Myers [7] proposed an efficient algorithm based on the idea of "bit-parallel [8]" for the approximate string matching problem. The speedup method of this paper is to compute another problem which can be solved faster than the original problem as a preprocessing, that is, the proposed method can be applied with the previous speedup methods simultaneously.

In this paper, the match-count problem [6] is considered as the preprocessing. The problem allows only replacement as the edit operation for the idea of distance. Although this approach makes no improvement of the computation time in the worst case, there exist significant speedup methods for this problem and a practical speedup is expected in some applications in which the occurrences of the pattern are not so many. While the time complexity of the standard algorithm for the approximate string matching problem is $O(n^2)$ for input strings of length n, the match-count problem is solved by the first Fourier transformation (FFT) in $O(n \log n)$ [5,6], and moreover, some improvements for the computation time were proposed [1,3,2]. This paper makes clear the relation between the solutions of the approximate string matching problem and the match-count problem, and proposes an algorithm which solves the match-count problem as a preprocessing for solving the approximate string matching problem.

2   Formalization

Let Σ be a finite set of characters. For an integer $n > 0$, Σ^n denotes the set of the strings of length n over Σ. Σ^* denotes the set of the strings of finite length over Σ and by ε the empty string. For a string u, $|u|$ denotes the length of u and u_i denotes the ith element of u for $1 \le i \le |u|$. The string $u_i u_{i+1} \cdots u_j$ is a *substring* of u, and denoted by $u_{i,j}$. In particular, $u_{i,j}$ is called a *prefix* if $i = 1$ and a *suffix* if $j = |u|$.

Let $Aa = \{ua \mid u \in A\}$ for $A \subseteq \Sigma^*$ and $a \in \Sigma$. An *edit transcript* from $u \in \Sigma^*$ to $v \in \Sigma^*$ is a string on $\{I, D, R, M\}$, such that, the set $T(u, v)$ of the edit transcripts from u to v is

- $T(u, v) = \{\varepsilon\}$ if $uv = \varepsilon$;
- $T(u, v) = T(u, v')I$ if $u = \varepsilon$ and $v = v'a$ for $a \in \Sigma$;
- $T(u, v) = T(u', v)D$ if $u = u'a$ and $v = \varepsilon$ for $a \in \Sigma$;
- $T(u, v) = T(u, v')I + T(u', v)D + T(u', v')R$ if $u = u'a$, $v = v'b$, and $a \ne b$ for $a, b \in \Sigma$;
- $T(u, v) = T(u, v')I + T(u', v)D + T(u', v')M$ if $u = u'a$, $v = v'b$, and $a = b$ for $a, b \in \Sigma$.

An edit transcript from u to v is *optimum* if the number of occurrences of I, D, and R in the edit transcript is minimum in $T(u, v)$. The *edit distance* $d(u, v)$ between u and v is the number of occurrences of I, D, and R in an optimum edit transcript.

Definition 1. *For $p, t \in \Sigma^*$ and an integer ℓ, the* approximate string matching problem *is to find the substrings t' of t, such that, $d(p, t') \leq \ell$.*

The *score vector* $S(p, t)$ between $p \in \Sigma^m$ and $t \in \Sigma^n$ (assume $m < n$) is the vector whose ith element s_i is the number of matches between p and the substring $t_{i,i+m-1}$ of t for $1 \leq i \leq n - m + 1$. Let δ be a function from $\Sigma \times \Sigma$ to $\{0, 1\}$, such that, for $a, b \in \Sigma$, $\delta(a, b)$ is 1 if $a = b$, and 0 otherwise. Then, for $1 \leq i \leq n - m + 1$, the ith element of the score vector is

$$s_i = \sum_{j=1}^{m} \delta(p_j, t_{i+j-1}). \tag{1}$$

Definition 2. *For $p, t \in \Sigma^*$, the* match-count problem *is to compute $S(p, t)$.*

3   Standard Algorithms

3.1   Approximate String Matching Problem

The edit distance between $u \in \Sigma^m$ and $v \in \Sigma^n$ is computed in $O(mn)$ time by the dynamic programming approach [11]. In this approach, the *cost matrix* $C(u, v)$ is evaluated, whose (i, j)-element $c_{i,j}$ is the edit distance between the prefix $u_{1,i}$ of u and the prefix $v_{1,j}$ of v. By the definition of the edit distance,

$$c_{i,j} = \min\{c_{i-1,j-1} + 1 - \delta(u_i, v_j), c_{i-1,j} + 1, c_{i,j-1} + 1\}$$

for $1 \leq i \leq m$ and $1 \leq j \leq n$. The base conditions are $c_{i,0} = i$ and $c_{0,j} = j$. The (m, n)-element of the cost matrix is the edit distance between u and v and obtained by computing the $m \times n$ elements of the cost matrix.

The approximate string matching problem is solved also in $O(mn)$ time by the previous approach on the base conditions $c_{i,0} = i$ and $c_{0,j} = 0$, which is clear from the idea of the Smith-Waterman algorithm [10]. $c'_{i,j}$ denotes the (i, j)-element of the cost matrix on these base conditions.

In the strict sense, the previous method finds the positions which the target substrings start (or end), and moreover there can exist more than two target substrings which start at one position. These problems are solved by a linear-time operation called a "traceback [6]". In the rest of this paper, we focus on finding the positions of the target substrings in the approximate string matching problem.

3.2   Match-Count Problem

A naive method for the match-count problem is, for $p \in \Sigma^m$ and $t \in \Sigma^n$, to make the $m \times n$ matrix $D(p, t)$ whose (i, j)-element is $\delta(p_i, t_j)$ and compute each s_k by Eq. 1 for $1 \leq k \leq n - m + 1$. Therefore, $S(p, t)$ is obtained by $m \times (n - m + 1)$ comparisons and $(m - 1) \times (n - m + 1)$ add operations. Thus, the time complexity of this naive algorithm is $O(mn)$.

The most straightforward method of parallel computation for the match-count problem is to part t or p into substrings. Intuitively, in this method, using k computers (processors, or cores) yields a k-times speedup. Clearly, by $t_{i,j}$ and p, $C(t, p)$ is obtained from the ith element to the $(j - m + 1)$th element. Therefore, by parting t into k substrings with overlaps of length $m - 1$ and combining the results, $C(t, p)$ is obtained by k distinct computations. If p is parted, the following is clear in general. Let c_i^p be the ith element of the score vector $C(t, p)$ and c_i^q the ith element of $C(t, q)$. Then, the ith element of $C(t, pq)$ is $c_i^p + c_{m+i}^q$, where m is the length of p. Therefore, we can also expect straightforward speedup except for the overhead.

Additionally, for the match-count problem, there exists an efficient algorithm using the fast Fourier transform (FFT) [6]. The convolution of two

$$w_i = \sum_{j=1}^{m} u_j \cdot v_{i-j} \quad (1 \le i \le m)$$

m-dimensional vectors u and v can be computed in $O(m \log m)$ time by FFT [4]. Therefore, the score vector between two strings each of length m is computed in $O(m \log m)$ time. By parting t into overlapping substrings and padding p with a never-match character, we obtain an $O(n \log m)$ algorithm.

4 Relation between Score Vector and Edit Distance

We make clear the relation between the score vector and the edit distance, and then propose an algorithm for the approximate string matching problem using the result of the match-count problem for a speedup.

We consider the score vector between $p \in \Sigma^m$ and $t \in \Sigma^n$ and the edit distances between p and the substrings of t. Now we extend the definition of the score vector. For $k \le 0$ and $n + 1 \le k$, we assume that t_k is a never-match character, that is, $\delta(p_j, t_k) = 0$ for any $1 \le j \le m$. Then, s_i in Eq. 1 is extended for $i \le 0$ and $n - m + 1 \le i$.

Lemma 1. *If there exists a pair of i and j such that $d(p, t_{i,j}) \le \ell$, then there exists r such that $\sum_{k=r}^{r+\ell} s_k \ge m - \ell$ and $i - \ell \le r \le i$.*

Proof. Let $g = |t_{i,j}| - |p|$. By the definition of the edit distance, if $d(p, t_{i,j}) \le \ell$, then $|g| \le \ell$ and there exist at least $m - \ell$ matches. Therefore, $d(p, t_{i,j}) \le \ell$ implies

$$\sum_{k=i-\lfloor(\ell-g)/2\rfloor}^{i+\lfloor(\ell+g)/2\rfloor} s_k \ge m - \ell.$$

Since $\lfloor(\ell+g)/2\rfloor \le \ell$ and $\lfloor(\ell-g)/2\rfloor \le \ell$ by $-\ell \le g \le \ell$, we have only to consider the summation $\sum_{k=r}^{r+\ell} s_k$ for $i - \ell \le r \le i$.

By the previous lemma, if $\sum_{k=r}^{r+\ell} s_k < m - \ell$ for $i - \ell \le r \le i$, then there is no pair of i and j such that $d(p, t_{i,j}) \le \ell$. That is, the candidates of the approximate string matching problem is reduced by the result of the match-count problem. The outline of an algorithm based on this idea is the following.

Algorithm A:
Input: $p \in \Sigma^m$, $t \in \Sigma^n$, ℓ
Output: $P = \{i \mid 1 \leq i \leq n, \exists k.d(p, t_{k,i}) \leq \ell\}$

for $(2 - m \leq i \leq n)$ compute s_i ;

$R := 0$; $Q := \emptyset$;
for $(3 - m - \ell \leq i \leq 1 - m)$ $s_i := 0$;
for $(2 - m \leq i \leq n)$ {
    $R := R + s_i - s_{i-\ell+1}$;
    if $(R \geq m - \ell)$
        $Q := Q \cup \{i - \ell + 1, i - \ell + 2, \ldots, i\}$;
}

for $(i \in Q)$ compute $c'_{m,i}$ and find P.

In the algorithm, s_i and $c'_{m,i}$ are computed by the standard algorithms for the match-count problem and the approximate string matching problem, respectively. Then, the following theorem is clear by Lemma 1.

Theorem 1. *Algorithm A solves the problem of approximate string matching.*

Intuitively, Q in Algorithm A is the set of the positions which can be the target of approximate string matching after the screening by match-count. Therefore, the algorithm is effective when the size of Q is extremely small compared with n. In the worst case, the number of positions is not decreased by the preprocessing, hence the time complexity of the algorithm is $O(mn)$.

5   Conclusion

An algorithm for the approximate string matching problem which uses the result of the match-count problem as a preprocessing was proposed. We made clear the relation between the results of the two problems, and thereby constructed the algorithm. The computation time of the algorithm is expected to be short in the case where the number of the occurrences of the pattern is small compared to the length of the text.

References

1. Atallah, M.J., Chyzak, F., Dumas, P.: A randomized algorithm for approximate string matching. Algorithmica 29, 468–486 (2001)
2. Baba, K.: String matching with mismatches by real-valued FFT. In: Taniar, D., Gervasi, O., Murgante, B., Pardede, E., Apduhan, B.O. (eds.) ICCSA 2010, Part IV. LNCS, vol. 6019, pp. 273–283. Springer, Heidelberg (2010)

3. Baba, K., Shinohara, A., Takeda, M., Inenaga, S., Arikawa, S.: A note on randomized algorithm for string matching with mismatches. Nordic Journal of Computing 10(1), 2–12 (2003)
4. Cormen, T.H., Leiserson, C.E., Rivest, R.L.: Introduction to Algorithms, 2nd edn. MIT Press, Cambridge (2001)
5. Fischer, M.J., Paterson, M.S.: String-matching and other products. In: Proceedings of the SIAM-AMS Applied Mathematics Symposium Complexity of Computation, New York, pp. 113–125 (1973/1974)
6. Gusfield, D.: Algorithms on Strings, Trees, and Sequences. Cambridge University Press (1997)
7. Myers, G.: A fast bit-vector algorithm for approximate string matching based on dynamic programming. J. ACM 46(3), 395–415 (1999)
8. Navarro, G.: A guided tuor to approximate string matching. ACM Comput. Surv. 33(1), 31–88 (2001)
9. Pearson, W.R., Lipman, D.J.: Improved tools for biological sequence comparison. Proc. Natl. Acad. Sci. USA 85, 2444–2448 (1988)
10. Smith, T.F., Waterman, M.S.: Identification of common molecular subsequences. J. Mol. Biol. 147, 195–197 (1981)
11. Wagner, R.A., Fischer, M.J.: The string-to-string correction problem. J. ACM 21(1), 168–173 (1974)

Applying Rules for Representing and Reasoning of Objective Product Use Information Exemplarily for Injection Molding Machines

Mareike Dornhöfer, Madjid Fathi, and Alexander Holland

University of Siegen,
Institute of Knowledge Based Systems & Knowledge Management,
Hölderlinstr. 3, 57068 Siegen, Germany
m.dornhoefer@uni-siegen.de,
{fathi,alex}@informatik.uni-siegen.de

Abstract. Information gathered during daily life can be generally categorized as either of objective or of subjective character. The given work focuses on the objective field of product use information and how to represent and reason the information with the help of Rules or a Rule Based System. The aim of the reasoning process is to infer new knowledge form the given product information and to use this knowledge for the improvement of a new product generation of the product. The application scenario detailed in this work focuses on the objective information gathered from an injection molding machine to improve not only parts of the machine, but indirectly the quality of the produced parts.

Keywords: Objective Product Use Information, Product Use Knowledge, Injection Molding Machine, Rules, Rule Based System.

1 Introduction

Rules or a Rule Based System (RBS) (defined e.g. in [3, 5]) are a generic applicable method from the field of knowledge management (adjacent to artificial intelligence) and knowledge representation methods. Rules are neither a new method nor are they limited to a defined application field. During former works Dornhöfer *et.al.* [1, 2] evaluated knowledge representation methods regarding their usability for representing and deriving of product use information (PUI) of an *objective* character. The evaluation based on a requirement catalogue consisting of over 30 requirements, the most prominent requirement being able to reason new knowledge from given product use information. The evaluation took place in the context of a project between the Universities of Bochum and Siegen (Germany) sponsored by the German Research Foundation. Overall 12 knowledge representation methods (Classical Logic, Frames, Case Based Reasoning, Semantic Network, Topic Map, Ontology, Fuzzy Logic, Rule Based System, Decision Tree, Bayesian Network, Neuronal Network and Support Vector Machine) were part of the evaluation process. The evaluation results illustrated *Bayesian Network* and *Rule Based System* as most appropriate in this problem context. The given paper presents an application scenario of a RBS with the background of an injection molding machine (IMM). The purpose of the RBS is to

A. Abd Manaf et al. (Eds.): ICIEIS 2011, Part II, CCIS 252, pp. 616–623, 2011.

represent and interpret product lifecycle information from the usage phase of the IMM. In consequence the reasoned product use knowledge (PUK) may be applied in the product development of a new product generation. The underlying goal is the improvement of the product quality of the machine and indirectly of the produced parts. Chapter 2 gives an overview which type of data are considered objective. Afterwards chapter 3 gives an introduction to the application scenario of the IMM, before chapter 4 presents an exemplary implementation of a RBS based on objective PUI from the IMM. Chapter 5 concludes this work.

2   Product Use Information (PUI)

Sääksvuori and Immonen [6] define product lifecycle information and indirectly a product life cycle itself with the words: *"The life cycle data of the product is always connected to the product and the stage of the product or order-delivery process. This [...] is connected to technological research, design and to the production, use, maintenance, recycling, and destruction of the product [...]."* According to the authors *"Product data can be roughly divided into three groups: 1. definition data of the product, 2. life cycle data of the product, 3. metadata that describes the product and lifecycle data."* This work focuses mainly on the lifecycle data of the product which is gathered during the use phase. Figure 1 shows an overview of possible objective PUI in this context.

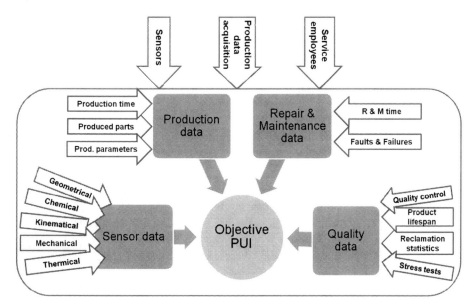

Fig. 1. Objective product use information (obj. PUI, also defined as objective feedback [3]) are gathered mostly via measuring technology and do not contain a personal opinion e.g. of a user of the product or another stakeholder (partner, supplier, ...). Obj. PUI may be gathered via sensor technology, methods of production data acquisition (e.g. number of rejected goods in a defined period of time) or via service employees who provide repair and maintenance services and gather input for product errors statistics. For this work a beneficial segmentation of obj. PUI are the four categories *measuring data*, *production data*, *repair & maintenance data* and *quality data*.

Measuring data: Based on [7] there are more than ten different measurement categories, whose indicators may be measured with the help of sensor technology or in a manual process. Figure 1 gives a few examples like: geometrical data (e.g. dimensions, sizes, and tolerances of the product structure), chemical data (e.g. material errors, surface structure), kinematical data (e.g. rotational speed, acceleration), mechanical data (expansion, pressure/mass of a product under certain conditions) or thermical data (e.g. behavior of the product in defined temperature ranges).

Production data (acquisition): Production data focuses on data which are acquired during the production process. This data may be the production time per product, possible production errors, production parameters/factors or requirements for an optimal production process. It is a category which is closely linked to measuring and quality data. The reason for adding this category (although it is not strictly PUI) is that consolidated results about errors during the production process may be optimized for a new product generation as well. A second aspect for adding this category is that a production machine is a product itself and therefore PUI may be gathered for example during the operation time of the machine. Information based on [8, 9].

Repair & Maintenance data: The third category of obj. PUI bases on DIN 31051 [10] and DIN EN 13306 [11], which focus on the different aspects of repair & maintenance of a product. There are different types of maintenance (e.g. preventive, predictive, corrective or scheduled) as well as actions which may be taken once there are failures or faults. To provide availability and reliability of a product, in this case a

production machine itself, service workers have to gather data about the machine and provide the right type of maintenance. This data may for example consist of the up-/ down-time of the machine, regular operation times, times between failures, the severity or criticality of failures, a failure analysis or regular scheduled maintenance processes. Except are possible subjective information of employees on maintenance sheets, as they would contain a personal opinion of the employee.

Quality data: The last category of obj. PUI is about quality data, which may be gathered during production steps, quality control, with the help of stress tests or indirectly from reclamation statistics (e.g. about fault frequency, average lifespan). For the production machine itself, quality is also about optimizing production parameters and factors for different production processes. A related topic is production management, planning and control illustrated in [8].

3   Injection Molding Machine (IMM)

An injection molding machine is a machine, which may be used for producing different plastic parts like water bottles, toys for children or interior parts of cars. The production process consists of several consecutive steps. Figure 2 divides the process into the three phases *liquefaction*, *injection* and *ejection*.

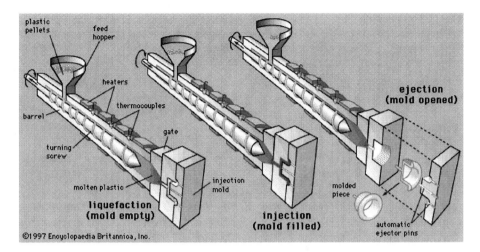

Fig. 2. Injection molding machine [14]. For the liquefaction a feed hopper filled with pellets of polymer material feeds the injection unit with said pellets. In the unit the material is melted with the help of different heaters and transported with the use of a turning screw. In the injection phase the now molten plastic is pressed into the mold. After a cooling down time, the last step of the production process is to eject the produced parts from the mold.

The reasons for choosing this type of machine for an application scenario are that it is a widely used type of machine in industrial production, the production method is relative easy to understand and it is easily possible to gather different obj. PUI from the machine. For the given scenario the gathered PUI are temperature values from different heating points. It could also be possible to gather e.g. the pressure of the turning screw. According to the short description of the scenario in [1] *"the aim is now to improve the temperature accuracy of the injection unit and the mold for the next generation of the machine to minimize the faulty output of the produced parts"*. Based on the figure above, the PUI is gathered at different heating points: 1) below the feed hopper, where the melting of the plastic pellets starts, 2) at a point shortly before the now molten plastic is injected into the mold and 3) in the mold itself, where the cooling down takes place. The gathered data will be stored in a database similar to Table 1:

Table 1. Examples of obj. PUI, based on [2]. Quality: 0 = rejected, 1= product quality ok.

Id	ProductionTime	Temperature1	Temperature2	Temperature3	Quality
1	15.10.2010 07:00:00	275.00	291.14	80.50	1
2	15.10.2010 07:01:00	273.75	289.29	81.88	1
3	15.10.2010 07:02:00	276.23	290.06	80.00	0
...	...	...	...	...	...
50.000	19.11.2010 00:19:00	277.32	287.47	81.66	1

The quality of the produced parts depends on the consistency of the molten plastic, which in turn depends on the optimal temperatures during the production process. Therefore the obj. PUI gathered for the following scenario consists of measuring data of the machine (the gathered temperatures) and of quality data of the produced parts.

For the quality data it is necessary to record if the quality of a produced part is acceptable (Table 1: Quality =1) or if the part had to be rejected (Table 1: Quality =0) after the production process or during quality control.

The following chapter shows how Rules may be used for representing and reasoning of this concrete obj. PUI. The background information about IMM base on the sources [12, 13, 14].

4 Representing and Reasoning Objective PUI with Rules

For the implementation of the scenario presented in the previous chapter in form of a Rule Based System, the JBoss Drools Expert [16,17] module has been used. The software is part of a business rules suite called JBoss Drools Business Logic integration Platform. *"Drools is a Rule Engine that uses the rule-based approach to implement an Expert System and is more correctly classified as a Production Rule System."* [16] The solution bases on Java technology. The rule scheme/syntax for JBoss Drools is defined as follows:

```
rule "name"
     attributes (optional)
     when Left hand side
     then Right hand side
end
```

There are different architectures which may be chosen for implementing a RBS based on business rules. Grässle and Schacher [15] document with the *service-architecture*, the *database-architecture*, the *generator-architecture* and the *layer-architecture* four different architecture models. The given work uses the service-architecture, where the host application is the central component of the realization. This application has got a connection to the database where the obj. PUI is stored according to the specifications named in chapter 3, as well as a connection to the business rules engine via a rule service API.

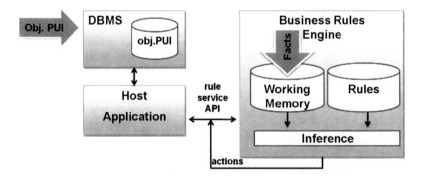

Fig. 3. Rules Service-Architecture based on [15], Business Rules Engine based on [16]. The engine consists of a rule base and a working memory, where the facts from the database are stored temporarily. *"The Inference Engine matches facts and data against Production Rules … to infer conclusions which result in actions."* [16] The actions, results or decisions gained during the inference process are available at the rule service API and may be used by the host application to display them for the user.

After discussing the buildup of a RBS for an IMM in theory, the following paragraph discusses two rules of an exemplary implementation. The deduced results should support finding temperature inconsistencies during the production process which led to rejected parts. In the consequence this knowledge may be used for the improvement towards a consistent temperature and the optimization of the quality of the produced parts. It is assumed that with the help of the host application, the user is able to define an optimal temperature for each heating point as well as a tolerance for the optimum.[1] As the Drools Expert module is a solution which allows the import of Java classes (and indirectly an import of variables of the classes) the three classes `MinMaxValues`, `DataRow` and `Number` are used for rule 1, while the classes `Checkfunction` and `Machine` are used for rule 2.

Table 2. Rule 1; rule scheme based on [16]; scenario adapted from [2]

Rule 1	Explanation

rule
`"number_rejects_t1_ok_t2_`
`too_low"`
	The idea is to determine with the help of the first rule, how many rejected parts of a batch have been produced while the temperature at heating point 1 ($t1$) of the IMM was in the optimal range and the temperature at heating point 2 ($t2$) was too low.

when
`MinMaxValues(`
`  min1: t1_min > "0",`
`  max1: t1_max > "0",`
`  min2: t2_min > "0",`
`)`
`DataRow(`
`  quality == "0" &&`
`  t1 >= min1 &&`
`  t1 <= max1 &&`
`  t2 < t2_min)`
	The **when** clause uses *MinMaxValues* to check, if the maximal values for the variables $t1\_min$, $t1\_max$ and $t2\_min$ are higher than 0°C as otherwise the temperatures are out of the predefined temperature range for the IMM. The values of these variables are allocated to the temporary variables *min1*, *max1* and *min2*. These variables are used to check whether $t1$ is within the optimal temperature range while at the same time $t2$ is lower than the minimal temperature threshold. The class used for this check is *DataRow*. During the import of PUI from the database each record is stored as an object of *DataRow* in the working memory. Based on *DataRow* it is also possible to determine whether the current quality of the part is 0, which indicates a rejected part.

then
`Number.reject_t1_ok_t2_`
`too_low ++;`
	For the **then** instruction there is a predefined variable *rejected_t1_ok_t2_ too_low* in the class *Number*. If the **when** clause for the current produced part is executed, the following action is an iteration of the variable. This way it is possible to determine how many parts where rejected given the temperature dependencies.

end	Each rule has to be closed with **end**.

---

[1] The minimal and maximal temperatures are calculated as `min= optimum - tolerance` and `max= optimum + tolerance`. This is rather rudimentary but serves the purpose of the given scenario.

The second rule uses the value of variable `reject_t1_ok_t2_too_low` from rule 1 as a condition for its own **when** clause.

Table 3. Rule 2; scheme based on [16]; scenario adapted from [2], rule quoted partly from [1]

Rule 2	Explanation

rule
`"significance_reject_t1_o`
`k_t2_too_low"`
	The rule determines if there is a significantly high number of rejected parts, while *t1* has been in the optimal range and *t2* has been too low.

when
`CheckFunction`
`(`
`  s:significance > 100,`
`  r:reject_t1_ok_t2_too`
`_low > s`
`)`
	The condition for executing this rule depends on the variable *reject_t1_ok_t2_too_low*, which has been calculated with the help of rule 1, and whether the value of the variable is higher than a significance threshold as indicated by *significance > 100*. This threshold may of course be changed depending on the examined batch size.

then
`Machine.checkPoint2();`
`Machine.setInfo("\n`
`Heater 2 may malfunction.`
`There were more than 100`
`rejected parts while`
`temperature 1: ok and`
`temperature 2: too low`
`");`
	The **then** clause contains two instructions. First a method called *checkPoint2()* of the class *Machine* is called upon. The results of this method have to be handled by the host application. The same applies for the second instruction, which allocates a user information to a variable of the class *Machine* with the help of the method *setInfo()*.

end	Each rule has to be closed with **end**.

Even though the two rules represent only an excerpt of an exemplary implementation, they show that it is possible to use a RBS for representing and reasoning obj. PUI. The main reason why this is possible is because the current state of technique allows it to (automatically) store obj. PUI in a structured way, which in consequence is accessible for the RBS. The application is a Java implementation. Regarding the performance of the system, there have been successful tests with sets of 10.000, 20.000 and 50.000 data records on a standard notebook (2.3 GHz, 2GB RAM, Windows 7).

5 Conclusion

Observing application areas of knowledge based methods in recent years shows that they are not necessarily only applied in the field of computer science but in other scientific, medical (e.g. [18]) or industrial (e.g. [19]) areas as well. The given paper discusses an application scenario for deriving new product use knowledge with the help of a rule based system. The input data are objective product use information from an injection molding machine. The IMM may be seen exemplary as the work shows that any other product or production machine, which provides objective data according to chapter 2, is applicable.

A question which has not been breached by this work, but gives an interesting research topic is whether it is also possible to represent PUI of a subjective character (e.g. customer product feedback) with a RBS and infer new knowledge in an efficient way. It stands to reason that the implementation is more complex given the natural language input, where necessary facts would have to be extracted without losing the opinion expressed by the user.

References

1. Dornhöfer, M., Fathi, M., Holland, A.: Evaluation of Advanced Knowledge Representation Methods for Reasoning of Product Use Information. In: German Workshop on Knowledge and Experience Management, Magdeburg (2011)
2. Dornhöfer, M.: Evaluation and implementation of knowledge representation methods to generate product usage knowledge, based on objective (machine based) feedback data (EvalIFeed), Diploma Thesis, University of Siegen (2011)
3. Neubach, M.: Wissensbasierte Rückführung von Produktnutzungsinformationen in die Produktentwicklung im Rahmen einer PLM-Lösung, Dissertation, Ruhr-University of Bochum (2010)
4. Lämmel, U., Cleve, J.: Künstliche Intelligenz, 3rd edn., Hanser München (2008)
5. Triantaphyllou, E., Felici, G.: Massive Computing - Data Mining and Knowledge Discovery Approaches Based on Rule Induction Techniques. Springer, New York (2006)
6. Sääksvuori, A., Immonen, A.: Product Lifecycle Management, 2nd edn. Springer, Heidelberg (2005)
7. Grote, K.-H., Feldhusen, J.: Dubbel - Taschenbuch für den Maschinenbau, 22nd edn. Springer, Berlin (2007)
8. Blohm, H., Beer, T., Seidenberg, U., Silber, H.: Produktionswirtschaft, Neue Wirtschafts-Briefe, Hamm, 4th edn. (2008)
9. Loos, P.: Grunddatenverwaltung und Betriebsdatenerfassung als Basis der Produktionsplanung und –steuerung. In: Corsten, H. (ed.) Einführung in das Produktionscontrolling. Vahlen, München (1999)
10. DIN 31051, Grundlagen der Instandhaltung, Beuth, Berlin (2003)
11. DIN EN 13306, Maintenance & Maintenance Terminology, Beuth, Berlin (2010)
12. Michaeli, W., Greif, H., Kretzschmar, G., Ehrig, F.: Technologie des Spritzgießens, Lern- und Arbeitsbuch, 3rd edn., Hanser, München (2009)
13. Jaroschek, C.: Spritzgießen für Praktiker, Hanser München, 2nd edn. (2008)
14. Injection molding: thermoplastic polymers. Art., Encyclopædia Britannica Online (1997), http://www.britannica.com/EBchecked/media/274/Injection-molding-of-thermoplastic-polymers
15. Grässle, P., Schacher, M.: Agile Unternehmen durch Business Rules. Springer, Heidelberg (2006)
16. JBoss Drools Expert, http://www.jboss.org/drools/drools-expert.html, JBoss Drools Expert User Guide, http://docs.jboss.org/drools/release/5.2.0.Final/drools-expert-docs/html_single/index.html
17. Browne, P.: JBoss Drools Business Rules. Packt Pub., Birmingham (2009)
18. Hu, Z., et al.: Ontology-Based Clinical Pathways with Semantic Rules. Journal of Medical Systems, PMID: 21445676 (2011)
19. Liu, Y., Lim, S.C.J.: Using Ontology for Design Information and Knowledge Management: A Critical Review. Global Product Development 12, 427–433 (2011)

Granular Computing Based Data Mining in the Views of Rough Set and Fuzzy Set

Yousef Farhang[*,**], Siti Mariyam Shamsuddin, and Haniyeh Fattahi

Faculty of Computer Science and Information System,
Universiti Teknologi Malaysia (UTM),
Skudai, 81310, Johor Bahru, Malaysia
yfarhang@yahoo.com

Abstract. Granular computing is a title of methodologies, techniques, and devices that make use of granules in the process of problem solving. The idea of granular computing has shown in a lot of areas, and it is likely playing a more and more important position in data mining. Rough set theory and fuzzy set theory, as two very important patterns of granular computing, are frequently used to process vague information in data mining. Combining rough set theory and fuzzy set theory, a flexible method is for processing imperfect information systems.

Keywords: Granular Computing (GrC), Data Mining, Rough Set, Fuzzy Set.

1 Introduction

Granular computing (GrC) is theories that create use of granules, groups, classes, or clusters of a world, in the procedure of problem solving. There is a fast growing and new attention in the study of granular computing. There are many basic problems in granular computing, such as granulation of the world, description of granules, relationships between granules, and computing with granules [1, 3]. Many models of granular computing have been proposed and studied. Each model only captures certain facets of granular computing. There is still a need for formal and compact models for systematic studies of basic issues of granular computing [5, 8].

Data are being collected and accumulated at a dramatic pace of across a wide diversity of fields. Data is necessary to get useful knowledge from large amount of information. Generally, data mining is considered as the nontrivial extraction of implicit, previously unidentified, and potentially useful information from information. That is to say, knowledge is generated from information [9]. But in our view, knowledge is firstly existed in the data, but just not understandable for human. In a data mining process, knowledge existed in a database is changed from data format into another human understandable format like law [4, 10].

The philosophy of granular computing has appeared in many charts, and it is likely playing a more and more main role in data mining. Rough set theory and fuzzy set theory are two very important paradigms in granular computing [7].

---

[*] This work is supported partially by the SCRG group in UTM of Malaysia.
[**] Corresponding author.

A. Abd Manaf et al. (Eds.): ICIEIS 2011, Part II, CCIS 252, pp. 624–629, 2011.
© Springer-Verlag Berlin Heidelberg 2011

The main objective of this paper is to discuss the granular computing based data mining in the views of rough set and fuzzy set, and introduce some applications of granular computing in data mining [2, 6].

2   Granular Computing

Solving of human problem involves the insight, concept and understanding of real world problems, as well as their solutions. Granular computing (GrC) is an emerging conceptual and computing pattern of information processing at different levels of granularity. It has been provoked by the increasingly urgent need for intelligent processing for huge quantities heterogeneous information (Zadeh, 1997; Lin, 1997; Yao, 2000; Skowron, 2001; Skowron & Stepaniuk, 2001). By taking human knowledge generation as a basic reference, granular computing offers a landmark change from the current machine-centric to human-centric approach for information and knowledge.

The first ingredients of granular computing are granules such as subsets, classes, objects, clusters, and elements of a world. The main notions and principles of granular computing, though under different names, have appeared in many related fields, such as programming, artificial intelligence, divide and conquer, interval computing, quantization, data compression, chunking, cluster analysis, rough set theory, quotient space theory, belief functions, machine learning, databases, and many others (Zadeh, 1998; Hu et al., 2005; Zhang & Lin, 2006). In current years, granular computing played an important position in bioinformatics, e-Business, security, machine learning, data mining, high-performance computing and wireless mobile computing in terms of efficiency, effectiveness, robustness and structured representation of uncertainty (Yao & Yao, 2002, 2002; Bargiela & Pedrycz, 2006).

Though extensive work has been done on granular computing, different researchers have various understanding on granular computing. Zadeh considers granular computing as a basis for computing with words. (Zadeh, 1997, 1998, 2006). Yao views granular computing as a triangle: structured thinking in the philosophical viewpoint, structured problem solving in the methodological viewpoint and structured information processing in the computational viewpoint (Yao, 2005, 2007). Bargiella and Pedrycz call attention to essential features of granular computing: the semantically transformation of information in the process of granulation and the non-computational verification of information abstractions (Bargiela, Pedrycz, & Hirota, 2004; Bargiela, Pedrycz, & Tanaka, 2004; Bargiela & Pedrycz, 2005, 2006).

Granular computing is a conceptual framework for data mining (Wang, 2006, 2007). The process of data mining is a transformation of knowledge in different granularities. In general, the original data is not understandable for human. That is because data is a representation of knowledge in the finest granularity. Human is sensitive with data in a coarser granularity. Thus, the process of data mining is to transform the data from a finer granularity to a coarser granularity. Also, it is variable to different problems how coarse a granularity is suitable. As well, the uncertainty of knowledge hiding in information cannot be changed in the process of transformation.

3 Fuzzy Set Theory and Rough Set Theory

Theories of fuzzy set (Zadeh, 1965) and rough set (Pawlak, 1982), as two important computing pattern of granular computing, are both simplifications of classical set theory for modeling ambiguity and dubiety, which is a key issue in data mining.

3.1 Fuzzy Set Theory

The notion of fuzzy set theory provides a convenient tool for representing vague concepts by allowing partial memberships.

In classical set theory, an object either is in a set or is not. That is:

$$A(x) = \begin{cases} 1 & x \in A \\ 0 & x \notin A \end{cases}$$

An object can partially belong to a set in fuzzy set. Formally, consider a fuzzy set A, its domain D, and an object x. The membership function μ specifies the degree of membership of x in A, such that $\mu_A(x) := D \rightarrow [0, 1]$.

In Figure 1, it means x does not belong to A when $\mu_A(x) = 0$, whereas it means x completely belongs to A when $\mu_A(x) = 1$. Intermediate values represent varying degree of membership, such as, $\mu_A(10) = 0.5$.

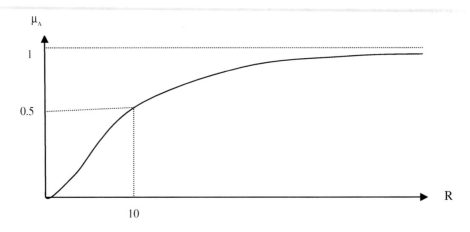

Fig. 1. The membership function $\mu_A(x)$ of x in fuzzy set A

The theory of fuzzy set provides an effective means for describing the behavior of systems which are too complex or ill-defined to be correctly analyzed using classical methods and tools. It has shown enormous promise in handling uncertainties to a reasonable extent, particularly in decision-making models under different kinds of risks, uncertainty and vagueness. Extensive applications of fuzzy set theory to various fields, e.g., control systems, expert system, pattern recognition, and image processing, have already been well established.

3.2 Rough Set Theory

The theory of rough set is motivated by practical needs to interpret, represent, characterize and process indiscernible of human. Defining concept X with the use of a finite vocabulary of information granules include lower bound (approximation) and upper bound (approximation). Lower approximation is $X_- = \{A_i \mid A_i \subset X\}$ and upper approximation is $X^- = \{A_i \mid A_i \cap X \neq \phi\}$. Also, accuracy of approximation is $\alpha(X) = \frac{X_-}{X^-}$.

In figure2, the upper and lower approximations shown for A_i set. U is a non-empty finite set of objects, called universe, A is a non-empty finite set of attributes.

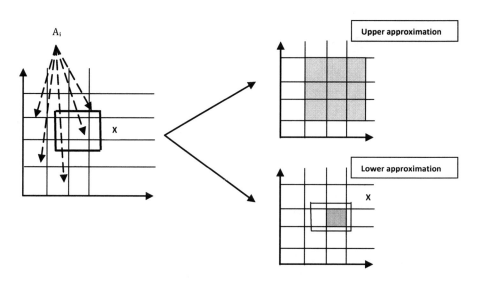

Fig. 2. Rough Sets; Upper and Lower Approximations

Rough set theory provides a systematic technique for representing and processing unclear concepts caused by imperceptible in situations with incomplete information or a lack of knowledge. In the past years, many successful applications can be found in various fields, such as process control, medical diagnosis, biochemistry, biology, economics, chemistry psychology, conflict analysis, emotion recognition, video retrieval, and so on.

To sum up, fuzzy set and rough set adopt different methods to address the boundary of an uncertain set. Fuzzy set uses imprecise method, but rough set uses classical precise method.

4   Granular Computing Based Data Mining

In granular computing, there are two important issues. One is the construction of granules, and the other is the computation with granules. Rough set uses equivalence relation to division the universe into a granular space. However, it is difficult to define an equivalence relation in an incomplete information system. So, it is required to extend the classical rough set theory to non-equivalence relation. Different from an equivalence relation, a non-equivalence relation induces a covering of the world. So, studying the covering based granular computing is significant. In addition, developing more efficient algorithms and increasing the generalization ability of knowledge are another two important issues in data mining.

Usually, the decision table to be processed is without any missing values or unknown values with each attribute, and many traditional data mining methods can only be applied to these cases, such as the classical rough set theory. But, due to inaccurate data measuring, inadequate comprehension or the limitation of acquiring information and so on, data systems with missing values or unknown values, called incomplete information systems, are really unavoidable in knowledge acquisition. In order to process incomplete data systems with rough set theory, two kinds of approaches were developed. One is filling the missing information, and then using the classical rough set theory to process it, but it may change the original information. The other is extending the classical rough set model to process incomplete information systems directly. Based on this idea, several extended rough set models are developed.

5 Conclusion

In this paper, a new understanding of data mining is introduced. Furthermore, its relationship with granular computing is analyzed. From the view of granular computing, data mining could be considered as a process of transforming the knowledge from a thin granularity to a huge granularity. Fuzzy set and rough set and are two important computing patterns of granular computing. For their facility in processing vague data, they were often used in data mining. Some purposes of granular computing in data mining are introduced in the views of fuzzy set and rough set. Though several problems in data mining have been partial solved by fuzzy set theory and rough set theory, there are some problems needed to be more studied.

Fuzzy set theory and rough set theory are two important expansion of classical set theory. The classical rough set theory is based on an equivalence relation, which restricts its application field. Although some extended rough set models have been proposed to process an incomplete information system, any one of them is developed for a special case. Therefore, fuzzy set theory and rough set theory were combined to get a supple way in processing an incomplete information system.

Acknowledgment. This publication is supported by a research grant (Research university grant) from Universiti Technologi Malaysia (UTM).

References

1. Calegari, S., Ciucci, D.: Granular computing applied to ontologies. International Journal of Approximate Reasoning 51(4), 391–409 (2010)
2. Herbert, J.P., Yao, J.: A granular computing framework for self-organizing maps. Neurocomputing 72(13-15), 2865–2872 (2009)

3. Lin, T.Y.: Introduction to special issues on data mining and granular computing. International Journal of Approximate Reasoning 40(1-2), 1–2 (2005)
4. Liu, H., Xiong, S., Fang, Z.: FL-GrCCA: A granular computing classification algorithm based on fuzzy lattices. Computers & Mathematics with Applications 61(1), 138–147 (2011)
5. Ma, J.M., Zhang, W.X., Leung, Y., Song, X.X.: Granular computing and dual Galois connection. Information Sciences 177(23), 5365–5377 (2007)
6. Pal, S.K., Shankar, B.U., Mitra, P.: Granular computing, rough entropy and object extraction. Pattern Recognition Letters 26(16), 2509–2517 (2005)
7. Panoutsos, G., Mahfouf, M.: A neural-fuzzy modelling framework based on granular computing: Concepts and applications. Fuzzy Sets and Systems 161(21), 2808–2830 (2010)
8. Qiu, T.-R., Liu, Q., et al.: A Granular Computing Approach to Knowledge Discovery in Relational Databases. Acta Automatica Sinica 35(8), 1071–1079 (2009)
9. Wang, D.W., Liau, C.J., Hsu, T.S.: Medical privacy protection based on granular computing. Artificial Intelligence in Medicine 32(2), 137–149 (2004)
10. Yeung, D., Wang, X., Chen, D.: Preface: Recent advances in granular computing. Information Sciences 178(16), 3161–3162 (2008)

Power Properties of Linearity and Long Memory Tests: A Simulation Study

Heri Kuswanto[1] and Philipp Sibbertsen[2]

[1] Department of Statistics,
Institut Teknologi Sepuluh Nopember, Surabaya, Indonesia
heri_k@statistika.its.ac.id
[2] Institute of Statistics, Leibniz Hannover University,
Hannover, Germany

Abstract. We show that specific long memory which is common in internet traffic data can hardly be distinguished from nonlinear time series model such as Markov switching by standard methods such as the GPH estimator for the memory parameter or linearity tests. We show by Monte Carlo that under certain conditions, the nonlinear data generating process can have misleading either stationary or non-stationary long memory properties.

Keywords: Nonlinear models, internet traffic, long - range dependencies.

1 Introduction

Long memory attracts attention among practical and theoretical communication technology in the recent years. In data communication network it is mainly applied to model the dynamic of the internet (ethernet) traffic data. The presence of long memory in internet traffic data has been well documented in many literatures such as [1], [2], [3], [4], [5] among others. However, so far it is not clear whether the evidence of long-range dependencies in the data is due to a real long memory or whether it is because of other phenomena such as nonlinearity. Recent works (mostly in econometrics) show that structural instability may produce spurious evidence of long memory. This phenomena can be observed also in internet traffic modeling as both long memory and nonlinear models are frequently applied to the traffic data. Diebold and Inoue [6] show that stochastic regime switching can easily be confused with long memory. Davidson and Sibbertsen [7] prove that the aggregation of processes with structural breaks converges to a long memory process. For an overview about the problem of misspecifying structural breaks and long-range dependence see [9]. Whereas these papers consider regime switching in the sense of a structural break in the mean of the process there can be many other ways of regime switching leading to the various nonlinear models such as Markov switching which is considered in this paper. Carrasco [10] shows that simply testing for structural breaks might lead to a wrong usage of linear models although the true data generating process is a nonlinear Markov Switching model.

A. Abd Manaf et al. (Eds.): ICIEIS 2011, Part II, CCIS 252, pp. 630–640, 2011.

Granger and Ding [11] pointed out that there are a number of processes which can also exhibit long memory, including generalized fractionally integrated models arising from aggregation, time changing coefficient models and nonlinear models as well. Granger and Tersvirta [12] demonstrate that by using the fractional difference test of [13], a simple nonlinear time series model, which is basically a sign model, generates an autocorrelation structure which could easily be mistaken to be long memory.

In this paper, we examine specific nonlinear time series model which is short memory and show by Monte Carlo that it can hardly be distinguished from long memory by standard methodology. In order to do this we estimate the long memory parameter by applying the [13] (further on denoted by GPH) estimator to the nonlinear Markov switching model. It turns out that not accounting for the nonlinear structure will bias the GPH estimator and give evidence of long memory. On the other hand we generate linear long memory time series and apply linearity test to this. We apply the general Tersvirta's Neural Network test of [14]. It turns out that the test cannot correctly specify the linear structure of the long memory process. The test is biased towards a rejection of linearity. As a result nonlinearity Markov Switching and long-range dependence are two phenomena which can easily be misspecified and standard methodology is not able to distinguish between these phenomena.

This paper is organized as follows. Section 2 presents briefly the concept of long memory, an overview of the nonlinear time series model used in this paper is given in section 3. The results of our Monte Carlo study are presented in section 4 and 5 and section 6 concludes.

2 Long Memory, GPH Estimator and Rescaled Variance Test

Long memory or long-range dependence means that observations far away from each other are still strongly correlated. A stationary time series $Y_t, t = 1, \ldots, T$ exhibits long memory or long-range dependence when the correlation function $\rho(k)$ behaves for $k \to \infty$ as

$$\lim_{k \to \infty} \frac{\rho(k)}{c_\rho k^{2d-1}} = 1 \tag{1}$$

Here c_ρ is a constant and $d \in (0, 0.5)$ denotes the long memory parameter. The correlation of a long memory process decays slowly that is with a hyperbolic rate. For $d \in (-0.5, 0)$ the process has short memory. In this situation the spectral density is zero at the origin and the process is said to be anti-persistent. For $d \in (0.5, 1)$ the process is non-stationary but still mean reverting. Further discussion about long memory can be found for example in [15].

A popular semi-parametric procedure of estimating the memory parameter d is the GPH estimator introduced by [13]. It is based on the first m periodogram ordinates

$$I_j = \frac{1}{2\pi N} |\sum_{t-1}^{N} Y_t \exp(i\lambda_j t)|^2 \tag{2}$$

where $\lambda_j = 2\pi j/N$, $j = 1, \ldots, m$ and m is a positive integer smaller than N. The idea is to estimate the spectral density by the periodogram and to take the logarithm on both sides of the equation. This gives a linear regression model in the memory parameter which can be estimated by least squares.

The estimator is given by $-1/2$ times the least squares estimator of the slope parameter in the regression of $\{\log I_j : j = 1, \ldots, m\}$ on a constant and the regressor variable

$$X_j = \log|1 - \exp(-i\lambda_j)| = \frac{1}{2}\log(2 - 2\cos\lambda_j). \tag{3}$$

By definition the GPH estimator is

$$\hat{d}_{GPH} = \frac{-0.5\sum_{j=1}^{m}(X_j - \bar{X})\log I_j}{\sum_{j=1}^{m}(X_j - \bar{X})^2} \tag{4}$$

where $\bar{X} = \frac{1}{m}\sum_{j=1}^{m} X_j$. This estimator can be motivated using the model:

$$\log I_j = \log c_f - 2dX_j + \log \xi_j \tag{5}$$

where X_j denotes the j-th Fourier frequency and the ξ_j are identically distributed error variables with $-E[\log \xi_j] = 0.577$, known as Euler constant. Besides simplicity another advantage of the GPH-estimator is that it does not require a knowledge about further short-range dependencies in the underlying process. Referring to [16] to get the optimal MSE, we include $N^{0.8}$ frequencies in the regression equation.

As an alternative to the GPH estimator we also apply a nonparametric V/S test proposed by [17] to the series. It tests the short memory process under null hypothesis against alternative of long memory process. The V/S statistic has better power properties than either the R/S statistic by [18] or the modified R/S of [19]. Defining $S_k^* = \sum_{j=1}^{k}(X_j - \bar{X})$ as the partial sums of the observations with the sample variance $\widehat{Var}(S_1^*, \ldots, S_N^*) = N^{-1}\sum_{j=1}^{N}(S_j^* - \bar{S}_N^*)^2$, the V/S statistic is given by

$$Q_N = N^{-1}\frac{\widehat{Var}(S_1^*, \ldots, S_N^*)}{\hat{s}_{N,q}^2} \tag{6}$$

with

$$\hat{s}_{N,q}^2 = \frac{1}{N}\sum_{j=1}^{N}(X_j - \bar{X}_N)^2 + 2\sum_{j=1}^{q}\omega_j(q)\hat{\gamma}_j. \tag{7}$$

$\omega_j(q) = 1 - \frac{j}{q+1}$ are the Bartlett weights. The classical R/S statistic of [18] corresponds to $q = 0$. We consider the statistic for several different values of q including the optimal q proposed by [8].

3   Markov Switching Process

Nonlinear time series models have become popular in recent years and are widely used in modeling internet traffic data. This paper analyzes a type of models that is commonly used in nonlinear modeling particularly in modeling the dynamic of the internet traffic series i.e Markov switching models. This model shares the property of being mean reverting with a long memory process and also mimics the persistence of long range dependent models by exhibiting only short-range dependencies. Therefore, this model is natural candidates to be misspecified with long memory. In the following the model is briefly introduced.

The regime switching model we consider in this paper are Markov switching models developed by [20]. In this model class, nonlinearities arise as discrete shifts between the regimes. Most importantly these shifts are breaks in the mean of the process. By permitting switching between regimes, in which the dynamic behavior of series is markedly different, more complex dynamic patterns can be described.

The general form of the model is given by

$$y_t = \mu_{s_t} + \mathbf{X_t}\phi_{s_t} + a_t \tag{8}$$

where $\mathbf{X_t} = (y_{t-1}, y_{t-2}, ..., y_{t-p})$, ϕ_{s_t} is the p x1 vector of AR coefficients , a_t follows $N(0, \sigma_{s_t}^2)$ and s_t is an m-state Markov chain taking values $1, \ldots, m$, with transition matrix P.

The switching mechanism is controlled by an unobservable state variable that follows a first order Markov chain. Thus, the probability that the state variable s_t equals some particular value j depends on the past only through the most recent value s_{t-1}:

$$P\{s_t = j | s_{t-1} = i, s_{t-2} = k, \ldots\} = P\{s_t = j | s_{t-1} = i\} = p_{ij} \tag{9}$$

The transition probability p_{ij} gives the probability that state i will be followed by step j.

Investigating whether nonlinear models can be misspecified as long memory contains two steps. First, we show that nonlinearity leads to a bias in estimators for the memory parameter. Second, we show that standard linearity test reject the null of a linear process when the data exhibits long-range dependence.

4   Testing for Long Memory

In this section, we simulate various data generating processes from the above nonlinear time series model, apply the V/S test and estimate the long memory parameter. The nonlinear model considered in our Monte Carlo study is

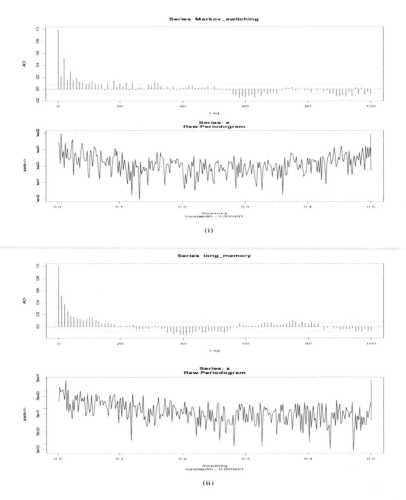

Fig. 1. Sample periodograms and ACF plots (i) Markov switching process (ii) Long memory with $d = 0.391$

stationary and short-range dependent. The autoregressive order is chosen to be one. The model is simulated with 1000 replications and different sample sizes of $N = 250$ and $N = 600$ after discarding the first 200 observations to minimize the effect of the initial value of the simulated series. The error terms are modeled to be $NID(0, 1)$.

This procedure is used to investigate whether the considered short memory nonlinear model could be detected as to exhibit long memory. We apply the V/S test to the models and compute the rejection probabilities. When applying the V/S test we do this for several values of $q = 0, 5, 10, 25$ and the q following [8]. They are denoted by q_1, q_2, q_3, q_4 and q_5 respectively. It should be kept in mind when interpreting the simulation results below that by construction of the V/S - test the rejection probability decreases for an increasing value of q.

We investigate the behavior of the GPH estimator when the true DGP is a Markov switching model. The DGP in this section is simulated based on the general Markov switching process:

$$y_t = \begin{cases} \phi_1 y_{t-1} + a_t \text{ if } s_t = 1 \\ \phi_2 y_{t-1} + a_t \text{ if } s_t = 2 \end{cases} \tag{10}$$

with $u_t \sim NID(0, 1)$.

We set $\phi_1 = -\phi_2$ in all of our simulations in order to generate a stationary nonlinear process. The transition probabilities are taken from [20], which are $P = (0.1, 0.25, 0.75, 0.9)$.

Table 1. Rejection probabilities of the V/S test for Markov switching processes

$\phi_1 = -\phi_2$	N=250					N=600				
	q_1	q_2	q_3	q_4	q_5	q_1	q_2	q_3	q_4	q_5
0.1	0.065	0.041	0.03	0.008	0.045	0.064	0.052	0.045	0.037	0.047
0.2	0.109	0.047	0.034	0.007	0.047	0.12	0.066	0.057	0.041	0.049
0.3	0.147	0.05	0.034	0.009	0.038	0.128	0.062	0.05	0.038	0.059
0.4	0.227	0.062	0.039	0.009	0.048	0.229	0.088	0.067	0.038	0.058
0.5	0.306	0.077	0.046	0.006	0.037	0.321	0.099	0.068	0.049	0.083
0.6	0.431	0.116	0.067	0.015	0.041	0.462	0.121	0.079	0.056	0.095
0.7	0.551	0.138	0.055	0.008	0.05	0.607	0.177	0.108	0.069	0.099
0.8	0.723	0.175	0.087	0.013	0.052	0.759	0.196	0.101	0.05	0.157
0.9	0.873	0.3	0.137	0.019	0.03	0.893	0.35	0.172	0.069	0.174

From Table 1 we see that the V/S rejection rate increases with increasing the parameters in almost cases. However, the rejection probabilities for q_5 are relatively higher and reach 0.174 for a sample size of $N = 600$.

The GPH estimator is biased towards stationary long memory and increases with the autoregressive parameter but with a relatively slow rate. However, the

Table 2. GPH estimator for Markov switching processes

$\phi_1 = -\phi_2$	$N = 250$		$N = 600$	
	d	$t - stat$	d	$t - stat$
0.1	0.024	11.871*	0.015	10.281*
0.2	0.058	27.790*	0.044	28.647*
0.3	0.090	40.437*	0.082	52.273*
0.4	0.123	51.219*	0.127	79.053*
0.5	0.158	61.040*	0.183	112.041*
0.6	0.195	70.967*	0.240	144.956*
0.7	0.232	80.574*	0.313	179.855*
0.8	0.269	91.512*	0.391	214.038*
0.9	0.304	97.464*	0.477	249.671*

bias increases with the sample size for a very small. These results therefore confirm [21] who shows that the GPH estimator is substantially biased for a stationary Markov switching process which does not contain long memory.

To investigate the impact of the transition probabilities to the GPH estimator, we consider another Markov process by considering the various P values given above and the parameter setting $\phi_1 = -\phi_2 = 0.9$. We use this autoregressive parameter, since it leads to a higher bias of the GPH estimator and therefore shows the relevant effect more clearly. Table 2 presents the results for the considered process.

Table 3. GPH estimator for the Markov switching process

$p_{11} = p_{22}$	$N = 250$		$N = 600$	
	d	$t - stat$	d	$t - stat$
0.1	-0.136	-61.264	-0.444	-223.591
0.2	-0.109	-45.272	-0.331	-156.937
0.3	-0.070	-27.990	-0.221	-102.034
0.4	-0.043	-16.533	-0.117	-52.100
0.5	-0.006	-2.408	-0.008	-3.733
0.6	0.034	11.958*	0.100	43.945*
0.7	0.076	26.163*	0.223	100.850*
0.8	0.120	39.935*	0.345	150.018*
0.9	0.173	58.814*	0.480	198.999*

Note that when $p_{11} = p_{22} = 0.5$ it implies that $p_{11} + p_{22} = 1$ and thus there is no persistence in the Markov process because the probability that s_t switches from state 1 to state 2 is independent of the previous state. This is a rather simple switching model. From Table 3 we see that for some values of the transition probabilities above 0.5 (close to one), they are biased towards stationary long memory and the process is detected as to be short memory when the transition probability is less than 0.5. It is natural since as the parameters approach the non-ergodicity point (when p_{11} and p_{22} are equal one), the AR component gets more persistent and causes the dominant component of the GPH bias (see [21] for details).

Similar to the other nonlinear models, periodogram which is generated from the Markov Switching model does not show much difference than those of the true long memory process (see Fig.1). On the other hand we see that the ACF of the Markov switching model does not decay as slow as the true long memory process.

From the above results, we come to the conclusion that although the process under the null is nonlinear but still a short memory process, the above results for the V/S test are consistent with [19] and [17], where the probability to reject the short memory null hypothesis is lower for large q, since the imprecision with which the higher order autocovariances can introduce considerable noise into the statistic is reduced. The classical R/S test fails to identify the short memory properties. The Andrews procedure also reject the null relatively often and might reach a probability of more than 5%.

The GPH estimator, which is also quiet popular as a semi-parametric procedure to detect long memory fails to distinguish the considered nonlinear processes from long range dependencies. Most of the processes are biased towards long memory. The periodogram of nonlinear and long memory processes behave quite similar near the origin. Thus, we can say that by these quite common tests, it is difficult to distinguish between nonlinearity and long memory. Long memory tests as well as point estimates can lead to a misleading inference. However, using a higher lag order in the V/S test gives more reliable results.

5   Linearity Tests

In this section we apply a general linearity test, namely the Neural Network test of [14]. This test is a special neural network model with a single hidden layer. This test is a Lagrange Multiplier (LM) type test derived from a neural network model based on the "dual" of the Volterra expansion representation for nonlinear series. We compute the rejection probabilities of the 5% significance level with 10000 replications and various sample sizes $N = 100, 500, 1000$ and 1500.

Let consider Fig. 2 for the results of this test. For a pure long memory DGP as well as for an ARFIMA $(\phi, d, 0)$ - process with a small autoregressive parameter $(\phi = 0.2)$, the values of the rejection probability increase with d and with the sample size. For an increasing autoregressive parameter the rejection probability collapses under the nominal size of the test and converges to zero. Since the test is Lagrange multiplier test, which involves the estimation of the autoregressive parameter to compute the statistic, the higher AR and d parameter are confounded as a simple AR(1) parameter. This leads to a higher sum of squared errors (SSE_0) in the denominator and the statistic tends to not reject the null hypothesis.

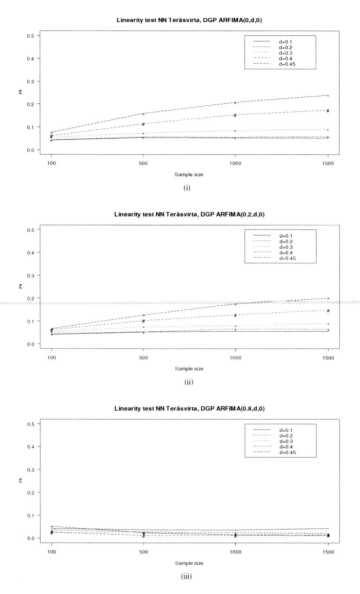

Fig. 2. Rejection probabilities of linearity test against Markov switching model (i) DGP is ARFIMA(0,d,0),(ii) DGP is ARFIMA(0.2,d,0) and (iii) DGP is ARFIMA(0.8,d,0)

6 Conclusion

In this paper we show by Monte Carlo that popular nonlinear model such as Markov switching models can easily be misspecified as long memory. We estimate the memory parameter for various specifications of the above models and find that the GPH estimator is positively biased indicating long-range dependence. However, applying the V/S test with an optimal lag-length as suggested by [8] seems to give reasonable results. On the other hand do linearity tests reject the null hypothesis of linearity when the true data generating process exhibits long memory with a rejection probability tending to one. The rejection probabilities increase with the memory parameter. However, a strong autoregressive root can collapse the rejection probabilities. Therefore, nonlinear models can easily be misspecified as long-range dependence and vice versa by using standard methodology.

References

1. Leland, W.E., Taqqu, M.S., Willinger, W., Wilson, D.V.: On the self-similar nature of ethernet traffic (extended version). ACM/IEEE Transactions on Networking 2(1), 1–15 (1994)
2. Karagianis, T., Molle, M., Faloutsos, M.: Long range dependence: ten years of internet traffic modeling. IEEE Internet Computing 8(5), 57–64 (2004)
3. Scherrer, A., Larrieu, N., Owezarski, P., Borgnat, P., Abry, P.: Non-Gaussian and long memory statistical characteristisation for internet traffic with anomalies. IEEE Transaction on Dependeable and Secure Computing (2006)
4. Brown, M.R., Bagocka, B.: WWW traffic data measure and its application. Intelegent Data Analysis 11(2), 137–154 (2007)
5. Song, L., Bordan, P.: A local stationary long memory model for internet traffic. In: Proceeding of 17th European Signal Processing Conference, Glasgow (2009)
6. Dieblod, F.X., Inoue, A.: Long memory and regime switching. Journal of Econometrics 105, 131–159 (2001)
7. Davidson, J., Sibbertsen, P.: Generating scheme for long memory process: Regimes, Aggregation and linearity. Journal of Econometrics 127(2) (2005)
8. Andrews, D.: Heteroskedasticity and autocorrelation consistent covariance matrix estimation. Econometrica 59, 817–858 (1991)
9. Sibbertsen, P.: Long-memory versus structural change: An overview. Statistical Papers 45, 465–515 (2004)
10. Carrasco, M.: Misspecifed structural change, threshold, and markov-switching models. Journal of Econometrics 109, 239–273 (2002)
11. Granger, C.W.J., Ding, Z.: Varieties of long memory models. Journal of Econometrics 73, 61–77 (1996)
12. Granger, C.W.J., Tersvirta, T.: Asimple nonlinear time series model with misleading linear properties. Economics Letters 62, 161–165 (1999)
13. Geweke, J., Porter-Hudak, S.: The estimation and application of long memory time series models. Journal of Time Series Analysis 4, 221–238 (1983)
14. Tersvirta, T., Lin, C.F., Granger, C.W.: Power of the neural network linearity test. Journal of Time Series Analysis 14(2), 209–220 (1993)
15. Beran, J.: Statistics for long memory processes. Chapman & Hall, New York (1994)

16. Hurst, H.: Long-term storage capacity of reservoirs. Transactions of the American Society of Civil Engineers 116, 770–808 (1951)
17. Giraitis, L., Kokoszka, P., Leipus, R., Teyssiere, G.: Rescaled variance and related tests for long memory in volatility and levels. Journal of Econometrics 112, 265–294 (2003)
18. Mandelbrot, B.B., Wallis, J.M.: Robustness of the rescaled range R/S in the measurement of noncyclic long run statistical dependence. Water Resources Research 5, 967–988 (1969)
19. Lo, A.: Long term memory in stock market prices. Econometrica 59, 1279–1313 (1991)
20. Hamilton, J.D.: A new approach to the economic analysis of nonstationary time series and the business cycle. Econometrica 57, 357–384 (1989)
21. Smith, A.: Why regime switching creates the illusion of long memory. Department of Agriculture and Resource Economics, University of California, Davis, mimeo (2005)

A Self Acting Initial Seed Selection Algorithm for K-means Clustering Based on Convex-Hull

S.M. Shahnewaz[1], Md. Asikur Rahman[2], and Hasan Mahmud[1]

[1] Department of Computer Science and Information Technology (CIT),
Islamic University of Technology (IUT), Dhaka, Bangladesh
{shawncit,hasan}@iut-dhaka.edu
[2] Memorial University of Newfoundland (MUN),
Computer Science, St. John's, NL,
A1B 3X5, Canada
asikur.rahman@mun.ca

Abstract. The classic k-means algorithm and its variations are sensitive to the choice of starting points and always get stuck at local optimal values. In this paper, we have presented a self-acting initial seed selection algorithm for k-means clustering which estimates the density information of input points based on the theory of convex-hulls. To reach into the core of actual clusters, we successively exploit the convex-hull vertices of given input set to construct new intermediate cluster centres. We also introduce a cluster merging technique which amalgamates the similar clusters to avoid getting stuck at local optimal values. Results of numerical experiments on synthetic and benchmark (*iris* and *ruspini*) datasets demonstrate that proposed algorithm is more efficient in terms of number of true cluster, purity and normalized information gain than the classic k-means algorithm. Thus, the feasibility of our algorithm in two dimensional space was validated.

Keywords: Clustering, K-means algorithm, Convex-hull.

1 Introduction

Clustering is a popular data analysis method and plays a momentous role in data mining. Now-a-days it has been widely applied in various fields, like web mining, pattern recognition, artificial intelligence, spatial database analysis, and so on. Clustering analysis is a kind of unsupervised learning method that groups a set of data objects into clusters. In this paper we have considered the partitioned clustering method. Because of the simplicity and efficiency, the classic K-means algorithm is the most popular partition clustering method. Though the K-means algorithm is widely used in many engineering applications including market segmentation, computer vision, geostatistics and astronomy to find a starting configuration, but it is very sensitive to initialization; the better initial centres we choose the better results we get. Much work has been done to find an optimal value for the initial seeds. To formulate the problem we have reviewed the main known methods for selecting initial centres of K-means algorithm.

A. Abd Manaf et al. (Eds.): ICIEIS 2011, Part II, CCIS 252, pp. 641–650, 2011.
© Springer-Verlag Berlin Heidelberg 2011

In Forgy Approach as written in [1], K instances are chosen randomly from the database and used as the seeds. In this approach it is assumed that centres will be chosen from the region where the highest density of points is located. But, there is no guarantee that we will not choose two centres from a single cluster. Likas et al. [2] presents a global K-means algorithm which aims to gradually increase the number of seeds until K is found. A recent Cluster Centre Initialization Method (CCIA) [3] based on Density-based Multi Scale Data Condensation (DBMSDC) [4] estimates the density information of data at a point and sorts the data according to their density. Finally, the author chooses the initial seeds from the list, which have the radius inversely proportional to the density of that point. Another k'-means clustering algorithm [5] is proposed recently that determine the value of K by minimizing a suggested cost function. The cost function has been determined based on the idea that the areas with dense samples strongly attract the centres. Different initialization method also has been discussed in [6], [7], [8] and [9]. But still there is no algorithm that can guess the exact value of K.

In this paper, we propose a new algorithm for k-means clustering which estimates the density information of input points based on the theory of convex-hulls. The new algorithm is able to avoid getting stuck at local optimal values as well as avoid the randomness of selecting initial cluster centre to detect the actual cluster. The rest of the paper is laid out as follows. Section 2 introduces the significance of convex-hull in cluster centre revelation. In Section 3, our new algorithm, Convex-hull Based K-means Clustering Algorithm is presented. Section 4 and 5 explains the datasets and the experimental results respectively. Finally, Section 6 summarizes the study and concludes.

2   Significance of Convex-Hull in Cluster Centre Revelation

In mathematics, convex-hull of a set of points is the minimal convex set that includes all the points. For a given two dimensional finite input set, the convex-hull is a convex polygon which detects the boundary region. We have the reason to believe that, if there exists some closely distributed points in convex hull vertices then the probability of having a cluster boundary with those points is higher. The typical edge point of the distributed dataset is the vertex convex-hull and initial cluster centre of the boundary clusters is chosen only from the closely distributed, convex-hull vertices.

In order to detect the inner cluster centres, we remove the points; those are already distributed among outer clusters. As a result, given problem space gets condensed and the obligation of exhaustive search is eliminated. Convex-hull vertices returned for the condensed input set have higher probability to touch the inner clusters. So our hypothesis of choosing initial cluster centre based on closely distributed convex-hull points has its basis. Once, we get the initial cluster centre, next we shift the initial centre into the actual core of the cluster with mean value of the assigned points of that cluster. Therefore, we apply the cluster merging technique to amalgamate the similar clusters, in order to guess the correct value of K and their initial centres for K-means algorithm.

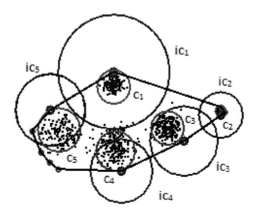

Fig. 1. Screen shoot of the 1st iteration of our proposed algorithm; clusters based on first convex-hull

To illustrate the significance of convex-hull, we use Fig-1 that demonstrates the result of first iteration of our proposed algorithm where initial cluster centre of intermediate clusters (ic$_1$, ic$_2$, ic$_3$, ic$_4$ and ic$_5$) are selected from the closely distributed convex-hull vertices. Finally, based on the distributed points of each intermediate clusters, we updates the centres and form the final clusters denoted by c$_1$, c$_2$, c$_3$, c$_4$, and c$_5$; which are almost at the core of actual clusters.

3   Convex-Hull Based Seed Selection Algorithm

3.1   Description of the Algorithm

Consider, a set of data points P is given in an m dimensional space, where p_j is the jth element of that set. A temporary copy of the input set P is required to calculate the intermediate cluster, which is denoted by TP. We denote the cluster set with C, which is initially empty. To choose the initial seeds of K-means algorithm, in the next step, we call the procedure *SelectIntermediateCluster* with a reference of temporary input set TP and denote the returned value with $C°$. Then, inside the *SelectIntermediateCluster* procedure; we must calculate the set of convex-hull points of TP, which is denoted by H. h_i denote the ith element of H. We denote the Euclidian distance between any convex-hull point and its neighbor with $d(h_i, h_{i+1})$. With the following equation we calculate the average distance among all pair of neighboring points present in H.

$$avg_{i=1.x}[d(h_i, h_{i+1})] \tag{1}$$

A subset of H with greater distances than $avg_{i=1.x}$ is used to construct the intermediate cluster centres. $c_k^{°c}$ denote the centre of the kth intermediate cluster. This process ensures that initial cluster centre is well distributed among the input data set P. To calculate the radius of an intermediate cluster, we choose half of the minimum distance between two neighbors of that intermediate cluster and express it as

$$c_k^{\circ r} = \min\left[d\left(c_k^{\circ c}, c_{k+1}^{\circ c}\right), d\left(c_k^{\circ c}, c_{k-1}^{\circ c}\right)\right] / 2 \tag{2}$$

Next, $c_k^{\circ p}$ denote the set of points distributed to k^{th} intermediate cluster. We select the elements of $c_k^{\circ p}$ from TP, those has less distance with cluster centre $c_k^{\circ c}$ than the cluster radius $c_k^{\circ r}$.

Based on the distribution of points in k^{th} intermediate cluster c_k°, we calculate the new cluster centre $c_k^{\circ c}$ with the mean value of $c_k^{\circ p}$. This mean value shift the centre of the intermediate cluster into the actual core of the cluster from the convex-hull region. Then, we remove $c_k^{\circ p}$ from TP to accelerate the next step of the algorithm. Finally, we store the first intermediate clusters into the empty cluster set C.

At this stage, again we invoke $SelectIntermediateCluster$ procedure to get the second intermediate cluster set C' for temporary input set TP. In the next step, we try to merge the newly generated intermediate clusters C' with previously generated cluster set C. In order to do this, we call the procedure $FindNearestCluster(C, c'_k)$ to obtain the nearest cluster c_k which has the minimum distance between two centres. If distance between c'^c_k and c^c_k is less than the radius of c_k then we merge those two cluster and c_k^p denote all points distributed to c_k and c'_k. We also, update the c_k^c and c_k^r accordingly. Otherwise, we add a new cluster c'_k into the cluster set C. We construct the intermediate cluster set C' until the value of TP is less than three. Ultimately, we construct the cluster set C that holds K cluster centres; those are applied to K-means algorithm to construct the final clusters. Our algorithm is summarized in Algorithm 1.

Algorithm 1. Convex-hull Based Seed Selection Algorithm

---

1.   *Initialization:*
     a.   *Let $P = \{p_j \mid j = 1, 2, \ldots., n\}$ a set of input points*
     b.   *Let $TP = P$, a copy of input data*
     c.   *Let $C = \phi$, a set of cluster, initially empty*
2. $C = SelectIntermediateCluster(TP)$
3.   *WHILE $|TP| > 2$*
     a. $C' = SelectIntermediateCluster(TP)$
     b. $C' = C' \cup C$
     c.   *For $k = 1$ to $|C'|$*
          i. $c_k = FindNearestCluster(C, c'_k)$, *where $c'_k \mathrel{!=} c_k$*
          ii. *if $d\left(c_k^c, c'^c_k\right) < c_k^r$*

          $$then\ c_k^p = c_k^p \cup c'^p_k, c_k^c = mean(c_k^p)\ and$$
          $$c_k^r = avg_{i=1\ldots x}[d(c_k^c, p_k^i)]$$

          else $C = C \cup \{c'_k\}$
4.   Return C.

$SelectIntermediateCluster(TP):$
1. $Let\ C^\circ = \phi, a\ set\ of\ intermediate\ cluster, initially\ empty$
2. $Let\ H = ConvexHull(TP), where\ H = \{h_i|\ i = 1,2,\ldots\ldots,x\}$
3. $C^\circ \subset H\ where\ c_k^{\circ c} = \{\ h_i|d(h_i,h_{i+1}) > avg_{i=1\ldots x}[d(h_i,h_{i+1})]\ \}$
4. $For\ k = 1\ to\ |C^\circ|$
    a. $c_k^{\circ r} = \min[d(c_k^{\circ c},c_{k+1}^{\circ c}),d(c_k^{\circ c},c_{k-1}^{\circ c})]/2$
    b. $c_k^{\circ p} \subset TP\ where\ c_k^{\circ p} = \{\ p_k^i|\ d(p_j,c_k^{\circ c}) < c_k^{\circ r}\ \}$
    c. $c_k^{\circ c} = mean(c_k^{\circ p})$
    d. $Remove\ c_k^{\circ p}\ from\ TP$
5. Return C°

---

4   Experimental Design

4.1   Synthetic Dataset

In order to measure the performance of our algorithm, we have used synthetic multivariate Gaussian dataset in 2D space. We construct each of our dataset with K Gaussian clusters; therefore we must choose the means and covariance matrices of each cluster. We used the interval $[-50, 50]$ to choose the mean m_k of the kth cluster, with a uniform probability. We have chosen n_k, number of points in each cluster, from a uniform random distribution over the interval $[50, 500]$. This large interval enables some clusters to contain up to 10 times more points than other clusters. Fig-2 shows two examples of 2 dimensional dataset with 5 and 10 clusters with different Gaussian distributions.

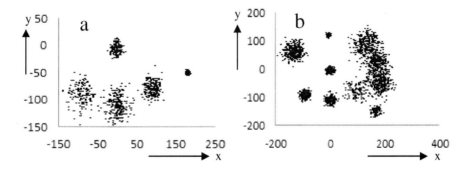

Fig. 2. Example plots of synthetic dataset (a) No. of cluster: 5, (b) No. of cluster: 10

4.2   Benchmark Dataset

In this research, performance of our algorithm was examined when applied to real world benchmark datasets. We use two real-world databases: one obtained from the UCI Machine learning repository [10] and another is a well-known benchmark dataset. Generally, in high dimensional data space, there are some difficulties when convex-hull is constructed. In our implementation we used Quickhull [11] algorithm to construct the convex-hull. Hence, we consider the convex-hull computation of high dimensional data space in our future work.

4.2.1 Iris Dataset

This data represents different categories of irises having four feature values. The sepal length, sepal width, petal length and the petal width in centimeters are the four features of *iris* dataset. It has three classes (with some overlap between class 2 and 3) with 50 samples per class. We chose two feature i.e. sepal length and petal length in our experiment.

4.2.2 Ruspini Dataset

The *ruspini* dataset is a popular benchmark problem in evaluating clustering methods. In statistics packages [12] it is incorporated as a built in data object. The dataset contains four classes and two features, where number of elements in each class is 23, 20, 17 and 15. This benchmark suits best in our experimental model because we considered only two dimensional space.

4.3 Metrics for Comparison

4.3.1 Purity

To measure of clustering algorithm *purity* is used as a simple and apparent evaluation method. In order to compute purity, each cluster is assigned to the class which is most frequent in the cluster, and then the accuracy of this assignment is measured by counting the number of correctly assigned points and dividing by total no of points n. Purity values close to 0 imply a bad clustering and a perfect clustering result has a purity of 1. We express it in equation 3.

$$purity(\Omega, C) = \frac{1}{n}\Sigma_k \, max_l |\omega_k \cap c_j| \qquad (3)$$

Where, $\Omega = \{\omega_1, \omega_2, ..., \omega_k\}$ is the set of clusters and $C = \{c_1, c_2, ..., c_k\}$ is the set of classes.

4.3.2 Normalized Information Gain

A qualitative performance measure of the clustering is that of information gain [13]. In the theory of Information gain, the concept of entropy is used as a measure of information. We let c_l denote the number of points in the class l, for $l = 1, 2 ... L$. $\Sigma_l^L c_l = n$ denote the total number of points in the dataset. To measure the average information in bits we use the following formula

$$EN_{Total} = -\sum_{l=1}^{L} \left(\frac{c_l}{n}\right) \log_2 \left(\frac{c_l}{n}\right) \qquad (4)$$

There are K clusters in the dataset and number of points in the kth cluster is n_k. We use c_l^k to denote the number of points belonging to each of the L classes, then the entropy of the kth cluster (EN_k) and Weighted Entropy(wEN) is expressed with

$$EN_k = - \sum_{l=1}^{L} \left(\frac{c_l^k}{n_k} \right) \log_2 \left(\frac{c_l^k}{n_k} \right) \tag{5}$$

$$wEN = \sum_{k=1}^{K} \left(\frac{n_k}{n} \right) EN_k \tag{6}$$

Finally, we define the Normalized Information Gain (NIG) as

$$NIG = \frac{EN_{Total} - wEN}{EN_{Total}} \tag{7}$$

If the value of $NIG = 0$ then no information is retrieved by the clustering, otherwise $NIG = 1$ means all information is retrieved.

5   Experimental Results

5.1   Synthetic Dataset

In Table-1, we present the results of the comparison between our proposed algorithm and k-means algorithm. We denote our proposed algorithm with *C-hull* and general K-means algorithm with *K-means*. To calculate the purity and NIG of K-means, we considered five runs of each setup and the average of those five runs was calculated because of the randomness of K-means algorithm. We have used actual total class as the value of K and randomly generate the initial cluster centres as the input of K-means algorithm.

Table 1. Results of synthetic dataset as described in sec 4.1

No. of Class	Input Size	Similarities In *C-hull*	Cluster *In C-hull*	Purity of *C-hull*	Purity of *K- means*	NIG of *C-hull*	NIG of *K-means*
5	1,182	1181	5	0.99	0.90	0.98	0.62
10	2,810	2728	11	0.97	0.86	0.82	0.55
15	3,172	2993	16	0.94	0.88	0.81	0.60
20	5,083	4991	20	0.93	0.85	0.80	0.53

Table-1 reflects that, performance of our algorithm is better than the classic K-means algorithm in each evaluation criteria. The value of NIG and purity near at 1ensures that initial seed selection was almost perfect. Hence, the number of cluster detected in two synthetic dataset is exactly equal to the number of classes present there. Constant better performance in dataset with different clusters ensures the robustness of the algorithm.

5.2 Benchmark Dataset

5.2.1 Iris Results

We summarize the result of our algorithm and K-means on *iris* data set in Table 2 and Fig 3.

Table 2. Result of real world dataset (iris) as described in sec 4.2.1

No. of Class	Input Size	Similarities In *C-hull*	Similarities In *K-means*	Cluster *In C-hull*	Purity of *C-hull*	Purity of *K-means*	NIG of *C-hull*	NIG of *K-means*
3	150	133	120	3	0.89	0.80	0.68	0.47

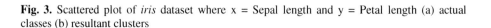

Fig. 3. Scattered plot of *iris* dataset where x = Sepal length and y = Petal length (a) actual classes (b) resultant clusters

Table-2 shows that our algorithm detects the exact 3 class of the *iris* dataset with a high purity and NIG value than classic K-means algorithm. Initial cluster centre was much accurate than randomly generated centres, which lead the K-means algorithm to identify 133 correct samples among 150 samples of *iris* dataset. Sometimes randomly generated initial centres aid the classic K-means to identify 133 samples correctly but not more than that. On the other hand, our proposed algorithm constantly provides the same result with 89% accuracy. The existence of two overlapping class of *iris* dataset degrades the NIG of both our proposed algorithm and classic K-means.

5.2.2 Ruspini Results

We summarize the result of our algorithm and K-means on *ruspini* data set in Table 3 and Fig 4.

Table 3. Result of benchmark dataset (*ruspini*) as described in sec 4.2.2

No. of Class	Input Size	Similarities In *C-hull*	Similarities In *K-means*	Cluster *In C-hull*	Purity of *C-hull*	Purity of *K-means*	NIG of *C-hull*	NIG of *K-means*
4	75	75	72	4	1.0	0.98	1.0	0.94

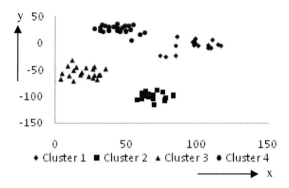

Fig. 4. Scattered plot of resultant clusters of *ruspini* benchmark dataset

Our algorithm persistently achieves 100% accuracy in *ruspini* dataset, which is better than the average purity and NIG of classic K-means. Fig-4 displays that *ruspini* dataset consists of 4 classes which are distributed in the boundary region and are correctly detected by our algorithm from the convex-hull vertices.

6   Discussion and Conclusions

Our new initial seed selection algorithm for K-means, use the full advantages of the theory of convex-hulls and overcomes the major drawbacks of K-means algorithm. Our main goal was to find an optimal value of K and their initial centres. In order to determine that, convex-hull helps to detect the boundary of a true cluster at any level of the input dataset, which lead us to an optimal value of K. From our analytical result, it is very evident that the number of detected clusters in every experiment is very close to the number of actual class presents there. It was very conspicuous that our algorithm is able to reveal the true clusters from the dataset and it does not stuck at local optima because of the cluster merging and forming technique. Hence, in this paper, we dealt with only two dimensional space and we believe our future work on multidimensional space will also provide much accurate result.

Acknowledgments. Thanks to Dr. Hasanul Kabir and to the anonymous reviewers for suggestions that improved the paper.

References

1. Anderberg, M.R.: Cluster Analysis for Applications. Academic Press, New York (1973)
2. Likas, A., Vlassis, N., Verbeek, J.J.: The global k-means clustering algorithm. Pattern Recognition 36, 451–461 (2003)
3. Khan, S.S., Ahmad, A.: Cluster center initialization algorithm for k-means clustering. Pattern Recognition Lett. 25(11), 1293–1302 (2004)
4. Mitra, P., Murthy, C.A., Pal, S.K.: Density-based multiscale data condensation. IEEE Trans. Pattern Anal. Machine Intell. 24(6), 734–747 (2002)

5. RizmanŽalik, K.: An efficient k'-means clustering algorithm. Pattern Recognition Letters 29(9) (2008)
6. Kaufman, L., Rousseeuw, P.J.: Finding Groups in Data. In: An Introduction to Cluster Analysis. Wiley, Canada (1990)
7. He, J., Lan, M., Tan, C.-L., Sung, S.-Y., Low, H.-B.: Initialization of cluster refinement algorithms: A review and comparativestudy. In: Proc. of Internat. Joint Conf. on Neural Networks (IJCNN), Budapest, Hungary, vol. 1, pp. 297–302 (2004)
8. Jiang, H., Yi, S., Li, J., Yang, F., Hu, X.: Ant clustering algorithm with K-harmonic means clustering. Expert Systems with Applications 37(12), 8679–8684 (2010)
9. Pe~na, J.M., Lozano, J.A., Larranaga, P.: An empirical comparison of four initialization methods for the K-Means algorithm. Pattern Recognition Letters 20, 1027–1040 (1999)
10. Newman, D.J., Hettich, S., Blake, C., Merz, C.J.: UCI repository ofmachine learning databases (1998), http://www.ics.uci.edu/~mlearn/MLRepository.html
11. Bradford, C., AberDavid, B.: The Quickhull Algorithm forConvex Hulls. ACM Transactions on Mathematical Software 22(4) (1996)
12. Pearson, R.K., Zylkin, T., Schwaber, J.S., Gonye, G.E.: Quantitative evaluation of clustering results usingcomputational negative controls. In: Proc. 2004 SIAM International Conference on Data Mining, Lake Buena Vista, Florida (2004)
13. Bradley, P.S., Fayyad, U.M.: Refining initial points for k-means clustering. In: Proc. 15th Internat. Conf. on Machine Learning, pp. 91–99. Morgan Kaufmann, San Francisco (1998)

Persian Text Summarization Using Fractal Theory

Mohsen Tofighy[1], Omid Kashefi[2], Azadeh Zamanifar[2],
and Hamid Haj Seyyed Javadi[3]

[1] Department of Engineering,
Islamic Azad University of Mashhad, Mashhad, Iran
[2] School of Computer Engineering,
Iran University of Science and Technology,
Tehran, Iran
[3] Department of Math and Computer Science,
Shahed University, Tehran, Iran
mohsen.tofighy@gmail.com, kashefi@{ieee.org,iust.ac.ir},
azamanifar@comp.iust.ac.ir, h.javadi@shahed.ac.ir

Abstract. The importance of text summarization grows rapidly as the amount of information increases exponentially. In this paper, we present new method for Persian Text Summarization based on fractal theory. The main goal of this method is using hierarchical structure of document and improves that for Persian language. The result shows that our method improves performance of extractive summarization.

Keywords: Text Summarization, Fractal Theory, Persian.

1 Introduction

The wave of information and the lack of time to read long texts make the modern society to look for abstracts and headlines instead of complete text. Human generated summaries are costly and time consuming. Therefore, many automatic summarization techniques have been proposed to solve the task of text summarization [1]. An automatic summarizer is a system that represents a compressed set of an input document displaying its important information [2].

Most of the automatic summarization methods are based on extracting the features of text. The main challenge is selecting the most suitable feature [3]. Automatic summarization techniques can drop into three major categories [4]: 1) sentence extraction, 2) bag-of-words headline generation, and 3) document compression. Sentence extraction as most popular summarization technique has been widely used since early works like Luhn [5] and Edmundson [6] till now. It is also used in fractal [7, 8] based summarizations that consider structure and hierarchy of the document [9]. It was shown that 80% sentences in summary were closely matched with input document [8].

In the past, fractal theory has been widely applied in digital image compression, which is similar to the text summarization in the sense that they both extract the most important information from the source and reduce the complexity of the source [7].

A. Abd Manaf et al. (Eds.): ICIEIS 2011, Part II, CCIS 252, pp. 651–662, 2011.
© Springer-Verlag Berlin Heidelberg 2011

The fractal summarization highly improves the divergence of information coverage of summary, user can easily control the compression ratio, and the system generates a summary that maximize the information coverage and minimize the dissimilarity from the source document [7].

Persian language differs from English language both morphologically and semantically. Some intrinsic problems related to Persian texts are categorized as follows:

- **Complex Inflection.** Persian language includes more than 2800 declensional suffixes [10]. Close fitting, non-close fitting or fitting with pseudo-space of affixes with words is another challenging issue in Persian [11]. For the word "vase" can -officially wrong but commonly spell as «گل‌دان», «گلدان», and «گلدان» in Persian. In some cases affixes and especially suffixes may change regarding lemma. As an example the word "bird" spelled as «پرنده» but the plural form is «پرندگان», where the lemma have deformed. This morphophonetic rules also affect the affixes intra-combination. These rules need phonetic attribute of words and so are hard to computationally implement [12]. For instance, single first person pronoun adjective «م» is inflects the word «شرکت» as «شرکتم», «خانه» as «خانه‌ام», «دانا» as «دانایم», and combine with plural suffix «ها» as «هایم» but with «ان» as «انم».
- **Multiple types of writing for a word.** In Persian some words have different correct spelling. As an example, words «اتاق» and «اطاق» are spelled correct, pronounce the same, and equally mean "room".
- **Homographs.** The same word may have different meanings. This is because of the lack of vowel in Persian writing [13]. Examples are «مَرد» which means «man», «مُرد» which means «died», but both of these words are written as «مرد».
- **Word spacing.** In Persian in addition to white space as inter-words space, an intra-word space called pseudo-space delimits word's parts. Using white space or do not using any space instead of pseudo-space (Zero Width Non-Joiner in Unicode character encoding), is a great challenge in Persian writing. The lack of a set of comprehensive writing rules, results in writing the same words and phrases in multiple forms by native Persian writers [12]. For example «آب‌سردکن» is a complete, correct and meaningful sentence means "Cool the water" but «آب‌سردکن» is a word and it means "water cooler".

In this paper we propose a method to summarize structured document based on fractal theory. We use the modified version of the method proposed by Yang [14] and we add other text features to achieve better result in sentences extraction.

2   Related Works

Text summarization consists of three major stages:topic identificatiom,text interpretation, and summary generation [15, 16]. Nowedays, most of the extracted summaries only embody stage one [17]. Topic identification is furthur devided to: text preprocessing, and text processing [18-20]. Methods are different from each other mostly in text processing step. Text processing can perform in three different levels of language, at 1) surface level, 2) entity level, or 3) discource level [16].

Some solutions rely on surface level methods such as sentence position [21, 22], paragraph position [23, 24], existence of cue words [25-27], and frequency of the words [21, 25]. Earliest summarization is constructed by Luhn [21]. It considers the frequency of the word and existence of cue words like the words that is used for conclusion. Each cue word has positive or negative score. tf [6] calculates the contribution of each word in a document. tf/idf [28] computes distribution of words in corpus. Title method is the other word-based methods [6] that is based on the assumption that title of the document indicates its content. So, each sentence is scored based on number of the words in the sentence that is also contained in the title of the text. Edmunson used the contribution of 4 features: title, cue, keyword and position and applied the linear equation of these features. The coefficient of this linear equation is calculated using training data [29, 30]. These methods can best employ to summarize *News* [31].

Entity level methods try to show an internal presentation of input text. It considers the semantic feature of the text and also the relationship that exists between different sections of the text. This relationship could be synonymy, similarity, consistency and co-occurrence. Entity level or Linguistic based method often tries to find the relationship between words by using lexical data base [32]. Co-occurrence method is based on the hypothesis that the words that occur in the same window (common context) are conceptually related to each other [33]. This method uses the concept of n-gram that is the sequence of n words [34]. Lexical chain based method is the other entity level method that uses the lexical database in order to determine the concept of the knowledge [35]. Barzilay [36] has proved the possibility of calculating lexical chains based on WordNet for the first time. Most of the methods that are based on creating lexical chain for English text summarization use the Brazily lexical chain but lexical chain disambiguation is different. Entity level methods require complex text processing but the outcome is always better than surface level processing.

Discourse level method tries to model the structure of the text. In other words it constructs the relations between sentences [37, 38]. It is based on the idea that coherent structure of the text could be constructed. Rhetorical structure theory (RST) represents text in tree-like structure in which internal nodes are relations [39, 40] and text segments are the leaves of the tree. These segments are nucleus and satellite. The former is the most important part of the sentences. The latter is the less important part of the texts [39]. The disadvantage of this method is that it is complex and expensive because it needs complex processing. It is not suitable for general purpose summarization too [41].

Besides traditional methods as mentioned above, there are some other methods that consider hierarchical structure of the text. Pembe [42] propose query based summarization for Turkish language that preserve the structure of the text. The sentences are scored based on heading, location, term frequency and query methods. Lawrie creates hierarchical summary based on important word of the text called topic terms and their related sub topic terms [43]. Fractal theory [44] was first used in digital image compression [45]. Fractals are mathematical objects that have high degree of redundancy like image. Image has some square blocks which are divided in to sub range block too. Fractal objects composed of different level of abstraction. First fractal based summarization was proposed by Yang [46]. The document is partitioned into range blocks based on document structure and fractal tree is constructed accordingly. The fractal value of each node is calculated based on weight of sentences in range blocks. The weight of each term is calculated based on combination of modified version of *tfIdf*, location, cue and heading methods which takes in to account the block in which the term is occurred.

Most traditional summarizations extract the sentences from input document based on some salient feature of the text, but the document has been considered as flat without considering its hierarchical structure. When humans write a document they use structure which is an important source of information [9]. We achieve a better understanding of information by using a structured text and text of different abstraction level has different level of importance. Documents are usually hierarchical and can be viewed as compositions of simpler constituents [47]. We are going to use fractal theory to transform the text document into a tree.

A novel model named fractal summarization has been applied [14] based on the idea of fractal view of H. Koike [8] and on the techniques of fractal image compression [46]. The main idea is to take into account the structure of the document in order to determine the important part of the text but this method is different from ours in the way that we score each part.

As it is shown in Figure 1, a document can be represented as tree which root node consists of chapters as children; a chapter consists of sections; a section consists of subsections, a section or subsection contains paragraphs; a paragraph consists of sentences, and a sentence is a group of terms. The smallest units which contain information are terms. We will refer to each level in the structure of a document depending on its position regarding title of the document. Then, the original document is represented as a tree according to its structure. The importance of each node is calculated as (1).

$$\begin{cases} F\ v_{root}=1 \\ F\ v_x=F\ v_{p(x)}\times CN_{p(x)}^{-1/D} \end{cases} \tag{1}$$

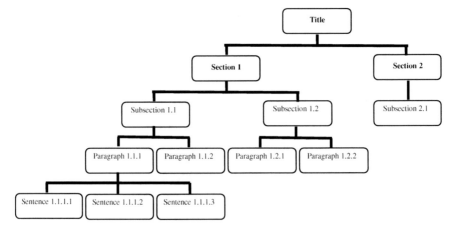

Fig. 1. Tree of document structure

Where Fv_x is the fractal value for node x. $P(x)$ is the parent node of node x, $N_{P(x)}$ is total number of child nodes of P(x), D is the fractal dimension, and C is a constant number that its value is between 0 and 1. When d=1 we have one tree and it is one branch, in most of the cases c=1. When d=c=1, the root value in N_{root} is divided to equal parts.

3 Proposed Method

Our proposed method is presented in Figure 2. Preprocessing steps includes HTML parser is used in order to extract hierarchical structure of document and constructing fractal tree. After that, Feature extraction is done by using automatic algorithms that extract feature and compute we score the documents at different levels (word, sentence, etc) based on these features.

3.1 Feature Extraction

We use 6 features for scoring sentences as following:

Length Feature. This feature is useful to filter out short sentences such as date and author names that are commonly found in news articles. The short sentences are not expected to belong to the summary. Length score of the sentence is the ratio of the number of words occurring in the sentence over the number of words occurring in the longest sentence of the document as in (2).

$$S_{F1}(x) = \frac{No.\ Word\ occurring\ in\ S\ of\ node\ x}{No.Word\ occurring\ in\ longest\ sentence\ of\ node\ x} \tag{2}$$

Term Weight Feature. The second type of scoring function is based on term frequency (tf). The frequency of term occurrences within a document has often been used for calculating the importance of sentence. The score of a sentence can be calculated as the sum of the score of words in the sentence. The score of word $i(w_i)$ at node x can be calculated by the traditional $tf.idf$ method as (3).

$$w_{ix} = tf_{ix} * log\frac{N}{n} \tag{3}$$

Where tf_{ix} is the frequency of term t_i at node x, N is the number of sibling nodes of x and n is number of nodes that contain the term t_i. The Sentence Thematic score at node x can be calculated as (4), where k is number of words in sentence.

$$S_{F2}(x) = \frac{\sum_{i=1}^{k} W_{ix}}{Max\ (\sum_{i=1}^{k} w_{ix})\ in\ all\ seiblings\ of\ node\ x} \tag{4}$$

Keyword Feature. The top 10 words with high TF-IDF score are chosen as keywords. The score for this feature is calculated as the ratio of the number of thematic words that occur in the sentence to maximum number of key words in the sentence. The keyword score of each sentence s is calculated as (5).

$$S_{F3}(x) = \frac{No.\,of\,Keyword\,ins\,of\,node\,x}{Max(No.\,Keyword\,in\,node\,x)} \tag{5}$$

Position Feature. Edmundson also considers the position feature [6] based on the assumption that topic sentences occur at the beginning or at the end of document or paragraph. The Position feature of node x is calculated as the inverse of the minimum distance between node x and first node and node x and last node in sibling nodes of x. Position score is calculated as (6), where n is the number of sibling nodes of x and i is ordinal number of node x regarding its position among other siblings.

$$S_{F4}(x) = \text{Max}\left(\frac{1}{i}, \frac{1}{n-i+1}\right) \tag{6}$$

Headline Feature. The word in sentence that also occurs in title gives high score. This is determined by counting the number of matches between the words in a sentence and the words in the title. We calculate the score for this feature as the ratio of the number of words in the sentence that also occur in the title over the number of words in the title of nodes in the path from the root to the node x. The headline feature score of sentence s is calculated as (7).

$$S_{F5}(x) = \sum_{s \in path\,from\,root\,to\,x} \frac{No.\,of\,Title\,word\,in\,s\,of\,node\,x}{No.\,of\,Word\,in\,Title} \tag{7}$$

Cue Feature. The last feature we have used is cue feature that is based on the assumption that the presence of pragmatic words increases the importance of a sentence. The cue score for each sentence is calculated as (8).

$$S_{F6}(x) = \frac{No.\,Cue\,word\,in\,s\,of\,node\,x}{Max(No.\,Cue\,Word\,in\,siblings\,of\,node\,x)} \tag{8}$$

As it is shown in Figure 2, in post processing stage, first, all features must be normalized because they have different range of values. For normalization we divide each feature by its maximum score in the whole document. The total score of node x is defined as (9) as summation of the 6 features score $S_{Fk}(x)$ multiplied by coefficient α_k, where α_k are positive real numbers between 0 and 1 that their summations equals to 1.They are the standardization factor to adjust the weighting of the different summarization features according to our preferences. For example, in newspaper, position and headline factor is more important than other factors. Therefore, $\propto_4$ and $\propto_5$ have greater values compared to others.

$$NS(x) = \sum_{\text{for each sentence } s \in x} \sum_{k=1}^{6} \propto_k S_{Fk}(x) \tag{9}$$

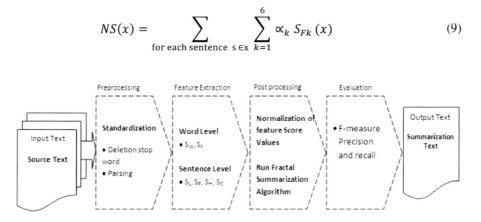

Fig. 2. Our Summarization method steps

3.2 Summary Generation

Figure 3 shows our proposed algorithm based on yang method. The fractal value of each node is calculated as (10).

$$\begin{cases} F\, v_{\text{root}} = 1 \\ F\, v_x = F\, v_{p(x)} \times \left(\dfrac{NS(x)}{\sum_y NS(y)} \right)^{-1} \end{cases} \tag{10}$$

Where $NS(x)$ is total score of node x that is calculated for each node according to equation 9, $P(x)$ is the parent node of x, and y is a child of $P(x)$. We define the compression ratio R. Compression ratio is the number of sentences of summary divide by the total number of sentence of document that can be determinate by user as it is shown in (11).

$$R = \frac{\#\ \text{sentence of output}}{\#\ \text{sentence of input}} \tag{11}$$

It has been shown that extraction of 20% sentences can be as informative as the full text of the input document [48]. The quota of the summary is the compression ratio times the number of sentences of the document and we calculate the quota of child nodes as (12), where $P(x)$ is the parent of node x.

$$quota_x = (Fv_{(x)}/Fv_{p(x)}) \times quota_{p(x)} \qquad (12)$$

The threshold value is the maximum number of sentences that we want to extract from the node. The optimum value is between 3 and 5 [49].

Pseudo-Code of Proposed Summarization Approach

```
1:   Choose a Compression ratio
2:   Choose a threshold Value.
3:   Calculate the total Sentence Quota of the summary
4:   Transform the document into a fractal tree
5:   Set the current node to the root of fractal tree
6:   Repeat
7:   foreach child node under current node
8:       Calculate the fractal value of child node
9:       assign the Quota of child node in proportion to fractal values
10:  foreach child nodes
11:          if the quota is less than threshold value
12:  begin
13:          Select the sentences in the node by extraction
14:          Set the current node to parent of current node
15:  Else
16:          Set the current node to the childe node
17:  until all the child nodes under current node are processed
```

Fig. 3. Algorithm of Our Proposed Summarization Technique

4 Experimental Result

We employ the standard measures (i.e. precision, recall and F-measure) to evaluate the performance of summarization. We assume that a human would be able to identify the most important sentences in a document most effectively. If the set of sentences selected by an automatic extraction method has a high overlap with the human-generated extract, the automatic method should be regarded as effective. Assume that *Sinput* is the manual summary and *Soutput* is the automatically generated summary, the measurements are defined as (13) to (15).

$$Precision(S_{Input}, S_{Output}) = \frac{|S_{Input} \cap S_{Output}|}{|S_{Output}|} \qquad (13)$$

$$Recall(S_{Input}, S_{Output}) = \frac{|S_{Input} \cap S_{Output}|}{|S_{Input}|} \qquad (14)$$

$$F - Measure = \frac{2 * precision * Recall}{precision + Recall} \qquad (15)$$

This section of evaluation uses a human-generated summary. The individuals involved in this process are the experts in Persian Language. The summary generated by experts would be used as a reference in obtaining the number of relevant sentences in a particular summary. We have used several different Persian news texts to construct the testing corpus. For example, the results of five papers are shown in table1. For each text, five graduated students have performed summarization manually. This task has been done in two different proportions of the original text: 30% and 40%. The ideal summary is constructed based on the majority voting of the manual results. Then we calculate the precision and recall of our work and other approaches. The results are presented in Table 1.

Table 1. Evaluation on persian fractal summarization

Article No.	Precision	Recall	F-Score
1	0.60	0.50	0.50
2	0.77	1.00	0.80
3	0.67	0.80	0.67
4	0.53	0.60	0.50
5	0.63	0.78	0.75
Average	**0.68**	**73.6**	**0.64**

Table 2 compares our method by other methods. It shows superior result compared to others.

Table 2. Result of our evaluation - Precision

Compression Rate	Our Approach	FarsiSum	Yang&Wang
30% - 40%	0.69	0.53	0.58–0.62

5   Conclusion

We proposed a method for summarizing Persian structured document based on fractal theory that considers both the abstraction level of document and statistical property of the text. Our result shows the superior result compared to flat methods and the other structured summarization method in literature.

References

1. Hobson, S.P., Dorr, B.J., Monz, C.: Task-Based Evaluation of Text Summarization Using Relevance Prediction. Information Processing & Management 43, 1482–1499 (2007)
2. Karimi, Z., Shamsfard, M.: Persian Text Aoutomatic Summarization System. International Journal of Computational Intelligence 4, 126–133 (2006)

3. Buyukkokten, O., Garcia-Molina, H., Paepcke, A.: Seeing the Whole in Parts: Text Summarization for Web Browsing on Handheld Devices. In: The 10th International Conference on World Wide Web, Hong Kong (2001)
4. Daumé, H., Marcu, D.: Induction of Word and Phrase Alignments for Automatic Document Summarization. Computational Linguistics 31, 505–530 (2005)
5. Luhn, H.P.: The Automatic Creation of Literature Abstracts. IBM Journal of Research and Development 2, 159–165 (1958)
6. Edmundson, H.P.: New Methods in Automatic Extracting. Journal of the ACM 16, 264–285 (1969)
7. Yang, C.C., Chen, H., Hong, K.: Visualization of Large Category Map for Internet Browsing. Decision Support Systems 35, 89–94 (2003)
8. Koike, H.: Fractal Views: A Fractal-Based Method for Controlling Information Display. ACM Transactions on Information Systems 13, 305–322 (1995)
9. Endres-Niggemeyer, B., Maier, E., Sigel, A.: How to Implement a Naturalistic Model of Abstracting: Four Core Working Steps of an Expert Abstractor. Information Processing and Management 31, 631–672 (1995)
10. Nasri, M., Kashefi, O.: Defects of Persian Official Writing Rules from Computational View. Technical Report PMF-1-I, SCICT (2008)
11. Kashefi, O., Mohseni, N., Minaei, B.: Optimizing Document Similarity Detection in Persian Information Retrieval. Journal of Convergence Information Technology 5, 101–106 (2010)
12. Kashefi, O., Minaei-Bidgoli, B., Sharifi, M.: A Novel String Distance Metric for Ranking Persian Spelling Error Corrections. Language Resource and Evaluation (2010)
13. Zamanifar, A., Minaei-Bidgoli, B., Sharifi, M.: A New Hybrid Farsi Text Summarization Technique Based on Term Co-Occurrence and Conceptual Property of the Text. In: Proceedings of the 2008 Ninth ACIS International Conference on Software Engineering, Artificial Intelligence, Networking, and Parallel/Distributed Computing. IEEE Computer Society, Thiland (2008)
14. Yang, C.C., Wang, F.L.: Fractal Summarization: Summarization Based on Fractal Theory. In: The 26th Annual International ACM SIGIR Conference on Research and Development in Informaion Retrieval. ACM, Toronto (2003)
15. Hovy, E., Lin, C.Y.: Automated Text Summarization in Summarist. Advances in Automatic Text Summarization 8, 18–24 (1999)
16. Mani, I., Maybury, M.: Advances in Automatic Text Summarization. The MIT Press (1999)
17. Hovy, E.H.: Automated Text Summarization. Oxford University Press, Oxford (2005)
18. Kyoomarsi, E., Khosravi, H., Eslami, E., Khosravyan, P.: Optimizing Text Summarization Based on Fuzzy Logic. In: The 7th IEEE/ACIS International Conference on Computer and Information Science, Portland, Oregon, USA (2008)
19. Xiao-Yu, J., Xiao-Zhong, F., Zhi-Fei, W., Ke-Liang, J.: Improving the Performance of Text Categorization Using Automatic Summarization. In: International Conference on Computer Modeling and Simulation, Macau (2009)
20. Sparck-Jones, K.: Automatic Summarizing: Factors and Directions. In: Mani, I., Maybury, M.T. (eds.) Advances in Automatic Text Summarization, pp. 1–13. MIT Press, Cambridge (1999)
21. Luhn, H.P.: The Automatic Creation of Literature Abstract. IBM Journal of Research and Development, 159–165 (1958)
22. Lin, C.Y., Hovy, E.: Identifying Topics by Position. In: The 5th Conference on Applied Natural Language Processing (ANLC). Association for Computational Linguistics, Washington, D.C., USA (1997)

23. Baxendale, P.B.: Machine-Made Index for Technical Literature: An Experiment. IBM Journal of Research and Development 2, 354–361 (1958)
24. Hearst, M.: Multi-Paragraph Segmentation of Expository Text. In: The 32th Annual Meeting of the Association for Computational Linguistics. Association for Computational Linguistics, Stroudsburg (1994)
25. Teufel, S., Moens, M.: Sentence Extraction as a Classifi Cation Task. In: The ACL Workshop on Intelligent Text Summarization Madrid, Spain (1997)
26. Elhadad, N., Mckeown, K.: Towards Generating Patient Specific Summaries of Medical Articles. In: NAACL Workshop on Automatic Summarization, Pittsburgh, Pennsylvania, USA (2001)
27. Sun, Y., Park, S.: Generation of Non-Redundant Summary Based on Sum of Similarity and Semantic Analysis. In: Asia Information Retrieval Symposium, Beijing, China (2004)
28. Salton, G., Buckley, C.: Term-Weighting Approaches in Automatic Text Retrieval. Information Processing & Management 24, 513–523 (1988)
29. Hassel, M., Mazdak, N.: Farsisum: A Persian Text Summarizer. In: The Workshop on Computational Approaches to Arabic Script-based Languages. Association for Computational Linguistics (2004)
30. Dalianis, H.: Swesum - a Text Summarizer for Swedish. Technical Report, Department of Numerical Analysis and Computing Science, KTH (2000)
31. Brandow, R., Mitze, K., Rau, L.: Automatic Condensation of Electronic Publishing Publications by Sentence Selection. Information Processing and Management 31, 675–685 (1995)
32. Zechner, K.: A Literature Survey on Information Extraction and Text Summarization. Term Paper, Carnegie Mellon University (1997)
33. Geng, H., Zhao, P., Chen, E., Cai, Q.: A Novel Automatic Text Summarization Study Based Term Co-Occurrence. In: The 5th International IEEE Conference on Cognitive Informatics, Beijing, China (2006)
34. Lin, C.Y., Hovy, E.: Automatic Evaluation of Summaries Using N-Gram Co-Occurrence Statistics. In: The Conference of the North American Chapter of the Association for Computational Linguistics on Human Language Technology (NAACL). Association for Computational Linguistics, Edmonton (2003)
35. Silber, H., Mccoy, K.F.: Efficient Text Summarization Using Lexical Chains. In: The 5th International Conference on Intelligent User Interfaces, New Orleans, LA, USA (2000)
36. Barzilay, R., Elhadad, M.: Using Lexical Chains for Text Summarization. In: The Intelligent Scalable Text Summarization Workshop (ISTS). The Association for Computational Linguistics, Madrid (1997)
37. Marcu, D.: The Rhetorical Parsing, Summarization, and Generation of Natural Language Texts. In: The 35th Annual Meeting on Association for Computational Linguistics. The Association for Computational Linguistics, Madrid (1997)
38. Marcu, D.: Improving Summarization through Rhetorical Parsing Tuning. In: The COLING-ACL Workshop on Very Large Corpora, Montreal, Canada, pp. 10–16 (1998)
39. Mann, W.C., Thompson, S.A.: Rhetorical Structure Theory: A Theory of Text Organization. Research Report, Information Science Institute, University of Southern California (1987)
40. Cristea, D., Postolache, O., Pistol, I.: Summarisation Through Discourse Structure. In: Gelbukh, A. (ed.) CICLing 2005. LNCS, vol. 3406, pp. 632–644. Springer, Heidelberg (2005)

41. Varadarajan, R., Hristidis, V.: A System for Query-Specific Document Summarization. In: The 15th ACM International Conference on Information and Knowledge Management (CIKM), Arlington, VA, USA (2006)
42. Pembe, F.C., Gungor, T.: Towards a New Summarization Approach for Search Engine Results: An Application for Turkish. In: The 23rd International Symposium on Computer and Informtion Science, Istanbul, Turkey (2008)
43. Lawrie, D., Croft, W.: Generating Hierarchical Summaries for Web Searches. In: The 26th Annual International ACM SIGIR Conference on Research and Development in Informaion Retrieval. ACM, Toronto (2003)
44. Mandelbort, B.: The Fractal Geometry of Nature. W.H. Freeman (1983)
45. Jacquin, A.E.: Fractal Image Coding: A Review. Proceedings of the IEEE 81, 1451–1465 (1993)
46. Yang, C.C., Wang, F.L.: Fractal Summarization for Mobile Devices to Access Large Documents on the Web. In: The 12th International Conference on World Wide Web. ACM, Budapest (2003)
47. Ruiz, M.D., BailÓn, A.B.: Summarizing Documents Using Fractal Techniques. In: International Conference on Enterprise Information Systems (ICEIS), Funchal, Madeira, Portugal (2007)
48. Morris, A.H., Kasper, G.M., Adams, D.A.: The Effects and Limitations of Automated Text Condensing on Reading Comprehension Performance. Information Systems Research 3, 17–35 (1992)
49. Goldsteiny, J., Kantrowitz, M., Mittal, V., Carbonel, J.: Summarizing Text Documents: Sentence Selection and Evaluation Metrics. In: The 22nd Annual International ACM SIGIR Conference on Research and Development in Information Retrieval, pp. 121–128. ACM, Berkeley (1999)

Supplier Selection: A Hybrid Approach Using ELECTRE and Fuzzy Clustering

Amir Hossein Azadnia, Pezhman Ghadimi,
Muhamad Zameri Mat Saman, Kuan Yew Wong, and Safian Sharif

Department of Manufacturing & Industrial Engineering,
Universiti Teknologi Malaysia, Skudai, Malaysia
azadnia.ie@gmail.com,
gpezhman2@live.utm.my,
{zameri,wongky,safian}@fkm.utm.my

Abstract. Vendor selection is a strategic issue in supply-chain management for any organization to identify the right supplier. Such selection in most cases is based on the analysis of some specific criteria. Most of the researches so far concentrate on multi-criteria decision making (MCDM) analysis. However, it incurs a huge computational complexity when a large number of suppliers are considered. So, data mining approaches would be required to convert raw data into useful information and knowledge. Hence, a new hybrid model of MCDM and data mining approaches was proposed in this research to address the supplier selection problem. In this paper, Fuzzy C-Means (FCM) clustering as a data mining model has been used to cluster suppliers into groups. Then, Elimination and Choice Expressing Reality (ELECTRE) method has been employed to rank the suppliers. The efficiency of this method was revealed by conducting a case study in an automotive industry.

Keywords: Supplier selection, Multiple Criteria Decision Making, ELECTRE, Fuzzy Analytical Hierarchy Process, Fuzzy C-Means clustering.

1 Introduction

An important concern in supply-chain management is supplier selection. Normally, above 60% of a manufacturer's total sales are spent on purchased items, such as components, parts and raw materials [1]. Moreover, purchases of goods and services by the manufacturer constitute up to 70% of product price [2]. So, selection of suppliers has gained an enormous extent of importance as a tactical issue in the area of supply-chain management.

Che and Wang [3] declared that enterprises must make an important decision regarding the selection and evaluation of suppliers in order to collaborate with qualified suppliers and eliminate those unqualified ones. Establishing a long-term cooperation with qualified suppliers can lead to rapid exchange of information which can provide beneficial support for supply-chain management. Lin *et al.* [4] mentioned that performance of outsourcing operations is greatly affected by vendor selection activities. Mafakheri *et al.* [5] pointed out that costs reduction and quality improvement

A. Abd Manaf et al. (Eds.): ICIEIS 2011, Part II, CCIS 252, pp. 663–676, 2011.
© Springer-Verlag Berlin Heidelberg 2011

of end products is highly dependent on choosing the appropriate supplier. Consequently, considerable amount of interests exist in development of suitable frameworks to evaluate and select suppliers. He *et al.* [6] suggested that selecting the suitable suppliers based on the characteristics of market and product features is a key factor in achieving good supply-chain management.

In order select a supplier, some different alternative suppliers should be evaluated according to different criteria. According to Degraeve and Roodhoft [7], price considerations in supplier evaluation were the main focus in supplier selection. Later, companies realized that being dependent on this single criterion in supplier selection could be harmful to their performance. A list of 23 criteria was indentified for supplier evaluation and selection process by a study done by Dickson [8]. In another study, Weber *et al.* [9] identified that the decisions to select the suppliers are influenced by some key factors. These key factors were derived from reviewing 74 related papers that appeared after Dickson's [8] distinguished research work. According to this well established review in the area of supplier selection, it was disclosed that price, quality and delivery performance are the most important factors to be considered in solving the problem of supplier selection.

Multi criteria decision-making (MCDM) is involved with the process of supplier selection. This process is mainly influenced by different intangible and tangible criteria such as price, quality, technical capability, delivery performance, etc. [10,11]. Many researchers solved the problem of supplier selection by different approaches which include linear programming (LP), integer non-linear programming, mixed-integer linear programming (MILP), analytic network process (ANP), multiple-objective programming, neural networks (NN), goal programming, data envelopment analysis (DEA), simple multi-attribute rating technique (SMART), analytic hierarchy process (AHP), cost-based methods (CBM), genetic algorithm, techniques for order preference by similarity to ideal solution (TOPSIS) and Elimination and Choice Expressing Reality (ELECTRE) methods [12-26].

The analytic hierarchy process (AHP) method plays a major role in MCDM methods which is based on pairwise comparisons as it was firstly developed by Saaty [27,28] but AHP would encounter difficulties in calculating the pairwise comparison matrix when there is a large amount of data. Likewise, Wang and Triantaphyllou [40] declared that ranking irregularities related to the AHP was found as a weak point in the TOPSIS method. Consequently, ELECTRE method was selected to perform the supplier ranking. This method plays a prominent role in the group of MCDM models which is based on the concept of appropriate employment of outranking relations [19]. It is obvious that MCDM methods have been widely used in order to solve the supplier selection problems but due to the huge amount of suppliers' information, analyzing the data using MCDM methods has become difficult. In order to lessen these problems, data mining techniques are being widely used by researchers to convert data into useful information and knowledge. Generally, digging out useful information from huge quantities of data is conceived as data mining [29]. Hidden patterns and relationships can help decision makers to perform better. Basically, this goal can be achieved by discovering those hidden patterns. Consequently, data mining techniques are utilized to address this issue [30]. One of the most popular techniques of data mining is clustering. It mainly focuses on constructing several clusters by dividing a great amount of raw data based on assessment rules. The outcome of this process can be helpful decision-making information for managers [3]. K-means [31], Fuzzy C-Means [32,33], Hierarchical clustering [34], Mixture of Gaussian [35] and Artificial neural network Self-Organization Maps (SOM) [36,37] are five of the most used clustering algorithms. In this research, Fuzzy C-Means (FCM) algorithm has been utilized which allows objects to belong to more than one cluster. This feature makes FCM more flexible than K-means method [38]. Also, in this research activity, Fuzzy AHP was used to weight the criteria. Then, FCM was utilized in order to cluster suppliers into clusters. After that, ELECTRE method was applied to rank the clusters. The final step was constituted of ranking the suppliers within the best cluster by means of ELECTRE method.

2 Basic Definitions and Notations

2.1 Fuzzy C-Means for Supplier Clustering

Fuzzy C-Means (FCM) clustering algorithm was firstly proposed by Dunn [33]. This algorithm has been further developed by Bezdek [32]. FCM algorithm allows objects to belong to more than one cluster with different membership degrees. As the core basis of this method, the following objective function should be minimized:

$$j_m = \sum_{i=1}^{N} \sum_{j=1}^{c} u_{ij}^m \left\| x_i - c_j \right\|^2 \quad 1 < m < \infty \quad (1)$$

Where, N and c are respectively the number of data and clusters. x_i is the ith datum, m is any real number greater than 1, c_j is the center of the jth cluster, u_{ij} is the membership degree of x_i belonging to the cluster j and $\|*\|$ is the Euclidean vector norm expressing the distance between j^{th} cluster's center and i^{th} datum. Fuzzy clustering is done throughout an iterative optimization of the j_m, with the update of u_{ij} and c_j by:

$$u_{ij} = \frac{1}{\sum_{k=1}^{c} \left(\frac{\|x_i - c_j\|}{\|x_i - c_k\|} \right)^{\frac{2}{m-1}}} \quad , \quad c_j = \frac{\sum_{i=1}^{N} u_{ij}^m \cdot x_i}{\sum_{i=1}^{N} u_{ij}^m} \quad (2)$$

If $\|U^{k+1} - U^k\| < \delta$, then the iteration will be discontinued, where δ is a prescribed accuracy level between 0 and 1, while k is the iteration step. This procedure converges to a local minimum or a saddle point of j_m. The algorithm steps are as follows [33]:

i) Initialize $U = [U_{ij}] \, matrix, U^{(0)}$

ii) At k-step: calculate the center vectors

$$C^k = [c_j] \, with \, U^{(k)} \, , c_j = \frac{\sum_{i=1}^{N} u_{ij}^m \cdot x_i}{\sum_{i=1}^{N} u_{ij}^m} \quad (3)$$

iii)   Update $U^{k+1}, U^k, u_{ij} = \dfrac{1}{\sum_{k=1}^{c} \left(\dfrac{\|x_i - c_j\|}{\|x_i - c_k\|} \right)^{\frac{2}{m-1}}}$

iv)   If $\|U^{k+1} - U^k\| < \delta$ then stop; Otherwise return to step ii

2.2   Elimination and Choice Expressing Reality (ELECTRE) Method for Ranking Suppliers

In this research, ELECTRE as a MCDM model has been used to rank the suppliers. Roy [19] firstly developed ELECTRE in order to solve the problem of insufficiency of existing decision making solution methods. Basically, two core actions are embedded in ELECTRE methods. First, one or several outranking relation(s) will be constructed [41]. After that, an exploitation process will be performed. Considering $A_1, A_2, \ldots, A_m$ are possible alternatives, $C_1, C_2, \ldots, C_n$ are criteria with which performances of alternatives are measured, x_{ij} is the rating of alternative A_i with respect to criteria C_j. Consequently, the steps of ELECTRE for ranking the clusters of suppliers are described as follows [19]:

1)   Obtain the weights, w_j of criteria, using AHP.

2)   Establish the data matrix $[x_{ij}]$ which shows the average score of suppliers in each cluster based on the criteria.

3)   Normalize the data matrix

$$R = \left[r_{ij} \right]_{m*n} \quad , r_{ij} = \frac{x_{ij}}{\sqrt{\sum_{i=1}^{m} x_{ij}^2}} \quad i = 1, \ldots, m; \ j = 1, \ldots, n \qquad (4)$$

4)   Establish weighted matrix

In this step, the weights of the criteria are taken into consideration. The weighted matrix, V, is calculated by multiplying the normalized rates by the relevant weights. Therefore, the weighted matrix is configured to be:

$$V = \left[v_{ij} \right]_{m*n}, \ v_{ij} = \left[w_j r_{ij} \right] \qquad (5)$$

5)   Establish Concordance and Discordance Sets

For each pair of alternatives A_p and A_q (p,q=1,2,...,m and p≠q), the set of attributes is divided into two different subsets. The concordance set, which consists of all attributes for which alternative A_p is preferred to alternative A_q can be written as:

$$C(p, q) = \{j, V_{pj} \geq V_{qj}\} \qquad (6)$$

In the above equation V_{pj} is a weighted score of alternative A_p with regard to the jth attribute. $C(p,q)$ is the set of attributes where A_p is better than or equal to A_q. The discordance set which is the complement of C (p,q), contains all attributes for which A_q is better than A_p. This can be shown as:

$$D\ (p,q) = \{j, Vpj\ < Vqj\} \tag{7}$$

6)   Calculate Concordance and Discordance Indices

The relative power of each concordance set is measured by means of the concordance index. The concordance index C_{pq} represents the degree of confidence in the pair wise judgments of (A_p, A_q). The concordance index of C (p,q) is defined as:

$$Cpq = \sum_{j*} W_{j*} \tag{8}$$

Where $j*$ are attributes which belong to concordance set C (p,q). On the other hand, the discordance index, measures the power of D (p,q). The discordance index of D (p,q), which indicates the degree of disagreement in (A_p, A_q), can be defined as:

$$Dpq = \frac{max|Vpj - Vqj|, j \in D\ (p,q)}{\delta} \tag{9}$$

Where Vpj indicates the performance of alternative A_p in terms of criterion C_j, Vqj indicates the performance of alternative A_q in terms of criterion C_j, and $\delta = max|Vpj - Vqj|, j = 1,2,3, \dots, n$.

7)   Determine the threshold value

In this step, two thresholds should be determined. Consequently, C^* and D^* as identified thresholds represent the average of C_{pq} and D_{pq} of suppliers, respectively.

8)   Determine outranking relationships

The dominance relationship of alternative A_p over alternative A_q becomes stronger with a higher concordance index C_{pq} and a lower discordance index D_{pq}. The method defines that A_p outranks A_q when $C_{pq} \geq C^*$ and $D_{pq} \leq D^*$.

3 Proposed Method

In this section, a hybrid approach of clustering method and MCDM have been proposed to deal with supplier selection problem. This problem would be intensified in the case of computational complexity when a large number of alternatives and criteria are considered. Moreover, wrong selection might be generated due to computational error. To address these limitations, a novel model namely supplier selection using Fuzzy C-Means algorithm and ELECTRE method is presented in this paper by integrating the Fuzzy C-Means (FCM) algorithm, Fuzzy Analytic Hierarchy Process (FAHP) and ELECTRE. The proposed method mainly uses FAHP, FCM and ELECTRE for solving the problem of supplier selection. The procedures of the proposed method are listed step by step as follows:

- **Step1:** Criteria selection. In this step, criteria for selecting the suppliers are selected based on the product and decisions of the company's experts.
- **Step 2:** Weighting selected criteria. FAHP is applied in order to perform the weightings.
- **Step 3:** Normalizing and weighting suppliers' data.
- **Step 4:** Clustering the suppliers based on their weighted normalized data in each criterion using FCM.
- **Step 5:** Ranking suppliers' clusters using ELECTRE method and identifying the best cluster.
- **Step 6:** Ranking suppliers in the best cluster using ELECTRE method.

4 Case Study

To illustrate the model, a case study was conducted. An automotive manufacturing company which is located in Iran was selected. G.G.S Company is a leading spare parts manufacturer in the automotive industry. This company supplies various components for the two great car manufacturers in Iran (SAIPA and IRANKHODRO). The aforementioned company utilizes an outsourcing policy for producing the components. In order to run its business, the company works with several small and medium automotive part manufacturers. Decision makers within the company wanted to ensure that the right manufacturers are selected to supply the fuel filter. For this study, 37 manufacturers of fuel filter were selected. Managers of the company wanted to select the best suppliers based on the four criteria (product price, quality, technical capability and delivery). They wanted to divide suppliers into four clusters based on their strategies. From the company's ISO 9001:2000 documents and suppliers' historical records, the data sets for suppliers' performance scores and products prices were collected.

4.1 Weighting Criteria Using FAHP

Product price, quality, technical capability and delivery were selected as the criteria for supplier evaluation based on the decision of experts within the company, ISO 9001:2000 documents and previous research activities in the literature. In this phase, FAHP has been used to weight the criteria. The steps of this phase are described as follows:

- *Step1*: *Pairwise comparisons.* In this step, using the fuzzy scale shown in Table 1, a group of three experts was asked to make pairwise comparison of the relative importance of the criteria. The group consisted of the owner, manager and chief executive officer of the company. The results are shown in Table 2.

- *Step 2*: *Calculating the weights of criteria.* In this step, Chang's FAHP [39] has been utilized for calculating the weights of criteria. The results are illustrated in Table 3.

Table 1. Triangular fuzzy scale

Triangular fuzzy scale	Linguistic scale
(1,1,1)	Just equal
(2/3, 1, 3/2)	Slightly more important
(3/2, 2, 5/2)	More important
(5/2, 3, 7/2)	Strongly more important
(7/2, 4, 9/2)	Very strongly more important

Table 2. Fuzzy pairwise comparison

	Price	Quality	Technical capability	Delivery
Price	(1,1,1)	(2/3,1,3/2)	(3/2,2,5/2)	(2/3,1,3/2)
Quality	(2/3,1,3/2)	(1,1,1)	(2/3,1,3/2)	(2/5,1/2,2/3)
Technical capability	(2/5,1/2,2/3)	(2/3,1,3/2)	(1,1,1)	(2/7,1/3,2/5)
Delivery	(2/3,1,3/2)	(3/2,2,5/2)	(5/2,3,7/2)	(1,1,1)

Table 3. Weights

Criterion	Price	Quality	Technical capability	Delivery
Weight	0.316284	0.487303	0.057591	0.138822

4.2 Normalizing and Weighting Suppliers' Data

Suppliers' data are shown in Table 4. Data inputs are measured in different scales. Therefore, a normalization process is required to put the fields into comparable scales and guarantee that fields with larger values don't determine the solution. In this paper, min-max approach was used which recalled all record values in the range between

Table 4. Data matrix

Supplier ID	Price	Quality	Technical capability	Delivery
1	8485	6	6	9
2	5061	3	4	7
3	8571	6	8	5
4	9465	7	5	8
5	7919	4	3	7
.	.	.	.	.
.	.	.	.	.
35	6793	7	4	6
36	5550	4	5	5
37	6540	7	6	6
Max	9960	9	8	9
Min	5046	2	3	4

zero to one. For the benefit criteria (quality, technical capability, delivery) the normalized value is equal to (record value- min value of field)/(max value of field-min value of field) and for the cost criterion (price), it is equal to (max value of field-record value)/(max value of field- min value of field). The normalized data have been multiplied by the weight of each criterion for achieving the weighted normalized data. The results are shown in Table 5.

Table 5. Weighted normalized data matrix

Supplier ID	Price	Quality	Technical capability	Delivery
1	0.094937	0.278459	0.034555	0.138822
2	0.315318	0.069615	0.011518	0.083293
3	0.089401	0.278459	0.057591	0.027764
4	0.03186	0.348074	0.023037	0.111058
5	0.131366	0.139229	0	0.083293
.	.	.	.	
.	.	.	.	
35	0.20384	0.348074	0.011518	0.055529
36	0.283844	0.139229	0.023037	0.027764
37	0.220124	0.348074	0.034555	0.055529

4.3 Clustering of Suppliers

The idea behind this approach is that FCM can make effective clusters containing similar data. So, the vendors who have a little deviation in points were considered in the same cluster. Thus, FCM groups the vendors into different clusters such as best vendors, better vendors, moderate vendors, and the worst vendors. After clustering the vendors into four clusters, they were ranked which is discussed in the next section. MATLAB 7.10 has been utilized for performing Fuzzy C-Means clustering. The results of supplier clustering using Fuzzy C-Means are shown in Table 6. It indicates four clusters; each with the related number of suppliers and their average four criteria values. The last row in addition shows the total average of product price, quality, technical capability and delivery for all suppliers.

Table 6. Clusters created by Fuzzy C-Means

	Average in cluster				
Cluster no.	Price	Quality	Technical capability	Delivery	No. of suppliers
1	7561.25	6.083333	5.416667	6	12
2	5448.090909	3.363636	4.727273	6.363636	11
3	7128.142857	4.285714	5.142857	7	7
4	9300.285714	7.428571	5.142857	7.285714	7
Total average	7359.44237	5.29031	5.10741	6.66233	

4.4 Ranking Suppliers' Clusters Using ELECTRE and Identifying the Best Cluster

In this phase, ELECTRE method has been used to rank the clusters. The steps of ELECTRE method are detailed as follows:

- *Step 1: Normalizing the Data Matrix.* As shown in Table 7, the data were normalized based on Equation (4) and R matrix has been developed.

Table 7. Normalized data

	Price	Quality	Technical capability	Delivery
1	0.505027009	0.551048239	0.529659	0.448991
2	0.363886005	0.304689188	0.462248	0.476203
3	0.476099146	0.388214024	0.502885	0.523823
4	0.621179763	0.672904308	0.502885	0.545204

- *Step 2: Establishing weighted matrix.* The weighted rating matrix was calculated. It was constructed based on multiplying the rates by the relevant FAHP calculated weights of the criteria. Therefore, according to Equation (5), V matrix was calculated.

- *Step 3: Establishing Concordance and Discordance Sets.* In Table 8 and 9, Concordance set and Discordance set were determined using Equations (6) and (7). This was followed by calculating Concordance and Discordance indices, C_{pq} and D_{pq}, using Equations (8) and (9).

Table 8. Concordance set

	Concordance set	Concordance index
C(1,2)	2,3	0.544894
C(1,3)	2,3	0.544894
C(1,4)	1,3	0.373875
C(2,1)	1,4	0.455106
C(2,3)	1	0.316284
C(2,4)	1	0.316284
C(3,1)	1,4	0.455106
C(3,2)	2,3,4	0.683716
C(3,4)	1,3	0.373875
C(4,1)	2,4	0.626125
C(4,2)	2,3,4	0.683716
C(4,3)	2,3,4	0.683716

Table 9. Discordance Set

	Discordance set	Discordance index
D(1,2)	1,4	0.371845
D(1,3)	1,4	0.130918
D(1,4)	2,4	1
D(2,1)	2,3	1
D(2,3)	2,3,4	1
D(2,4)	2,3,4	1
D(3,1)	2,3	1
D(3,2)	1	0.871978
D(3,4)	2,4	1
D(4,1)	1,3	0.618671
D(4,2)	1	0.453529
D(4,3)	1	0.330761

- *Step 4: Determine the threshold values.* C^* and D^* were defined as thresholds which represent the average of C_{pq} and D_{pq} C^* is calculated as 0.504799 and D^* is equal to 0.731475.

- *Step 5: Detemine Outranking Relationships.* According to ELECTRE model, A_p outranks A_q when $C_{pq} \geq C^*$ and $D_{pq} \leq D^*$. As shown in Table 10, among C_{pq} indices C_{12}, C_{13}, C_{32}, C_{41}, C_{42}, C_{43} are more than C^* and among D_{pq} indices, D_{12}, D_{13}, D_{41}, D_{42}, D_{43} are less than D^*.

Table 10. Outranking relationships

		$\geq C^*$			$\leq D^*$	Relations
C_{12}	0.544894	✓	D_{12}	0.371845	✓	$A_1 > A_2$
C_{13}	0.544894	✓	D_{13}	0.130918	✓	$A_1 > A_3$
C_{14}	0.373875		D_{14}	1		
C_{21}	0.455106		D_{21}	1		
C_{23}	0.316284		D_{23}	1		
C_{24}	0.316284		D_{24}	1		
C_{31}	0.455106		D_{31}	1		
C_{32}	0.683716	✓	D_{32}	0.871978		
C_{34}	0.373875		D_{34}	1		
C_{41}	0.626125	✓	D_{41}	0.618671	✓	$A_4 > A_1$
C_{42}	0.683716	✓	D_{42}	0.453529	✓	$A_4 > A_2$
C_{43}	0.683716	✓	D_{43}	0.330761	✓	$A_4 > A_3$
C^*	0.504799		D^*	0.731475		

So, the determination of outranking relationships was illustrated. Five outranking relations are described as follows:

1. Cluster 1 outranks cluster 2
2. Cluster 1 outranks cluster 3
3. Cluster 4 outranks cluster 1
4. Cluster 4 outranks cluster 2
5. Cluster 4 outranks cluster 3

According to these relations, it can be understood that cluster 4 is the best cluster followed by cluster 1 but the ranking of clusters 2 and 3 cannot be determined. Consequently, the threshold should be changed in order to reveal the ranking orders of clusters 2 and 3. So, the D^* has been changed to 0.9 which leads to a new determination of outranking relationships that are shown in Table 11. So, according to Table 11, six outranking relations are determined as follows:

1. Cluster 1 outranks cluster 2
2. Cluster 1 outranks cluster 3
3. Cluster 4 outranks cluster 1
4. Cluster 4 outranks cluster 2
5. Cluster 4 outranks cluster 3
6. Cluster 3 outranks cluster 2

Table 11. New outranking relationshipsï

	$\geq C^*$				$\leq D^*$	Relations
C_{12}	0.544894	✓	D_{12}	0.371845	✓	$A_1 > A_2$
C_{13}	0.544894	✓	D_{13}	0.130918	✓	$A_1 > A_3$
C_{14}	0.373875		D_{14}	1		
C_{21}	0.455106		D_{21}	1		
C_{23}	0.316284		D_{23}	1		
C_{24}	0.316284		D_{24}	1		
C_{31}	0.455106		D_{31}	1		
C_{32}	0.683716	✓	D_{32}	0.871978	✓	$A_3 > A_2$
C_{34}	0.373875		D_{34}	1		
C_{41}	0.626125	✓	D_{41}	0.618671	✓	$A_4 > A_1$
C_{42}	0.683716	✓	D_{42}	0.453529	✓	$A_4 > A_2$
C_{43}	0.683716	✓	D_{43}	0.330761	✓	$A_4 > A_3$
C^*	0.504799		D^*	0.9		

Consequently, the ranking of the clusters is 4, 1, 3 and 2. It means that cluster 4 is the best cluster, cluster 1 is the better cluster, cluster 3 is the moderate and cluster 2 is the worst cluster of suppliers.

4.5 Ranking Suppliers in the Best Cluster Using ELECTRE

In this step, seven suppliers from the best cluster have been ranked by ELECTRE method. The suppliers' information is shown in the Table 12. The process of outranking suppliers in the best cluster is the same as the previously done process for outranking the clusters. For summarization purposes, the final results of outranking suppliers are shown in Table 13.

Table 12. Suppliers' information

Supplier no.	Product price	Quality	Technical	Delivery	Cluster
4	9465	7	5	8	4
8	9960	8	3	6	4
13	8193	7	7	9	4
14	9692	6	7	9	4
27	8766	7	7	7	4
29	9670	9	3	4	4
33	9356	8	4	8	4

Table 13. Outranked suppliers

Rank	Supplier no.
1	33
2	29
3	8
4	13
5	27
6	4
7	14

5 Conclusion

In this paper, a new hybrid method based on clustering method and MCDM methods was proposed. It is shown that the new method can deal with supplier selection problem when the amount of suppliers' data increased. FAHP was employed to weight the criteria. After that, FCM clustering was used to group suppliers into four predefined clusters. Then, ELECTRE method as one of the MCDM methods has been used to outrank the clusters. From the best cluster, seven suppliers have been outranked by ELECTRE. A case study in an automotive manufacturing company was carried out to demonstrate the employment of the proposed model. The main contributions of this study are described as follows:

1. A new method of decision support system for supplier selection has been developed.
2. The pre-processing of suppliers' data is facilitated.
3. FCM integrated with FAHP has been used to cluster the suppliers.
4. FCM has been integrated with ELECTRE to solve the problem of MCDM when there are huge amount of data.

In spite of the fact that a large numbers of suppliers generate difficulties in the process of decision making; the proposed approach has overcome this problem by employing data mining methods to transfer the data into useful information. As a result, managers can benefit from the major advantage of the proposed method.

For future work it can be a good opportunity to combine other data mining approaches such as unsupervised methods with MCDM methods. Also, the resource allocation to suppliers could be considered by mathematical models.

Acknowledgement. The authors express their gratitude to the Ministry of Higher Education of Malaysia and Universiti Teknologi Malaysia for financial support of this research under Research University Grant Scheme (Vot: Q.J130000.7124.01J74).

References

1. Krajewsld, L.J., Ritzman, L.P.: Operations management strategy and analysis. Addison-Wesley Publishing Co., London (1996)
2. Ghodsypour, S.H., O'Brien, C.: A decision support system for supplier selection using an integrated analytic hierarchy process and linear programming. International Journal of Production Economics 56-57, 199–212 (1998)

3. Che, Z.H., Wang, H.S.: A hybrid approach for supplier cluster analysis. Computers & Mathematics with Applications 59(2), 745–763 (2010)
4. Lin, Y.-T., Lin, C.-L., Yu, H.-C., Tzeng, G.-H.: A novel hybrid MCDM approach for outsourcing vendor selection: A case study for a semiconductor company in Taiwan. Expert Systems with Applications 37, 4796–4804 (2010)
5. Mafakheri, F., Breton, M., Ghoniem, A.: Supplier selection-order allocation: A two-stage multiple criteria dynamic programming approach. Int. J. Production Economics 132, 52–57 (2011)
6. He, H.Y., Zhu, J.Y., Xu, L.H., Wang, Y.: Discussion and investigation of supplier selection method, Heibei. J. Ind. Sci. Technol. 22, 308–311 (2005)
7. Degraeve, Z., Roodhoft, F.: Effectively selecting suppliers using total cost of ownership. Journal of Supply-chain Management 35(1), 5–10 (1999)
8. Dickson, G.: An analysis of vendor selection systems and decisions. Journal of Purchasing 2(1), 5–17 (1966)
9. Weber, C., Current, J., Benton, W.: Vendor selection criteria and methods. European Journal of Operation Research 50(1), 2–18 (1991)
10. Onut, S., Kara, S.S., Isik, E.: Long term supplier selection using a combined fuzzy MCDM approach: A case study for a telecommunication company. Expert Systems with Applications 36, 3887–3895 (2009)
11. Ebrahim, R.M., Razmi, J., Haleh, H.: Scatter search algorithm for supplier selection and order lot sizing under multiple price discount environment. Adv. Eng. Softw. 40(9), 766–776 (2009)
12. Liao, C.-N., Kao, H.-P.: Supplier selection model using Taguchi loss function, analytical hierarchy process and multi-choice goal programming. Computers & Industrial Engineering 58, 571–577 (2010)
13. Xu, J., Yan, F.: A multi-objective decision making model for the vendor selection problem in a bifuzzy environment. Expert Systems with Applications 38, 9684–9695 (2011)
14. Xu, J., Ding, C.: A class of chance constrained multi objective linear programming with birandom coefficients and its application to vendors selection. Int. J. Production Economics 131, 709–720 (2011)
15. Kuo, R.J., Hong, S.Y., Huang, Y.C.: Integration of particle swarm optimization-based fuzzy neural networkand artificial neural network for supplier selection. Applied Mathematical Modelling 34, 3976–3990 (2010)
16. Wadhwa, V., Ravindran, A.R.: Vendor selection in outsourcing. Comput. Oper. Res. 34, 3725–3737 (2007)
17. Toloo, M., Nalchigar, S.: A new DEA method for supplier selection in presence of both cardinal and ordinal data (2011), doi:10.1016/j.eswa.2011.05.008
18. Zhao, K., Yu, X.: A case based reasoning approach on supplier selection in petroleum enterprises. Expert Systems with Applications 38, 6839–6847 (2011)
19. Roy, B.: The outranking approach and the foundations of ELECTRE methods. Theory and Decision 31, 49–73 (1991)
20. Chan, F.T.S.: Interactive selection model for supplier selection process: An analytical hierarchy process approach. International Journal Production Research 41(15), 3549–3579 (2003)
21. Bayazit, O.: Use of analytic network process in vendor selection decisions. Benchmarking: An International Journal 13(5), 566–579 (2006)
22. Chen, C.T., Lin, C.T., Huang, S.F.: A fuzzy approach for supplier evaluation and selection in supply-chain management. International Journal of Production Economics 102(2), 289–301 (2006)

23. Chang, B., Chang, C., Wu, C.: Fuzzy DEMATEL method for developing supplier selection criteria. Expert Systems with Applications 38, 1850–1858 (2011)
24. Barla, S.B.: A case study of supplier selection for lean supply by using a mathematical model. Logistics Information Management 16(6), 451–459 (2003)
25. Ding, H., Benyoucef, L., Xie, X.: A simulation optimization methodology for supplier selection problem. International Journal Computer Integrated Manufacturing 18(2-3), 210–224 (2005)
26. Almeida, A.T.: Multicriteria decision model for outsourcing contracts selection based on utility function and ELECTRE method. Computers & Operations Research 34(12), 3569–3574 (2007)
27. Saaty, T.L.: The analytic hierarchy process. McGraw-Hill, New York (1980)
28. Saaty, T.L.: Fundamentals of decision making and priority theory with the AHP. RWS Publications, Pittsburgh (1994)
29. Jiawei, H., Kamber, M.: Data Mining: Concepts and Technique. Morgan Kaufmann Publishers (2000)
30. Kumar, V., Chadha, A.: An Empirical Study of the Applications of Data Mining Techniques in Higher Education. International Journal of Advanced Computer Science and Applications 2(3) (2011)
31. MacQueen, J.B.: Some Methods for classification and Analysis of Multivariate Observations. In: Proceedings of 5th Berkeley Symposium on Mathematical Statistics and Probability, pp. 281–297. University of California Press, Berkeley (1967)
32. Bezdek, J.C.: Pattern Recognition with Fuzzy Objective Function Algorithms. Plenum Press, New York (1981)
33. Dunn, J.C.: A Fuzzy Relative of the ISODATA Process and Its Use in Detecting Compact Well-Separated Clusters. Journal of Cybernetics 3, 32–57 (1973)
34. Johnson, S.C.: Hierarchical Clustering Schemes. Psychometrika 2, 241–254 (1967)
35. Dempster, A.P., Laird, N.M., Rubin, D.B.: Maximum Likelihood from Incomplete Data via the EM algorithm. Journal of the Royal Statistical Society Series B 39, 1–38 (1977)
36. Kohonen, T.: Self-Organizing Maps. Springer, Berlin (1995)
37. Kohonen, T.: Self-Organization and Associative Memory. Springer, New York (1989)
38. Mingoti, S.A., Lima, J.O.: Comparing SOM neural network with Fuzzy C-Means, K-means and traditional hierarchical clustering algorithms. European Journal of Operational Research 174, 1742–1759 (2006)
39. Chang, D.-Y.: Applications of the extent analysis method on fuzzy AHP. European Journal of Operational Research 95, 649–655 (1996)
40. Wang, X., Triantaphyllou, E.: Ranking irregularities when evaluating alternatives by using some ELECTRE methods. Omega 36, 45–63 (2008)
41. Birgun, S., Cihan, E.: Supplier Selection Process using ELECTRE Method. In: International Conference on Intelligent Systems and Knowledge Engineering (ISKE), Hangzhou, pp. 634–639 (2010)

A New Approach to Multi-class SVM Learning Based on OC-SVM for Huge Databases

Djeffal Abdelhamid[1], Babahenini Mohamed Chaouki[1], and Taleb-Ahmed Abdelmalik[2]

[1] Computer Science Department, LESIA Laboratory,
Biskra University, Algeria
[2] LAMIH Laboratory FRE CNRS 3304 UVHC,
Valenciennes University, France
Abdelhamid_Djeffal@yahoo.fr,
Chaouki.Babahenini@gmail.com,
Taleb@univ-valenciennes.fr

Abstract. In this paper, we propose a new learning method for multi-class support vector machines based on single class SVM learning method. Unlike the methods 1vs1 and 1vsR, used in the literature and mainly based on binary SVM method, our method learns a classifier for each class from only its samples and then uses these classifiers to obtain a multiclass decision model. To enhance the accuracy of our method, we build from the obtained hyperplanes new hyperplanes, similar to those of the 1vsR method, for use in classification. Our method represents a considerable improvement in the speed of training and classification as well the decision model size while maintaining the same accuracy as other methods.

Keywords: Support vector machine, Multiclass SVM, One-class SVM, 1vs1, 1vsR.

1 Introduction and Related Work

The support vector machine (SVM) method is, in its origin, binary. It is based on the principle of separation between the samples of tow classes, one positive and one negative. In this form, the SVM method is very successful in several areas of application given the precision it offers. In practice, we find more applications with multi-class problems, hence the need to extend the binary model to meet multi-class problems. Existing methods currently try mainly to optimize two phases: a training phase and a classification phase. The first phase constructs the hyperplane, and the second uses it. The evaluation of the methods is based on the evaluation of the performances of the two phases. Among the well known methods, there are methods for direct solution without using the binary SVM model as Weston & Watkins model [1],but which suffers, always, from some slowness and weak accuracy. The widely used methods are based essentially on the extension of the binary model, namely, the one-against-rest (1vsR) and

A. Abd Manaf et al. (Eds.): ICIEIS 2011, Part II, CCIS 252, pp. 677–690, 2011.

the one-against-one (1vs1) methods. The 1vsR method learns for each class a hyperplane that separates it from all other classes, considering this class as positive class and all other classes as negative class, then assigns a new sample, in the classification phase, to the class for which it maximizes the depth. The 1vs1 method learns for each pair of classes a separating hyperplane, and uses the voting lists or decision graphs (DAG) to assign a new sample to a class [2, 3]. In [4–7] comparative studies are conducted to assess the performances of these methods. According to the authors, the 1vs1 method is faster while the 1vsR method is more accurate.

In this paper, instead of the binary SVM, we propose to use the one-class SVM (OC-SVM) that provides a hyperplane for each class that separates it from the rest of the space. For each class, we learn a hyperplane from only its samples. Then in the classification phase, we build for each class a new two-class hyperplane which separates it from all other classes. This two-class hyperplane is calculated from the previous one-class hyperplane and the closest sample of the other classes. The new two-class hyperplane is a shift of the one-class hyperplane, it is situated between the farthest misclassified sample, of the target class, from the hyperpaln, and nearest sample, belonging to other classes,to the hyperpaln. Our technique speeds up the training time and classification time, and reduces the decision model size compared to classic methods, while keeping very close accuracy. Our results were validated on toys and then on databases of UCI site [8]. The rest of the paper is organized as follows: section 2 introduces the binary SVM and Section 3 introduces the multi-class methods based on the binary model, namely, 1vsR and 1vs1. In section 4, we present the OC-SVM model and then we present our method in Section 5. The results and their discussion are presented in Section 6, and a conclusion in Section 7.

2 Binary SVM

The binary SVM solves the problem of separation of two classes, represented by n samples of m attributes each [9, 10]. Consider the problem of separating two classes represented by n samples:

$$\{(x_1, y_1), .., (x_n, y_n)\}, x_i \in \Re^m, y_i \in \{-1, +1\}\}$$

Where x_i are learning samples and the y_i their respective classes. The objective of the SVM method is to find a linear function f (equation 1), called *hyperplane*, that can separate the two classes:

$$\begin{cases} f(x) = (x \bullet w) + b; \\ f(x) > 0 & \Rightarrow x \in class + 1 \\ f(x) < 0 & \Rightarrow x \in class - 1 \end{cases} \qquad (1)$$

Where x is a sample to classify, w is a vector and b is a bias. We must therefore find the widest margin between two classes, which means minimizing $\frac{1}{2}w^2$. In cases where training data are not linearly separable, we allow errors ξ_i (called slack variables) of samples from boundaries of the separation margin with a penalization parameter C and the problem becomes a convex quadratic programming problem:

$$
\begin{cases}
Minimize & \frac{1}{2}\|w\|^2 + C\sum_{i=1}^{n}\xi_i \\
under\ constraints & \\
& y_i(w^T x_i + b) \geq 1 - \xi_i; i = 1..n \\
& \xi_i \geq 0
\end{cases}
\tag{2}
$$

The problem of equation 2 can be solved by introducing Lagrange multipliers (α_i) in the following dual problem:

$$
\begin{cases}
Minimize & \frac{1}{2}\sum_{i=1}^{n}\sum_{j=1}^{n}\alpha_i\alpha_j y_i y_j K(x_i x_j) - \sum_{i=1}^{n}\alpha_i \\
under\ constraints & \\
& \sum_{i=1}^{n}\alpha_i y_i = 0 \\
& 0 \leq \alpha_i \leq C
\end{cases}
\tag{3}
$$

Hence, we can have the following decision function (hyperplane):

$$
H(x) = \sum_{i=1}^{n}\alpha_i y_i K(x_i, x) + b
\tag{4}
$$

The function K is called *Kernel*, it is a symmetric function that satisfies Mercer conditions [4]. It can represent a transformation of the original input space in which data could be non-linearly separable to a new larger space where a linear separator exists. Solving the problem of equation 3 requires an optimization especially when the number of samples is high. Among the optimization methods most commonly used, there is the SMO (Sequential Minimal Optimization) where the problem is broken into several sub-problems, each optimizes two α_i [11].

3   Multi-class SVM

Several techniques have been developed to extend binary SVM method to problems with multiple classes. Each of these techniques makes a generalization of the abilities of the binary method to a multi-class field [2, 3]. Among the best known methods, we can cite 1vsR and 1vs1.

3.1   One-Against-Rest (1vsR)

Training. For each class k we determine a hyperplane $H_k(w_k, b_k)$ separating it from all other classes, considering this class as positive class ($+1$) and other classes as negative class (-1), which results, for a problem to K classes, to K binary SVMs. A hyperplane H_k is defined by the following decision function:

$$
f_k(x) = \langle w_k \bullet x \rangle + b_k
\tag{5}
$$

This function allows to discriminate between the samples of the class k and the set of all other classes.

Classification. A new sample x is assigned to the class k^* that maximizes the depth of this sample. This class is determined by the decision rule of the equation 6:

$$k^* = Arg_{(1 \leq k \leq K)} Max f_k(x) \tag{6}$$

Figure 1 shows an example of separation of three classes.

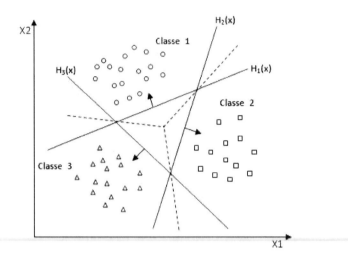

Fig. 1. One-against-rest approach

Interpreted geometrically, a new sample x is assigned to the class that corresponds to the farthest hyperplane. Thus, the space is divided into K convex regions, each corresponding to a class.

3.2   One-Against-One (1vs1)

Training. Instead of learning K decision functions, the 1vs1 method discriminates each class from every other class. Thus $K(K-1)/2$ decision functions are learned. The one-against-one approach is, thus, to build a classifier for each pair of classes (k, s).

Classification. For each pair of classes (k, s), the 1vs1 method defines a binary decision function $h_{ks} : x \in \Re^m \rightarrow \{-1, +1\}$. The assignment of a new sample can be done by two methods; voting list or decision graph.

a. Voting list

We test a new sample by calculating its decision function for each hyperplane. For each test, we vote for the class to which the sample belongs. We define, for this, the binary decision function $H_{ks}(x)$ of equation 7.

$$H_{ks}(x) = sign(f_{ks}(x)) = \{+1 \quad if \quad f_{ks}(x) > 0; \quad 0 \quad else\} \tag{7}$$

Based on the $K(K-1)/2$ binary decision functions, we define other K decision functions (equation 8):

$$H_k(x) = \sum_{s=1}^{m} H_{ks}(x) \tag{8}$$

The classification rule of a new sample x is given, then, by the equation 9:

$$k^* = Arg_{(1 \leq k \leq K)} Max H_k(x) \tag{9}$$

Figure 2 is an example of classification of three classes.

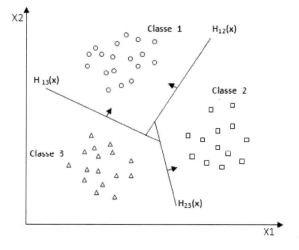

Fig. 2. One-against-one approach

b. Decision graphs

In this method, we define a measure E_{ks} of the generalization ability of the different obtained hyperplanes i.e for each pair of classes. This measure (equation 10) represents the ratio between the number of support vectors of the hyperplane and the number of samples of both classes.

$$E_{ks} = \frac{N_{vs}}{N_{exemples}} \tag{10}$$

Before deciding about new samples, we construct a decision graph. We start with a list L containing all the classes, then take the two classes k and s which E_{ks} is maximum, and we create a graph node labeled (k, s). We then create, in the same way, a left son of this node from the list $L - \{k\}$ and a right son from the list $L - \{s\}$, and continue until the list L contains only one class. This gives the decision graph of figure 3, whose leaves are the classes and the internal nodes are the hyperplanes:

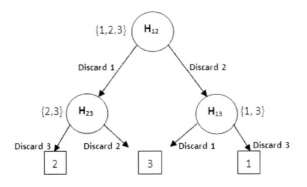

Fig. 3. Directed acyclic decision graph for three classes

A new sample x is exposed first to the hyperplane of the root, if the decision is positive then we continue with the left son, otherwise with the right son, until a leaf is reached. The reached leaf represents the class of the sample x.

4   One-class SVM

In the one-class SVM classification, it is assumed that only samples of one class, the target class, are available. This means that only the samples of the target class can be used and no information on other classes is present. The objective of the OC-SVM is to find a boundary between the samples of the target class and the rest of space. The task is to define a boundary around the target class,

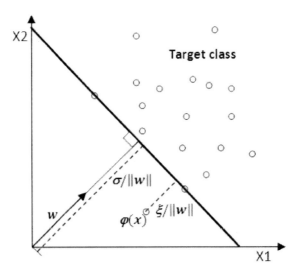

Fig. 4. One-class SVM with maximum margin

so that it accepts as many target samples as possible [12]. The one-class SVM classifier considers the origin as the only instance of negative class, and then tries to find a separator between the origin and samples of the target class while maximizing the margin between the two (cf. figure 4).

The problem is to find the hyperplane that separates the target samples of the origin while maximizes the distance between them. The problem is modeled by the primal quadratic programming problem of equation 11.

$$\begin{cases} min_{w,\xi,\rho} \frac{1}{2} \|w\|^2 + \frac{1}{vN} \sum_{i=1}^{l} \xi_i - \rho \\ \langle w, \phi(x_i) \rangle \geq \rho - \xi_i \\ \xi_i \geq 0 \quad i = 1, 2..l \end{cases} \tag{11}$$

Where N is the number of samples of the target class, (w, ρ) parameters to locate the hyperplane, ξ_i the allowed errors on samples classification, penalized by the parameter v and ϕ is a transformation of space similar to the binary case. Once (w, ρ) determined, any new sample can be classified by the decision function of equation 12:

$$f(x) = < w, \phi(x_i) > -\rho \tag{12}$$

x belongs to the target class if $f(x)$ is positive. In fact, solving the problem of the equation 11 is achieved by the introduction of Lagrange multipliers in the dual problem of equation 13:

$$\begin{cases} Minimize_{\alpha} \quad \frac{1}{2} \sum^{i,j} \alpha_j K(x_i, x_j) \\ under\ constraints \\ \qquad\qquad \sum_{i=1}^{n} \alpha_i = 1 \\ \qquad\qquad 0 \leq \alpha_i \leq \frac{1}{vl} \end{cases} \tag{13}$$

Where K is a kernel that represents the space transformation ϕ. Once the α_i are determined using an optimization such as SMO [11], the decision function for any sample x is given by equation 14:

$$f(x) = \sum_{i=1}^{l} \alpha_i K(x_i, x) - \rho \tag{14}$$

Where ρ can be determined from a training sample x_i having $\alpha_i \neq 0$ by the equation 15:

$$\rho = \sum_j \alpha_j K(x_j, x_i) \tag{15}$$

5   Multi-class SVM Method Based on OC-SVM (OCBM-SVM)

5.1   Training

The method we propose in this paper, extends the OC-SVM to multi-class classification. We propose to learn for each class its own hyperplane separating it from the rest of the space. We learn so for K classes, K hyperplane, but unlike the 1vsR method, we use to find each hyperplane H_k only the samples of the class k which speeds up considerably the training time. Table 1 shows the cost of different methods in terms of the number of used hyperplanes, the number of samples used by each hyperplane, and the estimated time of training depending on the number of samples of a class N_c. We assume, for the sake of simplicity, that the classes have the same number of samples. The estimated time is based on the fact that each hyperplane H_k using N_k samples requires a time of βN_k^2 (β represents the conditions of implementation such as CPU speed, memory size,...etc.).

Table 1. Comparative table of the training times of the different methods

Method	# Hyperplanes	# samples/Hyperplane	Estimated time
1vsR	K	KN_c	$K^3\beta N_c^2$
1vs1	$K(K-1)/2$	$2N_c$	$2\beta K^2 N_c^2$
OCBM-SVM	K	N_c	$K\beta N_c^2$

- The 1vsR method uses to determine each of the K hyperplanes all KN_c training samples, which leads to a training time of $K^3\beta N^2$, where K represents the number of classes and β a constant related to the conditions of implementation, based on the fact that the SMO algorithm [11] used here is of complexity $O(N^2)$.
- The 1vs1 method calculates a hyperplane for each pair of classes, i.e $K(K-1)/2$ hyperplanes, and to determine a hyperplane separating two classes, we use the samples of these two classes ($2N_c$), resulting in a training time of $2\beta K^2 N_c^2$.
- Our method requires the calculation of K hyperplanes, each separates a class from the rest of space. To determine each hyperplane, we use only the samples of one class, resulting therefore in a total training time of about $2KN_c^2$.

It is clear that:
$$K\beta N_i^2 < 2\beta K^2 N_i^2 < K^3\beta N_i^2 \tag{16}$$

This means that the proposed method optimizes the training time compared to methods 1VsR and 1vs1.

5.2   Classification

OC-SVM method allows to find a hyperplane separating one class from the rest of space, this hyperplane allows to decide on membership of a new sample to this class. If the sample is above the hyperplane then it belongs to the class, but if it is below, we have no information on to what other class the sample belongs. To correct this situation, we propose to modify the obtained hyperplane to enhance the decision information in the case where the sample does not belong to the class. We propose to find for for each hyperplane of a class, the closest sample among the samples of all other classes, then shift the hyperplane by a distance equal to half the distance between this sample and the misclassified sample, of the target class, that minimizes the decision function (the farthest one from the hyperplane) (cf. Figure 5).

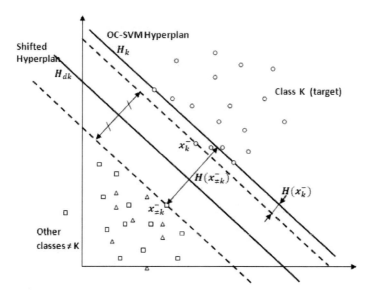

Fig. 5. Classification in OCBM-SVM method

More formally, let $H_k(x)$ be the decision function using the hyperplane of the kth class. And let x_k^- be the misclassified sample of the class k farthest from the hyperplane H, and $x_{\neq k}^-$ the closest sample to the hyperplane H, belonging to a class different to k. The distance of x_k^- from the hyperplane is given by $H_k(x_k^-)$ and the distance between the hyperplane and $x_{\neq k}^-$ is given by $H_k(x_{\neq k}^-)$. The proposed shift is $\frac{(H_k(x_k^-)+H_k(x_{\neq k}^-))}{2}$, and the new decision function for a sample x can be calculated by the shifted hyperplane H_{dk} of the equation 17:

$$H_{dk}(x) = H_k(x) - \frac{(H_k(x_k^-) + H_k(x_{\neq k}^-))}{2} \qquad (17)$$

After calculating all the K shifted hyperplanes, the decision about the class k^* of a new sample x can be given by the discrete decision rule of equation 18:

$$k^* = Arg_{(1 \leq k \leq K)} max H_{dk}(x) \qquad (18)$$

Table 2 shows a comparison between the time of classification of a new sample by different methods. This time is calculated based on the number of support

Table 2. Comparative table of classification time of the different methods

Method	# Used hyperplanes	Estimated time
1vsR	K	$K^2\beta N_c$
1vs1	$K(K-1)/2$	$K(K-1)\beta N_c$
DAG	$(K-1)$	$2(K-1)\beta N_c$
OCBM-SVM	K	$K\beta N_c$

vectors of each hyperplane, which is equal, to the maximum, the total number of samples used to find the hyperplane.

- The 1vsR method uses K hyperplanes, and to test a sample, it is evaluated for all hyperplanes. Knowing that each hyperplane contains a number of support vectors equal to the maximum total number of samples, the estimated time to find the class of a sample is $K^2\beta N_c$, where β is a constant that represents the conditions of implementation.
- For the method 1vs1 using the voting list, the classification estimated time is $K(K-1)\beta N_c$,
- For the method 1vs1 using decision graphs, the classification estimated time is $2(k-1)\beta N_c$.
- The estimated time for our method is $K\beta N_c$, because it tests the sample for K hyperplanes containing, at maximum, KN_c support vectors.

If we eliminate from the column of estimated time in Table 2 the factor βN_c, we note that the method OCBM-SVM optimizes the classification time. But this depends always on the number of support vectors obtained by the training method which can be very important compared to the number of classes K. Higher the number of training samples and the number of classes, the greater the advantage of the OCBM-SVM method, since it uses the minimum of samples, making it suitable for large databases.

5.3   Model Size

The size of the model is the amount of information recorded after learning to use in the decision model. Indeed, the obtained classifier contains, in addition to kernel parameters, information on the hyperplanes namely the values of α_i different to 0, the samples corresponding to α_i different to 0, and the bias (b or ρ). OCBM-SVM method also optimizes the size of the obtained classifier because it optimizes the number of hyperplanes and the number of support vectors for each hyperplane.

6   Experiments

6.1   Used Data

Our method was first tested on examples of Toy type (2 dimensions) that we have chosen of different complexities. Then we have tested it on benchmarks of

Table 3. Databases used for testing

Base	Domain	N_{att}	N_{class}	N_{train}	N_{test}
PageBlocks	Web	10	5	389	5090
Segment	Image processing	19	7	500	1810
Vehicule	Industry	18	4	471	377
Abalone	Industry	8	27	3133	1044
Letter	Character recognition	16	26	2000	10781
OptDigits	Industry	64	10	3824	1797

multi-class classification databases from the site "Machine Learning Repository UCI" [8]. The used databases are shown in the following Table 3:

N_{att} is the number of attributes, N_{class} is the number of classes in the database, N_{train} is the number of samples used for training and N_{test} is the number of samples used for testing.

6.2   Materials and Evaluation Criteria

The proposed method was tested on a Dual-core de 1.6 GHZ machine with 1GB of memory. The used kernel is RBF, and the optimization method is the SMO algorithm [11]. The evaluation criteria of the performances of our method are the training time in seconds $Tr(s)$, the classification time in seconds $Tc(s)$, the recognition rate R and the size of the obtained model.

6.3   Results

The first tests have been performed on toys of different complexities and have shown the advantages of OCBM-SVM method compared to other metods. In the example of table 4, we took 642 samples belonging to five classes. The results show that our OCBM-SVM method reduced training time to 0.109 second without losing accuracy, while the 1vs1 and 1vsR methods have given respectively 0.609 and 28.25 seconds. Even, the size of the resulting model was reduced to 18.290 KB. The classification time was 22.625 which is close to that of the method of decision graphs (DAG) with the remark that the number of samples and the number of classes are small.

The tests performed on the databases of the UCI site also confirm the theoretical results. Table 5 summarizes the results obtained on testing databases presented in the table 3.

Indeed, in all tested databases, OCBM-SVM method greatly improves the training time and model size, especially in large databases. For the *Abalone* database, our OCBM-SVM method reduced the training time from 3954.047 seconds to 1.5 seconds and the size of the model from 2996,002 KB to 226,954 KB. In the case of OptDigits database, training time was reduced from 16981.984 seconds for 1vs1 method and 68501.407 seconds (over 19 hours) for 1vsR method, to only 126,593 seconds while maintaining an accuracy better than the method

Table 4. Results on a toy

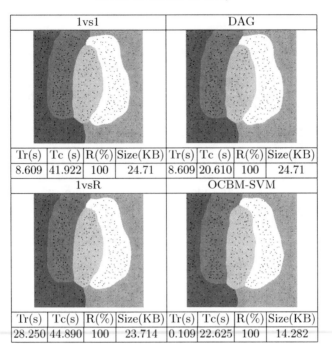

1vs1				DAG			
Tr(s)	Tc (s)	R(%)	Size(KB)	Tr(s)	Tc (s)	R(%)	Size(KB)
8.609	41.922	100	24.71	8.609	20.610	100	24.71
1vsR				OCBM-SVM			
Tr(s)	Tc(s)	R(%)	Size(KB)	Tr(s)	Tc(s)	R(%)	Size(KB)
28.250	44.890	100	23.714	0.109	22.625	100	14.282

1vs1. For the same database, the size of the model was also reduced from 3749.174 KB for the 1vs1 method and 2148,554 KB for 1vsR to 555,314 KB.

The proposed method keeps a classification time, in the case of large databases, close to that of the method DAG representing the fastest method in terms of classification time. Indeed, we note, in databases with a number of samples less than 1000 (case of *PageBlocks*, *Segment* and *Vehicule*) that the classification time obtained by some methods is better than ours. This is due to that in the databases of small size, the preparation work of classification structures (lists in DAG and shifts in OCBM-SVM) is important compared to the essential task of calculating the decision functions. In large databases, with number of samples greater than 1000 and number of classes greater than 10 (case of *Abalone*, *Letter*, *OptDigits*), the improvement of classification time is remarkable. Indeed, for the Abalone database, our method yielded a classification time of 5.282 seconds against 6.421 seconds for DAG method the best of the others. Also for the Letter database, the classification time was 10,766 seconds against 44.5 seconds for DAG. In the OptDigits database, the obtained time by the DAG method was better than the OCBM-SVM method, this can be explained by the number of support vectors obtained by each training method wich has an important influence on the classification time (see 5.2). With all its advantages, our method preserves a recognition rate in the range of rates obtained by other methods and sometimes better(case of *Abalone* database).

Table 5. Results on different databases

Base	Parameters	1vs1(Vote)	1vs1(DAG)	1vsR	OCBM-SVM
PageBlocks	$Tr(s)$	332	332	1105.516	8.531
	$Tc(s)$	6.922	4.718	7.906	8.109
	$R(\%)$	93.33	93.33	93.31	93.31
	$Size(KB)$	135.726	135.726	168.986	34.170
	$\#Hyperplanes$	10	10	5	5
Segment	$Tr(s)$	51.860	38.875	105.172	0.079
	$Tc(s)$	1.828	2.844	3.859	2.843
	$R(\%)$	78.23	77.79	76.85	76.24
	$Size(KB)$	266.346	266.346	177.522	78.162
	$\#Hyperplanes$	21	21	7	7
Vehicule	$Tr(s)$	481.313	481.313	1127.172	0.171
	$Tc(s)$	0.812	0.656	0.484	0.672
	$R(\%)$	69.41	69.41	72.07	71.80
	$Size(KB)$	202010	202010	259546	71066
	$\#Hyperplanes$	6	6	4	4
Abalone	$Tr(s)$	3954.047	3954.047	11324.652	1.5
	$Tc(s)$	14.125	6.421	9.322	5.282
	$R(\%)$	21.64	21.16	24.89	25
	$Size(KB)$	2996.002	2996.002	5478.347	226.954
	$\#Hyperplanes$	351	351	27	27
Letter	$Tr(s)$	4399.344	4399.344	34466.938	52.703
	$Tc(s)$	246.453	44.500	98.484	10.766
	$R(\%)$	82.91	82.91	84.83	79.59
	$Size(KB)$	6102.174	6102.174	2713.442	214.034
	$\#Hyperplanes$	325	325	26	26
OptDigits	$Tr(s)$	16981.984	16981.984	68501.407	126.593
	$Tc(s)$	54.022	14.500	32.15	24.578
	$R(\%)$	93.16	93.16	97.16	93.56
	$Size(KB)$	3749.174	3749.174	2148.554	555.314
	$\#Hyperplanes$	45	45	10	10

7   Conclusion

In this paper, we presented a new method for multiclass learning with support vector machine method. Unlike classic methods such as 1vs1 and 1vsR extending the principle of binary SVM, our method (denoted OCBM-SV) extends the principle of one-class SVM method. And to achieve the generalization ability of binary SVM, we changed the hyperplanes obtained by the one-class method to take into account information of other classes. The obtained results show great improvement in training time and decision model size. Our method also allows to improve the classification time (decision making) of new samples by reducing of the number of support vectors of the decision model. The obtained accuracy is very close to that of other methods and sometimes better.

References

1. Dogan, U., Glasmachers, T., Igel, C.: Fast Training of Multi-class Support Vector Machines, Technical Report no. 03/2011, Faculty of science, university of Copenhagen (2011)
2. Abe, S.: Analysis of multiclass support vector machines. In: Proceedings of International Conference on Computational Intelligence for Modelling Control and Automation (CIMCA 2003), pp. 385–396 (2003)
3. Guermeur, Y.: Multi-class Support vector machine, Theory and Applications, HDR thesis, IAEM Lorraine (2007)
4. Liu, Y., Wang, R., Zeng, Y., He, H.: An Improvement of One-against-all Method for Multiclass Support Vector Machine. In: 4th International Conference: Sciences of Electronic, Technologies of Information and telecommunications, Tunisia, March 25-29 (2007)
5. Seo, N.: A Comparison of Multi-class Support Vector Machine Methods for Face Recognition, Research report, The University of Maryland (December 2007)
6. Anthony, G., Gregg, H., Tshilidzi, M.: Image Classification Using SVMs: One-against-One Vs One-against-All. In: Proccedings of the 28th Asian Conference on Remote Sensing (2007)
7. Foody, M.G., Mathur, A.: A Relative Evaluation of Multiclass Image Classification by Support Vector Machines. IEEE Transactions on Geoscience and Remote Sensing 42, 1335–1343 (2004)
8. Frank, A., Asuncion, A.: UCI Machine Learning Repository. University of California, School of Information and Computer Science, Irvine, CA (2010), http://archive.ics.uci.edu/ml
9. Huang, T., Kecman, V., Kopriva, I.: Kernel Based Algorithms for Mining Huge Data Sets. Springer, Heidelberg (2006)
10. Wang, L. (ed.): Support Vector Machines: Theory and Applications. Springer, Heidelberg (2005)
11. Osuna, E., Freund, R., Girosi, F.: An improved training algorithm for support vector machines. In: ICNNSP 1997, New York, pp. 276–285 (1997)
12. Scholkopf, B., Smola, A.J.: Learning with Kernels Support Vector Machines, Regularization, Optimization, and Beyond. MIT Press (2002)

Developing a Team Performance Prediction Model: A Rough Sets Approach

Mazni Omar, Sharifah-Lailee Syed-Abdullah, and Naimah Mohd Hussin

Department of Computer Sciences,
Faculty of Computer and Mathematical Sciences,
Universiti Teknologi MARA, Arau Campus, 02600 Arau, Malaysia
mazni@isiswa.uitm.edu.my,
{shlailee,naimahmh}@perlis.uitm.edu.my

Abstract. This paper presents a rough sets approach in developing a team performance prediction model. To establish the prediction model, a dataset from an academic setting was obtained, consisting of four predictor variables: prior academic achievement, personality types, personality diversity, and software development methodology. In this study, four main steps in rough set, including discretisation, reduct generation rules, generation of decision rules, and evaluation were used to develop the prediction model. Two reduction algorithms; a genetic algorithm (GA) and a Johnson algorithm were used to obtain optimal classification accuracy. Results show that the Johnson algorithm outperformed the GA with 78.33% model prediction accuracy when using 10-fold cross validation. The result clearly shows that the rough sets is able to uncover complex factors in team dynamism, which revealed that the combination of the four predictor variables are important in developing the team performance prediction model. The model provides a practical contribution in predicting team performance.

Keywords: team performance, prediction model, rough sets, personality types, personality diversity, software development methodology.

1 Introduction

Working as a team is central part in every workplace. This is to ensure that organisational goals and strategies are met. Research in teamwork has been done extensively in management disciplines [1-2]. However, currently research of teamwork in software engineering fields is becoming more prevalent because software projects are mostly developed in teams. Research on teamwork especially in predicting team performance is vital because today's results will influence tomorrow's decisions. Team prediction model that indicate whether the team is effective or ineffective are vital to increase confidence in decision-making. Furthermore, the predicted results can serve as a preventive mechanism for decision makers to decide tactically their organisational strategic planning.

    In software engineering (SE), a main goal for teams is to produce quality software that meets clients' requirements on time within budget. When developing software,

A. Abd Manaf et al. (Eds.): ICIEIS 2011, Part II, CCIS 252, pp. 691–705, 2011.

good software practices are important steps to meeting the software organisational goals. However, the tasks are challenging due to the complexity of SE activities and factors influencing of team performance. Software engineering not only can be seen as a technical activity, it is also concerned with human skills such as communication, negotiation, and leadership to ensure the software project is successful. For this reason, this study is focused on the combination of four factors: prior academic achievements, personality types, personality diversity and software development methodology in determining team performance. Team performance is measured whether the team is effective or ineffective.

There are various techniques used to develop a prediction model. A classical statistical test such as a logistic regression and discriminant analysis is one of the most popular techniques. Mostly this research used parametric model [3], based on theoretical relationships amongst study variables and use algebraic equations in developing the model. However, it is difficult for these algebraic models to capture the relationships among all variables investigated in the study. Thus, this model may lack theoretical validity [4]. To overcome this, additional research on human factors used qualitative approach to explain the influence of the factors in affecting team performance. However, bias may exist in interpreting results using this approach. Technological advancement has resulted in the evolution of machine learning. There are various machine learning algorithms such as decision trees, artificial neural networks, and rough sets. These algorithms usually refer to supervised learning that attempts to learn and discover relationships based on historical data with available input (predictors) and target output (outcome). From the learning experience, machine learning is able to minimize differences between the observed and actual output. Machine learning in knowledge discovery in databases (KDD) becomes important because of its ability to automatically discover complex patterns from empirical data, thus giving useful knowledge to decision makers.

The importance of factors such as prior academic achievements, and personality types in determining team performance and the use of machine learning in building a prediction model, is extensively described in literature review; however, the integration of the two is not adequately addressed. Up to researchers' knowledge, no prior literature review exists that applies machine learning algorithms to build team performance prediction models based on the combination of four factors: prior academic achievements, personality types, personality diversity, and software development methodology. Thus, this study attempts to discover the applicability of rough sets in developing a team performance prediction model.

2   Related Works

2.1   Team Performance Modelling

Most research in predicting human performance has been carried out in academic fields. This is because data is easily accessible and available. Most studies aim to predict the performance of students on certain courses based on the students' backgrounds, Cumulative Grade Point Average (CGPA), and prior academic achievements [5-6]. Most of the prediction models are focused on the individual performance, but do not assess team performance. Therefore, research on team must be carried out to investigate significant factor that contribute to team performance.

Within team performance modelling, factors such as personality type's composition are commonly used to explain and predict team performance. Researches on team composition suggests that homogeneous teams experience more positive reactions because they have similar thinking pattern and able to communicate effectively, which bind the team members to accomplish high productivity and goal [7-8]. However, excessive cohesion can slow down the thinking pattern and therefore members are likely to interpret solution to the problem givens in similar ways. Heterogeneous teams need time to understand each others to make use of their differences to reach teams' goal. The team may enhance and bring new ideas and creative solutions to the teams [8-9]. An effective team is a team that can provide solution and hence develop creative and innovative quality software.

In situation where innovation solution is not essentials, heterogeneous teams can be at disadvantages because members must reconcile the diverse view point before they can complete a task. A team that is heterogeneous may work better than a group selected solely on technical ability [10-12]. However, when a heterogeneous team was given very simple tasks that do not demand high level creativity, conflicts occur among team members [13]. These resulted that there is no conclusive findings on team personality composition on affecting team performance. This may reflect of the different measurement used and expectation used in the studies.

Most techniques to determine relationships between personality types and team performance have been carried out using classical statistical techniques such as correlation [14-15], and multiple linear regression [16]. Based on these techniques, Acuna et al. [14] found a positive correlation between extroverted members and software quality, while Peslak [16] discovered that extroverted, thinking, and judging personality types improved project success. In addition, a qualitative approach is used when only small sample size is available. This was shown in [9] who pointed out that team personality type balance can determine team performance.

2.2 Rough Sets

Rough sets theory (RST) was introduced in the early 80's by Pawlak [17] for knowledge discovery. The rationale behind of RST is based on information representation and its granularity [18]. There are five basic concepts of rough sets theory. There are information systems, lower and upper approximation values, quality of approximation, reduct and core, and decision rules [19]. RST is derived on the concept of discernibility relationships of decision table. The decision table consists of condition attributes and decision attributes. In decision table, columns represent attributes and rows represent object or record of data. The decision table represents the information system (S) that can be defined as S = {U, C, D, f} where U is the set of objects in the table, C is a set of condition attributes and D is the set of the decision attributes. Consider B be any subset of C. Two objects x, y $\in$ U is refer to be B-indiscernible by the set of attributes $B \subseteq X$ *in S if and only if f(x,a) = f(y,a) for every a* $\in$ *B.*

RST deals with imprecise information in information system (S) by applying set concept of lower and upper approximation value. This concept is based on equivalence classes. The information system (S) = {U, A} and X/U be a set of objects and B/A be a selected of attributes. B-lower approximation is defined as $Bx=\{X \in U:[x]_B \subseteq X\}$ while B-upper approximation is $Bx=\{X \in U:[x]_B \cap X \neq 0\}$. Lower approximation of Bx set consists of objects that surely belong to the X set, whereas upper approximation of Bx set constitutes of objects that possibly belong to the X set with regard to knowledge provided by B. The boundary region of the set consists of objects that cannot be classified to the set.

Rough sets is capable in dealing with imprecise, uncertainty, and vague data sets [20; 4]. In addition, using rough sets does not require any assumptions of data size, data normality, and the algorithm is relatively simple to understand [19; 21]. Rough sets solely depend on the structure and information of data which are important [23]. This shows that rough sets is a non-invasive technique for knowledge discovery [23]. In addition, rough sets is an inductive approach in finding optimal solution from historical data to assist decision making.

Numerous applications have been used rough sets in developing a prediction model. These includes in the medical domain to predict cancer diseases [24]; in business to predict the bankruptcy of certain business [25]; in education to predict academic performance [26], and in bioinformatics application to predict protein function from structure [27]. Application of rough sets is widely used in bioinformatics applications. This is because the domain theories are not well understood [28] and thus, requires inductive approach such as rough sets to find relationship amongst variables investigated. This is similar to this study that investigates complex interrelated factors to predict team performance. Therefore, rough sets able to uncover hidden patterns in data.

3   The Modelling Process

Guidelines given by other researchers studying in knowledge discovery in databases (KDD) [29] suggested the use of machine learning techniques is adapted for developing the prediction model. KDD is a process of finding useful information and patterns of data [3] and is a widely accepted iterative process for building a prediction model. KDD is used in the present study because this approach allows researcher to discover data patterns and provide useful knowledge in building a prediction model. The five main stages of KDD approach are as follows:

3.1   Data Selection

Data was selected from empirical study conducted in [30-33]. The participants were third year undergraduate Information Technology students majoring in software engineering field. There were 120 students made up the sample, forming 29 teams. Each team consisted of three to five members. The teams have to develop a web-based application based on clients' need. In this study, data of individual members in a team was analysed according to the team. This is because team composition which consists of each member characteristics contributes to the team effectiveness.

Each team was randomly assigned to Agile and Formal Group. During this study, every participant was required to answer Jung Myers-Briggs (MBTI) Personality test.

MBTI personality types, is divided into four dichotomous pairs, which are Introversion (I) and Extroversion (E); Sensing (S) and Intuitive (N); Thinking (T) and Feeling (F); and Judging (J) and Perceiving (P). These four dimensions then make up 16 possible combinations of personality type as depicted in Table 1.

Table 1. The 16 MBTI Personality Types

ISTJ	ISFJ	INFJ	INTJ
ISTP	ISFP	INFP	INTP
ESTP	ESFP	ENFP	ENTP
ESTJ	ESFJ	ENFJ	ENTJ

A person can be classified into one of the 16 personality types based on the largest scale obtained. For example, a person scoring higher on Introversion (I) than Extroversion(E); Sensing (S) than Intuition (N); Thinking (T) than Feeling (F); and Judging (J) than Perceiving (P), would be classified as an ISTJ. The validity of this personality test has been demonstrated in other studies [12; 34]. Based on the personality type results, team personality diversity was calculated using team personality diversity formula [15], which is:

$$\text{Team Personality Diversity} = \sum_{i=1}^{4} f(K_i) \tag{1}$$

$$f(K_i) = \begin{cases} 0 & \text{if all team members have the same preferences in dimension i} \\ 1 & \text{if all but one team member has the same preferences in dimension i} \\ 2 & \text{otherwise} \end{cases}$$

where K = four dimension in personality types
(I-E, S-N, T-F, J-P)

Statistical correlation test has shown that only advanced programming course is significant to the software quality produced by the teams. Therefore, only this course was selected as prior academic achievement predictor variable in the prediction model. Software quality was assessed by the client and was coded as effective = 1 and ineffective = 0 (see Table 2). Effective teams were those that received 80 to 100 marks, all others being marked as ineffective.

3.2 Data Pre-process

Data was pre-processed to handle missing and noisy data such as outliers. This activity was carried out to rid of outlier data, which can affect the data quality, thus impacting further analysis and results. Data quality used in prediction model is critical in ensuring optimal model performance. However, data pre-processing can be time consuming, often accounting for up to 60% of data mining effort [35]. In this study, several functions in SPSS were used to prepare and analyse data. Box plot, scatter diagram, and cross tabulation were used to detect missing and noisy data.

For the purpose of the present study, missing data is defined as unavailable information in previous academic achievements and personality test results of some team members, whereas noisy data refer to data belonging to inactive members in a team. In addition, human inspection is also important to ensure data is consistent and thus, increase reliability and validity of data. From 120 data sets collected, all data are used to build the prediction model.

3.3 Data Transformation and Reduction

In this stage, the data is organised into required format to represent predictor and outcome variables to ensure that the input and output format representation does not negatively affect data quality [3; 36]. In this study, the collected data was transformed into appropriate categories as depicted in Table 2.

Table 2. Attributes and Categories

Predictor Variables			Category Level
1.	Prior academic achievements	Advanced Programming (TIA1023)	Grade A = 4 Grade B- = 3 Grade C = 2 Grade DF = 1
2	Personality type	Introvert (I) vs Extrovert (E)	Introvert (I) = 1 Extrovert (E) = 2
		Sensing (S) vs Intuitive (N)	Sensing (S) = 1 Intuitive (N) =2
		Thinking (T) vs Feeling (F)	Thinking (T) = 1 Feeling (F) = 2
		Judging (J) vs Perceiving (P)	Judging (J) = 1 Perceiving (P) = 2
3	Personality diversity	Team Personality Diversity	Between 0-8
4	Type of Methodology	Software Development Methodology	Agile =1 Formal =2

Outcome or Output variable			Category
1	Software quality (Q)	Team Effectiveness	Effective = 1 Ineffective = 0

3.4 Data Mining Using Rough Sets

Rough sets technique is the machine learning technique used in this study. Rough sets was chosen because this technique free from assumptions of data normality and data size. In this study, mostly data used is of nominal data type—personality types and software development methodology. Thus, normal data distribution criterion could not be achieved. In addition, rough sets can deal with small sample size.

Rough sets is available within the ROSETTA[37] tool, which can be used to analyze data using rough set theory. The tool is designed within rough set discernability framework and integrated with collection of rough set algorithms, which is appropriate tool for analysing research data. Therefore, in this study ROSETTA was used to analyse the data collected. There are four main steps in analysing data using ROSETTA as shown in Fig.1.

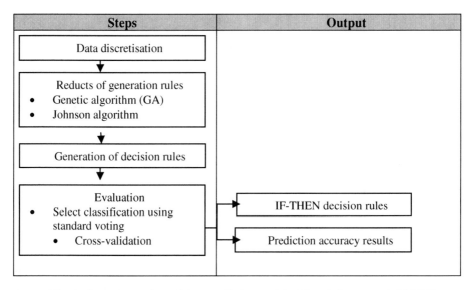

Fig. 1. General steps for building prediction model of Rough Sets using ROSETTA

Step 1: Data discretisation
Discretisation converts continuous data to discrete values for an improved pattern identification process. However, in this study, all the predictor variables and outcome variable are of ordinal and nominal data type, thus, discretisation process was not necessary.

Step 2: Reducts of generation rules
The next step in modelling using rough sets was computation of reducts. This process was conducted to identify minimal attributes that represent knowledge patterns present in the data. Thus, redundant and unimportant knowledge was first eliminated in order to generate a more reliable model. To reduct the generation rules, Genetic Algorithm (GA) and Johnson's were used. Genetic algorithm (GA) [38] is an efficient method in searching for optimal solutions and solving searching problems [28]. On the other hand, Johnson algorithm invokes a variation of a simple greedy algorithm to compute a single reduct only [39]. Both reduct generation rules were applied in order to identify the algorithm that can produce better classification accuracy. In this study, reducts using genetic algorithms (GA) was larger

than Johnson algorithms, with 70 for GA and 31 for Johnson. This has to be expected because GA was more heuristics for optimization of rules and find more reduct, whereas Johnson [39] has a natural bias towards finding a single prime implicant of minimal length. Example of reducts using Johnson algorithm is presented in Fig. 2.

```
{ie, diversity}
{sn, tf, diversity}
{gTIA1023}
{sn, tf, diversity, gTIA1023}
{ie, sn, tf, diversity}
{type, ie, sn, tf, diversity}
{type, diversity}
{diversity, gTIA1023}
...
```

Fig. 2. Sample of reducts using Johnson algorithm

Descriptive analysis of the attributes occurrence from the reducts using GA and Johnson algorithms was extracted from ROSETTA tool. Based on Fig. 3, the bar graph shows both algorithms reported that diversity has highest occurrences in the reducts. This reveals that team personality diversity has highest dependencies in determining of team effectiveness. Personality type, jp, which is judging-perceiving shows the lowest occurrences in the reducts for both algorithms, However, the percentage of occurrences for others attributes were not the same for GA and Johnson. This depends on how algorithm works on extracting the rules from rough sets.

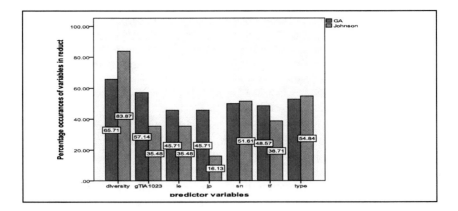

Fig. 3. Percentage occurrences of attributes in reduct using GA and Johnson algorithm

Step 3: Generation of decision rules

Based on the reducts, the patterns extracted from data were generated in the forms of IF-THEN rules, consisting of predictor variables and outcome variable. The rules contained four predictor variables (prior academic achievements, personality types, diversity, and software methodology) that predict team effectiveness and indicated patterns in the relationships among these variables. In this study, 157 rules were generated when using GA, and 50 rules generated when using Johnson reduction algorithm. GA generated more rules than Johnson. This is due to more reducts in GA as explained in Step 2. Table 3 shows sample of the most significant rules using Johnson algorithm. The most significant rules are the rules that highest support of objects in Left-Hand-Support (LHS) support. LHS support is number of objects in training data sets that match in the IF-part rules [28].

Table 3. Sample of most significant rules using Johnson algorithm

Rules no	Rules	LHS support
R1	type(1) AND diversity(5) => Q(0)	12
R2	type(2) AND diversity(3) => Q(0)	12
R3	type(1) AND tf(2) AND diversity(3) => Q(1)	9
R4	diversity(5) AND gTIA1023(2) => Q(0)	8
R5	type(2) AND sn(1) AND diversity(4) AND gTIA1023(3) => Q(0)	8

From Table 3, Rule 1 (R1) is the most significant rules. The rule shows that if the team using agile methodology (type (1)) with personality diversity is equals to five (diversity (5)), this team is predicted to be ineffective (Q(0)). The highest support for this rule is only 12 objects. In fact, it was found that more than 50% rules supported only by just 1 and 2 objects. This may because of small sample size that affects object coverage in the rule generated. Nevertheless, the rules show combinations of predictor variables are important in determining team effectiveness. The patterns generated provide information of association between variables in predicting team effectiveness.

Decision rules generated can be filtered based on rules strength and importance. Rules strength is measured based on how well each particular rule covered the data sets [40], where as rules importance refers to rules that occurred more frequently amongst the multiple rule sets [41]. In this study, most rules covered only by just 1 and 2 objects, and rules generated are unique. This is because of small sample size that affects object coverage in the rule generated. In addition, it is important to note that rule filtering must be performed carefully when sample data is small, as in that case, object coverage on certain rules is lower. Therefore, care was taken to avoid the reduction of model accuracy by rule removal. Thus, rules generated in this study were retained and not filtered.

Step 4: Rough set Evaluation
After rules have been generated, evaluation of model performance was carried out to ensure that patterns of rules generated can be generalized and produce a good prediction model. Rough sets was applied using ROSETTA tool, as it provides several classification procedures that can be applied, including standard voting, naïve Bayesian, and object tracking. However, in this study, only standard voting was used to assess the model classification accuracy. Standard voting is an ad-hoc classification technique, based on assigning a numerical certainty factor to each decision class for each object. This technique computes condition probability for each decision class that is correct [42].

Data was partitioned into two sets—training and testing sets by applying splitting technique, also known as split factor. Training set consists of sample of input data and its predetermined output for learning classification, whilst testing set is a new data used to evaluate model performances and ensure that the new data fits with the training set. Generally, in data mining process, 2/3 of data will represent training sets and the remaining 1/3 will be used for testing. In the present study, 70% (84 objects) of data was partitioned into training sets and 30% (36 objects) was used as testing sets. Moreover, in order to ensure that prediction performance was not due to chance; a k-fold cross validation technique was used as discussed in Section 3.5 Evaluation.

3.5 Evaluation

In k-fold cross validation, data was divided into k subsets, trained $k-1$ times, and tested k times, in accordance with the research done by [43]. This technique ensured that each data subset was tested once, and thus has the same proportion of data, reducing bias in the model evaluation. After dividing the data into selected fold, it is important to determine the accuracy of each fold. K-fold technique allows the average accuracy for each fold to be calculated. Most typical k-fold cross validation experiments used $k = 10$ [44]. However, depending on the data size, it is possible to divide, $k = 5$ and $k = 10$, to assess the model accuracy, which was the chosen approach in the present study. In this way, the fold with the highest prediction accuracy can be identified.

A criterion to choose the best technique to develop a team performance prediction model was assessed based on prediction accuracy. Accuracy is the most important factor to consider and is commonly used in assessing model performance [45] Therefore, a good prediction model is capable of obtaining highest prediction accuracy, thus ensuring that the model can accurately classify correct outcome, which is effective or ineffective team.

4   Results and Discussion

Hold-out and k-fold cross validation method were used to validate the prediction accuracy of the rough sets technique. Two reduction algorithms for rough sets rules generation were used; genetic algorithm (GA) and Johnson algorithm. Both algorithms were compared to determine the highest prediction accuracy.

Hold-out Method. Table 4 and Table 5 show the prediction accuracy for GA and Johnson algorithm of rough sets model. The accuracy is 80.56% for GA, and 75% for Johnson.

Table 4. Classification accuracy of GA using hold-out method

Actual Output	Predicted output		
	Ineffective (0)	Effective (1)	
Ineffective (0)	20	3	0.8696
Effective (1)	4	9	0.6923
	0.8333	0.75	**0.8056**

Table 5. Classification accuracy of Johnson using hold-out method

Actual Output	Predicted output		
	Ineffective (0)	Effective (1)	
Ineffective (0)	18	5	0.7826
Effective (1)	4	9	0.6923
	0.8181	0.6429	**0.75**

Table 4 shows that when actual output is ineffective, predicted output is 20 ineffective team members and 3 is classified as effective members. Therefore, specificity value is 86.96% (20/23). When the actual output is effective, predicted output is 9 for effective members and 4 is classified as ineffective members, thus sensitivity value is 69.23% (9/13). From these value, accuracy is obtained, which is 80.56% ((20+9)/36).

The result shows that GA with hold-out approach has highest percentage accuracy because rules generated by GA were more than Johnson algorithm as explained in Section 3.4. It shows that GA rules coverage is more and able to deal with pattern existed in new testing data set.

k-fold Method. Fig. 4 and Fig. 5 shows the accuracy of the rough sets model using the second cross-validation, where k-fold method, $k = 5$ and $k = 10$.

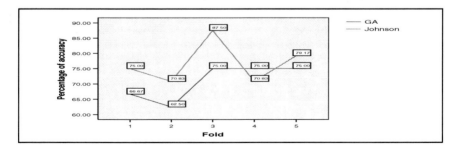

Fig. 4. Rough set model prediction accuracy using 5-fold cross validation

Fig. 4 shows prediction accuracy for each fold using k=5. The highest accuracy is 87.50% obtained by Johnson algorithm, and the lowest accuracy is 62.5% obtained by GA algorithm.

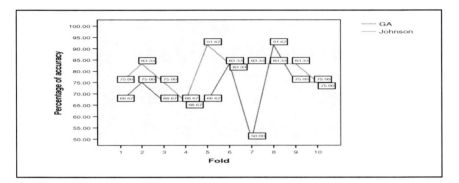

Fig. 5. Rough sets model prediction accuracy using 10-fold cross validation

Fig. 5 shows prediction accuracy for each fold using k= 10. The highest accuracy is 91.67% obtained by both algorithms, and the lowest accuracy is 50% obtained by GA. It was discovered that Johnson algorithm outperformed GA algorithm with 76.67% accuracy for k=5 and 78.33% accuracy for k=10. This indicated that Johnson algorithm has higher performance accuracy when using k-fold cross validation method. Although there was fluctuation of the accuracy for each fold, the difference was not statistically significant. This is indicated that the data set used is adequate to represent knowledge for predicting team effectiveness. The average accuracy results are presented in Table 6.

Table 6. Classification accuracy of rough set using k-fold cross validation

Rough Sets	Model Prediction Accuracy	
	k-fold (k=5)	k-fold (k=10)
GA	70.83%	71.67%
Johnson	76.67%	78.33%

This study shows that using different validation techniques resulted in different results of model accuracy for rough sets. GA achieved highest performance accuracy when using hold-out approach, but distinctively achieved lower accuracy than Johnson also when using k-fold method. Although accuracy of rough set using hold-out method is the highest (80.56%) using GA, this method has a drawback. In this study, the training data set is not fully representative of the real world application. Therefore, decision was made to use accuracy using k-fold cross validation, k=10 for both reduction algorithms, GA and Johnson for model accuracy comparison. Based on the results of cross-validation, it was revealed that k=10 are well suited in the model validation which is consistent with other study [43]. By using Johnson algorithm to reduct rules generated, the technique achieved 78.33% prediction accuracy, which is considered acceptable for new empirical data. Therefore, this technique is acceptable to develop the team prediction model.

This study shows that the four predictor variables are significant in predicting team performance. The team personality diversity is the most important predictor variable because team dynamism plays a role on how the teams interact and react to solve problem. This also indicated that a balance combination of personality types; introvert (I)-extrovert (E), sensing (S)-intuitive (N), feeling (F)-thinking (T), judging (J)-perceiving (P) are important in teamwork. In addition, a good programming skill is necessary in team to increase ability of members to write better software programs. Interestingly, findings show that types of methodology used by the teams affect the team effectiveness. This shows that treatment or intervention program may induce team to be effective. The factor may prompt decision makers to consider suitable training program for boosting a team to be productive and effective, thus achieving organisational goals.

5   Conclusion

This study attempts to develop a team prediction model using a rough sets approach. By using this technique, the model achieved an acceptable accuracy level with more than 70% accuracy. The result shows that using rough sets, knowledge pattern can be extracted from human empirical data. In addition, this technique is well-suited for data structure that contains multivariate discrete variables with small sample size. The knowledge can be used to understand effective teams, thus assisting decision makers to take necessary action and use preventive mechanism to improve team performance. Findings clearly indicate that using rough sets can reveal complex and vague relationship factors such as personality types and team diversity that play important roles in affecting team performance. Thus, this study provides a foundation and intention towards modelling human factors in team dynamism. The model provides a practical contribution to predicting team performance. In order to generalise the prediction model, future studies will be carried out using data collected in industrial setting [46] to validate the prediction model.

References

1. Bushe, G.R., Coetzer, G.H.: Group Development and Team Effectiveness: Using Cognitive Representations to Measure Group Development and Predict Task Performance and Group Viability. Journal of Applied Behavioral Science 43(2), 184–212 (2007)
2. Amato, C.H., Amato, L.H.: Enhancing Student Team Effectiveness: Application of Myers-Briggs Personality Assessment in Business Course. Journal of Marketing Education 27(41), 41–51 (2005)
3. Dunham, M.H.: Data Mining Introductory and Advanced Topics. Pearson Education Inc., New Jersey (2003)
4. Witlox, F., Tindemans, H.: The application of rough sets analysis in activity-based modelling. Opportunities and Constraints Expert Systems with Application 27(4), 585–592 (2004)
5. Nghe, N.T., Janecek, P., Haddawy, P.: A Comparative Analysis of Techniques for Predicting Academic Performance. In: 37th ASEE/IEEE Frontiers in Education Conference. IEEE, Milwaukee (2007)

6. Fan, L., Matsuyama, T.: Rough Set Approach to Analysis of Students Academic Performance in Web-based Learning Support System. In: Akhgar, B. (ed.) ICCS 2007, pp. 114–120. Springer, London (2007)
7. Gibson, C.B.: Building Multicultural Teams: Learning to Manage Homogeneity and Heterogeneity. In: Goodman, R.A., Boyacigiller, N., Phillips, M.E. (eds.) Crossing Cultures: Insights from Master Teachers. Blackwell Publishing (2004)
8. Neuman, G.A., Wagner, S.H., Christiansen, N.D.: The Relationship Between Work-Team Personality Composition and the Job Performance of Teams. Group Organization Management 24(1), 28–45 (1999)
9. Bradley, J.H., Hebert, F.J.: The effect of personality type on team performance. Journal of Management Development 16(5), 337–353 (1997)
10. Sommerville, I.: Software Engineering, 8th edn. Pearson Education, Essex (2007)
11. Rutherfoord, R.: Using Personality Inventories to Help Form Teams for Software Engineering Class Projects. ACM SIGCSE Bulletin 33(3), 73–76 (2001)
12. Karn, J.S., Syed-Abdullah, S., Cowling, A.J., Holcombe, M.: A study into the effects of personality types and methodology on cohesion in software engineering teams. Behaviour & Information Technology 26(2), 99–111 (2007)
13. Higgs, M., Plewnia, U., Ploch, J.: Influence of team composition and task complexity on team performance. Journal of Team Performance Management 11(7/8), 227–250 (2005)
14. Acuña, S.T., Gómez, M., Juristo, N.: How do personality, team processes and task characteristics relate to job satisfaction and software quality? Journal of Information and Software Technology 51(3), 627–639 (2009)
15. Pieterse, V., Kourie, D.G., Sonnekus, I.P.: Software Engineering Team Diversity and Performance. In: 2006 Annual Research Conference of the South African Institute of Computer Scientists and Information Technologists on IT Research in Developing Countries, pp. 180–186. ACM, Somerset West (2006)
16. Peslak, A.R.: The impact of personality on information technology team projects. In: ACM SIGMIS CPR Conference on Computer Personnel Research. ACM, Claremont (2006)
17. Pawlak, Z.: Rough sets. International Journal of Computer Sciences 11, 341–356 (1982)
18. Pawlak, Z., Slowinski, R.: Rough set approach to multi-attribute decision analysis. European Journal of Operational Research 72(3), 443–459 (1994)
19. Pawlak, Z., Skowron, A.: Rudiments of rough sets. An International Journal Information Sciences 177(1), 3–27 (2007)
20. Øhrn, A., Rowland, T.: Rough Sets: A Knowledge Discovery Technique for Multifactorial Medical Outcome. American Journal of Physical Medicine and Rehabilition 79(1), 100–108
21. Hui, Y.: Ad Hoc Networks Based on Rough Set Distance Learning Method. Information Technology Journal 10(5), 1038–1043 (2011)
22. Düntsch, I., Gediga, G.: Rough set data analysis: A road to non-invasive knowledge discovery, vol. 2. Metoδos Publisher, Bangor (2000)
23. Hassanien, A.E.: Intelligent data analysis of breast cancer based on rough set theory. International Journal of Artificial Intelligence Tool 12(4), 465–479 (2003)
24. Ruzgar, B., Ruzgar, N.S.: Rough sets and logistic regression analysis for loan payment. International Journal of Mathematical Models and Methods in Applied Sciences 2(1), 65–73 (2008)
25. Yahia, M.E., Arabi, N.D.A.: Rough Set Analysis for Sudan School Certificate. In: Wen, P., Li, Y., Polkowski, L., Yao, Y., Tsumoto, S., Wang, G. (eds.) RSKT 2009. LNCS, vol. 5589, pp. 626–633. Springer, Heidelberg (2009)
26. Hvidsten, T.R., Lægreid, A., Kryshtafovych, A., Andersson, G., Fidelis, K., Komorowski, J.: A Comprehensive Analysis of the Structure-Function Relationship in Proteins Based on Local Structure Similarity. PLoS One 4(7), e6266 (2009)

27. Hvidsten, T.R.: A tutorial-based guide to the ROSETTA system, 2nd edn. A Rough Set Toolkit for Analysis of Data (2010)
28. Fayyad, U., Piatetsky-Shapiro, G., Smyth, P.: From Data Mining to Knowledge Discovery in Databases. In: Fayyad, U., Piatetsky-Shapiro, G., Smyth, P., Uthurusamy, R. (eds.) Advances in Knowledge Discovery and Data Mining, pp. 1–34. AAAI/MIT Press, Cambridge, Mass (1996)
29. Mazni, O., Sharifah Lailee, S.A., Kamaruzaman, J., Azman, Y., Haslina, M.: Educational Approach of Refactoring in Facilitating Reverse Engineering. International Journal on Computer Science and Engineering (IJCSE) 2(3), 564–568 (2010)
30. Mazni, O., Sharifah Lailee, S.-A., Naimah, M.H.: Analyzing Personality Types to Predict Team Performance. In: CSSR 2010, pp. 624–628. IEEE, Kuala Lumpur (2010)
31. Mazni, O., Sharifah Lailee, S.A.: Identifying Effective Software Engineering (SE) Team Personality Types Composition using Rough Set Approach. In: International Conference on Information Technology (ITSIM 2010), pp. 1499–1503. IEEE, Kuala Lumpur (2010)
32. Sharifah-Lailee, S.-A., Mazni, O., Mohd Nasir, A.H., Che Latifah, I., Kamaruzaman, J.: Positive Affects Inducer on Software Quality. Computer and Information Science 2(3), 64–70 (2009)
33. Karn, J., Cowling, T.: A Follow up Study of the Effect of Personality on the Performance of Software Engineering Teams. In: International Symposium on Empirical Software Engineering, pp. 232–241. ACM, Rio de Janeiro (2006)
34. Pyle, D.: Data Preparation for Data Mining. Academic Press, United Kingdom (1999)
35. Kotsiantis, S.B., Kanellopoulos, D., Pintelas, P.E.: Data Preprocessing for Supervised Learning. International Journal of Computer Sciences 1(2), 111–117 (2006)
36. ROSETTA: A Rough Set Toolkit for Analysis Data, http://www.lcb.uu.se/tools/rosetta/index.php
37. Holland, J.H.: Adaptation in Natural and Artificial Systems, 2nd edn. MIT Press, Cambridge (1992)
38. Johnson, D.S.: Approximation algorithms for combinatorial problems. Journal of Computer and System Sciences 9, 256–278 (1974)
39. Al-Qaheri, H., Hassanien, A.E., Abraham, A.: Discovering Stock Price Prediction Rules Using Rough Sets. Neural Network World 18(3), 181–198 (2008)
40. Li, J., Cercone, N.: Discovering and Ranking Important Rules. In: IEEE International Conference on Granular Computing, pp. 506–511. IEEE (2005)
41. Øhrn, A.: ROSETTA Technical Reference Manual. Norwegian University of Science and Technology, Trondheim (1999)
42. Kohavi, R.: A Study of Cross-validation and Bootstrap for Accuracy Estimation and Model Selection. In: International Joint Conference on Artificial intelligence IJCAI 1995 2 (1995)
43. Whitten, I.H., Frank, E.: Data Mining - Practical Machine Learning Tools and Techniques, 2nd edn. Morgan Kaufmann, US (2005)
44. Rheingans, P., des Jardins, M.: Visualizing High-Dimensional Predictive Model Quality. In: 11th IEEE Visualization 2000 (VIS 2000). IEEE, Salt Lake City (2000)
45. Mazni, O., Sharifah-Lailee, S.-A., Azman, Y.: Agile Documents: Toward Successful Creation of Effective Documentation. In: Sillitti, A., Martin, A., Wang, X., Whitworth, E. (eds.) XP 2010. LNBIP, vol. 48, pp. 196–201. Springer, Heidelberg (2010)

Mining the Friendship Relation of Children from the Activity Data

Hirohide Haga and Shigeo Kaneda

Doshisha University,
Graduate School of Engineering,
1-3, Miyakotani, Tatara,
Kyotanabe, 610-0321, Japan
{hhaga,skaneda}@mail.doshisha.ac.jp

Abstract. This paper proposes a method to extract the friendship relations of children by using motion sensors. Children learn to fit into society through living in a group, and this is greatly influenced by their friendship relations. Although preschool teachers need to observe them to assist in the growth of children's social progress and support the development of each child's personality, only experienced teachers can watch over children while providing high-quality guidance. To resolve the problem, this paper proposes a mathematical and objective method that assists teachers with observation. It uses numerical data of activity level recorded by pedometers, and the authors make a tree diagram called a dendrogram based on hierarchical clustering with recorded activity level. Also, the authors calculate children's "breadth" and "depth" of friend relations by using more than one dendrogram. When the authors recorded children's activity level in a certain kindergarten for two months and evaluated the proposed method, the results usually coincided with the remarks of teachers about the children.

Keywords: clustering, dendrogram, friendship relation, pedometers.

1 Introduction

In nursery schools and kindergartens, children learn to fit into society through living in a group, and this is greatly influenced by their friend relations. Although preschool teachers need to observe them to assist in the growth of children's social progress and support the development of each child's personality, only experienced teachers can watch over children while providing high-quality guidance.

In particular, another issue is becoming a problem for unskilled preschool teachers: *Children with Special Needs*, who cannot form good friend relations in spite of having an average intelligence development level.[1]. The preschool

---

[1] The children with special needs include 1) unique character or legal condition at his/her home, 2) Autism-Aspergerfs Syndrome, 3) LD-Learning Disability, 4) ADHD-Attention Deficit Hyperactivity Disorder. A Japanese government survey in 2002 said that 6.3% of children in Japanese elementary schools and junior high schools have special needs.

A. Abd Manaf et al. (Eds.): ICIEIS 2011, Part II, CCIS 252, pp. 706–716, 2011.
© Springer-Verlag Berlin Heidelberg 2011

teachers have to identify the children with special needs in the early stages of development, and deal with the child in a proper manner. However, this is a very hard task for young and developing preschool teachers.

In a previous study[3], the authors demonstrated a new approach to analyzing friend relations by using activity level, recorded by pedometers, and tree diagrams called dendrograms based on hierarchical clustering. The pedometer detects child activity once every two minutes. For instance, let's assume that children play vigorously in the kindergarten yard for 20 minutes. The number of data is just 10 points and too small for clustering calculation. Thus, the proposed method should be applied for over a one-day period. The two-minute interval is not adequate for a detailed analysis.

Thus, this paper proposes a new approach to obtain more accurate and detailed behavior of the children by using new pedometers, detecting child activity once every four seconds. The proposed method finally clarifies "breadth" and "depth" of friend relations. The following Section 1 shows why the friend relation is important in early childhood education. Section 2 shows a conventional approach and its limitations. Section 3 proposes a new approach and the experimental evaluation is demonstrated in Section 4. Section 5 concludes this paper.

2 Importance of Friend Relation in Early Childhood Education

Children learn to fit into society through living in a group, and this is greatly influenced by their friend relations. A famous psychologist Mildred Parten[2] showed the following four categories of children's social play:

(1) Solitary play: the lowest level of social play. The child plays alone and independently even if surrounded by other children.;

(2) Parallel play: the child plays independently at the same activity, at the same time, and in the same place.;

(3) Associate play: this is described as common among three- and especially four-year-olds' play. The child is still focused on a separate activity but there is a considerable amount of sharing, lending, taking turns, and attending to the activities of one's peers;

and

(4) Cooperative play: this is described as a high level of play that represents the child's social and cognitive maturity.

Parten's categories have been frequently referred to for a long time. This theory is in excellent agreement with real friend relations. However, friend relations do not always change in accordance with Parten's theory. Child development depends on internal conditions (character, intelligence development stage) and external conditions (toys, influence of preschool teachers). Thus, preschool teachers have to read the dynamic change of the friend relation and support the development of each child in her/his daily nursery.

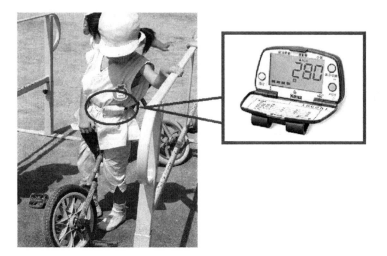

Fig. 1. Pedometer and Fixing Point

One class of 3, 4 or 5 year-olds in Japan is composed of up to 30 children. On the other hand, the competition among preschools is very severe, because the Japanese birth rate is very low and the number of children is decreasing. Thus, most preschool teachers work under irregular employment agreements and her/his work experience is usually less than three years for payroll reduction[2]. It is very difficult for these developing preschool teachers to grasp friend relations in the class.

3   Conventional Approach and Its Limitations

3.1   Conventional Approach

From the above viewpoint, the authors proposed an approach that uses numerical data of activity level recorded by pedometers, and the authors make a tree diagram called a *dendrogram* based on hierarchical clustering with recorded activity level[3]. Figure 1 shows the pedometer and its fixing point. The pedometer is a "Lifecorder Ex" manufactured by Suzuken Corp[4]', manufactured by Suzuken Corp[5]. The proposed conventional procedure is as follows.

1. Each child wears his/her pedometer in the morning. The pedometer is collected upon departure for home. This pedometer reports the activity once every two minutes. The activity score is an integer and from zero to nine.
2. The activity data is saved on PC. The activity data is a kind of *vector*. The vectors are clustered using the Ward Method and the distance is Euclidean Distance.
3. From the above clustering result, the friend relations and children with special needs are extracted.

---

[2] Japanese labor law prohibits that the length of irregular employment is more than three years. On the other hand, at least five years experience is required for preschool teacher growing-up.

3.2   Limitations of Conventional Approach

This conventional approach, however, has the following limitations. The first is the number of measured data. Let's assume that a child makes a stay of six hours, from 9 a.m. to 3 p.m., at his/her kindergarten. The number of elements in the measured vector is 180. This interval includes morning assembly, gymnastics hour, lunchtime, taking a nap, free playing, etc. There are many kinds of child-care efforts and most of them are not adequate for friend relation analysis. Free playing is suitable for relation analysis. However, the free playing is short and only a fraction of the total six hours of data. The clustering result is not accurate.

The second limitation comes from the Euclidean Distance. Let's assume that *Child A* performs one action. The movement is vigorous. On the other hand, another *Child B* performs the same action. However, the movement is quiet. In this case, the distance of the two vectors is large, in spite of *Child A* and *Child B* performing the same action. This phenomenon is a limitation of the conventional approach. On the other hand, Euclidean Distance may be suitable for the detection of "children with special needs." This is because of the fact that only he/she is quiet in a vigorous group, and this is meaningful for a child with special needs.

4   Proposed Method

4.1   Outline of Proposed Method

The authors employed a new Lifecorder EX pedometer manufactured by Suzuken Corp., detecting activity level once every four seconds. This increases the data density 30-fold. Thus, we can extract the pure "free playing" interval from the all-day data for friend relation analysis. Also, this paper proposes a new approach to figure out "depth" and "width" of child relations with several days' data. The outline of the proposed method is shown as follows. The details of Steps 2-4 are described in the following subsections.

Step 1: Activity Measurement; Activity Measurement. Each child wears a pedometer. The measured data are copied onto a PC.
Step 2: Clock Adjustment; The clock time of each pedometers is aligned.
Step 3: Data Extraction; Free playing interval data are extracted.
Step 4: Clustering; Friend relation is calculated from the extracted data by using a clustering algorithm.
Step 5: Depth and Width; Depth and width are obtained from several days' analysis. The definition of depth and width is given in a later subsection.

4.2   STEP2: Clock Adjustment

The clock of the pedometer is not accurate. Before the activity measurement, the accuracy was confirmed. The worst one delayed eight seconds for five days. This

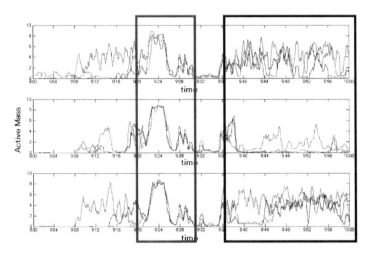

Fig. 2. Activities of 9 children from 9:00am to 10:00am

error cannot be negligible. To solve the problem, all pedometers were put into a bucket and the bucket was swung several times before the data measurement. Thus illegal activity datum peaks were detected and the temporal axis of each pedometer data was adjusted. As a result, the error of one day is under 0.5 second.

4.3   STEP3: Data Extraction

Figure 2 shows activity data for nine children, from 9 a.m. to 10 a.m., at a kindergarten in Osaka, Japan.[3]. The vertical axis shows the activity level and the horizontal axis shows time advance. As shown in the figure, nine activity data have similar values from 9:20 a.m. to 9:30 a.m. This time interval is the morning assembly, including preschool teacher speech and running in the kindergarten yard. On the other hand, nine activity data break apart in the interval from 9:35 a.m. to 10:10 a.m. This interval is "free playing."

The authors suppose that this free playing interval is best for extracting the friend relations in this paper. The "free playing" part is extracted with visual observation in the kindergarten. The extracted data are applied to the clustering step.

4.4   STEP4: Clustering

The clustering step consists of the following two sub-steps. 1) **Smoothing:** To avoid the influence of clock error or noise of the pedometer, the moving average is adopted. Figure 3 shows the effect of the smoothing. The interval of moving

---

[3] The number of children of this class is about 30. This figure shows a part of all data.

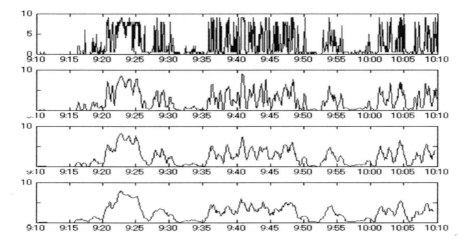

Fig. 3. Smoothing Effects by Moving Average (Top one is original)

average is 20, 40, and 60 sec. respectively from the second to the top in Figure 3. The top is original activity data. Experimentally, the moving average of 20 seconds was employed in this research. 2) **Clustering:** Hierarchical clustering with recorded activity and Pearson's product-moment correlation coefficient are employed. One dendrogram is generated for one "free playing." As mentioned below, the authors observed for two weeks.

5   Experimental Results

5.1   Outline of Experiment

To verify the effectiveness of the proposed method, the authors made the following social experiment. The visual observation records are written everyday by students.

Kindergarten: A kindergarten in Osaka, Japan.
Periode: From 11th to 26th Sept. 2007
              From 22nd, Oct., to 2nd, Nov., 2007. (28 days in total.)
Class: 29 members, Five years old

5.2   Clustering Results

Figure 4 shows a clustering result by using the Ward Method and activity record on Nov. 2, 2007. Also, figure 5 shows the result by using the Nearest Neighbor Method for the same data. The statistical package R[1] is employed for the calculation. The Ward Method minimizes the increase of the sum of squares in each group. The Ward Method is robust and suitable for group making. It is said that the Nearest Neighbor Method usually generates long chain-like clusters. To

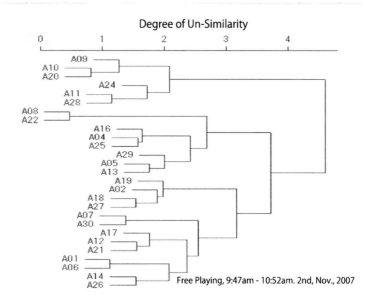

Fig. 4. A Dendrogram in Free Playing (Five years old, Ward Method)

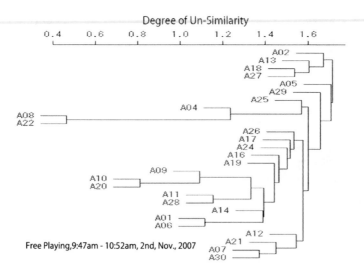

Fig. 5. A Dendrogram in Free Playing (Five years old, Nearest Neighbour Method)

evaluate the influence of the clustering algorithm, these two typical clustering algorithms are employed in this research.

In Fig.4 and Fig.5, the movements of children A08 and A22 are very similar to each other. The preschool teacher says that child A08 is a candidate for a "child with special needs" and child A22 is very interested in A08 and follows

A08. However, the authors, with their engineering background and having no expertise in the nursery domain, could not recognize that A08 is a candidate for a child with special needs. The dendrogram and the observation of the preschool correspond with each other for the other children.

There is a difference between the results of Fig. 4 and Fig. 5 In Fig. 4, there are many average sized clusters in the dendrogram. This is a typical result of the Ward Method, which is suitable for grouping analysis. here is only one big cluster in the Nearest Neighbor Method dendrogram, shown in Fig. 5. The Nearest Neighbour Method clarifies who is far from the other children. The method is suitable for children with special needs.

5.3   Analysis of Depth and Width

It was clarified that the clustering result is good information for observing friend relations in a class. However, the results possess lower reliability if only one day is analyzed. Thus, in this subsection, we discuss new concepts, *Depth and Width*. *Depth* evaluates how deeply one child has companionship with the other children. Also, *Width* represents how widely one child has companionship with the other children. Concretely, the following steps are employed.

Step1: Dendrogram Generation. Let children each wear a pedometer for a long time, such as one month, and dendrograms are generated for each free playing period.

Step2: Grouping. Each dendrogram is divided into eight clusters. The number eight is calculated from Parten's theory, which says that infant children ultimately form three- or four-member groups. Thus, the total number of 30 children is divided into eight groups.

Step3: Counting. Let K_j be an infant, where $j = 0, 1, 2, \cdots, n$, and n is the number of children in the class. Let's denote that $p(K_i, K_j)$ is a combination infants i and j, where $i \neq j$[4]. For each $i, (i = 1, 2, \cdots, , n)$, make all $p(K_i, K_j)$, where $j = 1, 2, \cdots, i - 1, i + 1, \cdots, n$. Count the number $Count_i$ for each i, where the initial value of $Count_i = 0$ and $Count_i = Count_i + 1$ when $p(K_i, K_j)$ are in the same cluster in each divided dendrogram of Step2 for all "free playing" intervals in one month.

Step4: Calculation of Depth and Width. Calculate the Depth and Width as follows.

Width: Median of all $Count_i$ for each $i, i = 1, 2, \cdots, n$. If the median is large, the child is always in large groups. On the other hand, the median is small, the child spends his/her preschool life in a small group, having a small number of children in the group.

Depth: Maximum value in all $Count_i$ for each $i, i = 1, 2, \cdots, n$. If this maximum value is large, this child always spends a time with a specific child or specific children. The specific children always act together in group.

---

[4] For instance, $p(A08, A22)$ is a pair for children A08 and A22.

5.4   Analysis and Discussion

Figures 6 and 7 show the results for the observation from 22nd, Oct. to 2nd, Nov. In these figures, a triangle indicates a male child, and a circle a female child. The horizontal axis is *Width* of the friend relation. Children in the right-hand side of these figures have many friends. Children in the upper area have specify friends and they always act together.

As mentioned before, A08 is a candidate of child with special needs. Figure 6 shows that A08 has a small number of friend. However, Fig. 7 shows that A08 is not a child with special needs now. A08 child spend much time with her friend.

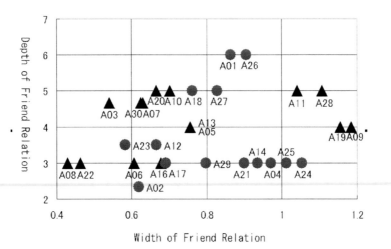

Fig. 6. Width and Depth Results (Five years old, Ward Method)

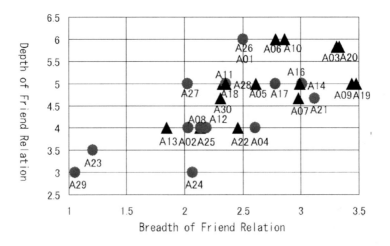

Fig. 7. Width and Depth Results (Five years old, Nearest Neighbour Method)

She may be a gentle child. The preschool teacher never handle her as a child with special needs and support her development in daily life.

Children A01 and A26 are plotted in the right-hand and upper areas in Fig. 6. The preschool teacher says that they are not leaders, but fair-haired boys. Figure 7 shows that the preschool teacher has to pay attention to children A29,A23,A24. Child A29 is a new classmate, and child A23 usually plays alone. A24 always chase after the preschool teachers. Also, the preschool teacher says that children A02,A20,A10 are "good" children having deep and wide friend relations.

Figure 6 shows that children of this class can be divided into the following four types.

Isolated: shows that children of this class can be divided into the following four types. Isolated: He/she has narrow friend relations. These children are plotted in the left-hand and lower areas in the figures. There are two types of children: one is a child with special needs and the other one likes solitary play. The preschool teacher never misread the solo-playing child as a child with special needs.
Social Community: The relation is rather shallow. However, he/she has many friends, and is plotted on the right-hand side of Fig. 6.
Intimacy: These children are plotted in the upper and left-hand areas of Fig. 6. They have a small number of friends, however, the relation is deep.
Mixed: They have deep and wide relations. They are plotted in the upper-right area of Fig. 6.

5.5   Related Works

This research is a kind of "life log" research. However, the target of these conventional life log tools is health care of a single user. In this research, the authors focus on acts in the group. This is a notable feature of the research.

6   Conclusion

This paper has proposed a new approach to grasping friend relations in kindergartens or nursery schools by using pedometers and hierarchical clustering. The authors conducted a social experiment for four weeks at a kindergarten of 5-year-olds in Osaka, Japan. The total number of children was about 30.

The obtained dendrogram and the human observations were in good agreement. Also, this paper has proposed a calculation method of the depth and width of child friend relations by using the dendrograms. These results determine the tendency of friend relations of the children in the class. Also, the results are in good agreement with the observations of an expert preschool teacher. Finally, the proposed method can be applied to supporting young and developing preschool teachers.

Acknowledgements. The authors deeply thank the director and teachers of a kindergarten in Osaka, Japan for their kind cooperation and guidance in the real world evaluation of the proposed scheme. Also, the authors thank Mr. Shinya Kihara for his contribution to this research work.

References

1. T. R. P. for Statistical Computing, http://www.r-project.org/
2. Hyun, E.: Making Sense of Developmentally and Culturally Appropriate Practice in Early Childhood Education. Peter Lang, New York (1998)
3. Kono, A., Shintani, K., Ueda, M., Kaneda, S.: New childhood observation method by active mass. In: Proc. of the the 4th IASTED International Conference on Web-Based Education, pp. 461–812 (2005)
4. Suzuken, http://www.suzuken.co.jp/english/whats/closeup/diabetes01.html
5. Suzuken, http://www.suzuken.co.jp/english/index.html

Practical Evaluation, Issues and Enhancements of Applied Data Mining

Wiesław Pietruszkiewicz

West Pomeranian University of Technology in Szczecin,
Faculty of Computer Science and Information Technology,
ul. Żołnierska 49, 71-210 Szczecin, Poland
wieslaw@pietruszkiewicz.com
http://www.pietruszkiewicz.com

Abstract. The wide popularity of Data Mining stimulated further expansion of spectrum of its methods and tools. However, the studies relating to this area usually focus on its scientific perception, and neglect other factors, being important in the practical evaluation of Data Mining and its applications, including stability of results, easiness of algorithms usage, demands on computational resources or speed factors. In this paper, we will provide the most significant limitations of applied Data Mining. Later, we will investigate how to perform the full evaluation of Data Mining methods and their results – beyond commonly used limited evaluation of results quality. The analysis will be done for two most popular types of tasks performed in Data Mining projects, i.e. feature selection and classification, but its results might be applied to other tasks. We will also provide information crucial to software applications based on Data Mining, including flexibility of knowledge representation forms.

Keywords: Applied Data Mining, Evaluation of Data Mining, Intelligent Software, Data–processing Software.

1 Introduction

The Data Ming (DM later) become very popular area of science as well as of industry. It has many methods suitable to be used in various data processing tasks. There are countless papers presenting high quality results achieved for various problems. However, there are many traps and problems when Data Mining is to be applied in practice and in such situations the evaluation of Data Mining methods should be done differently than the way proposed by the majority of papers. This is partially caused by a situation, when the majority of papers focus on DM and evaluates it only from the scientific perspective. Additionally, many specialised software tools/Data Mining frameworks exist and give an over–optimistic illusion that it's easy to perform Data Mining process. Even if delivering accurate results, they not necessarily will be satisfying in the real-life applications. Moreover, very often this process is done not paying any attention to the further usage of created knowledge, which is naively assumed

A. Abd Manaf et al. (Eds.): ICIEIS 2011, Part II, CCIS 252, pp. 717–731, 2011.

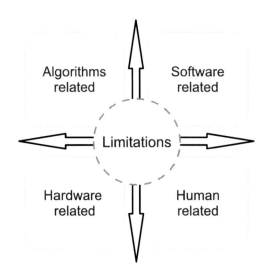

Fig. 1. Limitations of applied Data Mining

to be later deployed (inside software) without any issues. These mistakes will be high-lightened, explained and corrected by this paper. Its main idea is to present the problems of practical evaluation and usage of Data Mining by introducing factors important in practical deployment of DM and analysing deployment of DM in software.

2   Limitations of Computational Data Processing

The computational data processing, similarly to the other computing applications, is limited by different phenomena. They influence the capabilities, flexibility, usability or even economics of applied computational data processing.

Let's take a look at Figure 1 that represents the areas of Data Mining limitations established by us, which in our opinion constitute the most relevant factors. As it can be noticed Figure contains four types of limits relating to different areas:

- Algorithms–related — including, e.g. capabilities of algorithms to work with certain types of data or to produce a particular outcome form;
- Software–related — are results of software requirements on implementation of data processing applications, e.g. availability of data structures in programming languages, code efficiency in particular language or impossible scalability of software for a particular algorithm;
- Hardware–related —including, e.g. high demand on resources (memory requirements) or impossible to be implemented on a particular processing unit using standard tools (including programming languages and programming libraries);

– Human–related — are linked with expected behaviour of developed applications and contain, e.g. the easiness of usage, clearness of results or time of system's response.

The improvement of data processing methods, including Data Mining algorithms, can be done by the development oriented on any of these areas. It must be noted that this does not relate only to DM. This process is happening, even more dynamic, in the surrounding environment including, e.g. development of cloud computing or introduction of General Purpose Graphical Processing Units and their supporting technologies and languages. Therefore, algorithms capabilities can be extended onto more demanding or troublesome data, software can be build to support scalability (e.g. distributed processing), hardware limits are levied by deployment of more powerful and flexible processing units (e.g. 3rd generation of programming languages offered for embedded systems). Finally, the applied data processing is becoming less burdensome for people as they can use supporting computer environments, which automatise more tasks. The Data Mining is a particular example of computational data processing and it will be the subject of further analysis presented in the following sections of this paper.

3   Practical Evaluation of Data Mining

The practical evaluation of Data Mining will be presented herein for the two types of Data Mining tasks, being also the most frequently used types of algorithms:

– feature selection – reducing the size of dataset used to induct the knowledge, the results of this task are essential to the following stages of Data Mining,
– classification – attaching class memberships to data records; the observations taken for classification algorithms could be also applied to the regression or clustering algorithms.

These types of algorithms were selected as a resemblance of two major stages of Data Mining, i.e. pre–processing (preparing the data) and processing (doing actual data analysis). The third stage, i.e. post–processing (e.g. generation of reports) is optional stage and is not always performed.

According to [1] feature selection algorithms may be divided onto two major groups: filters and wrappers. Filters use a measure to evaluate the relationship between the input and output attributes, while the wrappers are multi-step procedures testing different combinations of features. It is also possible to add another group of feature selectors, i.e. embedded algorithms (see Figure 2). However, they aren't used particularly for the feature selection, but are incorporated by the others learning algorithms and deployed, e.g. in pruning or node selection (for more information about all three kinds of feature selection algorithms see [2]).

The process of feature selection was a subject of many researches e.g. [3] compared correlation based filters with wrappers. The other papers focussed on filters are [4] presenting an algorithm based on Information Theory and similarly

[5] compared different feature selection algorithms based on information entropy or [6] explained how both – feature and basis selection can be supported by a masking matrix. In another paper [7], the researchers compared different filtering algorithms, i.e. InfoGain, Chi2 and correlation.

The second kind of feature selection algorithms - wrappers - was a subject of research presented, e.g. [8] presented a sequential algorithm with low computational costs, being an example of general family of Forward Feature Selection algorithms. The other paper [9] proposed an algorithm of incremental feature selection. The most of feature selection algorithms use batch processing, however [10] presented a streamwise algorithm allowing to dynamically select the new-coming features. The research in [11] has shown a semi-supervised feature selection.

The usage of filters or wrappers causes two major problems. For wrappers it is an extensive searching through the different combinations of attributes. It forces the quality evaluation for each model build over each subset and every additional attribute increases the search space. On the other hand, the major problem we encounter using filters is an influence of measure selection on the quality of further developed model. The each evaluator used by filters, coming from information theory or statistics, may not be an optimal solution for various dimensions of subsets, i.e. a subset filtered by one algorithm may be inferior to a potential subset selected by another algorithm.

The second area of investigation conducted herein relates to the problems of classification. It was done using datasets extracted from SourceForge.net [12] by [13]. This data repository was a subject previous of research, e.g. [14] examined how machine learning algorithms like logistic regression, decision trees and neural networks could be used to analyse the success factors for Open Source Software. In the other paper [15] were presented similarity measures for OSS projects and clustering was performed. The other study done by [16] explained how to predict if OS project abandonment is likely. This dataset was used due to its character including: large size, number of classes (5) above average for common classification problems and presence of different attributes (numeric, nominal).

For the feature selection, the researchers usually limit their investigation to measures of quality, sometimes even to one, i.e. the accuracy of results. This is a basic factor used to comprehend the quality of results for datasets selected by various methods being compared. However, analysing this domain from the practical perspective, we will find additional factors influencing the evaluation of achieved results provided by Data Mining methods (see Figure 2):

- stability– indicates the spread of results, thus being a measure of selection risk (negative risk, i.e. selection of highly inferior subset of features).
- unbiasedness – biased selection is done by evaluating attributes using some arbitrary measure with a tendency to be suboptimal in the processing stage.
- scalability – for complex tasks it is desired feature to be able to divide and scale the calculations,
- flexibility – some methods do not work with all types of attributes and require additional conversions.

Evaluation of Data Mining

Fig. 2. Scientific and practical evaluation of Data Mining applications

When we examine the classifiers and their scientific applications, we will find that the factors important in a purely scientific evaluation of classifiers, which the most papers focus on and very often even limit to, are:

- quality – being the most common factor presented in the research papers that usually evaluate different DM methods from the perspective of results quality,
- stability – means that the results should be repeatable or very coherent during multiple runs of the DM method (with the same adjustments of internal parameters).

On the contrary, the practical usage of classification considers more parameters characterising the delivered outcome and involves factors like:

- speed/time of learning – as knowledge induction isn't one step process, the time–consuming methods increase the length of experiments that usually contain multiple run–test–adjust steps,
- number of adjustable parameters – influences the easiness with which a method could be used, higher numbers of parameters, increases space in which an optimal set of parameters should be found,
- speed/time of simulation – is the time taken by method to find an answer for the asked question (output for inputted data).

4   Experiments

4.1   Feature Selection

The first stage of experiments related to the feature selection. In this part of experiment we have compared the results of feature selection done for two datasets.

The majority of AI–oriented papers assume that the deployment of particular features cannot be decided at the data gathering stage (apart the rejection of obviously irrelevant features). Therefore, redundant features are collected and have to be filtered out later. Hence, it is required to reduce the data dimensionality as this process:

- Reduces the curse of dimensionality – the convergence of estimators used in the learning is much slower for problems with a higher dimensionality than for these with a lower number of dimensions.
- Lowers the memory requirements for data storage and processing – redundant or insignificant information increases the demand on memory, increasing storage costs or time span of stored data exceeding the possessed resources.
- Simplifies model's structure – which, being simpler, could become easily understandable by humans or software implementable.
- Speed-ups the process of learning – the complexity for machine learning methods usually is above linear complexity, i.e. quadratic or cubic.
- Removes unnecessary attributes being a noise – irrelevant features could "blur" the problem and cause lower quality of the results.
- Increases the generalisation abilities – unnecessary attributes limit model's generalisation abilities, i.e. capabilities to successfully work with the previously unseen data.

There are two solutions to the dimensionality reduction. At first, this task can be done by the recalculation of attributes into a smaller subset, e.g. using Principal Components Analysis or Discriminant Analysis methods. The other approach to space dimensionality reduction is the feature selection. This procedure generally return subsets of attributes, containing features being the most significant ones for the modelled process/system/object.

The main problems of feature selection done in advance, prior to the development of algorithm using these information attributes, are the two assumptions. The first one assumes that the characteristics of data used in selection (research phase) is identical to the data used in production (deployment phase). The second one, assumes that a particular — single — evaluation criterion reflects the quality of further–developed models. Unfortunately, these assumptions very often lead to not–optimal selection (some times highly inferior).

In this paper we compare typical filtering algorithms with a hybrid approach to feature selection, done by a parallel multi-measure filtering (later called by Multi Measure Voting - MMV in abbrev.). The main aim of this algorithm is to incorporate different measures on information usefulness and to limit probability of not-optimal selection. More information about MMV can be found in [17].

In this stage of experiments we have used two different datasets. The quality of feature selection done for them was evaluated using popular and flexible classification algorithms – C4.5 decision tree [18] and neural networks (in multi-layered perceptron variant [19]). During the experiments we have examined models with different numbers of attributes for each algorithm. To check their generalisation abilities, we have tested accuracy for 3–fold Cross-Validation and Training Set. An objective environment for the comparison of models was ensured by keeping

C4.5 parameters constant, otherwise adjustment could be done in favour of any algorithm. Hence, we set these C4.5 parameters to constant values:

- The confidence factor was set to 0.25,
- The minimal support of leaf was set to 2,
- The number of data fold was set to 3 (one of folds was used in error pruning).

Similarly, the neural networks were built and taught with these constant parameters:

- The learning ratio was set to 0.2,
- The momentum was set to 2,
- The net had one hidden layer with an adaptive number of neurons.

The first used dataset was the Personal (House–hold) Bankruptcy dataset [20]. This dataset contained 17 input attributes and 1 output class attribute (see Table 1). The input attributes were 8 numeric and 9 nominal attributes. All these features were divided into three groups:

- Behavioural features – Describing how the financial decision are being taken by household.
- Demographical features – Describing the family, i.e. the number of family members, their average age, education or family income.
- Geographical features – Containing the information about family's domicile.

The output attribute was a class feature, as all families were divided into three groups if family:

- Repaid or repay debts in advance or according to the schedule.
- Had or have slight problems in the repayments.
- Had or have significant problems in the repayments, stopped them or were a subject of any debt enforcement procedure.

This mixture of numeric and nominal attributes, having different characteristics, was selected as the testing data requiring feature selectors to prove their abilities to work with different types of data.

The results of the experiments present the accuracy for experiments with 3-fold cross-validation done using C4.5 Decision Tree and Multilayered Perceptron are in Figure 3 (C4.5) and 4 (Perceptron). It is possible to observe that MMV was in most of situations as accurate as the best single algorithm. Additionally, it was very stable comparing with the other algorithms and we expected and hoped to observe such behaviour. It must be remembered that there was not any globally optimal algorithm, therefore Multi-Measure proved to be a fast (comparing with the selection done using wrappers) and also effective approach to the problem of feature selection.

The second dataset used in experiments relating to the feature selection was Statlog Image Segmentation dataset, being popular machine learning benchmark available at UCI dataset repository [21]. This dataset contains 19 features with real values and 1 output class attribute. This dataset was selected due to different

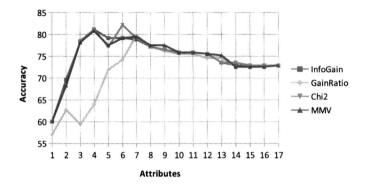

Fig. 3. The accuracy of 3–fold Cross Validation for House–hold bankruptcy dataset and C4.5 decision tree classifier

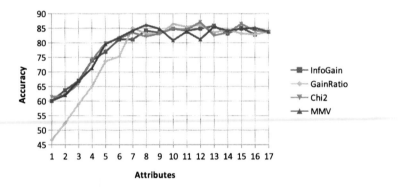

Fig. 4. The accuracy of 3–fold Cross Validation for House–hold bankruptcy dataset and Multilayered Perceptron

profile comparing with the household bankruptcy experiment, as the previous dataset contained mixed attributes, while this one had numeric real-valued features.

The Figures 5 and 6 present the accuracy of 3–fold Cross Validation performed by C4.5 and Multilayered Perceptron. It must be noted that GainRation filter was the worst algorithm for subsets of attributes in range from 1 to7, while this algorithm was the best in overall for household experiment. Therefore, a hybrid selection should be considered a robust and unbiased feature selection also for this task.

It must be pointed out that by analysing the primary evaluators we have observed that GainRatio was the most unstable method of features filtering as well as that the GainRatio-based models, sizing from 1 to 4, were highly inferior to all the others algorithms. It is possible to further extend the capabilities of MMV, e.g. by using other single evaluation criteria or introducing voting. However, the provided results of these basic experiments clearly explain the problems of feature selection done in practice.

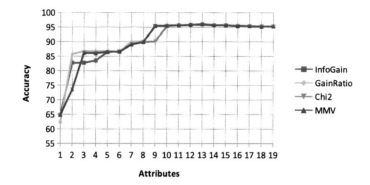

Fig. 5. The accuracy of 3–fold Cross Validation for Image Segmentation dataset and C4.5 classifier

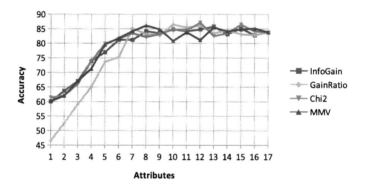

Fig. 6. The accuracy of 3–fold Cross Validation for Image Segmentation dataset and Multilayered Perceptron

4.2 Classification

The second stage of experiments was oriented on issues of classification. The dataset used in these experiments was [13] containing information extracted from SourceForge.net Web–based work environment. This dataset was used due to its character including: large size, number of classes (5) above average found for common classification problems, presence of different attributes (numeric, nominal) and these features were expected to cause problems for classifiers that would reveal the issues of practical Data Mining. More information about this data and its four parts (separate datasets) are in Table 1.

One of the first questions that must be answered during building the classification models is their size. Usually classifiers with higher dimensionality offer better quality of results, but increase of attributes space cause problems with memory requirements, increase cost of data gathering&processing or decreases

Table 1. Details for *Scope*, *Time*, *Costs* and *Effects* datasets used in Classification experiments

Dataset	Unique records	Reduced records	Objects	Attributes
Scope	167698	167698	2881	39
Time	233139	104912	77592	12
Costs	127208	20353	10889	18
Effects	96830	15492	64960	21

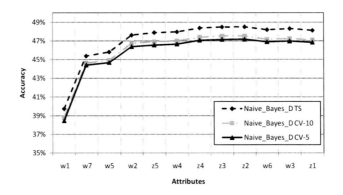

Fig. 7. The accuracy of classification vs used information attributes for *Time* dataset

speed of classification. Hence, in practical applications based on methods of classification a point of equity must be found, i.e. it is necessary to balance the increase of information available for classifiers with problems this increase causes. The Figure 7 shows this phenomenon for Time dataset and as it can be noticed there is number of attributes beyond which further increase does not significantly increase the quality of classification. It means that classifiers can be simplified without noticeable decrease of their quality.

Another typical problem of applied Data Mining is the time necessary to perform the experiments. Usually we cannot guess the optimal parameters for methods of classification, the size of models or even which method should be used. Therefore, a standard approach to Data Mining experiments is to perform cyclic operations of changes&testing. As the time taken differs very much for all algorithms it implies that the time of development process will also differ significantly. In the industry applications the resources available on development of DM applications usually are limited, with a small margin of reserves, and if time–consuming methods are applied they reduce chances to test other configurations or adjustments of parameters. The example of time of learning for different methods of classification was presented in Figure 8.

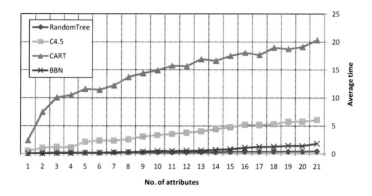

Fig. 8. The time of learning for different classifiers (*Effects* dataset)

5 Software Implementation

Another challenging task is the implementation of Data Mining based software. Again, when we investigate this domain we will find that it is not a trivial task. There are many important factors influencing the selection of proper Data Mining methods, among them we should distinguish:

- the understandability of results – the inducted knowledge might be or not easily understandable by humans, thus this feature defines the requirements for form of knowledge presentation,
- easy implementation – without a specialised programming library the knowledge and DM method must be programmed and there are large differences in the implementation effort for various methods,
- the demand for resources – after the implementation and during the usage in some situation, when datasets are large, a crucial issue might be the demand for resources beyond available level.

Therefore, method selection cannot be performed using only the quality of their results. The primary task of application is to deliver expected functionality. Hence, very often software can use knowledge in different forms (represented by different kinds of Data Mining algorithms) and, apart of additional implementational effort, this not influence the functionality of application. However, in some situations it is required to perform knowledge induction resulting in a form easily understandable for humans, e.g. according to the banking regulations all operations should be in explicit for bank staff, i.e. in form human–understandable procedures. This also applies to the procedures based on knowledge inducted by data analysis, e.g. credit scoring.

The standard approach to ease implementational problems is to optimise algorithms, unfortunately this might not work for software build over popular DM libraries (being already optimised) as they have a small potential of improvements done via code optimisation (not mentioning very high effort). However, for the production–ready systems it is possible to use three solutions:

- simplification – for many data processing methods it is possible to reduce their complexity (e.g. number of layers and neurons for neural networks) without a significant decrease of quality and it is required to perform analysis of quality&costs to find an acceptable compromise;
- GPU–supported processing – the deployment of General Purpose Graphical Processing Units results in three advantages, i.e. higher computational power, lower costs of processing and lower energy consumption (important especially in high–performance computing), and as GPUs offer parallel data processing, not task parallelism, they fit very well into the data mining algorithms;
- distributed processing clusters – the additional increase of processing power can be achieved by deployment of computing clusters; there are specialised technologies for distributed processing (e.g. Apache™Hadoop™) or even distributed Data Mining (Apache™Mahout™).

Another important feature of Data Mining–based software is selection of knowledge representation form. Evaluating them we've established the main advantages and disadvantages for four major forms:

- decision rules,
- decision trees,
- causual networks (Bayesian networks/belief networks),
- mathematical models.

Table 2 contains their main characteristics. Excluding features cause that generally–best form does not exist and the best suitable knowledge representation form must be selected according to the requirements of particular application.

6   Further Research

This paper does not cover all issues and aspects relating to the practical evaluation and deployment of Data Mining. Therefore, we have plans to further develop the research presented herein.

The first future aim is to prepare a set of benchmarks that could be used to measure introduced quality factors. The popular benchmarks, e.g. classification or regression datasets available at UCI contain information of accuracy achieved by researchers for these datasets. The new benchmarks should be oriented on applied Data Mining and used to measure and compare factors introduced in previous sections including memory requirements or speed.

The second aim is to create a practical guideline for usage of algorithms. It will provide an easy to use description of popular Data Mining methods. It must be noted that, opposite to the quality of processing, which must be checked for each dataset, it is possible to provide general observations for Data Mining algorithms regardless a particular dataset they will be applied.

Table 2. The basic characteristics of different knowledge–representation forms

Form of knowledge	Main advantages	Main disadvantages
Decision rules	Easy software implementation;	Delivers not–optimal structure in terms of size and speed;
	Obvious even for non–skilled users	Possible incoherency of rules
Decision tree	Fast functioning (learning and simulation);	Can be used only in classification tasks (or simplified quasi–regression);
	Intuitive visual representation	Non–resistant to noisy observations at run–time
Causual networks	Deal with partial information at run time;	Results depend on particular algorithms deployed;
	Work with partial observations	Suitable only to classification problems
Math models	Flexible form suitable to different tasks;	Even slightly complex results might be unclear for people;
	Usually fast at run–time	Very broad space of search for optimal model class

7 Conclusions

The paper presented the most important issues of applied Data Mining. It introduced and explained the differences between purely scientific Data Mining and its practical usage. Therefore, scientist could evaluate the results of their experiments beyond the scientific factors.

The second group of people that might be interested in the results presented herein are practitioners as paper provided a set of features that could help them understand what issues they will have to deal with when applying Data Mining in practice.

One of underestimated characteristics of Data Mining algorithms is the easiness of their usage. This feature is essential for applied data mining, where even the most accurate and sophisticated algorithms will be inferior the one being easy to use and giving average results. It is being caused by two factors: practitioners on average are not so highly skilled as the scientists and the resources available in industrial Data Mining project do not usually allow to perform try&seek experiments.

Analysing this subject from the perspective of development of intelligent systems it must be remembered that the most important factors influencing the successful design and development of Data Mining–based software include the speed of learning&simulations and the demand on computational resources. In some situations the method offering the best quality of results cannot be applied, due to unacceptable time of reply at run–time or too high memory requirements.

Finally, in our opinion the applied Data Mining requires different approach that presented by the majority of papers. While, for scientist a slight increase of classification quality is a main aim, the practitioners prefer solutions more robust, easier to be used or faster at run–time. Therefore, as the Data Mining is in the stage of maturity for a long time we – scientist and practitioners – must focus on its usage not on research aimed at building of more advanced algorithms, very often having a narrow specialisation. This is a main issue which must be solved to achieve wider audience and large spectrum of real–life Data Mining applications.

Acknowledgements. The research presented herein was a part of and funded by an internal West Pomeranian University of Technology research project.

References

1. Guyon, I., Elisseeff, A.: An introduction to variable and feature selection. Journal of Machine Learning Research, 1157–1182 (2003)
2. Saeys, Y., Inza, I., Larrañaga, P., Wren, D.J.: A review of feature selection techniques in bioinformatics. Bioinformatics 23 (2007)
3. Hall, M.A., Smith, L.A.: Feature selection for machine learning: Comparing a correlation-based filter approach to the wrapper. In: Proceedings of the Twelfth International FLAIRS Conference (1999)
4. Koller, D., Sahami, M.: Toward optimal feature selection. In: Proceedings of the Thirteenth International Conference on Machine Learning (1996)
5. Duch, W., Wieczorek, T., Biesiada, J., Blachnik, M.: Comparison of feature ranking methods based on information entropy. In: Proceeding of International Joint Conference on Neural Networks (2004)
6. Avidan, S.: Joint feature-basis subset selection. In: Proceedings of the 2004 IEEE Computer Society Conference on Computer Vision and Pattern Recognition (2004)
7. Zheng, Z.: Feature selection for text categorization on imbalanced data. ACM SIGKDD Explorations Newsletter Archive 6, 80–89 (2004)
8. Ververidis, D., Kotropoulos, C.: Sequential forward feature selection with low computational cost. In: Proceedings of European Signal Processing Conference (2005)
9. Liu, H., Setiono, R.: Incremental feature selection. Applied Intelligence 9, 217–230 (1998)
10. Zhou, J., Foster, D.P., Stine, R.A., Ungar, L.H.: Streamwise feature selection. Journal of Machine Learning Research 7, 1861–1885 (2006)
11. Ren, J., Qiu, Z., Fan, W., Cheng, H., Yu, P.S.: Forward semi-supervised feature selection. In: Washio, T., Suzuki, E., Ting, K.M., Inokuchi, A. (eds.) PAKDD 2008. LNCS (LNAI), vol. 5012, pp. 970–976. Springer, Heidelberg (2008)
12. Madey, G.: The sourceforge research data archive, srda (November 2008), http://zerlot.cse.nd.edu
13. Dżega, D.: The method of software project risk assessment. PhD thesis, Szczecin University of Technology (June 2008)
14. Raja, U., Tretter, M.J.: Experiments with a new boosting algorithm. In: Proceedings of the Thirty-first Annual SAS: Users Group International Conference, SAS (2006)
15. Gao, Y., Huang, Y., Madey, G.: Data mining project history in open source software communities. In: North American Association for Computational Social and Organization Sciences (2004)

16. English, R., Schweik, C.M.: Identifying success and abandonment of floss commons: A classification of sourceforge.net projects. Upgrade: The European Journal for the Informatics Professional VIII(6) (2007)
17. Pietruszkiewicz, W.: Unbiasedness of feature selection by hybrid filtering. International Journal of Computing 10 (2011)
18. Quinlan, J.R.: C4.5: programs for machine learning. Morgan Kaufmann, San Francisco (1993)
19. Rojas, R.: Neural Networks – A Systematic Introduction. Springer, Berlin (1996)
20. Rozenberg, L., Pietruszkiewicz, W.: The methodic of diagnosis and prognosis of household bankruptcy. Difin, Szczecin (2008)
21. Frank, A., Asuncion, A.: UCI machine learning repository (2010)

User Behavioral Intention toward Using
Smart Parking System

Amin Kianpisheh, Norlia Mustaffa,
Janet Mei Yean See, and Pantea Keikhosrokiani

School of Computer Sciences, Universiti Sains Malaysia,
11800 USM Penang, Malaysia
ak11_com040@student.usm.my, norlia@cs.usm.my,
janet_see@jabil.com, pantea.keikhosrokiani@gmail.com

Abstract. Car drivers may encountered difficulty in finding car park, improper parking, parking lot capacity overflow and wasting time in order to find car park. In order to satisfy the demand of users, Smart Parking System (SPS) is developed. SPS detects occupancy of each car park and concurrently display the number of vacant spaces and directional signage to the available car parks on the display boards. In order to assess user acceptance level toward using SPS, a research model is proposed by combining three different research theories which are Technology Acceptance Model (TAM), Theory of Planned Behavior (TPB) and Unified Theory of Acceptance and Use of Technology (UTAUT). An online survey with 150 respondents has been conducted to evaluate the user acceptance level based on perceived usefulness (PU), perceived ease of use (PEOU), subjective norm (SN) and performance expectancy (PE) variables. The result of the survey verified that SPS is going to be successful project because of the high proportion of respondents accept SPS due to its ease of use and usefulness for them.

Keywords: Car park, Multilevel parking lot, Directional signage, Perceived Usefulness, Perceived Ease of Use, Subjective Norm, Performance Expectancy.

1 Introduction

Growing urban population and improving human lifestyle, highlighted the importance of time value and one stop shopping. In modern daily life, most people prefer to receive more than one benefit and service at one time and from one location. Shopping behaviors are culturally different among countries. Visiting shopping mall as entertainment which is called "window shopping" is a type of "weekend activity" for Malaysian [1]. In addition to increasing rate of building new shopping complex means that major retail chains prefer to operate under one roof, rather than separate shops in different area [2]. Selecting appropriate technology for car park detection depends on objective and scope of the project. Monitoring parking lot vacancy is a significant technology which can be used for guiding car to vacant space and efficient use of parking spaces as well [3]. To help drivers in finding vacant parking space without much effort, intelligent parking systems should provide specific location of

A. Abd Manaf et al. (Eds.): ICIEIS 2011, Part II, CCIS 252, pp. 732–743, 2011.

vacant space and not just the total number of spaces [4]. In order to find vacant space, drivers need to look at the LED display board, which will show how many and which types of vacant spaces are available at each level of shopping complex by that time. After entering to the desired parking level, drivers are supposed to look at the internal signs which are hanging from the parking ceiling at each aisle. Each internal signage consists of two parts, one will show the number of the available spaces and the other one will show the direction (left, right or forward) of aisle which has vacant space.

Each individual parking space is equipped with LED lights which are located above the current space and can show green, red, blue or yellow color. The color of space indicates status of that space; green color means the space is vacant and ready to park, red color shows the space is full, blue color indicates that specific space is assigned for handicapped driver and yellow color LED indicates that car park is booked, VIP space or reserved for specific reason. Whenever the driver enter the one vacant space, the green light will change to red within a few seconds and counter of the aisle which the occupied space located in, will decrease one number simultaneously same as entrance information board counter.

The objectives of this research is to assess the users' acceptance level and demand towards SPS as described above and also to find out what are the users' most important needs to facilitate parking procedures for them. In line with this, another objective of this research is to find out important factors which can affect user acceptance toward using SPS. This paper will be organized as follows: the introduction section is about the importance of parking lot role in people's daily life and description of SPS, section II is about explanation and comparison of technology acceptance models, section III described how the research is conducted, section IV discussed how research hypotheses are created and lastly section V contain the analysis of the results generated from the data collected.

2 Background

For this section, a review of technology acceptance models used as a basis for research model is presented. The researchers have selected Technology Acceptance Model (TAM), Unified Theory of Acceptance and Use of Technology Model (UTAUT) and Theory of Planned Behavior (TPB) for this purpose.

A. Technology Acceptance Model (TAM)

Technology Acceptance Model (TAM) measures user acceptance toward new technology. TAM is derived from Ajzen and Fishbein's theory of reasoned action [5]. TAM main independent variables are perceived usefulness (PU) and perceived ease of use (PEOU) which will describe behavioral intention to use and system usage. In this model, PEOU and PU are the external variables which determine the intention to use a system. Here, PU is the level of individual's belief about usefulness of specific system and assess how new technology can enhance his/her performance. As for PEOU, it explains how system is convenient to use and requires minimal effort. PU refers to a person's feeling about the advantages that can be obtained by using an IT in an organization, whereas PEOU is related to how individuals evaluate the easiness or difficulty of using information system. The desire to use the information system demonstrates Attitude toward use (A) and willingness of an individual to execute a behavior translated to behavioral intentions (BI)[6]. Fig.1 presents Technology Acceptance Model (TAM).

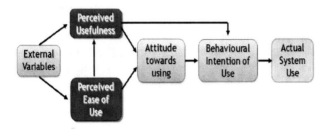

Fig. 1. Technology Acceptance Model (TAM)

B. Theory of Planned Behavior (TPB)

Theory of Planned Behavior (TPB) is completed form of Theory of Reasoned Action (TRA) with one more extra independent factor compared to TRA which is Perceived Behavioral Control (PBC). Indeed actual behavior is influenced by subjective norms, attitude, or perceived behavioral control or all of these factors. TPB is more powerful to illustrate behavior intention compared to TRA.

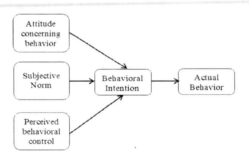

Fig. 2. Theory of Planned Behavior model (TPB)

Behavioral control is defined as one's perception of the difficulty of performing a behavior. PBC is related to individual's feel about ease of performing a behavior. If more resources and passions a person uses to execute the behavior then it is considered higher perceived behavioral control [7]. Fig.2 presents TPB model.

C. Unified Theory of Acceptance and Use of Technology (UTAUT)

UTAUT consists of two main dependent factors which are Behavioral Intention and Usage Behavior and aims to describe user behavior intention toward using a new information system technology. UTAUT is a consolidate form of TAM model and is a combination of eight previous models which used to explain user behavior intention (Theory of Reasoned Action (TRA), Technology Acceptance Model (TAM),

Motivational model, Theory of Planned Behavior (TPB), Combined Theory of Planned Behavior/Technology Acceptance Model, Model of PC Utilization, Innovation Diffusion Theory, and Social Cognitive Theory) [8]. UTAUT consists of eight independent variables. Four main independent variables of this theory are Performance Expectancy, Effort Expectancy, Social Influence and Facilitating Condition. In addition it has four moderating variables (Gender, Age, Experience and Voluntariness of Use).

Effort Expectancy (EE) shows how easy it is to work with new technology. Social Influence (SI) is almost the same as Subjective Norm factor in Theory of Planned Behavior (TPB) which describes how others will affect individual to use a new system. Performance Expectancy (PE) is the degree of user believe that using new technology and system will increase his/her performance. Facilitating Condition (FC) is related to show how technical support and organization will facilitate in using the new system.

To have a more accurate result about user behavioral intention toward using SPS, PE is used as one of independent variable of research. PE has important role to assess how individuals perceive using SPS will increase their performance. Fig.3 presents UTAUT model.

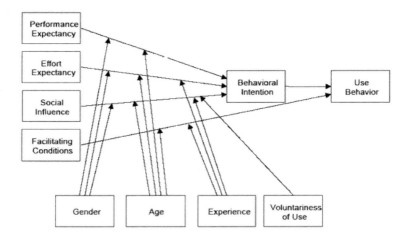

Fig. 3. Unified Theory of Acceptance and Use of Technology (UTAUT)

3   Proposed Research Model and Hypotheses

A. Research Design

Factors that are used to evaluate user behavioral intention to use Smart Parking System are perceived usefulness (PU), perceived ease of use (PEOU), subjective norm (SN) and performance expectancy (PE). The reason why these factors are chosen as proposed research model independent variables is described in Table 1.

Table 1. Research Factors and Functions

Factor	Source	Purpose of Choice
PE	UTAUT	- Line detection helps more people use parking. - Touch 'n Go helps to decrease queue up time. - Using SPS will lead to find car park quickly.
SN	TPB	- Searching for car park will make driver exhausted. - Waiting at parking ticket payment queue is time consuming. - Finding small changes and coin for payment is difficult. - Improper parking by others will make drivers irritate.
PU	TAM	- Using Touch 'n Go is useful. - Using different colors of LED light is useful to identify different types of car parks. - Improper parking detection (Line detection) is useful. - Place shops 'ads logos besides parking signage are useful.
PEOU	TAM	- Smart Parking System (SPS) require minimal effort to use. - Pay car park fee by Touch 'n Go system is easy. - Triggering alarm to inform those drivers who park wrongly to adjust car, is easy to understand. - Following signage to find vacant space is easy to use.

B. Hypotheses

Four hypotheses are stated to test whether the proposed research model and factors can interpret behavioral intention toward using Smart Parking System (SPS) or not. Research hypotheses related to the identified factors are listed as follows:

(H1): Positive Perceived Usefulness (PU) will increase user Behavioral Intention (BI) toward using SPS.

(H2): User Perceived Ease of Use (PEOU) about SPS will have positive effect on Behavioral Intention toward using SPS.

(H3): Subjective Norm (SN) has a positive effect on user Behavioral Intention (BI) to use SPS.

(H4): Positive Performance Expectancy (PE) will lead to more Behavioral Intention (BI) toward using SPS.

Proposed research model is based on mentioned factors as demonstrated in Fig.4.

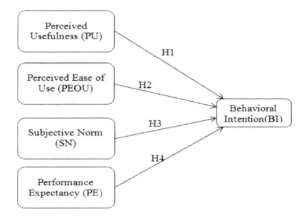

Fig. 4. Proposed Research Model to Measure User Behavioral Intention to Use SPS

4   Research Methodology

The first step of research methodology is to clarify problem of the research and then followed by second step where literature review on types of research models is done. The third step is designing research model based on previous step's result. The proposed research model is formed by combining three different research models which are TAM, TPB and UTAUT. Sample size and questionnaire are defined after proposing the research model. Last step of proposed research methodology is to collect and analyze the survey result. SPSS is used to analyze and evaluate questionnaire outcome. Fig. 5 shows the proposed research methodology. SPS's survey questionnaire consists of two categories of questions in six sections. First category contains fourteen questions in one section about respondents' demographic and their parking behavior such as age, gender, race, difficulty in finding car park, parking fee and etc.

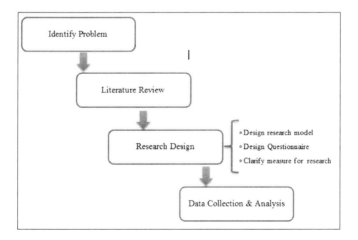

Fig. 5. Proposed Research Methodology

Second category contains twenty nine questions which are arranged in five sections and assess user acceptance about using Smart Parking System (SPS). Questions in section two are measuring Performance Expectancy (PE), section three Subjective Norm (SN), Perceived Usefulness (PU) and Perceived Ease of Use (PEOU) subsequently. Questions in last section measure a dependent variable which is Behavioral Intention (BI). All the second category questions are in 5 point Likert scale with 1= Strongly Disagree, 2= Disagree, 3= Neutral, 4= Agree and 5= Strongly Agree. Questionnaire is developed based on prior researches about parking problems and combination of acceptance factors based on the research models that have studied which is relevant to Smart Parking System (SPS).

To evaluate customer satisfaction, online survey in the form of questionnaire is conducted. This survey will be distributed through online method which includes sending email containing online survey hyperlink to students, friends from colleges and universities in Malaysia. In addition survey link is shared through researcher's Facebook profile to obtain more participants. To have more efficient method and saving time in collecting, keying in and organizing data, questionnaire is produced by Google spreadsheet through http://www.google.com/google-d-s/spreadsheets/. Online survey link is attached at www.arshantech.com , in order to gain more traffic to website, to increase reputation and to provide more information about SPS's features. The following hyperlink is the actual pages of SPS questionnaire. http://www.arshantech.com/index_files/Overview.htm.

5   Analysis of Result and Discussion

The results of the survey are explained in detail in this section. Analysis has been done to test research hypothesis. Different measures which are regression, correlation, reliability test and etc. are used to assess user intention about SPS. Total respondents are 155 which are collected from the online survey.

A.   Demographic Result

Fig.6 shows that 86% of the total 155 respondents have difficulty to find car park at multilevel parking. It highlights the user pain in finding the parking lot. It should take into account that most of the drivers have problem to find car park and thus there is urgent demand to develop a product which can fulfill their needs.

Fig. 6. Facing Difficulty in Finding Car Park at Multilevel Parking Lot

Fig.7 shows 59% of respondents (92 people) are female and the rest are male. Around 81% of respondents are between 18 to 33 years old and the rest of them are older as shown in Fig.8. Gender result shows that females are more interested to contribute in this survey. It reveals that females are more aware of the current parking lot problem more than males. Age of respondents can be interpreted as the 18 to 33 years old populations are more attentive to new technologies. Indeed they need the product, which has a high quality, usefulness and easy to interact. So it should take into account that SPS should be designed in such a way to fulfill the needs of users (e.g., technology, performance and minimal effort to use), especially for this age group.

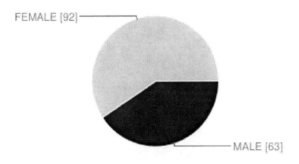

Fig. 7. SPS Survey Respondent's Gender

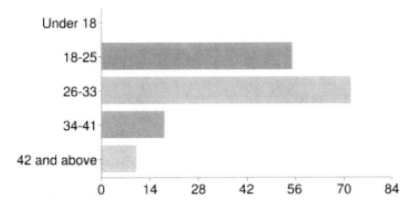

Fig. 8. SPS Survey Respondent's Age Group

Fig. 9 and Fig. 10 shows statistics that are related to different types of parking lots and the reason why drivers prefer to choose the particular parking lots. Around 60% of respondents would rather park at multilevel parking lots and 5% of the respondents which is the least among the respondents percentage choose roadside car park with Park-O-Meter. Safety reason is most important factor for choosing car park where 59% of respondents choose this reason and 48% choose weather condition which makes these two reasons with high percentage. It can be predicted in crowded city where drivers feel less safe to park at road side thus multilevel car park will be more acceptable. In addition, the area which has more raining season makes people has desire to use multilevel parking lot rather than outdoor and road side parking areas. Malaysia as a country with rainy season is projected to be a suitable market for SPS.

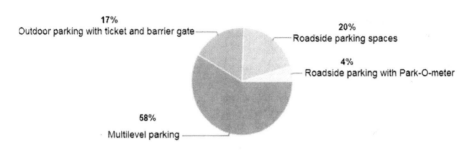

Fig. 9. SPS survey- Respondents Desire Parking Lots

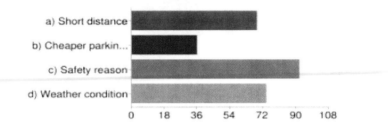

Fig. 10. SPS Survey- Reason Why Respondents Choose a Particular Parking Space

B. Descriptive Analysis

Descriptive analysis helps risk managers to determine variability of risk. The less dispersion of the distribution, the result is of a lower variability of risk and the greater the likelihood that actual results will fall within a specified range of that central tendency. On the other hand wide dispersion of results means less certainty in predicting a particular outcome. In fact company can rely on survey descriptive analysis result to predict users' perception and desire about Smart Parking System (SPS).

Table 2 provides information about mean and standard deviation of important survey's factors. PE1 confirmed using SPS will lead drivers to find car park more quickly. SN6 justifies searching for car park will make drivers exhausted. PU5 is another proof that vacant car park detection is useful to prevent wasting time in parking lot. Result of BI7 declares that most of the respondents are strongly agreed that those who have time constraint should use SPS. Based on all of these justifications, it can be concluded that time is important factor for grasping user behavioral intention toward Using SPS. So in developing SPS, it should take into account that this system must be developed in such a way that it can enable the drivers to find the car park quickly.

PU4 proves the perceived usefulness of using different colors of the LED lights to differentiate between vacant car parks, full car parks, handicap car parks and reserved car parks. In addition PE2 and PEOU2 prove that respondents agreed that by using SPS, finding handicap car park would be easy and required minimal effort. It can be concluded that using clear lights and notification to differentiate handicap car parks from normal car parks will be useful. It will lead to increase product performance and usefulness.

PE3 shows that on the average respondents agreed that the combination of shop advertisement with parking signage can be helpful to find nearest car park to that shop. With regard to improper parking and line detection feature of SPS, PE4, SN5 and PEOU3 are used to interpret the results of the survey. Based on SN5, most respondents feel irritated when they encountered a car park in the middle of two car parks. Result related to PE4 indicates that with line detection feature more people can use the parking lot. Based on the proportion of respondents in demographic section that stated they faced improper parking and also based on the descriptive analysis of PEOU3, it can be concluded that line detection feature must be considered as a feasible feature for SPS.

SN3 and SN4 are proof that there is parking fee payment problems for drivers when using the parking lot. Based on SN3, the waiting in parking ticket payment queue is time consuming and finding small change and coin for payment machine is considered troublesome according to respondents who answered questions related to SN4. PE5 shows that using Touch 'n Go module for car park payment will decrease payment queue up time. The high mean value of PU3 proves that Touch 'n Go method for car park payment is useful. PEOU1 shows that most of the respondents agreed with Touch 'n Go features for ease of use. In addition BI2 shows respondents have positive behavior intention to use Touch 'n Go feature a few days once it is launched.

Table 2. Detailed Descriptive Analysis

Question	Mean	Standard Deviation	N
PE1	4.21	.781	155
PE2	4.02	.879	155
PE3	4.01	.802	155
PE4	3.81	.988	155
PE5	4.25	.792	155
SN3	3.86	.861	155
SN4	3.87	.998	155
SN5	4.17	.804	155
SN6	4.18	.856	155
PU3	4.23	.653	155
PU4	4.20	.733	155
PU5	4.23	.737	155
PEOU1	4.28	.689	155
PEOU2	3.91	.768	155
PEOU3	3.86	.817	155
BI1	4.09	.724	155
BI2	3.95	.771	155
BI3	4.03	.760	155
B17	4.01	.837	155

BI3 refers to respondents' interest to recommend SPS to others to use. This means that SPS is considered as interesting product for users and the company which markets this product can take advantage of word of mouth in marketing SPS. So for this product, the system developer should consider to develop a unique, user-friendly and high performance product to attract users. BI7 confirms that user prefer to use SPS to find car park and users have positive behavioral intention toward it.

C. Regression Analysis

Result of regression analysis is used to test the proposed hypotheses. R square is an overall measure of the success of a regression in predicting dependent variable from independent variable. Adjusted R square measures the proportion of the variation in the dependent variable accounted for by the explanatory variables. Unlike R square, adjusted R square allows for the degrees of freedom associated with the sums of the squares. Adjusted R square here has value of 0.526 which means 52.6% of the variance in Behavioral Intention (BI) can be explained by variance in independent variables. The Durbin–Watson statistic test is used to detect the presence of autocorrelation in the residuals from a regression analysis. Durbin-Watson should be between 1.5 and 2.5 indicating the values are independent. Based on Table 3, Durbin-Watson values is below 2.5. Therefore, the regression residuals for all the hypotheses are positively serially correlated and have no problem of autocorrelation. So this analysis satisfies the assumption of independence of errors.

Table 3. Regression Analysis

Variable	Dependent = Behavioral Intention Standardized Coefficients (β)
Performance Expectancy (PE)	0.224**
Subjective Norm (SN)	0.082**
Perceived Usefulness (PU)	0.374**
Perceived Ease of Use (PEOU)	0.205**
R	0.734
R Square	0.538
Adjusted R Square	0.526
Durbin-Watson	2.380

6   Conclusion

Result of the survey that has been conducted shows positive behavioral intention toward using SPS. All the four hypotheses are accepted; and it is found that perceived usefulness with highest coefficient value (0.374) has most influence on behavioral intention toward using SPS. It can be concluded that more guidance and information are required by drivers inside the parking lots. The limitation of this study is that there is lack of information about smart parking bay detection systems. There is no study about SPS performance feedbacks which can be compared with camera based parking bay detection systems. Thus for future research, SPS can be compared with other detection technologies as well as to study elderly and handicap drivers' satisfaction level after using SPS.

It is hoped that the outcome of this study will assist in enhancing of SPS's usefulness and increase the performance on developing SPS. The outcome also has helped the researchers to assess the users' acceptance level of using SPS to find nearest car park with minimal effort and time in multilevel parking lots.

Acknowledgments. A special thank to Universiti Sains Malaysia for the support of this research under APEX Incentive Grant and to all those who contribute on this research.

References

1. Coopers, P.W.H.: From Beijing to Budapest - Wining Brands. Winning Formats 126 (2005)
2. Fishbein, M., Ajzen, I.: Belief, Attitude, Intention and Behaviour: An Introduction to Theory and Research (1975)
3. Huang, C.C., Wang, S.J.: A Hierarchical Bayesian Generation Framework for Vacant Parking Space Detection. IEEE Transactions Circuits and Systems for Video Technology 99 (2010)
4. Masrom, M., Hussein, R.: User Acceptance of Information Technology: Understanding Theories and Models. Venton publishing (M) Sdn. Bhd., Kuala Lumpur (2008)
5. Paynter, J., Lim, J.: Drivers and Impediments to E-commerce in Malaysia. Malaysian Journal of Library & Information Science 6, 1–19 (2001)
6. See, J., Yusof, U.K., Kianpisheh, A.: User Acceptance Towards a Personalised Handsfree Messaging Application (iSay-SMS). In: Proceedings of the 2010 International Conference on Science and Social Research (CSSR 2010), vol. 6 (2010)
7. Venkatesh, V., Morris, M.G., Gordon, B., Fred, D.: User Acceptance of Information Technology: Toward a Unified View. MIS Quarterly 27, 54 (2003)
8. Yamada, K., Mizuno, M.: A Vehicle Parking Detection Method Using Image Segmentation. Electronics and Communications in Japan, Part III: Fundamental Electronic Science (English Translation of Denshi Tsushin Gakkai Ronbunshi) 84, 25–34 (2001)

Author Index